NC

D1190389

Collins

Collins

Birds

A Complete Guide to all British and European Species

Dominic Couzens

Photographer and Photographic Editor, David Cottridge

Collins

To Emily and Samuel

First published in 2005 by Collins, an imprint of
HarperCollins Publishers
77–85 Fulham Palace Road
London
W6 8JB

www.collins.co.uk

Collins is a registered trademark
of HarperCollins Publishers Ltd

10 09 08 07 06 05

10 9 8 7 6 5 4 3 2 1

A catalogue record for this book is available
from the British Library.

ISBN 0 00 713821 0

Commissioning Editor – Helen Brocklehurst
Art Director – Mark Thomson
Editor – Caroline Taggart
Design and layout – Smith & Gilmour, London
Proofreader – Hugh Brazier
Index – Hilary Bird
Assistant Editor – Emily Pitcher
Editorial Assistant – Julia Koppitz

Colour reproduction by Colourscan, Singapore
Printed in Italy by LEGO, Vicenza

Contents

General introduction

This book is about the life histories of the birds of Europe. It's not an identification guide to be taken into the field and compared to the birds themselves, but rather a book to look up when you get home, to find out more about what you have seen. It covers almost every aspect of each bird's life, its ecology, feeding, breeding behaviour and migration for example, and points, hopefully, to what makes each bird special and unique.

Every species is treated in two ways, first as a member of its family, along with other closely related species, and then under its own heading. This enables us to make general points about each family first so that certain information – the number of eggs or the type of nest, for example – doesn't have to be repeated again and again, leaving room to give each species its own profile.

Ideally, despite this somewhat empirical description, this book will be more than a dry textbook. The hope of the team has been to produce something that is not only informative, but also captures the wonder of the birds of our continent.

Geographical spread and species covered

The region covered includes all of Europe east to about 35°E, taking in Finland in the north and the Crimean Peninsula in the south. It includes the northern island groups of Spitsbergen (Svalbard), Bear Island and Franz Josef Land, but not the Atlantic islands of Madeira, the Canaries or the Azores, nor Asian Turkey.

In theory, every bird that breeds within this area is included in the book, and so are the winter visitors and the commoner passage migrants. In practice, however, given that the eastern border is highly artificial, we have had to cull some of the more marginal breeders (e.g. Booted Warbler, Steppe Eagle) for fear of making too heavy a volume. Where the borders are blurred a bird's inclusion sometimes comes down to something as mundane as personal preference. Some very rare species that breed in the core of our region are also given sketchy treatment, sometimes as subsections of other species (e.g. Crested Coot). We do hope, nevertheless, that the roll call of species treated fully is representative of the birds of Europe as a whole.

Layout

The way this book is arranged is pretty simple. Every bird species in the world is part of a higher grouping known as a 'family' (scientific name ending in *–idae*), just as someone's son or daughter is an entity within a human family. In all its sections the book first describes the family and its characteristics, and then goes on to treat the various species within the families in their own right. The families, incidentally, are arranged in a sequence that corresponds to how early they are thought to have appeared in the fossil record (see page 8).

Family accounts

Within each account of the family is a description, often including diagnostic anatomical or behavioural features, followed by a table. Within the table the following questions are answered:

Name of family or bird e.g. WARBLERS family *Sylviidae*

Habitat In what sort of general environment does the family of birds live in Europe?
Food What are the main foods taken by members of the family? And how do they procure their food?
Movements Are members of the family sedentary (staying in the same place all year) or do they migrate? And if they migrate, where do they go, and when do they travel?
Voice What general sounds do the members of the family make?
Pairing style What sort of bond is formed between the sexes? Do one male and female have a formal relationship (monogamy), or does the arrangement involve a male with two or more females (polygyny) or a female with two or more males (polyandry)? Alternatively, are birds promiscuous, with either sex copulating with several different birds but not forming a pair bond as such?
Nesting Do members of the family nest in colonies or singly? Or do they form the halfway house of 'neighbourhood groups'?
Nest Where do the birds lay their eggs? If they build a nest, what shape is it and what sort of materials are used in its construction?
Productivity How many broods a year do the birds have? (This figure does not include replacement clutches, laid in response to the loss of the first, but only the number of possible successful clutches).
Eggs How many eggs constitute the normal clutch size?
Incubation Broadly speaking, how long is the period between laying and hatching?
Young When they hatch, are the young nest-bound (nidicolous) or can they run around (nidifugous)? Are they helpless and poorly developed (altricial) or are they mobile, self-feeding and well developed (precocial)? Are they naked or covered with down?
Parenting style How do the parents divide their labours? Who feeds, broods or tends the young once they have hatched?
Food to young What foods do the parent or parents bring to the young?
Leaving nest How soon after hatching do the young leave the nest, and in what circumstances (i.e. alone or with parents)? Do they remain for long with their parents?

It should be mentioned here that, on a few occasions, we have lumped families together (e.g. shearwaters *Procellariidae* and storm petrels *Hydrobatidae*) because of similarities between them.

Species accounts

The book then goes on to separate out the various species, presenting a mini-essay on each one. These mini-essays are not meant to be comprehensive, but instead attempt to draw on whatever is particularly interesting or 'different' about the bird. Beside each mini-essay is a photograph that has been chosen to give an instant impression, as far as is possible, of the character of the bird. The essays are accompanied by distribution maps and illustrative paintings.

Distribution maps

The distribution maps are a guide to where each bird is found at different times of the year. Although as accurate as possible, they can offer only a broad view of where a bird is found, and no indication of how common or rare it is in a particular location. As a rule, though, a bird is most abundant in the heart of its range and becomes progressively less numerous towards the edge.

The colours on the maps indicate the following:
Green represents areas where the bird is resident – i.e. it can be found there are any time of year.
Orange represents areas where the bird is present only in the breeding season, and migrates away in winter and back in spring.
Blue represents areas where the bird spends the non-breeding season after its migration.
Yellow represents areas where the bird is only a transient, passing through on migration, usually in spring or autumn.
In addition, the **arrows** show the direction of a migratory pathway where this is unusually concentrated or obvious. As a rule, only outward (post-breeding) pathways are shown.

Illustrative paintings and identification paragraph

This is not primarily a book of bird identification, but within each entry is a short paragraph about how a bird can be recognised in the field. It draws attention not just to plumage details but also, where appropriate and not mentioned elsewhere, to distinctive aspects of behaviour. When a bird is similar in plumage to a relative, the differences between the two are highlighted. And if there are major differences between the sexes, these too are mentioned.

On the whole the plumage patterns of young birds are not described.

Such details would hardly work without the accompanying illustrations. These show the major plumages of each species, and are designed to work in tandem with the photographs, to put each in context. The symbols and abbreviations used as labels for these illustrations are as follows: ♂ represents male; ♀ represents female; **br** represents breeding (summer) plumage; **non-br** represents non-breeding (winter) plumage; **juv** represents juvenile; 1st/2nd/3rd/4th winter refers to plumages for 1st winter and so on, and similarly 1st/2nd/3rd/4th summer refers to summer plumages over those years.

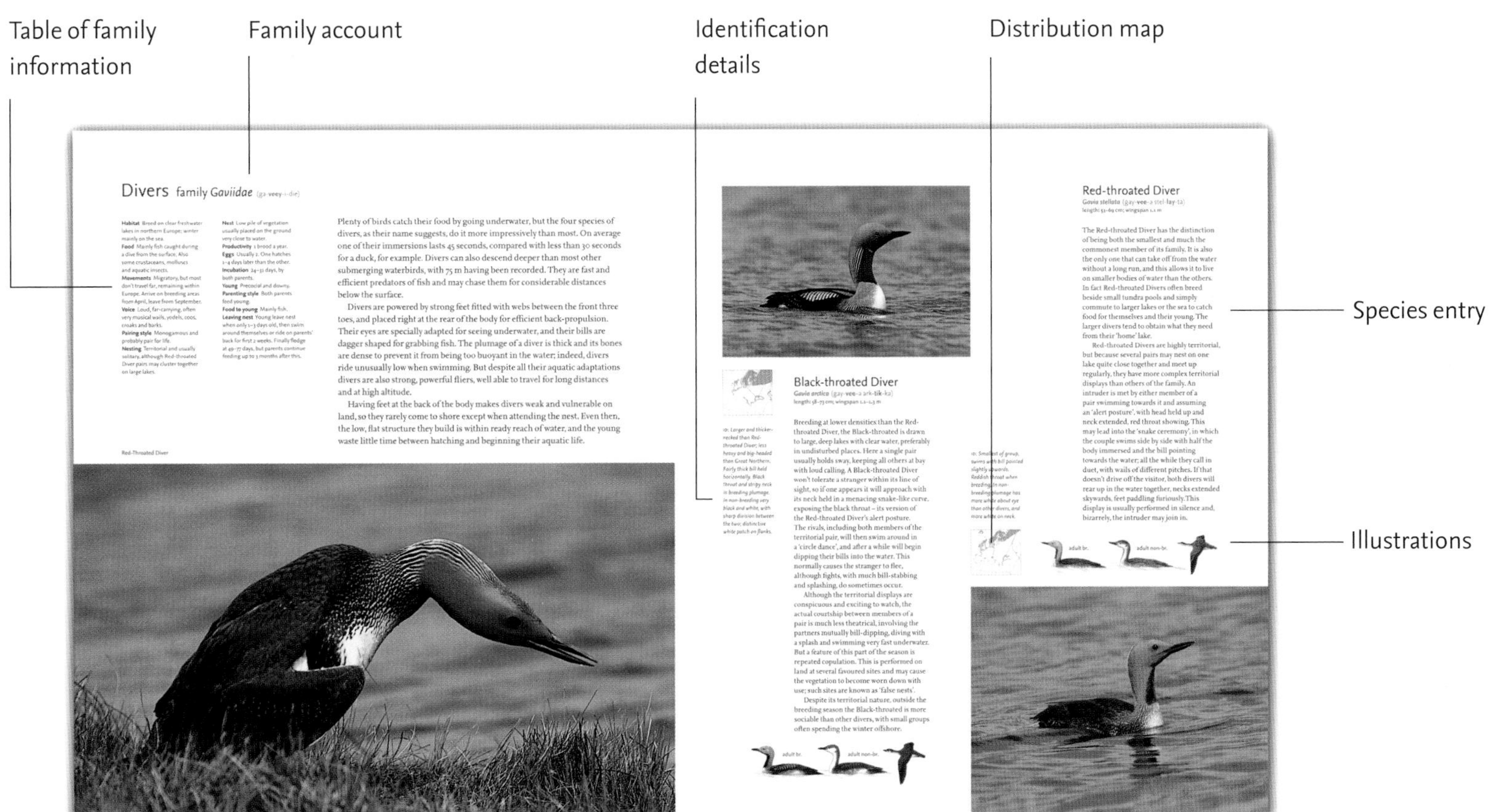

What shapes birds – evolution, anatomy and classification

One of the most famous fossils ever discovered came from Europe. It was a crow-sized creature uncovered in lithographic limestone in Bavaria, Germany, in 1861, and its appearance caused an immediate sensation in the scientific and political world. Unlike any other fossil previously found, this extraordinary specimen exhibited a mixture of bird-like and reptilian features – the wings and feathers of a bird, plus the teeth and bony tail of a reptile. Immediately heralded as the 'missing link' between birds and reptiles, its discovery gave unexpectedly quick momentum to the 'Theory of Evolution by Means of Natural Selection' that had been proposed by Charles Darwin and Alfred Russell Wallace just a few years previously. Evolution, as proposed and understood in the new theory, required creatures with mixed characteristics to occur in the fossil record, and *Archaeopteryx lithographica*, as the Bavarian fossil came to be known, fitted the bill perfectly. Darwin and Wallace changed the world with their bold new theory, and *Archaeopteryx* undoubtedly contributed to the revolution in thought.

Archaeopteryx: 150 million years old

We no longer live in times where evolutionary theory can cause shock waves in society, but, unbeknownst to many, there is no less of a revolution going on today in our understanding of the history of birds. Recent discoveries of fossils in China have begun to change our ideas of what a bird actually is. And it hasn't just been the discovery of new and outlandish birds that has caused this rumpus, but something far more fundamental – reptiles with feathers. The existence of specimens such as *Protoarchaeopteryx*, which clearly had feathers but was incapable of flight, and of *Sinosauropteryx*, which probably had the primitive beginnings of feathers, has blurred the historical distinction between the two camps of birds and reptiles. It is now hard to escape the conclusion that the birds of today are essentially highly modified reptiles.

Specifically, birds are thought to be descended from a group of reptiles called theropods. These include every child's favourite, *Tyrannosaurus rex* – indeed, some postulate that this fearsome creature might have been covered with feathers itself! The relationship with theropods, in fact, was suggested as long ago as 1860 on account of the anatomical similarities between *Archaeopteryx* and some theropod reptiles called coelurosaurs. Like birds, these walked on two feet. They had a strikingly similar design of the jaw, similar middle ear and other skull features, and the same position of the ankle between the tarsal bones, rather than below the tibia, as in mammals. This may all sound a bit abstruse, but each small feature was a piece of evidence nudging in favour of a common ancestor between birds and reptiles, the veracity of which was triumphantly confirmed by these much later fossil finds.

We can also look at modern birds to see the similarity between the two groups. Both have similar red blood cells (with nuclei, lacking in mammals) and a similar excretory and reproductive system. Both reptiles and birds lay eggs, of course, and these are of fundamentally similar design.

Interestingly, many early birds sported another reptilian feature: teeth. Not only was *Archaeopteryx* so endowed, so too were some of the most famous Cretaceous fossils, such as the diver-like *Hesperornis* and the gull-like *Ichthyornis*. It appears, though, that all the toothed birds died out in the infamous wave of mass extinctions that accounted for the dinosaurs in the late Cretaceous period, about 65 million years ago.

Well, not quite every dinosaur. Birds survived. And birds, it is now generally accepted, are the last surviving dinosaurs.

Modified reptiles

Birds may be modified dinosaur reptiles, but they do exhibit a good many features that make them readily recognisable as birds today. And although the various types of birds look distinctive on the outside, on the whole their body plan is astonishingly uniform. This summary roughly follows Proctor and Lynch (1993).

The great unifying feature of birds today is the presence of *feathers*. Feathers are possessed by all birds but by no other living creatures. Feathers were once thought to have evolved from modified reptilian-style scales, but it is now known that they grow out from the skin in quite a different way. They are made up of a protein called keratin (as are our fingernails) and are both very light and very strong. Most feathers consist of a central stalk (the rachis), from which close-lying branches grow (barbs). The barbs, in turn, are themselves branched and have 'twigs' that interlock with the twigs of other barbs, allowing the feather structure to be kept in shape, like a deluxe version of Velcro. There are many modifications of feathers for different purposes, for example for insulation (fluffy, downy feathers) and for flight (structurally strong, asymmetrical feathers). Feathers wear out and are exchanged at least once a year during the *moult*. The stunning coloration of some birds is achieved in two ways, by pigments and by the refractive properties of the feather structure, the latter being mainly responsible for iridescence.

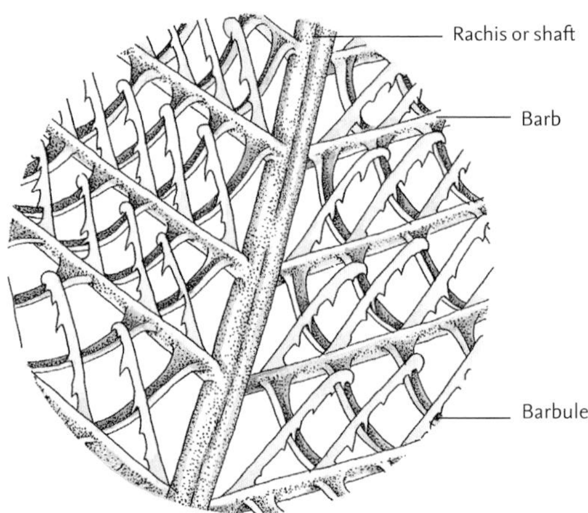

The next most obvious bird feature is a *lack of teeth* (but see above). Instead, birds have a horny bill which is a highly 'plastic' (modifiable) feature, with hundreds of different designs and variations, suited to the owner's dietary needs. The lack of teeth makes a bird's head much lighter than would otherwise be the case, and is all part of a bird's adaptation of weight loss for flight. A bird breaks down most of its food, therefore, not in the mouth but in the crop (a 'pocket' in the gullet) or in the gizzard, a muscular forward extension of the stomach. The gizzard mashes food, usually aided by small stones and grit that the bird ingests for the purpose.

A bird's forelimbs have, of course, developed into *wings* which are primarily used for flight. In common with bills, wings are among the most plastic attributes of birds (see below), exhibiting great variety in shape and size. Most of the wing bones are fused to make the structure rigid and light, and the maximum flexibility is at the 'wrist' rather than at the equivalent of our shoulder or elbow. Wings are powered by very large pectoral muscles in the breast. As modified forelimbs, wings are good for flight but not much else: think of the comparison with our hands and arms, for instance. So, to compensate for the loss of flexibility and dexterity, a bird's neck is long and supple, enabling the bird to use its bill for preening and dealing with food.

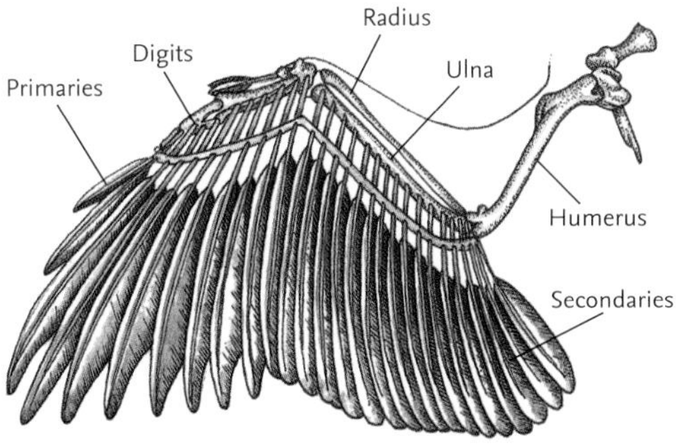

Birds are *bipedal* – they stand on two feet. Actually, not even this is quite true – they stand on their toes. What appears to be a bird's 'knee' is actually the equivalent of our ankle, and the lower part of the leg, known as the *tarsometatarsus*, is an amalgam of several bones of the foot. At the base of this are (usually) three remaining toes (of five, the others lost), plus a fourth, often backward-pointing 'toe' which is called the *hallux* and is not actually a toe at all. The toes and hallux have claws. The precise arrangement of foot and toes is often used to help to classify birds into families, as is a bird's ability to walk, run or hop.

The skeleton of a bird is truly special. To cut down on weight, the *fusion* and *reduction of bones* mentioned above for the forelimbs is a general feature throughout. A good example of this is the skull, which is essentially fused into one bone, without the usual filled 'cracks' (sutures) seen in the skulls of other vertebrates. Many of the bones of wing and tail have also simply been dispensed with. In addition to this, most of the major bones are *pneumatised*, which means that they are not solid but are hollowed out, with internal struts for support, a bit like a cave system. These hollow bones sometimes contain air sacs, which are part of a bird's respiratory system. Birds are the only vertebrates with this arrangement.

Two other features of birds should also be mentioned. Firstly, their bodies are *centralised* and compact, with most of the body mass packed tightly close to the centre of gravity. This helps a bird to be stable at all times, whether in flight, perched or on the ground. And birds are also, as a rule, rather *small* animals, a favourable attribute for creatures that frequently operate in the air.

Senses

Birds and humans have a similar emphasis on sight and sound in their sensory armoury, but little else in common. For, in addition to perceiving touch in some different ways to us, and having apparently very little sense of taste, birds also have several additional senses that we cannot perceive at all.

Almost all European birds rely on sight for the major tasks of life (a rare exception is the Barn Owl, which seems to hunt primarily by ear). A bird's eyes are comparatively large (constituting over 10 per cent of the mass of the head, compared to 2 per cent in people), and the receiving cells in the retina are more densely packed than ours, allowing birds to see perhaps twice as much detail as we can. Most birds see in colour and, in addition to seeing our visible spectrum, it has been proven that at least some species of birds can perceive the ultraviolet realm as well. With their well-spaced eyes on either side of the head, birds have a wide field of view of about 300 degrees; but this also means that they lose out on the span that can be perceived by both eyes simultaneously ('binocular vision'). Binocular vision, in which a single object is seen from two slightly different angles (i.e. from the two eyes) confers the ability to judge distance effectively. Only birds with forward-facing eyes, such as owls and harriers, have well-developed overlapping vision and binocular function. A bird's eyeballs are relatively immovable, so the head must be turned to fix a stare upon something; many species can move their heads in an arc up to 270 degrees.

Birds have a keen sense of hearing, but their ears are less complex than mammal ears. The range of frequencies they detect is more limited than ours, too, in the range between 1 and 12 kHz, but some birds, including pigeons, have recently been discovered to be able to perceive infrasounds (very low notes, inaudible to us) down to only 2 Hz. Some owls have a unique system of detecting sound three-dimensionally, thanks to having one ear placed higher on the skull than the other (see page 192).

Olfaction is generally thought to be a low priority in a bird's sensory armoury, with little of the brain devoted to it. Among European birds it is best developed in the family Procellariidae (see page 30), which includes the fulmars and shearwaters; these seabirds use smell not just to find food, but also to find their nest site. Some workers in the field of migratory studies have asserted that pigeons may use scents in the air to help them orientate, but not everyone seems to agree with this. It could well be, though, that future studies may show smell to be more important in birds' lives than is currently supposed.

Birds have an acute sense of touch all over their bodies. Besides the expected receptors in the skin, birds are also endowed with a unique armoury of special sensory bodies for detecting touch at the tip of the bill. These can be so finely tuned that they can detect vibrations as well as actual objects.

Finally, recent studies on migration have revealed that birds can detect some physical properties that we cannot. Most important among these is a sense of magnetic field, its direction and intensity; with the earth's magnetic field being fairly

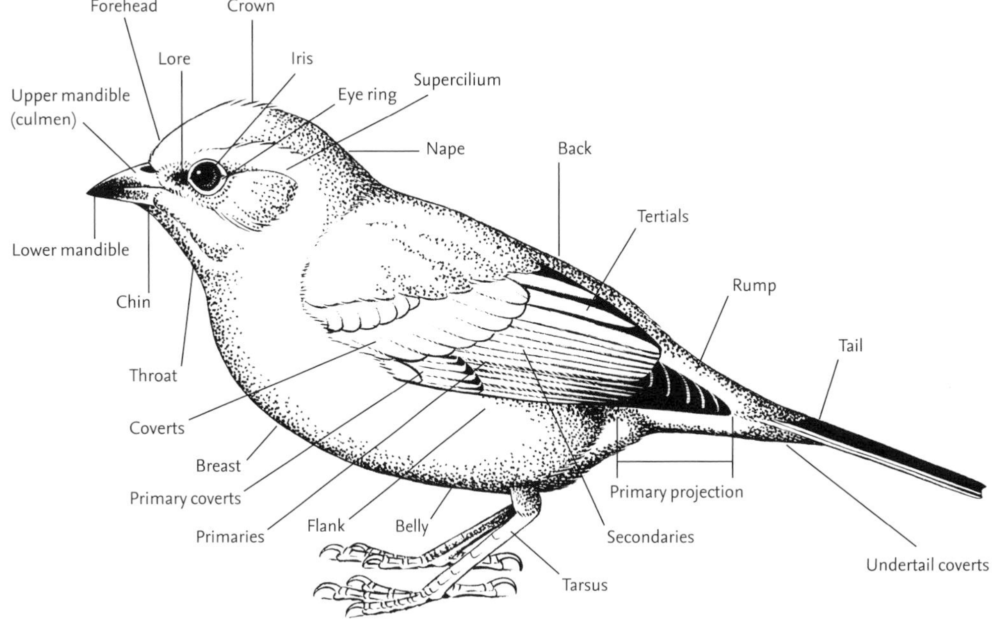

predictable, this has wide implications for a bird's still poorly understood ability to navigate over the earth's surface with pinpoint accuracy. Very recently some scientists have located material in the eye which is sensitive to a magnetic field, suggesting that birds might be able to 'see' field lines in some way. Birds are also sensitive to changes in atmospheric pressure, enabling them to have some short-term prediction of weather patterns. And they can also perceive lines of polarised light, invisible to us.

Metabolism

Birds have a higher metabolic rate than humans, and a higher internal temperature – about 40°C (range 38–42°) compared to about 36°. They are fast-moving creatures that burn energy rapidly and consume more food than other vertebrates of similar size. Some birds, in fact, can spend virtually all day feeding, especially in winter.

The high internal temperature is maintained not only by frequent feeding, but also by extremely effective heat regulation. As anyone who has slept under an eiderdown will attest, feathers make exceedingly good insulators and a good insurance against excessive heat loss. Providing birds can find food to eat, they do not usually get cold. Indeed, going around under several layers of feathers must be similar to passing the day wearing a thermal sleeping bag!

A note on classification and taxonomy: how the birds are arranged in this book

The sequence in which the birds are presented in this book is not random, but has biological significance. Simply put, the families are listed in the order in which they are thought to have evolved: the most primitive families are listed first and the most advanced families last. The choice of what is primitive or advanced is not easy to make, and is mainly down to best guesses (although highly informed ones) based on how simple or complex various details of the anatomy are. The fossil record helps: naturally one would expect the most primitive families to appear in the fossil record earlier than the more advanced ones, although, with such a limited record available, this does not necessarily follow. This, anyway, is the basis of the sequence.

Very recently, opinion about the origin of many families of birds has shifted, and current lists are now encouraged to begin with wildfowl (swans, ducks and geese) instead of divers, which appear much later. This change is only the tip of the iceberg. Recent taxonomic work, especially involving DNA, is continuing to unearth new evidence about bird evolution and the way in which families are related to one another. In the next few decades there will be some major and seemingly outlandish switches in opinion that will radically alter the systematic list. So for now, in this work, we are continuing to adopt the much better known sequence that has been followed in books for the last 30 years or so.

The sequence adopted within the families themselves is along the same lines, going from primitive to advanced. For example, the Chaffinch and Brambling have the least specialised bills among finches, and are listed first. However, owing to constraints of space and design, we have not always followed the precise sequences within families.

In this book we treat birds at two levels: at the family level and at the species level. However, the units of family and species are only two levels of detail that describe a bird's affinities. A more complete list is as follows, using the Pied Wagtail as an example:

Phylum: Chordata
Subphylum: Vertebrata (vertebrates)
Class: Aves (birds)
Order: Passeriformes (passerines, perching birds with well-developed vocal apparatus)
Family: Motacillidae (wagtails and pipits)
Genus: *Motacilla* (wagtails)
Species: *alba* (Pied and White Wagtails)
Subspecies: *yarrellii* (Pied Wagtail)

Most books, including this one, take the species as its basic, most widely understood unit. A Wren, a Cuckoo or a Swallow is a recognisable entity, enough to be given a name that distinguishes it from other birds. However, in some cases the differences between species are not so clear-cut. The Pied Wagtail, for example, is represented by at least two populations of birds with slight but consistent plumage differences. They have been given distinct English names: the Pied Wagtail in Britain and the Near Continent, and the White Wagtail in most of the rest of Europe. In behaviour and in ecology they are almost identical, so they are generally regarded as subdivisions of the same species (subspecies), with three-word scientific names: *Motacilla alba yarrellii* for the Pied Wagtail and *Motacilla alba alba* for the White Wagtail. However, their status as subspecies is a matter of opinion. Perhaps they are in fact two species?

Whether two populations are considered to be separate species or not has historically been judged on whether, when the two populations meet, they interbreed or not. If they do, they are subspecies; if they don't, they should be considered as species. However, it isn't that simple. Plenty of birds interbreed occasionally but are usually clearly separate – the Redwing and Fieldfare, for example. And even when birds interbreed quite regularly in the zone of overlap (e.g. Blue Tit and Azure Tit), consistent differences in their ecology, behaviour and morphology don't support the assumption that they are the discrete populations of the same entity. An informed judgement tends to boil down to a considered analysis of the entire range of their characteristics. But, in the end, it is a matter of opinion.

Or at least, it was. In recent years taxonomists have been given a new toy to play with – DNA. Now, by comparing the DNA 'fingerprint' of one bird to another, an empirical measurement of their similarity can be made. If two birds' DNA is very different, or very similar, we can make an easier judgement as to whether or not they are separate species. This work will probably eventually settle most arguments. In the meantime it is ongoing, and a few of the results are included in this book. DNA analysis has, for example, now suggested that the Marmora's Warblers of Sardinia and Corsica are different enough from the birds of the Balearic Islands for the two to be treated as separate species.

Those warblers are among the first of many. In 20 years' time we may need a few more pages of this book in order to include all the recently promoted species.

Flight and travelling

The wings of a bird are one of its so-called 'plastic' features. This means that a wing will vary a great deal in size and shape from bird species to bird species, rather than being consistently similar. In fact, the variation is not shown just within birds as a group, but within members of the same family. The Griffon Vulture, for example, has very long broad wings with 'fingered' tips, whereas the related Pallid Harrier has very narrow wings with sharp tips. Wings, it seems, are one of those variables that allow a bird to adopt and maintain a lifestyle.

Wings don't necessarily confer the ability to fly. Europe does have one native bird that is, or was, entirely flightless. The Great Auk (*Pinguinus impennis*) was a marine species that dived for its food and, when it came to land, nested among rocks close to the water. But this unworldly lifestyle made it vulnerable to humans. It was good to eat and easy to catch, and became extinct in 1844.

Some European birds become flightless, or nearly so, for short periods of the year. Wildfowl, including geese and ducks, as well as shearwaters and auks, get the moult of their flight feathers over

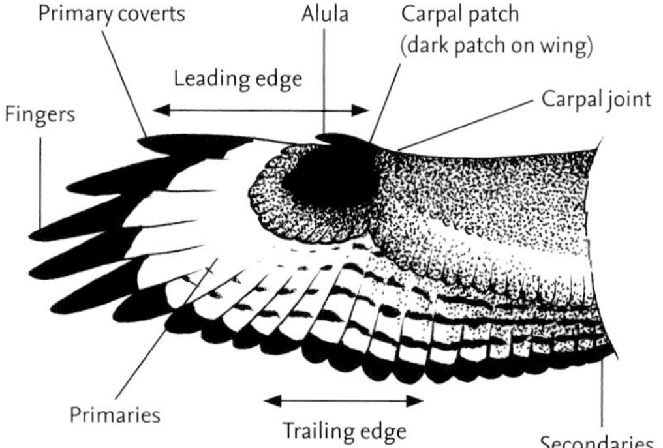

The 'fingers' on the ends of the wings of soaring birds, such as birds of prey, reduce turbulence at the wing-tip.

quickly by changing them all at roughly the same time. For a few weeks in July or August they can barely take off, so they retreat to very safe waters or mudflats and see their flight-impaired time out in a state of high caution.

But for most of the year all of our birds can fly, allowing them to move around with a freedom and efficiency almost unrivalled in the animal kingdom. Flight enables birds to escape predators, roam widely in search of food and colonise inaccessible places such as sheer sea-cliffs and tall trees with effortless ease. It also allows them to take advantage of temporarily benign conditions in climates which are normally inhospitable, and then to withdraw when the need dictates. In other words, birds can be migrants. Many of our birds are long-distance commuters, coming here just for the summer and retreating back to Africa for our winter months. Without flight this would be untenable.

To understand how birds fly, and how different birds fly differently, we need to dip our toes into the subject of aerodynamics for a moment. And we can begin by asking: how do birds get off the ground in the first place?

To answer this question, imagine air passing over a wing as the bird moves forward. The wing is shaped so that, at its leading edge, it is quite blunt, whereas the trailing edge is tapered (the shape is known as an *aerofoil*). The air passing over the wing, therefore, has to travel over a little 'hump' or 'hill' to get to the back, whereas the air below the wing has an unobstructed level passage and travels a shorter distance. Since physics dictates that the air streams must meet at the back of the wing at the same time, it follows that the air deflected over the hump must flow faster than the air below the wing in order to make its rendezvous. And because it flows faster, it is at a lower pressure than the air below the wing. The inevitable result of the difference in pressure is *lift* – the key to any sort of flight. The flapping of a bird's wings simply gives the bird forward momentum so that lift can come into effect.

A bird's life would be easy if the only force it had to contend with was lift, but there's an opposing force that comes along with flying, known as *drag*.

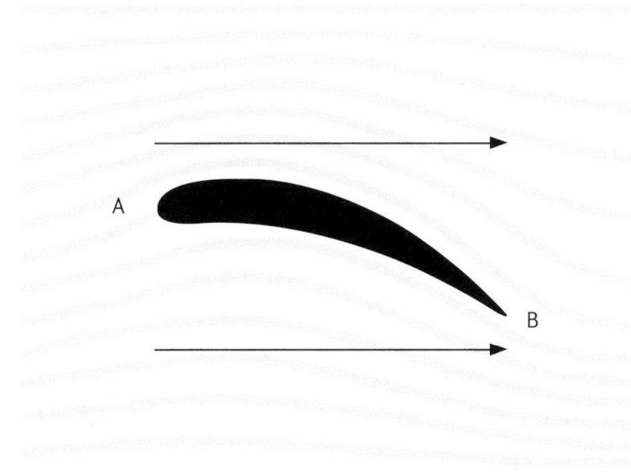

Air travelling from A to B over the wing has further to travel than under the wing, leading to lower pressure above than below, and hence lift.

Drag slows the passage of air over the wing and, therefore, reduces lift. Drag can be influenced by the nature of the surface of the wing, by the wing shape itself and by the complex patterns and flows of air created by the bird's movement, broadly known as turbulence. A bird's wing shape directly affects the degree of lift, drag and turbulence it will normally experience and, inevitably, defines its flight performance in different conditions. Not all birds need to be supreme fliers. Some require speed without efficiency; some require manoeuvrability and control; others require energy efficiency. It all depends on the bird's lifestyle.

There are two measurements that help us gauge a bird's wing dimensions in relation to its flying performance. They both have rather off-putting, technical names. *Aspect ratio* is the measurement of the wing length relative to its width. Birds such as shearwaters, with their long but narrow wings, have a high aspect ratio, whereas pigeons, with quite broad wings but low wingspan, have a much lower figure. Wings with a high aspect ratio give plenty of lift simply because they are long; the forces of lift operate all along the wing and give a powerful combined push, like the pulling from lots of members of a tug-of-war team. At the same time, drag is reduced because the wings are narrow, which reduces turbulence. This enables birds with high aspect ratios to fly long distances and expend little energy, but they tend not to be very manoeuvrable or fast. Long wings are more liable to break than shorter wings, too, which means that, despite the obvious advantages of a high aspect ratio, most birds have to compromise.

The other measurement of wing dimension is known as *wing-loading*. This is the ratio of a bird's overall weight to its wing area – the load the wings have to carry, in other words. Birds with a high wing-loading have relatively heavy bodies and small wings, therefore, whereas birds with low wing-loading have light bodies and large wings. A high wing-loading is not suitable for a bird that spends a lot of time in the air, but once it gets airborne a bird so endowed can often generate a lot of power and speed. Birds such as game birds and rails have a high wing-loading, and tend to move in short bursts of flight.

Birds exhibit many different styles of flight. A good number, especially the smaller ones, don't fly in a straight line when in normal flight but follow an *undulating* or *bounding* course. These birds include most of our familiar tits and finches, as well as woodpeckers and some owls. All these birds have a low aspect ratio and a high wing-loading, and their flight style is a way of saving energy. A few flaps give the bird lift; the bird stalls at its highest point and begins to fall until the next burst of flaps allows it to regain height, and so on.

In complete contrast, long-winged birds, with their higher aspect ratio, can glide – move forward in the air holding their wings out still. Gliding is inexpensive energetically, but it demands the occasional burst of flaps to keep up the flight speed. Soaring, a form of gliding in which a bird can actually gain height, makes use of the energy of wind and air currents to give the bird its extra momentum. There are two main kinds: *thermal soaring*, in which birds can use the energy of hot air rising from the ground in a temporarily stable system, and *slope soaring*, in which seabirds use the energy of the wind moving over waves to give them momentum. Both these types of soaring allow birds to travel enormous distances with negligible expenditure of energy.

Buzzard – With its long, broad wings, the Buzzard has a low wing-loading (33 N/m^2), allowing to it glide and soar, and a moderate aspect ratio of 5.8.

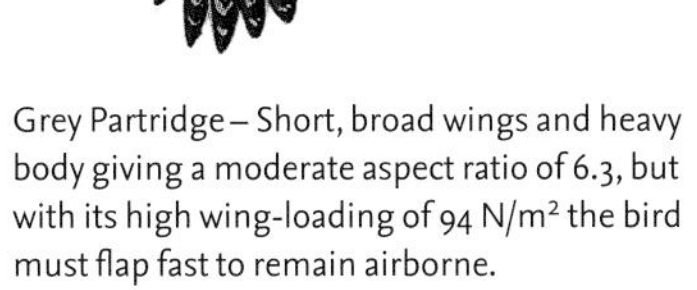

Grey Partridge – Short, broad wings and heavy body giving a moderate aspect ratio of 6.3, but with its high wing-loading of 94 N/m^2 the bird must flap fast to remain airborne.

Fulmar – The long, narrow wings give a very high aspect-ratio (11.4), allowing for exceptional gliding efficiency. The wing-loading is, however, quite high (73 N/m^2), so the bird needs to maintain speed and use the wind.

Wood Pigeon – A typical compromise of relatively high wing-loading (58 N/m^2) and relatively low aspect ratio (6.6) confers speed and manoeuvrability, but at some cost.

Where N/m^2 is newtons per square metre.

Have wings, will travel

Migration is one of the best known and celebrated of bird phenomena, yet most people, including birdwatchers, have a very narrow view of it. The general perception is that birds migrate south in autumn and return in the spring, having spent the winter in warm climates, often very far away. And whilst this is broadly true, it masks the remarkable diversity of migratory strategies shown by birds, and neglects the dynamic movements that take place within Europe itself.

In fact, if we try to define migration we immediately run into problems. One very important movement, undertaken by most birds at a predictable time each year, is called post-juvenile dispersal. This term refers to the movements undertaken by juvenile birds once they have left the nest. These journeys may take the birds only a few kilometres in all, and have no fixed destination, so they are perhaps not 'migrations' as such. But they are highly significant. It is important that a young bird leaves its parents' territory as soon as it can, for the short-term reason that the adults may wish to have a further breeding attempt, and for the long-term benefit of preventing either competition with its parents in later life or, in extreme cases, inbreeding with a sibling or even with a parent. Therefore, the majority of juvenile birds, including long-distance migrants, go on a journey of exploration to their wider neighbourhood and beyond in late summer. Even the juveniles of sedentary species that live in the same territories throughout their adult lives, birds such as Marsh Tits and Golden Eagles, disperse. And their dispersal distances can be considerable, up to 1000 km in some cases.

Martins gather on wires prior to migration.

Another poorly recognised movement is the seasonal shift between altitudes. A mountain top in winter may be as hostile as the Arctic, and a good many birds vacate their high-altitude breeding sites in favour of more benign climates in the autumn. Such species may not cover much distance – often only 50 km, for example – but the movement is no less vital for survival than a journey south of many thousands of kilometres.

The point of an altitudinal migration, though, is just the same as a latitudinal one. It is to avoid untenable conditions in the winter, those that would not enable a bird to survive. At the same time, migration is also a positive strategy: it enables birds to take advantage of seasonally favourable conditions in climates that would normally be out of reach. In places where the summer is short there is more space available and less competition for all breeding needs.

It is false to assume that a given bird species will have a migration strategy to suit all populations, or even all individuals. For example, Chaffinches are resident in many parts of Europe, but they evacuate parts of Fennoscandia and Russia completely in the autumn. In other parts of their range, however, some members of the population migrate and some stay put, a phenomenon known as *partial migration*. And there may be sexual differences or age-related strategies. Many ducks adopt a migration pattern in which the young travel the farthest, the females almost as far, and the males remain closest to the breeding grounds. This is known as *differential migration*.

Speaking of ducks, mention should be made here of a highly specialised migration that takes these and a few other birds to and from places simply for the purpose of moulting. The sites involved are often large lakes or other inaccessible sites which offer plenty of food and safety. Good moulting locations may be to the north of the breeding grounds, resulting in the birds apparently travelling in the 'wrong' direction in late summer. A *moult migration* is like a visit to some specialist hairdresser for an unusual cut, a journey with a purpose.

Another special form of journey is one that is not undertaken regularly, but only when events dictate. One such movement is known as an *escape movement*, when a population of birds simply evacuates an area in response to a sudden change in the weather, only to return when things improve. On a longer-term scale, eruptions from a place (or irruptions to a place) occur when a population of birds suddenly experiences unsustainable imbalances in supply and demand, and many individuals are forced into journeys they would not normally make. Most eruptive species occur in the north of Europe, and are often dependent on a certain type of food that may suddenly become scarce – e.g. fruits or seeds of a certain tree, or a species of animal that has years of boom and bust in its population. Eruptive species in Europe include the Waxwing, Coal Tit, Rough-legged Buzzard, Nutcracker, Rose-coloured Starling and Hawk Owl.

Breeding and family life

The birds of Europe exhibit a stunning diversity of breeding strategies, from laying one egg to laying 20; building no nest at all to constructing elaborate marvels that are at the centre of a bird's breeding system; having anything from one to seven broods a year; having a single mate a year to 18 mates at once; living in vast territories or dense colonies; and having a lifetime partner to having no relationship at all outside copulation. It could be said that no European bird is exactly the same as any other in its breeding behaviour.

In the light of this variety, this section attempts a few generalisations that will hopefully make sense of the great drama of reproduction in European birds.

Breeding seasons

In order to reproduce successfully any bird needs a lot of food to be available throughout its breeding attempt. This will not only ensure that the young can be fed, but will also enable the adults to be fit and up to their difficult task. A female, in particular, requires a great deal of energy to form eggs inside her and to keep them warm during incubation; only reliable and plentiful food will make this possible.

In winter, when many resources must be diverted into simply keeping a bird alive, and when the days are so short and the nights so long that the time available for feeding is highly restricted, breeding is seldom possible. Few types of food are available anyway – only fruits and seeds, plus a selection of vertebrate food, and invertebrates in certain special niches.

Most European birds, therefore, have a specific breeding season that is typically confined to the summer months. It is, properly enough, controlled internally, to avoid birds overextending themselves. After breeding, usually in the autumn, most birds enter what is known as their *refractory period*, when, among other things, their sexual organs stop functioning and may shrivel to almost nothing. During the early winter these organs lie barren and will not work again until they are 'switched back on', so to speak.

For most overwintering birds, the change from decreasing to increasing day length after the winter solstice in December is the switch that starts things off again. Birds detect this change in their brain (not through their eyes) and this triggers a chemical trip that sets off a chain of hormones charged with preparing birds for breeding. Gradually the gonads regrow (the ovaries may increase in size a thousandfold) and resume working. The moult into breeding plumage, if it occurs, will begin and the bird may also change its behaviour. A male may start singing in earnest, for example, and pairs may resume courting. These are outward expressions of the internal drive. What birds actually do in the late winter is fine-tuned by the weather. A warm, still day is more likely to stimulate song or courtship than cold or damp weather; but it is day length that exerts ultimate control.

Once the birds have been 'switched on', there is much individual variation as to when they begin the more obvious tasks of building nests and laying eggs. Older birds often begin breeding earlier than inexperienced ones, and birds that have survived the winter in the best condition can also begin sooner than those that require longer to attain peak fitness.

For a given species the start of the breeding season may be determined by many factors. Obviously many migratory species, having spent the winter in a different climate, cannot begin breeding until they have arrived back in their breeding areas. Even then, conditions may dictate that they must wait, for example for ice to melt in the Arctic. Birds in place at the right time of year may also find that they cannot breed, or must start late, because of a lack of food.

Birds may also time their breeding to take advantage of predictable gluts of food. Tits, for example, breed only when there is a bloom of caterpillars in the woods, and Sparrowhawks wait until those same broods of tits are leaving the nest and are available in quantity. Rooks, by contrast, breed early in the year so that the soil is moist and earthworms are easy to obtain; later in the season the ground is too dry for them. Many owls breed early so that they can seek food before seasonal vegetation has grown too high or too thick.

Finally, there are birds that breed at any time of year, or at unusual times. Pigeons may nest in any month, so their sexual organs clearly do not atrophy. Crossbills often breed in mid-winter when conifer cones are ripening, and Eleonora's Falcons breed in the autumn when the small birds on which they feed their young are migrating south.

Territories

A bird cannot just make a breeding attempt anywhere. It has to have a place to live, where it can build a nest and raise young. This place must provide nesting material, food and shelter, and must be a discrete location in which the family can grow as a unit. Such a place is usually called a territory. Territories may be large or tiny, and may provide all a bird's needs or just some of them.

The majority of birds live in discrete territories apart from other breeding pairs. These territories have borders that may be very clearly defined – a bird in its territory will be dominant, but when it strays into its neighbour's territory it will be subordinate. The boundaries are negotiated and fought over at the start of the season, but soon become generally recognised by both sexes of the adjacent pairs, so that at least an uneasy truce prevails and the birds can get on with their breeding attempt in comparative peace.

Some territories are all-purpose, providing a breeding pair with everything they need so that they never have to stray from them. Perhaps more often, though, it is only the immediate vicinity of the nest that is sacrosanct, and there is a certain amount of informal trespassing outside the inner core. This happens with many birds of prey, with Meadow Pipits and even with those fiercely territorial birds, Robins. But the territories as such remain intact.

An all-purpose territory tends to suit species whose food supplies are reliable, predictable and evenly distributed: normally only insects fit this description. Those species that feed on less abundant food, which may require something of a journey to find, tend to defend only the area around the nest. Finches, for example, feed their young on seeds, which are 'clumped' in their distribution: abundant in patches, absent elsewhere. They are unable to defend a territory wide enough to encompass scattered patches of their food plants, so they forsake the idea of an all-purpose territory altogether.

At the opposite end of the scale from holding an exclusive, all-purpose territory is colony nesting. In colonies birds do have territories, usually very tiny ones centred upon the nest, but their privacy for breeding is minimal. Colonies may be very large, incorporating thousands of breeding pairs, or they may hold only a handful, but they tend to exhibit a degree of synchronisation that may not be seen in other breeding systems. In other words, a given pair within a colony will display, copulate, lay eggs, incubate and feed its young at about the same time as the rest of the colony members; or at least it will be synchronised to the rhythm of its part of the colony (the so-called sub-colony). One of the advantages, then, of colonial nesting is that communal breeding activity gets everybody 'in the mood', as it were. There are other major advantages, too. Birds in colonies do not have to seek food on their own; instead the location of food resources will become 'common knowledge' and involve straightforward commuting movements. Another important benefit is that communal aggression against predators can be very effective. Gulls in packs can be highly intimidating, for example, and the remarkable dive-bombing of Fieldfares is a powerful deterrent to any predator.

However, colonies do attract predators, because they make food very easy to find for anything that can breach their defences. As a result, colonial nesters are much more vulnerable to catastrophic, unproductive breeding seasons than species that are well dispersed. They may also be prone to epidemics of disease.

The formation of colonies, though, is not always a matter of choice. A good many species nest communally because they are constrained by the availability of suitable habitat. Seabirds are a good example. Safe coastal nesting areas are always at a premium. Gannets might prefer to breed alone, but their need for predator-free, windy ledges close to the sea ensures that suitable sites are always densely occupied.

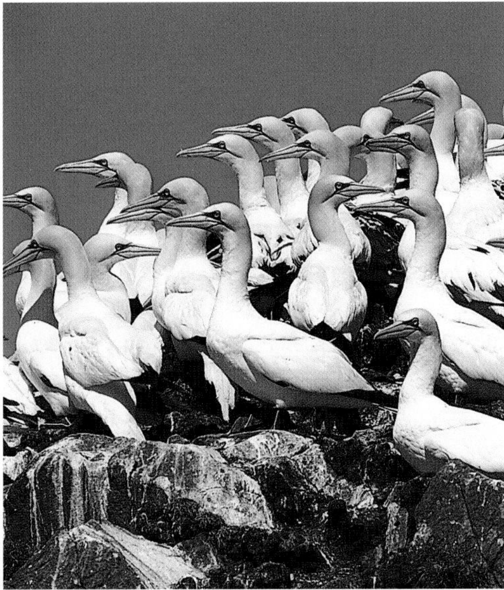
A colony of Northern Gannets.

In recent years the concept of the *neighbourhood group* has come into fashion. It's a halfway house between a colony and a well-dispersed population. If we think of a territory as being a detached house and a colony as being a terrace or block of flats, the neighbourhood group is a little like a cul-de-sac, a fairly intimate association between discrete households. Birds such as Short-toed Larks and Melodious Warblers exhibit unusually clumped distributions, with some parts of a habitat well occupied and other, apparently identical sections left empty. Clearly the members derive benefit from living close, but not too close, to each other.

Songs and displays

Territories are neither inherited nor divided equally; birds have to compete for them. A territory is treasured, and those birds that do not have them covet them. In theory, both the ownership of a territory and the details of its borders are under perpetual dispute during the breeding season, so there must be a mechanism for claim and counter-claim.

In many birds, the initial and continued claim is made by song, but it can also be made by a visual display or by both at once, depending on the species. If we listen to birds singing in a wood, we are listening to these claims. In most species the male is responsible for acquiring and maintaining a breeding territory, so the vocalists will be almost entirely males, and although the sound may be sweet to our ears, the real messages are not especially friendly. A singing bird, directing its

A Robin singing to assert his territorial rights

efforts to other males, is making it clear that the ground is occupied and will be fought for if necessary. The listeners may not like the message, but song actually civilises territorial males, keeping each in its place and offering a constant reminder of the status quo.

The tense stand-off is broken, however, when a male wishes to make a challenge. He might be a neighbour with ideas of expansion, or he could be a newcomer. His first task is to enter the rival male's boundaries uninvited and stay there, singing. A reaction is inevitable, and the resulting interaction will determine the ownership of the territory (or part of it). The dispute will often begin with a song duel – a trade of insults, if you like. This will be accompanied or followed by visual displays, in which the rivals can size each other up. Only if neither bird can be proven to be superior will a physical fight occur. This, then, is one function of those euphonious vocalisations we call songs.

Songs, incidentally, are only one type of vocalisation made by a bird. As outlined above, songs are very specific sounds used as the primary tool for territorial proclamation. As a result they are normally heard only in the breeding season. Birds may make a range of calls, though, at any time of year. The many vocalisations given the umbrella name of *calls* are usually rather short, simple sounds ('words') made in reaction to the prevailing situation: alarm, for example, or maintaining contact in a flock or mouthing sweet nothings to a mate. Calls are simple and reactive; songs are complex and proactive – trying to bring something about.

Besides the function of advertising territory, songs also play a role in attracting a mate (sometimes the same song does both, but some birds have different songs for differing purposes). A female, listening to the males allotting ground amongst themselves, finds herself in an ideal position to make a judgement on each one. She can determine how much and how vigorously a male sings and, especially among species that perform relatively complicated and individually variable songs, she can determine his repertoire size and other parameters. Armed with the information given in a song, a female can decide which males interest her and which do not, even before making contact.

Particularly in species that live out in the open, vocalisations are normally accompanied by visual displays. At any rate, whether or not songs are involved, interactions both between rival males and between potential mates are normally settled, sooner or later, by what can be seen rather than what can be heard. In these habitats, especially among larger birds, advertising and threat displays tend to replace song for both rival repulsion and mate attraction. In land birds with complex songs, visual displays take over once male and female have made the initial contact and are considering pairing up.

Although it is important to make a distinction between *threat displays* (aimed at keeping rivals away) and *courtship displays* (aimed at attracting and beguiling a mate), the actual postures involved are often quite similar. The observer cannot always tell what is aggressive and what is sexual, even when the gender of the object of the display is obvious. The fact is, though, that just as birds have a language of sounds, so they have a 'language' of postures and stereotyped manoeuvres. These choreographed movements are often species-specific and conventional, leaving no doubt as to the intentions of the performing bird.

Courtship displays are by no means confined to the period when birds of the opposite sex are choosing a mate. They continue, and often intensify, when birds have already paired up. A pair bond must be nourished in this way if it is to be maintained, and there are physiological as well as 'psychological' reasons for keeping up the dance. Males and females must get into breeding condition mutually and must synchronise their internal chemistry prior to copulation. In addition, the provision of food to a female by a male is a common element of courtship in many birds (*courtship feeding*). These extra meals may be very important in helping a female to get into peak condition for the energetically demanding tasks of egg formation and incubation.

Pair bonds

Birds form a surprising number of different types of pair bond. It was once thought that 90 per cent of bird species were monogamous and that the sexes were faithful to one another. We now know that birds exercise far more options than this.

It is true that most birds are monogamous, in that one male and one female co-operate in a given breeding attempt, and both have defined roles within the system. Usually the male is the main defender of the territory and he may also be a major builder of the nest or at least a provider of material. He will normally play little part in incubation or brooding, but contribute significantly to feeding the young (and often the female too). The female will be a nest builder, will incubate the eggs and brood the newly hatched young, sometimes bringing food to the chicks only later on when they are older.

But even birds that are fulfilling their roles wholeheartedly may not necessarily be 'faithful' to their partners. Many recent studies have shown that individual birds of monogamous species regularly practise extra-pair copulations (EPCs) outside the pair bond, presumably for the perfectly understandable reason that their neighbours may be better physical specimens than their partners and therefore likely to provide a better genetic template for their offspring. Such birds are described as being 'socially monogamous' but not 'genetically monogamous'. Among the many species in this category are the Swallow, Blue Tit and House Sparrow.

A minority of species enters into polygamous arrangements, in which a male or female inhabits a 'formal' (role-based) relationship with more than one member of the opposite sex. The hint of deception or secrecy implied in an EPC is usually missing, because the multiple partners are often well aware that they are sharing their mate with somebody else. The most frequent polygamous arrangement is *polygyny*, in which a male has more than one mate; the female equivalent is known as *polyandry*. Examples of regularly polygynous species include the Great Bittern, Hen Harrier, Woodcock, Great Reed Warbler and Pied Flycatcher (in this last-named species the different females may be unaware of each other's existence, at least at first). Regularly polyandrous species are far fewer in number, and most are waders: Red-necked Phalarope, Dotterel and Sanderling, for example. Polygamy implies a real relationship between male and female, in which the polygamous individual still plays a part in the breeding attempt beyond contributing its genetic material.

A few species exhibit systems, though, in which there is no real relationship between male and female at all; only copulation. The meeting between sexes is fleeting and physical, and individuals tend to copulate, if they can, with a number of members of the opposite sex. This is known as *promiscuity*. It is not the free-for-all that it might sound, though, because birds may be very choosy about whom they mate with, and there is no guarantee that an individual of a promiscuous species will copulate at all in any given year. At a *lek*, for example, males of a certain species gather in communal display and thereby force a visiting female to choose between them. But the arrangement of territories on a lek makes her choice easy: the best males tend to occupy the central positions, and it is to these that a female will go for her insemination. Peripheral territory-holders may have a completely blank breeding season. Examples of lek species include Black Grouse, Great Bustard, Ruff and Great Snipe.

Promiscuous and polygamous species tend not surprisingly to have inherently short-term relationships, but among (socially) monogamous species the length of the pair bond may be anywhere from very short (for just one brood among two in a season, as in the Whitethroat) to lifelong (as in swans, geese and sparrows). Partnerships that work in one season are often renewed in the next if both sexes survive, and this is the case even among such small and short-lived birds as Blue Tits and Blackbirds. Seabirds may meet each year at the breeding site after several months of separation at sea. Most birds, it would seem, prefer convenience to change, and seek to replicate any success they may have had in previous seasons.

Nests

Birds are unusual among vertebrates in that they spend considerable time looking after their eggs; this includes, notably, keeping them warm by incubation. This duty of care demands that they deal with all their eggs as a single unit, known as a brood. And if the brood is to be looked after, it must be kept in one place, known as a nest.

What constitutes a nest varies. Some birds don't make any constructions at all: auks, falcons and owls, for example, lay their eggs straight on to a substrate, such as a rocky ledge or soft patch of ground. Some birds that nest on the ground, such as waders and sandgrouse, may exhibit only token efforts towards nest building, such as making a shallow depression, known as a scrape, and perhaps adding a few items of lining around the area. Others make elaborate constructions. The Long-tailed Tit may spend three weeks building its domed nest, using at least four types of materials. The nests of Carrion Crows are multi-layered, and such birds as Swallows and House Martins may make thousands of commuting trips to collect suitable mouthfuls for their mud constructions. Among some species, such as Wrens, Penduline Tits, Blackcaps and Little Bitterns, the quality of the nest may play an important role in mate attraction.

Whatever the type of nest, it must confer certain advantages. Besides keeping the eggs or nestlings in one place, it must provide security and shelter for both adults and young. Discovery of a nest by a predator renders the whole breeding exercise fruitless, so birds seek to hide the nest or put it out of reach. Useful inaccessible sites include high cliffs, islands or overhanging branches. Many species place their nests in holes in trees or rocks, or secrete them in dense foliage, or otherwise conceal them by using inconspicuous materials. Many also ensure that their visits to the nest are as low-key as possible (they try to 'lose any tail') by keeping quiet and approaching the nest in a roundabout way. If a predator does make a close approach, some adult birds will attempt to cause a diversion by acting injured or monopolising the intruder's attention, behaviour known as distraction.

House Martin at the nest

Shelter is as important as secrecy. Adults can afford a certain exposure to bad weather, but the eggs, in general, cannot, so birds go to great lengths to ensure that their eggs are protected from wind, rain and excessive sunshine. Again, holes and, to a lesser extent, dense foliage offer protection, but users of other sites may have to be more inventive. Birds on the ground often orient their nests away from the prevailing wind, or use the entrance to mammal burrows; others ensure that the nest faces into or away from the sun, depending on the climate. Birds in the north tend to build more voluminous nests than individuals of the same species breeding in the milder south.

Eggs and incubation

All birds lay eggs, and for the most part these are rather similar in external and internal design. They are all thick-shelled and independent, but they are not completely enclosed systems, because the shell is porous enough to allow the exchange of gases. Bird eggs are relatively large compared to those of other animals, and, as a result, birds tend not to lay very many of them. In contrast to the hundreds or even thousands laid by fish or insects, birds rarely lay more than 20, and some only a single egg each year. A cluster of eggs is known as a *clutch*.

Most eggs are, of course, egg-shaped, with a narrow end. This helps them to turn in a tight circle if pushed by mistake, and also enables them to pack together under an incubating bird, narrow end in. They come in many colours or patterns, usually cryptic for camouflage purposes, but birds nesting in holes or cavities tend to lay white eggs, presumably because these are easier to see in the dark. Members of a given species usually (but not always) lay eggs of similar colour or pattern.

The number of eggs in a clutch varies from species to species, and in some cases from individual to individual. Birds of some species could theoretically lay many eggs, but don't because they are constrained by the number of chicks they are able to look after and/or feed. A bird 'tries' to lay the optimum number of eggs: not so many that it will be unable to feed all the resulting mouths, nor so few that there is a surplus of food and time. Some birds make only one breeding attempt a year, often timed to coincide with a glut of available food; others may lay several clutches in the course of a season, some containing more eggs than others.

In the majority of species incubation begins when the last egg is laid. This means that the eggs will hatch at approximately the same time, reducing the overall length of incubation and ensuring that, when they hatch, the chicks are at approximately the same stage of development. This gives each chick a roughly equal chance of survival and, in species whose chicks leave the nest soon after hatching, such as ducklings, it means that the brood can be kept together.

Some birds, though, begin incubation not with the last egg, but with the first, and the inevitable result is that the chicks hatch at different times and the brood contains youngsters of mixed ages. Being ahead of its siblings in growth, the first-born outcompetes the rest of the brood at each feeding visit and receives the lion's share of the food. Only when it is satiated will the rest be fed, and that happens only when supplies outside are good. This apparently cruel behaviour is necessary to ensure that, when food supplies are unpredictable, at least one chick will survive. The first-born is insurance; the survival of subsequent chicks is a bonus. This strategy, known as *brood reduction*, is typical of birds of prey and of swifts, among others.

Nestlings and fledglings

People often ask, 'Why do we never see baby pigeons?' The answer is that not all birds' babies follow our perception of what baby birds should look like: cute, fluffy and mobile.

Young birds actually fall into two main types upon hatching. The young of wildfowl, gamebirds and waders, for example, hatch after quite a long incubation and in a relatively advanced state. They are covered with fluffy down, their eyes open within hours and they are able to run and walk about and look for food themselves. These are the babies with which we are most familiar, such as ducklings and chickens. They are known as *precocial* young, and their ability to leave the nest almost immediately makes them *nidifugous*. They are still looked after by the parent or parents, but they are as mobile as inquisitive toddlers.

Most other birds are *altricial*. When they hatch these chicks are in a relatively poorly developed state after a short incubation. They are often naked, or covered only with sparse down. Their eyes are not yet open and they are completely immobile and nest-bound (*nidicolous*); they are often referred to as *nestlings*. It will be a number of days before they can regulate their own body temperature, so they require more *brooding* (warming by the adult, akin to incubation) than precocial chicks. They are fed in the nest and put on weight very quickly, soon approaching the size and mass of their parents. These chicks do not finally leave the nest until they have acquired their first set of feathers; once they graduate in this way they are known as *fledglings*. Altricial young, therefore, emerge resembling adults in size, and often in plumage too. That is why a baby pigeon is rarely recognised as such: it looks like a somewhat scruffy version of an adult.

Needless to say, not all birds fall precisely into one or other of these two camps. Young gulls, for example, are precocial but essentially nidicolous.

Once a youngster has left the nest the degree of parental care it receives varies from species to species. Some, such as Puffins and Swifts, leave the nest of their own accord and probably never see their parents again. At the other end of the scale, young geese or swans remain with their parents for months, even joining them for the migration south from the breeding areas. Young Starlings are independent within days, but for most other small birds parental feeding will last for a week or two. Those birds that require special skills for hunting, such as owls or birds of prey, tend to remain in the parental fold for an extended period of time.

A bird that has left the nest is usually known as a *juvenile*. It retains juvenile plumage until its first moult in the autumn, and then, having donned its first set of proper feathers, is described as being in *first-winter* plumage. After its spring moult it will be described as a *first-summer*, then a second-winter and so on, until it acquires adult plumage. The umbrella term *immature* describes any bird that is not yet wearing adult plumage.

Europe's habitats and their birds

One of the most obvious characteristics of any bird species is its habitat. We see ducks on water, tits in woods and larks in fields, and implacably associate one with the other. A habitat is the type of place in which a bird lives. Its niche is one of a species' most individual features, something that distinguishes it from all other birds, even closely related ones. So, for example, a Meadow Pipit lives in long grass and a Rock Pipit lives on seashores. Put a microscope to a species' requirements and its habitat may become ever more specific: not just woods, but woods with a particular kind of tree; not just rivers, but fast-flowing ones with well-oxygenated water; not just lakes, but those with a certain depth. A bird's identity is defined by where it lives and what use it makes of its habitat.

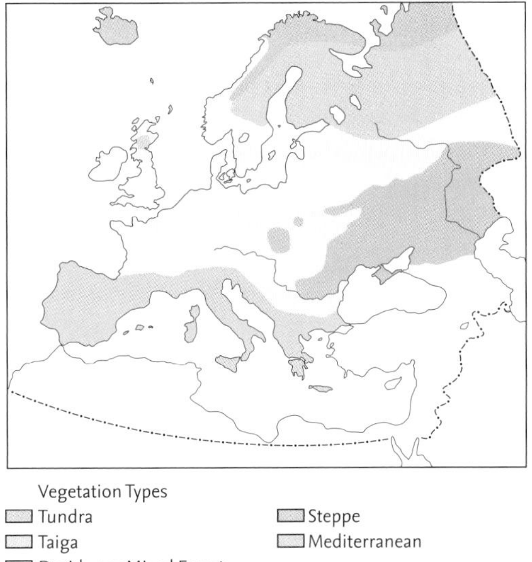

Vegetation Types
Tundra
Taiga
Deciduous Mixed Forest
Steppe
Mediterranean

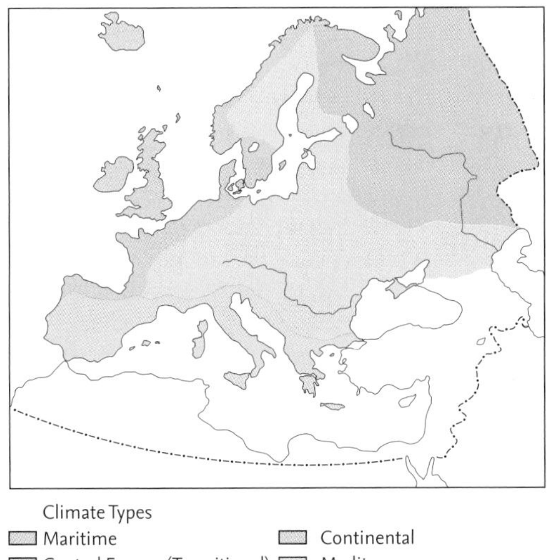

Climate Types
Maritime
Central Europe (Transitional)
Continental
Mediterranean

Zones

Besides being divided into habitats, Europe can also be divided into various vegetational zones according to the prevailing climate (see map). Many species are restricted to certain zones and even to areas defined by isotherms (lines drawn between places of similar average temperature). Two zones, though, are of special interest because they are so clearly defined.

Tundra

This is a mosaic of habitats found north of the 10°C summer isotherm, where tree growth is impossible and the soil is permanently frozen. Most is found above the Arctic Circle, but tundra is also found at high altitudes above the tree-line.

The breeding birds of the tundra are mainly visitors, coming for only the short and highly productive summer months. They arrive on territory late (often in June), to coincide with the melting snow, and leave as early as they can. Only a handful of exceptionally hardy species, such as grouse and a few birds of prey, remain in winter.

The predominant habitats of the tundra are wet ones: bogs and marshes, lakes, rivers and beaches. Naturally, most are very open habitats, so a high proportion of species sing and display in flight so that they can be conspicuous; these include most of the waders, plus pipits and buntings. A high proportion of tundra birds, including waders and even young ducks, feed on insects. Most of the rest feed on the zone's rodents, voles and lemmings. These small mammals have a pattern of boom and bust in their populations, and the numbers of predatory birds breeding go up and down accordingly.

Many of the Arctic species show adaptations against the cold, having larger bodies than their southern counterparts, and thicker layers of feathers. A few specialists, such as Ptarmigans and Snowy Owls, have feathering on their legs and feet.

Taiga

This term refers to the wide belt of mainly coniferous forest that borders the tundra to the south and creeps to the Deciduous Mixed Forest Zone at lower latitudes. The taiga includes habitats such as freshwater lakes, rivers and swamps, so by no means all taiga birds are forest birds. How open or closed the forest is will often determine the birds that occur there.

On the northern border is an intermediate zone of varying width characterised by a mixture of stunted forest and open habitats such as grassland. In more sheltered parts some trees may grow tall, as in true taiga. This intermediate zone goes under the name of *forest tundra*. See also the section on coniferous woodland on page 19.

Habitats

Open sea and ocean

The open sea is a specialised habitat with comparatively few birds. It provides no opportunities for breeding, so ocean-going birds have to return to land once a year for this purpose. Nevertheless, for its residents, the sea provides abundant resources and considerable personal security. Seabirds are often much longer-lived than land birds: a Puffin, for example, has a life expectancy of about 20 years, at least five times longer than a land bird of equivalent size.

One of the main problems of living on the open sea is that fresh water is not available. To get round this seabirds drink sea water and excrete the excess salt through special glands placed on top of the skull, usually in front of the eyes. They also hold on to what water they have in their body by removing almost all the moisture from their excreta before it is ejected, as indeed do many birds.

Seabirds also have dense body plumage for keeping warm. In a good many species, the feathers are pigmented so that the plumage is dark above and white (or pale) below. It is thought that this makes birds harder to see for potential prey species looking up and for potential predators or competitors looking down, although the large number of exceptions casts some doubt on this. White plumage in gulls and other species, such as Gannets, may make it easier for birds on the open ocean to see their peers from a long way off and register whether an abundant food source has been located – in the same way that vultures keep an eye on their colleagues. On the sea, feeding success often increases with flock size, as birds working together can unsettle prey and cause it to move about and become more conspicuous.

The ability to cover large distances is helpful to a seabird. Although some species travel by swimming, the majority are efficient fliers, with wings of high aspect ratio (see page 11). These birds make use of the action of the wind over the sea, harnessing the power of updrafts to take them thousands of kilometres without expending much energy.

It is actually quite misleading to consider the sea as a single habitat. Even amidst the deep ocean there will be features, including currents and upwellings, that make some areas more attractive to birds than others. The distance from shore, and the consequent depth of the water, is also significant and may be divided into zones. The *oceanic zone* is the farthest out, where the water is truly deep. Birds such as shearwaters and storm petrels are found here; they are often described as *pelagic* species. The *neritic zone* refers to the relatively shallow waters over the Continental Shelf, where a range of less specialised birds such as sea ducks, cormorants and divers can occur and feed on the abundant food near the seabed.

Sanderlings are unusual among waders for preferring sandy beaches to mudflats

The seacoast

Where land abuts the sea, all kinds of bird-rich habitats are created by the dynamic relationship of water and hard ground. These may include cliffs, beaches and sand dunes, to name but three, but there are others too, including estuaries, which are mentioned in more detail below.

The so-called *littoral zone* is good for birds not only in the variety of habitats created. It is also highly productive, providing rich and readily accessible feeding opportunities. And, perhaps more importantly than anything else, it supplies dry land close enough to the sea for birds to plunder the waters and breed within commuting distance.

Where elevated land meets the coast, cliffs are found, as well as offshore stacks and islands. These sites have the advantage of being relatively inaccessible to ground predators and are highly sought after by nesting birds, especially seabirds. In north and northwest Europe the Atlantic-facing cliffs have a community of many special birds, including some that, in the international context, are scarce. This community includes Gannets, Fulmars, Shags, Puffins, Kittiwakes, Black Guillemots and, at its northern edge, Little Auks and even Ivory Gulls. On cliffs topped by soft ground, Manx Shearwaters, European Storm-Petrels and Leach's Storm-Petrels breed. A few of these species make it into the Mediterranean, too, but this inland sea has its own special shearwaters, the Balearic and Yelkouan, as well as the wider-ranging Cory's Shearwater. The Black Sea, being relatively isolated, has no unique breeding species.

The species named tend to gather their food – fish, for example – from the sea. No species breeds in the littoral zone with the express intention of gathering food inland, although some gulls do this locally. Mediterranean Gulls on the Black Sea coast, for example, often commute inland to feed on swarms of insect food on fields, and Common Gulls will do this in northwest Europe. But for birds breeding close to the sea, the sea itself is usually the draw.

Cliffs are only one example of the littoral habitat. Beaches and dunes can also be popular breeding sites, although they do tend to be more accessible to predators than cliffs, and nests thereon may be liable to flooding as well as to predation. Most birds nesting in such areas – gulls and terns, for example – are colonial and depend on communal physical deterrence of predators, such as loud calling and dive-bombing; where possible, many of these species select islets and shingle banks to afford them protection. Other inhabitants of the low-lying littoral zone, such as Ringed and Kentish Plovers, have cryptic plumage and nest sites, and breed in scattered pairs. Among dunes, Shelducks often breed in rabbit holes and natural cavities.

Beaches and dunes attract many birds in the non-breeding season. These include many waders, such as the beach-loving Sanderling and various gulls. Among passerines, Snow Buntings and Shore Larks may be found in such sites in winter, picking off the seeds of shoreline plants.

Estuaries and salt marshes

At the mouth of a river, where the flow of water slows down as it reaches the buffer of the sea, the silt carried by the river is deposited and builds up. In some places the tide ebbs and flows over this mud periodically, producing what is termed the 'intertidal zone'. Being washed twice a day and being constantly supplied with nutrients, the intertidal zone is very rich in biomass and provides feeding for hundreds of thousands of birds, mainly in the non-breeding season.

The food available in the intertidal zone falls largely into three categories: worms, crustaceans and molluscs, all of which may occur in extraordinary concentrations. Some birds, such as Grey Plovers, feed from the surface, using visual clues such as the ejection of water from a worm's siphon, to find food. Others simply probe into the abundance, using their sense of touch to locate their prey. The rising and falling of the tide also provides opportunities, as fish can be found in the shallows to be fed on by gulls and ducks, and some previously recalcitrant animals, such as bivalve molluscs, open up their shells in order to feed when they are covered by water. Swimmers operate at high tide, waders when the mud is uncovered, a sort of shift system with some birds roosting and others feeding at every cycle of the tide.

Where the mud is more stable, salt marsh forms and adds vegetable matter to the food available in this ecosystem, mainly appreciated by Wigeon and geese.

Estuaries are not very suitable sites on which to build nests, although Redshanks may use the adjacent salt marsh and other birds may utilise fringe habitats such as beaches and pasture. Disturbance is often high, and spring tides may wash out the more ambitious breeding attempts.

Rivers

The habitat formed by a river depends on similar factors to those affecting a lake (see below). The difference, of course, is that the water is moving, and here it is the degree to which it moves that determines how many birds can use it. This factor, in turn, is affected by the prevailing gradient and the amount of water in the river.

Rivers can be understood to have 'lives'. Their young stages are close to the source, where they start as small streams and often flow quickly, even as torrents, especially in hilly areas. Later on, as a river is fed by more and more streams and tributaries, it swells in size and tends to slow down, especially when it reaches the lowlands, meandering in its middle age. It reaches maturity near its mouth, where it is usually at its widest. These different stages all have their characteristic birds.

Fast-flowing torrents have a few specialist species, notably the Dipper, Grey Wagtail, Common Sandpiper and Harlequin Duck. The Dipper and Harlequin immerse themselves in the water for aquatic larvae, often those that abound in these highly oxygenated waters. The other two feed along the edges, in the shallows and pebbles. Oddly, the Dipper, Grey Wagtail and Common Sandpiper all characteristically and habitually bob their rear ends up and down, for reasons that are unclear. When a river has become more substantial, Goosanders often dive into the deeper sections for fish.

Most of the birds that can be seen along 'middle-aged' rivers are species that also occur in lakes and other wetlands. Moorhens and Little Grebes live in the riparian shallows, for example, and Reed Warblers and Sedge Warblers are drawn to dense waterside vegetation. Three exceptions are birds that rely on riverbanks for nest sites – Kingfishers and Sand Martins widely in Europe and Bee-eaters in the south.

Species occurring in mature rivers are those typically associated with wetlands generally, such as Cormorants and Mute Swans. But several species are also found along the shingle banks of large rivers, including Little Ringed Plovers and Little Terns.

An interesting phenomenon among river birds is that many have linear territories. This means that a given pair of birds is allotted a certain stretch of water, including both banks, but completely ignoring the surrounding habitat.

Lakes

Bodies of fresh water can differ widely in their attractiveness to birds, so that some seem to be virtually lifeless, while others are permanently bustling with activity. The sorts of birds that a lake attracts will be defined by four more main properties: the shape and size of the water body; the depth; the productivity (related to underlying soil type); and the nature of the surrounding environment.

On the whole, larger bodies of water attract more types of birds, and ones that have irregular sides, with bays and channels, are more attractive than ones with straight edges or long sweeps – this is because the habitat the former provide is more varied. Nonetheless, some birds, such as Little Grebes, prefer small water bodies. Shallow lakes are often better for birds than deep ones, and the nature of the sides is very important. Deep lakes with steep sides (often man-made ones, such as reservoirs) are less good than water bodies with shallow sections. But ideally, a lake should present a range of depths. Dabbling ducks will be characteristic of the shallows, whereas diving ducks, such as Pochards or Goldeneyes, tend to prefer water at least 2 m deep. The depth, as well as the underlying soil, also determines a water body's productivity, or *trophic* status. *Eutrophic* lakes tend to be shallow and rich in aquatic vegetation. *Oligotrophic* lakes are those that are generally more than 8 m deep and not very fertile; they are often not very good for birds. Highly alkaline lakes in southern Europe have few birds but provide food for specialists such as Greater Flamingos and Avocets.

The surrounding environment can be a fact or in a lake's attractiveness, especially for breeding birds. Lakes in steppes and other dry areas may seethe with birds, whereas those in city centres will be relatively impoverished.

Lake birds consume fish, insects and their larvae, molluscs such as snails, and a few other invertebrates.

Marshes and other wetlands

Marshes can be thought of as wetlands that are mainly covered by vegetation rather than having open water. These habitats tend to be seasonally rich in birds, very active in spring and summer but rather quiet in winter, in line with the available food. They may also be ephemeral habitats, subject to drying out in hot weather. Many of the breeding birds of marshes are short-term visitors and include a number of warblers.

Common Snipe – a typical bird of freshwater marshes

Marshland birds live in dense, often tall-stemmed vegetation, which may or may not be in standing water. The many small passerines of marshes need strong legs and feet for grasping vertical stems, and they are often highly agile. Some species, such as the Savi's Warbler, hunt almost entirely at ground level, taking significant amounts of prey in or from the water. Others, such as Reed Warblers, hunt higher up and may flit from perch to perch in pursuit of prey.

Rails are highly adapted marshland birds with laterally flattened bodies, squeezed at the sides. Their small girth allows them to run through the 'forest' of stems at high speed, and their long toes spread their weight and allow them to walk on muddy ground without sinking.

Many marshland birds, such as the Bittern, not only have highly cryptic plumage, they also exhibit cryptic behaviour, rarely showing themselves. A good number are most active at dusk and dawn, suggesting that low vegetation is a risky habitat in which to live. Most inhabitants also have loud voices, which is often the only way to make contact with a mate or rival in the mass of dense vegetation.

Heathland and moorland

In many parts of Europe, mainly on poor soils, there grows a type of low (less than 50 cm tall) vegetation that is dominated by a small range of plants, notably heathers (Ericaceae). This habitat usually arises as a result of the degradation of previous habitats, such as forest, or by the abandonment of cultivation, and it is kept in place by, variously, grazing, deliberate husbandry or fire. The dry versions of this habitat, often found on acidic soils, are known as heaths, and the wetter versions characteristic of upland areas are known as moors. Both heaths and moors may play host to habitats within habitats, such as bogs or mires.

Heathland is not a particularly rich habitat, but it does have some interesting specialised birds. These include the Dartford Warbler, Stonechat, Wood Lark and Nightjar. Tree Pipits also occur on heathland, so long as there are scattered trees present as launch pads for song flights. These birds have different foraging methods, but they all feed on insects; Hobbies, too, often visit the wet parts of heaths for dragonflies.

Moorland is not a prime habitat either, and the Meadow Pipit can sometimes seem to be the only bird present. Various waders, though, such as Curlews and Dunlins, breed near the wetter areas.

Most moorland birds nest on the ground, including the typical predators Hen Harrier, Merlin (sometimes) and Short-eared Owl. In contrast to heathland, moorland rarely contains trees or even bushes.

Sclerophyllous scrub

The word *sclerophyllous* means possessing hard or stiff leaves, and such foliage is typical of the many spiny, evergreen, often aromatic plants that make up the varied scrub of the Mediterranean region. Two terms are often used for this type of community. *Maquis* is dominated by dense woody plants 1–3 m tall and grows on non-calcareous soils, and *garigue* refers to the lower-growing, less woody equivalent on chalk and limestone, but there are actually a bewildering number of different scrubby communities of this nature, each with slightly different vegetation. They often arise when woodland is cleared for agriculture and then abandoned, or after fires. Fires, indeed, perpetuate the scrub and release nutrients to reinvigorate the community.

Sclerophyllous scrub is a rich habitat, with the twin benefits of abundant insect and invertebrate life, and a good crop of small berries in the late summer and autumn. It supports many birds, including a particularly good representation of warblers in the genus *Sylvia*.

Grassland and steppe

Natural grasslands form where the rainfall is unable to support more abundant growth such as forests; unsurprisingly, grasses, rather than scrub, are dominant here. This is often an arid, waterless habitat and the number of birds it supports is relatively small. The main areas of grassland in Europe are the steppes of the continental east, and they support a distinctive range of birds.

Many grasslands are notably rich in large insects such as grasshoppers and crickets (Orthoptera), and these are often important in the diets of steppe birds such as the Rose-coloured Starling. Small mammals also occur in hordes and form the diets of Pallid Harriers and Lesser Spotted Eagles. The grass seeds are fed upon by such characteristic birds as larks.

Most grassland birds obviously tend to nest on the ground. Others, such as the Isabelline Wheatear, use rodent burrows, while birds of prey may use clumps of large, isolated trees if these are available.

Mountainous and hilly habitats

Mountains and hills often have a rich range of birds, for two reasons. The first is that they provide a varied habitat with the changing altitude, the second that they act as refuges from human encroachment on the land. Rugged hills are hard to cultivate and difficult of access, giving birds an advantage over people. Several large eagle species that are at heart primarily lowland birds, such as the Eastern Imperial Eagle, are now found mainly in mountains, having been forced there away from their preferred haunts.

Nevertheless the higher mountains do provide a habitat for some characteristic birds. The specialists occur above the tree line, where the air is thin and the climate harsh. Birds' haemoglobin is well suited to dealing with the lower oxygen levels, but mountain birds do show a number of adaptations against the cold that are analogous to those of birds at high latitudes. Many have thick plumage, for example, and are comparatively large-bodied (the Alpine Accentor, for example, is bigger than the closely related Dunnock).

Mountain birds often feed on berries from the low-growing shrubs and on seeds from the profuse plants of the alpine meadows. They are often highly adaptable as well as tough: Alpine Choughs, Snowfinches and Alpine Accentors, for example, may live in the vicinity of skiing complexes and high mountain villages, feeding off scraps and other waste.

A good many 'mountain' birds are really birds of rocky places. The Black Wheatear, Blue Rock Thrush, Rock Bunting and Black Redstart are examples of these, and so is the Red-billed Chough. The Wallcreeper, although confined to high altitudes for breeding, may occur on rocky outcrops at low elevations in winter. Rocky hillsides are often very good places for reptiles and large insects, and thus attract specialists such as Short-toed Eagles and shrikes.

Broad-leaved deciduous woodland

Deciduous forest is Europe's dominant habitat and often its richest in terms of species of birds. A high proportion of woodland birds has wide geographical ranges; among these are the most numerous species in Europe, the Chaffinch and the Great Tit.

At its best, a broad-leaved forest is multi-layered, with at least four strata going from bottom to top: the ground layer, the herb layer, the shrub layer and the canopy. Each has its own characteristic species. Where all the layers are present, as in open woodlands in which the regeneration of trees is natural, the bird diversity is greatest. Birds such as Woodcock favour the ground layer, Wrens and Robins inhabit the herb layer, Marsh Tits (the name is highly misleading) are often in the shrub layer and the Chiffchaff, Blue Tit and Lesser Spotted Woodpecker feed primarily in the canopy. Even within these layers the feeding opportunities are varied. Treecreepers, Nuthatches and woodpeckers search the bark at any level, for instance; various warblers glean leaves; and ground feeders may search the litter (Blackbird) or bare soil under shade (Nightingales). Other species catch flying insects in the canopy, be they Honey Buzzards or Spotted Flycatchers.

Of course, much of the character of a deciduous woodland is down to its component species of trees, and some are better for birds than others. Oaks are particularly rich, providing an exceptionally diverse invertebrate fauna. Beeches, with their thick foliage and poisoned ground layer, are less accommodating hosts.

It has been postulated that birds and flowering plants, including trees, have been evolving in concert since the early Tertiary period (about 50 million years ago). Unsurprisingly, interdependence is a common feature of deciduous woodland, with the result that a number of birds are strongly associated with certain types of tree: Jays with oaks, Hawfinches with wild cherry and hornbeam, and Redpolls with birch, for example. But in turn, trees require birds to spread their seeds, so everybody benefits.

Seeds, nuts, berries and other fruits are usually components of a woodland bird's autumn and winter diet. In the spring and summer invertebrates take over, and some woodland birds such as tits time their breeding seasons to coincide with the seasonal glut.

Coniferous woodland

Conifer forests are an extremely important part of Europe's landscape, making up the bulk of the taiga zone between 50° and 70°N and also cloaking many of Europe's mountainous areas up to the tree line. A healthy selection of species occurs in both departments (e.g. Tengmalm's Owl, Three-toed Woodpecker, Nutcracker); an equally significant number occur only in the taiga belt as defined by latitude (e.g. Pine Grosbeak, Siberian Tit, Waxwing); and only one, the endemic Citril Finch, is confined to mountain conifers. Some 32 of the taiga species are entirely restricted to conifers.

In general the bird population in coniferous woodland is lower than in broad-leaved woods. This is no doubt partly because of the latitude, but more importantly it is the result of the tree structure and relative paucity of tree species. As far as structure is concerned, the needles of conifers cast the ground in deep shade, restricting the growth of a field layer. Conifers also tend to be denser towards the canopy, leaving the lower strata rather bare of branches and leaves. For maximum diversity of birds there needs to be plenty of vegetation everywhere from the ground to the canopy, so coniferous woodland provides more sparing opportunities.

Woodland edge and scrub

Transitional vegetation between woodland and grassland is often called scrub. It consists of patches of shrubs up to about 5 m high interspersed with

The Capercaillie is mainly found in coniferous forests

grasses and open ground. A number of the birds of closed-canopy woodland (e.g. Bullfinch, Blackbird) occur in scrub as well, since the two habitats have much in common.

Scrub is a good habitat for birds, with strong invertebrate populations and often major concentrations of berry-bearing shrubs. The rich breeding population includes birds that forage principally among the bushes themselves, such as various warblers, plus birds that forage over the open areas nearby, including Yellowhammers and shrikes.

The density, height and other attributes of the scrub will often dictate what birds are present. Low scrub with tall herbs is good for the sun-loving Whitethroat, for instance, whilst taller scrub suits the more skulking Lesser Whitethroat. Barred Warblers appear to need clumps of vegetation at least 100 m long, and various birds are drawn to favoured bushes such as elders (Willow Tit in Britain), blackthorn or hawthorn.

Agricultural land

Farmland is one of the most important habitats in Europe and yet also one of the most diverse. There are hundreds of crops grown in Europe, and many sorts of livestock are kept, so there is no clear definition everywhere of what farmland actually is.

The best-known type of farmland is arable. Certain birds take to fields of crops better than others, but seed-eaters, which exploit both the grown crops and the 'weeds', are probably the most successful. Such birds include buntings (which feed mainly on grass seeds), Quails, partridges, pigeons, finches and larks. Livestock tend to require open grassy fields, and these are favoured by crows, wagtails and pipits; these birds, as well as Swallows, often utilise the swarms of insects that tend to surround cattle, horses and other animals. Waders such as Lapwings and Black-tailed Godwits use the wetter areas.

The breeding birds of farmland must, to some extent, follow the yearly working routine. Wood Pigeons alter their feeding habits in accordance with what crops are available at different times of year, and Skylarks have been known to change their breeding seasons around times of crop cutting. Many birds take advantage of ploughing and other disturbances in the ground. The harvest can be a boom period for seed-eating birds; the month of August is one the few times that House Sparrows move out of their territories to spend a few weeks on agricultural fields.

Gardens and urban landscapes

Throughout Europe a surprising number of birds have moved into that most extreme of man-made environments, the conurbation. Most are generalists that are adapted to woodland edge and have made the quick transition to suburban gardens – tits, Blackbirds and finches are examples. But there are some that are specialists, too. House Sparrows and Feral Pigeons, for example, do not occur in 'wild' habitats at all, but depend entirely on the presence of people.

Other city or town birds are drawn in by the buildings themselves. Such species as Swifts, Kestrels and Lesser Kestrels, House Martins and White Storks have found various types of buildings to their liking, usually because they are high above ground and inaccessible to predators. The Black Redstart, too, has adapted to some ruins and industrial sites because of their supposed resemblance to hilly terrain.

Rubbish tips are also an attraction, especially to gulls, crows and, in some parts of Europe, Black Kites. The provision of rubbish tips has changed the behaviour of some gulls in northwest Europe, bringing them inland to feed and, in some cases, even to breed.

The tit family (these are Blue Tits) are among the most enthusiastic visitors to artificial feeding sites in gardens

Watching birds

At its simplest, birdwatching means nothing more than watching birds. One of the hobby's major benefits is that it can be enjoyed wherever you are, which could mean in a lunch break, on a drive, in the street, in a garden or park, from a window or, of course, on a special trip for the purpose. It can also be interesting throughout the year, except perhaps in the dark Arctic winter. Birds are more or less everywhere – in deserts, on the sea, in cities and on mountain tops. They can break up the humdrum monotony of a day, by dint of being universal and yet unpredictable.

In common with any activity, birdwatching hones skills. You learn to use your eyes and ears. A major part of birdwatching, the identification of different species, is actually very difficult and can be frustrating at first. The secret, though, is to be thorough. The best bird identifiers are those that look (and listen) objectively: they observe first and ask questions later. When they watch a bird they note its features systematically and generally have a notebook to hand; they only refer to an identification guide afterwards. They learn quickly, and often on their own. The best birdwatchers are actually unusual people with special skills.

The rest of us learn by practice and determination. The slow but steady way to become a good bird identifier is to spend a great deal of time in the field and grow used to looking at birds. It's also useful to spend time immersed in identification books – an ideal way to wile away the hours of darkness when most birds are asleep! (For recommended websites and titles, see pages 22–23.) After a while you will develop a 'search image' for the species you know, and it is gained as follows. At first a new bird will perplex you. Look a few more times and you will learn its identification features, its 'field marks' – spots, streaks, a colourful rump and so on. After seeing it again you will begin to recognise it by the way it moves and behaves. Perhaps after years you will be able to identify it non-objectively and without effort. With experience, birdwatchers find that many species just look right and can be identified by a combination of shape and behaviour – and perhaps intuition – that is known in the hobby as 'jizz'. The bird's habitat, of course, will also prove to be a useful clue, and time spent in different habitats will introduce the birdwatcher to their typical inhabitants.

Time spent in the field can also lead one to learn about how birds can best be seen. For example, to the chagrin of many, birds are almost universally more active around dawn (especially) and dusk than at any other time of day, so the birdwatcher out early will always see the most birds. Light is important, too. Birds are difficult to identify in poor light, and silhouetted birds often look larger than they really are. Furthermore, if you are birdwatching, try to keep the sun behind you.

Birds are, of course, shy of people and instinctively flee even when they detect birdwatchers (they cannot discriminate). The most successful birdwatchers are quiet, talking only softly and moving around slowly; they will also tend to wear inconspicuous colours such as brown or green – red and yellow put the birds off. When you have a bird in sight, try to lift your binoculars up slowly, too, since sharp movements will often flush birds.

Not all birdwatchers are quiet in the field, and there is no law that demands that you should be; it will simply help you to see more birds. But in fact, you might find that you gain as much from being in the company of fellow enthusiasts as you do from watching birds. Birdwatching, as a rule, is well served by clubs and organisations, and being a member of a bird club is often a springboard to becoming involved in surveys and conservation work, if that is your thing. A list of the major birdwatching societies in the different European countries is given in the next section.

Once you are accustomed to birdwatching and have spent time learning to identify birds, you will hopefully begin to ask questions. Why is this bird here? What does it feed on? Why is it bowing its head? This is the sort of thinking that distinguishes the enthusiast. This book will hopefully answer some of those questions and, better still, provide plenty of fuel for that enthusiasm to grow and grow.

Conservation

There was a time when the activities of people undoubtedly increased the diversity of the birds of Europe. The continental hinterland was originally primarily forested, and the gradual fragmentation of the wildwood to make space for farmland and grazing land opened up opportunities for many bird species. In recent times, however, as humankind has spread over the continent and become the dominant force on the land, birds have, as a rule, been pushed out or otherwise harassed. Many have suffered large declines in population. Several, such as the Northern Bald Ibis (*Geronticus eremita*), have been lost as breeding species, although it is the subject of an ongoing reintroduction scheme. One, the Great Auk, as we have seen, has even become extinct.

Fortunately, in the last 50 years or so, people have begun to wake up and notice the effect of man's ravages upon the environment – and not a moment too soon. These pioneers have started to take measures to protect some of what remains and even to reverse some of the losses; and in so doing, their public profile has been greatly raised. Conservationists were once few in number and, although they have traditionally managed to punch far above their weight, they were, in the early days, encumbered by public and political apathy. But in recent years, thanks to tireless campaigning efforts by many conservation organisations, and greatly aided by an impressive tradition of representing wildlife well in film and print, conservationists have turned into Greens and have acquired notable political influence throughout the continent of Europe. The problems ahead are daunting, but it is now impossible to imagine our politicians ignoring environmental issues in the way that they once did.

What, though, are the threats that remain for our birds? Perhaps the greatest – and it has always been so – is still the wholesale loss of habitat. Where habitats are destroyed to make way for buildings, roads or industrial sites, the birds are driven out. Habitat destruction is an insidious menace because it usually happens on a small scale – environmentalists often win big battles – so that the habitat of even the most widespread bird can be whittled away until it is so fragmented as to be useless, or disappears altogether. Historically our marshland birds have often lost out in this way, and many sensitive species such as Great Bitterns and Spotted Crakes have had their ancient populations decimated.

Another major threat comes under the general term of pollution. When we hear this word we often imagine large-scale catastrophes, such as oil-tanker spills and industrial waste leaking into rivers. But again, the worst pollutants act by stealth. Fertilisers gradually seep into rivers and slowly strangle them; herbicides and pesticides gradually reduce the insect fauna of farmland and fields. It often takes years for the harmful effects of chemicals to become apparent.

Direct persecution is another problem but, generally, it is one trend that really is beginning to decline. Hunting and shooting are still major hobbies in many parts of Europe, but these days there is a climate of responsibility and regulation in many areas. And even in those countries where irresponsible and destructive shooting is endemic – such as Malta, Italy and parts of Spain and France – education is beginning to gain ground. May this continue until our migrant birds are safe in the skies.

A current live issue in conservation, which is related to pollution, is climate change. Potentially, this could cause more damage – or at least alteration in habitat and populations – than anything else. Particularly at threat are our specialist birds of the taiga and tundra, but who knows what else? We cannot entirely predict what will happen if Europe gets warmer, because it is such a complex issue. It is hard, though, not to be worried by the idea of the earth heating up by a process that is still out of control.

But we must not become too gloomy. As mentioned above, green issues are steadily gaining ground in the political arena, and there is cause to be optimistic about the fortunes of many European birds. The fact that virtually every European country now has National Parks, Nature Reserves and Protected Areas is to be celebrated, and so is the fact that a commitment to wildlife is enshrined in European Community laws and directives. Equally encouraging is that more and more people are studying birds and learning how best to conserve them.

It is particularly good to see that some of these measures are not just preserving birds and their surviving habitats, but are actually fighting back and gaining ground. In the last few years in Britain, the Royal Society for the Protection of Birds has been buying agricultural or commercial land to convert it into valuable habitat such as heathland or fenland, a reverse of hundreds of years of history. Special projects are also, Europe-wide, restoring lost species or consolidating their numbers by means of reintroduction schemes – Griffon Vultures in the Alps, Purple Gallinules in Mallorca, White-tailed Eagles in Scotland, Lesser White-fronted Geese in Fennoscandia and so on.

Another trend that is widespread and beneficial in Britain and increasing elsewhere is an interest in the birds of the garden. In industrialised countries the combined area covered by gardens is substantial and has the potential to provide refuge for a large number of birds.

Throughout Europe, though, it is often land use for farming that has the greatest effect of all on bird populations. In the West, intensification has created arable crops that are free of weeds and provide little habitat for birds; they are almost deserts. With the recent entry into the EU of countries with more traditional methods of farming (and more birds), it will be necessary to prevent the same thing happening there whilst at the same time enabling economic growth. This will be a huge challenge for politicians and lobby groups Europe-wide.

For more information on the conservation of European birds, please consult *Birds in Europe: Their Conservation Status* by Tucker, Heath, Tomialojc and Grimmett and *Important Bird Areas in Europe* by Heath, Evans, Hoccom et al (BirdLife International).

List of national organisations and websites

Albania
Albanian Society for the Protection and Preservation of Birds www.eeconet.org/eaf/albania

Andorra
Associacio per a la Defensa de la Natura, and@andorra.ad www.andorrasostenible.org

Austria
BirdLife Austria
birdlife@blackbox.at www.birdlife.at www.bird.at

Belarus
Akhova Ptushak Belarussi (APB)
apb-minsk@mail.ru. www.grsu.by/~zbtap
www.belarusguide.com

Belgium
BirdLife Belgium (BNVR-RNOB-BNVS)
www.natuurpunt.be www.rnob.be
www.protectiondesoiseaux.be

Bosnia-Herzegovina
Nase Ptice (Bosnia and Herzegovina Ornithology Society) naseptice@hotmail.com
www.zemaljskimusej.ba/english/natural_history.htm

Bulgaria
Eesti Ornitiliigiaühing (EOÜ)
bspb.hq@mb.bia-hg.com www.bspb.org
www.birdwatchingbulgaria.com

Croatia
Croatian Society for Bird and Nature Protection
jasmina@mahazu.hazu.hr

Czech Republic
Eeská Spoleènost Ornitologická (Czech Society for Ornithology) (CSO)
cso@birdlife.cz www.cso.cz www.birdlife.cz

Denmark
Dansk Ornitologisk Forening (DOF)
dof@dof.dk www.dof.dk

Estonia
Estonian Ornithological Society (EOU)
jaanus@linnu.tartu.ee www.eoy.ee

Finland
BirdLife SUOMI Finland
toamisto@birdlife.fi www.birdlife.fi
www.fmnh.helsinki.fi

France
Ligue pour la Protection des Oiseaux (LPO)
lpo@lpo-birdlife.asso.fr www.lpo.fr

Germany
Naturschutzbund Deutschland
Naturschutz.heute@NABU.de www.birdlife.de
www.do-g.de

Gibraltar
Gibraltar Ornithological and Natural History Society
gonhs@gibnet.gi www.gib.gi/gonhs

Greece
Hellenic Ornithological Society (HOS)
birdlife-gr@ath.forthnet.gr
www.ornithologiki.gr/en/enmain.htm

Hungary
Hungarian Ornithological and Nature Conservation Society (MME)
mme@c3.hu www.mme.hu

Iceland
Icelandic Society for the Protection of Birds
fuglavernd@simnet.is
www.fuglavernd.is/enska/home.html
www.ni.is/english

Ireland
BirdWatch Ireland
bird@indigo.ie www.birdwatchireland.ie

Italy
Lega Italiana Protezione Uccelli (LIPU)
lipusede@box1.tin.it www.lipu.it www.ciso-coi.org

Latvia
Latvijas Ornitologijas Biedriba (LOB)
putni@parks.lv www.lob.lv www.lza.lv/Zoo.htm

Liechtenstein
Botanish-Zoologische Gesellschaft
broggi@pingnet.li renat@pingnet.li

Lithuania
Lietuvos Ornitologu Draugija (LOD)
lod@birdlife.lt www.birdlife.lt

Luxembourg
Letzebuerger Natur Vulleschutzliga (LNVL)
secretary@luxnatur.lu www.luxnatur.lu

Macedonia
Bird Study and Protection Society of Macedonia
brankom@iunona.pmf.ukim.edu.mk

Malta
BirdLife Malta
info@birdlifemalta.org www.birdlifemalta.org

Netherlands
Vogelbescherming Nederland
birdlife@antenna.nl www.vogelbescherming.nl
www.dutchbirding.nl

Norway
Norsk Ornitologisk Forening
nof@birdlife.no www.folk.uio.no/csteel.nof

Poland
Polish Society for the Protection of Birds (OTOP)
office@otop.most.org.pl www.pto.most.org.pl

Portugal
Sociedade Portuguesa para o Estuda das Aves (SPEA)
spea@spea.pt www.spea.pt

Romania
Romanian Ornithological Society (SOR)
sorcj@codec.ro www.sor.ro

Russian Federation
Russian Bird Conservation Union (RBCU)
rbcu@online.ru www.rbcu.ru/union/en

Serbia and Montenegro
Liga za Ornitolosku akciju Srbije I Crne Gore
markorakovic@mail.com

Slovakia
Spolocnost Pre Ochranu Vtactva Na Solensku
sovs@chargenet.sk www.sovs.sk/eng_index.htm

Slovenia
Drustvo za Opazovanje in Proucevanje Ptic Slovenije (DOPPS) borut.mozetic@uni-lj.si www.ptice.org

Spain
Sociedad Espanola de Ornitologia (SEO)
asanchez@seo.org www.seo.org

Sweden
Sveriges Ornithologiska Forening (SOF)
birdlife@sofnet.org www.sofnet.org

Switzerland
Schweizer Vogelschutz (SVS)
svs@birdlife.ch www.birdlife.ch

Turkey
Dogal Hayati Koruna Dernegi (DHKD)
erdenoney@dhkd.org www.dhkd.org

Ukraine
Ukrainian Society for the Protection of Birds (USPB)
utop@iptelecom.net.ua www.utop.org.ua/eng

United Kingdom
Royal Society for the Protection of Birds (RSPB)
info@rspb.org.uk www.rspb.org.uk www.bto.org

Other useful websites
my.tele2.ee/birds (birds of eastern Europe)
www.fatbirder.com (general)
www.AERC.be/ (rarities)
www.euring.org/ (bird ringing)
www.ecnc.nl. (conservation)
www.guidedbirding.com (local guides)
www.birdforum.net (discussion, photographs and general)
www.birds-online.ch/ (general information)
www.megabytedata.com/MB064/ukbird.htm (bird names)
www.ornithomedia.com (general)
en.arocha.org (conservation)
www.birdlife.net (conservation)
www.ramsar.org (wetland conservation)
www.bl.uk/collections/sound-archive/wild.html (bird sounds)

Bibliography

Alerstam, Thomas. 1990. *Bird Migration.* Cambridge University Press.

Beaman, M. & Madge, S. 1998. *The Handbook of Bird Identification for Europe and the Western Palearctic.* Christopher Helm, London.

Berthold, Peter. 2001. *Bird Migration: A General Survey* (2nd edition). Oxford University Press.

Birkhead, T.R. 1991. *The Magpies.* T. & A.D. Poyser, London.

Brooke, M. 2004. *Albatrosses and Petrels across the World.* Oxford University Press.

Brown, L. 1976. *British Birds of Prey.* New Naturalist Series. William Collins, London.

Campbell, B. & Lack, E. (eds). 1985. *A Dictionary of Birds.* T. & A.D. Poyser, London.

Cannon, A. 1998. *Garden BirdWatch Handbook* (2nd edition). British Trust for Ornithology.

Coombes, F. 1978. *The Crows – a Study of the Corvids of Europe.* B.T. Batsford, London.

Couzens, D. 2003. *Birds by Behaviour.* HarperCollins, London.

Cramp, S. & Simmons, K.E.L. (eds). 1977–83. *Handbook of the Birds of Europe, the Middle East and North Africa: The Birds of the Western Palearctic, Vols 1–3.* Oxford University Press.

Cramp, S. (ed). 1985–92. *Handbook of the Birds of Europe, the Middle East and North Africa: The Birds of the Western Palearctic, Vols 4–6.* Oxford University Press.

Cramp, S. & Perrins, C.M. (eds). 1993–94. *Handbook of the Birds of Europe, the Middle East and North Africa: The Birds of the Western Palearctic, Vols 7–9.* Oxford University Press.

Cromack, H. and D. 2005. *The Birdwatcher's Yearbook.* Buckingham Press.

Davies, N.R. 1990. 'Dunnocks: cooperation and conflict among males and females in a variable mating system.' In Stacey, P.B. & Koenig, W.D. (eds) *Cooperative Breeding in Birds.* Cambridge University Press.

Del Hoyo, J., Elliott, A. & Sargatal, J. (eds). 1992–2001. *Handbook of the Birds of the World, Vols 1–7.* Lynx Edicions, Barcelona.

Del Hoyo, J., Elliott, A. & Christie, D.A. (eds). 2003–2004. *Handbook of the Birds of the World, Vols 8–9.* Lynx Edicions, Barcelona.

Ehrlich, P.R., Dobkin, D.S., Wheye, D. & Pimm, S.L. 1994. *The Birdwatcher's Handbook.* Oxford University Press.

Elphick, C., Dunning, J.B. (Jr) & Sibley, D. 2001. *The Sibley Guide to Bird Life and Behaviour.* Christopher Helm, London.

Ferguson-Lees, J. & Christie, D.A. 2001. *Raptors of the World.* Helm Identification Guides. Christopher Helm, London

Fjeldså, J. 2004. *The Grebes.* Oxford University Press.

Gaston, A.J. 2004. *Seabirds: A Natural History.* T. & A.D. Poyser, London.

Gibbons, D.W., Reid, J.B. & Chapman, R.A. (eds). 1993. *The New Atlas of Breeding Birds in Britain and Ireland: 1988–1991.* T. & A.D. Poyser, London.

Hagemeijer, W.J.M & Blair, M.J. (eds). 1997. *The EBCC Atlas of European Breeding Birds: Their Distribution and Abundance.* T. & A.D. Poyser, London.

Harrison, C.J.O. & Castell, P. 1998. *Collins Field Guide to Bird Nests, Eggs and Nestlings of Britain and Europe* (revised edition). HarperCollins, London.

Holden, P. & Cleeves, T. 2002. *The RSPB Handbook of British Birds.* Christopher Helm, London.

Michl, G. 2003. *A Birders' Guide to the Behaviour of European and North American Birds.* Gavia Science, Budapest.

Newton, I. 1972. *Finches.* New Naturalist Series, William Collins. London.

Ogilvie, M & Pearson, B. 1994. *Wildfowl.* Hamlyn Behaviour Guides. Hamlyn, London.

Olsen, K.M. & Larsson, H. 2004. *Gulls of Europe, Asia and North America.* Helm Identification Guides. Christopher Helm, London.

Perrins, C. 1979. *British Tits.* New Naturalist Series, William Collins. London.

Perrins, C. 1987. *Collins New Generation Guide: Birds of Britain and Europe.* William Collins, London.

Perrins, C. (ed). 2003. *The New Encyclopedia of Birds.* Oxford University Press.

Proctor, N.S. & Lynch, P.J. 1993. *Manual of Ornithology: Avian Structure and Function.* Yale University Press, Newhaven.

Shirihai, H., Gargallo, G., Helbig, A.J., Harris, A. & Cottridge, D. 2001. *Sylvia Warblers: Identification, Taxonomy and Phylogeny of the Genus* Sylvia. Helm Identification Guides. Christopher Helm, London.

Snow, B. & Snow, D. 1988. *Birds and Berries.* T. & A.D. Poyser, London.

Snow, D.W. & Perrins, C.M. (eds). 1998. *The Birds of the Western Palearctic,* concise edition (2 vols). Oxford University Press.

Svensson, L., Grant, P.J., Mullarney, K. & Zetterström, D. 2000. *Collins Bird Guide.* HarperCollins, London.

Turner, A. & Rose, C. 1994. *A Handbook to the Swallows and Martins of the World.* Christopher Helm, London.

Tyler, S.J. & Ormerod, S.J. 1994. *The Dippers.* T. & A.D. Poyser, London.

Wernham, C.V., Toms, M.P., Marchant, J.H., Clark, J.A., Siriwardena, G.M. & Baillie, S.R. (eds) 2002. *The Migration Atlas: Movements of the Birds of Britain and Ireland.* T. & A.D. Poyser, London.

Acknowledgements

Thanks are due to my wife Carolyn and children Emily and Samuel for putting up with me while writing such a long book. I adore them all for their love and vitality.

Thanks too to Dave Cottridge for being such an exceptional photographer and an energetic and dedicated photographic editor. His images make the book come alive. Thanks also to Norman Arlott for his artistic and accurate illustrations, which do the same.

I would like to thank my hard-working editor and manager, Helen Brocklehurst, for her professionalism, forbearance and attention to detail. The same applies to Caroline Taggart for editing such a long text so carefully and with such tact.

And many thanks are due to the designers at Smith & Gilmour for making such a great deal of information so easy on the eye.

Divers family *Gaviidae* (gah-**vee**-id-ee)

Habitat Breed on clear freshwater lakes in northern Europe; winter mainly on the sea.
Food Mainly fish caught during a dive from the surface. Also some crustaceans, molluscs and aquatic insects.
Movements Migratory, but most don't travel far, remaining within Europe. Arrive on breeding areas from April, leave from September.
Voice Loud, far-carrying, often very musical wails, yodels, coos, croaks and barks.
Pairing style Monogamous and probably pair for life.
Nesting Territorial and usually solitary, although Red-throated Diver pairs may cluster together on large lakes.

Nest Low pile of vegetation usually placed on the ground very close to water.
Productivity 1 brood a year.
Eggs Usually 2. One hatches 1–4 days later than the other.
Incubation 24–31 days, by both parents.
Young Precocial and downy.
Parenting style Both parents feed young.
Food to young Mainly fish.
Leaving nest Young leave nest when only 1–3 days old, then swim around themselves or ride on parents' backs for first 2 weeks. Finally fledge at 49–77 days, but parents continue feeding up to 3 months after this.

Plenty of birds catch their food by going underwater, but the four species of divers, as their name suggests, do it more impressively than most. On average one of their immersions lasts 45 seconds, compared with less than 30 seconds for a duck, for example. Divers can also descend deeper than most other submerging waterbirds, with 75 m having been recorded. They are fast and efficient predators of fish and may chase them for considerable distances below the surface.

Divers are powered by strong feet fitted with webs between the front three toes, and placed right at the rear of the body for efficient back-propulsion. Their eyes are specially adapted for seeing underwater, and their bills are dagger shaped for grabbing fish. The plumage of a diver is thick and its bones are dense to prevent it from being too buoyant in the water; indeed, divers ride unusually low when swimming. But despite all their aquatic adaptations divers are also strong, powerful fliers, well able to travel for long distances and at high altitude.

Having feet at the back of the body makes divers weak and vulnerable on land, so they rarely come to shore except when attending the nest. Even then, the low, flat structure they build is within ready reach of water, and the young waste little time between hatching and beginning their aquatic life.

Red-Throated Diver

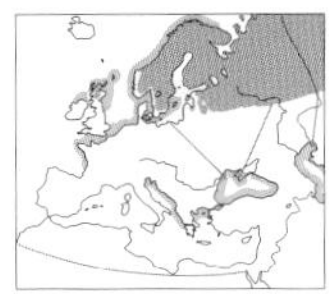

Black-throated Diver

Gavia arctica (gah-**vee**-a **ark**-tik-a)
length 58–73 cm; wingspan 1.1–1.3 m

ID: Larger and thicker-necked than Red-throated Diver; less heavy and big-headed than Great Northern. Fairly thick bill held horizontally. Black throat and stripy neck in breeding plumage. In non-breeding very black and white, with sharp division between the two; distinctive white patch on flanks.

Breeding at lower densities than the Red-throated Diver, the Black-throated is drawn to large, deep lakes with clear water, preferably in undisturbed places. Here a single pair usually holds sway, keeping all others at bay with loud calling. A Black-throated Diver won't tolerate a stranger within its line of sight, so if one appears it will approach with its neck held in a menacing snake-like curve, exposing the black throat – its version of the Red-throated Diver's alert posture. The rivals, including both members of the territorial pair, will then swim around in a 'circle dance', and after a while will begin dipping their bills into the water. This normally causes the stranger to flee, although fights, with much bill-stabbing and splashing, do sometimes occur.

Although the territorial displays are conspicuous and exciting to watch, the actual courtship between members of a pair is much less theatrical, involving the partners mutually bill-dipping, diving with a splash and swimming very fast underwater. But a feature of this part of the season is repeated copulation. This is performed on land at several favoured sites and may cause the vegetation to become worn down with use; such sites are known as 'false nests'.

Despite its territorial nature, outside the breeding season the Black-throated is more sociable than other divers, with small groups often spending the winter offshore.

Red-throated Diver

Gavia stellata (gah-**vee**-a stel-**lay**-ta)
length 53–69 cm; wingspan 1.1 m

The Red-throated Diver has the distinction of being both the smallest and much the commonest member of its family. It is also the only one that can take off from the water without a long run, and this allows it to live on smaller bodies of water than the others. In fact Red-throated Divers often breed beside small tundra pools and simply commute to larger lakes or the sea to catch food for themselves and their young. The larger divers tend to obtain what they need from their 'home' lake.

Red-throated Divers are highly territorial, but because several pairs may nest on one lake quite close together and meet up regularly, they have more complex territorial displays than others of the family. An intruder is met by either member of a pair swimming towards it and assuming an 'alert posture', with head held up and neck extended, red throat showing. This may lead into the 'snake ceremony', in which the couple swims side by side with half the body immersed and the bill pointing towards the water; all the while they call in duet, with wails of different pitches. If that doesn't drive off the visitor, both divers will rear up in the water together, necks extended skywards, feet paddling furiously. This display is usually performed in silence and, bizarrely, the intruder may join in.

ID: Smallest of group, swims with bill pointed slightly upwards. Reddish throat when breeding. In non-breeding plumage has more white about eye than other divers, and more white on neck.

Great Northern Diver

Gavia immer (gah-**vee**-a **im**-mer)
length 69–91 cm; wingspan 1.3–1.5 m

This is really a North American species, although it has a small outpost in Iceland, where about 300 pairs breed each year. Several thousand also winter at sea around the coasts of northwest Europe.

To breed successfully the Great Northern Diver needs large, undisturbed, deep lakes with a good population of fish. The fish don't necessarily need to be large; a length of 15–30 cm per catch is enough. There doesn't need to be much variety, either; a pair can sustain themselves and their young on just one fish species, so long as it is abundant. Diving conditions are also important on the home lake, because divers hunt by sight and need clear water. They often immerse the head and neck before a dive in a practice called 'snorkelling', checking whether any fish are within range.

The Great Northern Diver is famous for its territorial calls, which include a haunting tremolo wail, often heard, like many diver calls, in the depths of the night.

adult br.

adult non-br.

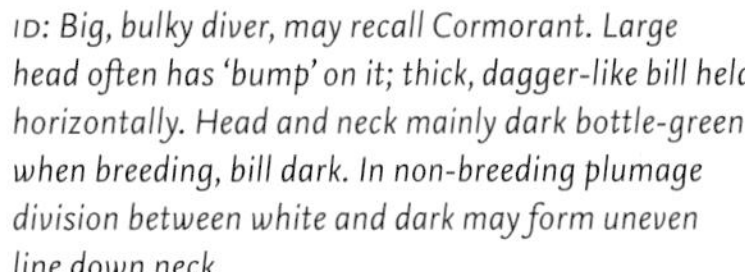

ID: Big, bulky diver, may recall Cormorant. Large head often has 'bump' on it; thick, dagger-like bill held horizontally. Head and neck mainly dark bottle-green when breeding, bill dark. In non-breeding plumage division between white and dark may form uneven line down neck.

White-billed Diver

Gavia adamsii (gah-**vee**-a a-**dams**-ee-eye)
length 76–91 cm; wingspan 1.4–1.5 m.

The occasional pair of White-billed Divers breeds from time to time in the extreme northeast of our region, in Russia, but this little-known High Arctic species is a peripheral bird in Europe. It summers every year in small numbers off the coast of Norway, and perhaps a few hundred regularly winter offshore in the North Sea as far south as the British Isles. It is the largest and bulkiest of the divers, breeding on lakes of any size surrounded by tundra, and also along rivers.

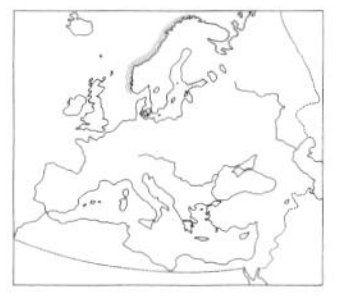

ID: Of similar size to Great Northern or larger; bill slightly uptilted and held pointing upwards. Plumages similar to Great Northern, although paler brown when not breeding. Bill always pale, not white but yellowish.

Grebes family *Podicipedidae* (pod-ee-si-**peed**-id-ee)

Habitat Lakes, rivers, marshes and other wetlands. In winter often found on the sea.
Food Fish and aquatic invertebrates and their larvae.
Movements Mainly migratory, although most species remain within Europe in winter, simply moving south.
Voice A variety of harsh and high-pitched sounds such as growls, braying, wailing and whinnying.
Pairing style Monogamous, usually pairing for one season.
Nesting Most species except the gregarious Black-necked are solitary and territorial, but all except Little Grebe may associate in loose colonies. Several species also nest among colonies of other birds such as gulls.
Nest A heap of waterweed or other vegetation, usually floating on the water and anchored to aquatic plants.
Productivity Normally 1 brood a year, but the Little Grebe regularly manages 2–3.
Eggs 2–6, usually 3–4.
Incubation 20–25 days, but 27–29 for the Great Crested Grebe. Both sexes contribute equally. The adults cover the eggs with nest material when taking a break. Eggs hatch asynchronously, so some chicks are older than others.
Young Youngsters hatch well formed and covered in down.
Parenting style Both parents bring food to the young.
Food to young Similar to adult food, but smaller items at first. The young are also fed large quantities of feathers, for reasons that are not yet fully understood.
Leaving nest The brood abandons the nest once the last egg has hatched; the young then ride on the parents' backs for the first 10 days or so. They become fully feathered by 44–79 days, but may still be fed for some time thereafter.

At first sight grebes could be mistaken for ducks, since they often share the same habitat. But grebes have pointed, not flattened bills and they almost completely lack a tail. Their legs and feet are also unique to the family; each of the toes is independent and lobed, not webbed to one another as in most waterbirds, and the legs are set right at the rear of the body for back-propulsion. The ankle joints allow for considerable movement about them, helping the grebe to make sharp turns under the water.

In common with divers, grebes have streamlined bodies and dense bones, allowing for efficient diving from the surface. The larger species chase after fish, but most of the others take smaller, slower-moving items such as aquatic insects and their larvae. In contrast to divers, grebes are rather poor fliers, moving along with very rapid, almost panicky wingbeats.

Grebes have unusually dense feathering, giving them good insulation and waterproofing; a large species such as the Great Crested Grebe may have 20,000 feathers, almost as many as a swan. These feathers are moulted almost continuously, allowing grebes to do an astonishing thing, unique to the family: eat them. It is not fully understood why they do this, but it has been suggested that feathers, once ingested, make a soft paste in which sharp fish bones can be wrapped up prior to expulsion as pellets. The feather 'plug' may also prevent parasites reaching the intestine.

In the breeding season grebes acquire smart, colourful plumage, often augmented by fine head plumes. These play a part in the grebes' spectacular courtship displays, each one unique to the species.

ID: Tiny grebe, often looking fluffy at the rear. Distinctive in breeding plumage, with chestnut neck and yellow-green gape. In winter black and brown, rather than black and white, with short neck and pale bill.

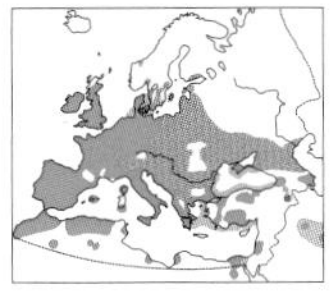

adult br.

adult non-br.

chick

Little Grebe

Tachybaptus ruficollis
(tak-ee-**bap**-tuss roof-ee-**koll**-liss)
length 25–29 cm

It's easy to overlook the Little Grebe, the smallest member of its family in Europe. It is highly adept at concealment, both by disappearing among the masses of shoots and leaves of aquatic plants, and by its habit of diving repeatedly with very brief visits to the surface. In common with other grebes it can expel air trapped between its feathers ('sleeking') and also empty its air sacs; both reduce its buoyancy, allowing it to surface at times with just its head and neck peeping above water, a bit like a submarine.

The smallest pools and ditches can support a pair of Little Grebes, so long as there is plenty of thick floating and fringing vegetation. These birds dive only to a depth of 1 m or so, scouring the mud and shallows for insects and their larvae, crustaceans and some small vertebrates, including fish. They also eat more snails and other molluscs than any other member of the family.

Pairs will sometimes occupy a small territory all year. They maintain the pair bond with a subtle display in which both sexes adopt a hunched posture and give tittering, whinnying calls. Other, more elaborate displays take place in the breeding season, including mutual presentation of weed – but these are often hidden from view.

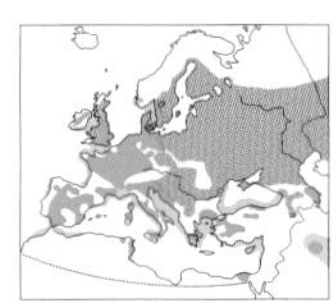

ID: *Largest grebe and most angular; long, narrow, pink bill. Distinctive in breeding plumage. In winter whitest grebe, and the only one showing white between eye and crown.*

Great Crested Grebe

Podiceps cristatus (**pod**-ee-seps kriss-**stay**-tuss)
length 46–51 cm, including neck; wingspan 59–73 cm

This is the largest of the European grebes, with the lengthiest neck and the longest, most dagger-like bill. Such a design is the mark of a confirmed fish-eater, and indeed Great Crested Grebes, in contrast to other grebes, catch many more fish than invertebrates. They take a wide range, too, from 3-cm-long sticklebacks to eels exceeding 20 cm. The Great Crested Grebe always requires plenty of open water for its underwater chases, so this limits it to less waterweed-clogged lakes than those beloved by other grebes. Often just a little fringing vegetation is enough – and that serves as an anchor for the nest.

Being open-water birds, Great Crested Grebes are easy to observe, and their spectacular water courtship formed the subject of one of the earliest in-depth studies of bird behaviour. The most common manoeuvre is 'head shaking', in which the members of a pair face each other and shake their heads from side to side; this may be interrupted by a quick ceremonial 'habit preen', in which the birds may shape as if to preen the feathers on their back, but merely ruffle them. Such motions may lead into more elaborate displays such as the weed ceremony, in which both sexes dive for weed, then swim rapidly towards each other and meet breast to breast, rearing up out of the water and shaking their heads from side to side, still holding the weed.

The Great Crested Grebe has a very long breeding season, with eggs recorded as early as February and young seen as late as October. At least one nest is built, although subsidiary platforms may be constructed for other purposes, including copulation. The young, stripy in pattern like old-time convicts, are perfectly able to swim as soon as they hatch, but for safety and warmth prefer to cling to either parent's back, fitting in between the wings. They might even hold on like this during an adult's dive.

Although newly hatched young will often be fed by one parent while resting on the other's back, a feature of later parenting is not teamwork but 'brood splitting', in which each parent takes sole custody of its allotted part of the brood, ignoring the others. Occasionally older chicks from an earlier brood will also join in the feeding of young, aiding the efforts of either parent.

Red-necked Grebe

Podiceps grisegena (**pod**-ee-seps griss-si-**jeen**-na)
length 40–50 cm

Although the Red-necked Grebe is quite a large species with a powerful, dagger-like bill, it is much less of a fish-eater than the Great Crested or even the Slavonian Grebe. Instead, at least in the breeding season, it tends to make do with feeding on aquatic invertebrates and their larvae.

More secretive than most other grebes, the Red-necked often conceals its floating nest deep in the vegetation. Sometimes, though, it will build near Coot nests, benefiting from these birds' aggression. It can be highly aggressive itself, too, and has been known to kill ducks in a fit of territorial pique.

In spring and summer the Red-necked Grebe performs eye-catching courtship displays on the water, including the 'penguin dance', in which the partners rear up breast to breast and may fence each other with their bills. But what sets it apart from other grebes in the breeding season is its extraordinary vociferousness. Some call sequences continue for 60 consecutive notes.

adult non-br.

chick

ID: *Only slightly smaller than Great Crested, but appearance recalls Slavonian or Black-necked Grebe; bill shorter and blunter than Great Crested's, yellow and black. More dusky than Great Crested in non-breeding, with grey cheek and little white on neck.*

Black-necked Grebe

Podiceps nigricollis (**pod**-ee-seps nig-rik-**koll**-iss)
length 28–34 cm

This is a bird of small, shallow, very productive and highly vegetated lakes. When diving it tends not to range far, instead searching among the submerged vegetation. It is adapted to capturing the tiniest prey and subsists mainly on insects.

It is highly sociable, tending to remain in small but close-knit groups in the winter. It also breeds in colonies, which may be substantial, and are often found within groups of other bird species, especially gulls and terns. Black-necked Grebes often breed at ephemeral sites such as floodlands.

Courtship displays include a 'penguin dance' routine like that of a Great Crested Grebe, but without carrying weed. In common with other grebes, the young frequently hatch within 30 minutes of first chipping through the egg, possibly as an adaptation to prevent drowning in the wet nest cup.

adult br.

chick

adult non-br.

ID: *Small grebe with very rounded head and short, slightly uptilted bill. In breeding plumage has golden, fan-shaped 'ears'. In non-breeding very black and white, but with dusky 'cheeks' reducing contrast between crown and side of head.*

Slavonian Grebe

Podiceps auritus (**pod**-ee-seps awr-**eye**-tuss)
length 31–38 cm; wingspan 46–55 cm

Small but dynamic, the Slavonian Grebe is a powerful underwater swimmer, with a top speed of 1 m per second when pursuing fish. It can also stay under for a long time – at least a minute – sometimes catching impressively large prey items in the process.

A pool occupied by a pair of these birds is the scene of some spectacular courtship in spring, especially the so-called 'weed rush'. Each of the pair dives to collect weed in its bill; the two then rise up out of the water, breast to breast, turn away from each other and rush across the water surface, side by side, the weed still dangling from their bills. This extraordinary feat may be repeated up to 15 times in succession.

adult br.

chick

adult non-br.

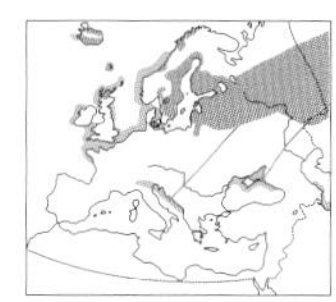

ID: *Small grebe with flattish head and straight bill. In breeding plumage has golden 'horns' on head. Very black and white in non-breeding, with clean demarcation between white cheeks and black crown; bill has white tip.*

Fulmars and Shearwaters family *Procellariidae* (pro-sel-lar-**ee**-id-ee) and Storm Petrels family *Hydrobatidae* (hie-dro-**bayt**-id-ee)

Habitat Much of the year on the open ocean, often far from land. Come ashore to breed, usually on cliffs or islands.
Food Fish, squid and crustacea (both groups); offal (shearwaters and Fulmar); plankton (storm petrels). At least some food is probably detected by smell.
Movements All migratory, leaving breeding colonies in late summer and sometimes travelling enormous distances across the oceans.
Voice Not musical, but often loud wails, growls and coos; storm petrels make purring sounds. Female shearwaters often have lower-pitched calls than males.
Pairing style Monogamous and probably pair for life, partners meeting up each year at nest site.
Nesting All colonial.
Nest Fulmars occupy an open ledge; shearwaters and storm petrels use burrows, which they may dig themselves. Minimal nest material.
Productivity 1 brood a year. Some pairs appear sometimes to take a 'sabbatical', not breeding at all in certain years.
Eggs 1.
Incubation 43–60 days in Fulmars and shearwaters; 40–50 in storm petrels. By both parents in long shifts.
Young Nest-bound chick hatches with eyes open and covered with thick down.
Parenting style Young brooded for first few days, then left alone while adults find food for it.
Food to young A mixture of partly digested adult food and stomach oil, regurgitated.
Leaving nest Shearwaters and Fulmars fledge at 43–97 days, storm petrels at 59–73 days. Food deliveries decrease before fledging; shearwaters may actually abandon chick to leave the nest itself. Young depart alone at night.

The species in these families spend most of the year far out in the open ocean, making them amongst the most difficult European birds to see. They do come to land to breed, but only to steep cliffs, remote headlands and offshore islands – sites where there are few or no ground predators. Even here the majority of species visit their nests only under cover of darkness. Outside the breeding season a few individuals may be glimpsed from land, but usually only when storm driven; such views tend to be brief and distant. If a birdwatcher wants to see a shearwater or a storm petrel in particular, the only answer is to meet them on their own terms, out over deep water.

Being confined to salt water, Fulmars, shearwaters and storm petrels must obtain their fluids from the sea, either directly by drinking or indirectly through their prey. All have well-developed salt glands above the bill that serve to freshen the body fluids, and the waste from this process passes down horny tubes on top of the bill. These tubes also encase the nostrils, and they can be seen clearly even from a distance, giving rise to an apt nickname for the families – 'tube noses'. The birds also have a good sense of smell, much better than that of most birds; they almost certainly use it for detecting prey on the high seas, perhaps following a scent gradient to home in on food.

Fulmars and shearwaters are medium-sized to large, up to the bulk of a large gull, and they all have wings with a high 'aspect ratio' – in other words, much longer than broad. This helps the birds to travel long distances over the sea, flapping then gliding in turn, while expending little energy, appropriating that of wind and wave instead – the term 'shearwater' refers to the way the bird skims just over the surface, wings rigid, playing the updrafts. Shearwaters have been known to travel 15,000 km on a single trip just to find food for the young.

Although shearwaters sometimes lunge into the sea while airborne, they usually seize their food – fish, squid or offal – while swimming on the surface. They will also dive underwater, using their wings for propulsion, and pursue prey there.

Storm petrels are the smallest seabirds of all, some no bigger than a sparrow, yet they are truly oceanic. Somehow they can cope with high winds and storms, despite their weak-looking, fluttering flight. In contrast to shearwaters, storm petrels obtain almost all their food while airborne, dipping down to the water surface to snatch minute fish and planktonic crustacea. They may patter the water with their feet, probably to maintain position above their prey, but possibly also to attract prey, or to disturb it so that it becomes more visible. It is thought that some storm petrels commonly feed during the hours of darkness, when their chosen prey comes closer to the water surface.

Northern Fulmar

ID: Gull-like seabird, but without relaxed flight of gull – instead stiff wingbeats and wings held rigidly out. Mainly grey with very white head and underparts, but these features both lacking in Arctic forms known as 'Blue Fulmars'.

Fulmar

Fulmarus glacialis (fool-**mar**-uss glay-si-**ay**-liss)
length 45–50 cm; wingspan 1–1.1 m

Several facets of the Fulmar's life set it apart from the rest of its family, not least that it breeds on open ledges on cliffs, not in burrows, and attends the nest site by day as well as by night. Its secret lies partly in its unprepossessing way of dealing with potential predators: if they get too close, the Fulmar spits foul-smelling stomach oil at them. Such a concoction can damage the plumage of a bird predator and, as far as humans are concerned, the smell can remain for days.

The Fulmar also breeds much further north than any other member of its family, from 50°N into the heart of the Arctic, as far as the polar pack-ice. The rich waters at these latitudes provide breeding Fulmars with plenty of squid, fish and plankton, which they seize from the surface of the water while swimming. The Fulmar's broad, heavy bill is also well adapted to dealing with offal and pulling flesh from carcasses, including those of whales, seals and walruses.

A taste for dead meat has enabled the Fulmar to prosper from some of man's commercial activities, including whaling in former times, and fishing. Large flocks of these grey and white birds are a common sight as they jostle over fish thrown out from trawlers, cackling like witches at a coven. Such sources of ready food have enabled the Fulmar's range and population to expand greatly for the last 200 years.

Fulmars are long-lived birds, with an annual survival rate of about 90 per cent, which is actually about standard for the family as a whole. Undoubtedly some individuals can attain the age of 50. With such a lifespan Fulmars can delay breeding until they are about eight years old, but some individuals have held out until they were twelve.

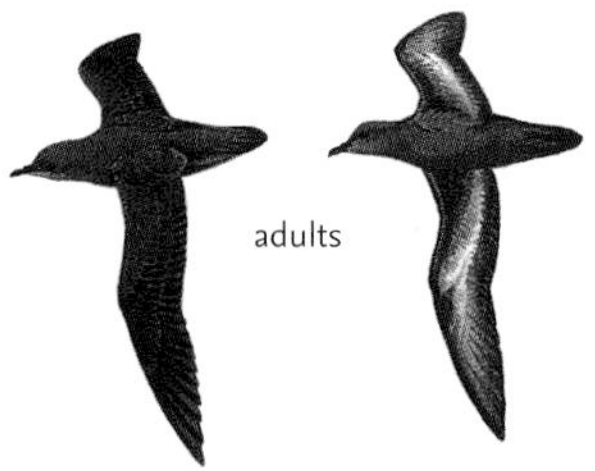

Sooty Shearwater

Puffinus griseus (puff-**eye**-nuss griss-**eh**-uss)
length 40–51 cm; wingspan 90–110 cm

The fact that the Sooty Shearwater is ever seen in Europe is extraordinary, for its nearest breeding colonies are no less than 10,000 km away, deep down in the South Atlantic Ocean. Yet it visits us annually, taking our waters in as part of a gigantic transequatorial feeding loop that it follows after breeding. The birds finish their nuptials each March and then stream northwards, passing first along the coast of South America, then that of North America, eventually arriving in the northwest Atlantic off New England and Newfoundland by June. A few weeks later they head east, using the prevailing westerly winds, and pass by our coasts in July and August, before heading south once again. On this long journey they eat cephalopods, crustaceans and fish, seizing these while swimming on the surface, or during a dive that may be as deep as 67 m.

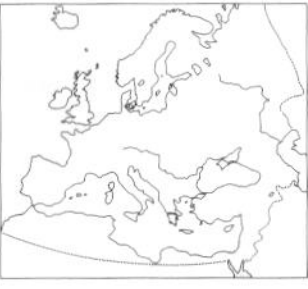

ID: Larger and longer-winged than Manx or Balearic Shearwater. Uniformly brown on whole of plumage; underside of wing often has silvery streak.

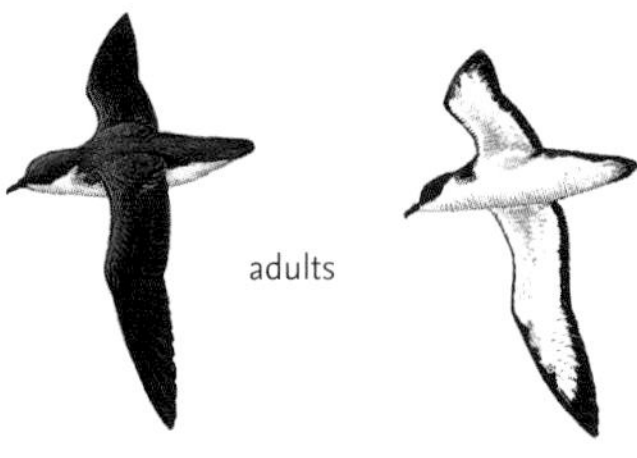

ID: Small shearwater with stiff-winged flight. Strikingly dark above, white below.

MAP: Manx only shown

Manx Shearwater

Puffinus puffinus (puff-**eye**-nuss puff-**eye**-nuss)
length 31–36 cm; wingspan 76–88 cm

This small, smart, black and white shearwater follows huge shoals of little fish, such as herrings and sprats, and catches them by plunging into the water from a modest height or by pursuing them in an underwater dive. In contrast to some shearwaters, it tends to do this in quite small parties, and often during the day.

Manx Shearwaters return to their flat-topped island breeding sites every March, and here the male and female meet again in their burrow after spending the winter apart. But newly formed pairs have the task of first finding their own burrow or digging one for themselves in the soft, grassy soil. Some pairs share theirs with rabbits or Puffins, although they obviously use separate chambers of the same burrow system. Once these preliminaries are over, the female goes out to sea again for a week or two to feed up and get into breeding condition.

These vulnerable seabirds come in and out of their nest sites only at night, so that they avoid the dangerous presence of gulls and other potential predators. If the other adult or the chick is in the burrow, they will find it by hearing its voice, but there is also evidence that each nest site has its own distinctive smell, so the bird literally follows its nose in the darkness.

Once breeding is over, Manx Shearwaters leave colony and island behind and travel right away from Europe, eventually finding their way to the east coast of South America, almost to the fringe of the Antarctic. The feeding is rich here and allows most of the birds to survive and return again the following spring.

Two newly recognised species, the Balearic Shearwater (*Puffinus mauretanicus*) and the Yelkouan Shearwater (*Puffinus yelkouan*), were once considered subspecies of the Manx and later lumped together under the umbrella term 'Mediterranean Shearwater'. The Balearic, as the name suggests, breeds in the Balearic Islands, with a world population of only about 5000 pairs. The Yelkouan breeds on rocky coastlines and islands from the south of France to the Aegean Sea and Crete. In appearance, it resembles the Manx Shearwater more closely than the larger Balearic.

Cory's Shearwater

Calonectris diomedea

(kah-loh-**nek**-triss die-oh-mi-**dee**-a)

length 45–46 cm; wingspan 1–1.2 m

Many of the important events in the Cory's Shearwater's life happen at night. This is the time when it usually feeds, snatching fish and squid while swimming, diving or in a quick plunge from flight. Night is also the time when breeding adults attend their colonies on rocky islands. They gather in huge flocks at dusk and then fly under cover of darkness to their burrows among boulder fields or soil. While gathering they make remarkable sobbing wails, but as soon as they reach their holes they fall silent.

Like other shearwaters, the Cory's is left alone in the burrow once it is about a week old and can regulate its body temperature; this allows both parents to find food for it. It soon fattens up until it is much heavier than the adult birds. Towards the end of its fledging period the parents bring less and less food, and may eventually abandon the youngster altogether. By then it is ready to depart on its first flight, alone and at night.

This is a large, powerful shearwater, at ease with strong winds and heavy waves. After breeding in late October, it travels rapidly south to winter in the South Atlantic and Indian Oceans. At this and other times it often makes a habit of following the movements of predatory fish or dolphins, mopping up the prey species as they flee.

ID: Large, stiff-winged shearwater with distinctive black cap; also variable small blotches on underside.

adults

Great Shearwater

Puffinus gravis (puff-**eye**-nuss **grah**-viss)

length 43–51 cm; wingspan 1–1.2 m

The journeys of this big, powerful shearwater mirror those of the Sooty Shearwater: breeding in Tristan da Cunha (where there are 5 million pairs), Gough Island and the Falklands, the birds leave the South Atlantic in April, first heading north to the east coast of the USA and Canada, then east across the North Atlantic towards Europe. Although sometimes abundant in our waters, Great Shearwaters are much less likely to be seen from land than are Sooties.

These are quite sociable birds, with a tendency to loaf on the sea in large parties. They feed on cephalopods and fish, obtaining what they need by surface seizing and diving underwater. They will follow the activities of whales and dolphins to take advantage of fleeing fish, and they will also scavenge near trawlers. In contrast to Sooty Shearwaters, they regularly follow ships.

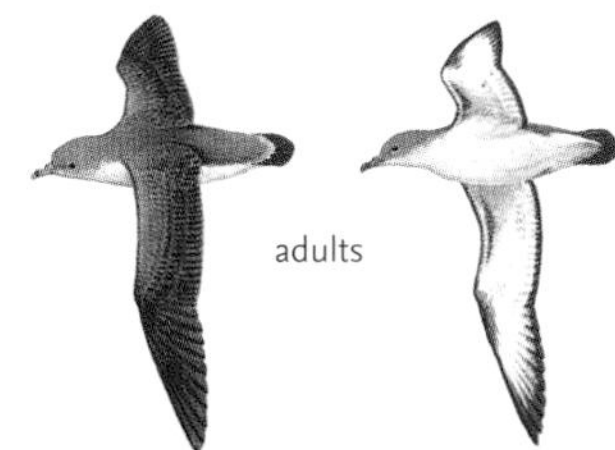

adults

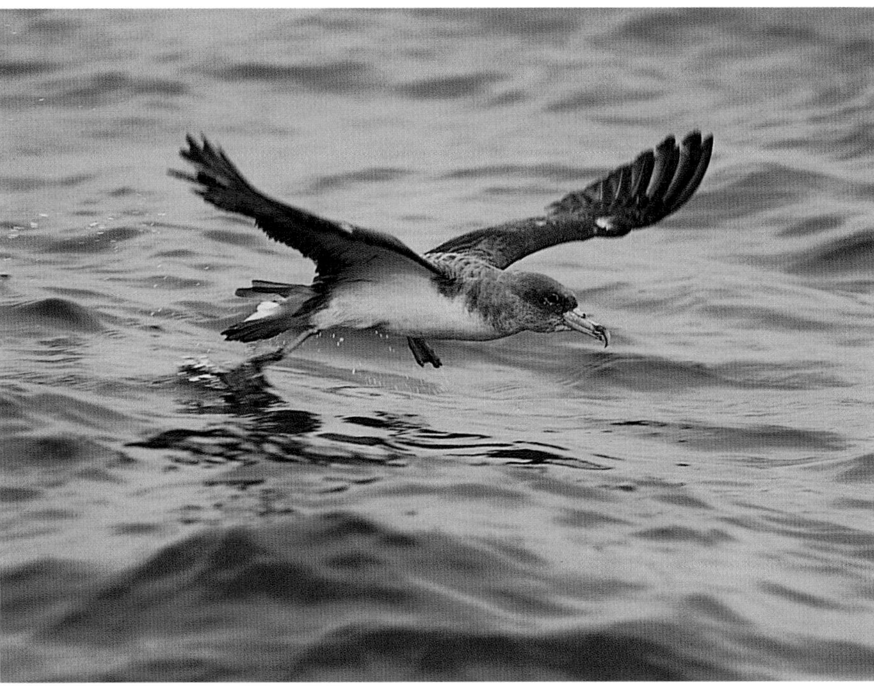

ID: Of similar size to Great Shearwater but with more languid, gull-like flight and bowed wings. Lacks black cap and has yellow, not black bill; also clean white on underside.

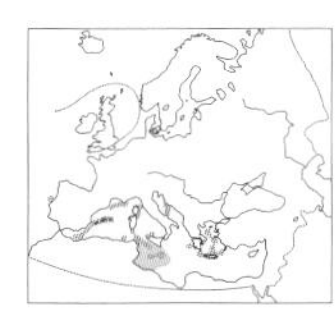

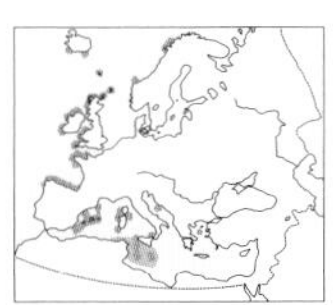

European Storm-Petrel

Hydrobates pelagicus

(hie-dro-**bay**-teez pel-**lah**-ji-kuss)

length 14–18 cm; wingspan 36–39 cm

ID: Small storm petrel with whirring, erratic, bat-like flight. White band under wing, square tail.

In the breeding season European Storm-Petrels are found on rocky islands or promontories, where they nest in crevices between boulders, under rocks or even in stone walls. Sometimes they choose burrows in the soil instead and may dig these themselves. European Storm-Petrel colonies are sociable places; the birds often nest close together, even in the same rock fissure. At night, the air may be filled with loud purring calls as they perform display circuits low over their breeding sites, usually in pairs.

Where possible, pairs meet up every year to breed. They lay a single egg that may weigh a quarter of the female's weight. Unsurprisingly, the male tends to take the first incubation shift to give the female time to recover from egg production; he may stay put for as long as six days. Although youngsters are fed by both parents and soon exceed them in weight, they are never abandoned or starved out of their burrows, as can be the case among some species of shearwater.

The European Storm-Petrel lives at sea outside the breeding season, and most of our birds travel to the coast of South Africa. While feeding they patter on the water surface, often with their wings far above their backs, holding position.

adults

Leach's Storm-Petrel

Oceanodroma leucorhoa

(oh-shan-oh-**droh**-ma loo-koh-**roh**-a)

length 19–22 cm; wingspan 45–48 cm

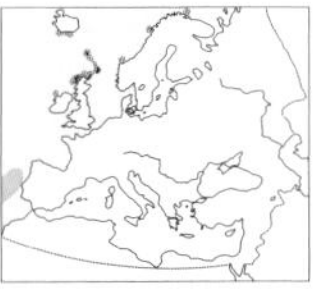

ID: Larger and longer-winged than European, with slower and deeper wingbeats; no white band under wing, but pale band on upper surface. White rump appears partially divided by dark streak.

Several hundred thousand pairs of Leach's Storm-Petrels breed in Europe, but their colonies are all on remote oceanic islands. Moreover, the birds visit their self-dug burrows only at night and are present only for the short summer season, so few birdwatchers ever see a Leach's Petrel unless one is blown towards the coast in autumn by a violent Atlantic storm, or their paths cross on the ocean.

Leach's Storm-Petrels are the largest of their family in Europe, although that is not saying much. They have longer wings than the others and are somewhat more aerial, manoeuvring expertly to snatch tiny fish or plankton from the water and less often pattering their feet on the surface.

adults

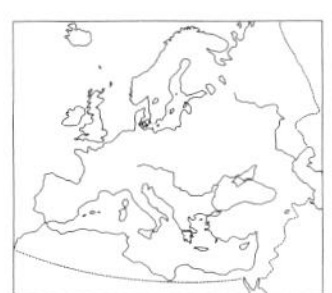

ID: Like Leach's but with more uniform upper wing, and more white on sides of rump.

Wilson's Storm-Petrel

Oceanites oceanicus

(oh-shan-**eye**-teez oh-**shah**-ni-kuss)

length 15–19 cm; wingspan 38–42 cm

ID: Similar to European Storm-Petrel but lacks white under the wing; pale streak on upper surface, like Leach's. Longer legs than other storm petrels, sticking out beyond tail.

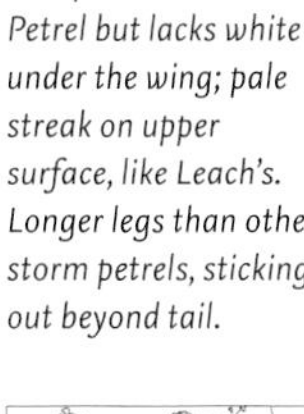

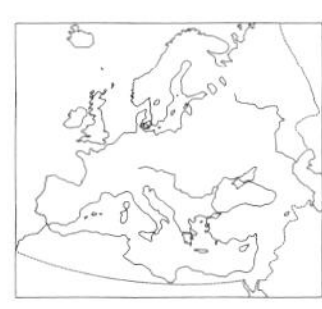

Although perhaps the most abundant seabird in the world, forming enormous colonies in Antarctica, the Wilson's Storm-Petrel was once considered a freak rarity in European waters. But recently birdwatchers making pelagic trips into the aptly named 'Wilson's Triangle' off southwestern Britain have discovered it to be a regular if rare visitor to the eastern Atlantic in late summer, and subsequently it has been found from Ireland to Portugal.

The Wilson's Storm-Petrel uses its feet more than other storm petrels to help it feed. It both patters its feet on the surface and appears to 'walk', holding position over food. It has yellow webs between its toes which may play a part in flushing food into view or perhaps even attracting it within reach.

Madeiran Storm-Petrel

Oceanodroma castro

(oh-shan-oh-**droh**-ma **kah**-stroh)

length 19–21 cm; wingspan 44–46 cm

There are only two small colonies of this seabird in Europe, both on uninhabited rocky islands off the coast of Portugal. Currently they number only 200-400 pairs between them, making the Madeiran Storm-Petrel one of Europe's rarest breeding birds. For most of its life this is a species of deep ocean waters and is seldom recorded by birdwatchers, partly because it is difficult to distinguish from other storm petrels and partly because individual birds are solitary, dispersing over a large area. The birds feed on fish, small crustaceans and squid, the capture of food being aided by the spiny tongue and palate.

In some parts of its range this species operates a unique shift system, with two separate populations breeding in exactly the same place, but six months apart.

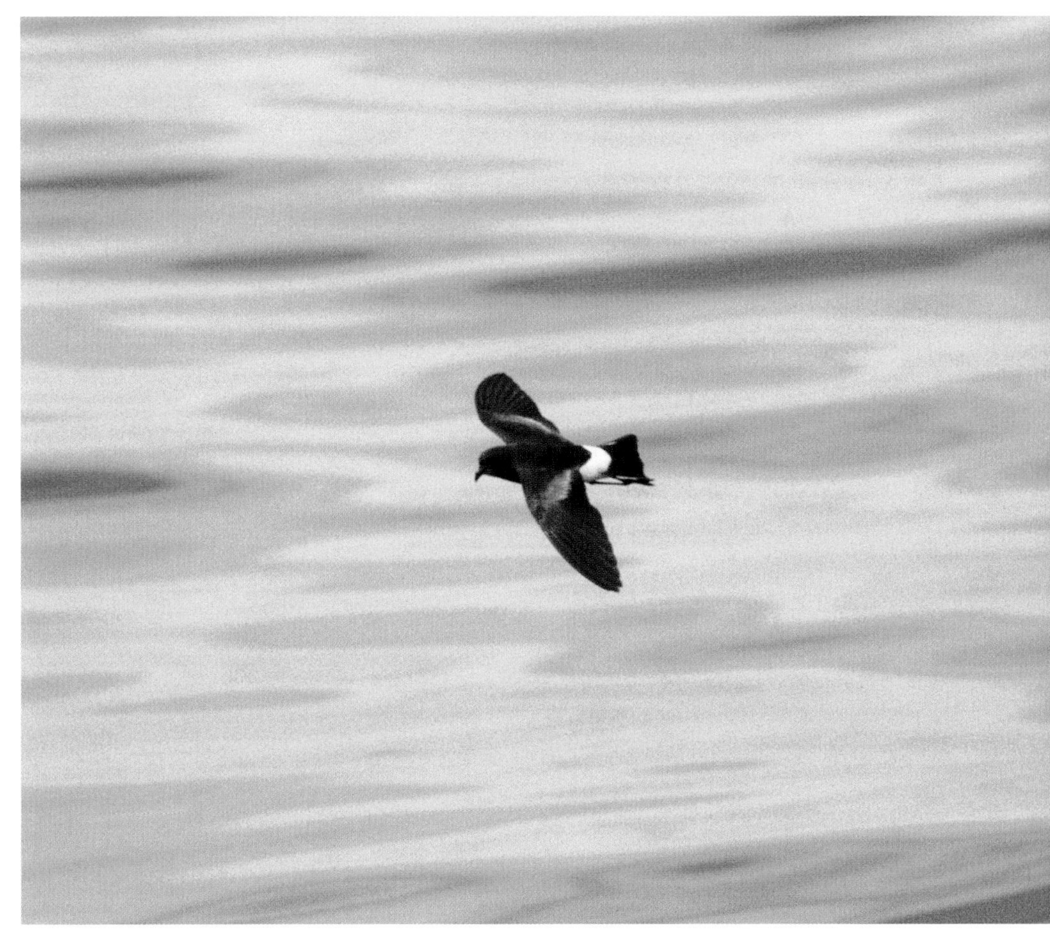

Northern Gannet *Sula bassana* (soo-la bas-san-a) family *Sulidae* (soo-lid-ee)

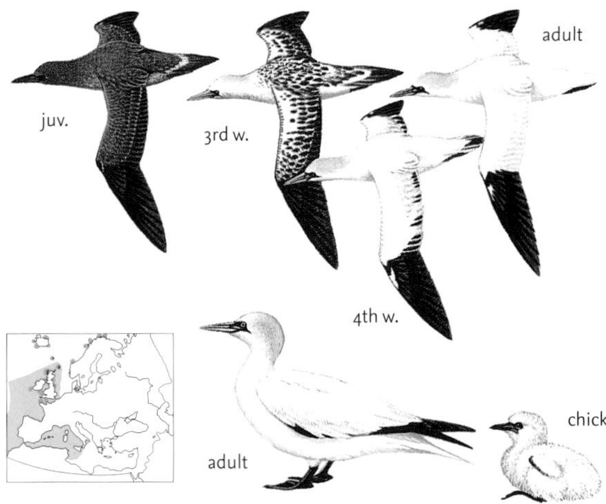

length 87–100 cm; wingspan 1.6–1.8 m
ID: *Largest seabird in Europe; adult unmistakable. Immature stages start brown, mottled in second year, adult plumage by fourth. With long, pointed wings and low, flapping and gliding flight over the waves, immatures may be mistaken for large shearwaters at a distance.*

Habitat Breeds on islands and sea stacks or cliffs. Winters at sea, mainly in shallow water above continental shelf.
Food Mainly fish, obtained in spectacular plunge dive.
Movements Partially migratory. Most attend breeding areas from January to about October. First-years and some adults disperse south to West African waters for winter, the former up to 5000 km, and the first-years may not come all the way back in the subsequent breeding season.
Voice A rumbling honking heard mainly at the colony.
Pairing style Monogamous and pair for life, renewing pair bond each year.
Nesting In large, densely packed colonies, from a handful to about 60,000 pairs.
Nest Large pile of seaweed, grass, feathers and earth, bound together with birds' excreta.
Productivity 1 brood a year.
Eggs 1.
Incubation 42–46 days, by both parents, under their feet.
Young Nest-bound and naked at first, but down acquired in first week.
Parenting style Both parents feed young by regurgitation, often travelling 150–200 km in a single trip, and occasionally 600 km.
Food to young Mainly fish.
Leaving nest Fledges at 84–97 days, having been left by the parents about 10 days previously. The newly fledged juveniles take to the sea alone and swim for their first few weeks, dispersing up to 72 km until they can fly.

The Northern Gannet is a truly spectacular bird, big, powerful and at home in the stormy waters of the North Atlantic. It is totally unmistakable to look at, with brilliant white plumage offset by smart black wing tips and a butterscotch-yellow head, a colour combination that makes it readily visible above the waves, even at great distance in the murk. Its distinctive flight profile – low over the water, with a series of flaps followed by a long glide – also makes it easy to identify. And when a Gannet begins feeding, any doubt about its identity soon disappears, even if the observed bird is a mere speck on the horizon.

That's because Gannets catch their food in a distinctive and lavish style. They are fish-eaters, like many a seabird, but have eschewed the majority method of submerging from the surface in favour of a more dramatic approach – a headlong plunge from high above the waves. They soar into the air to a height of 10–40 m, stall for a moment and then, with wings closed, plummet into the sea. They hit the water with a splash and their momentum takes them down a metre or two underwater, where hopefully the shoal of fish they had spied from above will still be swimming. With flaps of their wings and kicks of their fully webbed feet, they will grab a fish up to 30 cm long in their saw-edged bill before rising again to the surface.

Plunge-diving is quite a specialised pursuit, and the Gannet shows several adaptations for it. Its eyes are relatively forward-facing, giving it overlapping (binocular) vision, necessary for judging distance before taking the plunge. It also has nostrils that open inside, not outside, the bill – literally to prevent water rushing up its nose! And it is fitted with inflatable air sacs between its skin and muscle to reduce the impact of its momentous dives.

Gannets are highly sociable birds, often feeding in flocks several hundred strong (being on a boat among a flock of plunging birds is one of the great experiences of birdwatching). They also form colonies when breeding. The largest colony, on St Kilda off the west coast of Scotland, held 60,428 nests in 1994 and at least three other colonies in Britain also hold more than 20,000 nests. These are impressive numbers, but as a whole the Gannet's distribution is restricted, with fewer than 60 colonies in the world. Gannets are such large birds that they can breed only in places with enough constant updraft to allow them to take off, and such sites – on windy stacks and tall cliffs – are understandably at a premium.

In common with many seabirds, Gannets lay only one egg. Unusually, though, it is not incubated under the adult's belly, for Gannets have no brood patch (special patch of bare skin for incubation). Instead the parent bird literally stands on the egg, exposing it to the rich blood vessels in the webs of its feet, covering it up and keeping it at a temperature of 31.9°c. The egg duly hatches and the nestling then moves upstairs, so to speak, to rest on the surface of its parents' feet.

Pelicans family *Pelecanidae* (pel-li-**kah**-nid-ee)

Habitat Large wetlands such as lakes and deltas in warm regions.
Food Fish, obtained by scooping up in the pouch. Often hunts co-operatively.
Movements Migratory, leaving their breeding grounds at the end of the season. White Pelicans leave Europe, Dalmatian Pelicans move much smaller distances.
Voice Grunting, hissing and barking sounds.
Pairing style Monogamous, but for only 1 breeding season. Pair formation can sometimes be completed, from start to finish, in the course of a single day!
Nesting Large, dense colonies, often with discrete sub-colonies with synchronised laying of eggs.
Nest A large pile of vegetation in dense reedbed or on well-vegetated island.
Productivity 1 brood a year.
Eggs 2 (White), 2–3 (Dalmatian).
Incubation 30–36 days, by both sexes, on top of or below the feet.
Young Nest-bound and blind at birth, acquiring down within 3–8 days.
Parenting style Both parents feed young.
Food to young Fish by regurgitation.
Leaving nest Fledge at 65–85 days. 20–30 days after hatching, form crèches ('pods') with other young.

Looking at a pelican, it should not to hard to guess how it obtains its food, or what that food is; the huge bill and throat pouch act like a scoop-net to catch fish. The pouch is highly touch-sensitive, helping the pelican to detect food in the dark or in cloudy water; it is not simply a matter of immersing the bill and hoping. Pelicans indeed have some very sophisticated methods of hunting, including co-operative 'fish-driving', in which members of an informal group swim in a line towards the shore, chivvying their prey into shallower waters where they are more easily scooped up. To help them swim, pelicans have short, powerful legs and webs between all four toes.

Despite their large size and mainly aquatic habitat, Pelicans are highly efficient at flying high and even soaring. They use this ability to make long round trips from the colony to good fishing sites, often covering 150 km in the process.

Adult White Pelicans

Dalmatian Pelican

Pelecanus crispus (pel-li-**kah**-nuss **kriss**-puss)
length 1.6–1.8 m; wingspan 3.1–3.4 m

Slightly less sociable than the White Pelican, the Dalmatian forms smaller colonies of up to 250 pairs, and tends to feed on its own or in twos and threes, rather than in large groups. That said, it will sometimes hunt co-operatively and has on occasion been seen fishing in association with Great Cormorants; the latter dive from close beside the pelican, perhaps utilising its shadow to locate fish, and the pelican nets the fish that the Cormorants flush to the surface. This is possible because Dalmatian Pelicans typically feed in deeper water than their relatives the White Pelicans. Dalmatians depart their colonies earlier than Whites, in August, and disperse to the eastern Mediterranean or Caspian Sea region for the winter. A curious fact about the Dalmatian Pelican is that its divorce rate from one year to the next is 100 per cent.

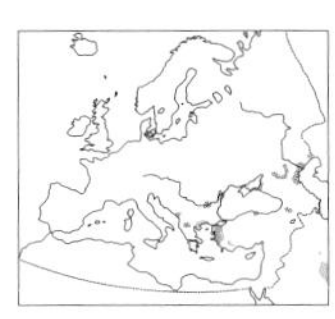

ID: *'Dirty white' plumage, shaggy crest; pale eye, reddish throat sac. Light underwing.*

White Pelican

Pelecanus onocrotalus
(pel-li-**kah**-nuss on-no-kro-**tay**-luss)
length 1.4–1.7 m; wingspan 2.7–3.6 m

Despite being widespread in Africa and Asia, the White Pelican is very rare in Europe, breeding in only a handful of colonies in Greece, Romania, Ukraine and Russia. Members of the colony, which may contain several hundred birds, arrive in March and April and leave from September, but it is still not known where they winter. Their favourite food is carp, which constitutes up to 25 per cent of their diet, and they tend to take fish of 300–600 g in weight.

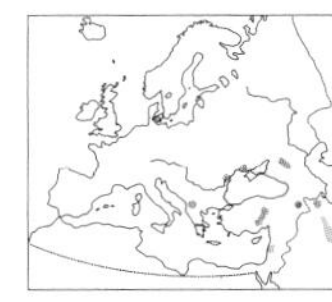

ID: *Clean white plumage, small neat crest; dark eye amidst pink skin patch; creamy throat sac. Contrasting black and white underwing.*

Juvenile White Pelican

Cormorants and Shags family *Phalacrocoracidae* (fa-la-kro-kor-**rah**-sid-ee)

Habitat Seacoasts, freshwater lakes and rivers.
Food Fish, caught during underwater pursuit, plus a few marine invertebrates.
Movements All species disperse in winter, often not very far, but both Great and Pygmy Cormorants may undertake long movements (Great up to 2400 km).
Voice Largely silent, but a few grunts and croaks.
Pairing style Mainly monogamous, but a small percentage of male Shags may be bigamous. Mates change from year to year.
Nesting Colonial, up to 2000 pairs (Great Cormorant). Pygmy Cormorants nest alongside other species.
Nest Large pile of sticks or seaweed, often held together by excrement, placed on rock or in tree.
Productivity 1 brood a year.
Eggs 1–6, usually 3–4, laid at intervals of more than a day.
Incubation 27–31 days, by both parents; eggs placed on top of feet to receive warmth through the feathers of the belly.
Young Nest-bound, altricial and naked; acquire down after a week.
Parenting style Both parents feed young, who must reach into parent's throat to grab food.
Food to young As adult diet.
Leaving nest The young may form crèches. Fledge at 42–58 days, but become independent after 3–10 further weeks.

Members of the cormorant family are waterbirds with a difference, because their plumage, surprisingly enough, is not very waterproof! Only the inner layer of down feathers keeps the skin dry, while the rest of the plumage periodically gets soaked. So, after a short fishing trip, a cormorant or shag must leave the water and hold its long, somewhat blunt-ended wings out to dry like washing on a line. This 'spread-wing' posture is highly characteristic of the family.

There is, of course, a point to having feathers that can get soaked: it reduces the birds' buoyancy in the water, making it easier and more energy- efficient to move around below the surface. Cormorants also have comparatively less body fat than many other birds and their bones are unusually dense. Some even ingest stones to keep them under the water. So once they are immersed they are masters of speed and manoeuvrability, with their streamlined, belly-flattened bodies, long, flexible necks and powerful, fully webbed toes. They steer with their tail and are propelled by their back-set feet, while the wings remain closed and out of the way. The prey – almost always fish – is grabbed by the strong bill, which is hooked at the tip.

Many waterbirds are awkward or helpless on land, but not cormorants and shags. They perch surprisingly well, on rocks, jetties, trees and even power lines. Individuals spend much of the day loafing at a favourite spot, the rights to which they defend with mild aggression. They are also superb flyers, perfectly capable of covering tens or hundreds of kilometres and even soaring high into the sky.

All cormorants and shags are sociable, roosting, breeding and sometimes fishing in groups. They lay more eggs than most other seabirds, breed at a younger age and have a much faster reproductive cycle than true seabirds; evidently the hazards of the inshore, within sight of land, are greater than those out in the deep ocean.

Pygmy Cormorant

Phalacrocorax pygmaeus
(fa-la-kro-**koh**-rakss pig-**mee**-uss)
length 45–55 cm; wingspan up to 90 cm

ID: Much the smallest cormorant, with the shortest neck and bill; tail rather long. Head and neck brown-tinged, with tiny white flecks when breeding.

adult br. adult non-br. juv.

Where the European Shag is marine and the Great Cormorant is catholic in its habitat requirements, this third member of the family is largely restricted to fresh water, at least for breeding. It occurs in wetlands with plenty of thick emergent vegetation, including deltas, rivers and swamps, and is therefore far more dependent on copious marshy plant growth than the other species.

It builds its nest among trees and shrubs growing in or close to the water, or in reedbeds, and it frequently rests just above the surface on logs, banks or even small islands of dead vegetation. It feeds on fish, mainly hunting in shallow water.

Like the European Shag, the Pygmy Cormorant is restricted in its distribution, occurring only in the lowlands of Eastern Europe and a few parts of Asia east to the Caspian Sea region. In the last century it suffered from widespread declines as its habitat was converted to agriculture, but now its diminished population is mostly stable.

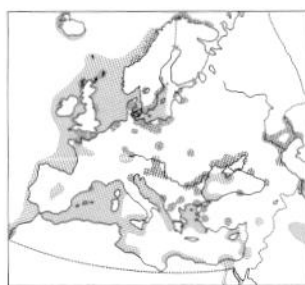

ID: Large, with long, thick neck and heavy bill. In breeding season adults have white thigh patch and throat, often with 'grey hairs' on head and neck; all lost in winter save pale throat. Juveniles brown, with white breast for some of first year; become increasingly dark over next three years.

Great Cormorant

Phalacrocorax carbo (fa-la-kro-**koh**-rakss **kar**-bo)
length 80–100 cm; wingspan 1.3–1.6 m

This is by far the most widespread member of the cormorant and shag family, occurring in eastern North America, Africa, Asia and Australasia, as well as in Europe. Such a wide distribution implies a degree of habitat flexibility and, as far as Europe is concerned, the Great Cormorant shows an interesting dichotomy of breeding site between east and west. In the northwest it breeds almost entirely on the coast, building nests on wide cliff ledges and rocky stacks; but in Eastern Europe it is equally at home on large freshwater lakes and wide rivers, nesting in trees to a height of 10 m.

Both of its main habitats provide the Great Cormorant with what it needs: sheltered, shallow water with a good supply of fish. It is almost entirely a bottom feeder, scouring both bare and vegetated parts of the sea or lake bed. It has a particular fondness for flatfish, but the range of species it takes is quite wide and depends on what is abundant locally. It has no special preference for size: it will tackle anything from a small sand eel to a large predatory species such as the freshwater pike. Its battles with eels can be spectacular to watch: these long-bodied, wriggly fish are a good but tricky meal, and a bird can spend many minutes attempting to manoeuvre them in its bill so that they can be swallowed. Even when the contest appears to be over, it may not be: eels have been known to wriggle to freedom even when some way down the bird's gullet.

Cormorants breed in colonies, usually of a few tens of birds. At the beginning of the season a male lays claim to a nest site, occupying a suitable ledge and intimidating any intruding rivals with a lunge forwards and a snake-like twisting of the neck, accompanied by loud calling. Once established, the male attempts to attract a mate with a 'wing waving' display. This involves folding the primary flight feathers behind the secondaries and raising its blunted wings rapidly up and down. As the wings are raised, the male's bright white nuptial thigh patch is revealed enticingly a couple of times a second, in a 'now you see me, now you don't' routine.

European Shag

Phalacrocorax aristotelis
(fa-la-kro-**koh**-rakss ar-ris-to-**tell**-iss)
length 65–80 cm, male larger than female; wingspan 1 m

The European Shag occurs only in the eastern Atlantic, the Mediterranean and the Black Sea. It has a more restricted habitat than the Great Cormorant, being confined to marine waters when breeding and hardly ever occurring inland. It can dive to greater depths, typically 15–40 m down but occasionally as far as 61 m, on or close to the seabed. It takes fewer flatfish than the Great Cormorant, and more small fish such as sand eels and blennies; it also takes some invertebrates such as shrimps.

The Shag has the longest breeding season of any European seabird. In Britain, young may be seen at colonies any time between April and October, and in the Mediterranean breeding may begin before the turn of the year. In nuptial plumage European Shags have wispy crests, and recent research has shown that the larger the crest (in either sex), the greater the breeding success. It seems, then, that in Shags, crests are an indicator of health.

ID: Smaller than Great Cormorant, with thinner neck and thinner bill; obvious angle between forehead and bill. Plumage has greenish hue. In breeding plumage lacks any white, but has obvious 'dried-hair' crest and yellow gape.

Herons, Egrets and Bitterns family *Ardeidae* (Ar-**deh**-id-ee)

Habitat Wetlands, including marshes, swamps, lakes and rivers; Cattle Egret on dry fields.
Food Mainly fish, but also insects, aquatic crustaceans, amphibians, reptiles, small mammals, occasionally birds.
Movements A few sedentary, but mainly migratory. Several are long-distance migrants to tropical Africa. Many are notably dispersive, moving long distances in any direction after breeding.
Voice Adults make various barks and croaks, but are not noisy as a rule. Cacophony from nests includes a range of unearthly sounds.
Pairing style Monogamous, but male Great Bittern may have up to 5 mates.
Nesting Most are strongly colonial (but not bitterns), nesting in 'heronries' with several species.
Nest Usually a platform of interwoven sticks placed in branches of a tree. Alternatively a pile of vegetation on the ground in a reedbed.
Productivity 1 brood a year.
Eggs 3–6.
Incubation 17–30 days, usually by both parents but by female only in Great Bittern. Eggs are laid at intervals of 1–3 days, and incubation begins with first egg.
Young Nest-bound and almost naked, with eyes shut. Soon acquire down.
Parenting style Both sexes feed and tend young (female only in Great Bittern).
Food to young Same as adult diet. Parents bring food in crop and are induced to regurgitate it by young pecking at bill.
Leaving nest Time in nest varies greatly, from 25 to 55 days. Young are usually fed for some time after leaving.

The birds in this family have their own special way of catching fish and other aquatic creatures. They don't swim in the water as many birds do, nor do they plunge in from a height; instead they simply wade in, stand still or walk slowly in the water, and then strike at prey located at their feet. It's a routine that demands considerable patience and generally a slow, cautious approach. The typical view of a feeding heron is of a tall bird standing motionless by the water, with its neck outstretched and pointed downwards, poised for a lunge.

Herons are ideally adapted for their wading and fishing. They have long legs for paddling, long toes for keeping their balance in mud or other unstable surfaces, a long neck for reaching down towards prey, and a long, dagger-shaped bill for making a grab. Although the neck of a heron doesn't look special from the outside, it is actually highly modified. The sixth cervical vertebra is elongated, allowing the neck to assume an exaggerated S-shape and snap forward with great speed. Remarkably, in the lower neck the windpipe and intestine actually run behind the vertebrae to keep out of the way and to prevent any damage. In flight the neck is held characteristically retracted.

The lifestyle of a heron puts unusual demands on its plumage, since the bird can easily collect oil and debris from both its prey and its immediate marshy environment. So herons have two exceptional adaptations for feather care. On the feet one claw is furrowed, or 'combed', while special feathers on the back produce 'powder down'. This down is administered to the plumage and absorbs filth, which is then combed out by the modified toe. Much time is spent on this plumage maintenance.

In the early spring many herons and egrets acquire special elongated plumes, and their bare parts generally change colour, too. These changes, coupled with ritualised courtship displays, seal the pair bond, which usually lasts only for a season and for a single brood. Herons and egrets are generally sociable when breeding and, perhaps unexpectedly for tall, lanky birds that are awkward when perched, they generally place their nests in trees, sometimes at considerable height. Frequently several species breed together in mixed colonies. The eggs are laid several days apart and, because incubation begins with the first egg, the young of a brood are of different ages. The youngest almost always dies early in life through lack of food, although its fellow siblings sometimes kill it themselves.

Great Bittern

Great Bittern

Botaurus stellaris (boh-**tow**-russ stel-**lah**-riss)
length 70–80 cm

In late winter and early spring, male Great Bitterns utter one of the lowest pitched of all bird sounds, a 'booming' easily imitated by blowing over the rim of a beer bottle. The sound advertises a bird's presence, both to rival males and to females, and is made by inflating the oesophagus. Each 'boom' is individually distinct, and can carry for as much as 2 km on a calm night. 'Booms' delineate territories and, should a male challenge another booming bird's borders, a fight to the death may ensue.

This territoriality is paramount because the Great Bittern, in contrast to other European herons, is polygamous. Each male attempts to attract more than one mate to his territory, and may, if he is highly successful, acquire as many as five. Within the male's borders, each female will build a nest, lay and incubate the eggs, and see the young through to fledging, all on her own. She will have no other obvious contact with the male, but will be free from interference by other birds by virtue of her mate's territorial protection.

The Great Bittern is a very fussy species ecologically. It breeds only in extensive, undisturbed stands of *Phragmites* reed, which are usually found at the edges of lakes or wide rivers. The reeds must be growing in shallow water, with little or no fluctuation in water level, and there must be both young and old stands present. In addition, the Bittern requires plenty of areas of open water within the reedbeds, beside which it can fish and catch frogs and small mammals. Such requirements are met only very locally, so the Great Bittern is rather patchily distributed in Europe, and in many places it is decreasing.

Few birds are so difficult to see. This is partly because Great Bitterns are stealthy in their movements and partly because they are active mainly at dawn and dusk. But perhaps above all, a Bittern's remarkable cryptic camouflage allows it to melt into the background, so that it may be impossible to spot even from only a few metres away. When sensing danger, it remains very still, standing with head and neck stretched vertically upwards, allowing its outline to blend into the reed stems. To complete the effect, it may even sway along with the plants and be lost to view.

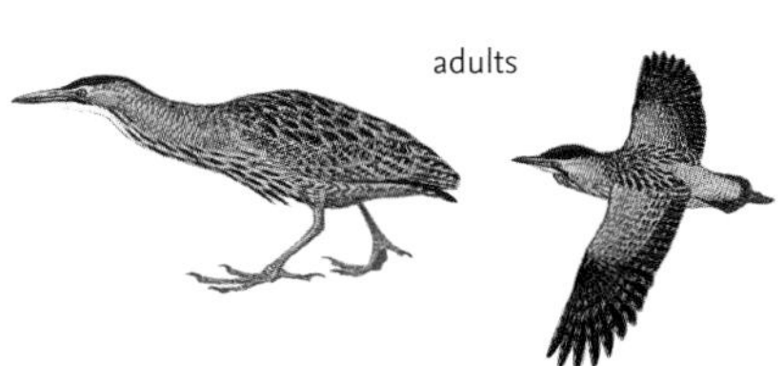

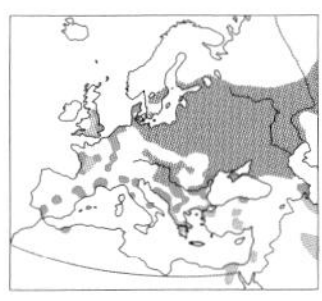

ID: Large, plump, thick-necked heron, with remarkably cryptic brown and black speckled plumage.

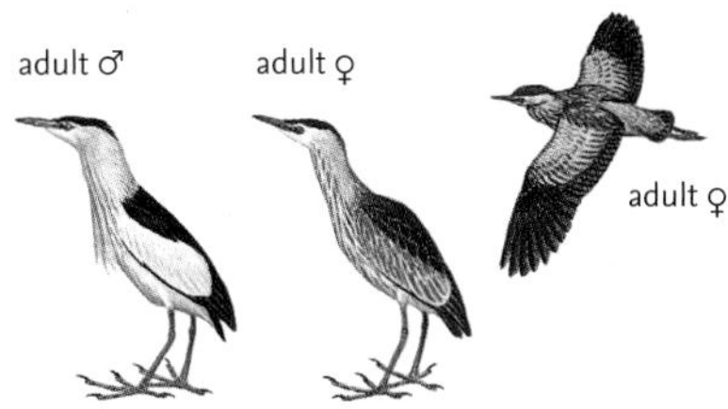

Little Bittern

Ixobrychus minutus (ik-so-**brie**-kuss mi-**noo**-tuss)
length 33–38 cm

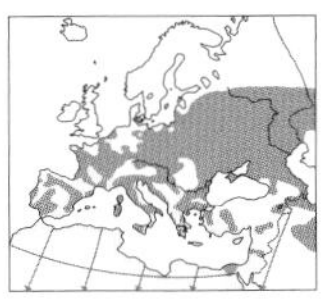

ID: Very small, rail-sized heron with long legs. Male distinctive, with clean black on crown and wings; female more streaked. Both have creamy-brown patch on wings, easily seen in flight.

No bigger than a Coot, the Little Bittern is the smallest of its family in Europe, and probably the most difficult to observe. It has little need to come out into the open or even to venture to the edge of a thick reedbed, for it climbs expertly, scaling reed stems with ease and navigating through dense vegetation without breaking cover. It feeds on small fish, amphibians and insects, which it takes either up in the vegetation or, in the case of fish, from small pools within the reedbeds. It hunts mainly at dawn and dusk.

In early spring male Little Bitterns advertise their presence day and night with a muffled barking sound, their 'song'. Uniquely among European herons, they build a nest as an inducement to the female to pair with them; if they are successful, copulation takes place on this platform. If no female is attracted, unsuccessful males may abandon their first nest and build another in order to improve their prospects. Once paired, male and female carry out breeding duties as a team, sharing incubation and feeding of the young. When members of the pair meet, they exchange greeting gestures that involve opening the bill and ruffling the neck feathers; it looks aggressive, but in fact helps to maintain the pair bond.

Little Bitterns are summer visitors to Europe, arriving in April, laying eggs in May, dispersing in July and departing for East Africa in August and September.

Little Egret

Egretta garzetta (ig-**grett**-ta gar-**zett**-ta)
length 55–65 cm

No other heron in Europe exhibits such a diverse range of feeding techniques as the Little Egret. It can remain motionless and stare down at its feet when appropriate, and it will also walk slowly to stalk prey. At times a more agile approach is called for, especially when chasing small fish in shallow water, and this elegant bird will then hop or break into a run; it then moves with surprising speed and often uses its wings to balance as it darts to and fro. Yet another trick is foot-paddling, in which the bird vibrates one foot on the surface of the water or mud, stirring up the substrate and presumably flushing food into view. This would appear to be the function of the Little Egret's very distinctive, otherwise incongruous yellow feet.

Little Egrets occur in a variety of wetland habitats, both fresh and saline. These include marshes, lakes, rivers, estuaries and also ephemeral waters such as flooded meadows. Here they hunt for smaller fish such as sticklebacks and loach, plus a range of aquatic insects, crustaceans, molluscs and amphibians. Normally, birds hunt by day and on their own, but on occasions they will be sociable; they will even mix with flocks of Cattle Egrets in dry fields.

adult br.

adult non-br.

In the breeding season, Little Egrets nest in trees, almost always alongside other species such as herons, Glossy Ibises and Pygmy Cormorants. Colonies are dense and crowded, and may number hundreds of nests in all, separated from one another by as little as 1–2 m. In common with several herons, these normally silent birds suddenly find their voice when breeding, the adults barking and growling as they come and go, the young making a comical bubbling gargle.

After breeding, Little Egrets, particularly the young, become markedly dispersive, moving in all directions well away from the colony. Many head north, in the opposite direction to their impending migration a few weeks later. This scattered dispersal means that birds radiate away from each other, preventing competition in the difficult dry summer period. Such movements may lead to colonisation in new areas and the Little Egret has recently been expanding its range considerably. It bred in Britain for the first time in 1996, and in the last few years has been finding its way increasingly to the Atlantic coast of North America.

ID: Small white heron with dark bill and legs but obvious yellow feet. A few plumes over neck when breeding.

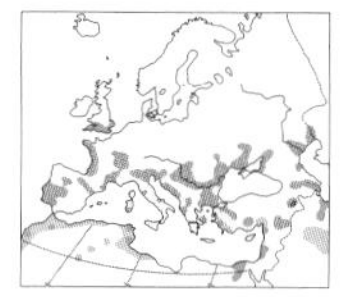

ID: *Stockier than Little Egret, with thicker neck and shorter legs; not very elegant. Bill short, yellow; legs pale, feet not yellow. In breeding plumage acquires colourful orange patches on crown, breast and back; very distinctive.*

Cattle Egret

Bubulcus ibis (byoo-**bulk**-kuss **eye**-biss)
length 48–53 cm

No heron has wandered away from the family norm quite so much as the Cattle Egret. Where most herons are confined to wet and marshy areas, the Cattle Egret is often found far from water, in dry fields and even semi-arid habitats; where most herons subsist at least partly on fish, the Cattle Egret is addicted to insects, particularly grasshoppers and crickets (in Russia, apparently, they eat little else); and where most herons are leggy and elegant, the Cattle Egret is rather short and sturdy, with plumper cheeks and a shorter bill than other members of the family.

What makes the Cattle Egret so different from the others is that its main means of gathering food is 'commensal' – that is, it takes advantage of the activities of another animal. In most cases, as the name implies, that means cattle. As these long-legged beasts graze and mill about, the herons gather around them and ambush any insects that are displaced by the cows' feet. To procure their prey they simply walk or run after it.

When breeding, Cattle Egrets form colonies that nest in trees, often alongside other heron species. The adults acquire colourful plumage and their bills change colour, as in other herons. The males perform short, circling flights to advertise their presence, and pair formation is inducted and maintained by various stereotyped displays. After breeding, they disperse in all directions, sometimes for enormous distances, and this habit has allowed the species to extend its range remarkably in the last hundred years or so. From its original base in tropical Africa it expanded to Europe. Then, early in the 20th century, it hopped across the Atlantic of its own accord from France to South America. Finally, in 1954, it made the comparable leap to North America, where it is now common.

adult br. adult non-br.

Great Egret

Ardea alba (ar-**deh**-a **al**-ba)
length 85–102 cm

If there is any European bird that can give a displaying peacock a run for its money, it is the Great Egret. In spring this species develops ornate plumes, called 'aigrettes', on its back, and these are used in many of its displays. From their resting position draped over the bird's back and tail, in the manner of an Ostrich, these feathers can be suddenly lifted into a fan and the effect is startling – to rival, mate or human observer.

The Great Egret is scarce in Europe and is more pernickety about its habitat here than in other parts of the world, being confined mainly to large wetlands and requiring extensive stands of reeds in which to make its substantial nest, placed just above water. Nonetheless, it is increasing in numbers, both as a breeding species and in its winter range.

In contrast to other egrets, Great Egrets usually hunt on their own and defend feeding territories from others of their species. Their preferred method of foraging is to walk very slowly in or by the water, stalking up to prey. But they will also stand motionless , waiting for a fish to come into range. In addition to fish they take large numbers of aquatic and terrestrial insects.

adult br. adult non-br.

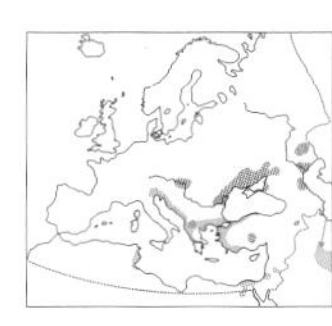

ID: *Much larger than Little Egret, size of Grey Heron. Bill yellow when not breeding, blacker otherwise. Legs usually dark, feet not yellow.*

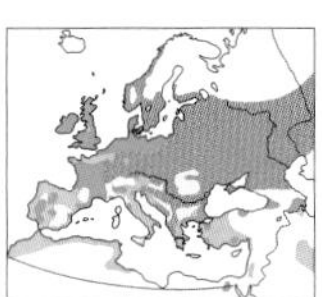

ID: *Large, lanky heron with thick bill and fairly thick neck; plumage mostly grey. In adult black stripe over eye, crown white; juvenile has dark crown.*

Grey Heron

Ardea cinerea (ar-**deh**-a sin-**neh**-ree-a)
length 90–100 cm

In Western and Central Europe this is by far the commonest species of heron, the one you see everywhere. It is also the one that reaches farthest to the north, to the fringes of the Arctic. It can flourish both in pristine, extensive wetlands and in areas with only a scattering of permanent water, which may be fresh or brackish. It will inhabit the corners of remote marshes far from human interference, yet can also reach into the heart of large cities, where it finds its food in park lakes and garden ponds. In much of its range, anyone saying the name 'heron' will be referring to this successful species.

This bird's hunting technique is typical of the family. It stands motionless over a pool of water, on a bank or immersed up to its thighs, and watches for movement below. In general, medium-sized fish, between 10 and 25 cm long, are the target, but the Grey Heron is not fussy. It will stand over molehills in fields waiting for a telltale twitch in the soil, or it will seize frogs and crabs in marshes.

Waiting patiently for fish is a technique that needs solitude, so individual Grey Herons vigorously defend their feeding territories from other birds, with violence if necessary. When the population is augmented by juveniles in the summer, pressure on good feeding sites becomes considerable and those birds that fail to keep their own patch don't survive for long.

In the milder parts of their range Grey Herons nest very early in the year, from February onwards. It's thought that this enables them to find fish more easily when the young hatch, before too much vegetation clogs the waterside. Typically they build their nests in the canopy of tall trees, often as high as 25 m, well above the height preferred by other herons. They are normally colonial, but isolated pairs can be found as well.

The nest of a Grey Heron starts off as quite a flimsy structure, a platform made of robust but not closely interwoven twigs. In its first year the eggs may be visible from below, but as the years pass the nest becomes larger and more massive. In most years between three and five eggs are laid, hatching at two-day intervals. The chicks remain on this open, lofty platform for three to four weeks before stretching their wings and beginning to perch on nearby branches, but it will be 50 days from hatching before they can finally fly. Even then youngsters tend to return to the nest regularly, at least for the first three weeks of flying free.

Purple Heron

Ardea purpurea (ar-**deh**-a per-pyoo-**ree**-a)
length 78–90 cm

Only slightly smaller than a Grey Heron, and resembling it in many ways, the more secretive Purple Heron is nevertheless very different in ecology and behaviour from its commoner relative. For one thing, it is exclusively a summer visitor to Europe, evacuating the continent by October and returning only in April. It is also much choosier about its habitat, being restricted to large wetlands with extensive stands of reeds. These reedbeds must be tall and without too many obstacles such as trees or dry land.

Purple Herons usually shun trees as nest sites, instead preferring to place a large pile of vegetation on the ground among the reeds. They are only loosely colonial; perhaps three or four nests will be placed in reasonably close proximity in the same part of the marsh.

When feeding, Purple Herons have a distinctive stance, holding their neck stretched out at 60 degrees above the horizontal plane as they stand in shallow water or on the shore. They are patient hunters, using their long, thin bills to grab large fish, amphibians and various insect larvae from the water.

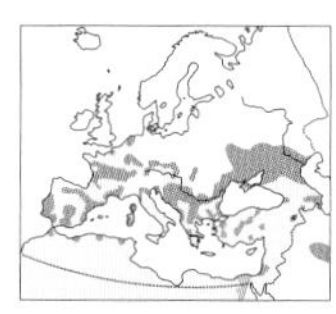

ID: *Thinner neck and longer, thinner bill than Grey Heron; more obvious stripes on neck. Colourful. Juvenile is washed-out version, much browner than juvenile Grey.*

Black-crowned Night Heron

Nycticorax nycticorax
(nik-**tik**-oh-raks nik-**tik**-oh-raks)
length 58–65 cm, male larger

ID: Small heron; adult unmistakably grey and black; juvenile spotted. Flies in half-light with faster wingbeats than other herons, thick bill apparent.

As it name suggests this small heron often feeds during the night, although its favoured times are dawn and dusk. It is thought that competition with other herons might prevent it hunting much by daylight, as it is perfectly capable of doing so. Fortunately, its large eyes are adapted for working in a wide variety of lighting conditions.

Night Herons often roost by day on the branches of dense waterside trees. They also nest in trees, often with other herons; when doing so, they keep slightly apart from other species, often constructing their platforms of twigs slightly higher up than the others'.

With its wide, relatively short bill, the Black-crowned Night Heron is an opportunist. It stands by the water and wades in, looking for amphibians (especially frogs), turtles, fish, snakes, lizards, insects, crustaceans and so on. Unusually, it will also raid birds' nests for eggs and nestlings in the appropriate season. Remarkably, they also occasionally use bait to attract food, placing an insect on the water surface and gobbling up whatever comes to eat it.

Squacco Heron

Ardeola ralloides (ar-deh-**oh**-la ra-**loy**-deez)
length 44–47 cm

A small, almost silent species, the Squacco Heron is confined in Europe to freshwater sites with thick vegetation. A creature of habit, it prefers to stick to its favoured method of waiting motionless beside the water, bill poised for a strike.

Although it almost always hugs rich waterside vegetation when feeding, and is most active in twilight, the Squacco Heron is not as secretive as the almost paranoid Little Bittern, with which it often shares its habitat. It lacks the Little Bittern's ability to climb about in vegetation and, in contrast to that species, will sometimes feed in small groups of well-spaced birds.

It is most sociable, however, when breeding. Pairs rarely nest in isolation, but form small enclaves within heronries dominated by other species, such as Little Egrets. The nests are often lower than those of other herons, regularly sited only 2 m above the water, and they are more carefully hidden within the foliage of overhanging trees. Both sexes build the nest, the male bringing material, the female arranging it.

The Squacco Heron is a migrant, arriving in April and departing between August and October for the northern tropics of Africa.

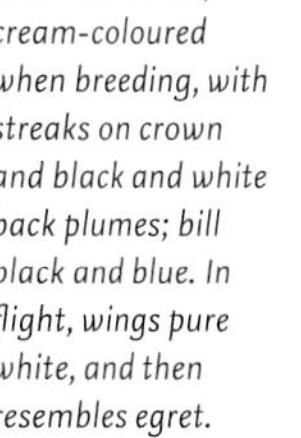

ID: Small heron, cream-coloured when breeding, with streaks on crown and black and white back plumes; bill black and blue. In flight, wings pure white, and then resembles egret.

Storks family *Ciconiidae* (si-kon-**ee**-id-ee)

Habitat Black Stork breeds in extensive, undisturbed forested areas; also on rocky crags. White Stork occurs in open areas with wet patches, including farmland.
Food Small animals, including fish, reptiles and small mammals.
Movements Migratory, wintering in tropical Africa.
Voice White Stork silent but for bill-clapping sounds; Black Stork makes gentle, breathy cheeps, with less incessant bill-clapping.
Pairing style Monogamous, but partners may change between seasons.
Nesting White Stork usually in small colonies up to 30 pairs, also often singly; Black Stork always singly.
Nest Large bundle of sticks reinforced with earth, grass or dung; lined with softer material such as moss and grass, and often with rags and other artificial materials.
Productivity 1 brood a year.
Eggs 3–5.
Incubation 33–36 days, by both parents.
Young Nest-bound and downy.
Parenting style Both parents feed young at the nest, regurgitating food onto nest.
Food to young Same as adult diet.
Leaving nest Young remain in the nest for 58–71 days, but may visit nest for feeding a little while afterwards.

Storks look like herons, but are larger and heavier and, when they fly, hold their head and neck extended in regal fashion, rather than retracted. They also feed in a different way, not adopting a heron's patient 'angler's' approach, but wandering steadily or even running over wet areas with open bill pointed downwards, ready to grab whatever comes within range. They are voracious predators, consuming a wide range of vertebrates and insects, and their breeding success depends largely upon whether food is available at the required density.

A few other details of stork breeding behaviour also distinguish these large birds from herons. For example, they incorporate mud, grass or dung into their nest structure, rather than using only sticks. And when feeding young, they regurgitate food onto the floor of the nest, rather than supplying it mouth-to-mouth.

Black Stork

Ciconia nigra (si-**koh**-nee-a **nye**-gra)
length 1 m, male larger; wingspan 1.5 m

This is a much more solitary, secretive bird than its better known relative. It usually breeds far away from human settlements, within large tracts of forest containing rivers and other wet areas where it can hunt for fish, frogs and salamanders in an undisturbed setting. Pairs are not colonial, but spaced well apart. Each nest is placed in a tree, up to 25 m above ground, or high on a cliff ledge, never on an occupied building.

The Black Stork is migratory (except in Spain), travelling to tropical Africa and back, but it doesn't go as far as the White Stork and its routine is slightly different. It invariably moves in smaller parties, up to a maximum of a hundred birds, and is less dependent on thermals, apparently expending less energy in flapping flight than the White Stork. It leaves its breeding areas a month later than its relative, in August and September, and arrives up to two weeks later in the spring.

adult

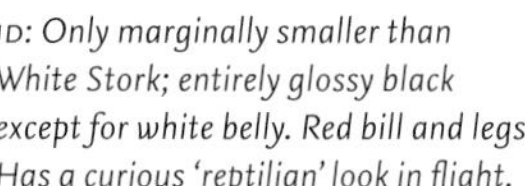

ID: Only marginally smaller than White Stork; entirely glossy black except for white belly. Red bill and legs. Has a curious 'reptilian' look in flight.

White Stork

Ciconia ciconia (si-**koh**-nee-a si-**koh**-nee-a)
length 1–1.1 m, male larger; wingspan 1.5–1.6 m

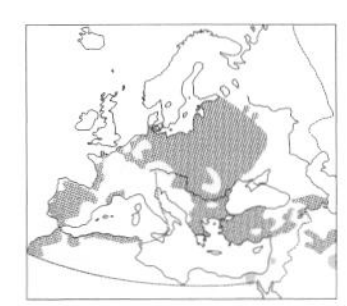

ID: Huge wading bird with white body, black and white wings, long red-orange bill.

Not many species of birds can be trusted to deliver human babies, but such is the White Stork's ability to return to its breeding sites at the same time each year that the legend arose, in Germany and Switzerland at least, that it was utterly reliable. Its migration and timing are indeed exceptional. Before and after a breeding season in Europe, it migrates to the southern tip of Africa, a round trip of some 30,000 km, one of the longest of all bird migrations. Yet somehow it manages to time its return perfectly.

White Storks don't bother to conceal their nests in any way, but place them out in the open on trees, chimneys, ruins, haystacks, pylons and poles; people also erect special platforms for them. The nests are huge structures, up to 2 m high and 1.5 m in diameter, and are made up of sticks, earth and grass, often decorated with rubbish. Where they are placed on chimneys, several to a village in small colonies, they become part of the rural landscape and local people often accept them with pleasure and pride.

Where White Storks are common it is not just the sight of these huge birds that is familiar, but the sound, too. When one of a pair arrives at the nest, both birds perform an 'up-and-down' display. Each lifts its head right up and over on to its back, all the while clattering the mandibles of its bill together to make a sound like a slow woodpecker.

Ibises and Spoonbills family *Threskiornithidae* (thres-ki-or-**nith**-id-ee)

Habitat Lowland wetlands with extensive shallow water, mainly in warm climates.
Food Mainly adult insects and their larvae, including caddis flies and water beetles; also leeches, molluscs, worms and crustaceans. Spoonbill takes a few fish and tadpoles. Both have special ways of touch-feeding.
Movements Migratory, wintering mainly in tropical Africa but with some remaining in the Mediterranean basin. Leave colonies September, arrive back in March and April.
Voice Both species largely silent, with some croaks and grunts.
Pairing style Monogamous, pair bond lasting 1 season.
Nesting Colonial. Spoonbill colonies are discrete from other waterbirds, but Glossy Ibis mixes with Pygmy Cormorants and various species of heron.
Nest Both build nest of reeds and/or twigs, lined with leaves, either placed in tree 5–7 m above ground, or on ground among dense vegetation.
Productivity 1 brood a year.
Eggs Usually 3–4.
Incubation 21 days (Glossy Ibis), 24–25 days (Spoonbill), by both parents.
Young Nest-bound but downy, eyes open at hatching. Young do not hatch at the same time.
Parenting style Young take food direct from throat of either parent.
Food to young Similar to adults' food.
Leaving nest Glossy Ibis leave nest at 25–28 days; Spoonbills at 45–50 days.

At first sight it seems strange that such visually different birds as the Glossy Ibis and the Spoonbill should be found in the same family. Yet although their bills are clearly very different, the two birds are similar in internal morphology and behaviour, and there are even recorded instances of them interbreeding!

Both these species can easily be distinguished from other tall wading birds by their method of feeding: both primarily use touch rather than sight. So they don't stand still and ambush prey like herons, nor do they indulge in head-down chases as storks do. Instead the Glossy Ibis immerses its long, curved bill into the substrate, and the Spoonbill places its bill in the water and moves it from side to side in a sweeping action. However, Glossy Ibises sometimes sweep and Spoonbills sometimes probe, further proving their similarities.

When flying, both species hold head and neck out, not retracted. They lack the heavy, laboured wingbeats of herons, but fly with a combination of stiff, rapid flaps and glides. Both species often fly in lines.

In common with other large wading birds, both Glossy Ibises and Spoonbills breed in colonies. Their nests are well built and strong, and are often placed very close together. In display, both species include mutual preening and bowing in their repertoire.

Eurasian Spoonbills

Eurasian Spoonbill

Platalea leucorodia
(plat-ta-**leh**-a loo-koh-**roh**-di-a)
length 80–90 cm; wingspan 1.15–1.3 m

ID: Adult unmistakable tall wading bird with black and yellow bill, flattened and swollen at the tip; crest; buttery yellow patch on breast.

A feeding Spoonbill is a distinctive sight, even discounting its large size and white plumage, for few other birds place their bills in the water and sweep them, slightly open, in a wide arc from side to side again and again, strolling forwards all the while. This is the Spoonbill's trademark foraging technique and the most efficient way to use its special bill. This bill is flattened in the horizontal plane, and at its broad tip are large numbers of sensitive internal touch receptors; when these fire, as the bill hits a moving object in the water, the mandibles snap shut at great speed and the prey can be captured and swallowed. It has also recently been discovered that the Spoonbill's bill, held open and moved rapidly through the water, acts as a hydrofoil, lifting food items off the surface of the water or mud so that they can be grasped more easily.

Spoonbills are not born with oddly shaped bills: the chick's bill is short and soft, with the tip beginning to flatten after nine days, and the shape clearly recognisable after 16. At this time, of course, the young are fed by the adults, so they do not yet require their specialised apparatus.

Not surprisingly, the Spoonbill is a bird of wetlands, requiring wide areas of open, shallow water of consistent depth in which to find its food. A muddy or sandy bed also helps, as this will ensure that the site is rich in prey and easy on the feet. In addition there must be reedbeds or low bushes nearby in which the birds can build their nests. So the Spoonbill is quite a localised species, patchily distributed in Europe.

Glossy Ibis

Plegadis falcinellus (pleh-**gad**-diss fal-sin-**nell**-uss)
length 55–65 cm; wingspan 80–100 cm

This is the one member of the family with a truly wide distribution; although rare and localised in Europe, it is found on every continent of the world except Antarctica – pretty impressive for a large wading bird. Its broad compass doubtless results from a tendency to wander nomadically after breeding, when adults and young form separate flocks and disperse widely.

The Glossy Ibis finds most of its food by pecking and probing into mud or water. Like the Spoonbill it has slit-like nostrils at the very base of the bill, so it can breathe while feeding in this way. It is mainly carnivorous and evidently not in the least fussy: insect larvae, worms, leeches, molluscs, crustaceans, fish, frogs and snakes all find their way onto its menu at various times. When feeding it is highly sociable, and a single bird on its own is an unusual sight.

Glossy Ibises nest on the ground or in trees, in colonies, usually with other large waterbirds. Early in life the chicks are given to wandering from the nest, making their parents follow them to various parts of the colony: a hint of what will happen later on.

ID: Medium-to-large dark wading bird with long decurved bill, larger, longer legged and much darker than Curlew. Glossy purple-brown plumage; neck spotted white in winter.

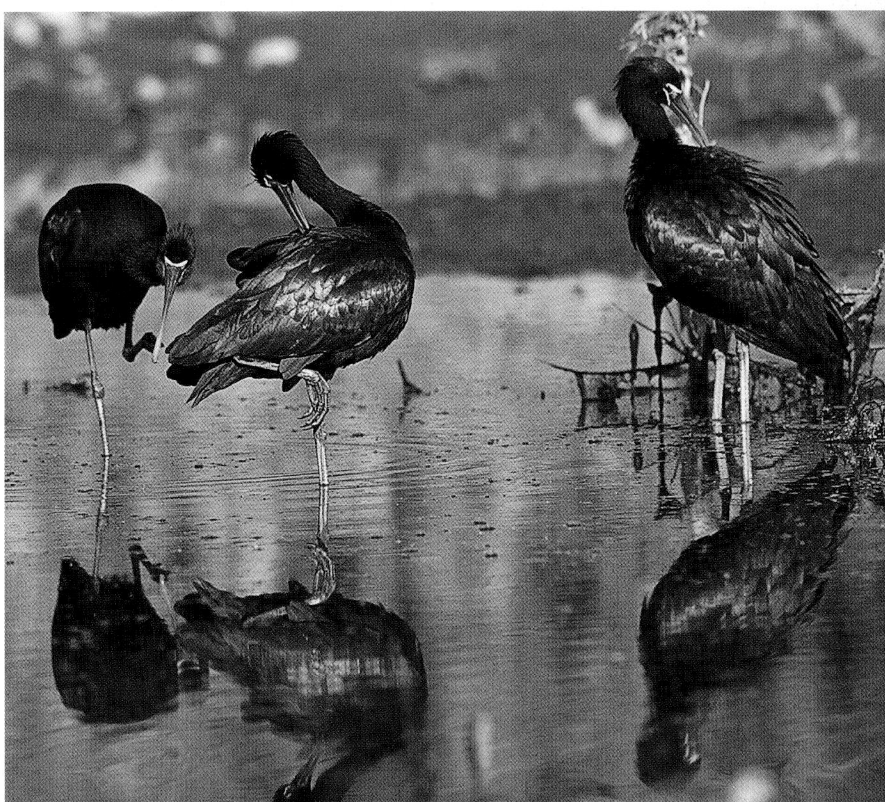

Greater Flamingo *Phoenicopterus ruber* (fee-ni-**kop**-ter-uss **roo**-ber)

family *Phoenicopteridae* (fee-ni-**kop**-ter-id-ee)

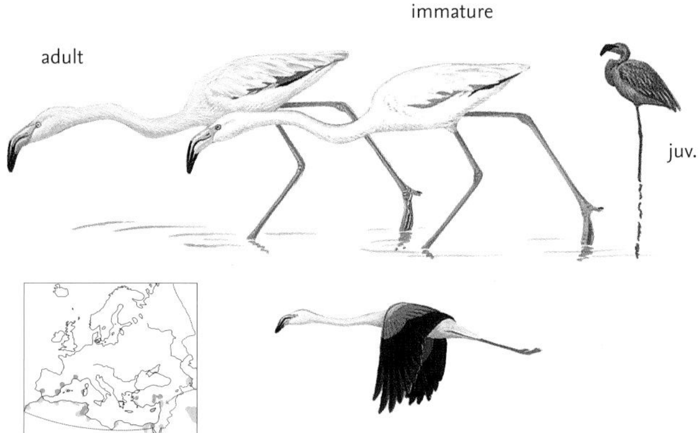

height up to 1.5 m, male larger than female; wingspan 1.4–1.7 m
ID: *Unmistakable tall wading bird, with long neck and legs, oddly small body, kinked bill, pink coloration.*

Habitat Open, extensive lakes or lagoons with shallow (less than 1 m depth) saline water.
Food A wide range of small or minute invertebrates filtered from the mud, including insects, crustaceans, molluscs, worms; also algae and diatoms. In recent years rice has become an important food source locally.
Movements Erratic, but present all year in some places. Doesn't necessarily breed every year – it depends on the water level and productivity of potential sites. May commute long distances to feed.
Voice A range of honking and cackling sounds.
Pairing style Monogamous, but pair bond probably for 1 breeding attempt only.
Nesting Highly colonial, in dense and often enormous colonies divided into sub-colonies.
Nest A cone of mud 30–40 cm high with a surprisingly slight cup on the top.
Productivity 1 brood a year.
Eggs 1.
Incubation 28–31 days, by both parents in long shifts.
Parenting style Both parents feed young at the nest and then at the crèche.
Food to young A unique type of milk (see text).
Leaving nest Young remains in the nest for 5–12 days; it is then able to walk and join a crèche. The parents continue to feed it, recognising it in the mêlée by voice, for up to 70 more days.

The Greater Flamingo is an odd-looking bird, but nothing in its strange design is wasted or incidental; even the pink coloration has its reason and purpose. Few birds are so distinctive, so peculiar and yet so fittingly adapted to an unusual way of life.

The flamingo is a tall, rangy bird, with long spindly legs and an equally long neck. The legs, bare right up to the body, enable it to wade in deep water, and the long neck ensures that, while wading, it can reach right down to the ooze on the lake bed at its feet. The front toes are webbed to give extra support when standing or walking in soft mud, but a flamingo is also quite capable of swimming when necessary. It feeds by filtering the water and mud for a limited range of invertebrates, during which process its head is immersed in the water, upside down and facing backwards.

The strange, bent bill never quite shuts, but leaves a permanent crack of 4–6 mm between the mandibles. When the bird is feeding, the tongue moves back and forth into the mouth cavity several times a second, and in doing so it draws water in and out through this gap to form the basis of a filtration system. Particles of 6 mm or more in diameter are excluded from entering, but smaller ones are drawn in. The inner edges of the mandibles are fitted with a network of tiny projections and hairs, and when water flows out these form a physical barrier to small particles in suspension, which are trapped. In this way the Greater Flamingo can filter out items as small as 0.5 mm in diameter. The characteristic kink in a flamingo's bill is necessary to maintain an even gap between the mandibles; if the bill were straight the gap would gradually increase along its length, and be too narrow for filtration at the base and too broad at the tip.

Greater Flamingos are drawn to highly saline or alkaline water; few other waterbirds can cope in this niche, so they have little competition. The range of food is limited; in Europe Greater Flamingos feed mainly on brine shrimps, which concentrate in vast numbers. A by-product of their unusual habitat is that the birds also ingest algae when feeding, and these make the carotenoid pigments that give flamingos their pink colour.

When feeding is good, the colour stimulates breeding. The first signs are spectacular group displays, in which the birds may, for example, lift their necks up in synchrony and then turn them rhythmically from side to side, a manoeuvre known as 'head-flagging'. Before long, the mood shifts towards nest-building, and the birds create sandcastle-like structures of mud, with a shallow top on which the single egg is laid. Uniquely, once the young hatch, they are fed on a fat- and protein-rich 'milk' made by the adults and secreted from the crop. This unusual food probably gives the young a good start in their challenging environment.

Swans, Geese and Ducks family *Anatidae* (an-**nat**-id-ee)

Habitat Almost any kind of wetland, from tiny ponds to large lakes and from totally fresh to highly saline water.
Food Swans and geese feed on aquatic vegetation and in winter will graze on arable fields. Many ducks also take some animal food when breeding. Seaducks eat various invertebrates and/or fish year round.
Movements Almost all highly migratory, with many breeding at high latitudes and wintering further south in very specific areas. Many also have traditional stopover areas on migration. Some journey to specific areas to moult. Males and females may winter in different areas.
Voice Bewick's and Whooper Swans utter honks and whoops or snorts; Geese make various honking, cackling and barking sounds. Ducks are famous for their quacks, typically louder and more frequent among females. Males make impressive range of unusual sounds.
Pairing style Swans and geese monogamous, usually pair for life. Ducks monogamous, for one season only, with extra-pair copulations often rife.
Nesting Usually solitary, though some (e.g. Mute Swan) are loosely colonial and others (e.g. Eider) more formally so. Swans often fiercely territorial.
Nest Swans a large pile of vegetation; geese usually a scrape in the ground out in the open, built up with vegetation and lined with down. Ducks usually a shallow bowl on the ground, lined with down; often well concealed; a few species nest in holes in trees.
Productivity 1 brood a year.
Eggs 3–8 (swans), 3–10 (geese), 3–14 (ducks).
Incubation 29–30 days in the Bewick's Swan, 35+ days in Whooper and Mute Swan; geese 24–30 days, ducks 21–32 days, usually by female only. Begins with last egg, so all hatch at about the same time.
Young Precocial, covered in down and with eyes open. Can feed themselves almost immediately and are soon highly mobile.
Parenting style Young feed themselves, but in swans and geese both adults lead and protect them. In most duck species male abandons female while she is incubating. Female leads brood from nest as soon as down of young dries, then broods and tends them.
Food to young As adult diet (swans and geese); young ducks generally gnats and other insects.
Leaving nest Young leave nest within hours of hatching and accompany one or both parents. Swans fledge at 40–150 days, geese at 35–75 days, ducks at 25–75 days, depending on species. Some species form crèches. Swans and geese remain with family into first winter.

Collectively known as 'wildfowl' or 'waterfowl', the swans, geese and ducks are an easily recognised group of birds with heavy bodies, rather long necks, strong wings and obviously webbed feet. In fact, only the front three toes are webbed, while the back toe is small and raised, but all members of the family are expert swimmers. Their ability on land varies considerably, depending on where the feet are set on the body. In swans, geese, Shelducks and dabbling ducks the feet are centrally placed, and the birds can walk well; diving ducks and seaducks have back-set feet, making them clumsy on land.

With their long, pointed wings powered by large flight muscles, almost all wildfowl are strong in the air. Many are long-distance migrants and ducks are probably among the fastest-flying birds of all, a speed of over 70 km/h having been recorded in level flight for the Eider. The majority of species breed in the northern half of Europe and vacate their breeding grounds in late summer. Female and immature ducks often travel further than adult males, a phenomenon known as differential migration. Swans and geese are unusual among birds in general for migrating in family parties.

Most members of the family are highly sociable outside the breeding season and may be encountered in large flocks, often in thousands. Representatives of all the groups mix freely with each other, so it is often possible to see several species of swans, geese or ducks together at the same time.

Wildfowl have an unusual way of moulting, which involves changing over all their flight feathers at about the same time, thereby becoming flightless for short periods. Most species congregate at special food-rich and safe areas to do this, and getting there may involve a considerable journey known as a 'moult migration'. Once they arrive it pays male ducks to go undercover, so to speak, so they abandon their perilously conspicuous coloration in favour of a special female-like plumage called 'eclipse plumage', which lasts until their flight feathers have grown back.

Wildfowl build rudimentary nests, a pile of vegetation at most and often just a shallow scrape. They lay quite high numbers of eggs and begin incubation with the last; this ensures that they all hatch at about the same time and the young can be led away from the vulnerable nest almost immediately. The young are very independent and can swim around and feed themselves almost straight away.

Swans genus *Cygnus* (**sig**-nuss)

Swans are the largest of the wildfowl, and among the biggest and heaviest birds in Europe. Their bulk can be explained in part by the need for a long and large gut to cope with a specialised vegetarian diet, but it also enables them to be intimidating and aggressive when confronted by predators or rivals. All swans are celebrated for their close family ties, especially between male and female. A pair mates for life as long as circumstances allow, and there is even a pre-breeding season of engagement for young prospective partners.

King Eider

Geese tribe *Anserini* (an-ser-**eye**-nee)

Geese are distinguished from the other wildfowl, and especially from ducks, in several ways. For one thing they are generally not very colourful, being either mainly brown (the so-called 'grey geese', *Anser*) or black and white ('black geese', *Branta*), although some certainly have bold markings. Importantly, the sexes do not differ in plumage, although males are usually bigger than females. In general geese are large wildfowl with long necks, rather triangular (not horizontally flattened) bills, relatively small heads, and legs that are positioned at the mid-point of the body. This last feature helps them to walk and run well, and many spend their days grazing on land rather than feeding in the water. All geese make loud, more or less cackling, grunting or yapping sounds. They form long-term, usually lifelong, pair bonds, and the young remain with the parents throughout their first winter of life.

Ducks subfamily *Anatinae* (an-**nat**-in-ee)

Ducks are amongst the most readily recognisable of birds, with their webbed feet, heavy bodies, horizontally flattened bills and familiar quacking voices. In most species, in contrast to swans and geese, male and female are coloured very differently, the male having bright and colourful plumage, the female being cryptically clad in brown or grey.

Bewick's Swan

Cygnus columbianus
(**sig**-nuss kol-lum-bee-**ay**-nuss)
length 1.15–1.3 m; wingspan 1.8–2.1 m

The Bewick's has by far the fastest life cycle of our three swans: the eggs hatch within a month of being laid and the young become fully feathered some five weeks after hatching, over twice as quickly as Mute Swan chicks. But for a bird of the High Arctic tundra, such speed is necessary. Summer at these latitudes is short.

The Bewick's Swan doesn't actually breed in Europe, but winters on a small number of selected, traditional sites in temperate regions in the northwest, mainly on floodplains and grassland, preferring fresh water. It tends to arrive late, often in October, and leaves in the early spring, in March. During this short stay it feeds on the roots, stolons and rhizomes of plants, either grazing on land or grubbing them up while swimming. While feeding or roosting it gathers in small flocks, within which family parties remain together; each individual can be recognised by the unique pattern of its bill. Bewick's are the noisiest of the swans, keeping up a continual babble on water and in the air.

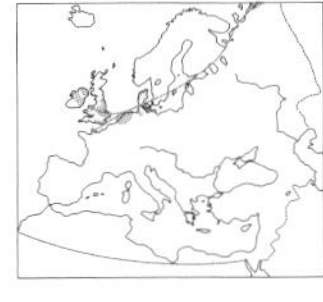

ID: Bill black and yellow in equal proportions, the yellow making a blunt shape against the black; smallest swan, with shortest neck, rounded head.

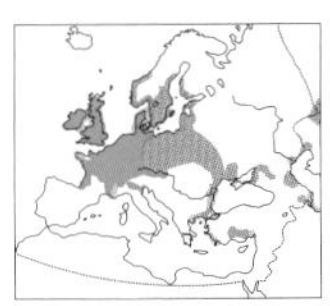

ID: Bill black and orange, usually held pointed downwards; neck often arched; relatively long tail; juvenile blotchy brown and white.

Mute Swan

Cygnus olor (**sig**-nuss **aw**-lor)
length 1.45–1.6 m; wingspan 2.1–2.4 m

When roused to threat a Mute Swan ruffles its neck feathers, arches its partially closed wings over its back and moves its head right back to rest between the wings. It then swims towards the source of its irritation with peculiar, two-footed strokes, jerking forward and frothing the water. This display, oddly enough, is called 'busking' and it is exclusive to the Mute Swan.

The Mute Swan is the largest of the swans and the least confined to the far north, at least as a breeding bird. Unlike the others, it has been successful in adapting to artificial environments and living alongside people.

Despite its name, the Mute Swan is far from voiceless; it will utter snorting sounds and, on occasion, even high-pitched, forlorn-sounding wails. But there is a time when, significantly, it doesn't call – in flight. Instead, the feathers on its wings are specially modified to produce a loud, far-carrying, singing swish when the bird is in the air, a sound that keeps a flock together and takes the place of a flight call.

Parental care is tender and long-lasting. In the first ten days of their lives the cygnets regularly ride on the back on an adult, usually the female, for both comfort and safety. During and after this time both parents pay close attention when the brood is on the water, fussing over the young and helping them to feed for themselves by uprooting vegetation and placing it under their cygnets' noses. The degree of care declines over time, of course, but most young Mute Swans remain with their parents well into the winter months.

Whooper Swan

Cygnus cygnus (**sig**-nuss **sig**-nuss)
length 1.45–1.6 m; wingspan 2.2–2.4 m

While many a Mute Swan leads a sedentary existence in Europe, the Whooper is more migratory, a herald of the changing seasons. Flocks depart from their breeding grounds in Iceland and Fennoscandia in September and return in late March or April, travelling in family parties and keeping together by means of their trumpeting, clanging flight calls, often uttered as three blasts. While migrating they can fly to extraordinary altitudes; one group was measured at 8850 m, close to the record for any bird anywhere.

Whoopers are less aggressive than Mute Swans and have a different threat display, in which a bird quivers its half-open wings and bows its head. Unlike Mutes, Whoopers don't carry their young on their backs; the cygnets must swim for themselves from the start.

In winter Whoopers are found more widely than Bewick's Swans and in a greater variety of wetland habitats, including those with an element of salt water.

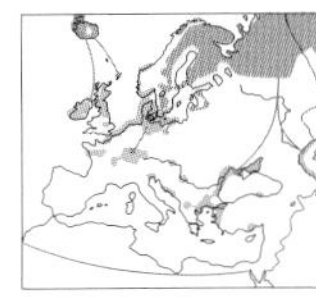

ID: Bill black and yellow, the yellow making a wedge with the black; larger and longer-necked than Bewick's; size close to Mute, but neck held straight and bill points forwards. Juvenile grey-brown, not blotchy.

ID: Large brown goose with dark head and neck and without any 'frosty' colour on wings and back. Legs dark orange-red.

Bean Goose

Anser fabalis (**an**-ser fa-**bay**-liss)
length 66–84 cm

If geese are generally thought of as waterbirds, the Bean Goose fits this description least well. As a wintering bird it takes to the water less than other geese, feeding mainly on dry agricultural fields. During the breeding season at least some Bean Geese hide their nests within birch scrub or even dense coniferous forest – an unusual habitat for a waterbird.

There has been speculation recently that the Bean Goose is not one species but two. The birds that nest in forests in the taiga belt are rather smaller than those breeding further north in more traditional, open habitats, and they have a different bill pattern. However, in the border between the taiga and the tundra, the 'forest tundra', the distinction breaks down and both forms, the so-called Taiga Bean Goose and Tundra Bean Goose, can be found breeding close to one another.

Of all the confusingly named 'grey geese', the Bean Goose is the least sociable, occurring typically in modestly sized flocks. It is also the least noisy, refraining from the incessant babble and overexcited clamour of other species.

Pink-footed Goose

Anser brachyrhynchus (**an**-ser brak-ki-**ring**-kuss)
length 66–75 cm

In their winter quarters Pink-footed Geese make spectacular commuting movements between their roost sites, on estuaries or large lakes, and their feeding sites on arable farmland, where they spend the day. To see them in action is one of the great experiences of birdwatching in Europe. The birds may travel as much as 30 km between the two sites, setting off at dawn and returning at dusk. They travel in huge groups, drawing V-shaped lines and waves across what is often a red sky, and all the while uttering perhaps the most musical of all goose calls, a staccato 'wick-wick' that fills the airwaves. Up to 40,000 birds may be involved in a single movement.

The winter day is short and the birds forage throughout without interruption where they can. The diet of grass, grain, winter cereals and potatoes is plentiful but not especially nutritious, so it's a case of graze until you drop. Sometimes, under a full moon, Pink-footed Geese will actually continue feeding into the night and roost nearby, amending their usual schedule.

At the end of winter Pink-footed Geese migrate to breeding areas in Iceland and Svalbard. Here they appear to be very fussy about where they nest. In Iceland pairs often select ledges on cliffs along the numerous river gorges, while others nest in more typical goose-like habitat among the tundra.

After breeding, Pink-footed Geese have a moult migration; in the case of Icelandic birds this can involve an apparently odd trip to Greenland, going north rather than south. They then return to their wintering areas, arriving in October and November.

ID: Smaller and shorter-necked than similar Bean Goose, with distinctive 'frosty' upper parts. Legs pink. Bill short, pink with black tip.

White-fronted Goose

Anser albifrons (**an**-ser **al**-bi-fronz)
length 65–78 cm

ID: *Small grey goose with two distinctive features: white band of feathering around the bill, and blotchy patches of black on the belly (not shown by immature birds). Bill pale orange or pink. Legs orange.*

A successful species that nests all around the Arctic, including North America, Greenland and Siberia, the White-fronted Goose is the most widely distributed of the 'grey geese'. It breeds on open, somewhat bushy tundra, often on islands amid lakes and rivers, and also on the raised parts of bogs. Any site chosen for breeding must afford reasonable cover, offer a view of any passing predators and be above the water level after the spring thaw. In contrast to many geese, White-fronted pairs usually nest on their own, at low density, far from other nest sites.

In Europe this bird is known mainly as a winter visitor. From October to March it seeks out low grassland, arable farmland and sometimes upland bogs, where it feeds on a wide variety of plant material. Birds from Greenland come to their winter quarters by way of a stopover in Iceland and are usually found in small flocks. Russian birds appear to have a more direct, transcontinental route and are much more sociable, often gathering in thousands to feed, loaf and roost.

Lesser White-fronted Goose

Anser erythropus (**an**-ser er-**rith**-roh-puss)
length 53–66 cm

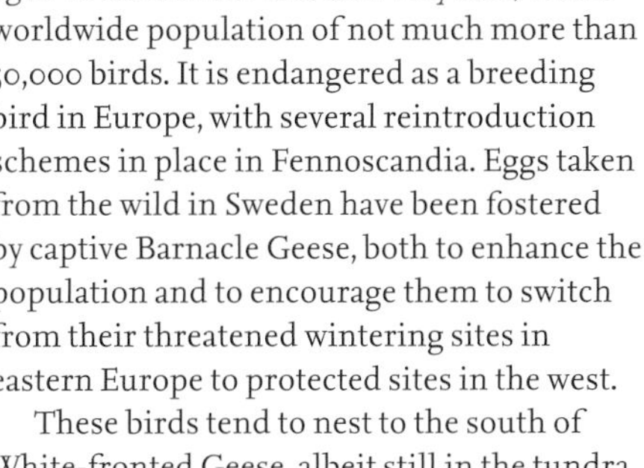

This is a smaller, daintier species than the very similar White-fronted Goose, with a faster feeding action and a greater tendency to run while grazing. It is also slightly more agile in the air. It is also now very rare, with a worldwide population of not much more than 50,000 birds. It is endangered as a breeding bird in Europe, with several reintroduction schemes in place in Fennoscandia. Eggs taken from the wild in Sweden have been fostered by captive Barnacle Geese, both to enhance the population and to encourage them to switch from their threatened wintering sites in eastern Europe to protected sites in the west.

These birds tend to nest to the south of White-fronted Geese, albeit still in the tundra or forest-tundra zone. They often place their nests among thickets and have a distinct preference for upland areas, slopes by streams and craggy cliffs. In common with the White-fronted Goose, pairs are not colonial, but well spaced.

Traditionally, the Lesser White-fronted Goose winters in far drier places than other 'grey geese', on steppes and semi-arid flats.

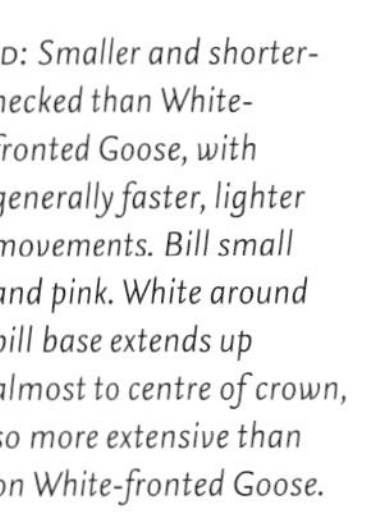

ID: *Smaller and shorter-necked than White-fronted Goose, with generally faster, lighter movements. Bill small and pink. White around bill base extends up almost to centre of crown, so more extensive than on White-fronted Goose. Diagnostic yellow eye ring.*

Greylag Goose

Anser anser (an-ser an-ser)
length 75–90 cm

If you eat goose for dinner you can be reasonably sure that, despite a few genetic twists and turns, your meal was essentially a Greylag in life. This is the best known of all geese, the one domesticated as a farmyard bird and the one that saved ancient Rome from the Gauls in 390 BC by doing what it does so well – spotting trouble and making a lot of noise. In much of Europe it is still an unsullied wild bird, inhabiting a broader spectrum of habitats and climates than other geese, including tundra, marshes and large lakes. But in some places, including southern Britain, the population originates from farmland birds that have gone wild and reverted, over a few generations, to the plumage pattern of their ancestors, if not to their natural timidity.

The Greylag Goose has been intensively studied, mostly in captivity. These studies have formed the basis for our understanding of imprinting, the process by which young birds in the wild recognise their mother almost from hatching and will instinctively follow her wherever she goes. Captive goslings can be made to follow not just non-parent birds, but also other animals, including people, and even simple objects. In the wild, imprinting helps the brood remain together under the protection of both parents.

In common with other geese, Greylags form long-term relationships and all pairs, migratory or otherwise, remain together all year. The bond is maintained by a complex vocabulary of calls and gestures. Of these, the most common and easily observed display is the 'triumph ceremony', in which the male launches an attack on a rival – real or imagined – and then returns to his mate to celebrate 'victory'. With head down and neck ruffled to show off the 'creases' that run down it, the male charges the foe. When he returns he holds his neck outstretched and the female follows suit; both call loudly, and although they may well face each other they will not actually meet front-on. That would be threatening; instead, the partners seem to peer past one another.

Another set of gestures ensures that, within flocks, birds have their own individual space where they can feed. In fact, since families remain together for many months after hatching, such a territory can be shared and all the members contribute to defending it. It's not a fixed territory but moves as the birds move, ensuring that the immature birds, those that would normally be bottom of the 'pecking order', are well fed.

The Greylag is the largest of the 'grey geese', the most powerful but the least agile in the air and the one requiring the longest run-up to become airborne. It feeds in the water more than other 'grey geese', often immersing its neck and upending its body to grasp submerged waterweeds and other plants. In winter flocks feed on agricultural land as well as on marshes and lakes.

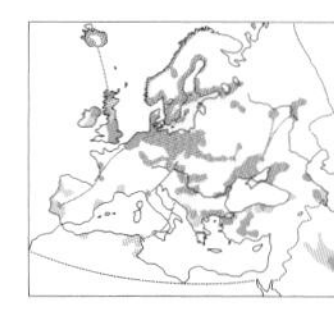

ID: Largest and heaviest of 'grey geese', with very large, triangular pink or orange bill. Little contrast between colour of head/neck and rest of body. Legs pinkish. In flight, prominent grey forward half of wings, contrasting with brown back.

ID: *Unmistakable large goose with brown body and black head and neck, the latter broken by white throat.*

Canada Goose

Branta canadensis (**bran**-ta kan-na-**den**-siss)
length 56–110 cm (highly variable)

There is no doubt that a few truly wild Canada Geese find their way to Europe each year from their native North America, tagging along with migrating Pinkfeet or White-fronted Geese. But we know this bird primarily as an introduced species: first released into the grounds of stately homes in England in the 18th century, it has been spreading, with continued introductions, ever since. Its rate of increase has accelerated in the last 30 years and it is now found in Fennoscandia, the Low Countries, Germany and France as well as Britain.

This is a large, long-necked goose, with a regal flight action that recalls that of a swan. It is aggressive and very noisy, making a rather discordant double honk that is not easy on the ear, but keeps family parties and flocks together day and night. The basic unit of a flock is the family group, and tussles between groups are common, with much nodding, head-lifting and aggressive head-down charges, accompanied by a cacophony of calls.

As an introduced bird, the Canada Goose lives rather differently in Europe to the way it behaves in North America. Far from being a bird of wild places such as tundra and large wetlands, here it seems happy to settle down on park lakes, gentle rivers and gravel pits, placing its nests on islands or riverbanks only a few metres from people and their dogs. It has also become far more sedentary, largely abandoning the celebrated mass migrations of American birds in favour of local movements. But there are signs that things are changing; some Fennoscandian birds now move south to continental Europe in winter and some significant moult migrations are undertaken in Britain.

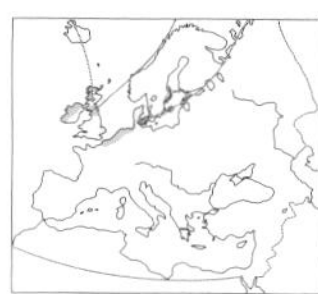

ID: Small goose with black neck, head mainly white or tinged yellow. Neat and strong contrast between black neck/breast and rest of grey-white underparts.

Barnacle Goose

Branta leucopsis (**bran**-ta loo-**kop**-sis)
length 58–70 cm

Most birdwatchers in Europe know this small goose from the densely packed wintering flocks feeding on salt marshes or coastal fields, and are perhaps unaware that its breeding season holds high dramas up in the Arctic. The Barnacle Goose is perhaps more restless than some of the others, though, continually moving around and bickering. Its flight call bears a striking resemblance to the yapping of a small dog.

In the Arctic of Greenland, Svalbard and Russia, the Barnacle Goose heads for the customary tundra zones of other geese in the breeding season, but one of its most regular breeding sites is rather unusual and at first sight would not appear to be very suitable. The birds specifically seek out precipitous places such as cliffs and rocky pinnacles, where they make a small depression in the ground and surround it with grass and copious down. Being placed high up and out of the reach of ground predators, the nest is safe for the period of incubation, but it presents a problem to the chicks when they hatch; their very first task is to make the leap from cliff ledge to ground, where the adults can lead them to rich feeding areas. With much vocal encouragement they launch out on what can be a fall of 20 m or more, and for landing they can depend only on the lightness of their bodies and a certain amount of luck. A good number perish, but presumably their overall chances are better than if they were raised in a more vulnerable, conventional ground nest.

In recent years the Barnacle Goose has spread as a breeding bird in Europe and now occupies quite a few islands in the Baltic, far to the south of its normal range.

Brent Goose

Branta bernicla (**bran**-ta ber-**nik**-la)
length 56–61 cm

This small dark goose is a bird of the extreme Arctic, breeding between the latitudes of 70° and 80°N. Here the weather is tempestuous and fickle, allowing the birds no more than three months to complete their breeding cycle of selecting a site, building a nest, laying eggs and raising the young to the flying stage. After this the door will be locked by the start of the long winter freeze. In order to get a head start the birds feed up heartily on the fresh spring growth of grass before they leave their wintering or staging areas, thereby increasing their weight by up to 20 per cent. Then, upon arrival, they can get on with their tasks without having to wait for the spring thaw to provide them with food.

The Brent Goose is unusual among geese in being something of a specialist in the winter. It shuns the inland waters favoured by most geese in favour of being strictly coastal and feeding on the estuarine plant *Zostera*, or eel grass, one of the few marine flowering plants in the world. This is not its only food; it will also take various salt-marsh plants and seaweeds, and in recent years it has come to use pasture and arable fields, eating the shoots of winter cereals and terrestrial grasses.

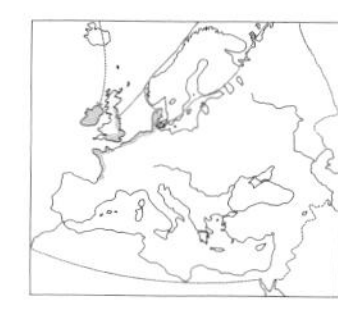

ID: Very distinctive small dark goose of estuaries and coasts; small white neck patch. Not much larger than Mallard.

juv. light-bellied race

adult light-bellied race

adult dark-bellied race

Egyptian Goose

Alopochen aegyptiacus
(al-**loh**-po-ken ee-jip-ti-**ah**-kuss)
length 63–73 cm

Only an honorary goose, the Egyptian is most closely related to the Shelducks. It can breed when only a year old, rather than three, the norm for 'real' geese. It is also perfectly capable of perching in trees, which is beyond the means of the rest.

The Egyptian Goose seems an unlikely candidate for introduction to Europe, being essentially an African bird adapted to warm climates. That said, from small beginnings in the 18th century ,there are now at least a thousand in Britain; it reached Holland in the 1970s and Belgium in the 1980s, and recent records in France and Germany suggest that it has not finished with its expansion yet.

This bird breeds earlier than true geese, laying eggs in March. Some nest on the ground under bushes, others use holes in banks and still others go for a hole in a tree.

ID: Oddly long-legged, curiously coloured 'goose'. Distinctive 'shades' around eye. Prominent white forewing obvious in flight.

ID: Unmistakable, although can be difficult to pick out among large flocks of Brent Geese.

Red-breasted Goose

Branta ruficollis (**bran**-ta roo-fik-**koll**-iss)
length 53–56 cm

Although this brightly coloured goose nests no nearer to us than central Siberia, on the Taymyr Peninsula – where, incidentally, its entire world population is found – it comes to Europe in winter, to the steppes and cultivated fields of the Black Sea region. In the 1990s there were about 70,000 birds, mainly in Romania and Bulgaria. It is a very late arrival here, appearing no earlier than November, having paused at several Russian stopovers en route. In contrast to most other geese, it acquires all its winter food by grazing on land, and is often found far from the nearest water.

When breeding, the Red-breasted Goose is known for its habit of nesting close to the eyries of fierce predatory birds such as Rough-legged Buzzards and Peregrines. The geese are watchful and the raptors aggressive, able to repel intrusions by large ground predators, so it seems as though both parties benefit. Even so, it is remarkable that a goose may nest as close as 5 m to a bird of prey.

ID: *Very distinctive long-necked waterfowl with bottle-green head and chestnut band around neck. Male has red bill knob; female lacks this and may show powder patch of white at base of bill.*

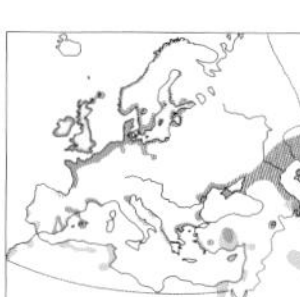

Shelduck

Tadorna tadorna (ta-**dorr**-na ta-**dorr**-na)
length 58–67 cm

The Shelduck occupies something of a grey area between ducks and geese, sharing certain characteristics of both. It is large for a duck or small for a goose, but it is more aquatic than most geese, feeding in water or mudflats rather than on fields. The sexes look much alike, as do those of geese, and the partners usually stay together for more than one breeding season. Yet it can perch in trees, which a true goose cannot, and nests in burrows. Finally it has a triumph ceremony and other displays that are more goose-like than duck-like. Decide for yourself!

The raucous laughter of the female and fast, breathy whistles of the male are familiar sounds in estuaries throughout northwest Europe, where the birds breed and winter. In these habitats Shelducks feed on a variety of creatures within the intertidal zone – their favourite appears to be a small marine snail called *Hydrobia*, which is abundant in soft mud. The birds feed in various ways; when the tide is out they will move their bill from side to side over the surface as they walk, hoping to detect something edible. When the mud is partially covered with water they will dip their head and neck into the water or upend to reach the bottom.

A few Shelducks occur in eastern Europe, on steppe lakes in the Black Sea region. These feed on freshwater creatures, using much the same techniques as estuary birds.

Wherever they occur Shelducks normally nest in burrows, although they can use the ground, buildings or even tree holes instead where necessary. A typical site is a rabbit hole within a dune system, and here the eggs are laid, sometimes as much as 3 m underground. It appears that the male always stays outside the burrow, keeping watch, and is not welcome if he tries to come in!

Almost as soon as they hatch, young Shelducks are led to water by the female, or by both parents. At first they are cared for privately, but it is not long before various families come together in informal groups. Then, after just two or three weeks, the adults fly far away to moult, leaving their young in crèches of up to a hundred birds. These are cared for by a handful of adults that remain behind and moult on site and may or may not have their own young within the crèche; so far it isn't known how or why certain individuals 'volunteer' for this duty.

The adults' moult migration is remarkable in itself. Almost every bird in northwest Europe leaves its breeding area and meets in one place, on the fantastically rich mudflats and shallow waters of the Helgoland Bight off northern Germany. With treacherous sands protecting them from predators, up to 100,000 birds moult here and become temporarily flightless in late July and August. In fact, they seem very reluctant to leave these vast food supplies and many do not reappear on their breeding grounds until late autumn or even the following spring.

Ruddy Shelduck

Tadorna ferruginea (ta-**dorr**-na fer-roo-**jin**-neh-a)
length 61–67 cm

Primarily a bird of the steppes of Central Asia, in Europe the Ruddy Shelduck breeds only in Turkey, Greece, Bulgaria, Romania and Russia. It differs in many aspects of its behaviour from the Shelduck, not least in occupying only inland sites far from the maritime coast and often well away from any large bodies of water.

While the Shelduck feeds preferentially on animal food, the Ruddy Shelduck is far more of an omnivore, grazing on plant material throughout the year. It will also wade in shallow water, pulling up plants and animals, and it will swim and reach food by upending. It habitually feeds at night as well as by day.

In common with Shelducks, these birds usually select holes for their nest sites, in banks, cliffs, trees and buildings. The young are led to water and often join other families, but there is no formal crèche system as in the Shelduck. And although there is a moult migration, all birds in the population join in once the young have learned to fly.

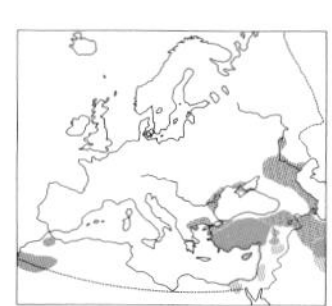

ID: *Easily identified by its distinctive coloration, dark chestnut with paler head; female has more white on head than male. In flight shows white coverts, like Egyptian Goose.*

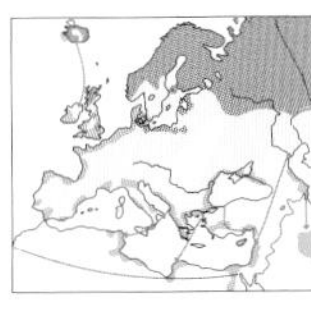

ID: Male very distinctive. Female is darker and less streaky brown than similar female ducks, and shows distinctive shaded patch around eye. Look also for white belly and small bill. With male, beware of Pochard, which dives and has black chest.

Wigeon

Anas penelope (**ann**-nass pen-**nell**-lop-pee)
length 45–51 cm

The Wigeon provides a good example of how a bird uses various features of its plumage in display. Look at a male Wigeon in flight and you will be struck by his brilliant white forewing. On the water, when rivals want to threaten each other, they casually lift their folded wings high above their backs for a moment, showing off the white markings to full effect. It is also hard to miss the male's straw-coloured forehead. Similarly, when the dominant male in a displaying group wishes to demonstrate his superiority to a female, he raises the feathers on his forehead and moves his bill slightly from side to side, exaggerating and showing off that choice feature. No other male ducks have similar plumage marks to the Wigeon, and no others perform these highly specific displays.

This attractively coloured duck belongs to the group known as surface-feeding or dabbling ducks, each of which is ecologically distinct from the others; the Wigeon is the consummate grazer of the group, feeding less on water than on land and eating grass, leaves, stems and roots. When foraging, Wigeons often gather in densely packed flocks, covering the grassy swards with their bodies and spilling forward like an incoming tide. They have the unusual combination of a small bill and an exceedingly strong jawbone, which enables them to pull up grass with great vigour and make use of the bill's cutting edge at the same time.

Sometimes Wigeons abandon their grazing habit for a short while and make use of other methods instead. They will readily swim, dabble and sometimes upend, although they perform this manoeuvre less often than most other ducks. Perhaps their most interesting secondary foraging method, though, is to be something of a pest to other birds. Quite a few wildfowl share the Wigeon's vegetarian diet, and Wigeons will, at times, feed off their scraps. Mute Swans, for example, can reach plant matter growing well down on the lake bed and in the process of bringing a mouthful to the surface they inevitably lose some from their grasp. To take advantage of this, Wigeons have been known to position themselves virtually under a swan's neck ready to catch the spillage, and they sometimes do the same to White-fronted Geese. Coots, for their part, dive to get food, but they must come to the water surface to swallow it, so they, too, often find themselves with a Wigeon in close attendance.

The Wigeon breeds only in northern Europe, although it is not closely attached to Arctic regions and avoids open tundra. In fact, it often nests in quite bushy habitats, so long as these are by lakes or marshes; and occasionally it will even select a site among trees. The nest is always on the ground, well concealed in low cover.

Few duck are as vocal, and memorably so, as the Wigeon. Throughout the pairing season in autumn and winter the males constantly utter an excited, almost surprised exclamatory whistle, while the females grunt approvingly.

Mandarin Duck

Aix galericulata (**ayks** ga-ler-ri-koo-**lah**-ta)
length 41–49 cm

The showy Mandarin Duck is not a native species in Europe, but an introduced alien from the Far East. It was first released in Britain in the 18th century, but never prospered before about the 1930s, when birds began breeding in the wild in earnest. Since then its population has grown to about 3500 breeding pairs, with a few others scattered around northwest Europe.

When breeding, this is a secretive species. Its habitat, unusual for a duck, consists of still or slow-flowing water surrounded by dense wood or forest, with branches overhanging the surface; most ducks prefer more open waters. The Mandarin is an agile, fast-flying bird, well used to twisting and turning between avenues of fringing trees. The nest itself is placed in a hole in a tree, especially an oak, and may be 15 m up. Hollow stumps are also frequently used.

In display the male Mandarin raises the orange 'sails' on his back and, with crest fully extended, dips his bill in the water and then passes it coaxingly behind a sail as a female watches. At the same time he makes an excited, breathy whistle. A group of males performing to a single female in communal courtship is an engaging sight, especially when the performance takes place, as it usually does, in the lifting mist of an early morning.

ID: Both sexes unmistakable.

Gadwall

Anas strepera (**ann**-nass strep-**pee**-ra)
length 46–56 cm

There are some characters that can only be appreciated in close-up, and one of these is undoubtedly the Gadwall. The male lacks any of the striking features or gaudy plumage of other drakes, and can look very dull at a distance, but get within a few metres of him and you will soon make out the attractive peppery markings on the crown and breast, and the pleasing brown plumes over the back.

There is one species, though, that hopes not to get too close to a Gadwall, and that is the Coot. Both are vegetarian, but the Gadwall is confined to feeding from the surface, while the Coot can dive. Gadwalls are not slow to take advantage of this and flocks may spend many hours intercepting feeding Coots as they rise to the surface, stealing their food. Wigeons also do this occasionally, but Gadwalls are much worse; thieving from Coots can, indeed, allow them to spend the winter on deeper water than would otherwise be the case. In North America the Gadwall parasitises the American Coot (*Fulica americana*) instead.

For the most part Gadwalls rely on highly productive, sheltered fresh water for their living. They tend to stick close to emergent vegetation and take plant material from the top few centimetres of the water, by head-dipping. They only occasionally upend or graze on land, and they do not normally feed from the water surface or on the mud.

Courtship begins very soon after breeding, from August onwards. The males have a 'head-up-tail-up' display that shows off their black hindquarters and they perform this communally, while the females mill around outside their 'ring'. Pairs form much faster than those of other dabbling ducks, because couples are dominant over single birds in access to food resources. It is also suspected that, in contrast to most other ducks, pairs may persist from year to year.

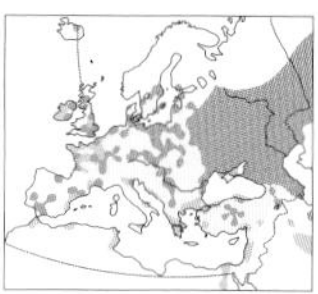

ID: Male and female both show white patch on wings (speculum) in flight and often at rest. Male has black rear end that directly abuts greyish lower belly. Female similar to Mallard but bill has neat orange sides. An elegant duck with rounded crown and upright posture.

Eurasian Teal

Anas crecca (**ann**-nass **krek**-ka)
length 34–38 cm

No duck in Europe is as small or as agile as the Teal. Flocks of these birds can rise vertically from the water, apparently with little effort. They don't need a run-up, but instead 'spring' into the air with a tremendous kick of the feet. Once airborne they can twist and turn, and they move with such quick wingbeats that groups are easily confused with tightly knit packs of waders.

Being so manoeuvrable has enabled the Teal to specialise in utilising small or very small bodies of water throughout the year. The typical breeding habitat is a tiny freshwater pool, bog or stream, often quite an isolated one, and sites surrounded by trees or bushes are perfectly acceptable. So long as the Teal has some shallow water available with ample fringing vegetation, the size of the area matters little and access is rarely a problem. When not breeding, the Teal is more catholic in its choice of habitat, visiting any type of water, large or small, and expanding into estuarine and even coastal waters.

When feeding, the Teal works the mud rather than the water itself. Typically it walks forward on a muddy surface with its head down and bill level with its feet, ingesting the ooze and filtering edible particles from it. Items taken include a wide variety of plants and animals, but in winter the diet narrows somewhat and most individuals get by mainly on seeds. Teal also swim to feed, both by picking from the water surface and by upending below it. This shallow-water habitat quickly freezes over when the temperature falls in winter and the birds then evacuate a non-breeding area to head west or south in search of milder conditions.

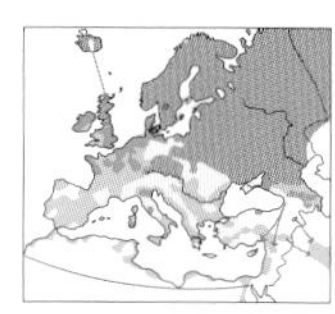

ID: Very small, with distinctive short neck. Male unmistakable. Female best recognised by size, and has a small bill with a faint orange base, not much of a pattern on the head, and a small white streak below the tail.

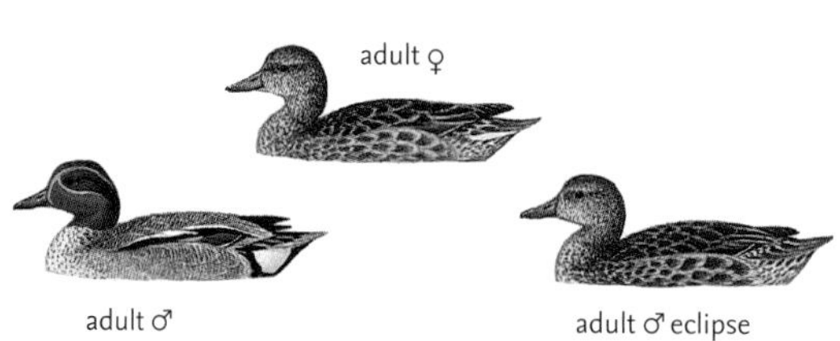

ID: Male unmistakable. Female paler brown than most other related female ducks, with plain grey bill; look for distinctive tapered shape.

Northern Pintail

Anas acuta (**ann**-nass ak-**kew**-ta)
length 51–66 cm

Tapered at both ends, the Pintail is an elegant duck. The male's long tail is mostly for show. The long neck enables both sexes to reach down well below the water surface for food, and they typically choose feeding areas with a water depth of 10–30 cm. They don't dive but do repeatedly upend, lowering their neck until they tip over, bottom up and head down, maintaining this position with furious paddling. Upending allows them to float on the surface and yet trawl the mud of the lake or estuary bed for small invertebrates and plant matter. No other dabbling duck upends as much as the Pintail. At times, though, it will also dabble on the surface of the water and even come on to land to graze, especially in winter. Much of its feeding activity takes place at night.

This is a very sociable species, gathering in large flocks in winter, although if disturbed the birds of a flock will split up into much smaller parties. Pintails often fly high, rather more so than other ducks, and they progress with very quick wingbeats. In autumn the two sexes have very different schedules and it is commonplace to find flocks containing only males or only females. The males leave the nest site during incubation and migrate away with other males to moult. The females and young follow, and it is not until late autumn that flocks start mixing again.

Pintails breed in flooded grasslands, meadows and marshes. Their nest is found in more open places than those of other dabbling ducks, quite often as much as 1–2 km from water, although 200 m is more usual. Suitable habitat is both scattered and often ephemeral, making the Pintail a rather sporadic breeder throughout its range.

Shoveler

Anas clypeata (**ann**-nass clye-pee-**ah**-ta)
length 44–52 cm

The Shoveler's outsize bill is its tool and its trademark. It is so long, so large and so greatly broadened at the tip that it dominates the bird's silhouette. It seems that the Shoveler can hardly swim without holding its head down with the bill resting on the water, as if it were carrying a heavy burden. But, of course, the bill is an adaptation for the Shoveler's main feeding technique, that of filtering or sieving. The tip is broadened to allow water in as the bird moves forward, and the bill itself is voluminous to allow plenty of water to be processed in one go. On the sides of the bill, both mandibles are fitted with comb-like projections called lamellae. These are found in most ducks, but in the Shoveler they are longer and denser than usual, forming a very efficient barrier to even the smallest particles as they attempt to flow out through the sides of the bill, pumped by the tongue. Despite eating very small items, the Shoveler can consume up to 10 per cent of its body weight in one day.

This sort of feeding requires shallow water with plenty of edible particles in suspension, so the Shoveler is drawn to productive freshwater marshes and lakes with plenty of fringing, but not stifling vegetation. It ingests all kinds of particles, including crustaceans, snails, insect larvae, seeds and plant debris. Its work is made easier if the mud can be stirred up first, so a particular feature of groups of feeding Shovelers is not that they require personal space, but that they benefit from being under each other's feet, so to speak. Birds in flocks often form a circle or circling huddle, each one taking advantage of the stirring caused by the bird swimming in front.

On productive waters Shovelers can find all the resources they need in one small area, which means that, in contrast to most ducks, they are highly territorial in the breeding season, defending their space from all comers by pumping their head up and down in threat with the bill pointing slightly upward. The male defends both site and female, enabling the two birds to form a stronger bond than is found in most ducks. There is less infidelity or rape than in most other species, and the male sometimes remains with the female right up to the end of the incubation period.

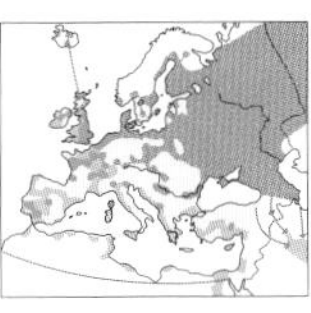

ID: Outsize bill diagnostic.

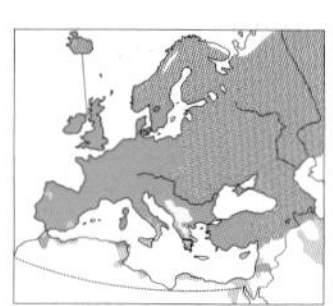

Mallard

Anas platyrhynchos (**ann**-nass plat-ti-**ring**-koss)
length 50–65 cm

ID: Male unmistakable. Female extremely variable, but look especially for purple speculum bordered by white. Quite a large duck, with fairly flat crown; bill pattern of female diffuse.

This is much the commonest and most familiar duck in Europe, remarkable in its adaptability and its ease with people. When children speak of 'ducks' they are referring to the Mallard, and many a lay person is unaware that any other sort exists – despite the fact that, worldwide, there are another hundred or so! This is the one that comes to bread at park lakes, and occupies the village pond. It is also abundant in wild habitats, from extensive marshes to small streams, and although it is primarily a bird of fresh water it will visit salt marshes in winter and even swim on the sea within sight of land.

Although the Mallard has a specific and recognisable plumage, with the drake sporting a fine bottle-green head and cute curling-up tail, centuries of domestication have produced a wide range of different breeds with different colours and characteristics. This meddling, together with extensive hybridisation with all manner of suitors in the wild and otherwise, has further mixed the genes to create a subclass of Mallard that looks nothing like the original. So you can find pure white ducks, glossy black ducks, ducks with crests, ducks with huge, bloated bodies and ducks with hideous thin necks, and they are all, essentially, Mallards. They often confuse birdwatchers into thinking that they have stumbled upon some special bird, so rare that it is not in the book.

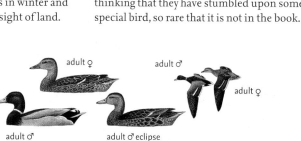

But this resilient species is still, in its original form, irrepressibly abundant. Part of that success is down to its ability to utilise just about every feeding method known to a duck, except for diving (but it occasionally does even this). So it can dabble with the best dabblers, it can upend, immerse just its head and neck, graze on grass and steal food from others. It takes a wide range of foods, both plant and animal, and is so opportunistic that it will simply indulge in whatever food item is most readily available on site. That, of course, is the recipe for a successful species.

For breeding, the Mallard is equally tolerant. It uses a wide variety of sites, placing its nest on the ground under various forms of thick vegetation, in the open on islands, in a hole in a tree, on the old nest of a large bird or on top of a building. Most Mallards are somewhat territorial, so the nests are well dispersed, but there are times when they can be placed only a few metres apart. In common with other ducks the female builds a rudimentary structure: just a hollow surrounded by fragments of plant debris and lined with a great deal of down from her own breast. During incubation the male leaves the area and the female broods and tends the young without his conspicuous presence.

Considering that the Mallard's pair bond breaks up during incubation and that most birds probably change their mates from year to year, the process of forming pairs in the first place is remarkably prolonged. It begins, in fact, in the autumn, when both sexes mix in winter flocks and the males are wearing smart new plumage. Courtship gets under way, as with other ducks, with a communal display by a number of males (usually no more than ten). It is easy to miss, because it consists of subtle gestures such as wags of the tail, shakes of the head and stretching, but there are also more elaborate routines, including placing the bill on the water surface and, with a flick of the head, throwing up droplets of water in the female's direction. This last 'water-flick' move is generally followed by a lifting of the front and rear of the body, the so-called 'head-up-tail-up' posture.

Eventually a female makes a choice and, often in the latter half of the winter, pair formation switches to repeated cameos in which the chosen male fights with and chases away rejected males, with the female's complicit encouragement. The male's proficiency at driving peers away is an important show of his fitness as a mate. As a reward, copulation is frequent from early spring onwards; both sexes approach each other and nod their heads up and down repeatedly, before the male eventually mounts.

adult ♀ adult ♂ adult ♀ adult ♂ adult ♂ eclipse

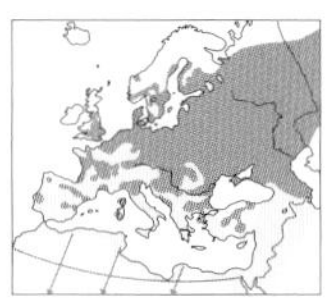

Garganey

Anas querquedula (**ann**-nass kwer-kwed-**doo**-la)
length 37–41 cm

ID: Only just larger than Teal. Male easily recognised. Female has larger bill than Teal and distinctive face pattern with dark supercilium and pale spot at base of bill. Bill is grey without orange base. No streak below tail.

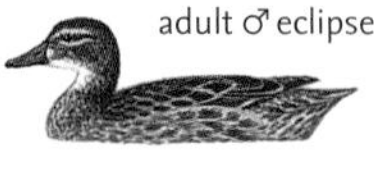

adult ♂ eclipse

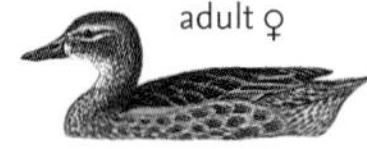

adult ♀

adult ♂ adult ♀

There is nothing unusual about a duck being a migrant – many species commute between breeding and wintering grounds in different parts of Europe. But the Garganey has the distinction of being the only duck to visit our continent only in the summer, like a Cuckoo or a Swallow. It arrives in March, having already paired in its winter flocks in West Africa, and leaves in October, not yet fully out of its eclipse plumage. Interestingly, Garganeys on southbound migration travel either through Spain or down the peninsula of Italy, but when they return all seem to use the Italian route.

The Garganey is a small and retiring duck, found principally in freshwater marshes, especially those bordered by steppe or grassland. It hugs the vegetation and can be difficult to observe, and it is also very shy, springing from the water at the slightest disturbance. It generally feeds by immersing its neck in the water, although it will pick from the surface, too, and occasionally upends. It eats both animal and plant matter.

When the males are displaying in communal courtship, they have a routine that is unique among dabbling ducks. They lean backwards so far that their crown touches their lower back and their bill points almost upwards; then, with a quick call like a dry rattle, immediately return to normal. Presumably this shows off the males' smart half-moon-shaped eyebrow to good effect.

Marbled Duck

Marmaronetta angustirostris
(mar-mar-ron-**net**-ta ang-goos-stir-**ross**-triss)
length 39–42 cm

ID: Highly distinctive duck with dark eye patch, crest and porridge-coloured plumage.

With its pale plumage, lethargic manner and muted vocabulary, the Marbled Duck is a highly unusual duck. It is extremely rare, too, being found in our region only in Spain, where less than a hundred pairs breed. It inhabits wetlands, both fresh and saline, and especially favours those that are shallow and surrounded with very rich, dense fringing vegetation. Although it is often seen sitting on logs or branches that just stick out from the water, the Marbled Duck is otherwise very difficult to observe, for it tends to hide away in thick shade and seldom flies or swims far.

The Marbled Duck occupies a space between typical dabbling ducks and typical diving ducks. It has centrally placed feet, like a dabbler, and only seldom dives. Yet it lacks the colourful wing pattern of a true dabbler and its pre-copulatory behaviour is closer to that of a diving duck, the usual head-nodding being replaced with both sexes dipping their bills into the water and sipping a drink. Having said that, though, male Marbled Ducks have communal courtship displays straight out of the dabblers' handbook.

Marbled Ducks usually nest on the ground in tall vegetation, although in some parts of Spain they use thatched buildings. And while some pairs are well dispersed and territorial, others come together to form small, densely packed colonies.

adult ♂

adult ♀

adult ♂ adult ♀

Red-crested Pochard

Netta rufina (**net**-ta roo-**fie**-na)
length 53–57 cm

Several aspects of the Red-crested Pochard's biology are highly unusual. It is, for example, the only species of duck to include courtship feeding as part of its pair-strengthening behaviour. This practice is common among many other birds from terns to tits, and in this species involves the male diving down to collect some waterweed, bringing it up and placing it on the water in sight of the female, who comes forward to consume it. The idea is presumably to provide the female with extra rations while she is forming eggs inside her body (that's its function in other birds), yet sometimes the male brings up an inedible object such as a twig instead!

Female Red-crested Pochards are also noted for 'egg dumping' – laying surplus eggs in the nests of other birds, Cuckoo style. The victims include members of its own species, plus Common Pochards and sometimes Mallards. The Red-crested Pochard and its chicks do not destroy the eggs or young of the host; the female simply steals in and, while the owner of the nest is not looking, increases the burden of parental care for the stranger while clandestinely improving her own productivity.

When not engaged in unusual breeding behaviour, the Red-crested Pochard has the best of both worlds when feeding. Although technically a diving duck and skilled underwater, it rides high when swimming and can both dabble efficiently and upend. It lives on large, relatively deep, reed-fringed freshwater lakes.

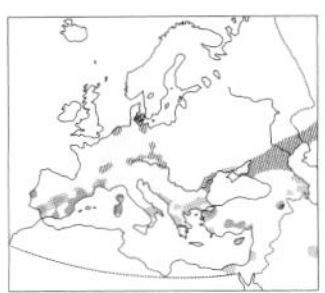

ID: Large, long-necked diving duck with very rounded crown. Male unmistakable. Female has long bill with pink spot at base, whitish cheek contrasting with coffee-brown crown. See female Common Scoter and Smew.

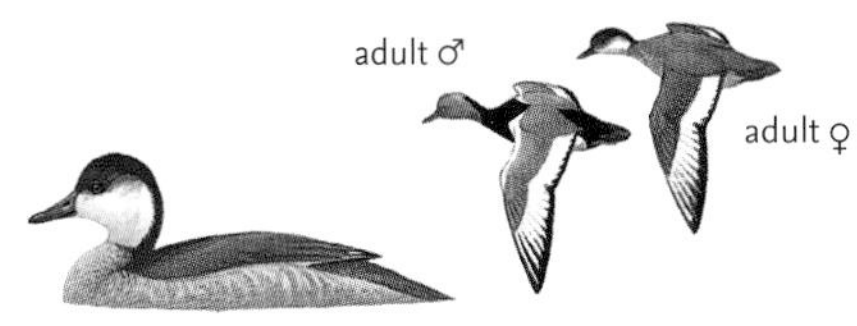

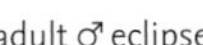

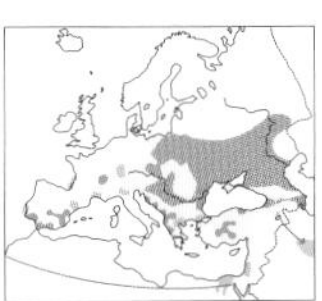

ID: Dark diving duck with very sharply defined white undertail patch. Head with high forehead and peaked crown. Male has white eye.

Ferruginous Duck

Aythya nyroca (**eye**-thi-a nye-**roh**-ka)
length 38–42 cm

'Ferruginous' means the colour of iron rust, which is a most appropriate name for this smart duck of continental Europe and Asia. It is a scarce and declining species, breeding on highly productive lakes with a great deal of emergent and fringing vegetation, interspersed with patches of open water. Although it is a diving duck, the Ferruginous also spends a lot of time swimming with its neck immersed, upending and even dabbling on the surface. A high percentage of its food is vegetable, including leaves, stems and seeds, but it is not averse to ingesting a variety of small aquatic creatures as well.

In common with several diving ducks, which are extremely awkward on land, the Ferruginous Duck usually builds its nest very close to the water's edge or even partially in the water, concealed within lush vegetation. Some pairs nest in close proximity to each other and the nest may also be placed among a colony of Black-headed Gulls or other marshland birds; the ducks benefit from the gulls' communal vigilance and aggression towards predators.

As ducks go, the Ferruginous is not very sociable, so it is hard to see more than a couple of pairs together at any one time.

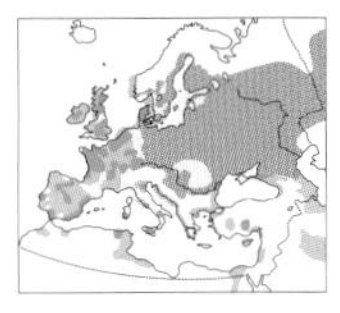

ID: Diving duck with peaked crown and sloping forehead. Male's three-colour pattern, with rusty red head, easily identified. Female has blotchy pale head with eye ring and slight whisker, rest of body grey-brown.

Pochard

Aythya ferina (**eye**-thi-a fer-**rie**-na)
length 42–49 cm

If you see a duck asleep in the daytime it is likely to be a Pochard, because this smart three-coloured bird usually shows a peak of feeding activity at night. It is common to see groups of them floating close together on a lake, their heads resting on their backs, while the more diurnally inclined Tufted Duck, with which the Pochard often shares the same waters, busies itself feeding nearby. Both species dive for their food but, while the Tufted Duck eats mainly animal material, the Pochard tends to be more of a vegetarian (though neither is restricted either way).

The Pochard obtains most of its nutriment from the bottom of a lake or pond. It specifically seeks fresh waters 1–2.5 m deep, with plenty of vegetation growing on the bottom but without too many obstacles cluttering its dives. Lakes with bottom-growing vegetation need to be clear enough to let sunlight through, so the presence of Pochards on a lake is often a good indicator of its depth, productivity and chemistry.

Pochards are highly sociable, sometimes gathering in enormous flocks, one of the features of which is the almost inevitable uneven sex ratio. Male Pochards migrate a couple of weeks before females, and settle in on their wintering grounds so completely that, when the females arrive, all the places are taken, so to speak, and the habitat cannot support any more bodies. The females are forced to move on and seek a wintering site further south. It's not very chivalrous!

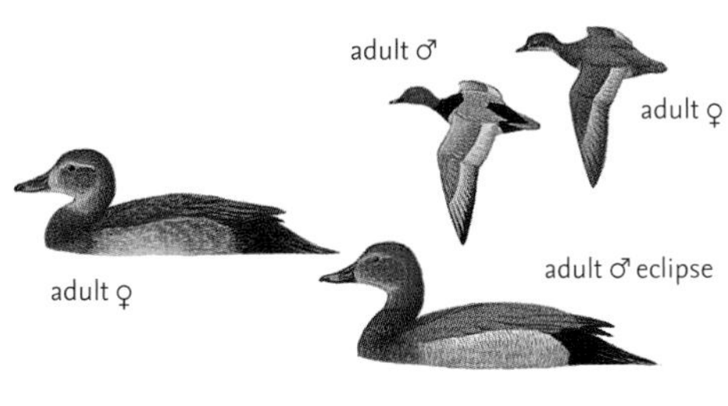

Greater Scaup

Aythya marila (**eye**-thi-a ma-**rie**-la)
length 42–51 cm

The Greater Scaup nests farther north than other diving ducks of the same genus, inhabiting freshwater lakes, large and small, within the tundra zone and on its fringes. It also has its own distinct winter habitat: while the rest are freshwater birds, the Scaup is very largely coastal.

Scaups are quite fussy about their wintering sites, tending to concentrate in large numbers at relatively few favoured locations. Here flocks of hundreds or even thousands may collect, feeding on productive mussel beds or near sewage outfalls with high concentrations of worms. Being diving ducks and bottom feeders, their feeding times are dictated by the tide. They don't like to dive too deep, only to 5–6 m, so at high tide they often simply roost or loaf. In many areas they also prefer to feed at night.

The nest of a Greater Scaup tends to be well hidden in low vegetation, very close to water. When they hatch, young Scaup are less independent than, for example, Tufted Ducks, and the mother – and occasionally even the father too – usually accompanies them all the way to the flying stage.

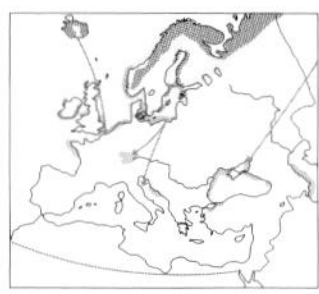

ID: Bulkier than similar species, with large head and evenly rounded crown. Back slopes down to water. Male has greenish tinge to head and has grey back. Female's most distinctive feature is large white patch around base of bill (this can be shown by Tufted Duck but is never as large or broad).

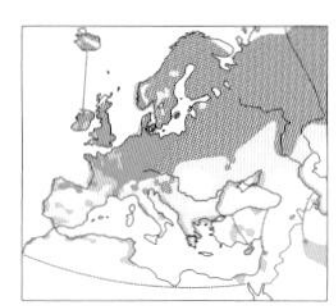

ID: Small diving duck with a tuft, although this doesn't always show prominently. High forehead but rather flat crown. Male black and white; at distance male Goldeneye similar but the latter has white breast. Female variable, generally brown with paler sides.

Tufted Duck

Aythya fuligula (**eye**-thi-a foo-**lig**-yoo-la)
length 40–47 cm

This is the commonest diving duck in much of Europe, although it avoids extremes of heat and cold. Its habitat requirements are simple: all it needs is reasonably clear water 3–14 m deep, plus at least some fringing vegetation. In such habitats it feeds mainly on still or slow-moving animal matter, which it collects from the lake bed. A favourite foodstuff is the zebra mussel, which was introduced into northwest Europe in the 19th century and has expanded greatly in numbers, benefiting the Tufted Duck along the way. Shrimps are also popular food items, as are spire shells and the larvae of various aquatic insects, especially caddis flies. Where suitable food is available the Tufted Duck will venture even into heavily populated areas, coming to bread alongside Mallards on lakes in urban parks.

For breeding, the Tufted Duck is particularly keen, as are many wildfowl, on islands in lakes. This can lead to many pairs nesting very close together, which they do amicably enough. Tufted Ducks also place their nests within colonies of gulls or terns, using the latter effectively as 'minders' by taking advantage of their vehement mobbing and harassment of predators.

Curiously, the Tufted Duck does not seem to use its eponymous tuft much in display. Instead, it performs a typical diving-duck routine, stretching its neck up as though peering over an obstacle, or throwing its head back to rest momentarily on its back. Drakes in communal display also make what sounds like a nervous giggle.

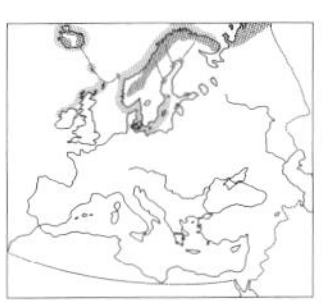

ID: *Small duck with variable plumage. Males easily recognised by their long tails and habit of diving. Females more difficult to identify, but head whitish with dark cheek spot. Distinctive flight with wings barely rising above horizontal, bird pitching from side to side; lands with a splash.*

Long-tailed Duck

Clangula hyemalis (**klan**-goo-la hie-ye-**may**-liss)
length 40–47 cm

One of the most successful of all Arctic nesting ducks, the Long-tailed Duck is found in the tundra zone throughout Europe, Russia and North America. It breeds on rivers, by pools, on islands, in fjords and along sheltered coasts almost anywhere north of the Arctic Circle, and its total world population is estimated at more than 10 million pairs. No wonder that its distinctive call note, 'Can cry I CAN!', is one of the most familiar sounds of the European tundra. In places it may be the commonest bird, let alone the commonest duck.

The Long-tailed Duck nests on the ground, its shallow, down-lined hollow usually well concealed by bushes or rocks. Pairs may be well dispersed or close enough to constitute a loose colony and, perhaps as a result, it is quite normal for several nearby broods to gather together and form a crèche. Young Long-tailed Ducks, therefore, quickly become sociable and remain so throughout their lives.

Once they have left their breeding areas, Long-tailed Ducks perform moult migrations (the males may fly an impressive 1000 km to a highly favoured area) and then move south to winter in waters well free of the ice. Here they remain in large, concentrated flocks, often far from shore and in heavy, rough seas. The Long-tailed Duck holds the record for any duck in terms of how deep it can dive, 55 m having been authentically recorded, so being a long way offshore does not hold too many difficulties for it. Indeed, it gives this bird a competitive advantage over other species that feed on similar foods in winter – molluscs and crustaceans from the seabed.

Later in the winter pairing takes place and shows several features that are unusual among ducks. For one thing, when the males begin making postures they do so almost entirely amongst themselves, shaking their black and white heads and performing other manoeuvres to work out who is better than whom. This means that the communal display phase is shorter than in other ducks and there is a rapid switch to one-on-one courtship. Once this begins, Long-tailed Ducks have many routines, but the most spectacular is the male's unsubtle demonstration of his best feature, the long tail. He suddenly thrusts his head and neck down towards the water and at the same time lifts his rear end upwards until the tail is pointing vertically; the position is maintained for a short while with a rapid kicking of the feet.

Harlequin

Histrionicus histrionicus
(hiss-tri-**oh**-nik-uss hiss-tri-**oh**-nik-uss)
length 38–45 cm

Fast-flowing rivers and torrents provide the specialised breeding habitat for this unusual duck, which in Europe breeds only in Iceland (no more than 3000 pairs). It feeds on shellfish, crustaceans and insect larvae, which it pulls off rocks while diving. When working such habitats it seems extraordinarily immune to the power of water, moving about against the current with ease and having little difficulty in taking off from the surface. It also manoeuvres expertly on nearby slippery rocks.

In common with many river ducks throughout the world, Harlequins are territorial, with pairs keeping apart, either physically or by ignoring their neighbours. Their nests are placed on the ground near water, usually concealed by rocks or bushes; islands in the river are favourite sites, and a few enterprising birds nest behind waterfalls.

In winter Harlequins move down from their mountain streams to exposed rocky coasts, where presumably rough seas and strong currents make them feel at home.

ID: *Rare duck of torrents. Male unmistakable. Female largely unpatterned dark brown, but with white spot behind eye and dusky white between bill and eye.*

Common Eider

Somateria mollissima
(so-ma-**teer**-ee-a mol-**lis**-si-ma)
length 50–71 cm

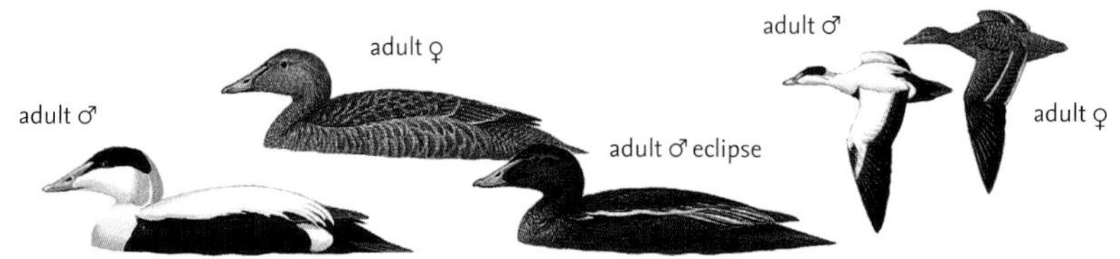

The female Common Eider provides a case study in dedicated incubation. She sits remarkably tight. Other female ducks customarily take breaks each morning and evening, but Eiders eschew this luxury and, especially towards the end of the period, will remain on their post all day and all night long. When the eggs hatch, the female can find herself in a state of near-starvation.

This, of course, is in addition to providing the eggs with the best insulation known. Eider down is famous for its lightness and resilience to the conductance of heat, and the female can build a nest on frozen ground, line it with down and be confident that the eggs are immune from the cold below. The feathers come from the female's breast, plucked with her own bill. Where Eider down is commercially farmed, for example in Iceland, the farmers actually remove the lining twice: first when the nest has just been completed and once at the end of the season, forcing the female to sacrifice twice the number of feathers.

Eider down still provides a few people with a livelihood, although these days it is mainly a luxury item, synthetic materials having long since replaced the real thing. It would never have worked in the first place if the Eider had not been a colonial species, with nests packed as close as two every square metre at times, making the down relatively easy to collect. Some colonies can hold as many as 3000 nests, and about a hundred nests will yield a kilogramme of down. It must be a hard way to earn a living.

The bird itself is very much a marine duck, rarely straying on to fresh water or inland. It is found in northern Europe from the High Arctic to more temperate regions, where it selects low offshore islands and flat ground near the sea for breeding. It doesn't migrate far in the winter, just dispersing to suitable feeding waters nearby. It is a large duck with powerful jaws and a formidable bill, used for crushing various hard-shelled invertebrates, including mussels, whelks, periwinkles and crabs. The birds dive for these creatures on the seabed, spending up to about 40 seconds underwater while they extract them from among the rocks and weed. Eiders prefer not to dive in water more than about 5 m deep and they have a particular preference for working while the tide is ebbing.

These are sociable birds and large flocks form in winter, providing ideal opportunities for communal courtship. The most familiar display is a throwing back of the head, common to many diving ducks but in this instance accompanied by the Eider's unique calls. The females make growling noises, while the males have a delightful musical three-note coo, saucy and suggestive; the sound is far-reaching, even in the cold wind and rain.

For a species justifiably famous for the care of its eggs, the Eider forms a remarkably loose attachment to the subsequent chicks. Within a few hours of their hatching, with the chicks swimming well and feeding for themselves, some females abandon them to the care of a few nearby colleagues, the so-called 'aunties'. The chicks soon join forces with other chicks and form crèches of up to about a hundred birds (500 has been recorded). Their subsequent care is the responsibility of another branch of Eider social services, the 'crèche guards', whose main function is to watch for predators. It may seem odd that the female should ditch responsibility for the chicks so quickly, but in her state of emaciation it is vital that she should go to feed as soon as possible.

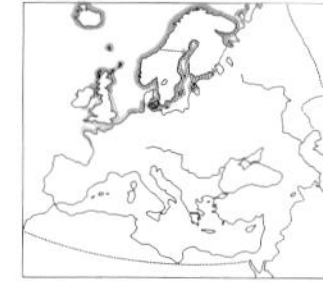

ID: Diving seaduck with extraordinary triangular head and outsize wedge-shaped bill. Male reverses pattern of most ducks in being dark below, white above; has green on head. Female lacks bold features, even a speculum, but shape distinctive.

King Eider

Somateria spectabilis
(so-ma-**teer**-ee-a spek-**tah**-bil-liss)
length 47–63 cm

Breeding in Europe only on Spitsbergen and in the Russian tundra, the King Eider is an exceptionally hardy bird of the extreme Arctic. It is one of the few ducks not to beat much of a retreat from high latitudes in winter, being rarely found south of Norwegian or Icelandic waters. Smaller but tougher than the Common Eider, it can live in deep waters and tempestuous seas far from land, and among all wildfowl is second only to the Long-tailed Duck in the depth of its diving, with over 50 m recorded (although disputed). Its diet, plucked from the seabed, includes molluscs, crustaceans and echinoderms such as starfish.

Besides its predilection for deeper waters, the King Eider differs from the Common Eider in several other respects. For one thing it usually breeds singly rather than in colonies, and the nest sites are often inland by freshwater lakes or rivers, not so concentrated along the coast. It is also more migratory, forming enormous moulting gatherings that may number 100,000 birds and moving away completely from its breeding areas in winter.

ID: Smaller and more square-headed than Common Eider. Male unmistakable. Female paler warm brown than Common Eider, with dark, not pale bill. Flanks have crescent marks, not bars. Odd 'smiling' expression caused by rounded gape.

Steller's Eider

Polysticta stelleri (pol-li-**stik**-ta stel-**lee**-rie)
length 43–47 cm

The Steller's Eider breeds no nearer to us than the eastern half of Siberia, so it is perhaps surprising that quite healthy numbers of this gaudy Arctic duck make the long journey to winter in our region. Some 40,000 Steller's can be found in the seas off northern Norway and adjacent Russia, and in the Baltic.

This eider has a smaller bill and a rounder head than the others, making it look more like a 'normal' duck. It usually feeds close to shore, in clear water among rocks, on the molluscs, crustaceans and echinoderms favoured by most eiders. Steller's are sociable and restless, often taking off and flying about, seemingly without warning. They are also notable for synchronised feeding, large parts of the flock diving in unison and returning to the surface at the same time.

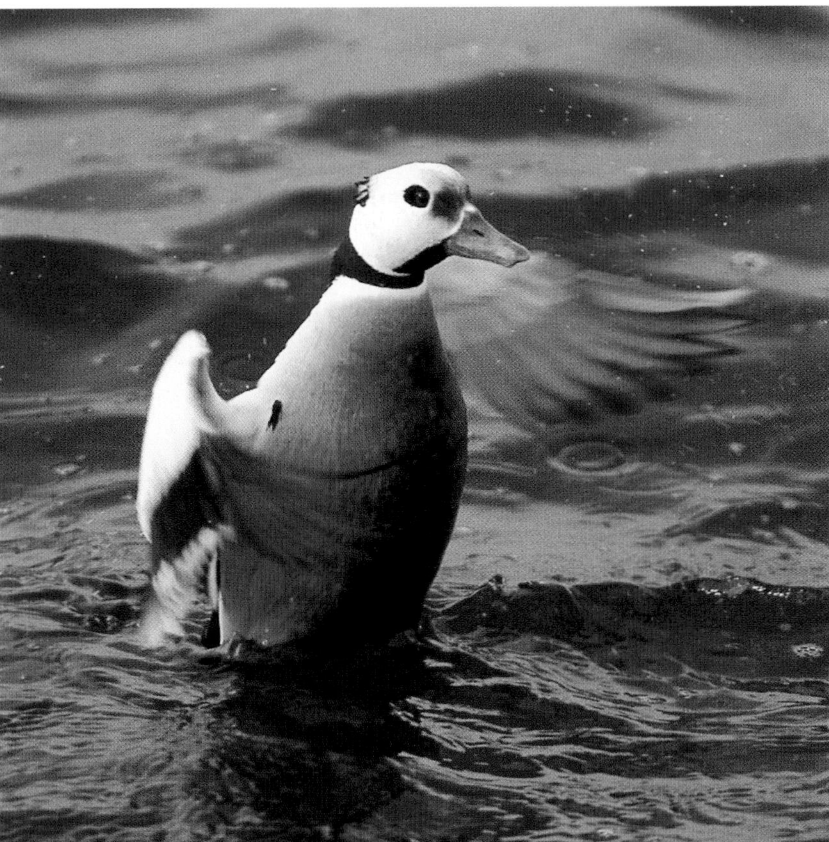

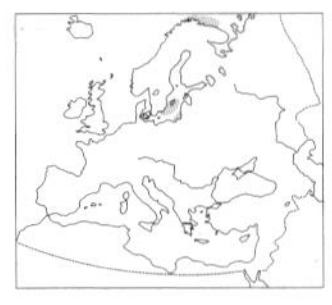

ID: Small eider with bill like dabbling duck. Male unmistakable, female distinctive. Latter dark with two white wing bars on either side of bluish speculum, a little like a very dark Mallard.

Common Scoter

Melanitta nigra (mel-la-**nit**-ta **nye**-gra)
length 44–54 cm

ID: Small seaduck with pointed tail and rounded crown. Male all black with small patch of orange on bill. Female dark brown with contrasting pale brown cheek and side of neck. Dives with a forward leap.

The name 'scoter' derives from the word 'sooter', or sooty duck, which is highly appropriate for this species – the male is the only duck with plumage of just one colour, namely black. The female, for her part, is brown with a distinctive pale cheek.

This is a common duck of the Arctic and sub-Arctic, breeding in quite a wide variety of habitats, including tundra lakes, riverbanks, islands and open moorland. The nest is the shallow hollow typical of most ducks and is lined with moss, grass and plenty of down. The domestic arrangements are also similar to those of most ducks, with the male deserting the female during incubation. The young hatch full of vitality and are soon feeding themselves. Occasionally broods meet together and effectively merge.

In the winter the Common Scoter seeks out shallow coasts no more than 10–20 m deep, preferably with a sandy bottom. Here it can obtain its primary food, molluscs and especially the blue mussel. Scoters on the sea are restless birds, forever flying about. When a large flock takes off and moves for any distance, some of the birds at the back often fly slightly higher than the others, presumably so that they can see where they are going, and give the whole flock a distinctive tadpole-like shape.

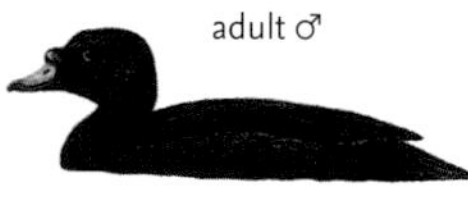

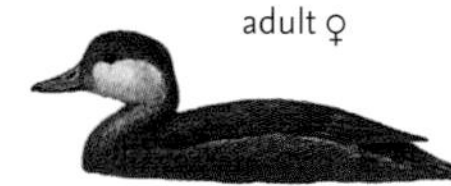

Velvet Scoter

Melanitta fusca (mel-la-**nit**-ta **foo**-ska)
length 51–58 cm

Larger and heavier than the Common Scoter, the Velvet Scoter rises from the water with more difficulty, needing a longer run-up and more foot-pattering to get itself airborne. It also dives in a different way; while the Common Scoter makes a preliminary leap and enters the water with wings closed, the Velvet sinks down without a leap and enters the water with wings half open. Both these differences can be useful in distinguishing these birds in winter flocks on the sea, because the two often mix together. Velvet Scoters are usually found in smaller numbers and they winter further north than many Common Scoters.

When breeding, Velvet Scoters may be found on open tundra, but are more often associated with wooded habitats such as lakes within the coniferous forest zone, where the nest is placed on the ground near the water.

During courtship and pair formation, males have a rushing display in which they patter very rapidly over the water, creating a pleasing splash behind them. Pairs also perform a special 'morning flight' routine, in which the female suddenly takes off and flies inland in a wide circle a few times, rapidly pursued by the male.

ID: Has much thicker neck than Common Scoter and heavier, wedge-shaped bill. Most easily distinguished from Common Scoter by white secondaries forming wing bar, best seen in flight but showing as a white blob on folded wing. Male has white half-moon below eye, female usually has a pale cheek patch.

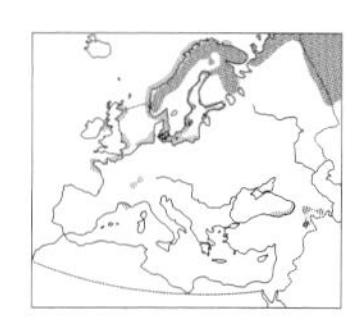

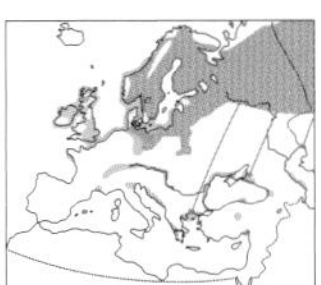

ID: Small, oddly shaped diving duck, with a bulbous head that looks too large for the neck. Male has bottle-green head with white spot between bill and eye, like a coin. Female very different, with mainly grey plumage and brown head.

Common Goldeneye

Bucephala clangula (boo-**see**-fa-la **klan**-goo-la)
length 42–50 cm

In the breeding season the Common Goldeneye requires a habitat of tall forest interspersed with lakes. The forest provides it with its rather unusual nest site, a large hole in a tree, and the lakes must be productive enough to hold enough food, deep enough for the bird to dive comfortably, and uncluttered with vegetation so that there is a clear run to the bottom, where the Goldeneye goes down to feed.

The practice of nesting in holes is a double-edged sword for any bird, and the Goldeneye is no different. On the one hand, holes above ground provide unrivalled security and concealment from predators. On the other, there is always a limited supply, which means that there is considerable competition for territories. The Goldeneye, furthermore, is quite exacting in its specifications. The hole must be big enough for a duck, which means that large rotten trunks are often required; otherwise the Goldeneye must rely on the presence of Black Woodpeckers to make their excavations. The hole should also be within at most a couple of kilometres of water; it must be no more than 5 m above the ground, so that the chicks can jump out unharmed; and there must be reasonably clear access for the birds to fly straight in.

Away from its nest site the Goldeneye is an inveterate diver. It can be an infuriating bird to watch, as one dive follows another with only a short space between. It is always easy to identify, however, as its bulbous head looks incongruously big for its neck and body, as if it had been donated by another species as a spare part.

In winter Common Goldeneyes move south, where they can be found both on large lakes and on the sea. In winter flocks the males begin displaying, a head-throwing routine, with the head resting on the back and the bill pointing upwards, being the most prominent feature.

Barrow's Goldeneye

Bucephala islandica (boo-**see**-fa-la iz-**lan**-dik-ka)
length 42–53 cm

One of two ducks confined in Europe to the island of Iceland (the other is the Harlequin), the Barrow's Goldeneye is chiefly a North American species. It is slightly larger and bulkier than the Common Goldeneye and generally less sociable, being found in smaller parties. It is also much less migratory; birds in Iceland do not go far for the winter, but seek out the nearest suitable ice-free waters, both fresh and saline.

There aren't many trees in Iceland, so rather than nesting in a tree hole, as it does over most of its range, the Barrow's Goldeneye must be content to use holes in the ground, bushy scrub or nest boxes. In some places it uses holes in lava floes, a rather special local habit.

To prevent interbreeding with the Common Goldeneye, Barrow's Goldeneye displays are somewhat different, most notably in the fact that the Common Goldeneye's frequent head-throw is entirely absent. These birds are highly territorial and nesting is always solitary.

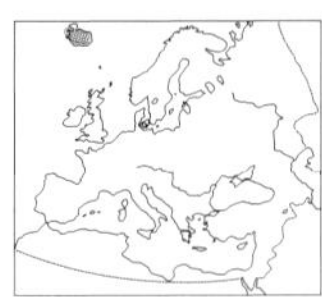

ID: Male similar to Common Goldeneye but has purplish, not green sheen on head, a white crescent (not a spot) between bill and eye, and several discrete white spots on its back. Female similar to Common Goldeneye but has smaller, shorter bill, sharper forehead and rounded crown.

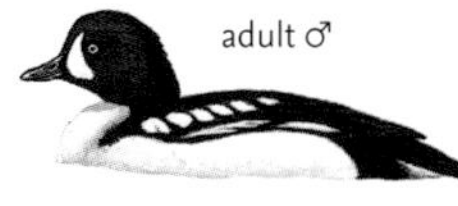

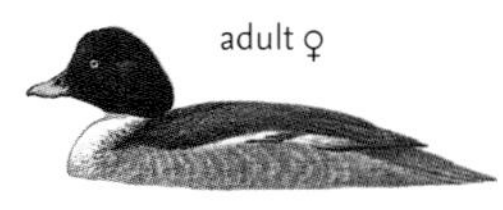

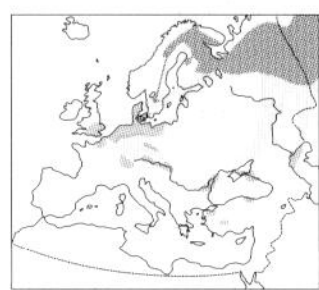

Smew

Mergellus albellus (mer-**jel**-luss al-**bel**-luss)
length 38–44 cm

ID: Male unmistakable. Female distinctive, with grey plumage and reddish-brown head with contrasting white cheek.

The Smew has much in common with the Goldeneye, despite looking very different and not being particularly closely related. The most striking similarity between the two species is in their breeding ecology: both use holes in trees as nest sites, particularly those made by Black Woodpeckers; both use down as virtually their only nest material; and both require the presence of large coniferous trees beside sheltered, productive lakes, where they feed on rather similar foodstuffs. Perhaps not surprisingly, there are several records of the two species hybridising.

There are differences, though. The Smew is much more restricted, in Europe breeding mainly in Sweden, Finland and Russia. The Smew also has a marked preference for quiet backwaters, flooded forest and other sites with plenty of tree cover; it is less drawn to open waters. And it has a more restricted diet; in the breeding season it favours insect larvae and for the rest of the year, particularly winter and early spring, fish.

In winter Smew migrate south, the females and immatures travelling further than the adult males. In early spring they begin to return and the sexes mix, triggering much display. The Smew's most obvious posture is the 'pouting display', in which the male puffs out his chest and retracts his head, keeping the bill horizontal.

Goosander

Mergus merganser (**mer**-guss mer-**gan**-ser)
length 58–66 cm

The Goosander is almost entirely a bird of fresh water, in contrast to the closely related Red-breasted Merganser. It nests along the upper reaches and fast-flowing sections of rivers and also beside large, clear lakes, and can be found in winter in rather similar habitats. Wherever it goes clear water is essential, because it hunts fish by sight. A bird swimming on the surface typically puts its head underwater for a quick look around before diving, a habit known as 'snorkelling'.

This bird also differs from the Red-breasted Merganser in that it typically nests in holes in trees (and also nest boxes), although it will use holes among rocks if necessary. If a tree has a rotten section, several females may use different holes in the same tree, forming a loose colony. The birds involved are remarkably calm and non-competitive, and will sometimes actually prospect for nest sites together.

Young Goosanders leave the nest when about two days old, an ordeal made worse by having to jump from the hole. If they land softly they make for the nearest water, following their mother. Once there, they occasionally have the luxury of riding on their mother's back for short periods. Among other wildfowl this unusual habit has been recorded only from the Mute Swan.

ID: Large, long diving duck with long, thin bill. Male is mainly creamy-white with dark green head. Female similar to Red-breasted Merganser but larger, with fuller crest with longer 'hair', a clean white chin and obvious border between brown head and creamy-grey body.

ID: Male's plumage distinctive. Female told from Goosander by thinner bill, 'blow-dried' crest and lack of obvious contrast between brown head and grey body.

Red-breasted Merganser

Mergus serrator (**mer**-guss ser-**ray**-tor)
length 52–58 cm

A certain amount of jargon surrounds this species, the Goosander and the Smew. These three ducks are known as 'sawbills', as they possess sharp, backward-pointing serrations on the side of the bill, fancifully recalling the teeth of a saw. The teeth are for holding on to fish. The Red-breasted Merganser takes a wide range of species, including the young of trout and salmon, plus perch, cod and sand eels, depending on the habitat. When under water, Mergansers use both feet and wings for propulsion, whereas the Goosander uses its feet only.

For breeding, the Red-breasted Merganser uses both fresh and saltwater habitats. It will select a site for its nest by a lake or river, or beside a coastal inlet or a sea loch. Oddly, perhaps, it also prefers having trees nearby: a favourite nest site is on the ground among a root system or under some sort of thick vegetation. Pairs may nest solitarily or in informal colonies, and in the latter situation the young sometimes form into crèches guarded by a small number of adults.

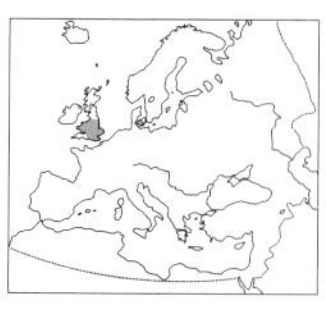

ID: Distinctive if tail is held up, as it usually is. Front of head forms obvious slope from crown down to bill. Male unmistakable. Female much less so, a very small duck with a diffuse pale stripe between dark crown and mottled ear coverts.

Ruddy Duck

Oxyura jamaicensis (ok-si-**oo**-ra jam-ay-**ken**-siss)
length 35–43 cm

If anyone told you that there was a bird somewhere that made bubbles as part of its display, you would probably think they were joking. But there is such a bird, the Ruddy Duck. Under the breast feathers of this unusual species is an air sac, and around it the feathers are very dense and capable of trapping air between them. If a male beats his breast hard and fast with his large bill, as if hitting a drum, a small spurt of bubbles collects on the water around the breast, and this, together with the associated slapping and croaking sounds – the latter probably made by the tracheal air sac deflating – serves to impress any nearby females.

This remarkable show is not home-grown, but came as an import – along with its performers – from North America. A few of these birds were accidentally introduced into Britain in 1953 and first bred in the wild in 1960. Finding conditions to their liking, they soon spread and there are now almost 1000 breeding pairs. In addition, further escapees and dispersing birds have begun to colonise several other countries in Europe.

The spread is of concern, because Ruddy Ducks have recently come into intimate contact with wild White-headed Ducks in Spain and produced fertile hybrids. With their population so low, the possibility of the White-headed Duck being interbred out of existence is very real, at least in Europe. So, as a counter-measure, a complete cull of Ruddy Ducks was authorised in Britain in 2003. It is an unpopular move and fraught with difficulty, so it will be interesting to see whether it is successful.

White-headed Duck

Oxyura leucocephala (ok-si-**oo**-ra loo-ko-**sef**-fa-la)
length 43–48 cm

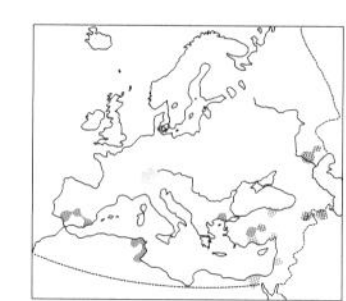

ID: Unmistakable on account of its bizarre swollen bill and rigid tail that is often held up at an angle of 45 degrees.

This strangely shaped duck is now perilously rare in Europe, with just 50–100 pairs breeding in Spain; it has a fragmented distribution elsewhere, too. For breeding it requires rich, shallow waters within arid regions, and these must have a substantial fringe of dense vegetation. Such sites tend to be at a premium and vulnerable to development.

The closely related White-headed Duck and Ruddy Duck belong to a small tribe of ducks known as the 'stifftails', named for their strengthened tail feathers, which are often held at 45 degrees, but can also be pointed straight up in display. The tail's primary function, however, is to help the bird steer while it is swimming underwater, propelled by its back-set feet. Stifftails feed in a way quite different to other diving ducks. They swim along on the lake bed and sift food from the mud and silt on site, moving their heads from side to side like an underwater Spoonbill. The process can keep them below the surface longer than other ducks, up to 40 seconds, and yet the White-headed Duck usually feeds in water no more than 2 m deep.

The nests of stifftails are more of a building effort than the customary sparsely lined hollow of other ducks. They consist of a cup of leaves and other plant material woven into the stems of emergent vegetation, half in and half out of water, and sometimes placed on top of a Coot nest. Tall plants nearby may be bent down towards the nest to make a 'roof' for extra concealment.

Birds of Prey families *Accipitridae* (ak-si-**pit**-rid-ee), *Pandionidae* (pan-dye-**on**-id-ee) and *Falconidae* (fal-**kon**-id-ee)

Habitat Just about every habitat bar the open sea is inhabited by a bird of prey.
Food All eat animals of one sort or another – mammals, other birds, reptiles, amphibians, insects etc, alive or dead. Very little plant material.
Movements Some are sedentary and do not move out of their home ranges (e.g. Golden Eagle). Some are partial migrants (e.g. Merlin) and some long-distance migrants (e.g. Eleonora's Falcon, Osprey). In contrast to many birds, raptors migrate by day, usually rising on thermals.
Voice Generally not good vocalists and often silent. Many utter simple trills and cheeps.
Pairing style Most are monogamous, but some, especially the harriers, exhibit polygyny, while vultures are occasionally polyandrous.
Nesting Usually solitary, living in a home range and defending only the immediate area of the nest site. A few are semi-colonial at times (e.g. harriers) and only a few are truly colonial (Griffon Vulture, Eleonora's and Red-footed Falcons, Lesser Kestrel).
Nest Members of family Accipitridae build nests, usually of sticks, that can become very substantial over years of re-use. Falconidae build no nests of their own, but lay direct on to substrate or appropriate old nests of other birds. Osprey (the only member of the family Pandionidae) very flexible (see entry).
Productivity 1 brood a year.
Eggs 1–7 (occasionally more). Often hatch asynchronously, leading to a wide age difference within the brood.
Incubation Usually exclusively by female.
Young Nest-bound, altricial and downy.
Parenting style Young are usually brooded by the female while the male hunts, delivering food that the female then feeds to the chicks. When chicks are older both sexes catch food.
Food to young As adults' prey. Normally brought to nest by male and fed piecemeal to the young. Vultures regurgitate their food for the young.
Leaving nest Young fledge any time between 25 and 70 days, depending on species.

Common Buzzard

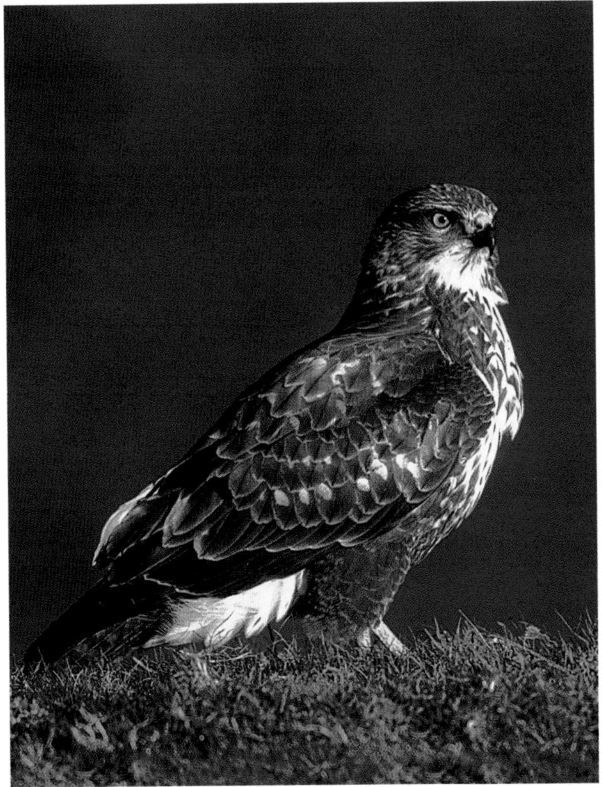

The term 'bird of prey' encompasses two main groups of birds: the day-hunting birds of prey, often known as 'raptors', and the night-hunting owls. Despite having similar killing apparatus – a hooked bill for tearing flesh and talons with long toes and sharp claws – the two groups are not closely related, and the owls are found later in this book, on pages 192–199.

Confusingly, the raptors are themselves divided into three families: the Osprey, the falcons and the rest. The **Osprey's** unusual diet of fish has made it very distinctive. The **falcons** have particularly compact bodies and pointed wings. Technically they also have some skeletal differences from the rest and moult in a different way. Their bill has a special notch to help them bite the neck of their victims. The falcons include the kestrels, Hobby, Merlin, Lanner, Saker and Peregrine.

The remaining diverse assemblage includes birds unified by the fact that they build their own nest and by internal anatomy, although outwardly many members of this family may look very different to each other. There are several well-known groups:

The **kites** are highly aerial raptors that feed on dead material (carrion) and also catch some of their own food. They have long wings and long tails, the latter forked. Kites often gather together where food is concentrated. The **vultures** are very large birds of prey that also eat carrion. Most have very broad wings and spend much of the day soaring on thermal updrafts. As food supplies are irregular, vultures can eat enormous amounts at a single sitting. Most have bare skin instead of feathers on their head, since they have to poke into bloody carcasses. The **harriers** are a small group of very long-winged, long-tailed raptors that specialise in flying low and slow over the ground ('quartering'). Harriers nest and roost on the ground and the males are often polygamous. The **buzzards** are medium-sized raptors with broad wings and short tails. They have a varied diet. **Hawks** hunt in woodland and other confined spaces, often ambushing their prey by using foliage as a screen. They have long tails and relatively short, blunt wings, making them highly manoeuvrable. The term 'hawk' is often used for raptors in general, which is both wrong and confusing. The **eagles** are regal-looking birds of prey with long, broad wings. They tend to have longer tails than buzzards and their head and neck stick out more in flight. Far more powerful than buzzards, they look more stable in the air, with slower, more powerful wing flaps.

Despite these differences, it is possible to make a number of generalisations about day-hunting birds of prey. As a rule they are neither very vocal nor vocally impressive. Although the Common Buzzard and Booted Eagle make far-carrying calls, the Golden Eagle makes pathetic cheeping sounds. Raptors are renowned for their hunting ability, and almost every species has its own favoured technique. But all hunt primarily by sight (although sound may be used by harriers). A raptor's eyes are large and densely packed with the visual cells that deal with detail, which helps them to pick out small prey from several hundred metres above ground.

Honey Buzzard

Pernis apivorus (**per**-niss ap-**piv**-or-uss)
length 52–60 cm; wingspan 1.35–1.5 m

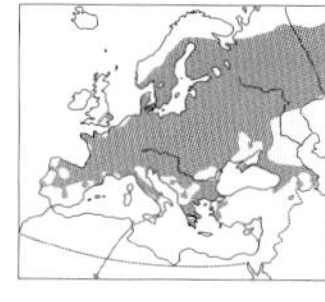

ID: Variable medium-sized bird of prey of similar build to Buzzard, but with more protruding head in flight and longer tail (longer than width of wing). Flies with slower, more fluid wingbeats and glides on flat or even slightly bowed wings (not raised in a V). Doesn't hover like Buzzard. Adults also distinguished by three clearly defined bars on undertail and normally a greyish head and orange-red (male) or yellow (female) eye.

There's no question that the Honey Buzzard looks like a raptor, with its hooked bill, large talons and long, broad wings – there is little to distinguish it from many a Common Buzzard, for example. Yet in its lifestyle, and particularly in its manner of feeding, the Honey Buzzard is cast in a different mould.

The main surprise is that the Honey Buzzard's principal summer prey is invertebrates – and very specific ones at that. It is the scourge of social insects, in particular wasps and hornets, eating adults, pupae, larvae and even the comb from their nests, the latter habit giving rise to the bird's name. It seems remarkable that it can sustain itself on such small pickings, yet it clearly can, since it is a widespread and fairly common species over much of central and northern Europe. It does supplement its diet with some larger food, especially birds and their eggs, but there is little to suggest that these are essential, except perhaps in the early part of the season, in May, when the birds have just arrived back from their wintering grounds in tropical Africa. For the most part, the Honey Buzzard is a consummate insect specialist.

Finding and catching wasps is hardly achieved by high flights and dramatic chases, so the Honey Buzzard's foraging is played out in secret under the forest canopy and along broad rides and woodland edges. It may fly slowly at no more than treetop height, scanning for flying insects, or simply sit on a perch and watch their comings and goings. Remarkably, it will also regularly search for nests by wandering along on the ground, and it has been observed hiking no less than half a kilometre for this purpose. Once it has located a wasps' nest it digs it out wherever it is lodged, often in a tree trunk or on the ground. It then consumes the insects or comb on site. The Honey Buzzard has reduced openings to its nostrils to prevent earth getting in while it is digging in the soil, and long, thick claws to do the actual work.

Not surprisingly, the wasps react angrily to this intrusion and attack the Honey Buzzard vigorously. Somehow, though, a bird working a nest always appears unmoved by the attempted stings. It has specialised scaly feathers on its face that act as a kind of armour against them, and its feet and legs are similarly protected. The only concession to a wasp's firepower is that before swallowing an adult, the Honey Buzzard snips off its sting first. Otherwise it seems quite unaffected.

The best wasp harvest lasts for a comparatively short season, peaking between June and August, and this is the time that Honey Buzzards breed. During pair formation the sexes perform a variety of aerial displays, one of which is unique to the species. It is based on a common bird of prey manoeuvre, flying up and then swooping down on an undulating course; but as the displaying bird reaches the top of its 'wave' it stalls for a moment, lifts its wings high over its back and shakes them rapidly, as if trying to dry them, before beginning its descent.

The nest is built high in a forest tree, often a beech, 10–20 m up. It is often placed on top of an old Crow or Common Buzzard's nest, and varies considerably in size. During its construction and beyond, the birds bring in a lot of sticks with leaves attached; it is not known whether this foliage is for camouflage purposes or helps with nest sanitation in some way. The two eggs are incubated mainly by the female, and not long after they hatch the chicks begin to ingest their unusual diet.

Black-winged Kite

Elanus caeruleus (ee-**lay**-nuss see-**roo**-leh-uss)
length 31–35 cm; wingspan 75–87 cm

Hugely successful in Africa, India and other parts of Asia, the Black-winged Kite is a scarce species in Europe. It is found only in Spain and Portugal, although there has been recent breeding in France and many records of wanderers as far as the Baltic. Where it occurs one can easily imagine it as an African bird: it likes open plains dotted with trees, steppe, arid areas and riverside woodland – places where one might expect an elephant to walk by!

The Black-winged Kite hunts mainly in flight, and is most often encountered hovering, holding position on the spot with wings beating rapidly and tail fanned. A distant bird may resemble a large grey Kestrel, although the Kite's short tail makes its trailing talons look much more prominent. Once prey is sighted it will typically drop down, check and hover closer to the target before the final plunge on to a small mammal, reptile or occasional bird. It will also fly low and straight over the ground, alternating soft flaps with low glides, its wings held up in a V. It can often look like an owl or harrier when doing this, especially when it hunts, as it often does, deep into the half-light of dusk.

Black-winged Kites live as pairs in a permanent year-round territory. Each year they build a new stick-nest on the branch of a tree, usually a thorny one. The birds will often perch by it and display, one raising its tail slowly upwards and down again; this signal also acts as a threat.

ID: Highly distinctive small (chunky Kestrel-sized) raptor of three colour shades. Not likely to be confused with anything else.

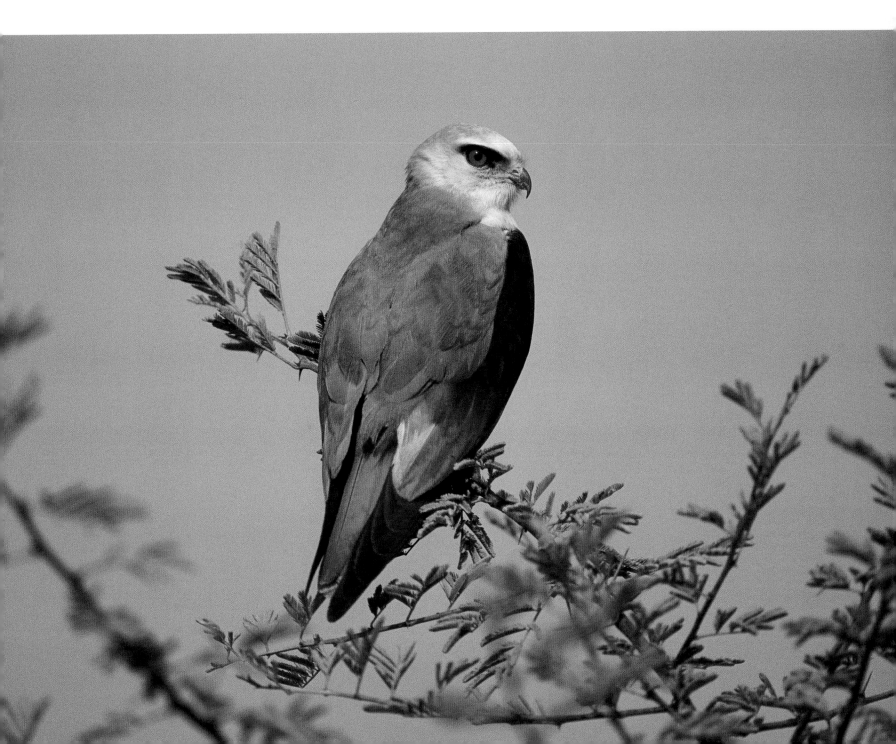

Red Kite

Milvus milvus (mill-vuss mill-vuss)
length 60–66 cm; wingspan 1.75–1.95 m

The Red Kite is a master of the air, riding the wind with consummate ease. In flight, it can turn sharply with a mere twitch of its tail and describe tight circles low over the ground without a wingbeat. It can make daring accelerations one moment, and then glide so slowly as almost to stall to a hover the next. Few birds of prey are so buoyant and agile, and few are so distinctive to look at. The long, narrow wings, held pressed forwards, make a distinctive kink, and the long, sharply forked tail trails behind unmistakably.

The Red Kite is almost confined to Europe; it appears not to compete well with the ultra-aggressive, highly adaptable and more sociable Black Kite. However, it does reach cooler and windier climates than the Black Kite, remaining in some temperate areas throughout the year. Ideally, it favours rolling country with open areas and small woods and copses intermixed.

Although Red Kites are probably best known as scavengers, they are also highly predatory, catching and eating large numbers of small mammals and birds. They catch far more live food than the Black Kite, especially in spring and summer. When hunting they tend to strike from a high, soaring position, making a rapid feet-first plunge down to the ground. Their aim is to take the prey by surprise; if they are seen approaching, they usually miss.

Breeding birds build a stick nest high in a tree and furnish it with all sorts of rubbish, including rags, paper, plastic, dung, sheep's wool and any kind of refuse. Sites are usually traditional and may be used by many pairs for successive generations.

adults

ID: This and Black Kite distinguished from other raptors by long wings and the forked tail which is often twisted around in flight. Fly with wings arched downwards. Red Kite has sharper fork and more conspicuous pale patch on 'hands'.

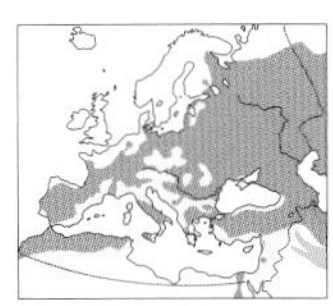

ID: Flight and shape similar to Red Kite, but tail more shallowly forked. Has darker plumage than Red Kite.

Black Kite

Milvus migrans (**mill**-vuss **my**-granz)
length 55–60 cm ; wingspan 1.3–1.6 m

The Black Kite has a strong claim to be the most numerous and successful bird of prey in the world, and the secret to its success is simple – it lives on the coat-tails of man. In many parts of Africa and Asia it is the commonest town scavenger, the one that frequents roadside rubbish tips and shanty towns, robs market stalls and steals scraps from the hands of unsuspecting human beings, and circles over docks waiting to pounce down on dead and dying fish. It occurs almost throughout the Old World and its ubiquity extends even to outposts such as Australia and Madagascar.

In Europe, with its relative cleanness and more suspect climate, the Black Kite is less abundant than in the fleshpots of the tropics. It is only a seasonal visitor, arriving in the first week of April and leaving in the course of August. Nevertheless, it encompasses a wide range of habitats and climates here, extending even into the boreal zone. In many parts of its range it is strongly associated with water, inhabiting lakes, marshes and industrial towns by the coast. But everywhere it follows people's activities and eats people's waste.

Black Kites have a simple hunting method: they fly slowly at a level 10– 20 m above the ground, scanning below them. What sets them apart from other birds of prey is their boldness and willingness to exploit almost every opportunity they find. They will feed unconcerned within a few metres of people; they will rob other birds of prey, even the largest and most fearsome; and they will enter colonies of fish-eating birds to pilfer fish from nests. They snatch carrion from both ground and water surface, group round carcasses like miniature vultures, yet also make rapid lunges at small live food such as chicks and rodents. There is little, it seems, that they will not try.

On the whole, Black Kites are highly sociable birds, gathering together to feed, loaf and roost – for an opportunist species, crowding is an inevitable consequence of having plentiful food nearby. Hundreds may congregate at favourite trees to spend the night, making quite an eerie sight as they crowd the branches. In some areas this sociability extends to breeding in loose colonies, but the normal pattern is for pairs to nest in isolation and to keep the same partners year on year.

Members of a pair have quite strongly defined roles. The male is very much a provider, bringing food in to the female on the nest as she incubates, and then also doing the bulk of hunting for the chicks when they hatch. In some cases, it appears, the female does not have to hunt for herself or her young throughout the entire nesting attempt. And, to make things even easier for her, the male also builds most of the nest structure, making a platform of sticks and decorating it with rags, paper and various other items of rubbish.

White-tailed Eagle

Haliaeetus albicilla
(hay-li-ee-**eet**-uss al-bis-**sil**-la)
length 70–90 cm; wingspan 2–2.4 m

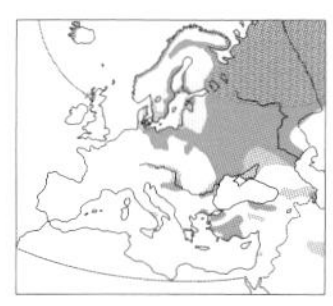

ID: Very large bird of prey with unmistakable shape: huge bill on protruding head, long, very broad wings and distinctively short, wedge-shaped tail. Adults have yellow bill and white tail.

This is a dramatic bird. With its vast bulk, outsize bill and imperious manner of flight, its very presence brings electricity to the birdwatching experience and panic to potential prey. When a White-tailed Eagle flies over a wetland area, every other bird near and far flies up in alarm, and mayhem reigns. It is dexterous enough to snatch prey from the surface of the water, so if it is in a position to isolate a swimming bird, it doesn't strike immediately but keeps it under surveillance until it begins to tire. The potential victim at first dives repeatedly, but the eagle can follow it underwater and harass it every time it comes to the surface. As the quarry runs out of energy, so the hunter waits for its moment.

These large eagles don't always opt for such harrowing tactics; they are inventive, adaptable hunters that veer towards the easiest option. They will often frequent abattoirs and fishing boats for scraps, and they take a high toll of defenceless chicks at seabird colonies. They steal food from Ospreys and other birds of prey, and they will wade into shallow water if there are enough fish to swim around their paddling feet.

Impressive and admirable though they are as hunters, nothing that White-tailed Eagles do quite matches the theatre of their courtship displays. Both sexes will make loud, challenging call notes, thrusting their head back and bill into the air, like outsize cockerels. Both soar high into the air, but the male climbs a little higher. He then dives down to the female, which turns over and presents claws. If both are so inclined, the two birds interlock their talons and then plummet downwards in a series of spinning cartwheels until they almost reach the ground. At the last moment the sky-dance partners separate and may soar up again to repeat the process – a royal couple at play.

Lammergeier

Gypaetus barbatus (jip-**pee**-tuss bar-**bay**-tus)
length 1–1.15 m; wingspan 2.66–2.82 m

It's hard to imagine a more unusual diet for any bird than the Lammergeier's. Believe it or not, up to 85 per cent of its food consists of nothing more than bones, hardly the most appetising prospect, you would have thought, for any living creature. But, armed with a powerful digestive system featuring high levels of acid in the stomach, this very large vulture manages to eke out a living. Even so, it is rare in Europe, found only in the Pyrenees and some high mountains in Greece. Reintroduction schemes are also underway in the Swiss and Italian Alps.

Being such a specialist, the Lammergeier doesn't need to become involved in any unseemly scrums with other vultures at a carcass. It can simply wait until they have finished and take away the rest, which might include skin and fur as well as the skeleton. The only potential competition would be from another Lammergeier, but these birds have such enormous home ranges (often over 1000 sq km) that they probably don't meet very often. In the Pyrenees, nests are on average about 11 km apart, giving everyone plenty of room.

Lammergeiers will take all kinds of carcass, large and small, but obviously a decent-sized sheep or chamois will provide the most sustenance. There is a problem with such a prize, though – the leg bones might be too long to swallow, and the delicious marrow inside will be hard to get at. But the solution is simple: the bird carries the offending bone to a height above 20 m, and drops it on to the rocks below, smashing it open. Favoured dropping areas, called ossuaries, can become littered with bones.

The Lammergeier doesn't take much live prey, but the bone-dropping method does translate rather well to tortoises. These unfortunate animals are dashed to their death and swallowed, shell, flesh and all.

ID: Has unique shape that should make it easy to identify: very large, with long wings and long, wedge-shaped tail. Adults also unmistakably coloured, but juveniles lack the ginger colour of the underparts.

Eurasian Black Vulture

Aegypius monachus (ee-**jip**-pi-uss moh-**nay**-kuss)
length 1–1.1 m; wingspan 2.5–2.9 m

Not many birds can intimidate a pack of feeding Griffons, but when this largest of European vulture comes down to feed, making a low glide with feet and tail up (Griffons come in with feet dangling), all other scavengers scatter. This rare bird has a massive bill and is highly aggressive at a carcass, ruffling its neck feathers to remind all of its dominance.

You might expect a bird of this size to feed primarily on the carcasses of grazing animals, but in fact this isn't the case. In Spain it now subsists primarily on dead rabbits and it can get by on small, isolated pickings. The exceptionally large bill, despite giving it first refusal when it does join other vultures, is actually adapted for taking the more difficult remains of dead animals: tough bits of muscle, skin and sinews. This adaptability has probably helped the Black Vulture to survive in an impoverished environment such as Europe, with its shortage of large mammals.

Black Vultures are much less sociable than other typical vultures; it is rare to see more than one or two at a time. They are also more territorial, working a large but well-defined section of country. They build a large stick nest in a tree, not very high up, only between 1.5 m and 5 m above ground; they rarely use cliff sites, as Griffons do.

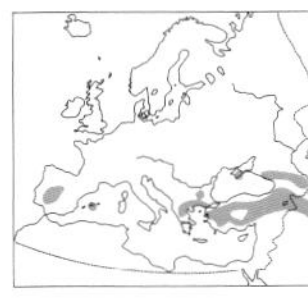

ID: Huge, all-dark vulture, lacking Eurasian Griffon's two-toned pattern below. Wings long and parallel-edged, with saw-toothed trailing edge. Not very sociable.

Eurasian Griffon Vulture

Gyps fulvus (**jips fool**-vuss)
length 95 cm–1.1 m wingspan 2.4–2.8 m

The Griffon is everyone's idea of what a vulture should look like, with its enormous size, long wings, huge bill and ugly, snake-like neck. It is also Europe's only truly gregarious vulture, the one that comes down in packs to dispose of the remains of sheep, horses, cows and wild deer and goats. The long, unfeathered neck gives a clue to its feeding style; it reaches far into a carcass, gobbling down the soft tissues, putting its head into places where feathers would quickly become matted with blood.

A Griffon Vulture's day starts late; there is no point in trying to become airborne before thermals or mountain winds start up in mid-morning, for flapping is not a sensible option for such a heavy, broad-winged bird. Once out, it spends much of the day soaring (as high as 3300 m has been recorded), keeping a keen eye out for signs of recent death below. It also watches its fellow colony members. Vulture hunting, in fact, is quite co-ordinated, with the birds spreading out over a wide area and remaining within eye contact of colleagues. When a carcass is seen, the message is passed down the line, so to speak, and the birds can congregate to feed.

When breeding, Griffons form colonies that usually contain fewer than 20 pairs. Cliffs are often used as a site, with each pair making a rather insubstantial cup-shaped twig nest. The female lays just one egg, and when the chick hatches it is fed on semi-digested carrion.

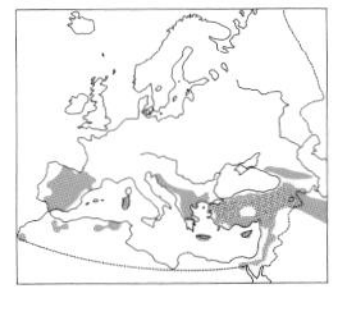

ID: Large broad-winged vulture, distinctively two-toned below. Also has white head and neck ruff. Soars with wings held up in a V. Usually seen in larger numbers than Black Vulture.

ID: Smallest of the vultures, but as big as an eagle. Adults have unusual plumage, easy to identify; young birds dark brown and less distinctive, but still show wedge-shaped tail, small head and odd thin bill.

Egyptian Vulture

Neophron percnopterus
(**nee**-oh-fron perk-**nop**-ter-russ)
length 58–70 cm; wingspan 1.5–1.7 m

Not a bird to discuss at meal times, the Egyptian Vulture has what one might kindly call a 'broad' diet. It discovered long ago that human refuse tips were a good source of scraps, and it will eat a wide range of organic waste, including dead animals of all kinds, rotting fruit and vegetables, and even human excrement. It is not averse to finishing off sick or injured smaller animals, including birds, small mammals and fish, and it will also eat living things as small as insects.

One might expect that such adaptability would be a recipe for success, but this species has suffered, as have many birds of prey, from long-term persecution and is now rather scarce in Europe. It is only a summer visitor here, arriving in March and leaving any time from July. It thus has a later start to its breeding season than other vultures, which are usually well underway by February.

The Egyptian Vulture nests solitarily, the pair selecting a site high up on a cliff or rocky outcrop. The birds prefer to use sheltered ledges or caves, as these have the double advantage of a commanding view and plenty of shade. Favoured sites are used year on year and the stick nest inside can become both very large and highly decorated with rags, bones, fur, rubbish and all the other trappings of the Egyptian Vulture's trade.

Marsh Harrier

Circus aeruginosus (**sir**-kuss eer-roo-jin-**noh**-suss)
length 48–56 cm; wingspan 1.15–1.3 m

Male birds of a good many species provision their mate during the breeding season, but none do it in quite such style as the Marsh Harrier (and indeed, other harriers). To make a food pass the male approaches the nest site carrying food and calls the female to him with a special signal; she flies up and both sexes manoeuvre in such a way that the male is flying just above the female. In an instant he drops the food and she flips upside down to catch it in her talons. It is a routine that must require considerable co-ordination, as well as practice. The transfer completed, the female usually returns to her nest to consume her meal, but sometimes goes instead to a so-called 'false nest' specially constructed by the male for the purpose.

The food pass is only one of the aerial routines of a Marsh Harrier's breeding season. The male performs many acrobatics on his own, soaring to heights of 75 m or more with odd, stiff wingbeats and then tumbling down erratically, turning about his axis, dropping as if dead and turning half over this way and that. These displays are designed to show off the bird's contrasting plumage to the full. Sometimes the female joins in the parade, too, the pair indulging in mock attacks and dancing around the skies.

With such command of flight it is not surprising that the Marsh Harrier is a dexterous and adaptable predator. In common with the other harriers, its main hunting method is to fly at a slow speed and low height over the ground – a method known as 'quartering' – and plunge down upon any nourishing prey it finds. Many vertebrates can be caught this way, particularly birds and their young, and small mammals. In general the Marsh Harrier moves over the ground a little quicker than other harriers.

The Marsh Harrier is the most aquatic of the harriers, requiring a minimum of 100 ha of marshy vegetation over which to hunt in the breeding season. In western and southern Europe it is resident or partially migratory, but northern and eastern birds winter in sub-Saharan Africa.

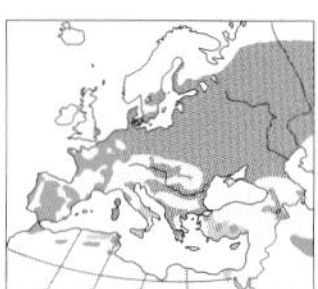

ID: Much the largest harrier with the heaviest body and bluntest wings. Mature female mainly sooty brown, with distinctive creamy forehead, throat and front edge to 'arm'; alone among female harriers completely lacks a white rump. Male is only male harrier with brown back, inner wing and belly.

adult ♂ adult ♀

Short-toed Eagle

Circaetus gallicus (sir-**see**-tuss **gal**-li-kuss)
length 62–67 cm; wingspan 1.7–1.85 m

This is the only eagle that regularly hovers, holding its position high above a rocky hillside by quick flaps of its rather broad wings. It will also fly slowly over the ground at 15–30 m up and will sometimes simply hang in the air on an updraft. This apparently lethargic method of operation is an adaptation for finding its major prey, snakes. At least 75 per cent of its diet may be made up of these reptiles, and much of the rest consists of lizards, with just the odd small mammal or bird taken occasionally. Once a snake is sighted the Short-toed Eagle goes into action, swooping down very fast and then, just before the strike, usually hovering low to fine-tune its assault. The reptile is seized on the ground and killed by gripping, or by crushing the skull. It is then swallowed whole and head-first or, if it is very large (snakes up to 1.2 m long have been recorded), it will be torn apart on site. After swallowing, the bird may sometimes be seen to fly off and resume hunting with the tail of the snake still showing in its throat.

Not surprisingly, given its diet, the Short-toed Eagle is a summer visitor to Europe and tends to occur in warm climates. Reasonably open habitats with rocks and scrub seem to suit snakes best, but the eagle also requires some tree cover nearby in which to build its inconspicuous and unexpectedly small nest.

This bird is more vocal than most other large birds of prey, making loud and frequent whistling sounds during the breeding season. Male and female indulge in some mutual circling routines, and the male sometimes carries a snake in his bill, but compared with many birds of prey the aerial displays are brief and unspectacular.

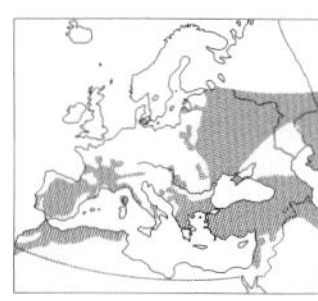

ID: Distinctive eagle with pale underparts, dark head and chest, and long wings and tail. Glides with carpal joints forwards. Often hovers and hangs in wind.

adult dark

adult pale

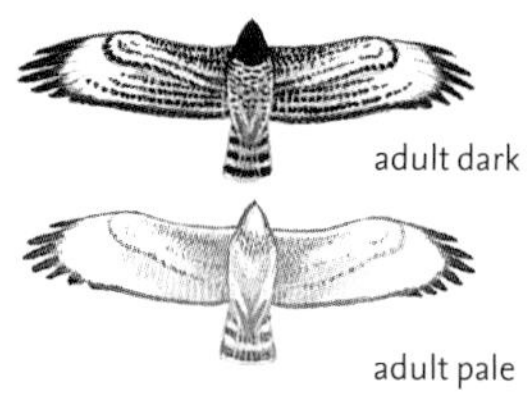

adult dark

adult pale

Pallid Harrier

Circus macrourus (**sir**-kuss mak-ro-**oo**-russ)
length 40–48 cm; wingspan 95–120 cm

No other harrier is found in such dry habitats as the Pallid, a bird of the rolling semi-arid grasslands of eastern Europe. It breeds only at the edge of our region, in Moldova, Ukraine and European Russia, where it is rare. It once occurred much further west, but has undergone a dramatic decline in range and numbers as grasslands have been turned into farmland, and its very existence as a species might one day be threatened.

The Pallid Harrier hunts much as other harriers do, in a quartering flight between 1 m and 5 m above ground. Its main prey items are small mammals, including voles, the steppe lemming, hamsters and ground squirrels, all of which show fluctuations in abundance along cyclical lines, so one season's feeding will be dominated by one species, another by another.

These birds winter in Africa, where they may lead a nomadic existence and feed on more insects than in Europe. In contrast to other harriers, males and females form pair bonds in their winter quarters and migrate north as a couple.

adult ♂

adult ♀

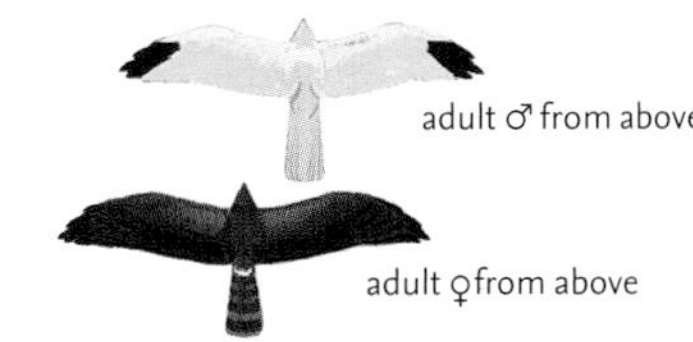

adult ♂ from above

adult ♀from above

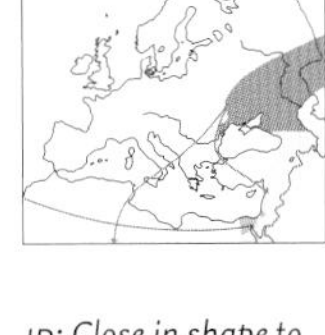

ID: Close in shape to Montagu's, with sharp wing tip and buoyant, tern-like flight. Male easily identified by pale grey colour and small wedge of black on wing tip (not the whole tip). Female formidably similar to female Montagu's, but with better-defined white neck collar and generally darker below.

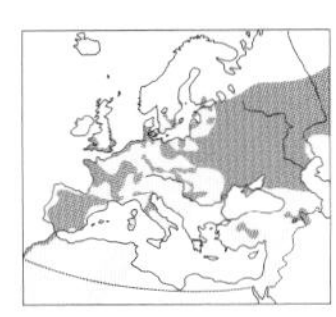

ID: Classic harrier shape of long wings and long tail, combined with the habit of flying slow and low. Sharp wing tips, thin wings and a flight so airy and buoyant that it has been compared to that of a tern. Male is only harrier with a black secondary band on upperside and uniquely also has dark brown speckles on underwing.

Montagu's Harrier

Circus pygargus (**sir**-kuss pie-**gar**-guss)
length 43–47 cm ; wingspan 1.05–1.2 m

Of the three widespread harriers, this is the lightest and most buoyant on the wing. Slight and angular, it can almost resemble a tern in flight as it floats low over the fields, heathlands or marshy areas where it breeds. It is a summer visitor to Europe, inhabiting drier places than the Marsh and warmer places than the Hen Harrier.

Its agile flight is ideal for catching manoeuvrable prey, and breeding Montagu's Harriers tend to concentrate on small, ground-nesting birds. They evidently ambush many of them as the latter are sitting, for eggs and nestlings also find their way into the diet. But the Montagu's is no specialist; some pairs rely almost entirely on voles, and any small ground-living animal that can be caught will be caught.

Montagu's breed amongst tall vegetation such as grass, low scrub or reeds; they usually find such sites near water, although arable fields containing crops such as wheat or oil-seed rape are increasingly used. It is not unusual for several pairs to nest together in loose colonies, but polygamy is rare.

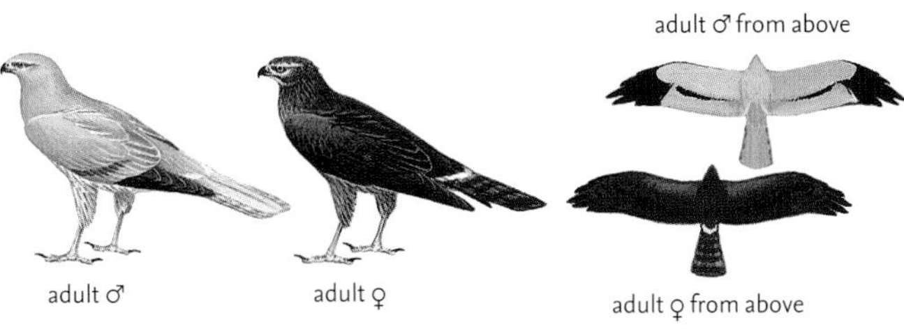

adult ♂ from above

adult ♂

adult ♀

adult ♀ from above

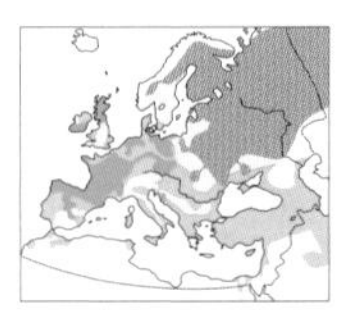

ID: Similar in shape to Montagu's Harrier and Pallid Harrier but larger, with broader 'arm' and blunter wing tips. Male has typical grey and black colour of other harriers, but clear demarcation between grey neck and white belly; whole wing tip is black and there is no secondary bar. Female has partial white neck ring but otherwise very little white on face; best identified by shape.

Hen Harrier

Circus cyaneus (**sir**-kuss sie-**an**-eh-uss)
length 44–52 cm; wingspan 1–1.2 m

Of all our four harriers, this is the only one that reaches into the Arctic to breed in large numbers, and does not retreat at all to tropical Africa for the winter. It is generally found in chilly, windswept places, including moorland, wetlands and the fringes of the tundra, but outside the breeding season it will also hunt over agricultural land.

In common with all harriers the Hen Harrier hunts by quartering low (less than 5 m) above the ground. At such heights it does not just look, but can also often hear prey and will interrupt its slow flight for a quick pounce into the vegetation. It takes a wide range of prey, including mammals, birds and insects, the local abundance of each being reflected in the diet. In some parts of the range up to 80 per cent of food may consist of small birds (almost half of these chicks), but in the far north the Hen Harrier depends more on voles and lemmings and its populations often mirror the rodents' three- to four-year cycle of boom and bust.

The breeding behaviour of this bird of prey is highly unusual. In some populations there is a marked tendency towards males having more than one mate, whereas in others monogamy is the rule. Where males are polygynous, most take just one extra mate, but there are records of exceptional individuals with as many as seven – these are almost always older, experienced birds. The nests of females making up a 'harem' can be as little as 50 m apart. In monogamous pairs the male does all the hunting and provisions female and young until the latter are at least two weeks old; where polygyny is practised the female must do some hunting for herself.

The Hen Harrier nest is usually little more than a low pile of vegetation, hidden in a thicket, but if the ground is wet it may be much larger, as much as 45 cm tall. The young usually leave it when they begin to grow feathers at about 15 days old, preferring to remain nearby in the vegetation. They keep contact with the provisioning adult by calling.

The Hen Harrier's displays are just as spectacular as those of the Marsh Harrier and others of this genus. The male's sky dance consists of a series of steep undulations, said to be steeper than those of any other harrier, and as he performs he often rolls over or rocks from side to side. Most birds rise and fall only three or four times, but one energetic male flew up and down no fewer than 149 consecutive times. Hopefully such a persistent individual was displaying to a harem of females.

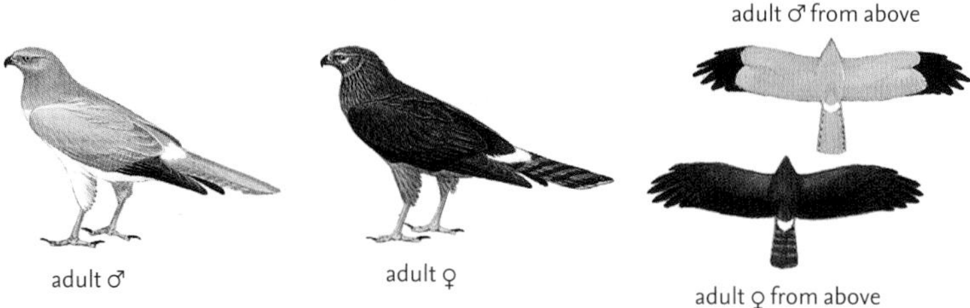

Goshawk

Accipiter gentilis (ak-**sip**-pit-er **jen**-til-iss)
length 48–62 cm; wingspan 93–135 cm

ID: Largest of the 'hawks', the male as big as a Carrion Crow, the female as big as a Buzzard. Looks hefty in flight, especially at the 'hips', and has bulging secondaries and rounded tail.

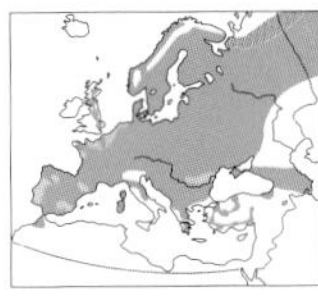

The formidable Goshawk and the Sparrowhawk resemble each other in appearance, hunt in a similar way and have almost identical nest sites and courtship displays. But in other ways this Buzzard-sized hawk is very much its own bird. It takes a wider variety of prey, encompassing not just birds but mammals, and these are often far larger than any attempted by the most audacious Sparrowhawk.

It is also hardier than the Sparrowhawk. Its range reaches well into the Arctic and some individuals have been found wintering at 70°N, where few other birds survive. In such places Goshawks feed almost entirely on grouse, and since these prey species often have cyclic fluctuations in abundance, the predators tend to follow suit, sometimes not producing many young in lean years.

The Goshawk hunts much like the Sparrowhawk, often striking in ambush from a concealed perch. Sometimes, though, it will rise to a great height and stoop down towards its intended prey in the style of a Peregrine, to gain speed; such a method is usually employed for catching highly mobile creatures such as pigeons. But if a Goshawk doesn't make an initial hit, it will often just give up, having a less persistent bent than many other predators. In contrast to Sparrowhawks, Goshawks usually reuse nest sites for at least two years running – again, perhaps part of their lazy streak.

Levant Sparrowhawk

Accipiter brevipes (ak-**sip**-pit-er brev-**vie**-peez)
length 32–38 cm; wingspan 65–75 cm

One of the features of the mysterious Levant Sparrowhawk is how dissimilar it is to the Sparrowhawk in many aspects of its ecology and behaviour, despite greatly resembling the commoner bird in appearance. For one thing it is exclusively a summer visitor to Europe, with a curious tendency to migrate in high, wheeling flocks of up to 20 birds, rather than following the Sparrowhawk's strategy, which, when it does migrate, is to travel singly and low down. It also has a very different method of hunting. Rather than waiting on a perch and setting out on an explosive ambush, the Levant Sparrowhawk simply flies along at moderate height above ground (6–10 m), breaking off from time to time to stoop down and seize prey.

Its diet, too, is very different from that of the Sparrowhawk and Goshawk. It seems to subsist mostly on lizards, plus large insects such as grasshoppers, locusts, beetles and cicadas. Being basically a feeder on more sluggish prey, the male and female are about the same size, in complete contrast to the Sparrowhawk.

The Levant Sparrowhawk occurs mainly in river valleys and other wooded areas, having a particularly strong attachment to broad-leaved trees. It is a scarce and secretive species, and much about its behaviour remains poorly known.

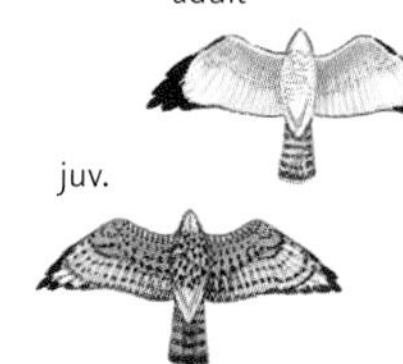

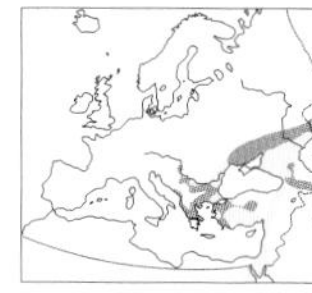

ID: Slighter in build than Sparrowhawk, with narrower wings, shorter tail and black wing tips. Grey cheeks and dark eyes.

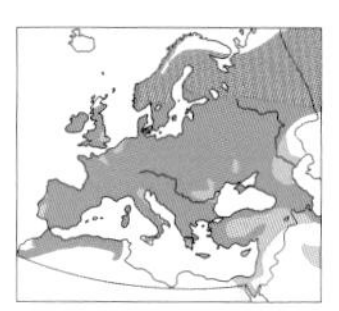

ID: Much the commonest 'hawk', smaller than Goshawk. May be confused with similar-sized Kestrel, but has blunt wing tips, and is barred across, not down breast. Distinctive flight consists of a few flaps followed by a glide.

Sparrowhawk

Accipiter nisus (ak-**sip**-pit-er **nie**-suss)
length 28–38 cm; wingspan 55–70 cm

Over much of Europe this is one of the commonest birds of prey, but it spends a great deal of time hidden in foliage, watching the comings and goings of potential prey. Only when displaying or soaring to scan the ground is it obvious, and then the sight of its long tail and broad, blunt-ended wings will provoke calls of alarm from small birds as they dive for cover.

The Sparrowhawk is small for a bird of prey, not much larger than a pigeon, but it is well adapted for rapid, manoeuvrable flight. To hunt it sets off from an observation perch and accelerates towards prey, with a few fast wingbeats interspersed with closed-wing glides; as it nears the target it usually keeps behind a screen such as a hedgerow or garden fence to conceal its approach. If all goes well it will be spotted too late, and the ambush is completed as the bird grips its prey in its talons. The claws administer the fatal wound and the prey is taken to a special perch to be plucked and eaten.

In common with several bird-hunting raptors, the sexes of the Sparrowhawk are of quite different size, the female being up to 25 per cent larger and heavier. In the majority of bird species males tend to carry the greatest bulk, so this grandly titled 'reverse sexual size dimorphism' in birds of prey is something of a puzzle. It is known that Sparrowhawks have gender-specific food preferences to prevent competition in the non-breeding season (males hunt tits and finches in woodland, females go for thrushes, starlings and pigeons in more open country), but this doesn't explain why it is the male that is the smaller. It might be related to the division of labour in the breeding season. The male Sparrowhawk takes on the majority of hunting, bringing food to the female and nestlings up to 20 times a day. Perhaps having a small, highly mobile bird rather than a larger, slower hunter to do this work is an advantage.

Whatever the reason, the female's size ensures that she is the dominant member of the pair and she initiates much of the courtship display. Soaring high above the territory, she fluffs out her undertail coverts, accentuating their white colour, and then either flies up and down in an undulating flight or dives spectacularly, breaking her fall just above the tree tops.

Sparrowhawk pair bonds officially last only one season, although couples will re-form if it is convenient to do so. The Sparrowhawk's stick nest, placed at any height in a tree, is also remade each year.

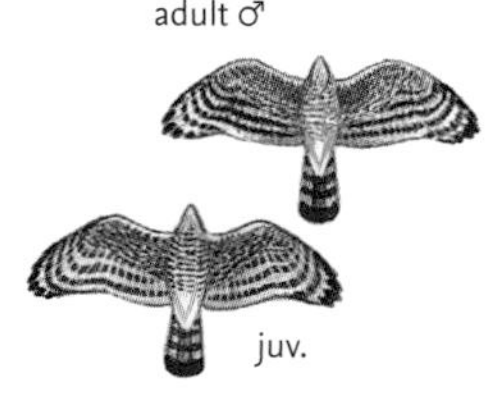

Common Buzzard

Buteo buteo (**boo**-teh-oh **boo**-teh-oh)
length 51–57 cm ; wingspan 1.13–1.28 m

Few birds of prey are as territorial as the Common Buzzard. Most others use a large area for feeding and breeding, a 'home range' that is defended only in the immediate vicinity of the nest. But the Buzzard is more formal. Individuals spend much of their time looking after their borders, sitting prominently on perches on the edge of the territory, watching for intruders, or soaring over it in tight circles, giving loud, mewing calls. Where land is disputed, many birds may circle in the air together, occasionally diving at each other and calling.

Optimum habitat for the Buzzard is a mixture of open ground for hunting and woodland for the nest. A whole array of habitats fits these requirements, so the unfussy Buzzard is widespread and often common. It breeds from the Arctic Circle, where the populations are migratory, to southern Spain and Greece. It is tolerant of high winds and rainfall, but on the whole Buzzards are not really mountain birds, rarely breeding far above 1000 m.

Individuals come in all sorts of colour variations. The dark brown forms are the commonest but virtually all-white birds are occasionally seen, too. The race found in eastern Fennoscandia and Russia, the so-called Steppe Buzzard, is strongly rusty red below and much less variable.

Buzzards are not specialised in what they eat, with small mammals, birds, lizards, insects and earthworms all being consumed at times. What a Buzzard eats and how is subject to what is available, what the individual prefers and the weather. A bird hunting voles (often a major food source) tends to sit on a perch a few metres above the ground and pounce when it sees movement below; it may have to wait many minutes before something stirs. Individuals hunting birds tend to perch closer to the woodland or even make short sallying flights along rides and edges. Those looking for invertebrates, especially earthworms, may spend hours on the ground simply walking about. If there is a brisk wind, many Buzzards will either hover or hang in the air up to 300 m above ground, plunging down when their eyes detect something. But if it is raining, most will return to their patient watch from elevated perches once more.

As might be predicted by their territorial nature, many Buzzards live quite settled lives. Pairs often stay in the same territory throughout the year and remain partners for the long term. Such pairs will build several nests over the course of time, switching sites between years or reusing structures, just as the fancy takes them. Most Buzzard nests are built in trees, but crags and cliffs will do if necessary. The structure is quite large, about 1 m in diameter, and is a platform of sticks and twigs lined with fresh green material.

ID: Common, widespread and variable raptor, the benchmark medium-sized species against which others are measured. Flies forward with distinctively stiff wing flaps followed by a glide; soars on wings raised in shallow V. Often hovers and hangs on wind. Highly variable in plumage pattern.

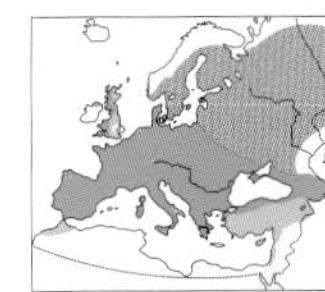

Rough-legged Buzzard

Buteo lagopus (**boo**-teh-oh **lay**-go-puss)
length 50–60 cm; wingspan 1.2–1.5 m

The fortunes of all raptors are determined ultimately by the abundance or otherwise of their prey, but few species show this quite as obviously as the Rough-legged Buzzard, a bird of the northern tundra feeding mainly on voles and lemmings. Both of these mammals have distinct cycles of abundance: on average there is a peak every three or four years, followed by a collapse. In boom years, when small mammals can literally be thick on the ground as they try to move away from their own untenable pressure of population, the buzzards respond by laying more eggs than normal (5–7 as opposed to 2–3). And because the rodents keep on producing litters throughout the summer, the resulting young are likely to prosper. In good years the Rough-legged Buzzard may breed far to the south of its normal range and at the end of the season may spill further down than usual to winter in temperate climates.

In lean years food may be hard to find and the Buzzards may then be forced to search for more difficult prey, such as birds. In these circumstances the older chicks within the reduced broods sometimes kill and eat their younger siblings to make up for the lack of food. Before they attempt to breed in poor years birds may travel far across the tundra searching for anywhere with a suitable rodent supply, and many do not even try.

In many other aspects of its life the Rough-legged resembles the Common Buzzard, although it hovers more while searching for prey and tends to nest on the ground, on a hummock or rocky outcrop.

ID: Larger than Common Buzzard, with less variation, longer wings and longer tail, giving hint of harrier-like shape. Flies with more fluid, slower wingbeats without stiffness of Common Buzzard, and also hovers much more often. White at base of tail often very conspicuous.

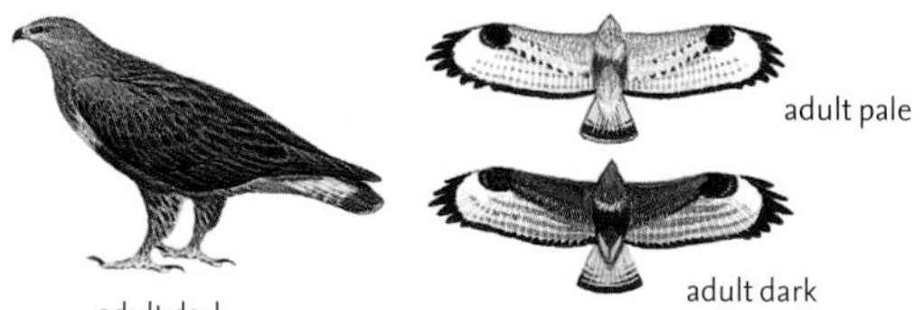

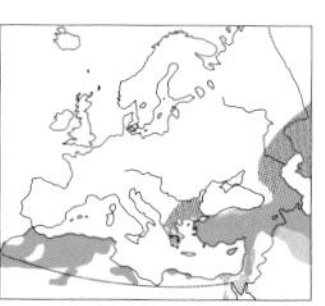

ID: Shares overall shape and manner of flight with Rough-legged Buzzard, though larger size, longer wings and slower wingbeats are usually enough to distinguish it from eastern race of that species.

Long-legged Buzzard

Buteo rufinus (**boo**-teh-oh roo-**fie**-nuss)
length 50–65 cm; wingspan 1.26–1.48 m

From what is known of the Long-legged Buzzard, it does not seem to be the most spectacular of hunters. It favours a slow version of the perch-and-pounce method, frequently spending hours on end sitting on a rock, earth mound or the ground, watching its immediate surroundings and waiting for something to happen. When it does, the bird will drop down on to a gerbil, rat, pika or small rabbit with unceremonious efficiency, sometimes intercepting a victim at the entrance to its hole. It will also wander along the ground looking for large insects such as grasshoppers and locusts; animals fleeing from bush fires are another easy target. When it does take to the air to forage, the Long-legged often hangs somewhat listlessly in the air, making the minimum effort.

This bird is found only in the extreme east of our region, where it is mainly a summer visitor. It prefers arid regions such as steppes and stony mountainsides, and usually builds its nest on a cliff ledge or slope.

Greater Spotted Eagle

Aquila clanga (**ak**-wil-la **clan**-ga)
length 65–72 cm; wingspan 1.55–1.82 m

Much the rarer of the two spotted eagles in Europe, this one is invariably found close to water bodies and wetlands. Otherwise it profits, as the Lesser Spotted Eagle does, from the juxtaposition of lowland forest, meadows and bogs, hunting chiefly over open terrain. It feeds in a similar way to its smaller relative, but probably takes more birds, sometimes snatching these from the surface of the water. It is neither a dynamic nor a spectacular hunter and rarely catches large, highly mobile animals.

The Greater Spotted Eagle is territorial and will keep an area of at least 15–30 sq km, and usually much more, as its own. Nests are widely dispersed, often in isolated clumps of trees rather than in the forest proper.

The migration of this species is complicated. At least some Greater Spotted Eagles remain in Europe in the winter, particularly in Turkey, whilst others apparently head for the Middle East. Breeding birds leave their breeding grounds somewhat later than Lesser Spotted Eagles, in November and December.

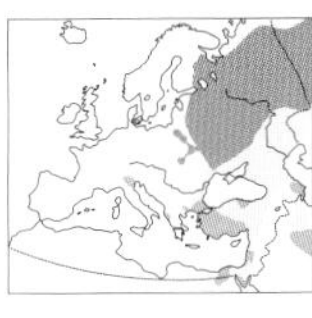

ID: Larger than Lesser Spotted Eagle, but equally compact; much shorter tail than Golden or Imperial Eagles. When gliding wings are more obviously bowed, with an angle between 'arm' and 'hand'.

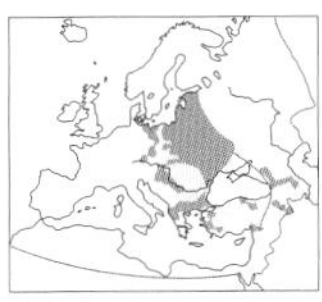

Lesser Spotted Eagle

Aquila pomarina (**ak**-wil-la poh-ma-**rie**-na)
length 60–65 cm; wingspan 1.34–1.59 m

ID: Adult rather featureless dark brown, but on upperwing there is a small but important white patch at base of inner primaries.

The Lesser Spotted Eagle is diminutive for an eagle, being not much larger than a Common Buzzard. Found mainly in the east of our region, it favours habitats where woodlands or forests abut fields and meadows. Where it is numerous pairs may nest as little as 1 km apart, hiding their structures in tall trees close to the woodland edge.

The Lesser Spotted hunts in three ways. It will quarter from up to 100 m up, diving down when it spies prey; it will perch on a tree limb and pounce down from there; and it will occasionally forage on the ground. Whatever method it uses the prey is taken on the ground, grabbed by the talons. Medium-sized vertebrates of various sorts may be taken, presumably in accordance with their abundance: in Greece snakes make up 70 per cent of prey; in Slovakia mammals such as voles are dominant.

This bird lays two eggs, several days apart. Since incubation begins with the first egg, one chick hatches before the other and has time to grow before it is joined by its sibling. The older chick then always kills the younger one, regardless of available food supply. This 'Cain and Abel battle' is one of the great puzzles of bird biology.

This species is a summer visitor to Europe, wintering in southeast Africa and making the journey via the narrow crossing of the Bosphorus.

Golden Eagle

Aquila chrysaetos (**ak**-wil-la krie-**see**-toss)
length 75–90 cm ; wingspan 1.9–2.27 m

ID: A very large, long-winged, long-tailed eagle, which soars with wings raised in shallow V. Inner wing not as broad as outer, producing inward curve into body. Golden-brown below, unlike any other eagle; head is reddish-brown. Tail is darker at tip, but no obvious tail band. From above, shows pale covert bar. Immatures distinctive, with white central patch on outer wing.

On the whole, people and Golden Eagles don't mix very well. This bird is most numerous in places with a sparse human population, in habitats such as high mountains, cliffs, large forests and wetlands. And many people don't like eagles: they accuse them of killing domestic animals or gamebirds and persecute them as a result. So in much of Europe the Golden Eagle has been wiped out, displaced by its nemesis.

It is certainly true that this magnificent raptor is a very effective hunter. It takes a wide range of live prey that includes a few gamebirds and there are reliable records of individuals attacking fawns of the roe deer. But in general the Golden Eagle takes rather modest prey for a bird of its size and power. It prefers rabbits, mountain hares, grouse, crows, seabirds and ducks. It is very unusual to see one killing anything larger, and the numerous tales of sheep and lambs being harried are probably mostly fictional or misinterpreted. That's not to say that Golden Eagles don't eat sheep or goats; they do. It's just that they take them as carrion when they are already dead, just as we do.

The Golden Eagle uses its 2-m wingspan to fly low and slowly over vast tracts of open countryside; it does not go in for hunting from a perch or making showy dives from a great height. In common with most birds of prey, it has very acute vision and will easily spot the movement of a quarry as far away as 1000 m or more as it quarters along and scans. Alternatively it might cause prey to stir by its very appearance; the sight of a low-flying Golden Eagle invites many a quarry to break cover and flee in panic. If so, the eagle can pick it off with a quick stoop.

Members of a pair sometimes hunt co-operatively, and there have been some remarkable observations of this in action. In its commonest form, one bird acts as the 'beater', flushing prey out by quartering low or even walking on the ground, while the other mops up. But there are also records of birds attacking deer fawns by separating them from their mothers, one bird distracting the adult, the other concentrating on the youngster. It is not known how often such teamwork is used.

To work so well together, the members of a pair need to know each other, so it's not surprising that Golden Eagles are both highly sedentary and faithful to their partners; they live a settled life. Most pairs live within a large home range, between 50 and 100 sq km in extent, and never go outside it unless forced to by extreme weather. Over the years they get to know their area well and find out the best places to hunt. Home ranges may pass down the generations.

Within the home range is the nest site, the eyrie, the only part of a Golden Eagle's patch that is vigorously defended from intruders. In fact a pair will usually have several nest sites (up to eleven), which can be used as circumstances dictate, and they will sometimes refurbish more than one nest in a single season. Most are placed on a cliff ledge, but tall trees are also used and may buckle under the strain of the structure being built up over many years: Golden Eagles nests have been recorded at 5 m tall and 3 m wide.

In early spring between one and three eggs are laid at three- to four-day intervals. With incubation beginning with the first egg, the resulting chicks are of different ages and, where there are two birds, the younger one fails to survive in 80 per cent of cases. This may be either because of inherent weakness or because it is intimidated or killed by its older sibling.

Once fledged, though, young Golden Eagles are looked after and tolerated by the parents for a considerable length of time. They often leave the home range during the winter or even hang on until as late as the following spring.

ID: *Similar in size to Golden Eagle, but with shorter tail and more parallel-edged wings, not pinched in towards body; soars on flat wings. Darker brown below than Golden Eagle, without the latter's rusty tones. Has clearly defined dark tail band.*

Eastern Imperial Eagle

Aquila heliaca (**ak**-wil-la hee-li-**ak**-a)
length 72–83 cm; wingspan 1.9–2.1m

The Imperial Eagle is at heart a bird of open steppe country, customarily nesting on tall isolated trees. It also occurs in forests and at present in Europe, with its range having been decimated by habitat destruction and persecution, it has almost entirely retreated to large tracts of hilly forested land.

In most of its range the Eastern Imperial feeds mainly on mammals, which it catches by pouncing, either from a perch (often a haystack) or from a plunge during soaring flight. Despite being not much smaller than the Golden Eagle, the Imperial tends to feed little and often rather than taking a few big meals. Hamsters, gerbils and susliks, which abound on the fields of Eastern Europe, usually suffice. Birds are less frequent prey.

The Eastern Imperial is mainly a migrant to Europe. At least some birds pair up in their Middle Eastern wintering grounds, where large eagles can be surprisingly sociable. In February or March they return and occupy home ranges, within which the large stick nest, 1 m or more in diameter, is built.

Spanish Imperial Eagle

Aquila adalberti (**ak**-wil-la ad-al-**ber**-tie)
length 78–82 cm; wingspan 1.8–2.1 m

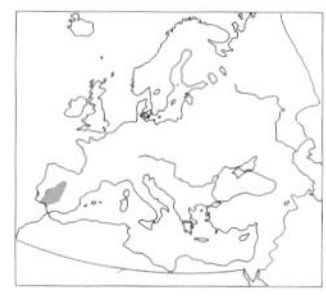

ID: *Very similar to Eastern Imperial Eagle, but adult has much more white on leading edge of the wing. Shows above and below. Flight feathers darker than those of Eastern Imperial, so underwing shows less contrast.*

Despite being geographically isolated from the Imperial Eagles of central and eastern Europe, and being larger and distinctively plumaged, the Imperial Eagles of Spain have been elevated only fairly recently to full species status. Their range is tiny and they are on the Endangered List, with only about 200 pairs left in the world.

Spanish Imperial Eagles differ from Eastern Imperial Eagles in several ways. They are non-migratory, with only the young dispersing at the end of the breeding season. Their main food is rabbits, rather than smaller mammals. And they are much less sociable, chasing rivals away from their territories rather than tolerating them. Otherwise they live in similar habitats and acquire their prey in similar ways.

The scene at the nest of a Spanish Imperial Eagle has a greater degree of harmony than is usual among eagles. The male, for example, feeds the young more often than in other species, and the young are less likely to do battle to the death with each other.

Bonelli's Eagle

Hieraaetus fasciatus (hie-ra-**ee**-tuss fa-si-**ay**-tuss)
length 65–72 cm; wingspan 1.5–1.8 m.

In some ways, the Bonelli's Eagle is unlike most other large birds of prey in character. It does not soar around lazily, but tends to fly with more purpose and usually somewhat lower down. Its primary feathers are less obviously 'fingered' than those of other eagles, making it less stable when riding thermals, but also faster and more agile. In common with its close relative the Booted Eagle it relies on fast ambush, either during a dive from the air or, less often, a burst from a perched position on to the ground. So it is unusually dynamic and energetic for its size.

The Bonelli's specialises in predating medium-sized mammals and birds. In Spain at least, it relies heavily on rabbits and Red-legged Partridges, but will switch to crows, pigeons and squirrels if the more regular prey is scarce or unavailable. Sometimes a pair hunts co-operatively together.

In some aspects of its ecology the Bonelli's Eagle differs sharply from the Booted. For one thing it remains within its home range all year round. It is more a bird of arid and mountainous zones than the forest-loving Booted. And it usually selects a cliff site for its nest, rather than a tree. The nest is very large for the size of bird, often 2 m in diameter and with individual sticks up to half this length. Most sites are very high off the ground, with a commanding view.

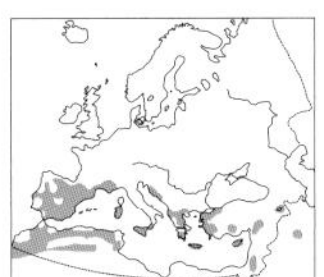

ID: Medium-large eagle with small, protruding head and long tail. Pair often seen together. Unique combination below of light body and head with dark wings and tail. Diagnostic black central wing bar.

Booted Eagle

Hieraaetus pennatus (hie-ra-**ee**-tuss pen-**nay**-tuss)
length 45–55 cm; wingspan 1.1–1.32 m

It might be small for an eagle, only slightly larger than a Common Buzzard, but the Booted Eagle is a formidable and dangerous predator, whose attacks are known for their speed and vehemence. When hunting it soars at a height of 200 m or more and then makes breathtaking rapid and forceful stoops down to the ground, crashing onto its prey. It will also plunge into the woodland canopy from lower flight and pursue birds among the foliage. Its agility enables it to manoeuvre quickly, even in tight spaces, and it can be persistent where necessary. To make matters worse for its prey, members of a pair regularly hunt co-operatively.

Birds are the usual victims, and they can be very small, no larger than a warbler – which suggests that the Booted Eagle can snatch them in mid-air – or as big as a Red-legged Partridge or Carrion Crow. The other principal targets are lizards, of which the large ocellated lizard is important in Spain.

Booted Eagles begin their breeding season by displaying in great style and calling incessantly. The male will soar very high and make a series of vertical closed-wing dives of up to 200 m descent, each time breaking off before reaching the ground and using his momentum to sweep upwards again. Later the female may join in, and the male will dive towards her with his wing tips touching his tail, before both plunge down to the tree-top nest site.

Mainly a bird of warm, sunny slopes and woodland, the Booted Eagle is a summer visitor to Europe, arriving in late March and leaving in September. It is not a sociable species and on its wintering grounds individuals are so thinly scattered that they seem to melt away into the vastness of Africa, with few concentrations anywhere.

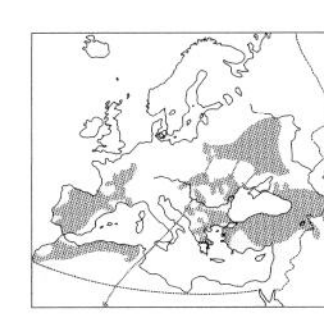

ID: Small Buzzard-sized eagle, and similar in shape to that bird. When soaring, wings are level, not raised, and Booted Eagle's 'hand' is broader. Tail square-ended, in contrast to Bonelli's.

Osprey

Pandion haliaetus (pan-**dye**-on hal-li-**ee**-tuss)
length 55–58 cm; wingspan 1.45–1.7 m

Several birds of prey catch fish to eat, but none do it more spectacularly or more effectively than the Osprey. This plunge-diving raptor is so successful that it occurs on every continent of the world except Antarctica, albeit locally in Europe. It is equally at home fishing over fresh or salt water, and it can nest anywhere from high in a tree to flat on the ground. So long as there are sizeable fish to catch in large areas of clear, unpolluted water, there are Ospreys.

Fish are difficult prey, tricky to catch and even more slippery to hold onto. Ospreys have several adaptations to cope with them, not least in their talons, their working tools. For one thing the Osprey's legs and feet are long, very big and fitted with sharp, hooked claws that have a wide reach. In addition, of the four toes, the outer one is reversible, meaning that two toes can face forward and two back, allowing an even spread (in most birds three toes point forwards and one back). The toes are also interesting in having short, 1-mm-long spines, or spicules, projecting from their lower surface; these stick into the fish's scales, helping the Osprey to keep hold of its meal.

Fish can be dealt with only after they are caught, of course, and the Osprey's method of hunting is simple enough. With its long wings designed for slow gliding and hovering rather than soaring, it rises to a height above the water where it can see fish coming to the surface – which can be as much as 70 m up – and simply moves along slowly, checking below it, like a golfer looking for a lost ball. Once it locates prey it hovers on the spot and, more often than not, moves down a little before hovering again, fine-tuning its bearings. Once committed to the attack the bird closes its wings, plunges towards the surface and then, just a few metres from the waves, suddenly lifts its wings and leads with its feet. The prey, which may be as much as 1 m below the surface, is grabbed upon impact.

Ospreys are not true waterbirds, and their first need upon procuring prey is to become airborne again. They have special oily plumage to prevent them being rapidly soaked, but they are not immune to drowning – there are several records of birds being dragged under by fish that were too big for them to carry. With a few powerful flaps they lift off the water and very soon manoeuvre the captive so that it is held under the belly with its head facing forward, torpedo-like. This reduces air resistance as the Osprey flies to a favoured feeding post to devour the meal.

Ospreys will catch any kind of fish they can, mainly in the range of 150–300 g (although up to 1.2 kg has been reported). They are limited by the degree to which a species comes up to the surface, and are therefore found mainly over shallow waters. Their strike rate varies from fish to fish: slow-moving species such as carp are caught, on average, on six out of ten occasions; fast ones such as trout only four times out of ten.

Ospreys are largely summer visitors to Europe, although a few do overwinter in the Mediterranean region. The bulk of the population leaves in September and arrives back in March, returning to the same eyrie and remaining with the same mate where possible. The nest is built up every year and after many continuous seasons it can become very large indeed.

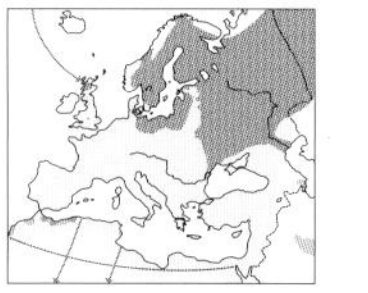

ID: Distinctive, long-winged raptor, with whitish plumage below making it resemble a large gull. Head white with dark stripe.

Kestrel

Falco tinnunculus (**fal**-ko tin-**nun**-kyoo-luss)
length 32–39 cm; wingspan 65–82 cm

To many people in Europe, the Kestrel is the only truly familiar bird of prey. It is the one that is easy to spot as it hovers over motorway verges or above waste ground in city centres. It is one of the few raptor species found in gardens or local parks, and in farmland. It doesn't need mountains or large forests or rocky hillsides in order to thrive, as so many others do. It is neither shy nor retiring, and it isn't difficult to identify. Its abundance brings it to people's attention.

A fair selection of other European raptors will hover, but none is as closely associated with this form of flying on the spot as the Kestrel. These birds fly at a moderate height over the ground, wings flapping rapidly and tail fanned, the head held extraordinarily still as they scour the ground for movement. If something appears they will often break from a hover, drop down slightly and resume hovering; the final strike is a quick plunge to the ground and a grab with the talons. At times they will perform a similar strike, but begin their plunge from a perch.

Although Kestrels have a catholic diet, most feed by choice on rodents, especially voles. These small mammals live in long grass and are active by day. It has recently been discovered that a vole's urine leaves an ultraviolet trail than Kestrels can detect, giving the hunters a distinct advantage in catching them. In the northern parts of the Kestrel's range the numbers of voles vary from year to year on a four-year cycle and the breeding success of the birds follows suit.

Although Kestrels are very much in the diurnal raptor group, they are far more successful than most others in the family at hunting in twilight or by moonlight. Males often do this in the spring when they are trying to feed both their mate and the nestlings, and their workload is heavy. At such times their prey changes: nocturnal mammals such as wood mice are taken, and occasionally young rabbits too.

It would be wrong to give the impression that Kestrels hunt only small furry mammals. Insects are often important, especially in the warmer parts of the range, and lizards make a good meal, too. A minority also seems to be adept at catching birds. When hunting, these experts use the same ambush technique as the Sparrowhawk – a surprise strike from a concealed perch. But most Kestrels are not very good at this.

The Kestrel will feed over almost any kind of open country, but it needs suitable nest sites nearby if it is to take up residence and breed. Three distinct types of site exist: some birds nest in holes in trees, others on cliffs and still others in the old nests of other birds such as crows. In recent times a fourth has been added: artificial sites. Kestrels have no problem at all in using large nest boxes, and the provision of these may lead to local increases in population.

It is possible to tell that a pair of Kestrels is intending to breed well before it does so: the birds start displaying in February, even though they may not attend the nest for another two months or more. Display flights are accompanied by hoarse trilling. High in the sky the male makes repeated mock attacks on the female; she dodges him by a rapid roll to the side. Later he may perform alone, flying along with erratic wingbeats and rolling from side to side to show off his whitish underwings. Kestrels form monogamous pair bonds and the male spends a great deal of his time bringing his incubating and brooding mate gifts of food.

Most Kestrels live in small home ranges and nest well apart, although in some areas colonies will form, like those of Lesser Kestrels. If the immediate countryside can support them, a pair will sometimes remain around the breeding site all year, but many move away to take up a feeding home range on their own. The Kestrel is a migrant in the northern and eastern parts of its wide range in Europe. Clever though it is in finding prey in the long grass, snow is an impenetrable barrier, forcing the bird to move away and hunt elsewhere.

ID: Small slender falcon lacking the obvious power of bird specialists such as Sparrowhawk or Merlin; has quite loose, 'flappy' wingbeats. Repeated hovering usually diagnostic. Sparrowhawk is of similar size but doesn't hover, and has blunt wing tips. Kestrel has longer tail than Merlin, Hobby or Peregrine. Kestrel also easily recognised by red-brown colour (but see Lesser Kestrel).

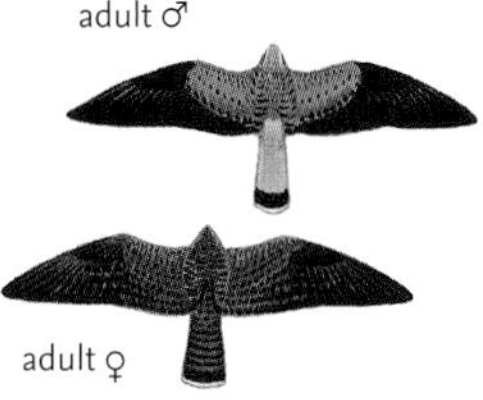

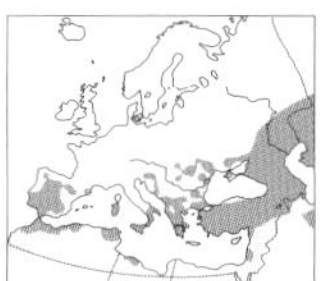

ID: *Very similar in shape to Kestrel, but has a shorter and thinner tail; at rest the wing tips nearly reach the tail tip. Male distinguished by unmarked grey head, red-brown back and diagnostic grey bar inside black outer flight feathers.*

Lesser Kestrel

Falco naumanni (**fal**-ko **now**-man-nie)
length 29–32 cm; wingspan 58–72 cm

Plenty of raptors incorporate insects into their diet, but none are as dependent on them as the Lesser Kestrel; some individuals eat nothing else all summer, while others take 90 per cent insects and 10 per cent other items in the course of their breeding season. These 'other items', curiously enough, often include centipedes, something of a speciality. The birds often hover and drop on their prey, but they can also catch insects in flight, or plunge from a perch to snatch them on the ground. When they do hover, Lesser Kestrels flap less than Common Kestrels and they have a tendency to break out of a hover, glide for a bit and then hover again.

The Lesser Kestrel is highly colonial. It shares this habit with the Red-footed Falcon, but the nest sites of the two species are completely different. Lesser Kestrels don't use old nests, but lay their eggs in holes in cliffs or, more usually, buildings. They particularly like old, crumbling buildings and are not put off if they find them within towns, so long as these are surrounded by open countryside. If there are feeding sites nearby, usually no more than 7 km away, the precise nature of the backdrop is immaterial.

Lesser Kestrels are migrants from Africa, with the males arriving first, in March and early April. They select a nest site and then advertise themselves by flying above their patch with food trailing from their talons, meanwhile giving a special call. This trophy is not usually an insect but a lizard, for reasons that only the Kestrels know.

Red-footed Falcon

Falco vespertinus (**fal**-ko ves-per-**tie**-nuss)
length 29–31 cm; wingspan 66–78 cm

Once Rooks have finished breeding early in the year, their tree-top nests often play host to new tenants later on in the summer: Red-footed Falcons. These migratory raptors arrive on the steppes, meadows and riverside trees of eastern Europe from late April onwards, and they have two main requirements for their stay: an abundant supply of large insects, and plenty of nests placed close together, the latter to cater for their habit of forming colonies. In common with other falcons, Red-footed Falcons don't build their own nest structure, so they have to make do with what is available. That's why Rooks' nests, placed high in a tree and near to fields and meadows, are ideal for them. If no such nests are available, they will breed as single pairs.

In terms of shape and behaviour the Red-footed Falcon is rather like a cross between a Kestrel and a Hobby. Although graceful in the air, well able to swoop and soar like a Hobby, it is also a habitual hoverer, like a Kestrel. It is in fact quite a versatile hunter, swooping low and catching insects in flight, hovering over and dropping down to the ground, perching on wires and scanning the ground, and sometimes trotting along on the ground itself. Adult Red-footed Falcons prey mainly on large insects, particularly grasshoppers, but for a short time in the breeding season they feed their young on small mammals such as voles and mice, or fledgling birds.

From August onwards Red-footed Falcons begin their long migratory flight back to southern Africa. Once there they often gather in large concentrations to feed on swarms of insects, in the company of Hobbies and Lesser Kestrels.

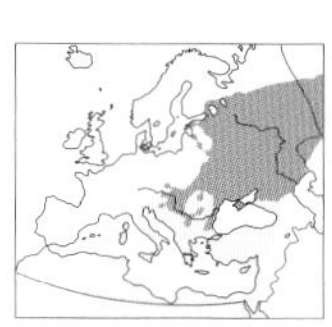

ID: *Smaller than Kestrel, about size of Hobby; slim build and thin, pointed wings recall Hobby, but tail longer. Male unmistakable, dark grey with chestnut undertail coverts; female grey above with barred wings, underparts buff with narrow streaks; small black face mask.*

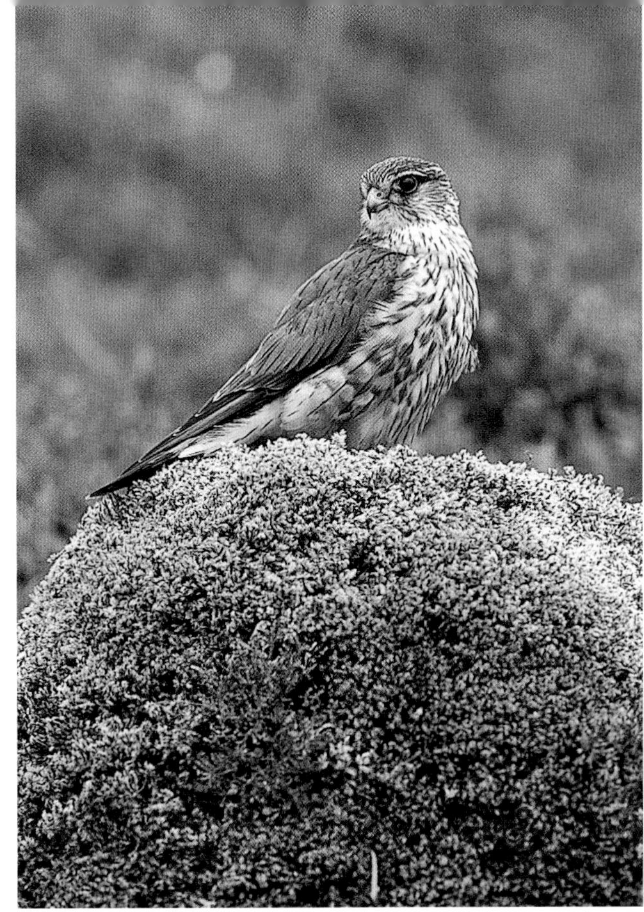

Merlin

Falco columbarius (**fal**-ko koh-lum-**bah**-ri-uss)
length 25–30 cm; wingspan 50–62 cm

It might be the smallest bird of prey in Europe, but the Merlin is a fearless hunter. It tends to catch its prey, usually a small bird, by approaching low to the ground and making a final burst at speed to surprise its victim, often using an acrobatic twist of body and talons to clutch onto its target at the last moment. Such single-minded pursuit can make it unheedful of danger to itself; some Merlins perish in the act of chasing, by hitting obstacles outside their tunnel vision.

It can also be a very persistent hunter. When a Merlin locks into a quarry it really locks; the two birds, hunter and prey, may twist and turn for minutes on end, the Merlin following every move of its victim's escape flight, occasionally breaking off to fly upwards to gain momentum before diving again. Again and again it will give chase, until one or the other bird becomes exhausted.

This small falcon is a bird of the north, occupying a variety of habitats from true tundra and mountain tops to moorland and dunes; also, in winter, farmland and wetlands. Almost any rough ground with an open aspect will do, although the Merlin is particularly drawn to rolling country and for its breeding site it often selects the head of a valley, where sitting or attending birds can survey their surroundings. The eggs are laid on the ground amidst vegetation, especially heather, or alternatively in an old crow's nest on the branches of an isolated tree.

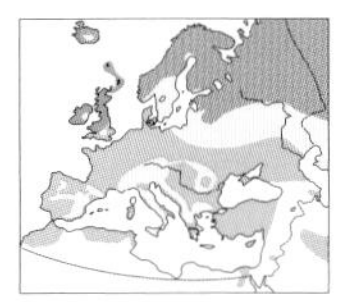

ID: Male no bigger than a Collared Dove. Shape like a miniature Peregrine, with short, broad-based wings and not especially long tail.

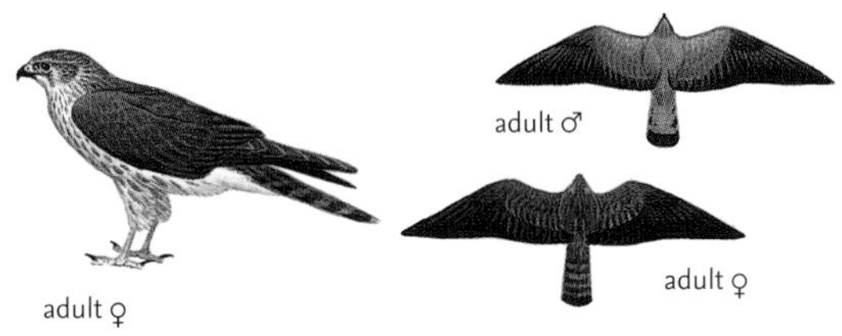

Hobby

Falco subbuteo (**fal**-ko sub-**boo**-teh-oh)
length 30–36 cm; wingspan 82–92 cm

It is no coincidence that a distant Hobby is frequently mistaken for a Swift, because these two unrelated aerial birds have much in common. Both have slim bodies, sickle-shaped wings and relatively short tails. Both spend much of their time aloft, sweeping high and fast around the open sky. And both are very much summer visitors to Europe, arriving only in the late spring, when the insects on which both feed start to become abundant.

On occasion the relationship is more direct, and a Hobby will actually catch and eat a Swift. This is quite a feat, for the Swift is fast, free-flying and highly manoeuvrable, and the Hobby is usually successful only if it can take its quarry unawares. And anyway, a Swift is a choice, irregular meal for a Hobby. It generally makes do with large insects such as dragonflies, beetles and moths, which it catches in its talons and consumes in flight.

In late summer, though, when the chicks require meat to grow, the Hobby switches mainly to catching birds. Open-country species such as Swallows, House Martins, larks and pipits are the most common prey items, but almost anything will do. Laying its eggs in June or July, the Hobby times its breeding season to ensure that plenty of recently fledged youngsters are about when the chicks are growing fast.

In contrast to the other European insect specialists, the Red-footed Falcon and Lesser Kestrel, the Hobby is a solitary nester. This enables it to occur in areas where there are not enough insects to sustain the other species, including temperate and even boreal parts of Europe.

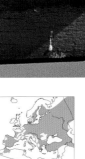

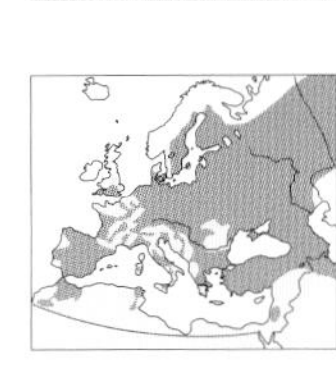

ID: Distinctive Kestrel-sized falcon with relatively short tail and narrow, pointed wings; often recalls large, slow-moving Swift in flight. Dark slate-grey above and heavily streaked below, with reddish thighs and prominent white cheeks.

Eleonora's Falcon

Falco eleonorae (**fal**-ko el-leh-oh-**noh**-ree)
length 36–42 cm; wingspan 90–110 cm

The Eleonora's Falcon has, to say the least, a highly individual lifestyle. Much is unique or unusual about it. It is the only species from Europe, for example, that finds its way to the distant Indian Ocean island of Madagascar for the winter. Birds migrating there leave their breeding grounds in October and travel east along the Mediterranean, across Suez and down the Red Sea, before following the East African coast to their destination.

Another exceptional feature of the Eleonora's Falcon's biology is its very late breeding season. It does not normally lay eggs until mid-July and August, months after most other species have finished. The reason, though, is simple. Their young are reared almost entirely on migrating songbirds, which are beginning to move south in large numbers by the time the eggs hatch in mid-August or September. Eleonora's Falcons breed in colonies, in places where small birds are easy to see as they travel, such as coastal cliffs and offshore islands. Here the members of a colony can intercept small birds flying over the sea. Working together, groups of falcons may form a barrier several kilometres long and 1000 m high, with birds posted at regular intervals, hovering, like border guards, ready to strike at any birds that try to get through. The predators hunt in the early morning and late evening when most migrant birds are travelling, and also sometimes by moonlight.

Eleonora's Falcon colonies are found only in a narrow band of latitude, six degrees from north to south, and only within the Mediterranean and on a few Atlantic islands. The bird is not only special, but also a great rarity. Only about a hundred colonies are known in the world, with a maximum of 300 pairs each; it adds up to only about 5000 pairs overall.

ID: Medium-sized falcon with noticeably long tail and long, pointed wings; very agile in the air; often hovers. Comes in several colour phases: dark morph is chocolate-brown all over; pale morph is Hobby-like, with white cheek, but underparts washed reddish-brown.

adult dark — adult pale

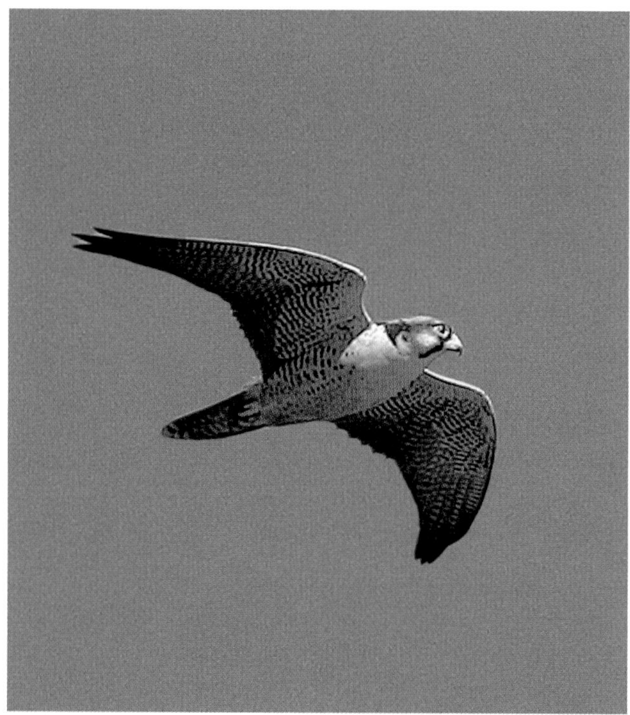

Lanner

Falco biarmicus (**fal**-ko bie-**ar**-mi-kuss)
length 35–50 cm; wingspan 90–110 cm

The Lanner invites comparison with the Peregrine, since both are large, powerful, highly aerial falcons. But where the Peregrine is all muscular power, the Lanner is slimmer, long-tailed and more elegant. Where the Peregrine is very much a bird specialist, striking its prey in mid-air, the Lanner also eats reptiles and mammals, snatching them on the ground. The Peregrine requires cliffs for nesting, whereas the Lanner can also use trees, adopting the old nests of crows and other birds, or sometimes requisitioning them from the current owners. And where the Peregrine is often found in cold and lush places, the Lanner copes with bleak, dry, barren landscapes holding a low density of potential food, and is often found in rugged mountains and on the edge of deserts.

Lanners live in large home ranges all year round, occupying them in pairs. The bond between male and female is very strong and the Lanner is noted for the frequency with which pairs hunt co-operatively, particularly in the winter. One bird will flush or chivvy prey, while the other delivers the fatal strike.

The Lanner is actually a flexible hunter, using a variety of techniques. Many birds are caught after a stoop from high above. Mammals and lizards are taken as the Lanner flies low and rapidly over the ground, interrupting its forward progress for a quick plunge to earth. But the technique suits the moment: for example, a Lanner has been recorded stooping 200 m straight down to snatch a bird from off a rock, showing not only remarkable flying skills but also audacious opportunism.

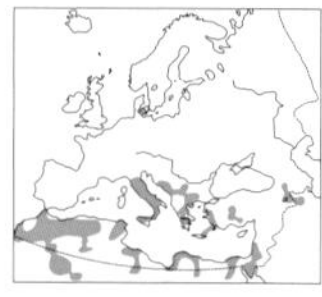

ID: Large falcon similar to Peregrine but with longer tail and less bulk at hips; may recall a large Kestrel, but flight is more powerful with shallow wingbeats. Much less bulky than Saker. Mainly white underparts, lightly spotted rather than strongly barred (Peregrine) or heavily streaked (Saker). Moustache is obvious.

adult — juv. — adult — juv.

ID: *Large stocky falcon, second largest after Gyrfalcon; wings rather broad with blunt tips. Adults strongly streaked on the underparts; whitish head contrasts with mainly dark body.*

Saker

Falco cherrug (**fal**-ko **cher**-rug)
length 45–55 cm; wingspan 1–1.3 m

With their streamlined bodies and fast flight, most falcons are bird-catchers; but not the Saker. It feeds predominantly on small mammals, one of only two European falcons to do so (the other is the Common Kestrel). Its favourite prey items are ground squirrels or susliks, which can constitute a major part of the diet, but it also catches gerbils, hamsters and some rabbits, as well as birds up to the size of sandgrouse. Such prey abounds on the steppes where this bird primarily occurs.

Most food is taken on the ground, although when a Saker does target birds, these can be snatched in mid-air. The usual view of a hunting Saker, though, is of a bird sitting for hours on a prominent perch on a rock or tree, watching for movement below. When something finally shows, the bird drops down quickly and silently, hoping to catch its prey by surprise.

In the breeding season, pairs of Sakers tend to breed either on cliff ledges or on the tops of isolated trees. Tree sites are usually 15–20 m above ground and are invariably within the abandoned nests of other birds such as Grey Herons, Ravens or other birds of prey. In recent years, showing welcome adaptability, the Saker has also taken increasingly to using artificial sites, particularly pylons.

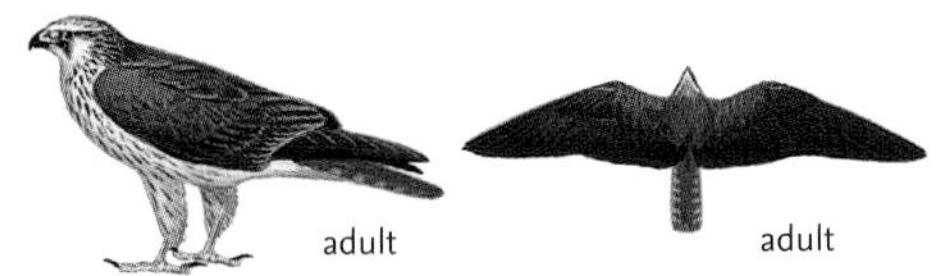

Gyrfalcon

Falco rusticolus (**fal**-ko russ-**tik**-oh-luss)
length 48–60 cm; wingspan 1.2–1.3 m

Many birds of the far north have great charisma, and the Gyrfalcon, the largest and bulkiest of the falcons, is no exception. It is scarce, very shy, an inhabitant of extreme habitats and often very distinctive to look at, especially the magnificent white morph from the High Arctic of Greenland. All this adds up to an exciting package.

The Gyrfalcon feeds mainly on medium-sized prey, especially birds. It usually catches them by flying low over the tundra or mountain top and attempting to flush them into flight; if it is successful, it then lifts into the air to give itself momentum and stoops down to strike from above. This policy is particularly successful in snaring grouse, and Ptarmigan and Willow Grouse can constitute a major part of the annual diet – after all, in winter there can be few other birds available at such high latitudes. A significant number of Gyrfalcon pairs also breed close to seabird colonies, especially those of auks, and gorge themselves on the adults. When hunting they can take some birds straight from the water surface.

A minority of Gyrfalcons feeds on voles and lemmings and these, as well as grouse, show distinct cycles of abundance: boom and bust every three to four years for the rodents and every ten years for grouse. This can make the production of young a complicated affair for the falcons, but if things look promising they will lay up to seven eggs, instead of the usual three or four. In good years, larger numbers than usual may move south from their breeding areas in the winter, often turning up in numbers in Iceland and other parts of northern Europe.

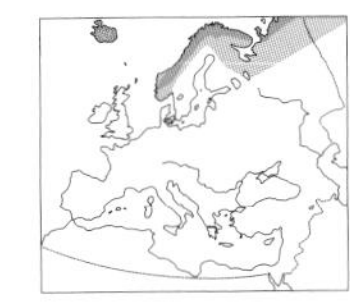

ID: *The largest falcon, almost as large as a Buzzard, but wings are not as broad. Much larger than Peregrine and even more bulky. Broader wings with a proportionally longer arm and blunter tips.*

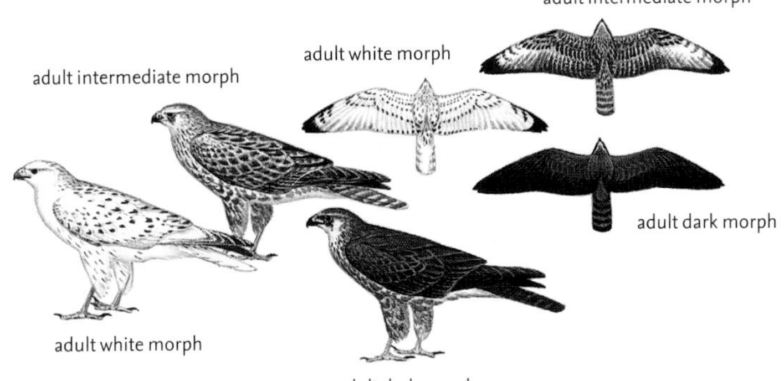

Peregrine

Falco peregrinus (**fal**-ko per-re-**grie**-nuss)
length 34–50 cm; wingspan 80–120 cm

The Peregrine is one of the world's most admired birds, revered by falconers, the general public and birdwatchers alike. It holds two impressive records. It is the world's fastest-flying animal – during its remarkable vertical plunges ('stoops') it has been reliably recorded doing a speed of 180 km/h (very much higher figures have been claimed). And it is also, arguably, the world's most widely naturally distributed land bird, occurring on every continent, in a wide variety of different habitats and in every climatic zone from the Arctic to the tropics. In this respect the Barn Owl is its main rival.

Seeing a Peregrine in the wild is never dull, not only because it is effortless and powerful through the air, but also because its appearance inevitably engenders terror. A flock of waders or gulls will one moment be at ease, with heads in wing and resting on one leg; the next minute they will be flying in all directions in a state of near-panic. Alarm calls will fill the air – and that is before the Peregrine has even mounted an attack.

Birds have reason to be cautious. For, although the Peregrine has favourite foods – pigeons, grouse and starlings, for example – it will kill almost any species, given the opportunity. In Britain, for example, it has been recorded killing birds of about 120 species, and in the northern hemisphere (mainly Europe and North America) over 300. These victims range in size from the very smallest (Goldcrest) to one of substantial proportions (Grey Heron); and they come, democratically enough, from almost every group of birds – even fellow raptors are at risk. However, to give the impression that a Peregrine sets out to log an impressive list of casualties would be wrong; many individuals concentrate on just one or a few abundant species, especially in the breeding season.

For hunting these birds require open country free of obstacles, so wetlands, moorland, tundra and the coast are all ideal. Their principal technique involves plummeting through the air and striking prey in mid-flight, disabling or killing it on impact, sometimes breaking its neck. The initial selection is made as the bird perches on a suitable lookout post, or circles high upwards. Then it positions itself above the quarry and plunges down, wings partly open, intending to take the chosen victim by surprise. However much you read about it or may anticipate it, a Peregrine stooping down at its outlandish speed and striking its target with a puff of feathers is a breathtaking sight. It is raw and shocking, yet admirable and impressive, too.

Although Peregrines are violent killers, there is little aggression about them in other ways. They are hardly territorial at all, with very few skirmishes reported; the occupancy of a home range appears to be enough to deter intruders. The young Peregrines in the nest are also non-competitive, lacking the murderous zeal of some other birds of prey.

Most individuals live in one area, with one mate, throughout their lives. All they require is a hunting and breeding area, the latter consisting usually of a cliff ledge but sometimes of a tall building. Peregrine home ranges are traditional and are passed down the generations. Some are known to have been occupied for 400 years or more.

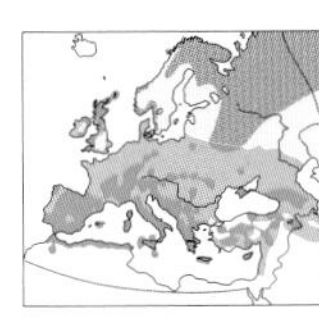

ID: A large falcon with broad-based, pointed wings, short tail and muscular body, especially about the chest; somewhat anchor-like shape in flight. Flies with stiff, shallow wingbeats. Black face mask with distinctive broad moustache. Slate-grey above, white below with dense, strong barring. Female much larger than male. Juvenile browner and streaked, not barred below.

Gamebirds families *Tetraonidae* (tet-ray-**oh**-nid-ee) and *Phasianidae* (fay-zee-**ay**-nid-ee)

Habitat Grouse mainly in northern latitudes, inhabiting open tundra, mountains and forest. The rest in temperate or Mediterranean climates, especially in open areas such as rocky mountain slopes and agricultural fields.
Food Mostly herbivorous, taking seeds, shoots, leaves and berries. Chicks usually feed on small invertebrates.
Movements Quail long-distance migrant, the rest mainly sedentary. Some hard-weather movements according to snow cover.
Voice Often loud and distinctive. Males have advertising calls and flocks may have 'rallying calls' to keep together.
Pairing style Remarkably varied, from monogamous to promiscuous. Black Grouse and Capercaillies have leks, pheasants have harems.
Nesting Solitary.
Nest Usually not much more than a scrape in the ground, lined with vegetation.
Productivity 1 brood a year, except the Quail and the *Alectoris* partridges. The latter may lay two clutches at the same time, one incubated by each sex.
Eggs 3–24, among the largest clutches of all birds, hatching synchronously.
Incubation 14–30 days, usually by female alone (sometimes by male alone).
Young Precocial and downy.
Parenting style Variable, depending on species.
Food to young In contrast to adults, mainly small invertebrates. Young are self-feeding.
Leaving nest Young leave nest within hours. They grow their wing feathers very quickly and some are capable of short flights within 7–10 days. All become independent between 3 and 12 weeks after hatching.

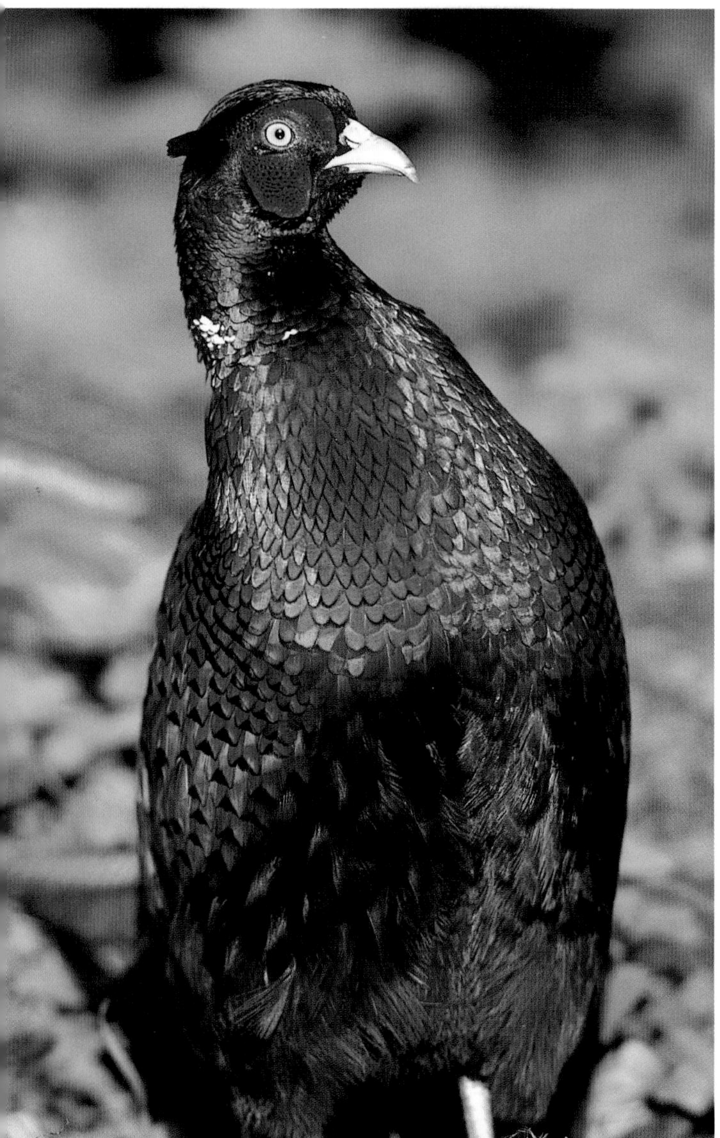

The gamebirds are economically among the most important of birds. One member, the Chicken, requires no introduction. Pheasants, partridges, Red Grouse and Quail are also all renowned for being good eating, and both pheasants and Red Grouse form the basis of whole industries involved with hunting, shooting and cookery. Being good to eat is, indeed, a group characteristic, and humans are not the only predators. Some birds of prey of northern Europe feed almost exclusively on grouse, and these are joined by carnivorous mammals such as foxes and martens.

As a rule, gamebirds are plump, short-bodied birds that live on the ground, although some, such as pheasants, may roost in trees. They have short, rounded wings designed for short bursts of rapid, powerful flight. When a gamebird is flushed it bolts away low, then alternates stiff flaps with glides as it makes its escape. It lands as soon as it can, with what looks like relief!

Gamebirds' legs and feet are strong and sturdy, fitted with three forward-pointing toes and a small hind toe, the latter raised to prevent extra friction with the ground. The birds use their feet for scratching in search of food, which is generally vegetable matter, such as seeds, berries or shoots. The bills of gamebirds are short, strong and down-curved.

The grouse are treated as a separate family from other gamebirds. In contrast to the rest they have feathers on their legs and over their nostrils, both of which are adaptations to the cold climates in which they are normally found. In addition they lack the 'spur' often found above the hind toe in other gamebirds, the function of which is unclear.

A number of gamebirds have been introduced into various parts of Europe and have self-sustaining populations in the wild. Most come from far-flung areas, but the Barbary Partridge (*Alectoris barbara*) occurs just across the Straits of Gibraltar, in Morocco. It has been introduced to Gibraltar, Spain and Sardinia, where it occurs on dry stony hillsides with scattered bushes. From North America come two species, the Northern Bobwhite (*Colinus virginianus*), a small quail-like bird living wild in Italy, and the California Quail (*Callipepla californica*), at large in France; both of these live in scrubby habitats. From Asia several pheasants have been introduced, the Golden Pheasant (*Chrysolophus pictus*) and Lady Amherst's Pheasant (*C. amherstiae*) to Britain and the Reeves's Pheasant (*Syrmaticus reevesii*) to France and the Czech Republic. All occur in large woodlands and forests.

Willow Grouse

Lagopus lagopus (la-**go**-puss la-**go**-puss)
length 35–43 cm

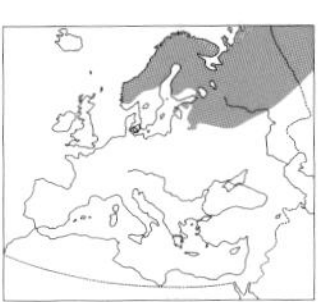

ID: In winter all white, except for black bill, eye and tail sides. From spring onwards, some warm rufous-brown colour on head, neck and back, increasing to cover all but wings and belly in late summer. Female always more delicately patterned, with scales. Red Grouse of Britain rich rufous all over throughout year.

In most families this would be considered an impressively hardy species, occurring as it does high into the Arctic in winter. But as far as grouse go it is always trumped by the more extreme Ptarmigan. The Willow Grouse prefers less exposed places, so it is often found around the edge of forests; it breeds well into the tundra, but requires the presence of bushes of willow and dwarf birch, rather than bare, rocky areas. It is also replaced above the tree line by the Ptarmigan. That said, it has similar plumage sequences to the Ptarmigan, including the all-white look for camouflage in the snow.

The diets of the two species are only slightly different, although the Willow, as its name suggests, sometimes takes willow in preference to anything else. But over its large range things may vary locally; the Scottish race, for example, the 'Red Grouse', feeds almost exclusively on heather all year round. Even the chicks begin to eat heather when they are less than three weeks old.

In early spring (or even during the autumn in Scottish birds) the males space themselves out into territories and perform advertising displays. They lift rapidly into the air with a burst of wingbeats, stall for a moment, then parachute down with more wingbeats and with tail spread. On landing they bob up and down, with wings drooped and tail fanned. This display is accompanied by a guttural call ending 'go-back, go-back, go-back…' The pair bond in Willow Grouse is relatively strong and, in contrast to most gamebirds, the male remains with the family until the chicks are fully grown.

Hazel Grouse

Bonasa bonasia (boh-**nay**-sa boh-**nay**-si-ah)
length 35–37 cm

Well camouflaged in the dappled shade of its habitat, and both quiet and shy, the Hazel Grouse is a difficult species to see. It occurs in large and relatively undisturbed forest areas, living part of its life on the ground and part up in the trees. If disturbed it takes flight more easily than other species of grouse and weaves away expertly through the trees.

Ecological studies have shown that the Hazel Grouse is mainly found in mixed woods with a rich understorey. The dominant trees may well be conifers, but they need to have three or four very important deciduous species intermixed with them: alder, birch, aspen and, of course, hazel. Several of these grow well near water, so Hazel Grouse, too, are often found near rivers and streams. Suitable habitat can be found anywhere between sea level and 2000 m.

In common with other grouse, the Hazel Grouse is mainly vegetarian and has a bland, unvarying diet in the winter. From December to March it eats the catkins and buds of the four trees named above. As spring sets in it switches to the leaves of the same trees, and will add leaves from the herb layer if snow conditions permit. In autumn the variety is very much greater, because berries become available in large numbers, and the birds feed mainly on the ground.

The male Hazel Grouse displays on the ground, beating his wings to make a loud drumming sound, sometimes adding a little jump into the air for effect. He also has a remarkably high-pitched, drawn-out whistling song, like a piccolo. Male and female form a monogamous pair bond.

ID: A small grouse of dense forest. If seen well, plumage distinctive, with many black and chestnut spots and chevrons densely packed on white breast and belly; grey back. Male has black throat, and both sexes have black tips to tail.

Ptarmigan

Lagopus mutus (**la**-go-puss **moo**-tuss)
length 33–38 cm

Only the toughest birds survive at 83°N, the northern limit of the Ptarmigan's range (in Greenland). And indeed, the Ptarmigan is like some madcap Arctic adventurer, positively drawn to snowdrifts, cold open areas with very low vegetation, rocky places buffeted by powerful and freezing winds, and high altitudes. For those that can beat the elements, there is little competition and even the predators are sparsely distributed.

One might say that the Ptarmigan wraps up well for its environment. It has thick plumage, especially in winter, and this covering extends to the legs and feet, to prevent heat loss. Even the nostrils are feathered. Moreover, the Ptarmigan's appearance closely follows the seasons. In winter, when its surroundings are white, the Ptarmigan is white, too, except for the jet-black sides of its tail, a delicate red ring over its black eye and a small ink spot behind its bill (the last-named in the male only). In spring, when the snow begins to melt and become patchy, the Ptarmigan turns brown and blotchy-white, seeking out snowdrifts in which to roost; and in autumn, when the tundra colour fades, the Ptarmigan's main colour becomes greyer. In order to retain its identity, though, the wings and lower belly remain white throughout the year.

Ptarmigans feed on the ground, and their rations can appear extraordinarily meagre. In winter, for example, they sometimes eat only twigs and buds from willows and birches, for months on end. The tedium is relieved in spring, with the emergence of shoots and other green parts of plants, and for a brief period in autumn there is a feast of berries to be had. But usually there isn't much variety or goodness. The guts of grouse generally are large and long, enabling the birds to cope with a nutritionally poor diet. Ptarmigans find most of it by scratching in the snow with their feet. In winter they grow special toenails twice their normal length to help this process along. What with feathered feet and long nails, they are virtually fitted with their own snowshoes.

In March and April the winter flocks split up and individuals form their own territories. Males advertise their patch with a curious call that sounds like running a stick over the slats of a picket fence, or like a long retching belch. The nature of the pair bond seems to vary: in some areas, birds are monogamous, in others the males are polygynous and in Iceland there is evidence that both sexes may have casual, short-term pair bonds. Whatever the nature of the relationship, it invariably splits up before the eggs hatch, and the young are tended only by the female.

ID: Slighter than Willow Grouse and with smaller bill. Male always distinguished by having black line between bill and eye (lores), even in otherwise identical white winter plumage. Male otherwise similar, but has greyer, less warm coloration than Willow Grouse, while female has yellower, lichen-coloured, more densely barred plumage than her counterpart.

Black Grouse

Tetrao tetrix (**tet**-ray-oh **tet**-rikss)
length 40–55 cm

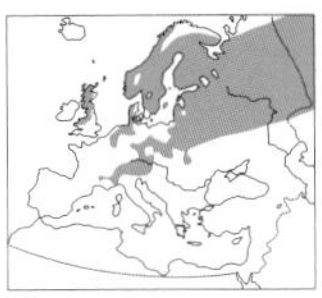

ID: Male much smaller than Capercaillie, with long forked/bent tail and white wing bar and undertail. Female similar to Capercaillie, but more plainly coloured and closely barred; underwing white.

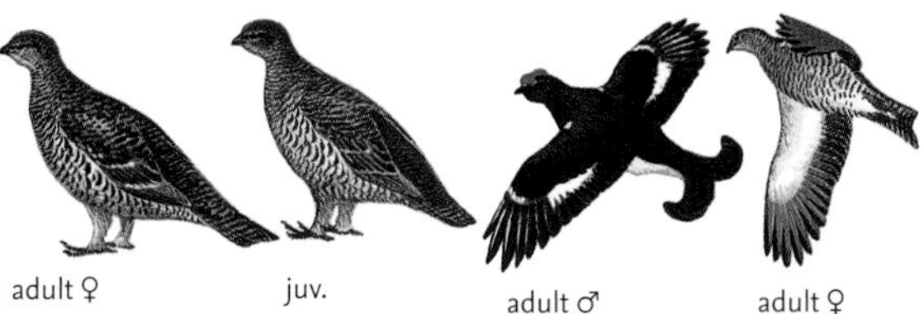

Filling in the niche between the tundra grouse (Willow Grouse, Ptarmigan) and the forest grouse (Capercaillie, Hazel Grouse), the Black Grouse is a bird of transition habitats between closed forest and open ground. A widespread species in northern Europe, it may be found on heaths, moors, bogs and forest clearings, so long as there are groups of trees nearby. Broadly speaking, it feeds on the ground in the summer months and up in the trees in winter, making use of its whole habitat.

You would be hard pressed to know that male and female Black Grouse were the same species just by looking at them; they are behaviourally and morphologically very distinct. They don't associate much, either. In winter the Black Grouse is a sociable bird (gatherings of up to a thousand have been recorded), but most flock with their own gender. Males have a shared home range and spend much time in each other's company – not all of it amicably. In fact, on many a morning in both autumn and spring, the males congregate at traditional areas known as arenas to display and fight each other. Usually selecting an open site such as a clearing, they droop their wings and lift up their tails to reveal their bright white undertail coverts. They participate in mock or real fighting and make a continuous dove-like cooing punctuated by sharp hissing sounds, like the release of volcanic gas.

On the arena the males' small territories are bunched together in close proximity, so that the arena acts as a communal display ground or 'lek'. Each male has a territory somewhere on the lek, but the choice ones are in the centre, and this is what the fighting and posturing is about. Knowing that all males aspire for the central territory, and therefore reasoning that the best male actually resides there, females ignore the attentions of marginal birds and go straight for the best genetic material. Marginal males may not copulate at all during the season.

This red-blooded system of mate selection confines copulatory activity to a brief peak of about ten days in the season. Each female may visit several leks and add variety to her brood of six to eleven eggs. She is then responsible for looking after eggs and young, while the males carry on as usual.

Capercaillie

Tetrao urogallus (**tet**-ray-oh oo-ro-**gal**-luss)
length 60–87 cm

Turkey-like in size and proportions, the Capercaillie is the largest grouse, but can still be a difficult bird to see. The females are well camouflaged for hiding on the ground, and both sexes spend much time feeding quietly high up in the trees. In addition, the Capercaillie is shy, so most encounters are of half-seen shapes careering away with a loud burst of wingbeats.

Capercaillies are almost entirely vegetarian, apart from a short period when, as chicks, they are insectivorous. In winter, when the ground is covered by snow, adults may spend up to five months in the tree canopy eating nothing but pine needles, shoots and a few cones. In summer they come down to the ground and search for a much broader diet, including the leaves and berries of ericaceous plants such as bilberry and bog whortleberry. These items are best found in rather open coniferous forest, with glades and boggy areas intermixed, although in Spain the bird can be found in deciduous forest with an understorey of holly.

In late winter male Capercaillies become territorial, defending their patch of land with a unique song that begins with tapping, accelerates to a brief drum roll and ends in a pop, like a bottle of champagne being opened; a few loud belches may be added for effect. The performers initially start singing in the tree tops, but later in the season they come down to ground once dawn has broken and strut about with wings drooped and tails fanned. Fights between rival males may lead to injury and even death. Birds intoxicated with aggression have been known to attack birdwatchers, cyclists and passing deer.

The reason for this aggression is the meritocratic 'lek' mating system (see Black Grouse). Capercaillies have much larger lek arenas than Black Grouse: they may be 1 km across, spread over an area of woodland. In common with other lek species, the sexes associate only for copulation; thereafter the female is responsible for eggs and young.

ID: Male heavy and very distinctive. Female told from Black Grouse female by rusty-brown colour on chest and tail and grey on the rump.

Red-legged Partridge

Alectoris rufa (a-**lek**-tor-riss **roo**-fa)
length 32–34 cm

The Red-legged Partridge, and possibly its close relatives in the genus *Alectoris* too, have the distinction of being among the few European birds to practise, on occasion, a double-clutch system of reproduction. The female sometimes lays two separate batches of eggs in two different nests and, while she incubates one, the male incubates the other. The hatching of each set of chicks is highly co-ordinated, and the adults and their charges often link up again once their broods are mobile. It sounds so efficient that it is perhaps surprising that more birds don't follow this system. Yet even the Red-legged Partridge doesn't always. More often than not, the female incubates one clutch alone and by the time they hatch the male may be off consorting with a different partner.

The Red-legged Partridge occurs in all sorts of open habitats, including dry mountain slopes, arable fields, open woodland and dunes, and on all types of soils. It ranges from the Mediterranean to temperate, from lowlands to 2000 m. It lives mainly on the ground, but also perches on trees, fence posts and rocks. There seems no end to its talents – it can even swim!

In common with other partridges, the Red-legged is highly sociable for most of the year. In late summer, after breeding, families often merge into 'coveys' of 20 birds or more and remain together throughout the winter. In early spring, though, the males begin to become territorial, announcing their ownership with a long-winded 'rallying call'. At its height this call sounds like the puffing of a steam engine, becoming faster and faster as the bird gets into its stride.

ID: Easily distinguished from similar Grey Partridge by white throat surrounded by black, and by lack of brown blob on chest. Told from Rock Partridge and Chukar mainly by black 'raindrops' falling from neck ring.

Chukar

Alectoris chukar (a-**lek**-tor-riss **choo**-kar)
length 32–34 cm

Rock Partridge

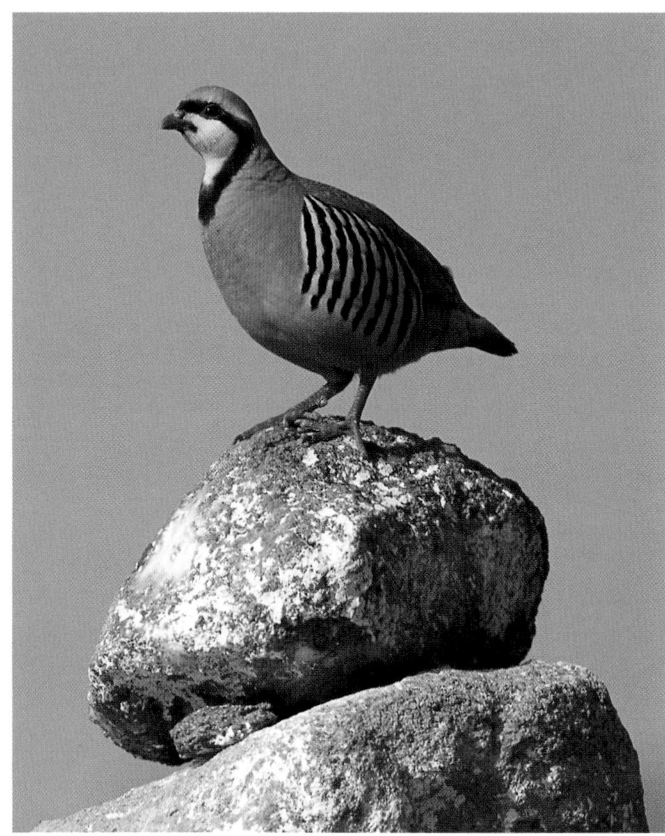

ID: Distinguished from similar Rock Partridge by its creamy throat and brown streak behind eye, and by lacking a thin white supercilium in front of the eye.

Principally a bird of Asia, the Chukar is found only in the extreme east of Europe, generally in arid habitats such as scree slopes, rocky hillsides and plains with short grass and a few scattered bushes. Such sites may be occupied at any elevation between sea level and 3000 m. The Chukar appears to have a more restricted diet than other partridges, subsisting largely on grass seeds, which it finds by digging into the soil with its bill. The bird has been recorded walking 3.5 km in a day simply to find water.

The name 'Chukar' comes from the bird's call, used to bring members of a flock back together. In spring, though, males use it as their territorial signal, and its purpose is thus to keep the birds apart.

At elevations of 900–2700 m from south-east France to Bulgaria and Greece lives the very similar **Rock Partridge** (*Alectoris graeca*). It is found mainly in regions of low humidity, and it prefers to have a mix of short turf, low scrub and a few scattered trees available.

Grey Partridge

Perdix perdix (**per**-diks **per**-diks)
length 29–31 cm

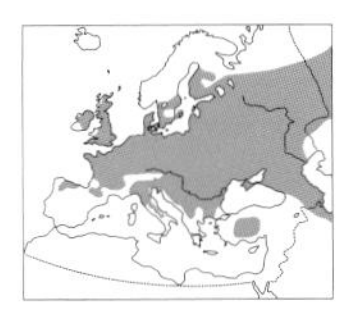

ID: Slightly smaller than Red-legged and other partridges. Orange throat without black border diagnostic. Large, heart-shaped breast spot more extensive on male than on female.

Ground-hugging in the extreme, the Grey Partridge is not very keen on flying. If it needs to move around, it goes on foot. If danger threatens, it will walk away or run, taking flight only when a predator is gaining. A pair was once observed for 15 hours continuously and in that period flew only four times, covering just 180 m.

Surprisingly, though, these birds are not particularly bad at using their wings. In the extreme east of their European range they are partial migrants, moving south for the winter and becoming nomadic for a few months. The deciding factor in migration is snow cover. If it lies for more than five months, or is more than 50 cm deep for over a month, the birds are forced to move out.

Their natural habitat is grassland, ideally just tall enough to cover the birds themselves. They also need patches of taller, thicker vegetation in which to nest, and some open earth to indulge in one of their favourite activities, dust bathing. Suitable grassland is a rare commodity in Europe nowadays, and most Grey Partridges are now found in agricultural areas.

Pair formation begins in February when flocks split up. Females stay put on their winter home range, while young males wander in search of a mate (the reverse of the arrangement in Red-legged Partridges). Courtship is initiated by the female, who approaches the male with head down and makes for his flank stripes, seeming to peer very closely at them. She then passes her bill over the male's flanks and back, without touching him, and circles him. The male, meanwhile, stands proud and erect, his neck fluffed out and his belly patch prominent.

For a nest the female makes a shallow depression under a hedge or thicket and lines it with a few bits of vegetation. She then proceeds to lay a remarkably large number of eggs, usually between 10 and 20. The average clutch size, which can reach 18 in the north of the Grey Partridge's range, is the highest for any bird in Europe, and perhaps the world. The record is 29.

When the chicks hatch, both parents attend them and move them around in search of insects, which constitute up to 90 per cent of their diet for the first two weeks of their lives. Later on the diet will change considerably, for the Grey Partridge is largely a vegetarian. In autumn and winter the birds eat the leaves of grasses, cereals and clover, mixed in with some weed seeds, of which the favourite appears to be knotgrass. The following spring they switch to the seed heads of chickweed and unripe grass seeds.

After the breeding season the whole family remains together to form a flock known as a covey, and this unit may be joined by a few unpaired birds, or perhaps another family. At night all the birds sleep in a rough circle with their heads pointing out and tails in; if flushed to flight, the covey usually remains together, whereas Red-legged Partridges in the same circumstances often fly off in different directions.

Quail

Coturnix coturnix (koh-**tur**-niks koh-**tur**-niks)
length 16–18 cm

ID: Very small, not much bigger than a Skylark; almost impossible to see unless flushed.

The Quail is the only profoundly migratory gamebird in Europe, but what a migrant it is! Its spectacular movements have been noted since Biblical times; and there is no doubt that huge numbers can arrive in an area without warning. Over the years the Quail has puzzled inhabitants of northern Europe by its wild fluctuations in numbers, odd arrival times and instances of overwintering. So if it is the only migratory representative of its family, it certainly does it in style.

Quail migrate at night, and do so in parties. They hate to go it alone, so much so that, before taking off, birds have a 'contact trill' to gather recruits together, and then a 'take-off whistle' to set the quorum off on their travels. They keep calling in flight and, just before dawn, they will often be stimulated to land by the sound of settled birds calling below.

But the Quail's most unusual migratory quirk has only recently been discovered. It appears that some birds arrive in North Africa early in the spring, breed, migrate north again and then breed a second time, which is almost unique among European birds. Even more remarkably, the offspring from the first broods can join the northward movement and breed themselves later the same summer, although they may have hatched only two months previously. Hence Quails may arrive through the breeding season in 'waves'. Such a system of relay reproduction is seen in several butterfly species as they move north from Africa each summer, but not in other European birds.

Young Quail can flutter when only 11 days old and fly at 19 days, and they reach sexual maturity at 12–15 weeks. Having such a quick turnover allows Quails to maximise their productivity when conditions are good.

The Quail breeds in open areas of grassland or cultivation, with vegetation that is tall enough to hide in, but not too tall. It feeds on the ground using its bill rather than its feet, and it eats the seeds of various weeds, as well as plenty of insects and other invertebrates – more than is usual for a gamebird.

Much of the breeding behaviour of Quails has also only recently been worked out. It appears that mature males and females cluster in specific shared 'mating centres' which act as communal breeding sites 4–12 hectares in extent. Birds are attracted to the centres by the male's highly distinctive 'wet-me-lips' call, which is usually given at twilight or during the night, when birds are migrating overhead. Within this common ground the males hold no territory, but meet up with the females and form a monogamous pair bond.

Common Pheasant

Phasianus colchicus (fay-zee-**ay**-nuss **kol**-chik-uss)
length male 70–90 cm (of which c.35–45 cm is tail); female 55–70 cm (tail 20–25 cm)

ID: Male unmistakable. Female smaller than male and without the gaudy plumage, but the long tail is usually sufficient to distinguish her.

Pheasants are such familiar birds that it is hard to appreciate that, as far as most of Europe is concerned, they are not native here at all, but were actually introduced by people. Those introductions were, admittedly, a long time ago – Roman times in Italy, for example – but many populations are still sustained chiefly by shooting interests, and it would be interesting to see how many birds would survive in the long term without being looked after, especially in the west. Some birds in the Black Sea region may well be native, and a small population along a valley in Greece has good credentials, too, but essentially the Common Pheasant's true centre of population is in eastern Asia.

Generally unappreciated by birdwatchers, the Pheasant is actually a spectacular species, especially the male, with his waxy red face, gaudy plumage and long, ladder-marked tail. They are usually seen striding along the edges of fields, but Pheasants also require wooded areas in their territories or home ranges if they are to thrive. They normally roost in trees and bushes, and the females spend much of their time in the undergrowth. The nest, too, is placed on the ground under bushes and shrubs.

Males and females often spend the winter in flocks of a single sex, which may be segregated by slight differences in habitat preference. Males occur in smaller flocks of up to ten in rather open areas, whereas the females collect in groups of as many as 30 in places with plenty of cover. Each flock has its own home range, with informal boundaries.

By February, however, males begin to walk around and look for territories. At first they merely scout, but in March and April they punctuate their rambles with bouts of proclamatory crowing. This is the familiar loud coughing sound so often heard from birds flying away, but made from a prominent perch on the ground to the accompaniment of wing flaps. Territorial flag-waves such as these may be challenged, and rival males may break into a fight at times; their combat is often prolonged and fierce-looking, but rarely fatal.

After these initial skirmishes, borders are firmly established.

Females select a mate by wandering into a male's territory and assessing his efforts at courtship. The male has a so-called lateral display, in which he weaves in semicircles around the female, drooping the wing nearer her, allowing it to touch the ground, like a courtier putting his cloak down for a lady. If all goes well, copulation soon follows.

Many male Pheasants acquire only one mate and may be attentive to the chicks when they hatch. But perhaps more often, males are polygynous, with several females paired to them exclusively in a harem, laying their clutches within a single territory. Few males acquire more than two or three females in all, but as many as 18 have been known in the wild. The males with multiple mates tend not to have anything to do with nests, eggs or chicks.

The clutch size is large, between 7 and 15 and, as in all members of the family, the female incubates her eggs assiduously. She relies on being still and camouflaged for her own protection and that of the brood, and on occasion female Pheasants have been known to sit tight until actually touched on the nest. After three of four weeks the eggs hatch and within 12–14 days the young are capable of flight. They feed on insects at first, but then graduate to grain, nuts and berries.

Rails and Crakes family *Rallidae* (ral-lid-ee)

Habitat Typically marshland birds, hiding away in dense vegetation. Corncrake only in dry meadows. Coot and Moorhen on open water.
Food Omnivorous, taking various plant fragments, including seeds and algae, and usually small animals such as insects and their larvae, worms and water snails. Water Rail sometimes kills vertebrates such as frogs.
Movements Water Rail, Moorhen and Coot may be sedentary or migratory, according to population; Coot performs moult migrations. Purple Gallinule sedentary. The rest are summer visitors, mostly wintering in tropical Africa.
Voice Living in thick vegetation, most have loud, distinctive songs and calls (see individual entries) and complex vocabularies.
Pairing style Most monogamous, but Corncrake often polygynous; Moorhen's mating system complicated.
Nesting Solitary, although Little Crakes and Moorhens may nest close together. Rare Purple Gallinule may form loose colonies.
Nest A cup of available plant material, on the ground in thick vegetation, or just above water level in marshes. Surrounding stems often pulled over to form canopy.
Productivity Most double-brooded, but Moorhen and Coot may rear 3 broods.
Eggs 2–12, usually hatching over several days.
Incubation 15–24 days. By both parents or, in Corncrake, by female alone. Often begins well before clutch is complete, leading to range of ages in brood.
Young Semi-precocial and downy.
Parenting style Both sexes feed the young.
Food to young As adults' diet, given bill-to-bill at first. Young are soon self-feeding.
Leaving nest Young rails can leave the nest within a few days, but often return to roost or rest (or visit specially constructed nest-like platforms). They fledge at 35–50 days.

The rails and crakes are a family of small to medium-sized birds of dense herbage and marshland. Apart from the well-known Moorhen and Coot, they are extremely secretive and hard to spot, although they tend to make up for this by having loud, far-carrying calls and songs, often the only clue to their presence. The bodies of most species are laterally flattened so that they can walk and run through 'forests' of reeds and other vegetation with great ease – where neither person nor predator can easily follow.

Rails and crakes have short, rounded wings and appear reluctant to fly – when disturbed they usually run for cover. Despite this, several are long-distance migrants, travelling at night, usually not very far above ground.

The legs are feet are relatively long, as is to be expected for birds that spend much time walking and running. The toes, too, are extended to help the birds stand on unsteady or unpredictable surfaces such as floating vegetation or mud. The Coot, which is primarily a swimming and diving bird, also has special lateral lobes.

Spotted Crake

Water Rail

Rallus aquaticus (**ral**-luss ak-**kwa**-tik-uss)
length 23–28 cm

A long red bill characterises this widespread species, distinguishing it from all our other rails. It's a useful tool, one that gives the Water Rail a chance to probe a little beneath the surface of water or mud, and also stab at more mobile prey. This is much the most predatory of our rails, taking not just a wide variety of small animals such as worms, shrimps, insects and molluscs, but also larger creatures, including frogs, small mammals, fish and even birds. These are despatched by fierce stabs behind the head, which paralyse them before they are eaten. The Water Rail also feeds on dead animals, and takes a significant amount of plant material, including berries. Among other feeding methods it has the curious habit of leaping up to 1 m above ground to grab insects from surrounding vegetation.

Of all our truly secretive rails, the Water Rail occupies the broadest range of habitats and is the least migratory. Almost any marshy ground with suitably dense vegetation will suffice, so long as there is some standing or slow-flowing water and open mud. Suitable sites may simply be narrow strips within a completely different habitat, and they are often used all year round. Being highly territorial in summer and winter, the Water Rail gets to know its patch well, sometimes wearing its own system of tiny tunnels through the stems of vegetation, a maze leading to favoured feeding sites.

Water Rails have loud voices and a rich vocabulary. The best known sound is the male's advertising call, which sounds like the grunting and squealing of a pig. When Water Rails meet they have an engaging courtship display, in which the male nods his head down, lifts his tail up and raises his wings to show the black and white pattern underneath.

juv.

adult

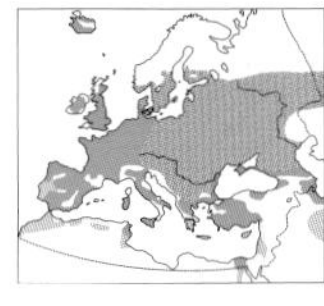

ID: Smaller and slimmer than the abundant Moorhen and usually much less ready to show itself. Easily distinguished from others in the family by its long red bill.

Spotted Crake

Porzana porzana (por-**zan**-na por-**zan**-na)
length 22–24 cm

The Spotted Crake returns invisibly to its breeding grounds in Europe between March and May each year, migrating at night and disappearing by dawn into damp vegetation. But it soon betrays its presence by the male's loud, distinctive song. Resembling a whiplash, the 'whit, whit' notes are repeated at about one-second intervals, often for minutes on end. They are heard from dusk, at intervals throughout the night, and at dawn.

One of several small rails with short bills found in Europe, this one occupies subtly different habitats to the others. In general it avoids reedbeds, occurring instead in thickets of sedge, rush, iris and tall grasses. It benefits most when conditions lead to a variety of water levels being found in a small area, allowing it forage on dry mud, wet mud and water up to 7 cm deep without moving far.

In general this species takes only small food items, but these cover a wide spectrum, including worms, snails, insect larvae, small fish, algae, shoots and seeds – the Spotted Crake has the distinction of being able to run the heads of grasses through its bill to get at the seeds, which other crakes appear not to do.

Males and females form a monogamous pair bond lasting only for a season, although two broods may result. The birds leave their breeding areas in July and August and most winter in sub-Saharan Africa.

adult ♂ adult ♀ juv.

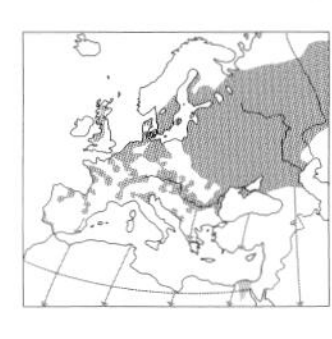

ID: Distinguished from other small, short-billed crakes by prominent white spots and streaks all over the underparts. Undertail buff, unstreaked. Also has a thicker bill than the rest.

Baillon's Crake

Porzana pusilla (por-**zan**-na poo-**sil**-la)
length 17–19 cm

Most rails are highly secretive, but they at least make loud, distinctive sounds to announce their presence. The Baillon's Crake is different. Its advertising call, a rasping rattle, simply melts into the noisy background of a marsh at night. The sound is quite loud, but easily dismissed as a frog or insect. Furthermore, no comparable call is recorded from the female . So perhaps it's no wonder that this is our least known, most elusive member of the rail family.

The Baillon's Crake also differs from the other small crakes in the nature of its habitat. It is drawn to quite low, often clumpy or tussocky marsh vegetation rather than tall stands. Favoured plants have thin stems, not thick like those of reeds, and light foliage. The surrounding water must not be especially deep, even though these tiny birds (which are smaller than Little Crakes, despite the name) can easily feed on floating vegetation or when swimming.

Although it has a characteristically weak flight, making it look 'like a fluttering ball', the Baillon's Crake is basically a migrant to Europe. Where it winters is still patchily known because of its secretive nature, but it is likely to be mainly in sub-Saharan Africa.

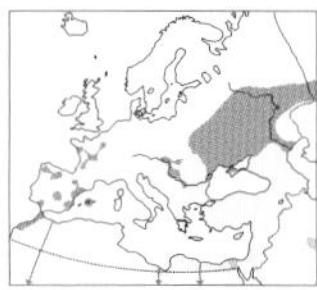

ID: Minute crake of wet areas; sexes similar. Short wings give truncated, ball-like shape. Extensively spotted white on back, unlike male Little Crake, and strongly barred black and white on flanks. Bill entirely green.

adult juv.

Little Crake

Porzana parva (por-**zan**-na **par**-va)
length 18–20 cm

This small rail has the distinction of having separate male and female plumages, one of the few members of its worldwide family to do so. The reason for this quirk is not yet known. The two sexes also have different voices (in common with most other rails) – the male a loud 'quack' which repeats for several minutes before ending in a flourish, and the female a short trill preceded by shriller version of the male's call.

The Little Crake's niche, distinct from that of other similar species in Europe, is in tall stands of dense vegetation growing in quite deep water. This can include reedbeds or growths of bulrush and various types of sedge. Suitable habitat sometimes occurs in flooded woodland. The Little Crake can climb stems and use bent or broken sections of plants as walkways to get around, and also regularly wanders over floating vegetation, but it freely enters the water, too. It can feed while swimming and apparently also dives, so it is much more aquatic than the Spotted or the Baillon's Crake. Its main foods are insects and their larvae, but it does take a variety of animal and plant food as well.

Little Crakes are territorial, but because of their size they can obtain their food within a relatively small area. In optimal habitat, nests may be only 30–35 m apart from each other. Both sexes build a shallow cup of nearby vegetation, often placing it in a tussock above the water surface.

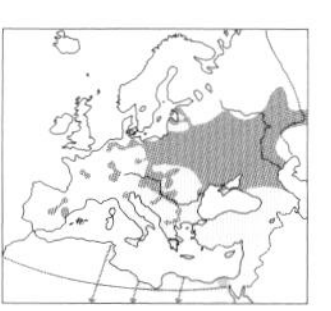

ID: Slightly larger and longer-winged than Baillon's Crake, and more of a reedbed bird. Female distinctive, with unmarked buff-coloured belly and warm brown, black-speckled upperparts. Male lacks Baillon's Crake's barring, but shares zebra-striped undertail.

adult ♂ adult ♀ juv.

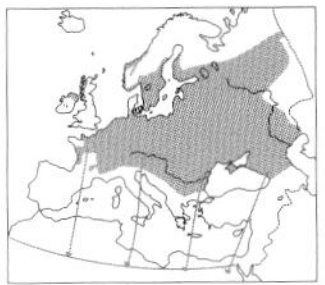

ID: A furtive rail of meadows and fields. Shows ashy-grey on head and throat, and chestnut wings when flushed.

Corncrake

Crex crex **(kreks kreks)**
length 27–30 cm

You won't meet a Corncrake in the same kind of habitat as the other rails. This is a dry-land species that avoids standing water and excessively wet vegetation. It prefers meadows, grasslands, the dry edges of wetlands, arable fields and ditches. Ideally the herbage should be no more than 50 cm tall, a little bit damp and thick enough to hide a medium-sized rail.

The Corncrake is a summer visitor to Europe, arriving in the second half of April and departing for Africa in September after breeding. It was once common and widespread in Europe, but has suffered a disastrous decline as a result of changing farming methods, especially the cutting and mowing of fields during the breeding season, and the general intensification of agriculture. It is one of the few European birds currently in genuine danger of global extinction.

In common with other rails, the Corncrake has a very distinctive voice. The scientific name *Crex crex* is a rendition of it; another way to appreciate is to imagine running a comb over the side of a matchbox twice in quick succession. This advertising call is mainly used at night, although it will also be stimulated by rainfall.

Recent research on the Corncrake has revealed an interesting side to its breeding behaviour – it is often polygynous, the males having two or more mates. It seems that each male starts the season with just one mate, but as the season progresses he will attract others by his continued advertising calls, and move his territorial borders a little to accommodate them.

Purple Gallinule

Porphyrio porphyrio (por-**fir**-ri-o por-**fir**-ri-o)
length 45–50 cm

About the size of a large chicken, the Purple Gallinule is the sort of bird that might have been dreamed up by a Hollywood movie producer, with its bright colours, dinosaur-like bill and ludicrously long legs. It has a habit of suddenly appearing from out of the rich waterside vegetation and then it surprises observers by climbing expertly up a reed stem, like a Bittern. In contrast to other rails it often uses its feet to hold food up to its bill while feeding, and also to pull vegetation toward it. The bill itself is a powerful tool for biting through and stripping tubers and other tough material.

This is a rare bird found in rich wetlands in Spain, Portugal and Sardinia. The total European population is about 4000 pairs.

ID: *Unmistakable. Very large; huge bill, long legs, violet coloration.*

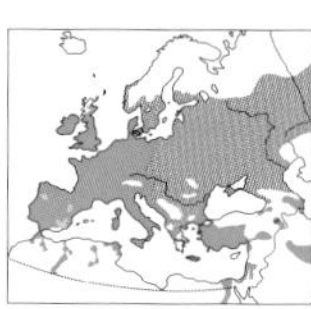

ID: *Common and distinctive rail with red frontal shield with waxy yellow tip. Legs greenish-yellow. Has broken white line separating wings from belly, and prominent white sides to undertail. Juvenile and first-winter birds have black bills. Swims but rarely dives, and is much more furtive than Coot.*

Moorhen

Gallinula chloropus (gal-lin-**noo**-la klo-**roh**-puss)
length 32–35 cm

The Moorhen is a very amphibious bird, trotting over grass, mud and piles of waterside vegetation with ease and ascending expertly into the branches of trees – yet also regularly swimming out in the open water. Admittedly it makes heavy weather of its swimming, nodding its head exaggeratedly with each stroke of its feet, like a cyclist labouring uphill. But there is no doubt that it is an adaptable and able species. It occurs throughout Europe in all types of well-vegetated habitats with open fresh water. It has also conquered the Americas, Africa and much of Asia.

The range of food taken is very broad. Plant material includes pondweeds and duckweed, as well as the leaves of a great many waterside plants. Animals include the usual worms and insects, plus occasional birds' eggs. The Moorhen rarely dives, but picks from the surface of the water while swimming, and gleans vegetation, often climbing high into bushes and even trees in order to do so.

The Moorhen has a very flexible mating and nesting system. Many a pair produces eggs and young by themselves and without incident, but co-operative breeding is quite common. It has long been known that young birds from early broods will assist their parents with offspring later in the year, helping to incubate eggs, brood, refurbish the nest and feed the young, for example. But recently it has been discovered that family ties can be stronger still. Two or more females can use the same nest, each contributing her own eggs and sharing parental duties, and it has emerged that these are often blood relatives, mother and daughter, sharing the same male, which may be the younger bird's father! On other occasions unrelated birds will also co-operate with a nesting attempt, making for a rather complicated social structure in the breeding season.

Another common practice among Moorhens is known grandly as intraspecific brood parasitism – that is, the laying of eggs in the nest of another individual of the same species. This is not co-operative, but the clandestine version of sharing a nest. Effectively the eggs are planted without permission and the burden of parenthood shifted onto unsuspecting birds.

It is easy to find a Moorhen nest. It is quite a bulky structure, an open platform of vegetation built into waterside vegetation or placed on the ground near the water's edge. Usually the male brings the materials and the female builds, and each pair may build several platforms, one for the eggs and others for the care of the chicks.

Coot

Fulica atra (**foo**-lik-ka **at**-ra)
length 36–38 cm

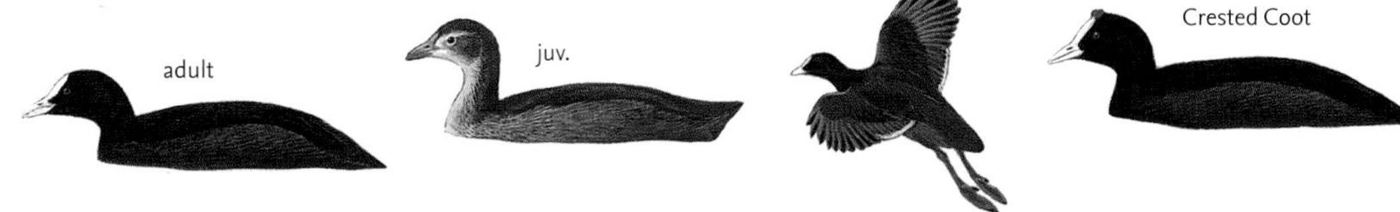

With its habit of swimming around on the surface of open water and diving down to get its food, it is easy to assume that the Coot is some sort of duck. But a quick look at its legs and feet soon dispels such a notion: rather than being webbed like those of the duck, the toes are individually lobed and the Coot's legs are long, enabling it to run along the ground like a sprinter. This is no duck. But then it is no ordinary rail, either.

Most rails are shy and retiring, but the Coot is easy to see. It is numerous, tame, noisy and astonishingly irritable. Wherever it goes, the air is filled with its short-tempered 'kut' calls (giving it its name), and other clucks and discordant trumpets. Many quarrels are accompanied by splashes. An important threat display is an aggressive charge across the water – the 'splattering attack' – and adult Coots also lean back in the water and strike each other with their long legs, as if they were kicking hard in the backstroke.

An important icon of Coot society is the frontal shield. This prominent feature, set off by the coal-black plumage, is larger in the male than in the female, and larger in some individuals than in others. It offers something of a challenge to other birds, especially when the head is lowered towards a rival.

The aggression of the Coot sometimes goes beyond adult rivalry into something more sinister. Coots are normally attentive parents, dividing the labour evenly between them: for the first few days the female broods while the male brings food; later the brood may be 'split' between the two parents, with each adult feeding only its selected half. But occasionally, and incongruously, a parent can be seen to attack a chick, grabbing its head and shaking it, sometimes fatally. The very opposite of parental care, this extreme behaviour may be related to food supply, ensuring that there are not too many chicks taking meagre resources.

Watching Coots in the breeding season, one might facetiously suppose that the youngsters bring about murderous passions in their parents by their incessant cheeping pleas for food. The chicks look remarkably unlike the adults: they are fluffy, with minute, stunted wings, heads stained with red or yellow, and red bills. The period of parental care is much longer than in most rail species, with the young feeding themselves only after about 30 days.

This bird is mainly vegetarian and has diverse feeding methods. It will graze on land, swim with its head and neck immersed (often scraping algae from the rocks and vegetation), pick from shallow water and, of course, dive – although its diving is rather limited, as it is somewhat buoyant. Its submersions are brief (20 seconds maximum), it doesn't go very deep and it does not swallow its food underwater. As a result, it is a favourite victim of bullying ducks such as Gadwalls, which requisition the Coot's hard-won pickings as soon as it reaches the surface. At times, though, Coots may use their aggression to turn the tables on their persecutors or take it out on members of their own species that have found food nearby.

In southern Spain there occurs the very rare **Crested Coot** (*Fulica cristata*). It is primarily an African species and there are no more than 25 pairs in our region, concentrated in a few highly productive wetlands. Much of its behaviour is very similar to that of the Common Coot, but it is said to be shyer.

ID: Distinctive (but see Crested Coot) swimming rail of open water, with black plumage and white frontal shield with pinkish hue (bluish in Crested). Wings have thin trailing edge of white (absent in Crested). Often seen swimming with ducks, and dives for food. Juvenile is smoky-grey with whitish throat and belly.

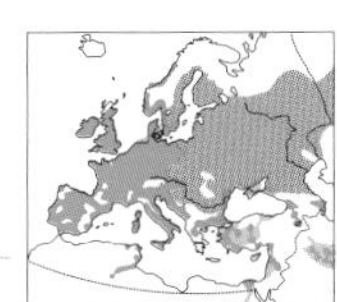

Crane *Grus grus* (grooss grooss) family *Gruidae* (groo-id-ee)

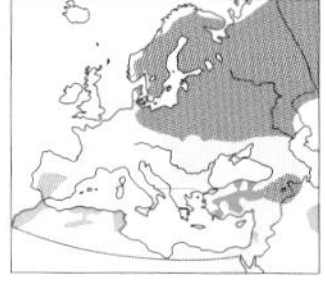

length 1.1–1.2 m; wingspan 2.2–2.45 m
ID: Unmistakable on the ground. See main text for differences from other long-legged wading birds.

Habitat Breeds in shallow wetlands, including swamps in forest clearings, bogs and artificial waters. Winters on farmland, roosting by wetlands.
Food Omnivorous, but mainly plant material, including grass shoots, roots, seeds, fruits such as acorns and olives. Animal material (mostly invertebrates) especially in summer.
Movements Migratory, with well-defined staging and wintering areas.
Voice Complex. Includes a remarkably loud clanging call that carries for many kilometres.
Pairing style Monogamous.
Nesting Territorial and solitary.
Nest A large heap of vegetation about 80 cm wide with a shallow cup on top. Placed on the ground, usually on a slight rise.
Productivity 1 brood a year.
Eggs Usually 2.
Incubation 28–31 days, usually 30. By both sexes, but the bulk by the female with male guarding nearby. Hatch 2 days apart.
Young Precocial and downy.
Parenting style Both parents tend the chicks.
Food to young As adults' diet, but smaller items at first. Adults bring food and deliver it to the ground or towards bill of youngster.
Leaving nest Fledge at 65–70 days, but wander around with parents after only a few days. Family remains together throughout the next winter. Mature at 4–6 years.

At first sight the Crane seems to resemble any one of several kinds of tall, long-legged birds. It is, however, somewhat taller than the rest and has a very distinctive bushy 'tail' (actually the tertial flight feathers) that is very much its own. In contrast to a heron or egret its flies with its neck outstretched, giving a majestic profile, and it flaps its long, broad wings with slow, powerful wingbeats. It can be told from a stork by its much smaller head and bill. These differences are superficial and there are many other technical, anatomical ones, too, which ally the Crane to the very different-looking rails and crakes.

Another difference between Cranes and the rest, though, is particularly striking: the Crane's remarkably loud, trumpeting voice. The other wading birds are very quiet, but Cranes are always calling, and their clarion-like sounds carry for many kilometres. The strength of sound is achieved by a quirk of anatomy. The trachea coils all around the sternum and its rings fuse with this bone to create a series of plates that vibrate and amplify the sound. The loudest calls are made by the pair in duet: these 'unison calls' are almost deafening.

Cranes don't communicate with their voice alone; they also carry out a series of ground displays that are so elegant and varied that they are often described as 'dancing'. There are many versions, but birds will often run along the ground in circles or figures of eight, beating their wings without necessarily lifting off. They may also leap into the air and kick their legs or head forwards, or spontaneously bow or bob their heads, or throw plant material exuberantly into the air. The precise function is not always clear, since dancing may break out among birds in winter flocks, as well as between pairs. But whatever its function it is highly infectious and will spread quickly from one end of a feeding flock to the other.

Cranes are highly migratory, moving on a narrow front between their specific breeding, resting and wintering areas, and they are rarely seen outside their usual routes. They breed in many northern European countries and winter mostly in France, Spain and Africa.

Bustards family *Otididae* (ot-**tid**-id-ee)

Habitat Open plains with short grass, often in undulating or rolling country. Also agricultural fields, but very vulnerable to disturbance.
Food Both animal and plant material picked up during slow walk. Animals mainly invertebrates, but Great Bustard takes occasional small vertebrates.
Movements Sedentary except for some French Little Bustards that are summer visitors to north of country.
Voice Heard only during display; both make snorting or flatulent sounds, and Little Bustards make a swishing sound with their wings.
Pairing style No formal pair bond; males are promiscuous, and probably females too.
Nesting Intermediate between territorial and colonial. In Little Bustard, up to 3 nests in single territory; Great Bustard nests are usually close to display ground, but not always.
Nest A shallow scrape on the ground, with minimal or no lining.
Productivity 1 brood a year.
Eggs 2–3 (Great), 2–6 (Little).
Incubation 21–28 days (Great), 20–22 days (Little), by female only. Females desert nest if alarmed.
Young Downy and able to walk and feed within hours of hatching.
Parenting style Only female tends chicks.
Food to young Self-feeding, with high proportion of small invertebrates.
Leaving nest Leave nest as soon as they can, and fledge after 25–35 days. Little Bustards are fully grown at 50–55 days, Great Bustards at 80–120 days, but young of both species may remain with female into their first autumn of life.

The bustards are ground-dwelling birds that spend much of their time standing still, or walking around at a leisurely pace. They have heavy bodies, long necks and long, strong legs, and a feature of the family is that they lack a hind toe and are thus incapable of perching. They can fly, but the Great Bustard has the distinction of being the heaviest flying bird in Europe, so it rarely goes far. Bustards are grassland birds, with highly cryptic camouflage to match their surroundings. They are nervous and difficult to approach, and suffer greatly from disturbance.

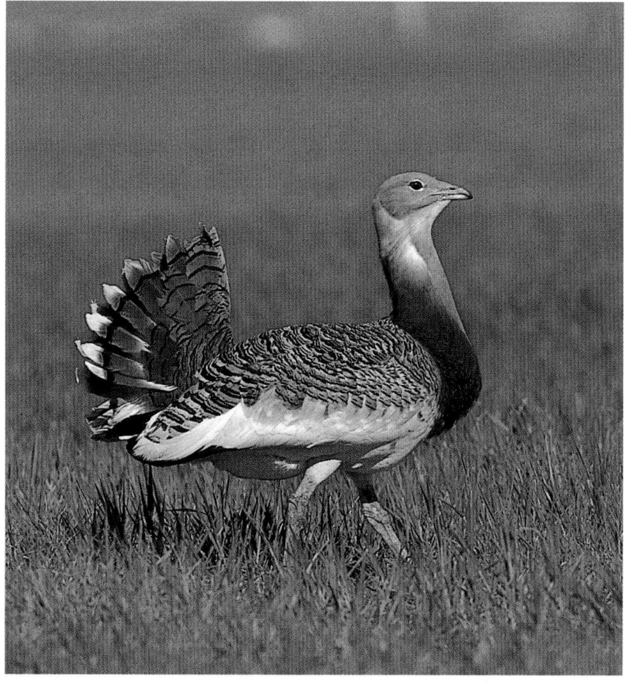

Great Bustard

Otis tarda (**oh**-tiss **tar**-da)
length 75–105 cm

On a few favoured plains and fields in undisturbed parts of Europe, male Great Bustards stand in scattered groups and perform one of the most eye-catching displays of any bird. With a few contortions of wing and tail, they transform themselves into a seething mass of white feathers, recalling, as has been irresistibly suggested, a foam bath. With no vocal accompaniment and just the odd stamp of the feet, dominant males show off in this way to females. These performances are part of a 'dispersed lek': a communal show, attracting many visiting females in search of the best mates. Normally on a lek the female makes a beeline for the central territory and mates with the incumbent, but at the Great Bustard's dispersed lek the males wander around, so the females must assess them on their performance alone.

ID: Unmistakable huge ground bird; flies magnificently, with majestic slow, powerful wingbeats.

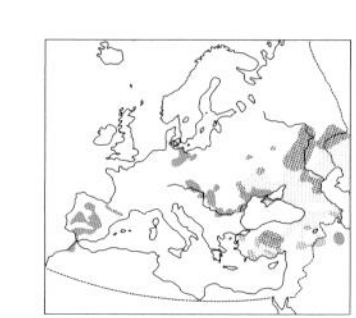

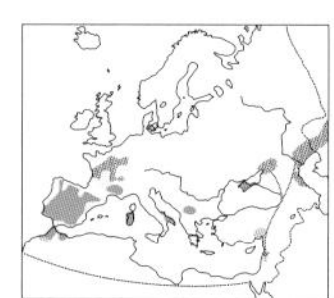

ID: Shape is distinctive, rather like a gamebird with long legs. Male unmistakable. Flies with fast wingbeats, similar to style of Mallard.

Little Bustard

Tetrax tetrax (**tet**-rax **tet**-rax)
length 43 cm; male heavier than female

It may not match the Great Bustard in appearance, but the Little Bustard is no slouch when it comes to displays. It has at least four of them, one only vocal – a short flatulent snort. In the half-light of early dawn a ritual foot-stamping is heard, as the feet beat alternately on the ground up to five times each. Another signal is a wing flash, a showing-off of the white on the wing as it is beaten quickly; this is accompanied by a swishing sound from the flight feathers. And finally and most stylishly, a male may combine the displays: he foot-stamps and then leaps up to 1.5 m into the air, flashing his wings as he does so, and snorting. Such a performance may well stir up a passing female's juices, and copulation may take place without any further displays.

Oystercatcher *Haematopus ostralegus* (hee-ma-**toh**-puss os-tra-**lee**-guss)

family *Haematopodidae* (hee-ma-toh-**pod**-id-ee)

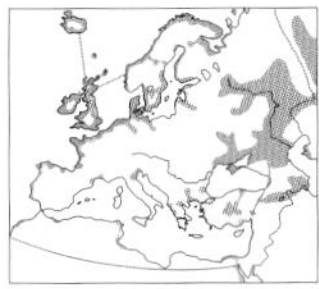

length 40–48 cm
ID: Unmistakable.

Habitat Coastal marshes and seashores. Less often by lakes and rivers and nearby agricultural land.
Food In seashore habitats, mostly bivalve molluscs, plus some polychaete worms and crustaceans. Inland, earthworms predominate, with some insect larvae.
Movements Most populations are migratory, usually moving a relatively short distance, although some make it to West Africa.
Voice Many different calls, but usually loud and piping. Main call is 'ke-BEEK'. When several birds meet for piping display, the noise is one of the loudest made by a European bird.
Pairing style Monogamous, with occasional bigamy by the male. Pair bond is very long-lasting – remarkably, 20 years has been recorded.

Nesting Solitary and territorial.
Nest A scrape in open ground or short vegetation, 20 cm in diameter and 5–7 cm deep. Built by both sexes.
Productivity 1 brood a year.
Eggs Usually 3 (range 1–5).
Incubation 24–27 days, by both sexes.
Young Downy and precocial, but fed by adults.
Parenting style Both sexes tend and feed the young.
Food to young As adult food. Uniquely, Oystercatchers feed their young until after fledging, even though the chicks are fully precocial (see text).
Leaving nest Young leave nest at 1–2 days, but fledge only at 28–32 days.

The Oystercatcher is considered to be different enough from the other waders to be placed in its own special family. The main reason for this is its unusual and eye-catching bill, which is straight, blade-like and unmistakably bright orange.

This tool is specially adapted for dealing with shellfish. It is so laterally thin that it can be poked between the half-open shells of bivalves, and some Oystercatchers have a special hunting method that makes maximum use of this feature. It is called stabbing, and consists of creeping up on grazing molluscs and snipping their adductor muscle before the latter can squeeze the two valves shut. Rendered gaping and helpless, the shellfish can then easily be consumed.

There are actually two parts to an Oystercatcher's bill, an inner bony core and a strong outer protective sheath called the rhamphotheca. The latter is strongest near the bill tip, and is so tough that it has allowed an alternative method of processing shellfish to develop. Called hammering, it is the manual-labour equivalent to the skilled task of stabbing; the bird extracts the shellfish from the sand or from its place on the mussel bed and simply hammers it open until, once again, the adductor muscle can be reached and severed. In an Oystercatcher population individuals become specialists of one art or another; usually as youngsters they pick up their principal technique by watching their parents in action. Birds that normally feed on mud tend to be stabbers and have a pointed bill to match; hammerers have chisel-shaped bills.

These arts are so specialised that they must be learned, an apprenticeship that takes some time; young Oystercatchers cannot feed themselves until well after fledging. Yet being wader chicks, they hatch fluffy and mobile and leave the nest almost immediately. This is a unique state of affairs among birds: chicks that are raring to go, but are incapable of obtaining food. It puts quite a strain on adult and chick alike, and as a result the Oystercatcher's nesting success is usually extremely low.

Nevertheless, it is a common and familiar bird in Europe, found on coasts throughout the north and northwest of our region and also far inland in the steppe country of the east. It is hard to overlook anywhere, being both highly conspicuous and extremely noisy. The piping display, for defence of territory, consists of birds lining up alongside one another and pointing their bills down, as if shouting at the mud. It is so loud that it easily drowns out a human voice.

Avocets and Stilts family *Recurvirostridae* (ree-kur-vi-**ross**-trid-ee)

Habitat Shallow wetlands, both of fresh and, especially for Avocet, saline water.
Food Invertebrates obtained from water or mud, by sight or touch.
Movements Black-winged Stilt principally a summer visitor to Europe, wintering in Africa north of Sahara. Avocet migrant in very north of its range and resident but dispersive in south, neither population travelling very far.
Voice Black-winged Stilt has loud, whining 'kek-kek' call, resembling a tern; Avocet gives slightly breathy, fluty 'kluut'.
Pairing style Monogamous, with pair bond lasting for 1 season.
Nesting Usually colonial, but sometimes solitary. Colonies of Avocet 20–70 pairs, Black-winged Stilt 10–40.
Nest Black-winged Stilt nest varies from shallow scrape to cup of vegetation, often among vegetation. Avocet nest a shallow scrape on bare ground.
Productivity 1 brood a year.
Eggs 3–4.
Incubation 22–25 days, by both sexes.
Young Downy and precocial. Fed by adults at first.
Parenting style Both sexes feed and tend the young.
Food to young As adults' food.
Leaving nest Young fledge at 35–42 days (Avocet) or 28–32 days (Black-winged Stilt).

The Avocet and the Black-winged Stilt are large, slim waders with unusually long, spindly legs that enable them to venture into deeper water than most of their wading competitors. Both have long, thin bills – of greatly different shapes – and hence both are able to forage at every level from the water surface down to the muddy bottom. When bottom-feeding they readily immerse their head and neck. Both walk with long strides, fly with rapid, powerful wingbeats and are similarly clad in bold black and white.

Black-winged Stilt

Himantopus himantopus

(him-**man**-toh-puss him-**man**-toh-puss

length 35–40 cm

The bright pink legs of the Black-winged Stilt are so long that it can wade into deep water without swimming. It has no need for fancy feeding techniques; it simply uses its needle-thin bill for picking aquatic invertebrates from the water.

This is a highly conspicuous and often very tame bird, found principally around the Mediterranean region. It occurs in wetlands with plenty of open water of consistent depth. It is not fussy about the chemical composition, covering the whole range between fresh and highly saline. Its only demand is that the waters round about are biologically productive and rich in food.

Where Black-winged Stilts occur it is easy to watch their eye-catching displays. They breed in small colonies which throb with activity and noise, and interactions are common. When one bird threatens another, it will walk slowly towards it with neck craned upwards and feathers sleeked – the aptly named 'giraffe display'. This is just a prelude; more serious attempts to supplant another are known as 'head-and-legs-down' flights, in which one bird hovers over another and would seem to be trying to land on its back. In lighter mood, males have an advertising flight that takes them low over the marsh, stopping at intervals to hover with legs dangling but head up. Although it is called the 'butterfly' display, it makes the bird look like a tiny helicopter.

The pre-mating ritual is prolonged. For the whole minute that it lasts, all the action is by the male, the female remaining virtually motionless in a leaning-over, soliciting posture (males will sometimes attempt to copulate with logs and other artefacts that resemble the female's shape). In a routine that seems to suggest that the male is trying to pluck up the courage to mount, he will dip his bill into the water and preen his breast on several hesitant occasions, sometimes walking around the back of the female as well. At last he takes off and hovers over the female, settling gently on her back. Both birds have such long legs that balance appears to be a problem; as the male falls off, he copulates very quickly, 'on the way down', so to speak.

Black-winged Stilts use a wide variety of nest sites. On the whole, they are satisfied with more vegetation around them than are Avocets, but will use bare ground, too. After breeding, most of the European population moves to Africa north of the Equator.

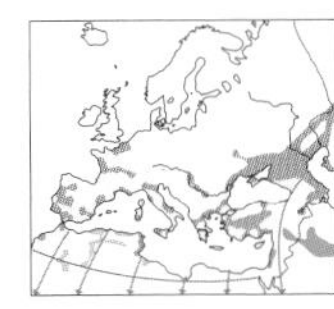

ID: Unmistakable. Male has green gloss on back, female has brownish back. Male often also has more black on head and neck.

Avocet

Recurvirostra avosetta

(ree-kur-vi-**ross**-tra ah-voh-**set**-ta)

length 42–45 cm

ID: Unmistakable, but at a distance might blend in with flocks of gulls or Shelduck.

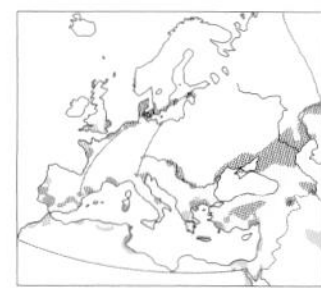

Very few birds in the world have strongly uptilted bills, so one can guess that the Avocet has one for a good reason. This is indeed the case: its bill is a tool for sifting through water while wading in it. If you can imagine that, when feeding, an Avocet is leaning forward and down, you will realise that where the bill hits the water it will be approximately horizontal. This exposes a greater surface area of touch-sensitive bill to the water than would be the case if the bill was straight, especially since the bird holds its bill slightly open when feeding. Another advantage is that the bill will open to the same width throughout its length, rather than being open widest at the tip, a design feature also utilised by flamingos for filtering out large inedible items of detritus. When feeding, the Avocet moves its bill through water or soft mud with a scything action, turning its head from side to side as if watching a tennis match. As the bill moves through the substrate it touches crustaceans, worms and insects in suspension, which can then be manoeuvred and swallowed.

Avocets not uncommonly feed alongside flamingos, although they have a much wider distribution in Europe – they will breed as far north as southern Fennoscandia. All they require for success is relatively large expanses of still, usually saline water below 15 cm in depth, with soft mud around the edges, the whole area packed with high concentrations of invertebrates. If these conditions are present, the Avocet can breed nearby on the open flats.

Avocets are sociable, usually occurring outside the breeding season in groups of 10–30, although concentrations of several hundred birds may be found on estuaries in winter. They are also colonial. In the early season they indulge in group ceremonies, in which pairs face each other like boxers in a ring and call, bow and trample their feet. The function of these ceremonies is unclear.

Stone Curlew *Burhinus oedicnemus* (boo-**rie**-nuss ee-dik-**neem**-uss)

family *Burhinidae* (boo-**rie**-nid-ee)

length 40–44 cm

ID: Distinctive but cryptically coloured wader with brown striated plumage, a large, staring yellow eye, thick legs with knobbly 'knees' and a yellow and black bill.

Habitat Heaths, grasslands, fields, dunes and arid stony desert and semi-desert.
Food Invertebrates and small vertebrates caught mainly on the ground at twilight or at night.
Movements Migratory in the north and east of its range, grading to partial migrant and resident further south. Most don't go far, to North Africa at furthest. In breeding areas March–November.
Voice Loud ringing call with slightly strained quality, usually 2 notes with emphasis on the second. Has both Curlew- and Oystercatcher-like tone.
Pairing style Monogamous.
Nesting Solitary and territorial, but nests may not be far apart.
Nest A scrape in the ground in the open (5–7 cm deep, 16–22 cm in diameter), sometimes with thin lining of grass and 'decorated' on the outside with pebbles or other fragments.
Productivity 1 brood a year.
Eggs 1–2.
Incubation 24–26 days, by both adults.
Young Precocial and downy.
Parenting style Both parents feed and tend the young. Apparently the latter may sometimes involve the adults carrying the chicks to safety in the bill.
Food to young Presumably much as adults'.
Leaving nest Young leave the nest within 24 hours, then may be taken up to 1 km away. They are fed for the first few days, eventually flying at 36–42 days.

It might technically be classed as a 'wader', but one thing you are unlikely to see a Stone Curlew doing is wading. It is very much a bird of dry, stony places and, although it prefers to have water close to its breeding sites, it rarely occurs by lake shores and never in tundra or on estuaries, the sorts of places where 'normal' waders occur.

The Stone Curlew's odd appearance merits its being placed in its own special family, along with a few related species from other parts of the world. The group is often collectively known as 'thick-knees' for reasons that will be obvious from the photograph; the 'knees' are, in fact, correctly termed the tibiotarsal joints, equivalent to our ankles. The Stone Curlew's large head and somewhat sinister staring eye are also key features shared by all members of the family. The large eye helps the bird see in low lighting conditions, since all thick-knee species are primarily nocturnal, taking advantage of invertebrate activity on warm nights

Stone Curlews often spend much of the day sitting motionless in the shade of a tree, but dusk sees a burst of activity. Local pairs often meet up for a short group display (clearly a knees-up) in which birds call loudly, bicker and jump up and down; and then each pair goes off to feed. The Stone Curlew's foraging method is like that of a plover: watching for prey and then running after it, often with a final lunge or a leap into the air after a moth or flying beetle. Other items on the menu include ground-living invertebrates, small mammals or reptiles, and the eggs or chicks of other birds.

The pair bond is probably lifelong, and each season the pair begins its breeding activity by choosing a scrape. The male points his bill to a likely spot and the female starts scraping a shallow hollow; later both sexes contribute and they may make several hollows before choosing their favourite. The female lays two eggs and both sexes contribute to incubation. If disturbed, Stone Curlews lie low at first, but if danger stalks close to the nest they will act aggressively towards the intruder, flying at it and, on the ground, spread their wings in a belligerent posture. Stone Curlews do not, it seems, have a 'broken-wing' display to distract the predator's attention away from the nest, as most waders do.

Pratincoles family *Glareolidae* (glay-ri-**oh**-lid-ee)

Habitat Areas of flats or very low herbage near water, always in warm, dry climates.
Food Predominantly flying insects, especially locusts, grasshoppers, crickets and beetles. Caught on the wing or on the ground, often in the evening at swarming time.
Movements Summer visitors and long-distance migrants to Africa.
Voice Sharp nasal calls such as 'kit' or 'ket', similar in style to those of terns.
Pairing style Monogamous.
Nesting Colonial, but nests may be some distance apart.
Nest Simple scrape (7–10 cm diameter) that may be lined with dry plant debris. Sometimes in hoof-print of large animal.
Productivity 1 brood a year.
Eggs 3 (Collared); 3–4 (Black-winged).
Incubation 17–19 days, by both sexes (Collared; unknown period for Black-winged).
Young Downy and precocial.
Parenting style Both sexes feed and tend young.
Food to young No appreciable difference from adult food; presented directly or regurgitated.
Leaving nest Young leave nest 2–3 days after hatching and are fed by parents for first week; fledge at 25–30 days.

An eclectic mix of wader and swallow, the pratincoles are highly distinctive waders that spend most of their time hawking in the air for flying insects. They have long, sharply pointed wings and long, forked tails, making them look and behave more like swallows or terns than waders. Nevertheless, pratincoles can run fast along the ground in typical wader fashion; they also make wader-like scrapes for their nest and lay the 'right' number of eggs.

The bill of a pratincole is unusual for a wader, being relatively short and distinctly arched; it is the uniting and distinguishing feature of the family. At its base is a wide gape, ideal for snapping up insects mid-flight.

Collared Pratincole

Glareola pratincola (glay-ri-**oh**-la pray-**tin**-koh-la)
Length 22–25 cm

This is the commoner of the two pratincoles in Europe, although it is still a very local species with exacting and specific habitat requirements. Any breeding site must invariably be in a warm climate, preferably near water, and it must provide an abundant supply of large flying insects, especially of the swarming kind (the birds often hawk them in the twilight and after dark). In addition to that, the Collared Pratincole has an almost pathological dislike of obstacles on the ground, even though it is essentially an aerial bird. So colonies are invariably on bare, flat ground with the minimum of grass or other vegetation, no large rocks and without the soil being too broken up. That leaves dried-out floodlands, semi-desert and salt flats as favoured sites, and not much else. The Collared Pratincole does admittedly hunt some insects on the ground, where it is easier to chase them unencumbered, but its fussiness is still hard to understand.

Collared Pratincoles nest in small, loose colonies of a few tens of pairs, in which each couple maintains a territory of about 10–100 sq m. There is much dispute over boundaries at first – in threat a bird ruffles its feathers, spreads its tail to show off the white base, and half-opens its wings – but equally there is great solidity in defence against predators, with many pairs co-operating in open attack against the intruder. When one member of a pair lands on the territory the greeting display is attractive: the male runs enthusiastically towards the female, the birds meet, stand still alongside each other, bow down slightly and then each droops the wing nearer its partner.

ID: Distinctive, the only likelihood for confusion being the Black-winged Pratincole, which is entirely black under the wing. This species has chestnut under the inner part of the wing, and also a white trailing edge to the upperwing, which Black-winged Pratincole lacks.

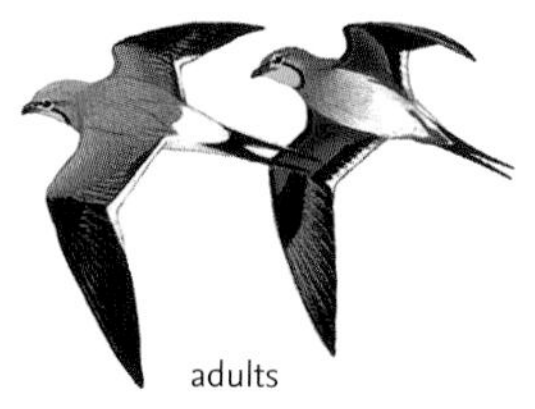

adults

Black-winged Pratincole

Glareola nordmanni (glay-ri-**oh**-la **nord**-man-nie)
Length 23–26 cm

The differences, ecological and behavioural, between this species and the closely related Collared Pratincole are slight. The Black-winged Pratincole is more a bird of steppe country than the Collared, so it will tolerate more grassy conditions and taller herbage for its breeding colonies, and is less confined to flats and bare fields. It also has a tendency to be more sociable than the Collared Pratincole, forming larger colonies (up to several thousand pairs) and larger post-breeding and migrating flocks (10,000 has been recorded). On the steppes it often nests close by other wader species, such as Lapwings.

One major distinction between the two lies in their respective migration routes and wintering areas. The Black-winged Pratincole is a very long-distance migrant, travelling 10,000 km to sub-equatorial (mainly southern) Africa, whereas the Collared goes only as far as the southern fringe of the Sahara Desert. There are so few records of the Black-winged Pratincole between its breeding and wintering areas that it seems likely that the birds cover the distance in just one or two non-stop flights at high altitude. Once there, most individuals settle on high grassy plateaux, the southern-hemisphere equivalent of their 'home' steppes.

adult

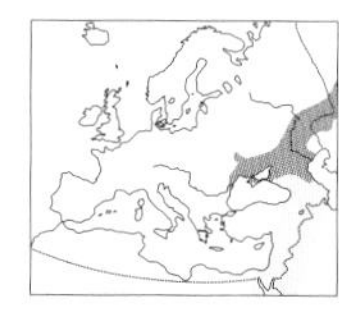

ID: Has a shorter tail than Collared Pratincole, not reaching the wing tips when the bird is at rest. Also has longer legs. Slightly less red at base of bill.

Plovers family *Charadriidae* (kar-ra-**drie**-id-ee)

Habitat Open habitats for breeding, including fields, tundra, marshes, beaches and mountain tops. When not breeding, usually grasslands or estuaries.
Food Insects, worms, molluscs, crustaceans, plus a few berries and seeds, obtained visually from the surface.
Movements Most are highly migratory, often travelling long distances between breeding and wintering areas.
Voice Greatly variable, but often loud and musical; used extensively in display. The Lapwing has a remarkable whining sound and makes a throbbing with its wings. Dotterel rather silent.
Pairing style Some form lifelong pair bonds, others are seasonally monogamous. Kentish Plovers of either sex may acquire two or more mates; Dotterel females regularly polyandrous.
Nesting Most defend exclusive territories, but occasional groupings of Lapwings and Kentish Plovers occur.
Nest Usually a shallow scrape with minimum of lining of nearby vegetation.
Productivity 1–3 broods a year.
Eggs 3–4, usually hatching at about the same time,
Incubation 21–29 days, by both sexes (except Dotterel).
Young Precocial and downy.
Parenting style Typically both adults tend the chicks at first, but one (usually the female) leaves before they fledge.
Food to young Self-fed, similar to that of adults.
Leaving nest Chicks can leave nest almost immediately and may be led far from the nest to special feeding areas. Fledge at 19–45 days.

The plovers are waders with rather a uniform shape, not exhibiting the gallery of bill and leg variations shown by the other main group of waders (Scolopacidae, page 137). They are all plump, short-necked and large-headed, with short bills that are never any longer than the head and hence are rarely used for probing. Instead, a plover's foraging method is simple and standardised: the bird stands still and scans the nearby ground or mud for movement. If it sees something it runs toward it, stoops down and grabs it, then resumes its scan. That's all there is to it, and it's called the 'stop-run-peck' method. Among large flocks of feeding waders, plovers are often easy to pick out because they are the only ones that stand still for any length of time. In contrast to other waders, the plovers have minute, useless hind toes, a loss that is good for running about (it reduces drag), but prohibits them from perching.

To feed in the plovers' stop-run-peck manner requires space and privacy, so plovers don't forage in the dense flocks often formed by touch-feeding waders. Their eyes are large and well adapted for keen vision, with high numbers of rod cells (those responsible for detecting contrast and detail) in the retina, so they can feed by both day and night.

The nests of plovers are similar to those of other waders, not much more than a scrape in the ground. Birds in both families lay the same number of eggs – three to four – and all may lead predators away from the nest by using an advanced array of distraction displays, although plovers are also notably aggressive in nest defence. Interestingly, recent DNA evidence suggests that, despite their similarities to other waders, plovers are actually most closely related to gulls and terns.

Eurasian Dotterel

Little Ringed Plover

Charadrius dubius (kar-**rad**-ri-uss **doo**-bi-uss)
Length 14–15 cm

Three very clear features separate the Little Ringed Plover from its close relatives the Ringed and Kentish Plovers: it shuns seacoasts when breeding; it is not very sociable; and it is exclusively a summer visitor to Europe. Plumage-wise, though, it is very similar to the Ringed Plover, and the chicks have such similar patterning that, where both species forage in the same places, broods can become hopelessly mixed up and chicks inadvertently swapped around.

The natural breeding habitat of the Little Ringed Plover comprises the edges and banks of freshwater lakes and rivers, plus brackish flats and lagoons. In recent years, however, the bird has also spread to artificial sites, such as gravel pits and sewage farms. As a species it is used to changing conditions and setbacks – a female will replace up to three lost clutches in a season, for example – so it has managed to thrive in these unlikely places. Young from first broods may leave their natal area from late June onwards and wander locally, perhaps uncovering potential sites for future colonisation.

Little Ringed Plovers are aggressive on their breeding grounds and have a special 'hostility flight' directed at rivals. More often, though, advertising males simply fly at low altitude over the territory and beyond, describing wide circles or figures of eight, with exaggerated slow wingbeats and occasional tilts from side to side. Yet, despite their obvious hot-headedness, some pairs allow a third bird to live within the territory. It may help in territorial defence and even take a turn at incubating the eggs.

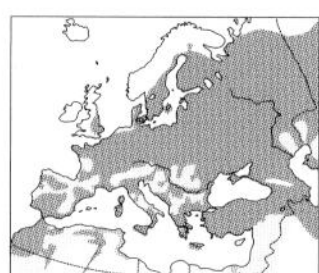

ID: Small plover, one of three with black markings on the face. Has complete breast band, mainly black bill, distinctive yellow eye ring and no wing bars.

Ringed Plover

Charadrius hiaticula
(kar-**rad**-ri-uss hie-ay-**tik**-koo-la)
Length 18–20 cm

This is much the most widespread of the three small plovers with black and white heads, and the only one whose range stretches up into the tundra zone. It breeds in a variety of habitats, including seacoasts, riverbanks, lake shores and artificial sites, but in the south of its range coastal breeding birds greatly outnumber the rest. In contrast to the other two species, large numbers of Ringed Plovers winter in northwest Europe; these are mainly birds that have not travelled far. Those breeding in the extreme north overfly mainland Europe to winter in Africa, a classic case of 'leapfrog migration', in which the further north a population breeds, the further south it winters.

A Ringed Plover's bold markings are a case of disruptive camouflage, breaking up the bird's outline and allowing it to melt into a 'busy' background of stones or detritus. This enables it to nest out in the open on, for example, well-drained beaches, with a well-defined high-water mark. Such breeding sites are fraught with hazards and it seems that, at least in temperate areas, well over 60 per cent of nests fail.

Ringed Plovers cannot avoid poor weather or exceptional tides, but they make huge efforts to defend the camouflaged nest and eggs from predators. To this end they employ a whole range of distraction displays, including pretending to be busy and hence unaware of a predator, feigning injury and imitating the actions of a palatable rodent.

Along with the usual stop-run-peck feeding action so typical of plovers, Ringed Plovers are one of several species to employ 'foot-pattering' – standing on one leg and vibrating the other against the surface of the sand or puddle. The technique causes prey such as crustaceans to become active, possibly by mimicking the moving water of an incoming tide, or perhaps by causing a tiny area of mud to become less sticky and thereby less suitable for its inhabitants.

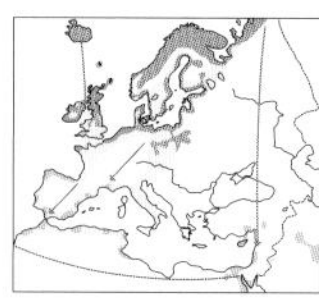

ID: Small plover with a complete black collar. Larger and dumpier than Little Ringed Plover, with heavier bill which is orange with a black tip in summer. No obvious eye ring. In flight shows white wing bar.

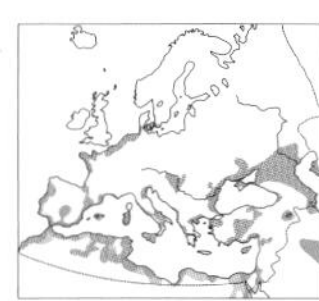

ID: *The only one of the small plovers with an incomplete breast band (disruptive camouflage is unnecessary against the plain, unpatterned sand on which it nests). Long, dark legs; long, thin, dark bill.*

Kentish Plover

Charadrius alexandrinus

(kar-**rad**-ri-uss al-leks-an-**drie**-nuss)

length 15–17 cm

Not many birds like to nest on sandy beaches, but the Kentish Plover is one that does. It likes to be able to run over smooth surfaces free of obstructions and can show an impressive turn of speed, its legs becoming a blur. When feeding normally it utilises the plover stop-run-peck method, watching motionless for movement on the surface, then running to grab whatever it sees. It feeds on crustaceans, worms, molluscs and, where it breeds inland, insects too.

Most of the Kentish Plover's breeding sites are on the coast, though a few birds can also be found inland on salt flats, by lakes and near various man-made workings. But as a species it has taken to these less than the Little Ringed Plover and does not travel far in order to find them.

Kentish Plovers are territorial, but less aggressive to each other than the other two small plovers. This is just as well, because the nests of these birds may be as little as 2–5 m apart, within locally dense populations. The males don't have a threatening song display, and they use their advertising song flight infrequently or not at all. Feeding sites of breeding pairs are away from the territory, on neutral ground. In common with other small plovers, Kentish Plovers regularly nest close to aggressive and demonstrative birds such as Lapwings, Oystercatchers and, notably, Collared Pratincoles. By doing so they greatly enhance their nesting success.

Most Kentish Plovers are monogamous, but some birds desert the young of their first brood to pair up with a second mate. Males or females may do this, usually about six days after the eggs have hatched, and they may not necessarily remain in the area. There is a record of a male abandoning an incubating female mid-season and moving 280 km south to breed with a mate from a previous season. And yet, conversely, some pairs re-form and breed year after year.

Males display to females by performing a 'scraping ceremony' on a potential nest site. The eggs are laid on bare ground and may be partially covered with sand to protect them from the sun. The male incubates by night, the female by day, and both sexes have elaborate distraction displays to lure predators away from the nest.

Spur-winged Plover

Hoplopterus spinosus

(hoh-**plop**-ter-russ spie-**noh**-suss)

Length 25–28 cm

This is a common species in Africa that just squeezes into our region in Greece and European Turkey, where there are only a few hundred pairs at most. In most of its range it is resident, but in Europe it is a summer migrant, present between March and October. It breeds in marshes that are neither entirely fresh nor completely saline, selecting open sites on dry ground for its nest. It often nests in loose neighbourhood groups.

ID: *Unmistakable within its limited European range.*

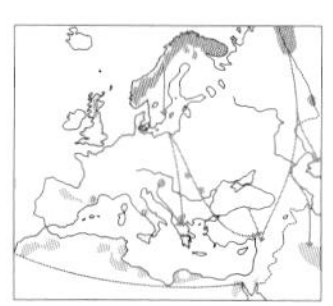

Dotterel

Charadrius morinellus
(kar-**rad**-ri-uss mor-ri-**nel**-luss)
length 20–22 cm

ID: Very distinctive in breeding plumage, with chestnut breast and belly delineated above by white breast band. Broad white supercilium. In non-breeding plumage, supercilium still present, but turns buff; white breast band remains but belly pale grey. In flight, wings entirely plain. Very tame.

The Dotterel has turned some of the norms of bird breeding behaviour on their head. The roles of the sexes are reversed, with the larger and more colourful female taking on most of the duties traditionally linked to the male, and vice versa. The system has arisen to allow the females time to lay two or even three clutches with minimum investment of energy and resources, and is ideal for high egg production in a bird constrained by the short breeding seasons of the far north.

Although some Dotterels arrive on the breeding grounds already paired, it is often the females that turn up first, in flocks known as 'trips'. If this happens they gather on a display arena and await the arrival of the males, who keep their distance at first, like shy teenagers at a dance, spending their days feeding. Soon, though, the trips mix and the females initiate courtship. They move among the males, attempting to isolate a desirable one, like a sheepdog sorting sheep, and they continually lift then fold their wings in an enticing manner to make their intentions clear. They might also run away from the male and pretend to be incubating or brooding. Eventually, if the male is interested, the two will launch into the air and perform a mutual display flight.

From then on the male is responsible for most or all of the incubation of the eggs and the brooding and tending of the chicks. It is a considerable investment of his time and so, during his brief association with the female as she is forming the eggs, he keeps her away from other males and copulates with zeal, protecting his paternity. The female typically abandons him once the clutch is complete and goes in search of another mate, although most probably fail to acquire one.

There are variations on this theme. For example, the females often share some of the incubating duties for second or third clutches. And acquiring a second male after the first ('serial polyandry') works only when there are plenty of males around. In some years females could outnumber males and, in a complete turnaround, these males may then pair with more than one female. On occasion they have been recorded incubating two clutches of eggs in the same nest.

All this takes place in Arctic or mountainous habitats, where it is cold, windswept and often misty. Dotterels are keen on open, flat terrain, often interspersed with rocks and boulders and with grass kept short by climate or grazing. Here they feed on insects and spiders, acquiring them in the usual plover's stop-start manner.

Dotterels are summer visitors to Europe, wintering on the steppes and plateaux of North Africa and the Middle East. They have a habit of migrating in short bursts, stopping off en route on traditional staging areas and often remaining on these for many days.

ID: *In breeding plumage black throat and underparts combined with intricate gold-spotted upper parts make it easy to recognise. Black colour lost after breeding, but golden wash to plumage remains. Has thinner bill than Grey Plover, and pale underwing.*

Golden Plover

Pluvialis apricaria (ploo-vi-**ay**-liss ah-pri-**kay**-ri-a)
length 26–29 cm

Golden Plover flocks show solidarity. When these birds are flushed alongside other feeding waders, they invariably separate from the other species and form their own tight-knit units, often acquiring an oval outline of packed birds. The units wheel around endlessly, shaping to land on numerous occasions before finally doing so, as if just too nervous to take the plunge, finally settling long after the other waders have recommenced feeding.

You won't normally find Golden Plovers on winter estuaries – or at least, not in the middle of the intertidal zone where Grey Plovers hold sway. Golden Plovers are very much grassland birds that like to feed on stubble or close-cropped pasture, sharing these habitats with Lapwings. Both birds eat beetle larvae and insects, and not infrequently search for them at night under a full moon.

Golden Plovers breed on upland moors and bogs, and in the tundra. They revel in cool, misty and windy places where their crystal-clear calls and songs, pleading and tragic, seem entirely appropriate. The males often sing in flight, rising as high as 300 m above ground and flying with an exaggerated upstroke to show off their glistening white underwings. Pairs usually last from year to year and divorces are few.

Pairs are highly vigilant on their breeding territories and react promptly to the appearance of potential predators. They either slip quietly off the nest or make a noisy commotion to distract the intruder. Dunlins, great admirers of the Golden Plover's effective detection, often nest close by.

Grey Plover

Pluvialis squatarola
(ploo-vi-**ay**-liss skwat-**tar**-oh-la)
length 27–31 cm

A few breeding Grey Plovers flirt with the very eastern border of our region, nesting on dry, hilly tundra at low density. But most Europeans know this bird only as a passage migrant and numerous winter visitor to coasts and estuaries on the Atlantic and Mediterranean seaboard. It is one of our larger wintering waders and often a somewhat bolshy one. It prefers to be alone, gathering into small flocks only at high tide to roost with other waders.

In contrast to many waders, but in common with all plovers, the Grey Plover hunts almost entirely by sight. It uses the usual stop-run-peck technique to find insects and their larvae on the tundra, and large worms, molluscs and crustaceans such as crabs on estuaries; it has a heavy bill and strong muscular stomach to deal with hard-shelled items.

But the technique of using sight carries the strong disadvantage of constant interruption. Muddy estuaries in winter may teem with waders going about their business, and their close proximity can not only upset the concentration of this sight feeder, but flush its potential prey as well. So Grey Plovers are a little like over-fussy park keepers trying to keep kids off the grass, forever chivvying birds away and getting hot under the collar. Many individuals hold permanent feeding territories on the mud-flats and keep competing birds away. Only at high tide when their territories are covered can they relax.

Those Grey Plovers that are territorial – and there are those that protect their precious mud year after year – risk losing up to 10 per cent of feeding time while they defend their borders. But the effort is worthwhile. These fussy individuals get into condition earlier than their peers and migrate to the breeding areas in advance of the rest, greatly enhancing their chances of breeding success. In their late-season absence a resourceful individual may take over the vacated territory and gain short-term benefit. Clearly, there is nothing like having your own private mud.

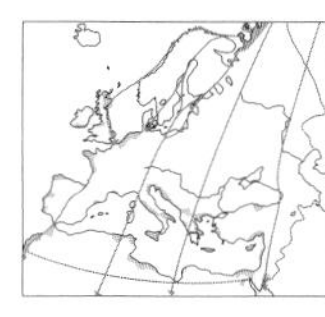

ID: *Unmistakable in breeding plumage, a black and white version of Golden Plover. In non-breeding plumage most easily distinguished from other waders by black 'armpits' seen in flight. Otherwise portly wader with heavy, short bill, white spots on upperparts.*

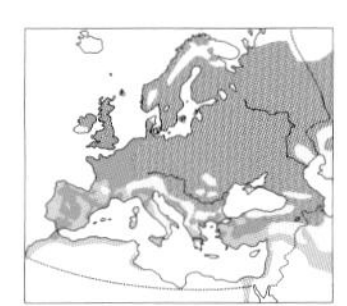

ID: *Highly distinctive wader with obvious crest; iridescent green above, white below. Rounded wings and noticeably laboured, floppy flight.*

Lapwing

Vanellus vanellus (van-**nel**-luss van-**nel**-luss)
length 28–31 cm

When a male Lapwing is wrapped up in his song flight, diving and rolling wildly in the sky and making mewing, squealing sounds, he can have the look of a bird exuberantly out of control. But in reality he is more like a dancer, following definite, specific routines choreographed in advance and common to all Lapwings. As he performs, all eyes are upon him; he is being judged and marked, metaphorically, by an audience of rival males and potential mates.

The full display begins with a gradually ascending flight low to the ground powered by deep, slow wingbeats – the so-called 'butterfly flight'. If a female is watching intently, the display may end here, but usually the acrobat suddenly accelerates into the next part of his routine, the 'alternating flight', in which he flies forwards rapidly, rolling his body from side to side like a boat caught in a storm, and with wings throbbing. After this he will change tack, making several brief ascents followed by dives, and to make this section more interesting he will sometimes flip over on his back in mid-air. A relatively normal, level 'low flight' follows, taking the bird 10–50 m forwards without doing anything spectacular, but this abruptly ceases as he increases the speed of his wingbeats and gains height quickly, introducing loud calls that sound a little bit like a yodel. Having reached the top of his ascent he maintains altitude and accompanies his flight with excited 'weep weep!' calls. Finally he plunges dramatically towards the ground in a vertical dive, sometimes turning over completely as he does so, and makes a sound somewhat like the peeling of Sellotape. He then levels off in an alternating flight and lands.

Naturally, some males perform their routines better than others and, although most are monogamous, some will attract two females to nest within their defended territory. Most females strive to prevent this happening, however, acting very aggressively towards any of their gender that might dare to breach their borders. They do not wish to compromise the male's paternal assistance. The relationship between paired birds lasts only for a season, but both sexes contribute to incubation and looking after the chicks, and this often includes distraction displays and the harassment of marauding predators.

This is a bird of open pastureland and one of the few waders to breed over almost all of Europe, from the sub-Arctic to the Mediterranean fringe. In historical times it has shifted away from natural habitats to colonise agricultural land. It not only breeds on farmland but winters there, too, feeding on soil invertebrates such as insect larvae and worms.

Lapwings are only short-distance migrants; their very rounded wings are not suitable for long flights, so they tend to remain within Europe in winter, perhaps popping over to North Africa at the very most. Being dependent on feeding in moist soil, they are extremely vulnerable to frost and snow, so the moment conditions deteriorate they hasten away to warmer and wetter climates.

adult ♂ non-br.
juv.
adult ♂ br.
adult ♀ br.

Snipes, Sandpipers and Phalaropes

family *Scolopacidae* (skoh-loh-**pay**-sid-ee)

Habitat For breeding the whole range is covered, although wetland and boggy habitats predominate. In winter, many are found on estuaries, some in freshwater habitats and a few on rocky shores.
Food Invertebrates are most important, notably insects in the breeding areas and worms, molluscs and crustaceans in winter. Food type and feeding method closely correlated with the shape of the bill.
Movements Most highly migratory; passage generally at night. Several species fly enormous distances, sometimes at great heights; speeds of 60–70 km per hour are usual. Many breed at high latitudes and winter from Europe down to the Equator.
Voice Varies from incessantly noisy (Redshank) to almost silent (Ruff). Sounds are often fluty and clear; vocabularies complex.
Pairing style The family is noted for its extraordinary range of pairing methods. Polyandry is notably frequent, especially in the Arctic.
Nesting None is truly colonial, although aggregations of nests and territories are quite common. The majority nests solitarily.
Nest Usually nothing more than a depression in the ground, perhaps lined with nearby plant fragments.
Productivity 1 brood a year, but Dunlin and possibly Jack Snipe can have 2.
Eggs 3–4; pear-shaped to fit neatly into the centre of the nest. Usually all hatch within a short time.
Incubation 17–32 days, beginning after clutch is complete. By both, or occasionally by one bird of either sex.
Young Precocial and downy. Walk and feed within a few hours of hatching.
Parenting style Often both tend the chicks at least at first, but one of the pair may desert the other before the young can fly.
Food to young Young self-feeding, the exception being Snipes and Woodcock, in which adults bring food (e.g. worms) to young. Mostly invertebrates.
Leaving nest Young leave the nest as soon as their down dries. Fledge at 14–45 days.

Black-tailed Godwit

This is a large family encompassing a good many birds that look superficially rather different to each other, especially in the length and shape of the bill, neck and legs: a large Curlew, for example, towers over a Little Stint and its bill is actually longer than the Stint itself. But both often feed on mud by the waterside, giving rise to the name wader, or shorebird, that is used for the family as a whole. Both have long, pointed wings, share many skeletal features, have bills rich with touch receptors, well-developed pectoral flight muscles, short tails and brown streaky plumage. Their calls are somewhat similar in pitch. Both sing in flight, lay four eggs and build similar rudimentary scrape-type nests. On closer inspection this heterogeneous family shows a surprising number of unifying features.

With the exception of the Sanderling, the scolopacid waders treated here differ from plovers in possessing a clearly visible raised hind toe; a few species have small webs between their front toes, which tend to be quite long. They have relatively smaller heads and eyes than plovers, and their bills are generally longer and thinner. The bills are often complex structures, with internal strengthening in some species and the ability to move some parts relative to others (rhynchokinesis) in others. Although many species regularly feed by sight, a feature of the family is its ability to find food exclusively by touch, often by probing the bill far into the mud or other substrate. Most bills are slightly swollen at the tip; impulses from the touch receptors feed to a special portion of the brain that is better developed than in the plovers.

Most members of the Scolopacidae breed in swampy or marshy areas, and a high number of species have their headquarters in the northern parts of Europe where there are extensive wet bogs and tundra. Typically, many waders swap these habitats for coastal mudflats and salt marshes in winter, and the distances between summer and winter quarters can span the globe. With their long, pointed wings, waders are designed for fast and efficient flying; many can fly for several days and nights non-stop, often at altitudes as high as 7000 m.

This family of waders exhibits dizzying variation in pairing systems – everything from lifelong partnerships to momentary meetings culminating in and ending in copulation. Some waders are polyandrous, a few polygynous and others promiscuous. Either partner may incubate on its own, or both will share the task – sometimes within the same species! In contrast to this great variation, many waders have rather similar displays (song flights, for example, are often of the rising and falling 'switchback' type) and, as mentioned above, nests and eggs are somewhat standardised.

In the vast majority of species the young are precocial (able to move around and feed themselves within hours of hatching) and self-feeding. The only exceptions to this rule are the Woodcock and Snipe, whose advanced form of probing clearly requires a lot of practice.

Knot

Calidris canutus (ka-**lid**-driss kan-**noo**-tuss)
length 23–25 cm

A great world traveller, the Knot is one of the few species to move to and fro between the Canadian Arctic and western Europe. Birds breeding at high latitudes on barren plateaux on islands or coasts in the New World cross via Greenland to winter on selected muddy estuaries in northwest Europe. In addition, populations from Siberia pass Europe on their way to West Africa, and a few halt their journey here, too. In order to complete these vast journeys, some requiring several days and nights of continuous flying (for example, over the Atlantic), the Knot may build up fat reserves totalling 80 per cent of its body weight.

The switch from Arctic tundra to temperate estuaries is wholesale. On the tundra Knots nest solitarily and feed almost entirely on insects, which they obtain by picking from the surface. On the intertidal mud they pack together in flocks that may number 10,000 individuals. Each bird feeds on a small range of mud-dwelling molluscs, obtained not from the surface but below it, using the sense of touch.

In the winter the Knot is devoted to its hard-shelled prey: individuals have been known to eat 700 Baltic tellins in a single day, finding many of them by inserting their bills into the mud and pushing them forwards, making a furrow ('ploughing'). Since everybody is finding prey by touch, it is feasible to feed in large, compact groups without one bird distracting another. The Knot ingests the molluscs whole and breaks the shells down in its muscular stomach.

Obviously, since they take their food in the intertidal zone, Knots cannot forage when the tide is high. At such times they roost above the high-water mark, often in enormous, dense flocks. Before settling they frequently indulge in aerial manoeuvres, individuals flying remarkably close together, the whole flock wheeling from side to side and up and down, ever-shifting like a huge plume of smoke, sometimes showing their dark upper sides, the next moment their white undersides. Altogether they make a spectacular sight on a dreary winter's day.

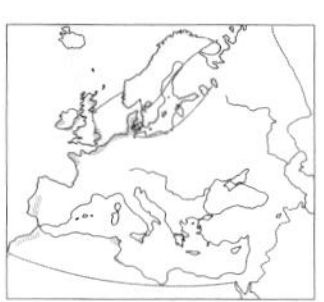

ID: Medium-sized dumpy wader with short legs and characteristic head-down posture. Summer plumage unmistakable. When not breeding turns cold grey, like Dunlin. Characterised by obvious white supercilium, pale green legs and shortish, stout bill.

adult non-br.

adult br. adult non-br. juv.

Sanderling

Calidris alba (ka-**lid**-driss **al**-ba)
length 20–21 cm

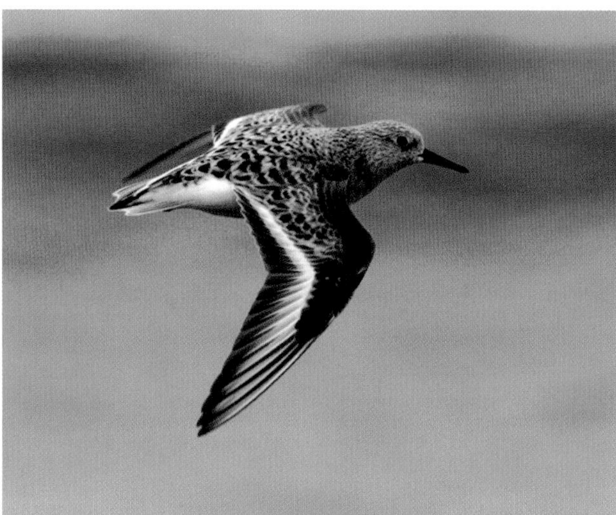

Watching a Sanderling feeding can be exhausting. Its main technique is to pick small prey items from the shallow water of retreating waves., which demands a great deal of dashing about along beaches, in and out with the breakers, with legs moving as fast as clockwork to avoid being swamped by the fast-moving water. It looks hard work, but this method of foraging isolates the Sanderling in the non-breeding season from the heavy competition among waders in the softer, humdrum, muddy intertidal zone of estuaries. So flocks of feeding Sanderlings normally have the beach virtually to themselves.

The Sanderling has a clear physical adaptation to its lifestyle of fast running: it lacks a hind toe, a modification that cuts down drag on the hard ground as it moves forwards; it is the only wader so designed. It also has an extremely sensitive bill to help it find prey concealed in the sand. The touch receptors at the tip are so efficient that they can detect the vibrations of worms 2 cm away; they don't have to touch something to know it is there. In addition to worms, the bill also picks up tiny crabs, shrimps and sandhoppers, among other items.

Away from its more familiar winter haunts the Sanderling is one of the extreme Arctic nesters among waders, breeding way north of any other species except the Knot. Even the northernmost parts of Fennoscandia are too warm for it; it prefers Arctic islands almost hugging the polar icecap. In this forbidding zone it selects a dry, open site on the chilly tundra, never far from water, usually on the coast. Its only shelter comes from sparse, low-growing vegetation.

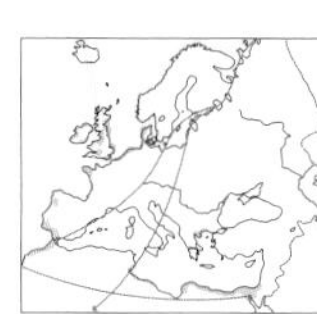

ID: Usually seen in winter plumage when similar to Dunlin, but much whiter and often with small black spot at shoulder. Stronger white wing bar. Bill shorter, stouter. Summer plumage notable for clear contrast between white belly and peppery spots and reddish colour on chest.

adult br. adult non-br.

juv.

adult non-br.

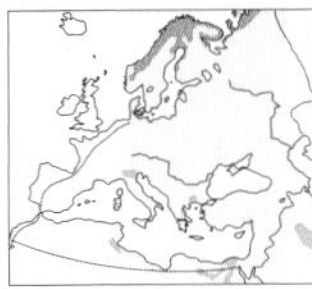

ID: Recognised as a stint by small size and short, straight bill. Legs green. Clear demarcation between white belly and greyish chest, with slight white nick going up shoulder, recalls miniature Common Sandpiper. Breeding and non-breeding plumage similar.

Temminck's Stint

Calidris temminckii
(ka-**lid**-driss tem-**min**-kee-eye)
length 13–15 cm

This is one of the few waders that remains faithful to much the same habitats throughout the year: sheltered fresh water with plenty of low, fringing vegetation. It is thus a bird of less extreme Arctic conditions than the Little Stint, found well inland and far to the south of that species' range, especially along rivers and inlets.

The high-pitched trilling song, almost as sustained and overlooked as that of the Grasshopper Warbler, is highly distinctive. It is usually delivered in a simple song flight, in which the male bird describes a circle low to the ground whilst fluttering its wings very quickly in a raised position. But it may also be delivered from a perch (the wings fluttering nonetheless), which is unusual for a small wader.

The breeding behaviour of Temminck's Stints is geared to rapid, efficient production. Each female typically lays two clutches of eggs, one for herself to incubate and the other for a male, a system that ensures that plenty of eggs will hatch within a short period; some females, indeed, begin laying the second clutch only two days after finishing the first, although a week is a more typical interval. The first clutch will be incubated by the male that fertilised it, but the second will have a different father. This is because any male tends to spice up his incubation stint by seeking out and mating with a second female between sits.

Little Stint

Calidris minuta (ka-**lid**-driss min-**noo**-ta)
length 12–14 cm

No bigger than a House Sparrow, the Little Stint is Europe's smallest wader and also, perhaps, the most feverish in its movements. Among a family well known for its lightning flight and fleetness of foot, the Little Stint stands out for the ease of its take-off when disturbed and its high rate of pecking when feeding. A foraging bird keeps its head down, picking minute items from the mud, several to a second. It is completely focused on the task in hand and may allow a very close approach from people. It catches prey on the surface by sight, rather than probing, and sometimes defends short-term territories from rivals to prevent its feeding being disturbed. The overall effect is of a bird that never stops moving.

A small population breeds in the High Arctic tundra of Norway and Russia, nesting on the drier parts near the coast, usually at low altitude. The social organisation there is such that the birds have very short-term pair bonds and are often polygamous. Both males and females sing to attract the opposite sex, and neither keeps a clearly defined territory. In common with the Temminck's Stint, females sometimes lay two clutches of eggs, incubating one themselves and commandeering a male to incubate the other, usually the first, clutch.

Otherwise, the Little Stint is a common passage migrant in Europe and a few birds also overwinter. In general, non-breeding Little Stints are found on more coastal, open sites than Temminck's Stints.

ID: Very small wader with noticeably short, sharp bill. Fast feeding action often separates it from Dunlin. Breeding plumage 'cereal-coloured', with white belly; pale V marks down back. Legs black.

ID: Breeding plumage very distinctive. At other seasons has notably long legs and long, evenly curved bill; shows clear white supercilium, in contrast to Dunlin. Tends to wade deeper than other closely related waders.

Curlew Sandpiper

Calidris ferruginea (ka-**lid**-driss fer-roo-**jin**-eh-a)
length 18–19 cm

Europe is only a small part of the Curlew Sandpiper's migratory 'empire'. From its limited headquarters in central Siberia, it spreads out remarkably far to winter over a broad swathe of the southern hemisphere, including coastal Africa, India and Australia, taking in Europe as part of its journey. Some birds fly to West Africa via the western coasts of Europe, while others travel overland across eastern Europe and cross the Mediterranean; a few also take in the Black Sea en route to East Africa. Europe is a mere stopover, like a motorway service station. Interestingly, birds don't use the western coastal flyway at all in the spring, but take a more direct route instead.

For male Curlew Sandpipers, the breeding season is wild and short. Having travelled from the southern hemisphere to get to the right place, they may stay as little as two weeks. Throughout this time they chase females frantically all day long in an attempt to copulate. Then they depart, leaving the females as sole incubators.

On its passage through Europe the Curlew Sandpiper visits coastal and freshwater flats, marshes and pools. It has longer legs, a longer neck and a longer bill than the Dunlin so, not surprisingly, it is more of a true wader and can be found feeding further out in deeper water.

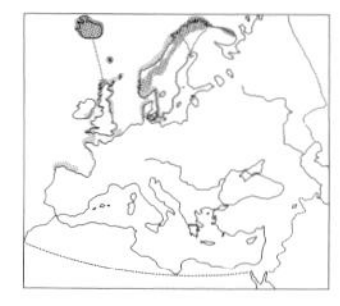

ID: Dark, dumpy wader with rather long tail that projects beyond wing tips. Summer plumage dark and unremarkable, with little or no 'purple' colour. In winter characterised by yellow legs and bill base.

Purple Sandpiper

Calidris maritima (ka-**lid**-driss mar-rit-**tie**-ma)
length 20–22 cm

There is nothing particularly unusual about where the Purple Sandpiper breeds: primarily on Arctic and sub-Arctic tundra, as well as on beaches and islands. Where it winters, though, is curious. It does not travel far, only to rocky shores and man-made coastal artefacts within and to the south of its breeding range. Here it has little competition from other waders except the Turnstone, and thrives. While the rest probe into the mud, the Purple Sandpiper examines rock fissures and beds of seaweed for hard-shelled molluscs, crustaceans and a few worms. It also, unusually for a wader, ingests significant amounts of algae. The Purple Sandpiper has several adaptations for its littoral lifestyle: a strong but slightly decurved bill, a large muscular stomach to grind down shells, and an ability to swim should it be caught by the waves.

The two sexes divide incubation equally between them, but as soon as the eggs hatch the female deserts and leaves the brood in the studious care of the male. Both give their all to nest protection when on duty, and include in their armoury some remarkable distraction displays to deflect predators. The most famous is the 'rodent run', in which the bird literally pretends to be a lemming or similar and runs along low to the ground, making rodent-like squeaks. Beguiled by easy food, the predator follows this new trail, away from the nest, and must be extremely surprised when, at a safe distance, the 'rodent' takes off and flies away!

Broad-billed Sandpiper

Limicola falcinellus
(lie-**mik**-koh-la fal-sin-**nel**-lus)
length 16–17 cm

The fussy Broad-billed Sandpiper is highly selective of its breeding habitat. What it likes best are sub-Arctic bogs at moderate or high altitude (up to 1000 m), where there is plenty of soft mud or peat. It conceals its nest in the wettest parts – the sort of place where ground predators should fear to tread.

These waders are loosely colonial, but within the broad boundaries of the colony the males defend their own sections vigorously. Their eye-catching song flight consists of slow passes about 20 m above ground, interspersing wing shivers with descending or ascending glides on wings lifted high. The whole performance speeds up considerably when borders are challenged.

This bird does indeed have a broad bill, much more so than that of similar species such as Dunlins or Stints. It is used for picking items from mud or vegetation and also, especially, for probing into the ooze. At times the bird will move along with its bill immersed, 'ploughing' a furrow and detecting buried items by touch.

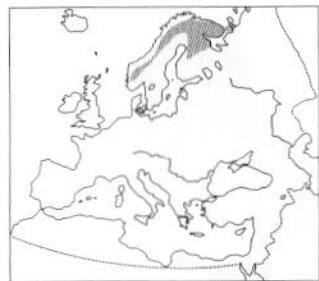

ID: Slightly smaller than Dunlin with shorter, green (not black) legs. Bill quite broad at base, but with obvious downward kink at tip. Belly quite heavily streaked.

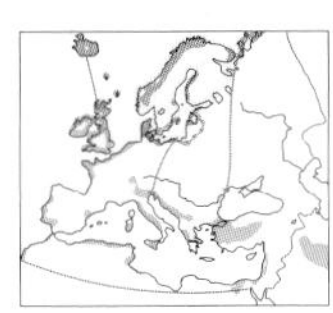

ID: In breeding plumage easily recognised by oily black belly. At other times often nondescript: look for bill, of equal length to head and slightly down-curved. White wing bar, white sides to rump and upper tail.

Dunlin

Calidris alpina (ka-**lid**-driss al-**pie**-na)
length 16–22 cm long.

The field guides say that one of the keys to identifying small waders is to get to grips with the Dunlin. This says much about this successful species: it is one of the most wide-ranging of Europe's breeding waders and perhaps the commonest of all here in the wintertime, occupying a wide range of habitats at both seasons. It is also one of the most variable of waders, with a tricky trio of races visiting Europe and showing subtly different characteristics.

The bill, though, is quite distinctive. Regardless of which race the bird belongs to, the bill is about as long as the head and slightly down-curved, thus ruling out a good many similar species with shorter or straighter bills. Unsurprisingly, given its length, the bill is used for probing as well as surface picking; Dunlins often practise a type of feeding known as 'stitching' – inserting their bills several times in succession as if they were sewing. At these times the birds are using touch as their primary sense and can gather in large, dense flocks without fear of getting in each other's way. Outside the breeding season, and especially on large, muddy estuaries, Dunlins are well known for forming huge flocks that wheel around and make spectacular aerial movements prior to roosting.

During the breeding season Dunlins occupy moist, boggy ground, especially if there are small pools interspersed. This requirement is met by tundra, moorland and salt marshes, among other habitats, so the Dunlin would be considered quite catholic for a wader in its choice of breeding site. Males and females usually form a monogamous pair bond, although some females pair with a second male once their first clutch has hatched. It is not uncommon for pairs to re-form from year to year, which presumably puts such bigamous females in something of a quandary as to which male to choose next year.

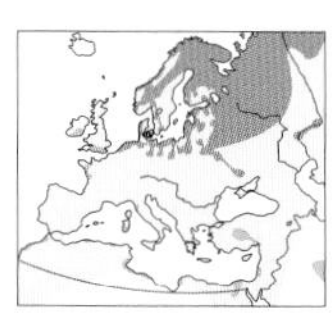

ID: Males in breeding plumage unmistakable. Outside breeding season an oddly shaped wader with a head that appears too small for its body. Bill short, slightly down-curved, often with white feathering at the base ('sheepskin noseband'). Scaly upper parts. Red or green legs. In flight, white ovals either side of rump.

Ruff

Philomachus pugnax (fil-**lom**-mak-kus **pug**-naks)
length 20–30 cm; a remarkable degree of variation

The Ruff is the embodiment of a prejudice that one occasionally hears from exasperated female humans. The male's testes are relatively enormous, accounting for 5 per cent of his entire body mass; and they are, indeed, heavier than his brain.

This is a bird in which males and females differ more than most. The differences are sharpest in the breeding season, but even at others times of the year the males are nearly 25 per cent larger than the females. The breeding plumage differs between the two so radically that the sexes are more different in appearance than many species are from each other. At the same time, the breeding behaviour of each sex has been polarised to the limit.

The Ruff operates a promiscuous mating system in which the relationship between male and female begins and ends for good in the act of copulation. The female is henceforth responsible for all the affairs of nest, eggs and young, so the male's contribution to breeding is merely genetic. Nonetheless, it is important to the female that these genes are good ones, and the Ruff's unusual 'lek' system enables a female to find a high-quality male quickly and efficiently.

A lek is a communal display in which males perform against each other, as if they were competing for limited places in a football team. A Ruff lek forms on flat ground. Here the local males fight it out between themselves who will occupy each small section of the display arena, effectively a territory of about 1 sq m. A hierarchy develops because some territories are better than others – the central one being the best – and it is ground out by much posturing, in which the colourful 'ruffs' come into their own, and pugilistic skirmishing. No Ruff owning a central territory will get there without having earned the right to occupation, and the rewards are such that a lek is very much a meritocracy. A visiting female, knowing this, will normally go straight to the central territory and copulate with the owner, ignoring the attentions of all other performers. Males forced to the margins of the arena are the weakest birds and pay dearly by spending the breeding season with a limited chance of copulation. These birds, sometimes called independent marginals, sometimes change lek.

Instead of suffering such a fate, some male Ruffs shun territoriality altogether and commute between leks, attempting to steal copulations from under the nose of an incumbent. Such birds are markedly different in colour to most males. While territorial or 'independent' males have colourful ruffs of a blackish, brownish or reddish hue, each bird having its own unique 'costume', these 'satellite' Ruffs have pale or white plumage. It is thought that they are not merely tolerated, but actually recruited to the arena, possibly because their white plumage enables females to locate the lek more easily. Their breeding success is, in any case, higher than that of independent marginals. One might expect the latter birds to want to change behaviour, but they cannot just become satellites. To be a satellite you must be born a satellite, with your signature white plumes and ruffs; an unsuccessful independent cannot go under cover. Its genetically inherited plumage marks out its behaviour for life, and it will never be tolerated by another independent. Thus the Ruff's mating system is a consequence of plumage, genetics and individual ability.

Ruff leks start in the early morning and may continue for much of the day. They are silent places for, despite the high stakes, Ruffs do not vocalise during their display; noise might make them too vulnerable to predators.

The outlandish plumes and ruffs are worn only between April and the end of June, by which time all breeding matters are long settled. The males leave the breeding grounds in June and the females and juveniles follow a month or so later. Before and during its migration (usually to Africa), the Ruff moults, the males reverting to a rather traditional appearance not unlike that of any other wader. At such times it is hard to credit them with their bizarre behaviour and appearance on the breeding sites.

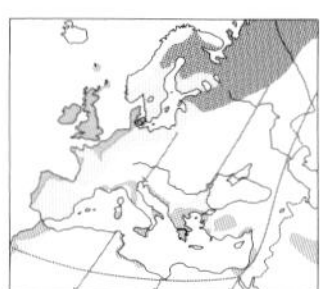

ID: Smaller than Snipe with a habit of rocking up and down as if on springs. Shorter bill than Snipe. Centre of crown dark, lacks stripe, but there is an extra eyebrow-like stripe over eye. Underparts striped. Two broad straw-coloured lines on each side of upperparts.

Jack Snipe

Lymnocryptes minimus
(lim-noh-**krip**-teez **min**-ni-muss)
length 17–19 cm

Much still remains to be discovered about the Jack Snipe, perhaps the most skulking and retiring of all the waders. Small, cryptically camouflaged, an inhabitant of thick cover and most active in the half-light, it is difficult to see at all and almost impossible to study. When flushed it does not fly away in mad zigzags like a Snipe, but instead shifts reluctantly only at the point of being trodden upon, and then flops down again a few metres ahead, as if it were ill or injured. The Snipe calls in protest as it flies away; the Jack Snipe remains silent. It seems to try everything not to be detected.

Except for one thing. The Jack Snipe has a very odd habit, sometimes shared by other snipes (but never as much): when feeding, it rocks its body up and down by flexing its legs, making it look as if it were on springs. At times this habit breaks the Jack Snipe's cover, and the point of it is far from clear.

For breeding, Jack Snipes visit marshes and bogs on the interface between tundra and taiga, often being found alongside Broad-billed Sandpipers. A typical nest site is on a moss-covered mound. Unusually for a wader the nest has something of a structure, being a loose cup of vegetation. From the sketchy observations made so far, it appears that the female tends the chicks, but the Jack Snipe's mating system is unknown.

Where Jack Snipes occur, a very strange sound can be heard at dawn and dusk in the breeding season. It sounds like the distant beating of horse's hooves on a hard surface and its transmission is sometimes clear, sometimes muffled, at once near, then far away again. This is the Jack Snipe's flight song, uttered as the bird rises often as high as 60 m and plunges earthwards once more. The flight path is wild, reckless and free, as if this skulker had finally been unleashed to be itself in the safety of the night sky.

Great Snipe

Gallinago media (gal-lin-**ay**-go **mee**-di-a)
length 27–29 cm

Only slightly larger than a Snipe, and with great similarities in plumage, the Great Snipe can be hard to tell apart from its more abundant cousin. One clue, though, is in the way it flies off at the approach of predators. The Common Snipe creates a bit of a palaver, bolting out with a kissing call and flying far away with great zeal and dash. The Great Snipe, by contrast, is more laid-back. When disturbed it does fly off, but makes a slight sound with its wings and little else. The beats are slower, the flight line steadier and it tends to land less than 30 m away from where it was originally flushed.

The Great Snipe is scarce in Europe, found mainly in meadows, bogs and tundra edge, often with tree cover nearby. Its numbers have declined severely over the last hundred years through habitat loss and shooting, leaving it to survive mainly in the east and north of our area. It feeds on similar foods to the Snipe, but it occasionally picks as well as probes and will also utilise somewhat drier habitats.

On spring evenings male Great Snipes conduct a remarkable communal display in the semi-darkness. Gathering at traditional arenas, each bird defends his own hollow or tussock from other males, mock-fighting, performing 'flutter jumps' to about 1–2 m and making a highly complex song that involves a twittering phase (called 'bibbling'), a section like a bouncing table-tennis ball coming to a stop and an odd whizzing like a spent firework. The females enter the arena to mate and assess the males by their appearance (apparently the males showing off the most white on the tail are most desirable). They copulate with the male of their choice and this is the extent of the relationship between the sexes; thereafter the female looks after eggs and young alone.

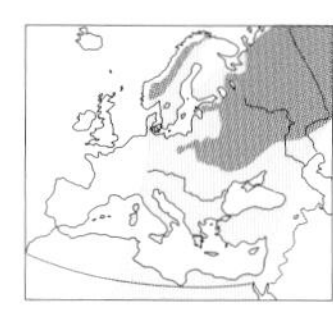

ID: Slightly larger and plumper than Common Snipe, with shorter bill. Stronger and more intensive barring on breast, flanks and belly than Snipe, without white patch. Underwing darker. Outer tail feathers extensively white.

Snipe

Gallinago gallinago (gal-lin-**ay**-go gal-lin-**ay**-go)
length 25–27 cm

The Snipe's long, straight bill is the perfect tool for probing deeply into the soft mud, and it will feed wherever the substrate is not too hard, especially favouring the edges of pools and puddles. Where the earth or mud is rich it will stand still in one place for some time, making a series of insertions on the spot, leaving behind a semicircle of small holes. And once the bill is in place, the Snipe will often vibrate it a little and pull it up and down, feeling around in the mud for movement a few centimetres below its feet.

The bill is a feat of biological engineering. At the tip it is fitted (as are the bills of most of this family) with millions of tiny touch receptors that are wired to a special part of the brain. These provide the Snipe with an exceptionally fine sense of touch at the bill tip, easily enough to pick up the presence or movement of particles nearby in the mud. The Snipe's bill also demonstrates another, more unusual trick: it can be opened only at the tip, so that food can be picked up and swallowed without the bird having to remove its bill from the mud. The bill structure is not especially rigid; the component bones and connectors can move relative to one another, an arrangement known as rhynchokinesis. The trick then is mechanical: if the bill is bent slightly at its near end, the bend can be transmitted to the tip such that the rest of the bill remains closed. In this way the Snipe's bill tip can pinch a worm or insect larva *in situ*, and the long tongue can then transport the food item up towards the mouth.

The bill is not the only unusual anatomical feature of the Snipe; it also has a modified tail. Most waders have 12 tail feathers, but the Snipe has 14 or sometimes more. The outermost of these are stiffened and attached to the body by independent muscles, such that they can be splayed out from the rest of the tail. When a Snipe indulges in one of its rising and plummeting display flights, the wind passing by these feathers causes them to vibrate and to make a distinctive buzzing sound ('drumming'), a little like the bleating of a sheep. The sound adds an instrumental dimension to the display, without the bird having to go to the trouble of singing. The sound made by the feathers varies according to how susceptible to wear they are; worn-out feathers presumably make a less attractive sound than intact ones.

The display marks out the territory and serves to lure females. If it works, any pair bond may have a fragile beginning, with promiscuity commonplace in both sexes. However, out of necessity, things soon settle down. Once the eggs hatch, both parents become fully occupied with feeding the chicks. In contrast to most wader chicks, young Snipes cannot feed themselves at all, and the adults divide the small brood between them in order to cope. For a week or two neither parent has any time for the luxury of promiscuity.

The Common Snipe is widespread through much of the northern half of Europe, where it occurs in any freshwater habitats with plenty of fringing vegetation and soft mud. A broader range of similar habitats is occupied in winter.

adults

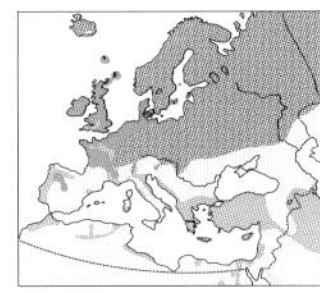

ID: Small, cryptically coloured wader with very long, straight bill, half as long as its body. Very fast wingbeats in level flight; zigzags away in panicky escape flight when flushed, gives kissing call. In fresh or brackish water, not usually found in the intertidal zone.

Woodcock

Scolopax rusticola (**skoh**-loh-paks russ-**tik**-oh-la)
length 33–35 cm

There's no point looking for a Woodcock on an estuary or on the muddy margins of a pool. This is a wader with a very unusual habitat: the woodland floor. It lives a life of amazing secrecy, hidden in undergrowth for much of the time, sitting tight, protected by its intricate 'leaf-litter' camouflage. It comes out mostly at night and in twilight. Should you flush it in daylight, it will rocket away with a volley of wingbeats, twisting through the trees and far out of sight.

It is also quite impossible to creep up on a Woodcock without being detected. This is because the bird has a remarkable gift for surveillance. The eyes are placed high on the skull (so high, in fact, that the brain case is below them) and very much to the sides. This means that, without turning its head, the Woodcock can see in a complete 360-degree circle, with some overlapping ('binocular') vision immediately in front and behind. Its vision also covers everything above it in the vertical plane. As a Woodcock probes its long bill into damp patches in the litter layer, finding all its food by touch, it can theoretically see everything around it.

Woodcocks eat primarily worms, plus a few beetles and other insects. Their main method of feeding is to find a patch of soft mud and probe into it. On occasion, though, worms are encouraged to come to the surface with a little pattering with the feet.

The breeding behaviour of the Woodcock is intriguing and unusual. Waders tend to be monogamous, polyandrous or promiscuous, the last of these implying no prolonged pair bond. But the Woodcock employs a system known as successive polygyny, in which a male will have several mates (up to four), yet spends a respectable amount of time with each one. This period probably adds up to only a few days, but is long enough to ensure that a female is disinclined to call the attention of any other male.

To obtain a mate in the first place, a male undertakes display flights at dawn and dusk. These are completely different to the rising and falling 'switchback' flights of most waders; instead they follow a wide circular course over the tree tops, several kilometres long. On the way the bird adopts an odd flight style, with bursts of double wingbeats giving a flickering appearance. He also gives a vocal accompaniment, a series of soft croaking notes terminating in a loud squeak. The whole performance is known as 'roding' and it catches the attention of any receptive females waiting below, who either fly up and join the male briefly and silently, or give a sneezing summoning call from down below. Either way, both sexes end up on the forest floor, enshrouded in the darkness, where they continue their courtship in privacy.

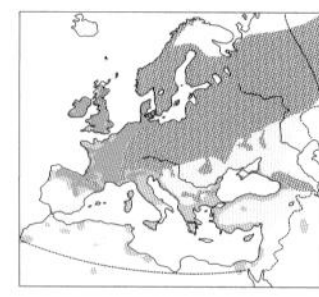

ID: Distinctive. Much larger and fatter than any Snipe. Similar long, straight bill. Wings much more rounded than on any similar wader. Usually seen in woodland.

adults

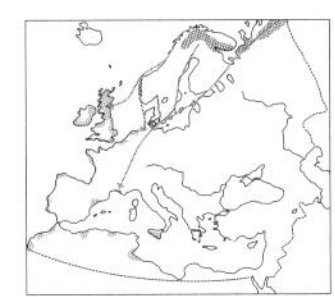

ID: *Similar to Black-tailed Godwit but with shorter legs, especially section between 'knee' and belly (the tibia); also more uptilted bill. In breeding plumage reddish colour extends down to under-tail coverts. In non-breeding plumage Curlew-like, with streaks on back; longer supercilium than Black-tailed.*

Bar-tailed Godwit

Limosa lapponica (lim-**moh**-sa lap-**pon**-ni-ka)
length 37–41 cm

A small number of Bar-tailed Godwits (under 15,000 pairs) breed in the peat bogs of Lapland and adjoining Russia, but most of us know this bird only as a common passage migrant and winter visitor. At these seasons it is found almost exclusively on selected muddy estuaries, often in large numbers, where it feeds on the intertidal mud for worms and bivalve molluscs. The females are larger than the males and their bills may be up to a third longer. As a result the sexes are often segregated on an estuary, with the males foraging on the open mudflats and the females paddling along the waterline, getting their feet wet and probing into the soft mud.

Two different populations of birds use European estuaries, and their migration strategies are subtly different. Those from Lapland and western Siberia spend the winter on the estuaries of Europe's western seaboard. They leave in March and April to travel to the Low Countries and the Baltic to fatten up and moult prior to migrating to their breeding grounds. The birds from central and eastern Siberia winter mostly in West Africa. On their return they don't fly direct, but use western Europe as a stopover, a habit that may add very considerably to their migratory journey. A single flight takes them to the same fattening sites as those used by the western birds, but they arrive later, in early May.

Birds of the eastern population moult in Africa before departing for the spring staging posts but, intriguingly, some carry out a further partial moult as soon as they arrive, making themselves look still finer and redder. This is probably physiologically unnecessary, but it speaks volumes for their fitness. A bit of showing off may well help them find a mate more quickly.

ID: Godwits second only to Curlews in size among estuary waders. Taller and more elegant than Bar-tailed, with longer legs and straighter bill. In breeding plumage has bars on belly, and reddish colour fades towards lower belly and flanks. In non-breeding plumage fairly plain, without streaks on back.

Black-tailed Godwit

Limosa limosa (lim-**moh**-sa lim-**moh**-sa)
length 36–44 cm

Both the godwit species are large waders with more or less straight bills. They are built for proper wading, having long legs and also partly webbed feet to enable them to walk on soft mud without sinking. They are at home in the water and often wade in up to their bellies; characteristically they immerse the whole of their head and neck below the surface as they feed. A foraging godwit tends to walk slowly forwards, leaning down to make shallow, exploratory probes; then without warning it switches to much deeper, more jabbing probes and triumphantly pulls out a worm or similar large morsel.

The Black-tailed Godwit inhabits gentler climates than the Bar-tailed. It is not a tundra bird, but instead thrives in damp meadows, poorly drained fields and wet moorland within our continental and temperate zones. It is one of the few waders to have increased in Europe in recent times, having been able to take advantage of the spread of farmland and fields under cultivation. In winter, in contrast to the marine Bar-tailed Godwit, it tends to favour freshwater meadows inland. But the Icelandic race is unusual in this respect; it winters on intertidal mudflats, mixing with its Bar-tailed equivalents.

In spring Black-tailed Godwits perform an impressive array of noisy display flights, made all the more eye-catching by the birds' highly contrasting black and white wing pattern. The 'ceremonial flight', carried out by males advertising their availability, consists of a preliminary rapid rise with fast wingbeats, a tumble, a strange flight with the wingbeats alternated and taking the bird in an erratic course ('limping flight'), and then a nose-dive towards the ground. All these manoeuvres may take place above occupied territories, but at this stage Black-tailed Godwits seem to consider the airspace above them to be neutral and communal.

Whimbrel

Numenius phaeopus (noo-**mee**-ni-uss **fee**-oh-puss)
length 40–42 cm

Remarkable though it may seem, the arrival date of some Whimbrels on their European breeding grounds is correlated to the rhythm of the moon: the full moon brings their pre-migration food supply, fiddler crabs, out in large numbers to look for a mate. The birds gorge on them, fuel up and fly from West Africa to Europe. The earlier the full moon occurs around the birds' general departure time (March and April), the earlier they set off.

Upon arrival here, Whimbrels settle on open tundra, on moorland with short vegetation or in peaty bogs among forests. Their centre of distribution is well to the north of that of the closely related Curlew. In the first few days of their stay Whimbrels often feed on berries, but then revert to a diet of insects, spiders, worms, snails and slugs. Wherever they occur they tend to pick from the surface rather than probing deeply as the Curlew does, although their kinked bill is handy for reaching down the short burrows of crabs in the non-breeding season.

The nest site itself is usually on dry, open ground. Both parents share incubation and tend the chicks, although the brood may be split early on, with the male tending the older chicks while the female stays on the nest. Some broods may eventually amalgamate into crèches, giving both adults the chance to begin their migration early. The crèche members stay together and migrate as a juvenile group.

ID: Very similar to Curlew but smaller, with a kink-tipped, rather than evenly curved bill. Flies with faster wingbeats and doesn't need a run to take off. Curlew has less patterned head. Distinctive call includes fast whistle of about seven evenly pitched notes.

adults

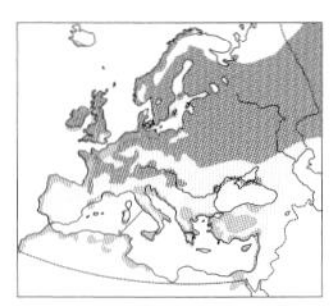

ID: Large wader with long, evenly curved bill. Unlikely to be confused with any other wader except Whimbrel.

adults

Curlew

Numenius arquata (noo-**mee**-ni-uss ar-**kway**-ta)
length 50–60 cm

You cannot miss the marvellous slim, curved bill of the Curlew – it defines the bird itself. But what is it for? On a simple level the answer is obvious: it allows the Curlew to reach into places that other waders cannot reach, and thus confers upon its owner a competitive advantage when foraging. But it takes a closer look to see just how useful the shape is. When the bill is poked through a narrow entrance – the burrow of an animal, for example, or the gap between rocks – the tip can investigate a greater surface area than a straight bill could. Another advantage is that, when a curved bill is probed into a soft substrate, such as mud, its turning circle at the tip is much wider than at the tip of a straight bill, so the Curlew can touch-detect prey over a relatively wider volume. Thirdly, the curved bill is slightly better for reaching prey on the surface.

But if a curved bill is so useful, why doesn't every wader have one? The answer is that the structure has its disadvantages, too. A curved bill is inherently much weaker than a straight one. It must be strengthened by a series of internal struts and thickenings. This is all very well, but it allows for only a narrow passage inside, and the tongue's operation is therefore limited to the part of the bill nearest the mouth, which means that the Curlew can swallow larger items only if they are brought to the surface.

Female Curlews have longer bills than males, and they are also larger and heavier-bodied. This means that in the wintertime the two sexes can segregate, where possible, into subtly different niches, the females occupying the muddy intertidal zone, the males utilising nearby pastureland and grassland. The females frequently hold feeding territories throughout the non-breeding season and may return to them year after year.

For breeding the Curlew occupies a wide range of sites in many climatic zones, from the fringes of the Arctic to the steppes of eastern Europe; these include moorland bogs, uplands and the edge of the tundra. Its only requirements are that that each site provides both damp places and dry patches, and that disturbance is reasonably limited. The nest is placed on the ground, often in an exposed place, but also sometimes on a tussock.

On arrival in spring, male Curlews defend discrete territories by means of a stereotyped song flight, consisting of a steep rise on fluttering wings, followed by a slow, parachuting descent with the wings held above the horizontal. It is not much different from many wader routines, but its accompaniment – the long, bubbling song – elevates it into an experience not to be missed. After a slow start the song builds up to an ecstatic fluty climax, one of the familiar, atmospheric sounds of lonely moorlands.

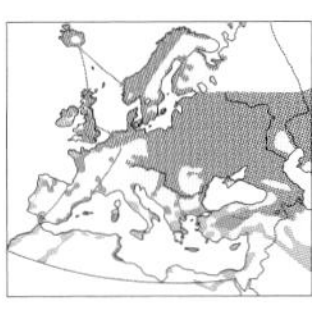

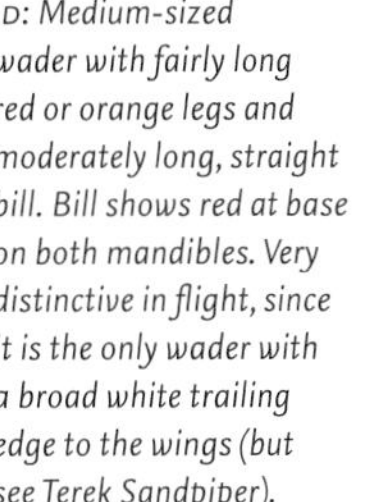

ID: Medium-sized wader with fairly long red or orange legs and moderately long, straight bill. Bill shows red at base on both mandibles. Very distinctive in flight, since it is the only wader with a broad white trailing edge to the wings (but see Terek Sandpiper).

Redshank

Tringa totanus (**trin**-ga toh-**tay**-nuss)
length 27–29 cm

Nobody entering the breeding territory of this exceptionally noisy bird is likely to leave without knowing what they have done. Latin in temperament, the Redshank reacts with vehemence to the slightest intrusion, making its loud whistling 'pew, pew' calls so persistently and angrily that, after a while, even the most determined of predators must begin to grow weary of the din. To make matters worse, the Redshank's alarm call is very much a rallying cry, so the air is soon thick with birds, all sounding off at maximum volume. It is an effective defence strategy and, indeed, other species of birds often breed near Redshanks, knowing that their nest site comes fitted with an early-warning system.

Birdwatchers are used to seeing hordes of waders using salt marshes in winter, but in the breeding season few of these birds remain – except, that is, Redshanks. Salt marshes are a major stronghold and in Britain, for example, over half the total population breeds in this habitat. Elsewhere the Redshank will occur anywhere with a high water table and saturated soil, and that may include freshwater marshes, wet grasslands, bogs and floodlands. It has a wide range in Europe and, although it does occur on the Arctic fringe, it is not, unlike most waders, a bird of the north.

Most pairs breed semi-colonially, which helps the birds make their concerted defence against predators. Display sites are often used communally, and there may be special pre-breeding zones used both for feeding and for meeting potential mates, a bit like clubs or restaurants. Redshanks have two methods of courtship; one, the song flight, a typical up-and-down 'switchback' routine on rapidly beaten wings, is performed by males advertising their bachelor status. The second is ground-based and is essentially a chase at low speed. One bird pursues the other, keeping a constant distance behind it so that if it loses ground it must fly along a little to keep up. If all goes well, the two birds will eventually progress to their pre-copulatory display, in which the male lifts his wings and beats them for quite a time before mounting. The wing lift and chase are common to courtship and aggression, so that in the early stages of pair formation it can be difficult to ascertain the gender of either bird.

Outside the breeding season some Redshanks occur inland, but the majority are found on estuaries and other coastal sites. Here they may use their medium-length bills to gather a variety of foods, but typically they exhibit a strong preference for a limited choice of great favourites. For example, in estuaries, Redshanks are particularly fond of a small shrimp-like crustacean called *Corophium volutator* and will eat it preferentially even when it occurs at low density. Not surprisingly, however, the birds tend to concentrate where it is abundant (there may be 6000 per square metre) and feed on the larger examples, finding them by spying them as they emerge from the mud. A single bird has been seen to eat about 50,000 *Corophium* over a 24-hour period.

Redshanks can feed by day or night, using both sight and touch, either in flocks or singly, with a minority of birds holding feeding territories. Essentially the Redshank, then, is an adaptable species, a fact that helps to explain its abundance and success.

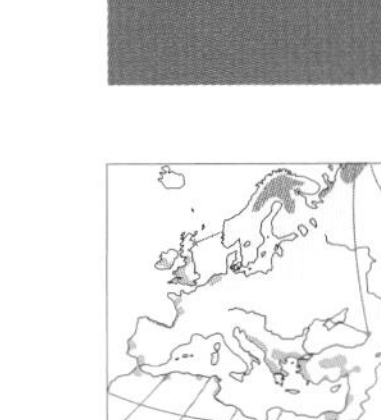

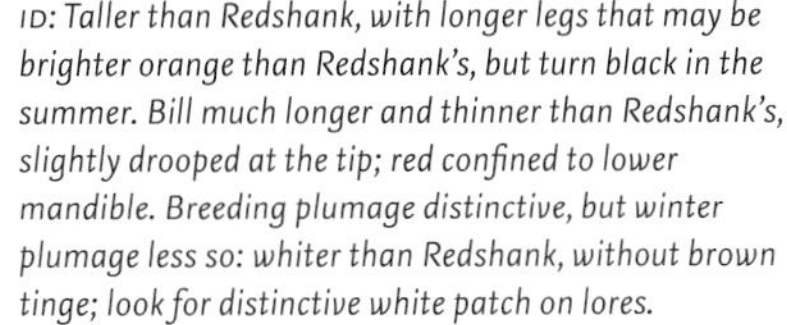

ID: Taller than Redshank, with longer legs that may be brighter orange than Redshank's, but turn black in the summer. Bill much longer and thinner than Redshank's, slightly drooped at the tip; red confined to lower mandible. Breeding plumage distinctive, but winter plumage less so: whiter than Redshank, without brown tinge; look for distinctive white patch on lores.

Spotted Redshank

Tringa erythropus (**trin**-ga er-**rith**-roh-puss)
length 29–31 cm

The Spotted Redshank is one of the best timekeepers among waders, or indeed among any birds – in Finland, for example, these birds invariably arrive on their breeding grounds between 1 and 8 May (usually on the 4th). They then breed and leave at intervals according to age and sex; the females depart on or about 10 June and travel down to the Waddensee off northern Germany to moult. Males and juveniles leave the breeding areas in the second half of July and in August and join them. Everyone travels south, mainly to Africa, in September. Few other bird species follow such rigid timetables.

Taking in the detail, you might have noticed that female Spotted Redshanks stay in the breeding areas for less than six weeks. That is a light burden for any reproducing bird, and the females work it by delegating most of the incubation and all the chick-rearing to the male – they simply lay the eggs, sit for a few incubating stints and take off. It's quick, it's efficient and there isn't much of a pair bond to leave behind anyway.

Spotted Redshanks avoid competition with Redshanks by feeding in deeper water. They have longer legs and longer bills, and are better able to wade, swim or even upend, like ducks, with head and neck submerged. They often feed socially, many individuals moving this way and that in an effort to panic and confuse shoals of small fish. At times they will also perform co-ordinated rushes, with many birds running abreast, bills half submerged in the water.

ID: Tall, pale wader with long, stout bill, slightly uptilted. Legs green. No wing bar, but rump and lower back white, tail white with faint markings. Often looks dark above, especially on wings, and pale below. In winter, wings dark and head very pale.

Terek Sandpiper

Xenus cinereus (**zee**-nuss si-**nee**-ri-uss)
length 22–24 cm

A rare breeding bird in Finland, Russia, Estonia and Belarus, the Terek Sandpiper reached our area only in the last hundred years or so and has been regular here only since about 1950. It occurs in boreal river valleys, especially in places with extensive wet grasslands dotted with scrubby bushes.

It shares many characteristics with the Common Sandpiper, such as the habit of bobbing its tail up and down and skimming low over the water. Its long, uptilted bill, however, is diagnostic and is used for probing into mud. In the non-breeding season it hunts burrowing crabs, but in the summer it appears to subsist mainly on gnats.

Greenshank

Tringa nebularia (**trin**-ga neb-boo-**lay**-ri-a)
length 30–33 cm

There's nothing like a good breeding site and, once a Greenshank has obtained one, it will return to it year after year. As a bonus, it might find last year's mate waiting for it upon arrival, for some pairs enjoy a continuity that is unusual among waders. Admittedly a few male Greenshanks will mate with more than one female in a season, but this is unusual and the rest are solidly monogamous.

Greenshanks breed in moorland and tundra, often not far from tree cover. Upon arrival on site the males perform an impressive rising and falling display flight, in which they first gain height with laboured wingbeats and then, with a wing shiver, glide down with bowed wings, describing a series of circles. This flight may take them up to 300 m above ground, and once they reach their personal summit the displaying birds begin a fluty repetition of double notes to accompany their slow descent.

Somehow, in between displays, the busy males also find time to build several nest scrapes within the territory, one of which will be selected to hold the eggs. These nests are often placed close to stones or logs of wood, presumably to enable the adults to find them. The female incubates the eggs and tends the chicks in their early days, but before long she abandons the family and migrates south. Male and young follow later, sometimes together.

The Greenshank is the largest 'shank' and has the heaviest bill, which is used extensively for probing into soft mud. That's not the only feeding technique, though: the Greenshank will also move its bill tip from side to side over mud, or pick straight from the surface. Birds also chase fish, by lunging at them, herding them or detecting them by running the bill tip through the water.

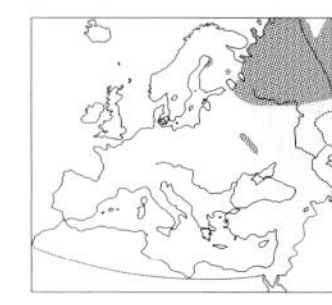

ID: Distinctive, dashing small wader with unique, slightly uptilted bill. Short legs yellow. upperparts grey-brown, underparts white. Thin white trailing edge to wings.

Wood Sandpiper

Tringa glareola (**trin**-ga glay-ri-**oh**-la)
length 19–23 cm

With its longer legs and longer, thinner bill, the Wood Sandpiper has more strings to its bow when foraging than the Green. While the latter mainly picks, the Wood Sandpiper can pick from the surface, probe into submerged mud and sweep its bill from side to side in the water. It will also run after flying insects and snap them up, often after a jump. So, not only does it eat the usual insects and their larvae (beetles are especially important), but it can also acquire such exotic extras as seeds, fish and even small frogs.

It breeds in north and northeast Europe, where it inhabits marshy, waterlogged ground with copious rich vegetation, not necessarily with a growth of shrubs or trees (so the English name is misleading). It typically sites its nest deep in the vegetation, either on the ground or on some raised clump such as a tussock. Raised sites may be surrounded by water, giving the birds their very own 'moat'. Birds with further delusions of grandeur lay their eggs inside the abandoned nest of another bird, stealing the thunder of the Green Sandpiper.

It vacates its breeding areas entirely in the wintertime, migrating to tropical Africa. Those that breed in shrubby habitats forsake these for more open areas and, in contrast to the secretive Green Sandpiper, Wood Sandpipers readily feed in small flocks far from cover and with the sun on their backs.

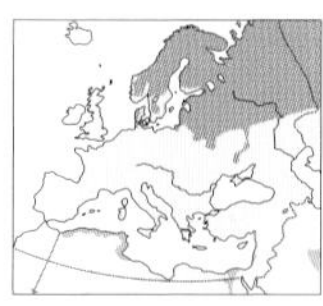

ID: Small but tall, with bright yellow-green legs. Always looks browner above than Green Sandpiper and has prominent pale supercilium. Chest lacks prominent white/dark contrast of Green Sandpiper. In flight, no wing bars; narrow black and white bars on tail.

Green Sandpiper

Tringa ochropus (**trin**-ga **oh**-kro-puss)
length 21–24 cm

Wader nest sites are often nothing to write home about, but the Green Sandpiper's is truly unusual. It lays its eggs well above ground, the only European wader to do so habitually (Wood Sandpipers occasionally do). It uses abandoned nests of thrushes, Wood Pigeons or even squirrels and lays its eggs straight inside, usually with a minimum of modification to the structure, or material added. The nest is often 10 m or more above ground, in a thick pine or spruce tree. So young Green Sandpipers have an extra hazard to add to the usual ones faced by their peers – an early jump down to the ground!

This species is widely distributed in the taiga belt of northern Europe, breeding in swampy wooded areas and boggy open forest. On migration and in winter it leaves behind its attachment to trees and moves to treeless freshwater sites with thick waterside vegetation and ditches, where it can hide away and pick for insect larvae and other invertebrates. When flushed it has a panicky, zigzagging escape flight, similar to that of the Snipe.

Green Sandpipers form monogamous pair bonds but, almost as soon as the young have hatched, one bird – usually the female – abandons the family and migrates. In some years, then, the first autumn migrants are recorded south of the breeding range as early as the second half of June.

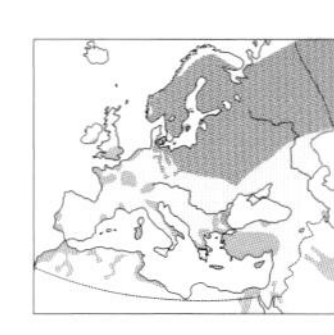

ID: Very dark above, clean white below, with sharp contrast between the two on breast. Bill fairly long and straight, legs green. Lores white, but no supercilium beyond eye. In flight no wing bar, and rump shows brilliant white. Zebra-crossing pattern to tail, bars broad.

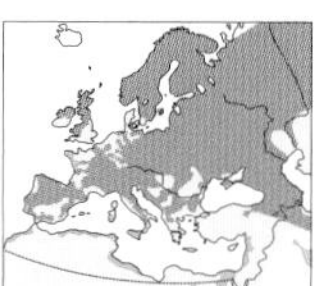

ID: Horizontal or crouching in posture, with small head and medium-length straight bill. Legs greenish. Tail projects beyond wing tips. Clear border between white belly and grey-brown chest, and a tongue of white reaches up to the shoulder. White wing bar.

Common Sandpiper

Actitis hypoleucos (ak-**tie**-tiss hie-poh-**loo**-koss)
length 19–21 cm

The Common Sandpiper is unusual among small waders in being easy to identify, mostly by features that are purely behavioural. When feeding, for instance, it cannot stop bobbing its rear end up and down, and when it takes off it has a flight style all its own.

The bobbing up and down ('teetering') is curious. Several other waders wag their tails and hindquarters, but none do it to the same exhaustive extent as the Common Sandpiper. It is suggested that the motion makes the birds more obvious, and is perhaps an individual's signal to its peers that a part of the river is occupied. Another theory is that it mimics the swaying of plants in flowing water and thus makes a bird less obvious. Both cannot be right, of course!

The flight style of the Common Sandpiper takes it very low over the water, with wings held rigid and the beats in bursts, irregular and stiff; the bird intermittently glides. The wingbeats, moreover, are oddly curtailed; the wings never reach above the horizontal, so there seems to be very little upstroke. It is a flight method that takes the Common Sandpiper along more slowly than other waders, only to 30–40 km/h, about half the usual value. But it also accommodates an unusual escape response. If a dangerous bird predator gets too close, a Common Sandpiper will dive into the water, then swim in safety to the shore using kicks of its feet and a rowing action of the wings.

It is easy to understand, then, the Common Sandpiper's choice of habitat. It breeds beside lakes, rivers and streams, and is particularly drawn to the fast-flowing sections of the upper reaches. Within this habitat it is tolerant of climate and altitude, breeding from sea level to 4000 m and from the Arctic fringes almost to the Mediterranean. In winter those that remain in Europe (primarily in the south) encompass a wider range of habitats, including rocky shores.

The Common Sandpiper is almost entirely insectivorous, detecting its prey by sight and not using its bill to probe. It is a busy feeder, moving quickly along, picking from the shore, searching in cracks or taking excursions into grassland. It often creeps up on prey, stalking with its body crouched. Its feeding methods demand a certain privacy, and individuals often maintain feeding territories to ensure this.

Pairs are monogamous and defend a linear territory along watercourses or shorelines. The nest is built on the ground, often concealed by thick, hanging vegetation. Sometimes it is just a scrape, one chosen from several made by both sexes; at other times it can be a more substantial, better-crafted cup.

Marsh Sandpiper

Tringa stagnatilis (**trin**-ga stag-**nay**-til-liss)
length 22–24 cm

Some birds have a look and a character all of their own, and the Marsh Sandpiper is one of these. Its delicate feeding style, in which it picks invertebrates from the water surface or mud with meticulous stabs of its needle-thin bill, nicely complements its smart profile of slim body and long legs. It is a true wading wader, able to move sedately through even quite deep water, up to its chest at times but, in contrast to the other leggy sandpipers, it doesn't normally swim. It will scythe its bill from side to side through the water like a miniature Spoonbill, hoping to detect food items in suspension by touch. And although usually elegant to a T, it will sometimes leave its dignity behind on fast dashes in pursuit of agile prey, rather like a Little Egret.

Marsh Sandpipers are sociable in an informal way, never forming huge, dense flocks, but preferring company nonetheless. But they are perhaps more notable for their reliance on other species. When feeding they have no hesitation in following ducks, herons and other waders, picking up what these birds disturb. And when breeding, pairs may nest among colonies of large waders, gulls and terns, taking advantage of the communal vigilance against predators.

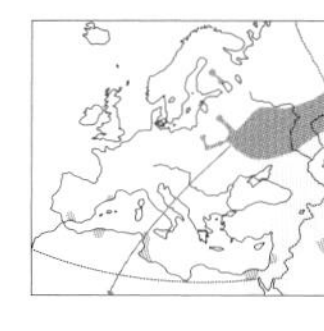

ID: Distinctive shape with very long, pale green legs and fairly long, straight, needle-thin bill. In flight, pattern similar to Greenshank, but smaller and more slender. Neatly spotted and streaked in summer plumage.

ID: *Small but plump wader with short orange legs and short stout bill. In winter, white below, dark and scaly above, with messy pattern on head and bold breast band. Summer plumage tortoiseshell-coloured, distinctive.*

Turnstone

Arenaria interpres (ar-ree-**nay**-ri-a in-**ter**-preez)
length 22–24 cm

The Turnstone is very much the beachcomber among waders. Not for it a sissy slender bill with curves and supreme tactile efficiency – it has a thick, short bill and exceptionally strong neck muscles to go with it. Its typical foraging method is summed up by its name: it turns over stones and debris to reveal edible items underneath, or pushes them aside, a technique that requires strength and resourcefulness. At times, several Turnstones will line up and, with a metaphorical 'heave-ho', pool their resources to overturn a large item such as a dead fish.

The word 'edible' can be stretched to its limit, as evidenced by the record of one Turnstone consuming soap. Its diet is more varied than that of any other wader, including fish, crustaceans, insects, molluscs, starfish and scraps thrown out in human rubbish. There is even an infamous record of one feeding from a human corpse. Turnstones almost invariably nest among colonies of other seabirds and 'reward' the latter for their vigilance and protection by eating their eggs.

Individual birds often have their own specialisations and preferences for feeding, but these may be modified by group dynamics. Turnstones have been studied outside the breeding season, when they gather into close-knit flocks of 10–30, and it transpires that the dominant members keep a keen eye on their subordinates and prevent them from feeding in the most effective manner – that is, by flicking or nudging debris to the side by the bill. Instead, as most females do, they must turn over pebbles and other small items. If they contravene their duties, they may be attacked and even killed. And there is no hope of fooling anyone, because an individual is recognisable by its own unique pattern on the face, and experiments have proven that these birds are indeed able to tell their associates apart.

Male and female Turnstones also have characteristic head patterns, and this, no doubt, helps them to re-form pairs each breeding season, if both members survive. Otherwise there is little in the way of courtship display, except for chases on the ground and in flight. The male does perform a display flight, but it is mostly silent and used less often than in most other waders.

Once pairs are formed the male and female are rarely apart, and her mate's close presence enables the female to feed up effectively for egg formation and incubation, often trying out thorough foraging techniques that might be too dangerous to attempt alone. The nest is a shallow depression lined with leaves, and both sexes contribute to the tending of the young. There is some evidence that Turnstones have a truly extraordinary method of nest defence: apparently they may peck into the anal opening of the unfortunate intruder.

Turnstones are highly migratory. Birds breeding in Fennoscandia and western Russia migrate via Europe to West and North Africa; those breeding further east winter in the eastern Mediterranean; and the birds found on rocky shores and jetties in northwest Europe are part of the breeding population from Greenland and Canada.

Red-necked Phalarope

Phalaropus lobatus (fa-la-**roh**-puss lo-**bay**-tuss)
length 18–19 cm

The Phalaropes are strange waders that are often placed in their own special family. Unlike the rest they are essentially swimmers, whose breast plumage is so dense that they float on the water like ducks – or perhaps more like corks. They have small webs between their feet, and their laterally compressed legs each have several lateral lobes that aid in swimming (the same arrangement as a Coot). Although principally aquatic ,they are highly capable of walking on land and perform impressive migratory flights, sometimes at considerable altitude.

The Red-necked Phalarope breeds in northern marshes and tundra, selecting sites where there are plenty of small pools. Its main food items at this season are gnats and other flying insects, plus a few snails and worms. The Red-necked Phalarope employs several methods of feeding, including picking food from the surface of the water or vegetation, and fluttering after flying insects, but its most celebrated trick is known as spinning. This technique is much as it sounds: the swimming bird rotates in a circle on the spot, hoping to swirl food particles up to the surface and within reach.

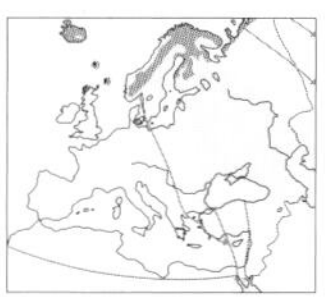

ID: Breeding plumage unmistakable; male slightly less colourful than female. In non-breeding plumage best distinguished from Grey Phalarope by much thinner, needle-like bill.

At the high latitudes where Red-necked Phalaropes live, the breeding season is very short, so these birds are among a handful of Arctic species that reverse the normal sex roles. The female is 10 per cent larger than the male and she initiates display. Both sexes take part in nest building, but the male then undertakes the bulk of the incubation and all the brooding and tending of the young, allowing the female, where possible, to seek out another mate and produce another clutch. Role reversal is a key way to reduce the female's load during breeding.

After their brief flutter with the northern tundra, Red-necked Phalaropes undertake an extraordinary overland migration. First they head south or southeast and stop off on large water bodies in western Asia, including the Black and Caspian Seas, performing this transfer in a non-stop flight. Then, after a pause of a few weeks, they move on south, and winter out of sight of land in the Arabian Sea.

Grey Phalarope

Phalaropus fulicarius
(fa-la-**roh**-puss foo-li-**kay**-ri-uss)
length 20–22 cm

The Grey Phalarope lives the life of a seabird that somewhat reluctantly comes ashore seasonally to breed. It is a rarity in our region, nesting only in Iceland and Svalbard, on coastal marshy tundra with plenty of pools or on dry sandy ground near the sea. During its stay it practises the same role-reversal strategy as the Red-necked Phalarope, and the females sometimes lay two clutches for different males. It is less colonial than the Red-necked Phalarope.

The moment the young have taken flight the male and his family make straight for the sea. Here they will spend the next eight months or so, migrating over the ocean to the rich oceanic upwellings that occur off West and South Africa. Grey Phalaropes do not, therefore, take an overland route as Red-necked Phalaropes do, but on their way south they are vulnerable to westerly gales that can whisk them to inshore waters or even a long way inland. Their buoyancy, such an advantage at most times, is a liability in a powerful wind.

On the ocean Grey Phalaropes feed on plankton and tiny fish. They have unusually broad bills for scooping plankton from the water, and this may be transported up the bill, captured in a droplet, by surface tension. To feed effectively, Grey Phalaropes need water containing 50,000 organisms per litre or more. Such densities are found near debris such as floating seaweed, and also near marine mammals; Grey Phalaropes have been recorded picking organisms off a whale's back!

ID: Brilliant breeding plumage unmistakable, although male less colourful than female. More frequent in non-breeding plumage in Europe than Red-necked Phalarope; has relatively thick, laterally flattened bill that is yellow at the base; doesn't look needle-thin. Grey back without pale stripes.

Skuas family *Stercorariidae* (ster-koh-ra-**rie**-id-ee)

Habitat For breeding, mainly tundra and islands. At sea for the rest of the year.
Food Almost anything, but mainly meat, obtained by catching mammals, birds and fish, or by harrying birds to steal a meal from them. They are also scavengers.
Movements Highly migratory, dispersing far into the oceans, often crossing the equator.
Voice In contrast to gulls and terns, not very vocal, and silent at sea. On breeding grounds a few grunts, mewing calls and wails.
Pairing style Monogamous.
Nesting Pomarine and Long-tailed Skuas solitary and highly territorial. Great and Arctic Skuas sometimes solitary but also form colonies, defending a small area around the nest but feeding outside the territory.
Nest A scrape in the ground.
Productivity 1 brood a year.
Eggs 2.
Incubation 23–29 days, by both sexes.
Young Semi-precocial and downy.
Parenting style Young are fed and tended by both adults. Female skuas are larger than males, so when the chicks are young they defend the territory while the males hunt for food. If ground intruders, including people, threaten the nest, they are dive-bombed fiercely. A skua usually strikes at the head, and can draw blood.
Food to young Regurgitated meat.
Leaving nest Any time between 24 and 44 days.

Great Skua

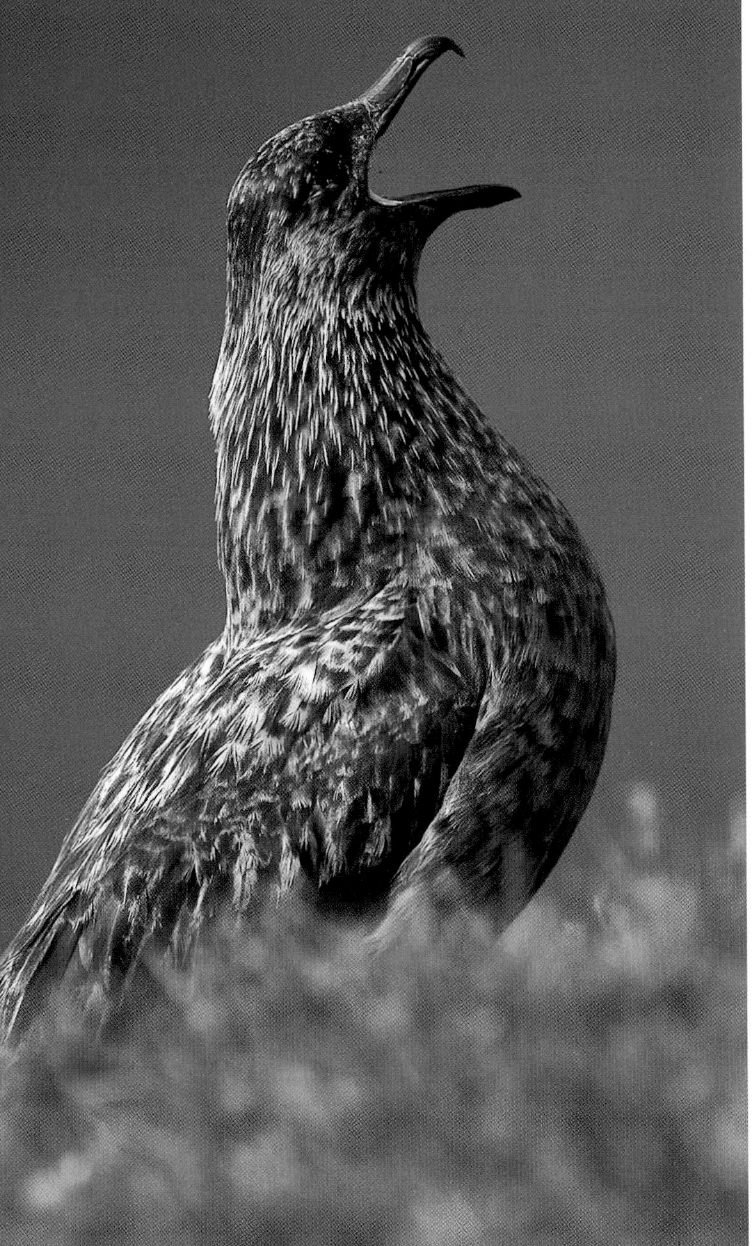

Skuas are superficially similar to gulls, but they differ by having the most extraordinary feet. These are webbed to help the birds swim in the water, but they are also fitted with murderous, predatory claws. The skuas are the only birds in the world to have such a combination.

Seabirds to the core, our four species are birds of cold latitudes. They have dense plumage, heavily protected feet and a high metabolic rate, all of which exclude them from breeding much below about 59°N. This must come as a relief to the gulls, terns and auks that nest further south, because the skuas, as a family, are both predatory and piratical, both dangerous and a pest: one of their features is a tendency to chase after other birds and harass them in order to steal the food that they are bringing to their young. Skuas are hawk-like in shape, with long, narrow wings, enabling them to fly with great skill after their victims, tailgating close behind to intimidate them and following every twist and turn. After a few minutes of such treatment most birds drop or disgorge their catch, and the skua mops it up.

Skuas are also killers. The Great Skua, for example, will catch and eat such birds as Storm-Petrels and Puffins, and the Long-tailed and Pomarine Skuas subsist largely on lemmings when breeding. Skuas have a strong bill with a hook at the tip which, together with the claws, does the damage.

A curious feature of skua plumage is the existence of different colour schemes, something which is most obvious in Arctic and Pomarine Skuas. Both these species have both dark and light 'phases', which occur at consistent levels within each population, although the percentage differs between populations – there tend to be more light birds the further north you go. It is thought that light-phase birds, with their pale underparts making them difficult to see from below, are mainly predatory in nature and can swoop down on lemmings, whereas the dark-phase ones, hard to see against the sea as they come in low, are mainly robbers of seabirds.

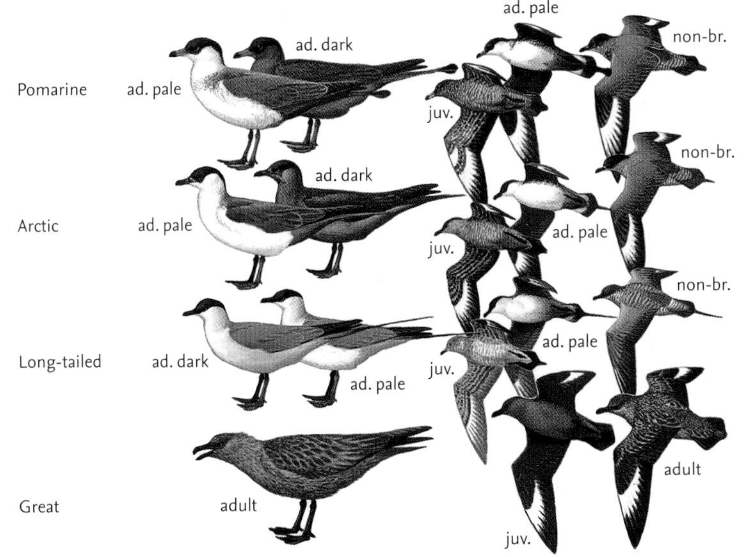

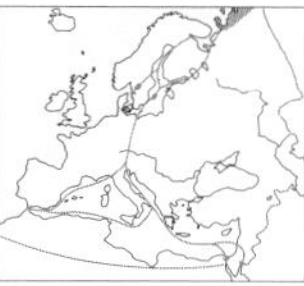

ID: *A large, heavy skua, about the size of Lesser Black-backed Gull and with characteristic blob-tipped tail feathers. Much bulkier than Arctic, with ample chest. Flies with shallow wingbeats and may recall Great Skua at a distance, which Arctic seldom does. In breeding plumage light phase has more yellow on face than Arctic, a breast band and a pink-based bill, latter feature shared by dark phase. Dark phase scarce.*

Pomarine Skua

Stercorarius pomarinus

(ster-koh-**ray**-ri-uss poh-mar-**rie**-nuss)

length 46–51 cm

The Pomarine Skua is very similar to the Arctic Skua to look at, but appearances deceive. Recent genetic studies have shown that the Pomarine is extremely close to the very different-looking Great Skua – so close, in fact, that their DNA is almost identical. The more imaginative theories hold that the Pomarine might have arisen through hybridisation between Great and Arctic Skuas when the forebears of the Great Skua broke through into the northern hemisphere as recently as the 15th century. More mundanely, the Pomarine might simply have nicked some DNA off a Great Skua when the two hybridised.

This species breeds on the very northeastern fringe of our area, in the tundra. It has a more strictly coastal distribution than the Long-tailed Skua, but shares that species' fanatical taste for those hard-pressed northern rodents, the lemmings, which can account for 90 per cent of its summer diet. In contrast to the Long-tailed Skua, the Pomarine hunts for these mostly on the ground and is perfectly capable of digging them out of their burrows. The remaining 10 per cent of the diet is made up of the eggs and young of neighbouring smaller birds.

Pomarines are extremely aggressive to other skuas in defence of their territory, protecting every corner of it from all comers. Strangely, though, they are rarely aggressive toward human intruders. Theirs is a multi-purpose territory, used for courtship, nesting and most of their foraging. Not surprisingly, Pomarines lack the colonial tendencies shown by some other skuas.

Outside the breeding season Pomarine Skuas move out to sea and migrate down to West Africa. Here they subsist mainly on fish, but will also catch and eat smaller seabirds such as gulls and phalaropes. Occasionally they will harass seabirds for disgorged food instead, and have been seen forcing them into the ocean to drown.

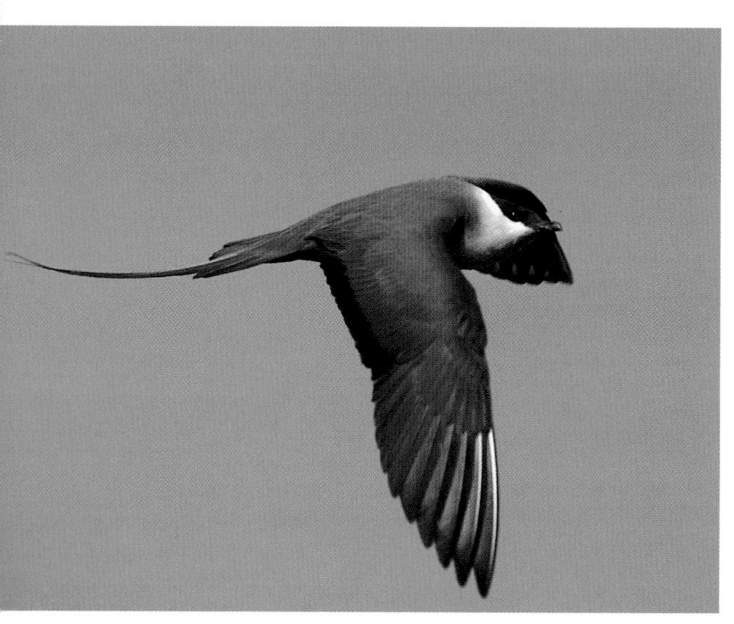

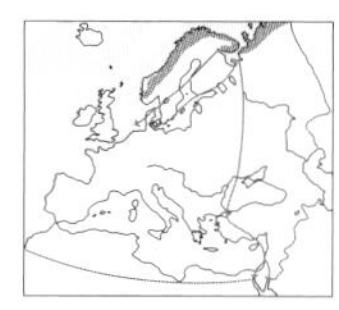

ID: *Very light skua with almost tern-like flight. Adults easily distinguished from other skuas by the long, pointed tail, and also by relatively narrow wings. Lighter above than other skuas. Dark phase almost unknown.*

Long-tailed Skua

Stercorarius longicaudus

(ster-koh-**ray**-ri-uss lon-ji-**kow**-duss)

length 48–53 cm (including tail streamers up to 22 cm long)

Of the three similar skuas, the Long-tailed is the smallest, lightest and most elegant in flight. It does not make a career out of chasing birds and robbing them of food, but instead is an effective predator of small mammals in the tundra of the Arctic and sub-Arctic. It finds these by hovering in the air 20–50 m over a likely spot and diving down to intercept the rodents on the ground. Once it has cornered prey the Long-tailed Skua does not apply the *coup de grace* with its claws, but instead pecks the victim to death, keeping its feet out of the way. And then, oddly, having taken the trouble to acquire a good meal, it often shakes out the rodent's entrails and eats only these, leaving the rest behind. In some areas lemmings constitute 99 per cent of the summer food.

The Long-tailed Skua's ability in the air does allow it some flexibility in diet when required. It can hawk insects by swooping around, for instance, and on the unusual occasions when it pursues birds for scraps it does so with great expertise. It will eat eggs, berries and even songbirds. Away from its breeding areas, on the oceans, it is thought to feed on fish and offal, and will at times grab these from the surface while swimming.

It is not known precisely where Long-tailed Skuas winter, but they are often recorded in the Atlantic off South Africa and South America at the right time of year. They are certainly transequatorial migrants, departing from Europe in July and August and travelling far out to sea, out of reach of most observations.

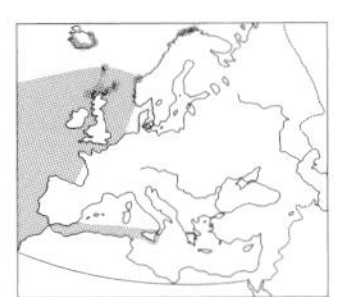

ID: A heavy-bodied bird, about the size of a large gull. Dark brown plumage with light speckles and a thick, dark grey bill with a slightly hooked tip. In flight identified by its broad wings, very short tail and prominent white bases to the primaries producing 'wing flashes' above and below. Not much variation in plumage, unlike other skuas.

Great Skua

Catharacta skua (kath-ar-**ak**-ta **skoo**-a)
length 53–58 cm

To other birds Pomarine Skuas are a threat, Arctic Skuas a nuisance and Great Skuas just plain dangerous. The last named are much the most predatory of their family, and often eat other birds instead of bothering to rob them. There are astonishing records of Great Skuas killing birds as large as geese, and mammals up to the size of blue hares. Great Skuas commonly consume Kittiwakes and Puffins, ambushing the latter as they exit their nest holes, and some have taken to feeding at night, picking off Storm-Petrels on their way to their burrows.

Adaptability in diet and hunting method is a key talent of the Great Skua, and there is evidence that birds learn from others so that colonies have their own local speciality. In Iceland, for example, Great Skuas tended to avoid bothering Fulmars until 1940, but then a few broke the mould and the habit spread. And it is safer to be an adult Kittiwake on Foula in Shetland, where you are usually left alone, than on the nearby island of Noss, where your life is in constant danger. Being a Great Skua yourself does not necessarily confer immunity, because these birds have a distasteful habit of catching and eating their neighbours' chicks.

Battles between Great Skuas and Gannets can be spellbinding to watch, and prolonged, neither bird wanting to give way. Gannets are large birds with sharp bills, and they should be a good match for a skua; furthermore one would not expect them to be keen on the idea of giving up a fish meal that they might have travelled 200 km to catch. But Great Skuas fly at them and attack them physically, attempting to grab them by the wing tips and sometimes, in so doing, forcing them into the sea. Usually, to escape the Great Skuas' attentions, victimised Gannets will reluctantly regurgitate their hard-won catch.

The Great Skua has a restricted world distribution, being confined as a breeding species to Europe. It has several close relatives in the southern hemisphere and curiously, in contrast to these species, it has not managed to conquer the polar hinterland, a place where it might be expected to thrive.

ID: *About the size of a kittiwake, with narrow-based wings and a pointed tail. Pale phase lacks breast-band and has smaller cap than Pomarine Skua, with rather little yellow on the cheek; bill black. Both phases (both common) have smaller wing flashes than Pomarine. Has dashing flight in comparison to more ponderous and powerful Pomarine and Great Skuas.*

Arctic Skua

Stercorarius parasiticus

(ster-koh-**ray**-ri-uss par-ra-**sie**-ti-kuss)

length 41–46 cm

This, the commonest of Europe's breeding skuas, has adopted two quite different ways of life in different parts of its range. In the Arctic it may live at low density on the tundra, feeding on small birds and their eggs, plus berries and insects, but not, in contrast to Long-tailed and Pomarine Skuas, taking very many lemmings. Elsewhere, breeding on coastal moorland and offshore islands, it feeds itself and its young almost entirely on food stolen from other seabirds. Its chief victims are Arctic Terns, Kittiwakes, Puffins and Black Guillemots, and these are forced to drop fish that they are carrying whole to the young or, in the case of Kittiwakes, to disgorge the meal that they would feed to the young by regurgitation.

When an Arctic Skua robs a fellow seabird it does not ask nicely. It approaches the target in purposeful flight, similar in manner to that of a bird of prey, sometimes diving from above like a Peregrine and taking the victim by surprise. Many birds are startled into dropping their food, which the skua may field in flight before it reaches the water. Other species are hassled repeatedly, the skua invading their personal space and following on their coat-tails. An Arctic Skua is a fast and skilful flier, with plenty of stamina, and is hard to shake off. It also projects a clear threat of violence and has the ability to carry it out, although usually intimidation is quite enough.

These miscreants often breed on the wetter parts of moors, especially when their distribution overlaps that of the Great Skua, which claims the dry spots. Pairs that are well spaced obtain most of their food inside their borders, whereas those in loose colonies defend only the immediate vicinity of the nest and commute to the nearest seabird colony. Whichever strategy they choose, Arctic Skuas are highly aggressive in defence of their nest. Intruding humans are attacked by dive-bombing, and unsuspecting birdwatchers may sustain minor injuries.

In common with other skuas, the Arctic Skua is principally a summer visitor to Europe, leaving in autumn and wintering south of the equator. On the first leg of their journey some individuals travel overland and may be seen in central Europe and the Black Sea. Others, cunningly, escort flocks of Arctic Terns as these move south along the coast, and rob them every step of the way.

Gulls family *Laridae* (lah-rid-ee)

Habitat Breed in almost any maritime habitat, including cliffs and cliff tops, islands, salt marshes and beaches. Inland, may use lakes, marshes and steppes. In winter they often spend more time at sea, but also visit rubbish dumps, docks, towns, farmland and pasture.
Food Essentially omnivorous, taking many food types over a lifetime, but often concentrating on a few sorts of abundantly available food. Many take fish, and inland species often eat insects.
Movements Most are migratory, but often do not travel far. All species that breed in Europe winter here, too.
Voice Very noisy and may dominate a neighbourhood; it is their calls that, above all others, convey seaside atmosphere. A wide variety of sounds, including the multi-syllabled, laughing 'long call' and various wails and mews.
Pairing style Monogamous, often for the long term. There are occasional instances of polygynous trios and female–female pairs (see introduction).
Nesting Almost exclusively in colonies, but some species may nest as single pairs in the colony of another species. Some species nest singly at times.
Nest A cup of vegetation, such as seaweed, varying considerably in dimensions, even within a species. Usually on the ground or on a cliff.
Productivity 1 brood a year.
Eggs 2–3 (Kittiwake usually 2).
Incubation 21–35 days, by both adults.
Young Semi-precocial and downy, with cryptic coloration.
Parenting style Both adults tend and feed the young. To beg, the young may peck at the orange spot that is present at the tip of some adult gulls' bills.
Food to young Regurgitated fish and other matter.
Leaving nest Any time between 3 and 7 weeks.

Herring Gull

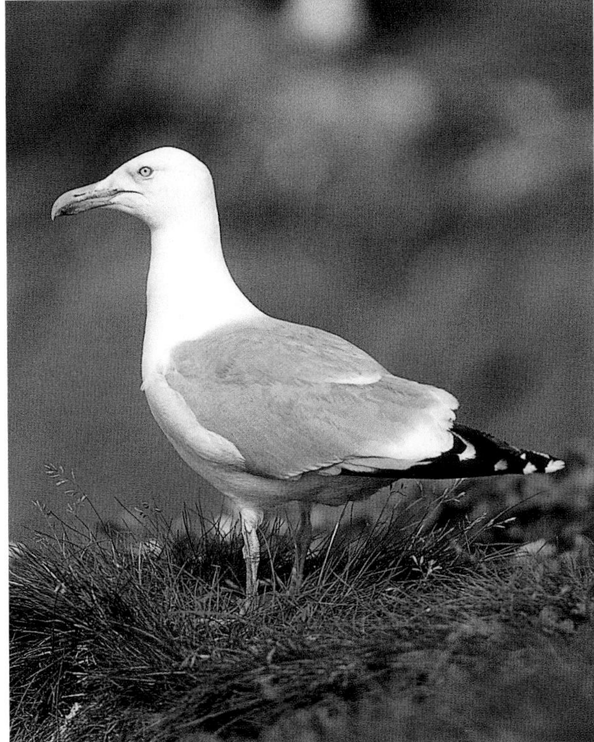

Gulls are among the most successful and visible of all the birds in Europe. They are hard to miss, especially on the coast. It would be wrong to call them 'seagulls', though, as many people do, because many species preferentially breed inland, near lakes, and others come inland to feed on pasture, farmland and rubbish tips in the winter.

The gulls are professional generalists. They can eat almost anything (fish, though, are usually important) and employ a wide variety of techniques to obtain their food. They are excellent fliers, excellent swimmers and they run well on land, making them remarkably flexible in terms of locomotion. Add to this boldness and considerable intelligence, and you can begin to understand why the family is so successful.

Gulls are easy to recognise as such, since they all have much the same shape, with heavy bodies, fairly long legs and webbed feet. All adults are predominantly white below, grey or black above. Some have smart black or brown heads in the breeding season, and most have black wing tips (this reduces plumage wear, because granules of the black pigment melanin fortify the keratin of the feathers and make them resistant to abrasion) with white spots at the end, known as 'mirrors'. The bare parts, at least, are far more colourful than the rest, and it is often these that change colour in the breeding season to make a gull's juices flow. The sexes are invariably identical in plumage and, in order to prevent too many misunderstandings, gulls have developed a wide range of gestures at their colonies to represent aggression, appeasement and courtship. A colony of gulls in the breeding season, with all its nodding, shaking and strutting, resembles a convention of Freemasons.

A few of these displays are easy to understand. A bird leaning forward and belting out its so-called 'long call', as uninhibited as an opera singer, is being territorial. A gull tugging at the grass is deflecting its anger. And a male arriving at his territory and throwing up on the ground is being a good provider; his female will readily accept the offering.

On the whole gulls are monogamous and their pair bonds often last for life. There are records of trios, usually with a male paired to two females, and different species of gulls sometimes hybridise. A very unusual facet of mating behaviour, though, seen in Herring Gulls among others, is the occasional but regular existence of female–female pairs. They have no sexual relationship as such but, having enlisted the grateful help of nearby males, the two may lay eggs and bring up the resulting chicks together.

Young gulls could have been designed to confuse birdwatchers. They take a number of years to mature, and during this time they moult twice a year, changing slightly on each occasion. A gull chick is fluffy at first and then obtains its first feathers, its juvenile plumage. A few weeks later, in the autumn, it moults into first-winter plumage, and then into first-summer plumage the following spring. When just over a year old it moults into second-winter plumage, then second-summer and so on. Gull enthusiasts adore identifying each one of these guises and gleefully discuss tertial steps, feather fringes, gonydeal angles and other such exotica.

Sabine's Gull

Larus sabini (**lah**-russ sab-**bie**-nie)
length 27–33 cm

A smartly plumaged gull of the High Arctic, the Sabine's nests sporadically on Svalbard, but is a regular autumn passage migrant to the northeast Atlantic, passing well offshore. Most individuals seen in European waters are actually breeding birds from Greenland and Canada, which have crossed the Atlantic Ocean and are skirting our waters on their way down to the productive ocean west of southern Africa. The peak of passage is between late August and mid-October, the adults appearing before the juveniles. If these migrants encounter westerly gales en route they may be found in large numbers off our coasts, especially in the Bay of Biscay.

The Sabine's is an expert at picking small fish and invertebrates from the surface of the sea, perhaps even more so than the Little Gull. But it practises a range of other feeding techniques, including plunge diving, picking from the surface while swimming and running along beaches in a stop-start manner, rather like a plover.

The moult sequence is unusual. The autumn moult is late and may even overlap with the spring one. As a result, the autumn adults seen in Europe are dark-hooded and the young birds still in juvenile plumage.

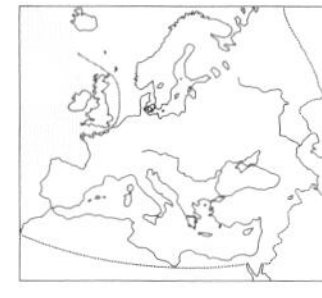

ID: Smaller than Black-headed Gull, with small head and long, sharply pointed wings. Uniquely, tail is slightly forked, but this can be difficult to see.

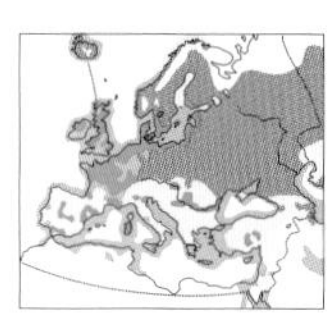

ID: One of Europe's commonest gulls. Small, with a slender bill and narrow, pointed wings that tend to beat fast for a gull. Easy to recognise in breeding plumage (February–July) by the chocolate-brown (not black) hood and white nape.

Black-headed Gull

Larus ridibundus (**lah**-russ rie-dib-**bun**-duss)
length 34–37 cm; wingspan 1–1.1 m

Undoubtedly the most successful of all the small gulls, the Black-headed is found virtually throughout our region; it is the only gull that breeds extensively in inland continental Europe as well as widely on the coast. Birds breeding by the sea are found on salt marshes, sand dunes and offshore islands, whereas those inland occupy marshes, lagoons and the margins of rivers and lakes. Interestingly, almost all inland breeding birds migrate to the coast for the winter, while some coastal birds move in the opposite direction, seeking out lakes, agricultural fields and man-made habitats, including towns and cities.

For breeding, the Black-headed Gull requires the presence of sheltered, shallow water, where it can indulge in its favoured foraging methods, such as flying low over the surface and dipping down or plunging in after prey. Scientists have shown that being white below aids the capture of waterborne prey; birds dyed black on their bellies were more conspicuous to fish and invertebrates, and their foraging success diminished as a result. Birds also snatch food as they swim and, in many places, they leave the water to search for insects and worms on land. In addition to these conventional feeding methods, Black-headed Gulls will also hawk high in the air, scooping up swarming insects, and they are among the few gulls that may land on trees and bushes to take a meal of berries. In short they are omnivores and opportunists, like all the successful gulls.

Colonies are dense and often large, with hundreds or even thousands of pairs. The birds keep the peace with a wide range of displays and gestures, one of the most prominent being the 'swoop-and-soar' display, in which rival males indulge in a chase that culminates in one bird almost hovering over the other, calling loudly. The ground displays tend, as might be expected, to involve the prominent head markings. A bird challenges another by lowering its head to show off the brown hood, and if it wishes to be somewhat more threatening it performs the evidently rather rude 'head flagging' display, in which the bird turns slightly away from its rival to show its prominent white nape. But these are just some of the many displays – a few nouns in a complex language.

adult br.

adult non-br.

1st sum.

1st w.

juv.

Slender-billed Gull

Larus genei (**lah**-russ je-**nee**-eye)
length 42–44 cm

If you have a long neck and a long bill it's sensible to use them, and the Slender-billed Gull employs a selective range of foraging methods to do just that. It has a particular fondness for swimming in the water and dipping down to snatch fish from the shallows at its feet or upending like a duck; in so doing it can reach further below the surface than other similar gulls, giving it a competitive advantage. It will persistently plunge into the water from a low flight not much more than 1 m above the surface, again reaching further down than its competitors. When swimming it assumes a distinctive shape, with its long neck stretched forward at 45 degrees to the water, as if it were straining to reach a finishing tape in a race, and with its tail sticking up at the back.

The Slender-billed Gull also has long legs, which makes it an effective paddler. In the shallows where it normally feeds, it is the only gull of its type that can run through the water after prey. And its special party trick is for a group to wade forward in a line, herding fish toward the shallower water, before each bird takes off and plunges into the shoal. In some parts of their range Slender-billed Gulls swim or trot at the feet of Greater Flamingos, fielding fleeing shrimps.

With all these advantages one might expect the Slender-billed Gull to be a common and widespread species, but it is not. In Europe it is climatically restricted to a narrow zone of latitude around the Mediterranean and Black Seas. Part of this can be explained by its dislike of choppy and cold water. For breeding it selects beaches or islands by shallow tidal water or, alternatively, settles by the edges of saline lagoons. The large, densely packed colonies are usually on bare mud or among *Salicornia* plants or other very low vegetation.

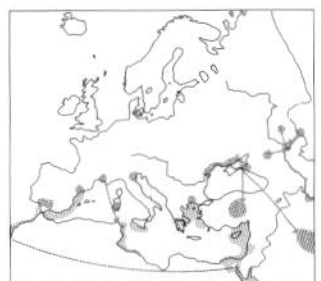

ID: A larger and distinctly elongated version of Black-headed Gull. Has longer bill, longer wings, longer neck and much longer legs. Usually given away with characteristic front profile, with long, sloping forehead leading down to lengthy bill.

adult br. | adult non-br. | 1st sum. | 1st w. | juv.

Audouin's Gull

Larus audouinii (**lah**-russ ow-doo-**in**-nee-eye)
length 48–52 cm

In a family where many species are characterised by their abundance and adaptability, the Audouin's Gull provides an exception by being rare and specialised. It typically breeds on uninhabited offshore islands no more than 50 m in elevation, often with a covering of boulders, grass and bushes. Some breed more conventionally on sandy beaches, but all colonies are in the Mediterranean region in a narrow climatic zone. The world population is no more than 20,000 pairs, with 78 per cent concentrated into just two Spanish colonies.

These birds are specialists in eating fish such as sardines. They have a characteristic way of searching for them, too, which is to fly back and forth along a transect in the water, usually close to shore. They flap slowly and low over the surface, quartering with legs dangling like an owl. When one of these gulls spies a fish below, it exercises a neat down-and-sideways flick of the bill to snatch the fish from the water, the same movement that a flying bird might use to pluck a berry from a bush. Only the bill gets wet; the plumage remains immaculate.

It requires considerable flying ability to perform this feat and, of all the larger gulls, none can match the Audouin's for grace in the air. It is highly manoeuvrable and can greatly outperform the Yellow-legged Gull, with which it shares much of its range. These two species, in fact, have quite a fraught relationship, Yellow-legged Gulls regularly robbing their more skilful neighbours of their expertly caught food. Perhaps to avoid this, Audouin's Gulls do most of their hunting at night.

ID: A medium-large gull with a distinctive shape: sloping forehead, long, distinctly pointed wings (an important field-mark) and long legs. Adult easily recognised by combination of black legs and red bill; rather smoky grey in colour.

adult br. | 2nd sum. | 1st sum. | 1st w. | juv.

Mediterranean Gull

Larus melanocephalus
(**lah**-russ mel-lan-noh-**sef**-fa-luss)
length 36–38 cm

Sixty years ago it would have been possible to pigeonhole the Mediterranean Gull as a species of the steppe region of eastern Europe (albeit wintering mostly in the Mediterranean). It remains a bird of that area, breeding on scattered lakes, marshes and lagoons near inland seas, and commuting to feed over grassland, where it chases insects on the ground and often hawks for them in flight. It commonly follows the plough and has regularly been seen feeding on swarms of locusts, which are a speciality of that area. Since the 1940s, however, the Mediterranean Gull has undergone a major expansion in its range, breaking out of its continental mould to breed on temperate coastal sites, such as salt marshes, in northwest Europe. That expansion is continuing, and seems to show that this smart-plumaged species has acquired an impressive ability to colonise new places with different climates.

It is a sociable species, breeding in large, dense colonies of at least a hundred pairs (45,000 is known). Nests can be a mere 8 cm apart, although 63 cm appears to be average. To defend their small territories the birds usually threaten rivals on the ground, not in the air; the Mediterranean Gull lacks the Black-headed Gull's 'swoop-and-soar' display, for instance. During terrestrial interactions the black hood is an important 'badge', and birds will often sleek or ruffle feathers to change the shape of their head, according to their emotions and motivations. The Mediterranean Gull also has a threatening 'squinting' display, shutting its dark eyes, presumably to show off its bright white eye crescent to advantage.

The nests are usually placed on flat ground with sparse vegetation, rather than on bare sand. Colonies are often found close to those of Sandwich Terns and Slender-billed Gulls, and the Mediterranean Gulls may steal the eggs of both these neighbours. Insidiously, unmated adults are also known to eat the eggs of established pairs, although whether this is a deliberate form of destructive infanticide is not yet known.

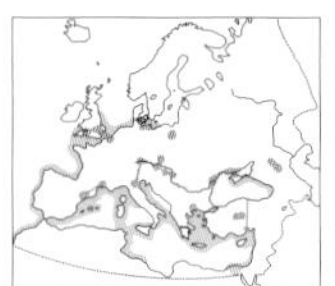

ID: Larger than Black-headed Gull, with a heavier body, shorter, decidedly blunter wings, longer legs and a noticeably thicker bill. Flies with stiff, shallow wingbeats and glides more than other medium-sized or small gulls. Breeding adult is only common European Gull with combination of truly black head and apparently entirely white wings.

adult br. | adult non-br. | 1st sum. | 1st w. | juv.

Little Gull

Larus minutus (**lah**-russ min-**noo**-tuss)
length 25–27 cm; wingspan 75–80 cm

Success as a gull does not always require adaptability and a wide range of feeding methods; the Little Gull proves this by using just a few foraging styles highly successfully. Its small size and thin bill makes scavenging ineffective, stealing food unworkable and trying to eat other birds or mammals potentially hazardous. Instead it contentedly feeds on insects (e.g. dragonflies, mayflies, caddis flies) and other invertebrates in the breeding season, and marine invertebrates and fish at other times.

Its most commonly observed method of feeding is to fly back and forth over the water up to about 5 m in height, and to drop down to the surface, snatching its meal in mid-flight. This is very much the feeding style adopted by a tern, and the Little Gull indeed often feeds alongside terns, in both fresh and salt water. It will nest among terns, too; behaviourally it lies in the grey zone between the two groups.

In contrast to other gulls, the Little Gull is confined to freshwater sites for breeding, usually marshes with lush vegetation where plenty of insects can hide. Its nests (which are almost always in small colonies) are placed on plants growing in shallow water or close by, and during the course of the season these plants may grow up and conceal the sitting adults almost completely. Occasionally the nest, an accumulated pile of dead plant material, is actually placed on a raft of vegetation floating in the water. In common with most gulls, the chicks, which can swim, leave the nest within a few days.

The displays of the Little Gull are very similar to those of the Black-headed Gull and have an important aerial element missing from those of most other species of gull. In early season, for example, birds will chase each other gracefully over the water and make 'long calls', holding their heads up as they do so.

adult br. | adult br. | adult non-br. | 1st sum. | 1st w. | juv.

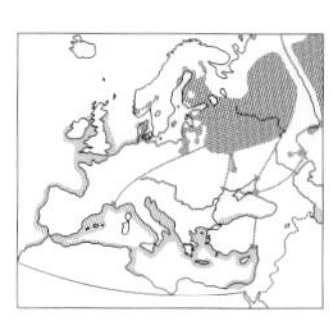

ID: The smallest gull, with distinctly short, blunt-tipped, almost rounded wings. Rides buoyantly on the water surface and flies in more tern-like manner than most gulls, with quick changes of direction and frequent dips to the surface.

Common Gull

Larus canus (**lah**-russ **kay**-nuss)
length 40–46 cm; wingspan 1.1–1.2 5 m

No other European gull is as flexible in its breeding habits as the Common Gull. This medium-sized species often nests abundantly on seacoasts, inhabiting cliff ledges, grassy slopes, sand dunes and islands; yet it is also perfectly at home on lakes and marshes a great distance from the sea, and even breeds in dry habitats, such as moorland and farmland, nowhere near water. It is sometimes colonial, albeit modestly so, with no more than a few tens of pairs; but it is also regularly a solitary breeder, to a greater extent than the other gulls. Finally, it builds its nest in a remarkable variety of sites, including the expected ones such as open grass, dunes and rocks, plus more exotic ones including floating vegetation, roofs, tree stumps and the branches of trees up to 10 m above ground.

One look at a Common Gull's gentle expression and small bill would lead you to predict that this is not the most predatory of gulls, and indeed it hardly ever feeds on adult birds, chicks or small mammals. Much of its time is instead spent absorbed in working the ground, where it eats earthworms, insects and various other invertebrates. It typically forages on well-drained soil and, on the coast, often on sand. It has a habit of foot-paddling, standing on one leg while the other agitates the substrate, a technique that often makes worms come to the surface and causes other food to become more obvious.

The Common Gull is mainly a bird of the northern half of Europe. It is easily overlooked among flocks of other species, but may come out of hiding by uttering its very high-pitched squealing call which, with some artistic licence, has earned it its American name of 'Mew Gull'.

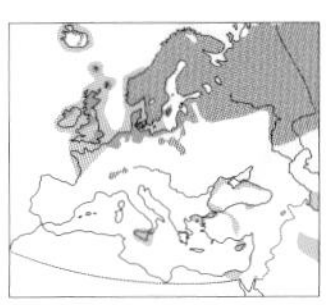

ID: Medium-sized gull with fairly intense grey back, darker than Herring Gull or Black-headed Gull. Often seen with Black-headed Gulls, but distinguished by larger size, broader wings and smoother flight, with slower wingbeats. Bill yellow, legs yellow/grey.

Lesser Black-backed Gull

Larus fuscus (**lah**-russ **fooss**-kuss)
length 52–67 cm; wingspan 1.35–1.55 m

Despite its similarity in plumage to the Great Black-backed Gull, this species is actually much more closely related to the Herring Gull, and very close to the latter in size. It shares the Herring Gull's ability to nest on flat grassy slopes, sand dunes and low islands, and the birds often mix together in colonies, the Lesser Black-back tending to inhabit any parts with denser ground vegetation. It is much less enthusiastic than the Herring Gull about cliffs and cliff tops, though, so the latter's neighbour in such places is more likely to be the Great Black-backed Gull.

In mixed colonies of Herrings and Lesser Black-backs there is very little interbreeding, and part of this can be explained by slight differences in the two species' territorial and courtship displays. The most obvious distinction is in the 'long call' display, a routine that accompanies the prolonged, open-mouthed proclamations made by birds laying claim to their territory. Herring Gulls finish their long call by looking upwards at an angle, whereas Lesser Black-backs point vertically towards the heavens. Such subtleties in display are a feature of the social and sexual life of gulls.

Lesser Black-backs often forage further away from their nesting colonies than Herring Gulls and this reflects their overall superiority in the air. They are strikingly elegant and often indulge in effortless sailing glides. Where the dominant, food-robbing Herring Gull frequently appropriates its neighbour's meal, the Lesser Black-back may be forced to use its talents to make foraging flights to much deeper water, far offshore. Here it often plunge-dives for fish (often herrings) and invertebrates.

After breeding, Lesser Black-backs, being essentially migrants, leave their colonies and fly south. In the northeast of Europe this may involve a trip of up to 7500 km to East Africa, but western birds travel far shorter distances. Many breeding birds of northwest Europe, especially Britain, have virtually abandoned their migration to the Mediterranean in the last 30 years, remaining close to their breeding areas instead. Immature birds, though, often migrate further than adults.

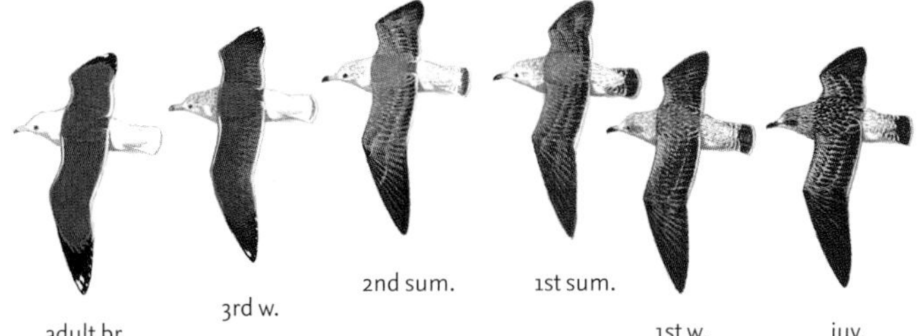

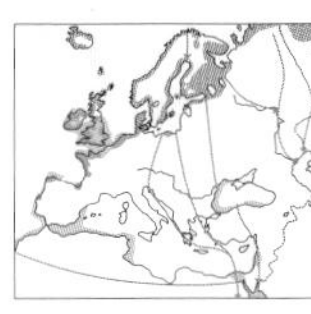

ID: One of two gulls with intense dark backs, the other being the Great Black-backed. Adult distinguished from that species by yellow legs.

Herring Gull

Larus argentatus (**lah**-russ ar-jen-**tay**-tuss)
length 55–67 cm; wingspan 1.38–1.55 m

Noisy and boorish, the Herring Gull is a dominant personality on the coasts of northern Europe. It is the most abundant of the large gulls, and often the most inquisitive and bold. It is the gull that wakes people at dawn by making ear-splitting calls from the rooftops of genteel seaside towns, and the one that has the cheek to fly down and steal sandwiches out of the hands of unsuspecting tourists. It is an extraordinarily successful bird, but too 'in-your-face' ever to be popular with people.

This is essentially a coastal gull. It dislikes being out of sight of land on the ocean and seems to be reluctant to go inland, either, although it can be lured there by large bodies of water and by rubbish dumps. By the sea, though, it is everywhere, foraging on beaches for shellfish and scraps, swimming to grab surface-living invertebrates, flying down to snap up items from the water surface, even plunging in for shoaling fish. It feeds on the intertidal zone in estuaries, often picking up shellfish, flying up to 5 m or so and then dropping them onto a hard surface to break them open. It will find carcasses washed up by the tide, and feed on scraps from overflowing seaside rubbish bins. It will paddle its feet in soft mud to find worms and crustaceans. And it will harass all and sundry, especially other gulls, to steal from them. Each individual has its own feeding regime and its own preferences, and the net result is an overwhelming dominance of the habitat by this one species.

The Herring Gull is also highly adaptable about where it nests. Trusting that colonies of large, aggressive gulls are an intimidating prospect for most predators, it audaciously uses flat ground with easy access, including sites such as dunes, cliff tops and beaches. An unusual habit of nesting on flat-topped buildings is a comparatively recent and still localised one, but roofs make good, safe substitutes for shingle and sand.

Colonies are often very large and may overlap with those of other gull species. They tend to divide into sub-colonies anyway and within these divisions activities such as egg laying and chick rearing are highly synchronised, producing localised baby booms. In the early part of the season birds attempting to form or re-establish pairs visit so-called 'clubs' on the edge of the colony, where they can go about their business without causing friction.

Once paired, the birds spread out and maintain their own personal territories within the body of the colony. Individuals resemble each other closely, so an elaborate series of commonly understood gestures and displays has arisen to prevent anarchy between competing birds at this stage. Initially an individual – usually a male – can lay claim to a territory, in the full hearing of the neighbourhood, by uttering its 'long call', a 20-note sentence belted out with full force, like an operatic aria. Then, should a bird be directly challenged, it takes up posturing. First, it stands still in an upright pose, pointing toward its rival, its plumage sleeked. Then it will become more animated, pointing its bill down and opening its wings slightly at the carpal joints, like a cowboy ready for the draw. The last ritual before a fight is known as grass pulling, in which frustrated birds take their aggression out on the nearby vegetation. If that doesn't work, physical combat will ensue.

Courtship entails more gestures and ceremonies. Among these courtship feeding is particularly important, because it not only strengthens the pair bond, but also nourishes the female during the egg-laying period. She requests food by adopting a hunched posture, with body crouched and head slightly up. She might also pester the male by pecking at his head and bill, until finally he regurgitates his offering onto the ground beside her.

For a young gull, life in the colony can be difficult. The adults make a point of feeding each chick carefully, but that does not prevent some harassment between competing siblings, and occasional murder. Wandering away from the territory is far more hazardous, though, because adult Herring Gulls routinely kill and eat their neighbours' itinerant offspring. Yet chicks are also sometimes adopted by neighbours, despite the fact that they are recognised as strangers. Remarkably, the urge to be adopted comes from the chick itself, in response to inadequate food provision by its parents. Boldly, it seeks out a family slightly younger than itself and risks death in order to be incorporated into it. Perhaps this is simply an early-stage example of the resourcefulness of this irrepressible species.

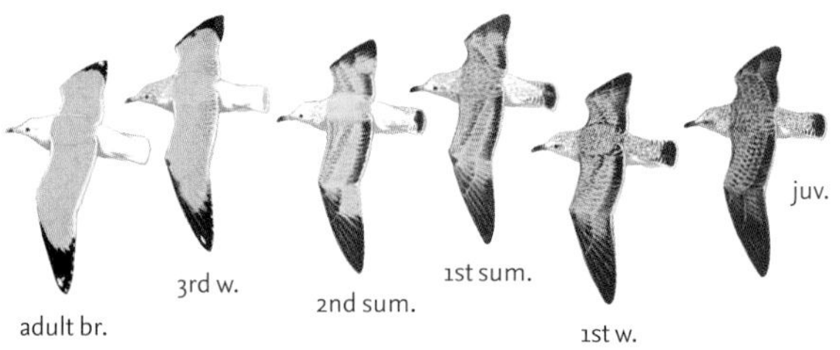

ID: Large, 'frowning' pink-legged gull with pale eyes and paler back than most similar gulls. Tends to be abundant where it is found.

Yellow-legged Gull

Larus cachinnans (**lah**-russ **kak**-kin-nans)
length 59–67 cm ; wingspan 1.4–1.6 m

A few years ago the Yellow-legged Gull languished in the obscurity of being regarded as a subspecies, nothing more than the Mediterranean version of the all-conquering Herring Gull. It then spread north along the Atlantic coast and met the Herring Gull as the latter moved southward. Colonies of the two remained separate and the few cases of hybridisation resulted in chicks that did not survive. Added to the evidence of some plumage differences and distinctly different tones of call, the Yellow-legged Gull was born.

It is now in danger of being split into two species in its own right. The Yellow-legged Gulls of the oceanic west are ecologically different from those of the east. The western birds breed on offshore islands, cliffs and salt-marshes, while the eastern ones ('Caspian Gulls') site their colonies on the banks of large rivers, lakes and inland seas, or on islands therein. The western birds take fish and offal, while the eastern birds often commute to the nearby steppes to catch ground squirrels and insects. However, both types share some food preferences, including the eggs and chicks of birds, and show some overlap in their choice of habitat.

This is still very much a close relative of the Herring Gull, and most of the territorial and courtship displays are identical in the two species. However, when the birds are uttering their challenging territorial 'long call' the accompanying display is slightly different. It involves bowing down until the bill points to the feet ('throw-forward') and then lifting the head upwards as if to look towards the summit of a low hill ('throw-back'), calling all the while. Yellow-legged Gulls throw forward with their chin closer to their breast than the Herring Gull, and throw back with their head pointed more to the sky, so their display is the more emphatic of the two.

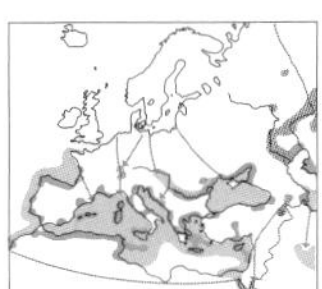

ID: Very similar to Herring Gull, but has rather longer and narrower wings with slightly more pointed tip. Legs bright yellow, not pink. Grey on back is slightly darker than that of Herring Gull, and wing mirrors are a bit smaller.

adult br.

Iceland Gull

Larus glaucoides (**lah**-russ glow-**koy**-deez)
length 52–60 cm

The Iceland Gull is a winter visitor to Europe from its breeding grounds in Greenland. It occurs in small numbers in Britain and Fennoscandia, but is most abundant, as its English name suggests, in Iceland, where it is found along the coast by cliffs, in harbours and near rubbish dumps. It resembles the Herring Gull in size and the Glaucous Gull in plumage, the latter so much so that each corresponding stage is virtually identical in the two species. The Iceland Gull is a lighter bird on the wing than the lumbering Glaucous and shows great agility when snapping up food in flight from the water surface. It will also plunge-dive in a manner strikingly similar to that of a tern, even occasionally immersing itself completely, which is unusual among large gulls.

On its breeding grounds in Greenland the Iceland Gull nests on broad, roomy ledges on tall sea cliffs which are often shared with Glaucous Gulls and Kittiwakes. Where this happens, the site is divided and stratified. The Glaucous Gulls invariably take to the top of the cliffs like puffed-up executives, relegating the Icelands to the lower sections, where they may mix with the Kittiwakes. Below the quarrelsome Glaucous Gulls is a buffer zone occupied by nobody. The arrangement is a headache for Iceland Gulls because humans often eat their eggs, every year accounting for 20 per cent or more of the population.

Where they are not persecuted a few Iceland Gulls nest on the ground, among rocks. The chicks of these birds wander freely, whereas those of cliff-nesting birds wisely stay put in the nest.

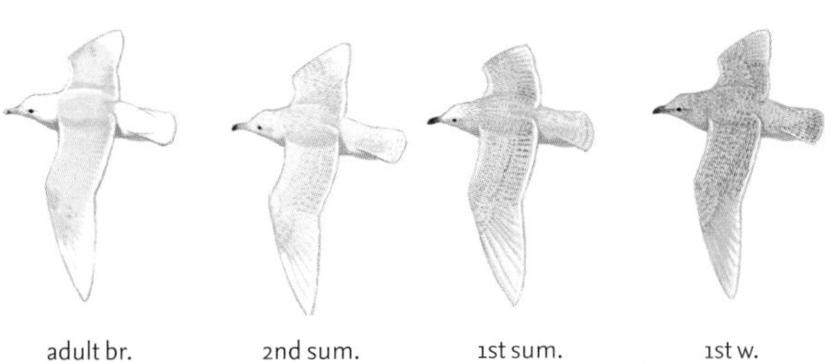

adult br. 2nd sum. 1st sum. 1st w.

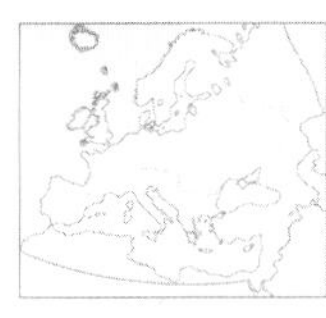

ID: About the size of Herring Gull, but with more 'gentle' expression and always distinguishable by the lack of any black on the wings.

Glaucous Gull

Larus hyperboreus (**lah**-russ hie-per-**boh**-ree-uss)
length 62–68 cm; wingspan 1.5–1.65 m

The brutish Glaucous Gull is very much the predator among the guild of gulls that are predominantly found in the far north of our region. It is a large, aggressive, domineering bird armed with a fearsome bill. Among its predatory habits it regularly eats large numbers of eggs and young at seabird and goose colonies, and pairs of Glaucous Gulls may actually have the temerity to divide sections of Brünnich's Guillemot 'cities' between themselves, so that each has private predation rights over a vertical slice of cliff below its nest. Within this feeding territory a member of the pair will repeatedly fly slowly forwards into the wind, scouring its section for unguarded nests. In this way the gulls take a heavy toll on the smaller birds.

But to say that the Glaucous Gull is only a predator would be wrong; it has other talents, including food piracy or 'kleptoparasitism'. In winter, individual Glaucous Gulls compete amongst themselves for access to feeding flocks of Eiders, intercepting the ducks as they come to the surface with shellfish or fish. The Glaucous Gull is also an effective scavenger, the only northern gull that can break open corpses floating in the water. If you add in grabbing food while swimming, scavenging at refuse tips and searching for pickings on beaches and mudflats, you have the feeding profile of an adaptable, opportunistic and not very squeamish species.

The Glaucous Gull is a fierce predator, but at least in Iceland it is loved by somebody, for it very often interbreeds there with the Herring Gull, with which it shares many displays and other breeding behaviour. Usually, though, it nests alone or in pure colonies on rocky outcrops and cliffs, even occasionally upon ice or snow. In colonies nests are usually 10–20 m apart and, unusually, the young are taken away when a few days old to special rearing territories close to the sea.

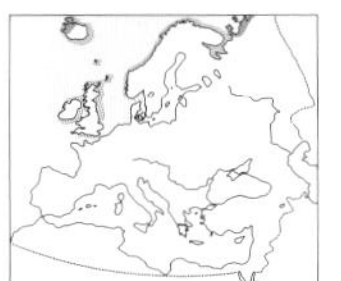

ID: Second to Great Black-backed Gull in size, with same heavy bill, sloping forehead, bulky chest and blunt rear end. Plumages at all stages similar to Iceland Gull, but it has a long bill and the wing tips barely project beyond the tail.

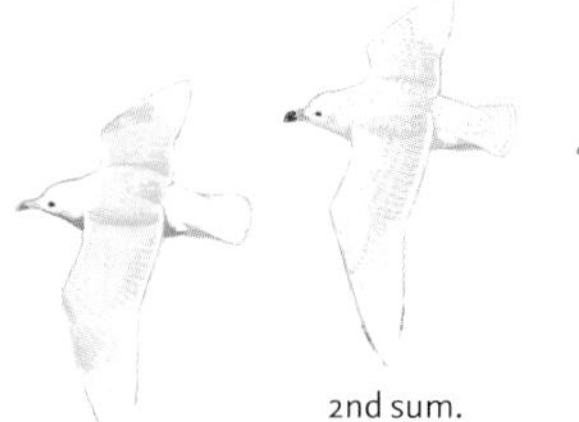

2nd sum.

1st sum.

1st w.

adult br.

Great Black-backed Gull

Larus marinus (**lah**-russ mar-**rie**-nuss)
length 68–79 cm long; wingspan 1.52–1.67 m

The menacing Great Black-back is the largest gull in the world and would be perfectly capable of swallowing the smallest, the Little Gull, whole if the opportunity arose – although there are no records of it doing so. It has a heavy body and a slightly lumbering build, and it flies with slow, laboured, almost heron-like wingbeats. The bill is large, strong and slightly hooked, and is used both as a weapon and as a tool. The Great Black-backed Gull is top of the gull hierarchy and often builds its nest on the highest point of a cliff or pinnacle, above the other gulls, its minions.

There are many examples of this bird's predatory tendencies. It catches Puffins and Manx Shearwaters in flight and stabs them and shakes them to death. It has been known to catch rabbits and treat them the same way. It has a particular taste for seabird chicks and young, and where it is common it can seriously impair nesting success of other species. Its victims are often young gulls, including Herrings and Lesser Black-backs, which it may drag into the air and drop onto a hard surface, the same technique it and other large gulls employ to crack open the shells of molluscs and crustaceans. The Great Black-back's power, aggression and intelligence make it a formidable hunter.

Strangely enough, it shows much less ease with people than most other gulls. It has been among the last of the common species to take up the habit of nesting on roofs, and this practice is still very unusual. It tends to select inaccessible sites for the nest, although it will also mingle with other gulls in large colonies (and must be a very unpopular neighbour). Pairs of Great Black-backs often breed well apart from one another and where colonies form they are usually rather small. It seems that these fierce birds don't benefit from being close together; the breeding success of dense colonies is usually very low.

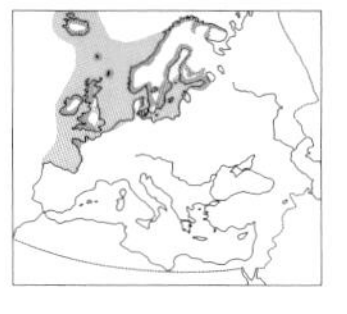

ID: The largest gull of all, with a massive bill, thick neck and large, bulky body. Adults black on the back and wings, with flesh-pink, not yellow legs. Has very heavy flight action, with slow wingbeats sometimes even recalling a heron.

1st sum.

juv.

2nd sum.

1st w.

Ivory Gull

Pagophila eburnea (pay-**gof**-fil-la ee-bur-**nee**-a)
length 40–43 cm; wingspan 1.08–1.2 m

This is a true Arctic gull that in Europe breeds only on Svalbard, with just a couple of hundred pairs present, and on Franz Josef Land, where it is common. It nests on level ground or broad cliff ledges up to 300 m high, often sharing the cliffs with Kittiwakes. It tends to be closely associated with Arctic pack-ice, around which it feeds, eating the excreta of polar bears and seals and scavenging from carcasses.

Curiously, this seabird seems to hate the water. It swims badly and, when foraging on shore, tends not to get its feet wet!

Another Arctic gull, the Ross's Gull (*Rhodostethia rosea*), does not breed in Europe but appears in the same places as Ivory Gulls in late summer. It flies buoyantly in the manner of the Little Gull, using surface dipping and hovering as feeding methods. It will also pick from the water like a phalarope.

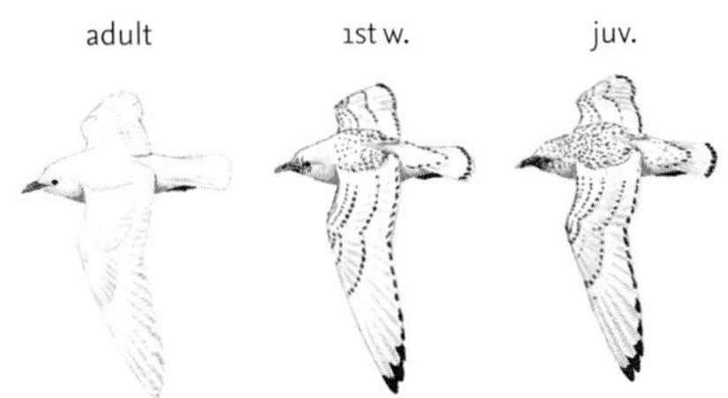

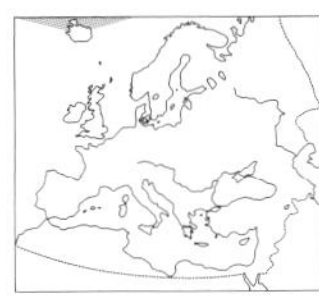

ID: Perhaps the only unmistakable gull! Has broad-based but pointed wings and heavy, almost pigeon-like body. Adult pure white but for black legs and strangely coloured bill: greenish with yellow and orange tip.

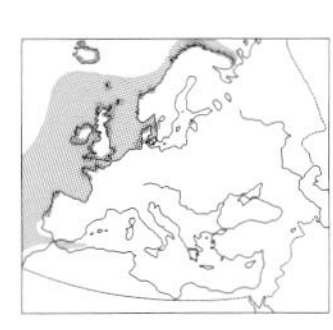

ID: Slightly larger than Black-headed Gull, with slightly broader and noticeably 'parallel-edged' wings. Flies with stiff wingbeats. No white mirrors on wingtip.

Kittiwake

Rissa tridactyla (**riss**-sa trie-**dak**-til-la)
length 38–40 cm; wingspan 91–97 cm

No Kittiwake is at home inland; this is a truly marine gull, occupying coastal cliff ledges for breeding and afterwards dispersing out into the open ocean for the rest of the year. It feeds mainly on fish and marine invertebrates, including plankton, which it gathers by snatching from the water surface or by plunging to a depth of 1 m. It often follows whales as they bring food from the depths, and at times it will forage near trawlers, too. A Kittiwake can fly into the strongest winds, often harnessing their power by gliding low over the waves in a manner similar to a shearwater. Storms don't normally perturb it, although the most ferocious of them will cause the birds to settle on the water to ride out the worst conditions. Outside the breeding season many Kittiwakes cross the open ocean to feed over rich waters off the Newfoundland coast. Young birds often remain hereabouts until, at two years old, they are ready to breed. So the open ocean holds no terrors for Kittiwakes except, that is, for the larger gulls and skuas that often intercept them and attempt to rob them of their food.

Kittiwakes form colonies on precipitous cliffs, although a few have also taken recently to using window ledges on buildings or piers. Most colonies are very large – 10,000 or more pairs – and the din from them is both distinctive and deafening. Each bird repeatedly calls out its English name 'kitti-wake' in a loud, drawn-out, insistent manner and in a nasal, trumpeting voice. Even Herring Gulls seem muted by comparison.

The nests are often built on what looks like a slender foundation, just the merest projection out from a rock. Precariously perched above a sheer drop, some nests must give way with disastrous results; yet, placed where they are, they and their tenants are uniquely safe from ground predators. The nests are made of mud, seaweed and grass, often lined with feathers and far more elaborate than most other gull structures.

Young Kittiwakes differ from other gull chicks in being greyish-white and lacking cryptic coloration. By necessity they do not wander about on the nest, unlike other gull chicks; or at least, if any ever did, the trait would have soon died out by an extreme form of natural selection!

Terns family *Sternidae* (stern-id-ee)

Habitat Coastal habitats and freshwater rivers, lakes and marshes.
Food Mainly fish, insects or crustaceans, often caught by plunge-diving.
Movements Highly migratory, wintering mainly along the coast of Africa. The Arctic Tern has the longest migration of any bird known.
Voice Harsh screeches and mutters.
Pairing style Monogamous.
Nesting Colonial, sometimes with more than one species mixed in. Terns also mix with other species of birds (e.g. gulls) and other birds mix in with them.
Nest A shallow hollow on the ground.
Productivity 1 brood a year.
Eggs 2–3.
Incubation 19–26 days, by both parents.
Young Semi-precocial and downy.
Parenting style Fed and tended by both parents.
Food to young As adult food, brought in bill.
Leaving nest Sandwich Terns leave the nest and form crèches by about 7 days old. The rest fledge at 15–32 days. Learning to fish is difficult and young terns remain with their parents for several weeks after learning to fly. Unusually among birds, they migrate with their parents and may even be fed along the way.

Roseate Tern

At first sight terns look very like gulls, but closer scrutiny reveals that they are more angular in profile, much slimmer and, you might say, more elegant and refined. They lack the blunt-instrument bills of gulls and have instead sharp, dagger-like tools used to snatch prey from the water (usually fish) or in mid-air (insects). Their wings are slimmer than those of gulls, and so sharp at the tip that you would imagine you could impale paper on them. Their tails are long and often so deeply forked that they have been dubbed 'sea swallows' in several languages. They have full, deep wingbeats that are buoyant yet far from effortless: terns rarely glide along in that imperious, confident way that gulls do. A gust of wind unsettles a tern much more than a gull.

Terns are not all-rounders. They fly well – enough to make plunge-diving their main form of procuring food, for example – but they almost never swim, despite having webbed feet and the ability to use them. They can stand and walk well enough, but for some strange reason they dislike moving far along the ground. If you approach a tern it will invariably fly off, whereas a gull might perhaps walk or run away. Terns do have relatively short legs, which might explain their terrestrial reticence.

Most terns have black caps, but otherwise the plumage is white or grey. The exceptions to the rule are marsh terns, all of which have some sooty-black coloration. The Roseate Tern has a distinct wash of pink to its breast, a feature that it shares, oddly enough, with several species of gulls. In common with gulls, it is often the bare parts, the bill and legs, that most easily distinguish one species from another.

All terns are more or less colonial and suffer in the breeding season from being timid and overwrought. They are susceptible to disturbance and may abandon colonies after just one episode of intrusion. They need little in the way of inducement to fly up in panic and often do so, as a colony, without any provocation at all. When faced by predators terns will often mob the interloper en masse, screeching in chorus, dive-bombing and throwing up regurgitated fish. The vigilance of terns and this communal aggression makes their colonies attractive as cover during the nesting season for other, less demonstrative species.

Terns are phenomenal migrants and contain among their number the Arctic Tern, the greatest traveller of all birds. Every species is a summer visitor, and most winter close to or south of the equator.

Gull-billed Tern

Gelochelidon nilotica
(jel-lo-kee-**lie**-don nie-**loh**-ti-ka)
length 35–38 cm

With a shorter, thicker bill than the rest of the terns, the Gull-billed has a rather different diet to that of its relatives. It does eat fish – it could hardly be a tern if it didn't – but it also catches a uniquely wide range of other animal foods, including insects, earthworms, crabs, frogs, reptiles and occasionally even small birds. In one Italian study nearly two-thirds of the diet consisted of lizards! Insects are also regularly important, but as far as food is concerned the Gull-bill is an opportunist.

While every other tern in the world feeds predominantly over water or wet places, the Gull-billed sometimes transfers its main foraging method to dry ground. As it quarters over grasslands, orchards or agricultural fields with no water evident nearby, it looks completely out of place.

With such varied and plentiful feeding preferences one might expect Gull-billed Terns to be everywhere, but they are not. They are decidedly scarce, with a European population of no more than 4000 pairs. They require islands, dunes, shores and pasture on which to nest, and are very susceptible to disturbance, but perhaps the main reason is that Europe lies at the very north of their range and they prefer warmer climates.

Most Gull-billed Terns in Europe breed in small numbers among colonies of other gulls and terns. Display involves less aerial activity than in most other terns, and nests are usually close to vegetation.

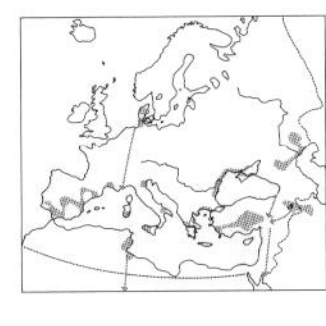

ID: A relatively large, white-looking tern. The wings look forward set in flight and the bird flies with stiff wingbeats, holding the wings out relatively straight. Doesn't normally plunge-dive, but hawks for insects over land.

Common Tern

Sterna hirundo (**ster**-na hir-**run**-doh)
length 31–35 cm

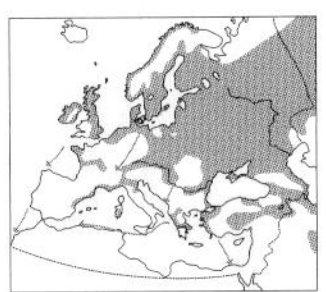

ID: This and the Arctic Tern look greyer than Roseate or Sandwich Terns in flight. Breeding adult has long red bill with a black tip and red legs. At rest, tail does not reach wing tips. Fairly white about the head, and pale grey on the belly, paler than Arctic. In flight, distinguished from exceedingly similar Arctic Tern by subtle difference in wing pattern: from above, contrast between dark outer primaries and paler inner ones obvious, forming a 'nick' into wing.

The Common Tern is by far the most widespread of its family in Europe, and the most flexible in its breeding habitat. Although it is primarily a coastal bird, it has ventured further than the other terns into inland habitats, penetrating into the heart of Europe, primarily along river systems such as the Rhine, Loire and Danube. Here it breeds in freshwater marshes, riverine shingle and on islands or artificial structures in lakes, whereas on the coast it selects beaches, islands and the upper parts of salt marshes, which are all rather typical tern habitats.

The Common Tern is also flexible in its feeding preferences and can react to severe shortages of its favourite fish by turning to other species found in slightly different places, or to crustaceans or insects. Its main feeding method is to plunge-dive decisively after a hover, but it will also dip down to snatch items on or just above the surface.

These birds nest in colonies, usually of a fair size: the average in Britain, for example, is 263 pairs. Inland colonies are smaller. Nests are rarely less than 50 cm apart and usually rather more, allowing the birds to hold a territory of 2–3 sq m. The boundaries are vigorously defended at first, but once incubation is underway things relax somewhat, although chicks wandering around may be attacked. Pairs can be extraordinarily faithful to their breeding site, and there is a record of one couple returning to the same place for 17 consecutive years.

Fish play an integral role in pair formation and maintenance. Males in early season often perform 'low flights', flying over the colony with fish in bill, showing it off to the females and calling loudly. Alternatively there may be 'high flights', in which a fish-carrying male suddenly rises up to about 200 m into the air, joined by the female, while they both glide and hold their wings in a V. Once the pair has begun to establish, they enter a 'honeymoon' period, during which the male presents fish to the female about six times an hour, to keep her in condition. This time is crucial to the partnership because, by monitoring her male's efforts, the female can decide whether or not he is a suitable provider–and she may leave if she deems not. It's an important decision, because for a while before the first egg is laid the female may be entirely dependent on her male's offerings. The better she is fed at this time, the larger eggs she will lay, leading to higher-quality young.

ID: *Of similar size and shape to Common and Arctic Terns, but much whiter in overall colour. Tail streamers are very long and project a long way beyond closed wing tips; they also look obviously long in flight.*

Roseate Tern

Sterna dougallii (**ster**-na doo-**gal**-lee-eye)
length 33–38 cm

This rose-tinted tern is more specialised than its overbearing close relatives the Common and Arctic Terns. It takes a narrower range of food items (almost entirely marine fish), employs fewer feeding methods (just plunge-diving) and has more specific habitat requirements, at least in Europe, than the others. This does not mean, though, that it necessarily avoids their company: it usually breeds in mixed colonies with one or both species and finds them useful when in the mood for stealing fish.

When hunting for themselves Roseate Terns are a little more daring and fuel-injected than the other two. They fly higher over the sea when seeking food, descend at more of an angle when they dive, make more of a splash when they hit the water and immerse deeper and for longer before emerging with their catch. Instead of hovering they break into a dive as they fly along, like a marathon runner grabbing a drink without breaking stride. Their dynamic style carries them more widely over the fishing area, up to 1 km in a wide arc, and as a result they rarely form dense flocks. They often follow large predatory fish, including tuna, taking advantage of stampedes of panicking small fish making for the surface. The sea is very much the Roseate Tern's habitat, and it is virtually never recorded inland, even after storms.

The Roseate Tern's favourite breeding sites are rocky islands near shallow, calm water. In contrast to other terns it seeks out cover and may tunnel into marram grass on dunes, find suitable shelter among rocks or even use the entrance to burrows. With its nest site duly hidden, the Roseate is much less aggressive toward predators than either the Common or the Arctic Tern.

Arctic Tern

Sterna paradisaea (**ster**-na par-ra-**diz**-zee-a)
length 33–35 cm

No species of bird performs a longer migratory journey than the Arctic Tern. From its breeding grounds in northern Europe it coolly transfers to the waters of the Antarctic for the winter, travelling at least 17,500 km in the process. Having fed among the penguins for a few months these terns return north, using much the same route – except, that is, in the latter stages, where evidence from birds recovered in the Ural Mountains suggests that some may take an extensive overland route, probably at great altitude. So they return to their colonies having had many adventures and, taking into account their Antarctic jaunts, travelled as much as 50,000 km in a year. And in that same year they will have seen more hours of daylight than any other animal on earth.

Despite being exposed to so much daylight, and with it so much opportunity for feeding, the Arctic Tern adheres to quite regular foraging times, usually being most active in the early morning and evening. It has a fairly varied diet, with crustaceans and insects being consumed along with the usual fish. In recent years the bird has expanded its range in the Baltic Sea by feeding on midges, which themselves are increasing because of silting up. In these areas it is trespassing into territories previously occupied only by the Common Tern. When diving for fish, Arctic Terns are characteristically more hesitant than Common Terns, often hovering several times at different heights before literally taking the plunge.

The breeding behaviour of Common and Arctic Terns is so similar that it seems remarkable that the two species hardly ever hybridise. Admittedly, the courtship of the Arctic Tern has more of an aerial element to it, with the females, for example, typically taking flight as soon as they are approached by a male. But perhaps the nesting sites are a more important factor. Arctic Terns usually nest on more barren beaches or islands than Common Terns and, where the two mix, the Common take the grass and the Arctic the bare rock (they have shorter legs). There is a climatic difference, too, with the Arctic Tern reaching into far more extreme latitudes than the Common – indeed, 60 per cent of the breeding population is found in Iceland.

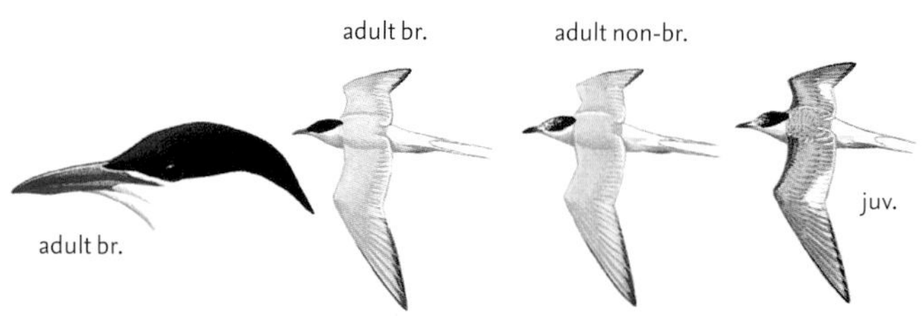

ID: *Very similar to Common Tern, with same greyish body, red legs and red bill. Bill is shorter, without a black tip, and legs are also noticeably shorter. Has slightly more rounded head, and at rest the tail sticks out well beyond the wing tips.*

ID: *A fairly large tern with, in breeding plumage, a distinctive crest and a long black bill with yellow tip. Flies with heavy but regular wingbeats, with wings angled back and head down.*

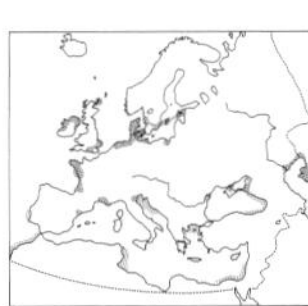

Sandwich Tern

Sterna sandvicensis (**ster**-na sand-vis-**sen**-siss)
length 36–41 cm

When dealing with predators terns have two possible strategies. They can either take to the skies in a communal protest to dive-bomb and mob the attacker, the method employed by most smaller terns, or they can follow the Sandwich Tern's way and simply stay put on the ground, displaying a closely packed colony armed with spiky bills and solidarity. It is typical for the larger, more intimidating terns to follow this stay-put strategy, and as a rule these species have the most densely packed colonies. The nesting density for a Sandwich Tern colony in Europe can be as high as twelve nests per square metre.

Despite this, Sandwich Terns have a reputation for being easily disturbed. If alarmed by an intrusion from a human or fox, they will quit the area and find somewhere else. Their method of settling on a nesting site allows for this eventuality, because they don't do this until shortly before egg laying: pairing preliminaries are carried out at a roosting area nearby.

In common with most other terns, Sandwich Terns frequently undertake manoeuvres known as 'dreads', in which most members of the colony suddenly and silently take off from their territories and fly off over the sea. When they have gone a respectable distance away they all start calling, and amble back in no great hurry. These dreads may be triggered by something as innocent as a change in the rhythm of the waves, or have no obvious trigger at all, and their function is quite unknown.

When the chicks hatch they are fed by the adults on the territory, but at about a week old they usually leave the site and gather with other chicks into crèches on the edge of the colony. These crèches are guarded by a few adults, and the youngsters face threats by running away from them while still closely packed, like a very large rugby scrum. The idea is, as with dense colonies, to present a show of solidarity and reduce each chick's chance of being predated. While their young are in a crèche both parents can go out foraging; when they return they simply call their young out, like parents arriving at a nursery.

The crèche is not a stepping stone to rapid independence, because parental care is exceptionally long in this species and in other terns. Almost uniquely among birds, adult terns may actually continue provisioning their young during their migratory journey. In Sandwich Terns this has been seen as late as August.

Sandwich Terns winter off the west coast of Africa. When the adults return in spring the first-year birds remain behind to spend the summer in these rich fishing grounds. When almost two years old they may visit a colony; although not arriving until June, which is too late for breeding, they may be enlisted by a pair to bring a few fish to their latest brood. Only when they are about four years old do they breed for the first time.

adult br.

Caspian Tern

Sterna caspia (**ster**-na **kass**-pi-a)
length 47–54 cm

The largest tern in the world, and one of the most aggressive, the Caspian can easily hold its own among gulls and other seabirds. More than that, it can displace them. There are consistent records of Caspian Terns evicting Herring Gulls from sites where they wish to nest – and Herring Gulls are not pushovers. The Caspian Terns do it by arriving on a desirable spot en masse and simply staying put.

Watching a Caspian Tern feed is a spectacular sight. In common with most terns it is a plunge-diver and will enter the water with an impressive splash, sometimes immersing itself completely. It tends to subsist on larger fish than other terns, usually at least 9 cm long (which is towards the upper limit for a Sandwich Tern) and up to 25 cm at times. Larger specimens are typically taken to shore, where they are despatched with a few blows of the outsize bill.

In Europe most of the colonies are medium-sized (10–200 pairs) and some are known to have been occupied for at least a hundred years. One of the regular sights of early in the breeding season is 'high flying', in which birds lift up more than 100 m above the ground with slow, deliberate wingbeats. The Caspian Tern's high flight differs from that of smaller terns in that only one or two birds are ever involved, and they never carry fish.

adult br.

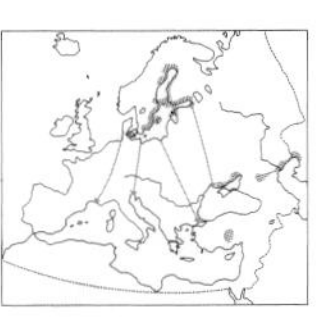

ID: *A huge tern with a massive red bill, making bird look as though it is carrying a carrot. Pretty unmistakable, as big as a large gull. Flies with slow, strong wingbeats.*

Little Tern

Sterna albifrons (**ster**-na **al**-bi-fronz)
length 22–24 cm

The smallest of the terns, Little Terns prefer to breed close to their feeding sites. Where some species may commute up to 60 km to find fish for their young, Little Terns will go 4 km at most and preferably only a few metres. In fact, most colonies are 1.5 m or less from the high-water mark, with clear water very much at hand. The majority of colonies are found on beaches and low islands and, while most are coastal, a significant proportion of birds can penetrate inland and breed along the shingle beds of large rivers.

It is easier to observe Little Terns fishing than perhaps any other tern. They hover over shallow water, with rapid, almost butterfly-like wingbeats, and often follow an ebbing or flowing tide, taking them unconcernedly close to people. The hover is followed by a plunge-dive from about 5–7 m. It is on record that, while providing for its chicks, a bird may make as many as 109 dives per hour and visit the young 63 times in the course of a day. The fish that Little Terns take are mostly between 3 cm and 6 cm in length. The birds are not especially fussy, and in some areas they may catch shrimps or insects instead – it all depends what is available nearby.

These terns are extremely susceptible to disturbance, and this can greatly affect their breeding success. In one study a colony of 87 pairs managed to raise only 9 young in a certain year; later, after wardens were installed to guard the site, 154 pairs raised 177 young.

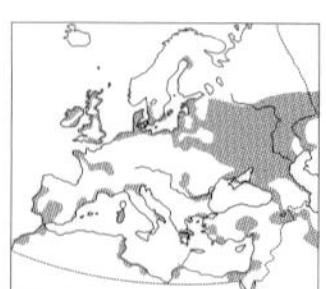

ID: Very distinctive small tern that flies with rapid, butterfly-like wingbeats; often hovers for long periods. In breeding plumage, long bill is yellow with a black tip (reverse of Sandwich).

Black Tern

Chlidonias niger (klie-**doh**-nee-ass **nie**-jer)
length 23–28 cm

ID: Small tern with short, shallowly forked tail. Flies with agile jinks and dips. Easily recognised in breeding season by smart coal-black head and breast, with plain grey wings above and below. Legs and bill black.

The Black Tern is the commonest of the three dark-plumaged terns collectively known as marsh terns. These differ from the other terns, sea terns, in typically breeding inland and in placing their nests on floating vegetation instead of on islands, beaches and sand dunes. The Black Tern is less restricted in habitat than the other two, the White-winged Black Tern and Whiskered Tern, in that it may use both freshwater and brackish marshes, and it also ranges over a broader climatic range. Although it normally follows the marsh tern code by building its nest on floating vegetation in 50 cm or more of water, it will also sometimes use much shallower sites and might even place its heap of weeds on the ground.

The feeding of marsh terns is quite different from that of sea terns. The main diet in the breeding season is almost invariably insects. The method of catching is also different, the marsh terns rarely plunging into the water, but instead dipping down elegantly and snatching food from the surface or just above it. The appearance of this foraging is leisurely and effortless, with lots of rising and falling, and lacks the earnest and purposeful style of sea terns. Marsh terns also hawk in mid-air for flying insects, looking rather like outsize Swallows.

Black Terns nest in colonies. On arrival on the breeding grounds in April they typically scout around for a couple of weeks to check for suitable conditions. Then, once they have selected the site, they act like a shy teenager asking for a date, landing on it for only a short time each day before flying off. Only a few days before first egg laying do they finally occupy the site and then rapidly build their nests. Black Terns pair up in a similar way to sea terns, with 'high flying' forming a major component of courtship, often with as many as 20 birds taking part.

After breeding, virtually the whole population of northern and eastern Europe gathers to moult and prepare for migration in just one place, the IJsselmeer in the Netherlands. Between 150,000 and 200,000 birds spend two to three weeks here in July and August, before resuming their journey.

In complete contrast to the other marsh terns, the Black Tern rather changes its spots in the winter and assumes the mantle of a marine tern. Its winter distribution is entirely coastal and it feeds almost exclusively by dipping to the surface of the sea for small fish.

Whiskered Tern

Chlidonias hybridus
(klie-**doh**-nee-ass **hie**-brid-duss)
length 23–25 cm

A fussy species which likes the sun on its back, the Whiskered Tern is the patchiest in distribution of the marsh terns, occurring mainly in the catchments and deltas of a few mighty rivers such as the Volga, Danube and Guadalquivir. Here it breeds in the usual marsh tern habitat, still or slow-flowing water with copious floating vegetation, although it will also take to man-made habitats such as fish ponds and rice fields. Its food is similar to that of the other marsh terns, consisting more of insects than of fish, and with the occasional amphibian such as a newt thrown in.

Whiskered Terns do, though, have their own distinctive feeding technique. More often than not they simply fly up and down again and again over the same patch of water, usually into the wind and only 2–4 m above the surface. When they see something they break the marsh tern mould by plunging down to the surface, getting their feet and bellies wet, and then resume their quartering. They also regularly dip down to the surface to snatch an item without immersing, and will sometimes catch beetles by dropping onto them on the ground.

Most European colonies are small, with fewer than 20 pairs. In fact, should a colony ever exceed more than a few pairs, the birds will divide themselves, somewhat antisocially, into discrete sub-colonies with synchronised breeding. Whiskered Terns are equally snooty towards other species, too, because although they often nest alongside Black-headed Gulls and other marsh terns, they won't actually mix with them. The only exceptions to this appear to be grebes. In central Europe, Little, Great Crested, Red-necked and Black-necked Grebes may all be drawn to Whiskered Tern colonies like fans to a pop star's home, nesting there in preference to anywhere else. The grebes obtain safety by breeding close to the aggressive terns, but it's not all to their advantage. The terns sometimes take over the grebes' floating nests, and at times the broods may be mixed, leading to confusion all round.

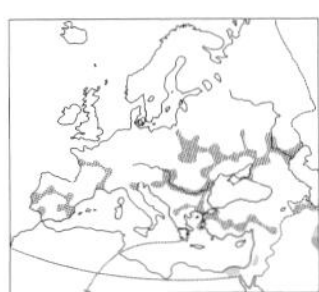

ID: Slightly larger than Black and White-winged Black Terns, with broad wings and a notched tail. Resembles a Common or Arctic Tern but has darker grey plumage, making a sharp contrast with the white cheeks, and has less forked tail.

adult br. adult non-br.

White-winged Black Tern

Chlidonias leucopterus
(klie-**doh**-nee-ass loo-**kop**-ter-russ)
length 23–27 cm

The White-winged Black Tern has a more restricted distribution in Europe than the Black Tern, being found mainly further east, in the steppe zone. It shares the Black Tern's regard for freshwater habitats, but does not take regularly to man-made environments. The precise description of its prime habitat would be natural flooded grasslands and meadows adjacent to large freshwater lakes or rivers. Not surprisingly, such places often appear only sporadically, so the White-winged Black Tern tends to move about from year to year in search of the right conditions. In drought years it may not breed at all, and in other years may be quite abundant.

The White-winged Black Tern has a diet typical of all the marsh terns, namely insects. It greatly favours flies and dragonflies. One would expect it, therefore, to be extremely agile in the air, and so it proves. It is quicker and more decisive than the Black Tern, making rapid skims over the water as well as frequent dips to the surface and, although it can hover, it tends to do so less than the Black Tern. It also, uniquely for a marsh tern, will periodically land on the surface of the water and wade.

These birds breed in small colonies, usually of 20 pairs or less and well spread. They sometimes nest among Little Gulls and Black-necked Grebes and, although they will breed close to other terns, they will not form mixed colonies with them. The nest, as in other marsh terns, is usually placed on floating vegetation.

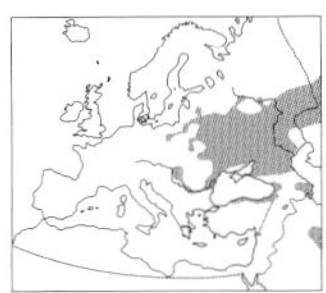

ID: Similar to Black Tern but tail barely notched and with broader, blunter wings. Easily distinguished in breeding plumage by bright white forewings contrasting with black belly and dark grey back at rest; legs also red, not black.

adult non-br. juv.

Auks family *Alcidae* (al-sid-ee)

Habitat Marine, usually breeding on cliffs facing the sea, occasionally inland. At sea in winter.
Food Mainly fish or plankton.
Movements Most disperse southwards but not very far, remaining in European waters at least. Black Guillemot doesn't go far from its breeding site, whereas Puffin may cross the Atlantic.
Voice All have low-pitched growling or purring noises except Black Guillemot, which utters 'electronic' sounding bleeps, and Little Auk, which twitters.
Pairing style Monogamous.
Nesting Colonial, often in vast assemblages.
Nest On ledge, in crevice, in burrow or under boulder. Little or no material, although Little Auk and Puffin bring in some furnishings such as feathers.
Productivity 1 brood a year.
Eggs 1 (except Black Guillemot, 1–2).
Incubation 28–43 days, by both sexes in long shifts.
Young Nest-bound, altricial and downy.
Parenting style Both adults feed and tend the young.
Food to young As adults' diet, brought in bill except for Little Auk, which has special food pouches in the throat.
Leaving nest Considerable variety. May leave when fully fledged or less than half grown, alone or in company of male parent.

Guillemot

The auks are often called the 'penguins of the northern hemisphere' and the label is useful if not entirely accurate. Both groups contain about the same number of species of marine birds that catch fish by swimming underwater, propelled by both their kicking webbed feet and their flapping, paddle-like wings. The legs are set so far back on the elongated body that, when they come to land, members of both groups must stand upright rather than perch. In both families the principal plumage colours are the same, black above and white below, to make them inconspicuous to predators above and prey below respectively. Each group contains some of the deepest divers among all birds. And each family is a dominant force among seabirds in its respective area, including among its number some of the most abundant of any birds anywhere, nesting together in vast, crowded colonies.

One major difference between the two families, though, is that auks fly. Not very well, mind you – they have to flap very fast and they are not very manoeuvrable. In fact it can be highly amusing watching them land at their breeding ledges, especially in a high wind; they just don't look comfortable. But flight enables them to colonise cliffs and other precipitous sites, where ground predators are excluded.

The centre of auk diversity in Europe is the Arctic, where all six species occur and where two species, the Little Auk and the Brünnich's Guillemot, are confined. Arctic waters tend to be exceptionally rich in food, with not just fish, but also plankton and crustaceans available. The precise type of food consumed by an auk is related to its bill shape, with the sharp-billed Guillemots specialising on small fish, for example, and the stubby-billed Little Auk preferring plankton.

Auks breed in colonies, form monogamous pair bonds, build little or no nest and lay just one or two large eggs. One of the most remarkable features of the family is the extraordinary variation in the development of the young. They may leave the nest one-quarter grown in company with an adult (Guillemot, Razorbill) or fully fledged and independent (Puffin). No other family in the world shows such variation.

Guillemot

Uria aalge (yoo-**rie**-a **al**-jee)
length 38–43 cm

A breeding colony of Guillemots is not a place for introverts. No bird colony in the world is as crowded. Packed along narrow ledges on high sea cliffs, or standing shoulder to shoulder on top of sea stacks, breeding Guillemots may assume a density of 20 pairs per square metre on flat rocks, or up to an incredible 70 pairs where the surface is uneven. The birds stand in physical contact like commuters in rush hour, and the noise, smell and constant movement must be quite overwhelming.

Nevertheless, precipitous cliff faces are safe. No ground predator would risk scaling such dangerous rock walls, and any aerial marauder would be faced with a row of sharp bills. Once the egg has been laid, at least one parent Guillemot will be in constant attendance, on guard against danger. A little discomfort is a small price to pay for a successful breeding season.

Guillemots follow the typical pattern of low productivity for a long-lived species (they regularly live up to 20 years), by laying just one large egg a year, to which they devote all their energies. Being laid on bare rock high up on a ledge, the egg is pear-shaped rather than round, ensuring that, should it roll, it will have a tight turning circle and not fall off the cliff – although, since Guillemots are clumsy birds, this does happen quite often. The egg is highly patterned with all kinds of spots, speckles and squiggles, and each one is recognisable, which may ensure that the parents incubate the correct egg. It is also possible that at times, if both adults do need to vacate the nest simultaneously, the unique egg can be found again as surely as an individually marked house.

The adults feed the youngster on fish, and they have a somewhat laborious way of doing it. They go out to sea, sometimes as far as 50 km, catch a single fish and return three to eight times a day, carrying the prey lengthways in the bill so that the bony head is embedded deep in the Guillemot's mouth, possibly so that it can be pre-digested. Such paltry efforts add up to about 28 g of food per day.

This goes on for three weeks and then the youngster, still flightless but highly capable of swimming, leaves the nest site. This is a fraught process, usually taking place just before dusk, when the colony becomes a tense, agitated place, ringing with the braying calls of anxious adults. Departure is risky, for several reasons. For a start the youngster must jump off the cliff ledge, to descend as much as 300 m before it hits the water. Its wings are weak, its downward progress fluttery and poorly controlled, and it must avoid hitting any rocks below. Secondly the departure of chicks is an opportunity for easy meals for gulls or skuas; they may pick the youngsters off from their 'diving ledge' (not all jump from the nest site), intercept them on the way down or field them from the water when they surface. And thirdly the youngster must rendezvous with its father when it gets to the sea, because otherwise it will starve. It cannot yet catch enough fish to sustain itself, so for the moment must be provided for.

If father and young meet up successfully, they swim out to sea together and remain as a unit for about a month. During this time they may cover 700 km or more while the youngster serves its fishing apprenticeship. The female parent, meanwhile, spends a couple of weeks resting at the colony and then disperses out to sea to moult.

ID: Commonest and most numerous auk, with long, pointed bill and very short tail. Southern birds chocolate-brown above, white below; northern birds blacker above. Both have diagnostic streaks on the flanks. In flight looks blunt-ended, as legs trail. Birds on water lack long tail of Razorbill.

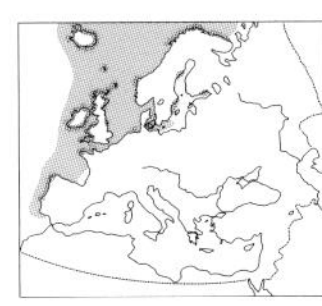

Little Auk

Alle alle (**al**-lee **al**-lee)
length 17–19 cm

This is the smallest of the European auks, and also the one most confined to Arctic waters. Not one breeding colony lies south of latitude 65°N and some are up above 80°N. Various islands off the north coast of Norway hold most European breeders, with 100,000 pairs in Svalbard, for example. There is also a minute and decreasing colony in Iceland, with just a handful of pairs.

Plankton forms the main diet of this small, stubby-billed species, but it will also eat fish fry at times. The young are fed mainly on copepod crustaceans, which are transported from the fishing areas in a pouch in the throat. En route these are covered in mucus and delivered as a form of planktonic paste, which may include as many as 600 stewed items, all between 1 mm and 17 mm long. Little Auks feed mainly where convection currents around the ice bring food towards the surface, and normally don't dive much deeper than 20 m.

Little Auks breed on boulder-strewn slopes facing the sea, selecting crevices up to 1 m long. The outside may still be covered in snow even when the chicks are hatching, and very well hidden, but this does not stop many birds falling victim to humans, Arctic foxes and even polar bears. If they survive, the young leave the nest fully fledged.

After breeding some birds drift south, where, during severe, prolonged gales, they may be beached in large numbers and perish. Such phenomena are known as 'wrecks'.

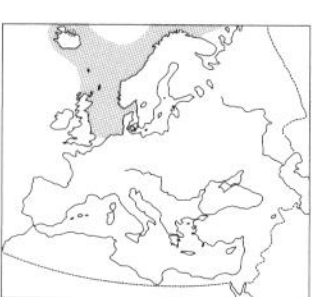

ID: Easy to identify at all times so long as the minute bill can be seen. Flies very fast and low, and may resemble a Starling more than an auk. Wings rather narrow. Has white streaks in mid-wing. On water, usually looks neckless.

Razorbill

Alca torda (**al**-ka **tor**-da)
length 37–39 cm

When Razorbills and Puffins are fishing the same waters, the former sometimes cause their smaller counterparts a shock. Like bullies in a swimming pool they will sneak up on the Puffins from under the water and attack them, attempting to steal fish from their bills. This approach often works and, for the Razorbill at least, it is an energy-saving way of acquiring food for themselves or their young.

Normally, though, few Razorbills are such miscreants; instead most spend their time diving down into the shallows to catch fish of their own. They don't dive as deeply as most other auks, rarely descending below 5–7 m, and they liberally sprinkle their diet with crustaceans, something that their cliff-ledge neighbours the Guillemots rarely do. In another contrast to the Guillemots they may catch several fish before taking them up to the chick – 20 has been recorded – and they hold these crosswise, not lengthways in the bill.

Although sharing the cliff-nesting habit with Guillemots, Razorbills are found at much lower densities, with most nests a few metres apart. They shun the precipitous cliffs beloved of the stunt-nesting auks, instead selecting broader ledges, often with overhangs, or settling among boulders in less elevated locations. Some Baltic colonies, especially, are on low rocky islands.

The young leave the nest about 18 days after hatching and they do it in daring Guillemot style, jumping off the cliff and meeting their father on the sea. In contrast to Guillemots, though, the youngsters leave after dark, usually between 9 and 11 p.m. on an August evening.

Once fledged the young swim out to sea and, in contrast to all the other auks, may go a long way south, dipping into the Mediterranean or reaching the Atlantic coast of Africa, where they spend the winter.

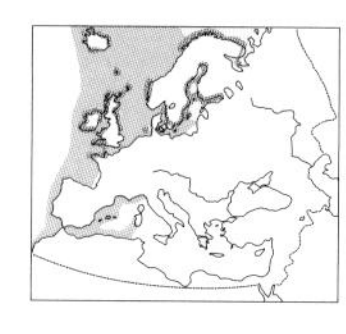

ID: Distinctively shaped auk with thick, blunt bill. Bill has single white band and a thin white streak runs from eye to the top of the bill. Has longer tail than Guillemot which extends beyond feet in flight and may point upwards when bird is on water.

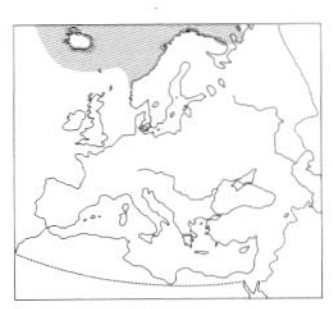

ID: Similar to Guillemot, but has much thicker bill with a white streak along the gape. Always black above. White below, lacking the streaking of Guillemot, and in breeding plumage this white meets to make sharp point below.

Brünnich's Guillemot

Uria lomvia (yoo-**rie**-a **lohm**-vee-a)
length 39–43 cm

The Brünnich's Guillemot has a thicker bill than the Guillemot and is much less of a specialised fish-eater, especially in the winter. It regularly consumes squid and crustaceans, plus smaller numbers of marine worms and molluscs. It is the record holder among auks for the depths of its dives, with an impressive 210 m having been recorded. Although 20–50 m is more regular, there is no doubt that this species is no stranger to the seabed, frequently consuming the special fish that occur there.

Confined to the Arctic and sub-Arctic, the Brünnich's Guillemot breeds only where precipitous cliffs overlook waters teeming with life; these are usually found near marine upwellings. It selects ledges that are, if anything, narrower than those chosen by Guillemots, and the cliffs occupied may be 200–450 m above the sea. Colonies are often enormous, rarely with fewer than a hundred pairs, and typically well into the tens of thousands (300,000 is known). These birds pack in less densely than Guillemots, with a maximum nest dispersion of 37 pairs per square metre, and usually much less.

Young Brünnich's are raised in a similar way to Guillemots, dispersing to sea with their father after being fed by both adults on the ledge for three weeks.

Black Guillemot

Cepphus grylle (**sep**-fuss **gril**-lee)
length 30–32 cm

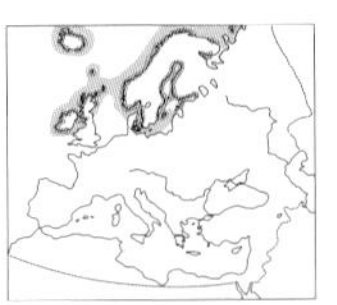

ID: Distinctive in both plumages. In breeding plumage black with large white wing patches. In winter much whiter than other auks, lacking standard black above/ white below pattern; head almost white.

The Black Guillemot is the only European auk to specialise in foraging on the seabed itself, rather than from the middle or subsurface levels. To do this it needs shallow water, tending not to stray very far out to sea and often remaining within 15 km of its breeding grounds throughout the year. It rarely dives below 8 m, swapping depth for thoroughness, working its way along the bottom and often surfacing a long way from where it went down. The seabed offers not just its own range of fish, but a wide variety of other invertebrates, too.

Because it finds its food in shallow water close at hand, the Black Guillemot is a more efficient provider of food than the other auks, and this enables it to go out on a limb by audaciously laying two eggs. It feeds its young mainly on fish, making 3–15 visits a day, sometimes bringing in several snacks at once. In common with the Puffin and Razorbill, it carries these fish crosswise in its bill.

These birds breed in crevices, sometimes among boulders not far from the lapping waves, but also sometimes in deep holes in high-rise cliffs. Although primarily colonial, Black Guillemots don't pack together in large numbers, 20 pairs being normal and a thousand pairs exceptional. In fact they often nest singly, too, with both members of a pair typically being faithful to both the site and the mate – the divorce rate is only 7 per cent.

The young fledge after being fed by both adults in the nest for 34–39 days, leaving well feathered and without the adults' knowledge.

Puffin

Fratercula arctica (fra-**terk**-yoo-la **ark**-tik-ka)
length 26–36 cm

Few birds are as instantly recognisable as the Puffin, yet comparatively few people have seen them in the wild. They are largely confined to the western edge of Europe, on the Atlantic coast, from the Brittany region of France to northern Norway and Svalbard, and they are distinctly fussy about their habitat. They need loose soil in which to dig their nesting burrow, so maritime cliffs or coasts with grassy tops are favoured, although in places they will nest among boulders, too. Another consideration is safety, and Puffins are always found in places where ground predators cannot get access, such as on islands, or where getting to them is difficult or risky, such as sea cliffs.

Once they have settled upon a locality, however, Puffins may occur there in vast numbers. Several colonies in Europe have 100,000 pairs or more, and in prime locations these may be found at densities of one or two pairs per square metre. In Puffin colonies the earth is riddled with small burrows 1–2 m long, most of them dug out by the birds' feet. Where possible, though, Puffins use rabbit burrows or tunnels made by Manx Shearwaters, sometimes sharing them with the rightful owners!

Early in the breeding season male Puffins defend the nesting burrow by an engaging territorial display known as a pelican walk. Puffing their breasts out, standing erect like guardsmen and with bill resting on chest, they strut back and forth in comical fashion, lifting their red feet high like children pretending to be giants. Displays between the sexes, on the other hand, take place not on land but on the water, where adults gather before moving into the colony in the spring. In contrast to Guillemots, copulation also takes place on the water.

Puffins lay a single egg at the bottom of their burrow and incubate it in shifts lasting, on average, 32 hours. Once the chick hatches the parent or parents bring in food about six times a day – but it's usually a decent meal, because Puffins are able to carry a good many fish in one go, crosswise in the bill. The record for one delivery is, remarkably, 62 fish – quite a mouthful! The fish are kept in place by the bill's backward-pointing edges and by the bird's tongue. One reason why Puffins bring in so much food is that, in contrast to other auks, they tend to chase after shoals, rather than individual fish.

The young Puffin leaves the nest once it is anything up to 60 days old. It leaves at night, unaccompanied, and swims out to sea. In contrast to other auks Puffins regularly disperse over very deep water and birds in their first winter often cross the Atlantic.

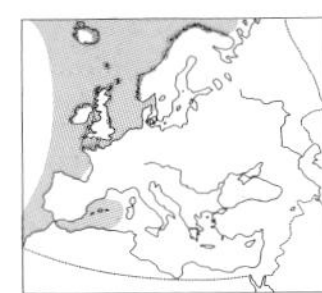

ID: Unmistakable in breeding plumage, with huge, brightly coloured triangular bill. In winter bill smaller and less colourful, face smoky-grey. When seen in flight, smaller than Razorbill and Guillemot, with shorter front and rear end; underwings dark.

adult br.

adult non-br.

juv.

adult non-br.

Sandgrouse family *Pteroclididae* (ter-roh-**klie**-did-ee)

Habitat Dry, arid areas, including semi-desert, steppe, plateaux (Black-bellied) and cereal fields.
Food Mainly seeds, especially of the pea family.
Movements Resident, with some nomadic movements.
Voice Black-bellied has a bubbling call, that of Pin-tailed is harsh, grating and descending.
Pairing style Monogamous.
Nesting Solitary, but not territorial. Nests are often not far apart, though.
Nest A scrape on the ground.

Productivity 1 brood a year.
Eggs 2–3, hatching at the same time.
Incubation 19–24 days, by the female during the day and the male at night.
Young Precocial and downy.
Parenting style Both adults tend the young.
Food to young Young are self-feeding, but depend on male parent for water brought soaked in his breast feathers.
Leaving nest Leave nest on first day, as soon as down is dry. Independent about 2 weeks later.

The sandgrouse are a small family of slightly mysterious birds that look a bit like both waders and pigeons, with an element of gamebird thrown in. The feet are feathered like those of grouse (hence the name), the sharp-pointed wings are borrowed from waders and the squat bodies with short neck, bill and legs are similar to those of pigeons. The most recent biochemical research links them most closely with waders, but nothing is settled quite yet among the specialists.

Sandgrouse are highly adapted to living in arid and desert environments. The feathers on the feet dull the extreme heat of burning sand, and the soles are specially thickened to cope with a life of walking along rough ground. The birds are remarkably cryptic in both appearance and habits, wearing intricately patterned, mainly brown plumage and keeping the lowest of low profiles. A sandgrouse's day consists mainly of quietly wandering along the ground, eating seeds, leaves and a few green shoots. If it gets excited, or angry with a colleague, the sandgrouse never shows it; the argument is buried and the birds remain alive.

Only at certain times are sandgrouse demonstrative, and that is on a daily or twice-daily basis, when they visit water. This is a group activity occurring at precisely the same time of day, usually an hour or two after dawn. Birds from all around come together and fly around the site in circuits before landing, calling excitedly. If the coast is clear they settle nearby and run down to the water, in their exuberance emancipated for a moment from their understated lives, like a bunch of company executives skinny-dipping. Then, after a few moments of gulping down water, they are off to anonymity again.

Sometimes a departing male sandgrouse carries a very special load: water for the chicks. A male's belly feathers are specially adapted for carrying water, rather like a sponge, so a father makes sure that at the waterhole he immerses well. He then flies off to the nest, often many kilometres away. The young run towards him and drink from his belly like a brood of suckling piglets.

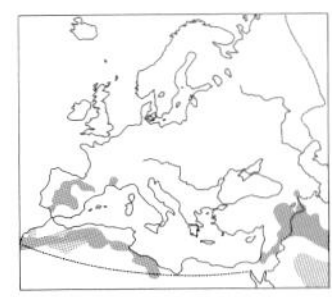

Pin-tailed Sandgrouse

Pterocles alchata (**ter**-ro-kleez al-**kay**-ta)
length 31–39 cm

ID: Slimmer than Black-bellied Sandgrouse, with longer tail and white underside. Male greener on top than female, with less barring; rusty colour on head and breast more intense.

The Pin-tailed Sandgrouse's visits to water are noisy and exciting events. The drinkers all arrive 2 hours 45 minutes after sunrise, streaming in from different directions, like commuters arriving at work, and forming into one large mass, which may contain a thousand birds. They habitually fly several times around a potential site before alighting, and will at times perform aerobatic displays first too, like roosting Starlings, the whole flock looking at a distance like smoke billowing in the wind. On hot days they may need a second drinking visit, and come about an hour before sunset.

This is a bird of lowland arid habitats – dry grassland, plains, cultivations and dried-out mud. In optimum habitat there may be four nests to every hundred hectares. The nests themselves are merely scrapes in the ground, often in hoof prints. Normally the Pin-tailed waits at least until June to breed, when seeds are just becoming available.

After breeding the birds collect in flocks. When they can they often mix with groups of foraging Little Bustards, which act as lookouts for sandgrouse when they enter vegetation that is too high for them to peer over, something they would not normally do.

Black-bellied Sandgrouse

Pterocles orientalis (**ter**-ro-kleez oh-ri-en-**tay**-liss)
length 33–35 cm

The larger and plumper of Europe's two sandgrouse, the Black-bellied is a bird of plains, steppes, plateaux, grasslands and cereal cultivation. It has a preference for rolling country and is often found at altitudes up to 1300 m. In farming areas its survival depends on tracts of fallow land remaining within low-intensity cultivation, so not surprisingly its future in Europe looks precarious. There are perhaps 50,000 pairs in total, but the species is in sharp decline.

This is a less gregarious sandgrouse than the Pin-tailed. Flocks rarely number more than 25 birds and the excited pre-landing displays at waterholes are lacking. These birds do, however, arrive from nest sites as much as 60 km away and they all show up at the same time, about three hours after dawn. On hot summer days their second appointment at water, if appropriate, is an hour before sunset. They usually do not immerse much, but there are records of them being swallowed by large fish.

The nest of a Black-bellied Sandgrouse is a shallow scrape, often in a small depression and, unlike that of the Pin-tailed, often not far from cover. When the eggs are being incubated, the male's shift lasts from an hour after sunset until four hours after sunrise, while the female takes over by day; these long stints are designed to draw as little attention to the nest as possible.

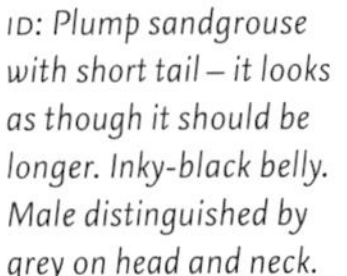

ID: Plump sandgrouse with short tail – it looks as though it should be longer. Inky-black belly. Male distinguished by grey on head and neck.

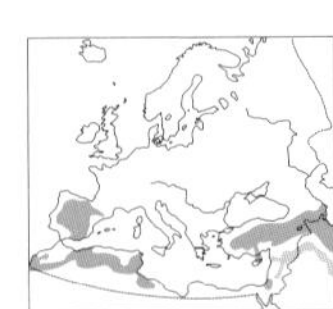

Pigeons and Doves family *Columbidae* (koh-**lum**-bid-ee)

Habitat All except Turtle Dove occur around human settlements, the Feral Pigeon and Collared Dove almost entirely so. Also woodland edge, sea cliffs, farmland.
Food Mostly grain, but many other parts of plants, including shoots, leaves, berries and tubers.
Movements Collared Dove and Feral Pigeon resident, although Collared Dove young highly dispersive. Stock Dove and Wood Pigeon migratory in north and east, not travelling far. Turtle Dove long-distance migrant to Africa.
Voice Variations on a coo, but Turtle Dove purrs and Collared Dove has a trumpeting call.
Pairing style Monogamous.
Nesting Solitary and territorial.
Nest Poorly made platforms of sticks.
Productivity Usually 2–3 broods a year, but 4 or 5 is not unusual and 6 has been recorded.
Eggs Usually 2.
Incubation 16–18 days, by both parents.
Young Nest-bound, altricial and downy.
Parenting style Both adults tend and feed the young.
Food to young A form of milk manufactured in the crop.
Leaving nest Young leave any time between 15 and 37 days after hatching, earlier if the nest is disturbed. They may then be fed by the parents for a few further days.

Stock Dove

There is no official distinction between a pigeon and a dove, even though many people might say that doves are small, slimmer versions of pigeons. But the term is interchangeable. In Europe, for example, one of our five species, the one with the scientific name *Columba livia*, has two English names – Feral Pigeon and Rock Dove.

This family is one that everybody recognises. Many of its members are abundant and live in close proximity to people. A pigeon or dove is a plump, squat bird, with a small head, short bill, short scaly legs and broad but pointed wings. Part of its frontal solidity is explained by the fact that very large pectoral flight muscles are housed beneath the breast. These muscles power the wings highly efficiently and can move the birds along at more than 70 km/h, sometimes for enormous distances. The staring eyes seem to give these birds a permanently rather gormless expression, especially when they bob their heads in time with their steps on the ground, like a chicken, but it would be foolish to write them off as 'bird-brained'. Pigeons and doves may not have the cognitive skills to read a map, but they do have highly sophisticated ways of finding their way about (see Feral Pigeon).

Two behavioural features of pigeons and doves are highly unusual. They are among the few birds in the world, and the only ones in Europe, that can suck up water instead of raising their heads to let gravity do the work. Contrary to expectation this is not an adaptation to drinking more efficiently, but rather a mechanism by means of which pigeons and doves can sip from the most minute water sources, such as accumulations of drops on vegetation or shallow, ephemeral puddles.

The other adaptive trick is to feed their young on milk, a habit shared among other birds only by flamingos and the Emperor Penguin (*Aptenodytes forsteri*). This means that the parents manufacture the food for their young rather than feeding it direct from the wild, so to speak. Cells in the adults' crop walls fill up with nutrients from the food they have taken, thicken and then break off, making a paste-like substance full of protein and minerals. The chicks grow quickly and are immune to the unpredictability that so blights many a young bird's development.

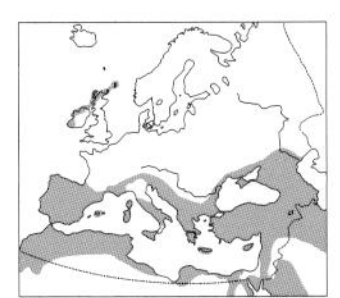

MAP: Does not include the distribution for the widespread Feral Pigeon.

ID: *Feral Pigeon flocks have mixtures of birds of all colours and individual plumage patterns, in contrast to any other pigeons. These and Rock Doves have red eyes. Rock Dove has two complete black wing bars, white rump and pale undersides to wing in flight. Ashy-grey above. Slim, with relatively long wings.*

Rock Dove/Feral Pigeon

Columba livia (koh-**lum**-ba **liv**-vee-a)
length 31–34 cm

Few birds in Europe have been neglected as wild study subjects in the same way as this species, the bird variously known as the Rock Dove, the Street Pigeon or the Feral Pigeon. As a result we know rather little about its population and distribution in Europe, and much less than we should about its ecology and behaviour.

One problem is that the species is represented by two very different strands of population. We are all familiar with the pigeons in our cities and towns, the ones that come to be fed at people's feet at such celebrated sites as Trafalgar Square in London or St Mark's Square in Venice; these are such icons of city life as to be overlooked as part of the scenery. But much less well known are the birds which live remote from people on sea cliffs and precipitous mountains, the wild 'Rock Doves'. That they are actually the same species, with the same origin, requires some explanation.

Originally all Feral Pigeons were Rock Doves, so to speak; they all looked alike and they lived in wild places. But some time between 5000 and 10,000 years ago they crossed paths with grain farmers, being attracted from their hideaways by the prospect of easy food on cultivated fields. People soon recognised that the young pigeons or 'squabs' were highly edible and encouraged them to breed near settlements. Little by little the Rock Dove was brought into domestication, aided by its ridiculously undemanding diet of grain, its liking for simple breeding ledges and its phenomenal year-long reproductive rate. The population now flowed along two streams: the wild Rock Doves continued their lifestyle as they had before and remained unchanged, but the domesticated birds began to be selectively bred for characteristics such as edibility, homing ability and attractive plumage. Thus a whole range of pigeon breeds arose – white pigeons (or doves), homing pigeons and pigeons with feathered feet, long tail plumes and curious head adornments; they became as diverse as breeds of dog. But at heart they were still all the same species.

The story turned full circle as domesticated birds escaped; some flew from dovecotes, others did not return to their lofts. A significant newly wild or 'feral' population built up, comprising individuals of many colours and plumage patterns, metaphorically wearing their prison clothes on the outside. With their new-found licence to roam, these birds did not, as one might expect, return to their origin on the cliff tops, but instead settled comfortably into built-up areas, using building ledges instead of rocky cavities or caves, and feeding on bread and grain instead of wild seeds. Thus under the same heading we have two camps – the Rock Doves with their ancestral plumage, and the Feral Pigeon with its new-fangled colour schemes – living well apart.

Until recently Feral Pigeons have rarely been studied in their semi-wild state, let alone censused. Clearly the population in towns and cities in Europe, and indeed elsewhere, is very large: in Barcelona, for example, a recent count came up with 2849 birds per square kilometre. This goes to show how remarkably well a shy bird living in remote places has been converted into a world-beater.

One aspect of Feral Pigeon biology is truly astonishing. Pigeons are renowned for their homing ability, accomplishing barely credible feats of pinpoint navigation (flying from Guernsey in the Channel Islands to the correct address in Brazil, for instance) and achieving enough reliability to be entrusted with carrying important human messages. Research has confirmed that they orientate by means of the sun's position together with an accurate internal clock, and that they are highly sensitive to magnetic fields. In addition to this they use landmarks, low-frequency sounds (infrasounds) and possibly smells to find their way. They are also sensitive to atmospheric pressure, so they even have a built-in weather-forecasting system to help them along the way. And yet this most famous of travelling birds is not actually a migrant. Most birds live within a very small area and never leave it.

Stock Dove

Columba oenas (koh-**lum**-ba **een**-ass)
length 32–34 cm

Easily overlooked because of its similarity to two domineering relatives, the superabundant Wood Pigeon and the streetwise Feral Pigeon, the Stock Dove is nonetheless a successful species, occupying most of Europe except for the extremes of north and south. Its habitat is a little more restricted than the others', however, because it usually requires tree holes in which to nest, and these are always a limiting factor. In some places it will use crevices in rocks and buildings, and a few enterprising birds even take over rabbit burrows, but for the most part the Stock Dove is a conservative species. It will thrive where tall, mature trees are found not far away from short-grass fields and bare ground, where the birds feed. In many parts of Europe its presence is promoted by the excavating work of Black Woodpeckers, especially in beech woods.

Pigeons do not show off a spectacular range of feeding techniques and the Stock Dove typically just wanders along the ground, pecking. Occasionally it will feed among bushes or in trees, too. However, it takes a wider range of food items than most other pigeons, including many types of wild seeds, nuts and fruits, preferring not to concentrate on one abundant foodstuff in competition with the tunnel-visioned Wood Pigeon.

Males advertise their presence with a gentle, questioning series of coos, a sound easily lost in the tree tops. They also embark on a somewhat unimaginative display flight, taking off and landing without much ceremony and simply gliding in an arc or a circle with the wings held up in a V. A rather more vigorous display, though, and one that is shared with other pigeons, is known as 'driving'. This is a chivvying routine, designed to help the males keep their mates firmly monogamous, by depriving them of time to admire alternatives. On the ground a driving male continually chases after his mate, often pecking at her to keep her moving and never losing sight of her; even in flight the chase and close attendance continues. Driving may last for many days, finishing only once the two eggs are laid and the male's paternity is assured.

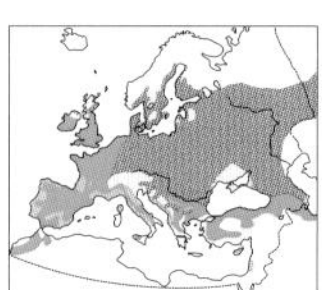

ID: Small pigeon/dove with short, stubby wings; looks compact. Fast, flickering flight. Eyes black. Thundercloud grey above and on wings, which each have two very small black inner wing bars. Wings black at tips, grey inside; no white.

adult juv.

Wood Pigeon

Columba palumbus (koh-**lum**-ba pal-**lum**-buss)
length 40–42 cm

In many farming districts of Europe, a flock of Wood Pigeons feeding on a field is a familiar sight. The birds stick close together as they forage, the flock often assuming an oval shape as all the members slowly advance forwards together, picking up their beloved grain. Within the flock is a rigid hierarchy: the dominant birds stay in the centre, enjoying a faster feeding rate by having plenty of bodies between them and potential danger; subordinate birds march along on the edges of the group and at the back, where they are more likely to become victims of a strike.

The Wood Pigeon also roosts in groups, gathering in trees and shrubs to spend the night. When disturbed a bird often clatters away noisily, leaving behind a displaced feather or two to float to the ground. Although this looks like a panic response it isn't; the sudden noise is intentional, designed to startle a predator and give the bird half a second's extra time to get away.

If any bird leads an easy life, a Wood Pigeon breeding near a farming area would probably count as one that does. It can acquire most of what it needs in a few short foraging sessions, of which the main one is in late afternoon, prior to roosting. It eats all kinds of foodstuffs, including many that man has thoughtfully provided for it. Among its favourite snacks are wheat, barley, oats, sugar beet, cabbage, Brussels sprouts and turnip. Not surprisingly, many farmers consider these birds to be a pest, and something like 9.5 million are shot every year in Europe.

But the Wood Pigeon is not found only in rural areas. Its exceptional adaptability has enabled it, since about 1800, to colonise towns and urban areas, where it eats all kinds of scraps in addition to seeds and other grain. It has moved here from the woodland edge, and most nests are still found on the branches and forks of various types of trees. These nests are flimsy, cost-cutting structures made from sticks collected on the ground and from below it's often possible to see the eggs placed on the end result.

Wherever it occurs, the Wood Pigeon's advertising call, five coos on a quick-slow-slow-quick-quick rhythm, is a very common, atmospheric sound. Equally familiar is the male's roller-coaster display flight, in which he rises up at a shallow angle, claps his wings loudly together, stalls as if shot and then glides down with wings and tail spread. The manoeuvre follows a straight line and may be repeated up to five times in succession. The bird lands, lifts his tail up and down slowly and then usually resumes cooing.

Wood Pigeons may breed at almost any time of year, but their peak season tends to be July, just in time for the harvest.

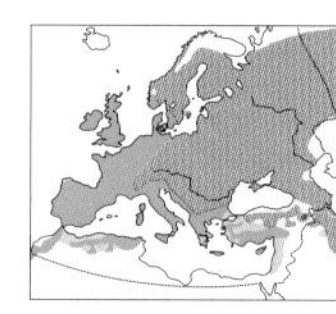

ID: Hefty pigeon with relatively long tail. Diagnostic white patch on neck side, and white bands on wing (where engines on aircraft's wing would be). Eyes yellow. Primary feathers white-fringed (not in other pigeons). Juvenile lacks neck adornments.

adult juv.

Turtle Dove

Streptopelia turtur (strep-toh-**pee**-li-a **toor**-toor)
length 26–28 cm

'Turtle' or '*turtur*' might seem a strange name for a dove, but it arises from this bird's repetitive advertising call, 'trrr, trrr', a soporific purr that emanates from some hidden perch any time between late April and August. When making the sound the birds bow their heads with their lower neck swollen and make slight nodding movements in time with the sounds. The performance has three peaks – the early morning, late afternoon and, perhaps surprisingly, around midday. Its main function is to attract females.

Turtle Doves are also vigorously territorial and will fight if necessary to hold on to what they have. To prevent this happening, though, they have a display flight which is performed at the slightest sign of another bird. The occupier takes off at a sharp angle, sometimes with a few wing-claps, gets to about 20 m, stalls and spirals down, spreading his tail to ensure that the white border is shown off to advantage, often not landing immediately but gliding along for a final flourish. These display flights may also be performed as part of the courtship display, but with somewhat more eager and faster flaps at the start.

The nest is built low down in a shrub or a hedge, and consists of the flimsy platform typical of pigeons; but as if the Turtle Doves were acknowledging their lack of nesting prowess, it is sometimes placed on top of the structure of another bird. The female lays two eggs and, as is the pigeon way, both the squabs are fed on crop milk. Uniquely among pigeons, once one brood has left the nest there is a biologically enforced hiatus, ensuring that the birds do not rush into the next breeding attempt too quickly.

There is something else unusual about the Turtle Dove and that is that, alone among our pigeons, it is a summer visitor, departing for Africa in September and returning in April. The birds migrate by day on a broad front, often in large numbers; 20,000 have been counted passing Malta in a single day.

The Turtle Dove is our only pigeon to avoid built-up areas. It is still a common bird, though, wherever there is light woodland or hedgerow, especially in warm, sunny, sheltered spots.

ID: Small, colourful dove, distinctive with its zebra-crossing neck ring and tortoiseshell pattern on back. Tail is contrastingly white-tipped. Belly white, in flight contrasting conspicuously with dark underwing.

Collared Dove

Streptopelia decaocto
(strep-toh-**pee**-li-a dek-ka-**ok**-to)
length 31–33 cm

Perhaps more than any other bird species in Europe, the 20th century belonged to the Collared Dove. Starting almost exactly in 1900, it began one of the most rapid and far-reaching expansions ever recorded for a bird working under its own steam. Making its way roughly northwest from Turkey, it had settled in most of the Balkans by 1928, much of central Europe by 1957, Britain, France and Italy by 1963 and northern Spain and southern Fennoscandia by 1977. It is estimated that between 1930 and 1970 it colonised 2,500,000 sq km of land; but it had not finished yet. Having taken over the west it turned its attentions eastwards and by the end of the century had made it to the Caspian Sea and beyond. Few areas of Europe have been left untouched. And wherever it has gone it has consolidated its position, progressing from being a complete stranger to being a common and familiar species within just a few years. Compared to none at all in 1900, the population in Europe at the beginning of the 21st century could be as many as 14 million pairs.

It is no less remarkable that, despite the magnitude of this expansion, we don't know why it took place or how it was triggered. It is simplistic to suggest that, by some sort of genetic mutation, it managed to fill a previously unoccupied niche, but that is as good an explanation as we have. We do know that the spread was carried out by young birds dispersing after fledging and then not returning, but the degree of dispersal is now slowing down in some areas. It could well be that this amazing spread, an unparalleled incident that has taken place in front of our eyes, will never be entirely explained.

As to the Collared Dove itself, its needs are well served by rural and suburban landscapes. It will nest in a small tree, bush or hedge and feed on grain from farms and bird tables. Chimney pots and aerials provide excellent perches for bouts of calling, and bird baths, ponds or gutters sort out its need for water. It seems to belong there.

The Collared Dove has a highly repetitive call suitably rendered 'un-i-ted', as chanted by a football fan. Bouts of calling often cease without warning, as the male launches into a display flight that takes him up to 20 m or so at a steep angle before he stalls and, with wings and tail spread, glides down on a spiralling path. After this show of territorial prowess the bird often lands, lifts up his tail and utters an excited trumpeting call. It could be the trumpet of a victorious invader.

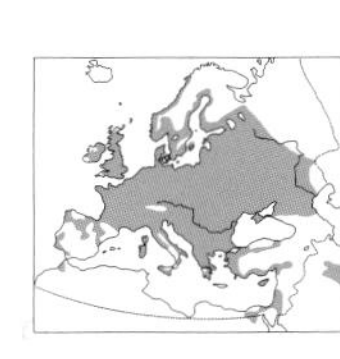

ID: Small, anaemically coloured dove/pigeon with long tail; distinctive flicks of wings in flight, without consistent beat. Thin but conspicuous white-edged black neck ring. Underside of wing of uniform pale colour, not contrasting with belly.

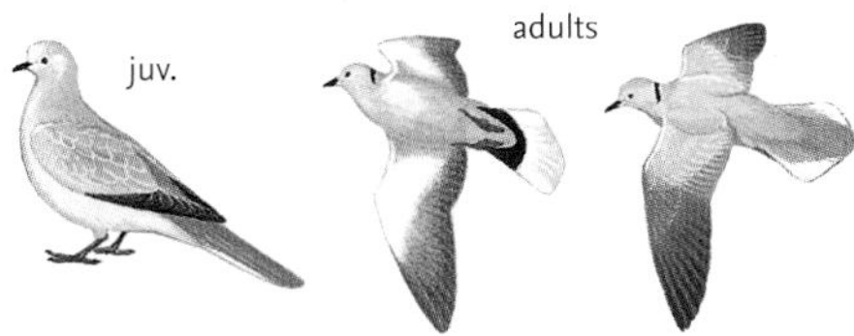

Rose-ringed Parakeet *Psittacula krameri* (sit-**tak**-oo-la **kray**-mer-eye) family *Psittacidae* (sit-**tas**-sid-ee)

adult ♂

length 38–42 cm

ID: *Unmistakable medium-sized, long-tailed green bird. Red parrot bill (brown in juvenile). Female head relatively unadorned. Male has black throat and rose-pink/blue neck ring, edged with black.*

Habitat Gardens, parks and orchards.
Food Although basically vegetarian it appears to be omnivorous in its introduced range, often taking scraps from bird tables.
Movements Sedentary.
Voice A typical loud screech, often uttered in series.
Pairing style Monogamous.
Nesting Solitary, although pairs will nest close together, sometimes in the same tree.
Nest In a tree hole; no structure, but the eggs are laid on a carpet of wood chips.
Productivity 1 brood a year.
Eggs 3–4, hatching at different times.
Incubation 22–24 days, by female only.
Young Nest-bound, altricial and naked.
Parenting style Fed and tended by both parents.
Food to young Vegetable matter, delivered bill to bill.
Leaving nest Young fledge at 40–50 days.

Europe is one of the few places in the world with no native parrots, but in recent years the Rose-ringed Parakeet has managed, thanks to human introductions, to gain a foothold. Having been released deliberately or accidentally in numbers in the 1970s, it has managed to build up some self-sustaining wild populations in locations as widely scattered as England, the Netherlands, Austria, Spain and Italy. All these populations are reportedly increasing steadily, and the English one now numbers about 5000 birds. The situation in all these countries needs to be monitored closely, because the Rose-ringed Parakeet is often an agricultural pest in its native range of Africa and India (it is the only parrot to inhabit both continents) and could potentially become one here.

At the moment a greater concern is competition with native birds. The Rose-ringed Parakeet is a hole-nesting species and, to borrow parlance from estate agents, the market for holes easily outstrips the slender supply, even without parakeets. If Rose-ringed Parakeets, which are aggressive and may start breeding exceptionally early in the year (January sometimes), were to increase beyond their current status as a curiosity, the fortunes of such competitors as Jackdaws, Starlings and Great Spotted Woodpeckers could be affected.

Another species of parrot, the Monk Parakeet (*Myiopsitta monachus*), has also established itself from introduced stock in Europe, notably in Barcelona, where there are perhaps 200 birds. This species has the distinction of being one of the few colonial parrots in the world, making large 'apartment blocks' of sticks, each shared by several pairs.

Cuckoos family *Cuculidae* (koo-**koo**-lid-ee)

Habitat Common Cuckoo in almost any habitat except built-up areas and unbroken dense forest. Great Spotted Cuckoo in open oak and pine woodland and almond groves.
Food Invertebrates, especially caterpillars.
Movements Both migrate to Africa for the winter.
Voice Common Cuckoo famously calls its name; female has startled ringing, bubbling trill, always given after she has raided a nest and also at other times. Great Spotted Cuckoo has cackling call.
Pairing style Common Cuckoo promiscuous, with short-lived, non-exclusive pair bond at best. Great Spotted Cuckoo monogamous.
Nesting Builds no nest.
Nest None; instead, it sublets that of host – various small insectivorous species for Common Cuckoo, Magpies and Crows for Great Spotted Cuckoo.
Productivity Have no broods as such (see below).
Eggs Each female Common Cuckoo may lay up to 25 eggs (8–12 more usual). Great Spotted Cuckoo up to 16, sometimes several in one host clutch.
Incubation By foster parent(s) only. Egg of Common Cuckoo hatches after 11–13 days, that of Great Spotted Cuckoo after 12–14.
Young Nest-bound, altricial and naked.
Parenting style None at all.
Food to young Mainly insects, delivered by foster parents.
Leaving nest Common Cuckoo chick leaves nest at 20–30 days, but makes sure that eggs or young of host are evicted much earlier, within 2–3 days. Great Spotted Cuckoo chick or chicks leave nest at 16–21 days, not ejecting host young.

Cuckoos are more celebrated for deeds than looks, but both our species are slender-bodied, long-winged, long-tailed birds with an unusual arrangement of the toes – two facing forward and two facing back, like those of a woodpecker. Their bills are moderately long, slightly curved and fairly thick, and the wings are pointed, making them look fairly hawk-like in silhouette. For this reason, or because of their parasitic habits, or both, they are frequently mobbed by other birds.

Both our cuckoos are what the scientists call 'brood parasites', never building their own nests, but instead deceptively farming their eggs out to other birds to look after, usually to the detriment of the hosts' young. Despite the fact that cuckoos are celebrated for this form of parasitism, the majority of cuckoo species in the world actually do make the effort to raise their own young themselves.

Our two species have an unusual diet, consisting mainly of hairy caterpillars, especially of the colonial type. Secondary in importance are beetles, spiders and other invertebrates, and the Great Spotted Cuckoo eats some lizards. Cuckoos have a special mechanism of the gizzard to deal with the hairs and noxious poison of the caterpillars: the lining periodically sloughs off and is then ejected as a pellet, thereby ensuring that the hairs do not pass through to the rest of the gut.

Great Spotted Cuckoo

Clamator glandarius
(klay-**may**-tor glan-**day**-ri-uss)
length 38–40 cm

The Great Spotted Cuckoo is very much Europe's 'other' cuckoo, restricted to the Mediterranean region and commonest in Spain. A migrant like the Common Cuckoo, the adults depart Europe in July while the juveniles hang contentedly around in the breeding areas and drift away, somewhat grudgingly, by November. Since the adults reappear as early as February, the species is missing only for a few weeks each year.

Although it is a brood parasite like the Common Cuckoo, the Great Spotted has very different hosts: not small insectivorous birds, but Magpies and Carrion Crows. Many aspects of its behaviour also differ markedly from the Common Cuckoo. The approach to a nest is performed not by the female alone, but by a pair. The case for having two raiders is readily apparent: the male appears in full view and distracts the hosts' attention, while the female advances through the thick branches unnoticed to lay her egg. She is taking a big risk, because if intercepted nearby or even inside the structure, she could be attacked and badly injured. Without the presence of the male it is doubtful whether many raids would be successful.

When laying in a Magpie's nest the female Great Spotted Cuckoo is usually in and out within ten seconds; for Carrion Crows, which have open, not domed nests, it can be as quick as three seconds – again, to avoid attack. In contrast to the Common Cuckoo the female does not remove and eat a host egg, but she might chip one or two of the Magpie's clutch to make sure they don't hatch, or ensure that she lays her harder-shelled egg on top of them, to crack them this way. Great Spotteds regularly lay more than one of their own eggs in the same nest.

Naturally, the eggs hatch before those of the host: the Magpie's incubation period is 18–22 days, the Cuckoo's only 12–14 days. However, in contrast to the Common Cuckoo, the youngster does not evict any of its nest fellows, neither eggs nor young; this is because Magpies calibrate the amount of food they bring in to the size of clutch, and a Cuckoo on its own might not receive enough food. Instead, the youngster, having at least four days' start on its host's young and a faster growth rate to boot, can normally out-compete them for the parents' offerings, causing the host chicks eventually to starve. The begging routine of the Great Spotted Cuckoo specially mimics the begging levels of an extremely hungry Magpie chick, duping the parents into thinking that its needs are paramount, even when it is in fact satiated.

ID: Unmistakable if seen well, with long tail and clear white spots on dark grey wing. Pale below, throat tinged buttery. Juvenile has chestnut on outer wing and black, not grey cap.

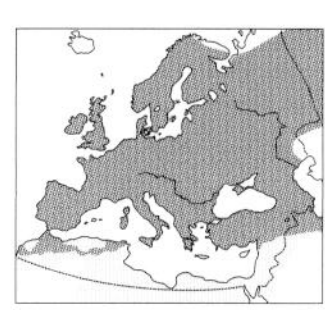

ID: Medium-sized, hawk-like grey bird with long tail and pointed wings. In flight, wings do not appear to rise above horizontal. Mainly grey, but barred on breast; tail spotted. Some females have tinge of buff on breast, otherwise look like males (but a few mainly rusty brown). Juvenile barred above and below, white nape spot.

Common Cuckoo

Cuculus canorus (koo-**koo**-luss ka-**noh**-russ)
length 32–33 cm

Perhaps no other bird in Europe is as infamous as the Cuckoo, a bird that invariably outsources the fundamental task of looking after its own chicks to an unrelated foster parent. Moreover, this happens to the detriment of the foster parent's own brood, without its permission and sometimes without its knowledge. This is brood parasitism on a grand scale.

The drama begins in April, when the Cuckoos arrive from their African winter quarters and the males begin making their loud advertising calls. Few sounds are so resonant of the season. The less demonstrative females, whose call is a loud but infrequent bubbling trill, cannot fail to make contact with such noisy operators, but once met the sexes have no need of much co-operation, so relationships are brief and both sexes are probably promiscuous. The males hold 'song territories' to attract females, while the latter hold their own exclusive 'egg territories', containing a supply of the nests of their host species.

A female instinctively seeks out the nests of the same species that reared her, a trait that is passed genetically along the female (but probably not the male) line. A club of females specialising in the same host is known as a 'gens' (plural 'gentes'). The gentes present differ from place to place. In Britain, for example, the main hosts and their gentes are Reed Warbler, Meadow Pipit, Dunnock and Robin, whereas in Fennoscandia they are Redstart and Brambling, and in some parts of Central Europe Great Reed Warbler and Pied Wagtail are important. A species' degree of vulnerability to becoming a regular host depends on several factors. Reed Warblers, for example, have rather variable eggs, so they are relatively poor at noticing the intruder. If a species has eggs of consistent colour the Cuckoo will often mimic them, but this does not necessarily mean that the host will accept them – it depends on how 'wise' a certain species has become to parasitism. Cuckoos and hosts are set in a sort of permanent 'arms race', with the hosts working towards the rejection of all Cuckoo eggs and the parasites aiming for full acceptance.

A Cuckoo with plans for its hosts is a birdwatcher. It spends much time hidden away on a high perch in a tree, observing the stage that certain pairs have reached and working out where the nests are. It is important that it remains concealed because it doesn't want its cover to be blown; nor does it wish to evoke a mobbing response from the local community, which can be dangerous. On some occasions, however, to be mobbed is useful. If a host such as a Meadow Pipit has widely spaced, well-hidden nests, the only way to find them might be to make a full-frontal approach and gauge where the nest was by monitoring the degree of agitation – a bit like the game we play as children, leading someone to a hidden item by saying they are 'warmer' or 'colder'.

Ideally the female needs to act when the clutch is incomplete; that way, an egg can be added and a host's egg removed before the host starts incubating. The timing is careful, too. Most small birds lay their eggs at dawn, but the Cuckoo strikes in the afternoon, at a time when, with incubation not yet begun, both adults may be away from the nest regularly. The female steals in and lays her egg within a few seconds, departing with a host egg in her mouth in exchange; the latter egg will be eaten. In the course of a season, she may lay in as many as 20 nests.

As long as it is not rejected the young Cuckoo develops faster than its host's chicks, having been given a head start by beginning its growth in the female Cuckoo's oviduct. Once it hatches it has a long rest and then, as is known throughout the world, it ejects all its nest-bound competition there and then. It hauls eggs or nestlings to the rim of the nest in the small of its back and, with a final effort it despatches them over the side, to certain death. Occasionally two Cuckoos hatch in the same nest and then a real battle is joined.

The young Cuckoo goes on to drain every drop of effort from its overworked foster parents, begging constantly for more with the bottomless pit of its gape opened wide. It grows fast on their labours and, since its beseeching calls are such a powerful stimulus, it will often enlist the efforts of other small birds roundabout which, against their better judgement, find themselves queuing up to take part in food deliveries, too. Finally, gorged on ill-gotten gain, it takes leave of these services and goes out to prepare for its lone migration southward. All Cuckoos, adults and young, are gone by the end of September.

Owls families *Tytonidae* (tie-**toh**-nid-ee) and *Strigidae* (**strie**-jid-ee)

Habitat Most habitats are covered, from open tundra and moorland to deep forest.
Food All are predatory, catching a wide range of foods, especially small mammals and birds. Voles almost invariably seem to come off worst. Indigestible material, in the form of bones, skin and chitin (from insects), is expelled as pellets, 1–2 times a day.
Movements Many are highly sedentary, living in 1 territory all their lives; others are nomadic, seeking good populations of their food animals; some, such as Long-eared and Short-eared Owls, are relatively short-distance migrants. Scops Owl migrates to Africa for the winter.
Voice Famous for their far-carrying, low-pitched hoots, the advertising calls of the males. Various other noises, including squeals, screams and laughs.
Pairing style Usually monogamous (Tengmalm's not always).
Nesting Solitary and territorial. Long-eared and Scops Owls sometimes nest close together, but not really in the colonial sense.
Nest Typically either in a crevice or in the old nest of another bird. No structure, except in some Short-eared Owls.
Productivity Usually 1 brood a year, but occasionally 2 (Barn Owl, Long-eared, Short-eared and Tengmalm's) and often none (Snowy, Ural, Great Grey) in bad rodent years.
Eggs 2–8, hatching asynchronously.
Incubation 21–35 days, by female only, fed by male.
Young Nest-bound, altricial and downy.
Parenting style Both adults feed the young, tended mainly by female.
Food to young Same as adults', brought in bill.
Leaving nest Young leave nest any time between 21 and 36 days, often well before they are able to fly. Fledging is any time between 28 and about 90 days, but the young may remain dependent for many weeks afterwards.

Little Owl

Europe's predatory birds operate something of a shift system, with the diurnal birds of prey terrorising small animals by day and the owls coming out to hunt during the twilight hours and at night. The two groups are therefore kept separate and competition between them is reduced.

Everyone knows an owl, with its upright, fluffy body, large head, flat facial discs and huge, expressive eyes. Few groups of birds are so distinctive or so well known. To us they look 'wise', but this is a myth; their brains are so caught up with sensory perception that there probably isn't much left for cognitive thought!

Not surprisingly, the night vision of owls is good: their eyes are large, to allow plenty of light in, and the types of cells most prominent in their retina are those charged with detecting contrast. This allows them to see just a little better than we humans do in the dark (and we should not underestimate our considerable nocturnal abilities). The birds also look to the front in a similar way to us – the eyes are close set and give overlapping (binocular) vision, which confers a good perception of depth and distance. To enhance this still further, an owl frequently bobs its head up and down, enabling it to assess a target from different angles. The eyes are set in immovable eye sockets so that, if a bird wishes to look at something to the side, it must turn its head. Most owls can rotate theirs about 270 degrees in the horizontal plane. Contrary to popular belief, owls are perfectly capable of seeing in the daytime, although they probably cannot detect much colour.

The hearing of owls is exceedingly acute and in fact most species probably locate prey more by hearing than by sight. Their ear openings, which are found behind the outer edge of the owl's facial disc, are very large and the facial discs themselves reflect sound towards the ears. Remarkably, most owls also have an asymmetrical arrangement of the openings, with one ear higher up the head than the other; this means that sound in the vertical plane will reach one ear faster than the other, enabling the bird to assess the difference and calculate where the sound is coming from. In this way owls can find food in complete darkness.

Owls also need the means to despatch the prey that they catch. For this they have sharp talons and a sharp, hooked bill, both features shared with diurnal birds of prey. An owl's feet are, however, different from those of a raptor, having two toes facing forwards and two back, giving a symmetrical grip for holding squirming prey. In common with raptors, owls strike with their feet and then, if necessary, finish their victims off with a few bites of the bill.

Since owls live, at best, in the half-light, they tend not to have spectacular displays or plumage. Instead, as everyone knows, they make far-carrying, low-pitched hooting sounds and have a wide vocabulary of other, more intimate calls associated with pair formation. Each owl species' calls are highly recognisable, from the screeching of the Barn Owl to the quavering hoot of the Tawny and the sonar-like blips of the Scops.

On account of its heart-shaped face, short, V-shaped tail, comb-like inner claw and various other anatomical features, the Barn Owl is placed in a different family to the rest, the *Tytonidae.*

Barn Owl

Tyto alba (**tie**-toh **al**-ba)
length 33–35 cm

The Barn Owl has the most acute hearing of any animal known. The heart-shaped face, with a ridge separating two concave discs, means that the stiff feathers of the facial disc reflect sound, especially high-frequency sound, towards the ear openings, thereby magnifying the signal. The openings themselves are large and asymmetrical, with the left ear slightly higher up than the right; this means that, by detecting minuscule time differences between the sounds arriving at each ear, the owl can register where the noises are coming from both horizontally and vertically. This allows it to locate the source of the sound with incredible accuracy – when flying down to catch prey in total darkness, for example, it will not deviate off course by more than one degree. It can also hear prey moving under the cover of grass or snow, hidden from view. The mere rustling movement of a tiny mouse in the leaf litter is enough to give it away.

The Barn Owl is an active hunter, meaning that it obtains most of its prey while on the move. Typically it flies low over the ground, the optimum foraging height being 3 m, moving slowly forward with wavering flight and deep wingbeats, listening for movement below. Once it hears something it may hover above the disturbance first and then strike with its feet. Not surprisingly this technique is ruined by extraneous noise, making hunting in wind and rain difficult. The wings of the Barn Owl are also specially modified to make flight as quiet as possible: the main flight feathers have a downy surface, the leading edges of the wings have comb-like fringes and the trailing edge has a hair-like fringe to reduce turbulence.

Over most of its range the Barn Owl feeds primarily on small mammals, with the proportion of these reaching 90 per cent or more. It has been recorded eating a bewildering range of other items, as well, though, including dozens of species of birds, rabbits, moles, weasels, grass snakes, slow worms, frogs, fish, insects and earthworms. It is particularly keen on rats and mice, and in some parts of the world Barn Owls have replaced the domestic cat as the primary controller of these rodents.

It is almost as adaptable in its choice of habitat and nest site. Basically requiring rough grassland over which to hunt, the Barn Owl will occur in many such open areas, especially where these abut hedgerows, rivers or ditches along which it is easy to hunt for the abundant rodents that live there. The density of Barn Owls is restricted by the availability of nest sites, meaning that, in certain places, the birds have to be quite flexible. Cavities in old buildings and, of course, barns are particularly favoured, but hollows in trees and cliff faces may also be used, along with more unusual sites such as burrows in the ground and the abandoned nests of large birds.

A very unusual feature of Barn Owl breeding behaviour, one rarely seen in birds, is that the male is the choosing sex, having the final say in whether the pair is formed. Normally the female assesses a male on the basis of looks, display performance, song or territory quality (and who knows what else?), but in the Barn Owl the assessment is his. Apparently he often makes it on the basis of the degree of black spottiness on the female's lower flanks, which is individually variable. If a female is well spotted her offspring will have superiorly symmetrical wing feathers, fewer external parasites and a higher degree of immunity to infection than the offspring of poorly spotted females.

adult pale   adult dark

ID: Distinguished from all other European owls by heart-shaped facial disc and very small black eyes. Has wavering flight like Long-eared and Short-eared Owl. Mainly nocturnal.

ID: Usually unmistakable on size alone; also has prominent ear tufts as a contrast to all other large owls.

Eagle Owl

Bubo bubo (**byoo**-boh **byoo**-boh)
length 60–75 cm

Quite simply the biggest owl in the world, the Eagle Owl takes some impressively large prey. Young deer and chamois, foxes and martens, herons and buzzards have all been recorded in its diet, although it is more dependent on rabbits and hares over most of its range, and even on mammals as small as water voles.

One strange feeding technique has been reliably recorded on a number of occasions, and that is cannibalism. Young Eagle Owls hatch out at intervals of a day or so, leaving some chicks well behind the others in their development, and it is fairly common for these backmarkers to be eaten by their siblings or even by their parents. More extraordinary still, it is also known for adult Eagle Owls to be killed by their own kind.

The Eagle Owl is primarily a nocturnal species, becoming active after sunset. Birds hunt mainly within a home range that they occupy all year, and know the best sites to look for food. This area is usually 12–20 sq km, but when the male and later the female are seeking food for the young, they tend to remain within a kilometre or so of the nest site. Eagle Owls defend their territory by giving a deep and somewhat authoritative hoot, in keeping with their stature, but they also make a wide range of other sounds.

The pair starts breeding very early in the year, often having eggs in the nest in February even in Fennoscandia. They use all sorts of different sites, but rocky ledges and cave entrances are probably the favourites, with tree holes and abandoned open nests as alternatives. At the nest they are extremely sensitive to human disturbance and have been known to abandon quite well-grown young when subject to intrusion.

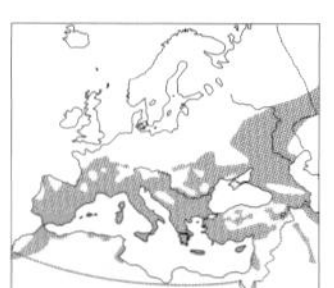

ID: A small, slim owl, not much bigger than a large thrush, easily distinguished from all other small owls in Europe by prominent ear tufts. When not raised, these still appear as bumps on crown. Flies on straight course. Nocturnal.

Scops Owl

Otus scops (**oh**-tuss **skops**)
length 19–20 cm

In contrast to most European owls, which are hardy, the Scops Owl is a bird of warm climates, with its centre of distribution around the Mediterranean and Black Sea. Being largely insectivorous, it is also the only European owl that is a regular trans-equatorial migrant, like a Swallow or a Cuckoo, although some Short-eared Owls may also cross the Sahara. Birds normally arrive on their breeding grounds in March and leave again in September, and their migration is pretty impressive. All the signs are that in autumn they overfly most the Mediterranean and the Sahara in a single long flight. Unusually among bird migrants, they are reported to do so in family groups. In some parts of Europe an element of the population stays put in winter.

It's not difficult to detect a Scops Owl, because in spring the males utter a very distinctive, sonorous, whistling 'tiu' as their advertising call and repeat it every few seconds with great regularity and stamina, seemingly for hours on end. The females can make this call, too, and may advertise to males early in the season, in a reversal of the normal roles. When male and female meet, they often put their calls together and make a duet.

The Scops Owl's favourite foods are insects, especially crickets and beetles, which it normally catches by ambushing them on the ground, having spotted them from an elevated perch first. Moths, being pesky, uncontrollable things, can often only be caught by some clever footwork in mid-air after a rapid aerial chase. The Scops also eats worms, small birds and mammals, including, occasionally, bats. As this indicates, it is very much a nocturnal forager.

These birds are quite adaptable in the habitats they select for breeding and the sites they adopt for nesting. All they require for the former are plenty of insects, some fallow ground and some old trees for roosting, and for the latter they will use a variety of holes (including the burrows of Bee-eaters) as well as the old nests of birds such as crows. This flexibility has allowed them to inhabit parks and gardens, where they are common, and even penetrate into urban areas.

Hawk Owl

Surnia ulula (**sur**-nee-a **yool**-yoo-la)
length 36–39 cm

The Hawk Owl is at home in the sunshine and goes to roost after dusk, so it does the opposite of what you'd expect for an owl. It is also shaped differently, with a relatively slim body, short wings and long tail, and it flies in a manner more resembling the direct style of a Sparrowhawk than the more wavering efforts of many in its family. At least it has a typical diet for an owl, though, feeding almost entirely on voles in the breeding season, with a few other small mammals and birds added on, especially in winter.

To hunt it practises the 'perch and pounce' method, observing prey from an elevated vantage point and gliding down to grab it. Long-term studies have come up with an interesting insight into the details of this: apparently a bird must change vantage points 13.5 times for each successful capture, using five different perches in all. Low perches are also more profitable than high perches, all of which suggests that the smaller the distance between prey and predator, the higher the capture rate.

Being vole specialists, the Hawk Owl's fortunes and movements are determined by the availability of these small mammals, which have a three- to four-year cycle of abundance. In good vole years the birds may breed further south than usual, whereas in poor years they may not breed at all. As a result, the Hawk Owl is one of Europe's few truly nomadic birds, with individuals moving in any direction in search of food. Normally they maintain neither territories nor pair bonds beyond one season.

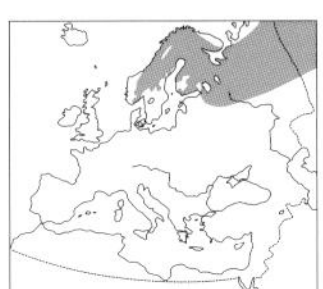

ID: Primarily diurnal. Unusual shape, with long tail and narrow wings with blunt tips – so recalls a Sparrowhawk. Flies with short bursts of flaps with straight glides, again resembling a hawk.

Snowy Owl

Nyctea scandiaca (nik-**tee**-a skan-dee-**ay**-ka)
length 55–70 cm (male 55–64 cm, female 60–70 cm)

The unique silky-white plumage of the Snowy Owl gives a very obvious clue to where it might be found. This is a bird of the Arctic, breeding only between 60°N and 83°N, mainly on the open tundra. As an adaptation to its way of life it has a special dense covering of feathers for its legs and toes to keep out the extreme cold, and it also has such acute hearing that it is able to pick up the noises of prey moving beneath the snow.

Its most important food items are lemmings, which may constitute the entire diet when plentiful. In good lemming years a pair of Snowy Owls can find enough food in a home range 1–4 sq km in extent, whereas in less favourable years that area increases to 8–10 sq km and breeding activity may be greatly reduced. Outside the breeding season the Snowy Owl may add birds to its diet, sometimes snatching them from the water surface, which is unusual for an owl. It will also snare them in aerial pursuit, showing a remarkable and unexpected turn of speed and manoeuvrability.

The Snowy Owl catches rodents primarily by watching the ground from a rock or ridge, and then flying out to get them. If it is successful, it does not do what most owls do, which is to take the food to a hidden place for private consumption and eat it piecemeal. Instead the Snowy Owl eats its prey on the spot, or nearby in the open, usually gulping it down whole, although if it has a full stomach it will pick at the corpse like a child unenthusiastically eating greens.

Pairs are usually formed just for a season because of the Snowy Owl's unpredictable lifestyle on the lemming train – the owls not only follow the lemmings' lead individually in the winter, causing pairs to split up, but the males, which are smaller than the females, tend to move further away from the breeding areas to retreat from the Arctic winter.

Prior to breeding the male may take to the skies with a spectacular display flight, in which the wings are held up in an exaggerated upstroke, causing the bird to drop down, and then swept equally far down, to produce renewed lift and, overall, an undulating flight. Later, as the pair bond is formed, the male brings food to the female, as is the case with most owls. He does, though, make his presentation in style, dropping the lemming down while holding his wings up by the carpal joints as if they were hanging from a washing line, and bowing his head forward. This posture is known as the angel display.

ID: Unmistakable very large owl.

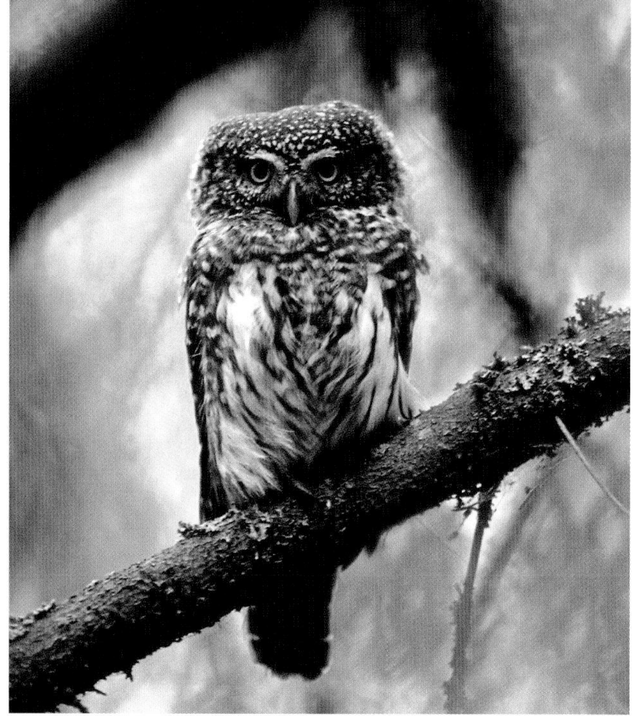

ID: Smallest European owl, smaller than a Starling. Compact, with oddly small, rounded head, medium-length tail that is often jerked up and down. Flight distinctive, highly undulating. Crepuscular.

Pygmy Owl

Glaucidium passerinum

(glow-**sid**-di-um pass-ser-**rie**-num)

length 16–17 cm

Despite its status as Europe's smallest owl, no bigger than a large finch, the Pygmy Owl shares the northern coniferous forest zone, harsh winters and all, with several of the larger species. One way it survives is to cache food, and Pygmy Owls have been known to have 200 items stored away at any one time, in holes or nest boxes.

The Pygmy Owl is an agile hunter and besides feeding on voles and other small mammals, as so many owls do, it also catches a substantial number of birds. In the breeding season, researchers have found that birds constitute about 40 per cent of the diet, and that figure probably rises in the winter. Pygmy Owls have different ways of catching mammals and birds. The former are taken by sitting out in the open on a high perch and then flying down to pounce on what is seen. Birds, on the other hand, are ambushed, the owl flying out from a hidden position and often catching its prey on the wing. Food is usually eaten piecemeal, with the head typically being bitten off first.

Most captured birds are small, but sometimes bumper strikes are made, for example against woodpeckers. This is somewhat ironic, because the Pygmy Owl relies on woodpeckers, especially Great Spotted, Grey-headed and Three-toed Woodpeckers, to make a nesting or caching hole. Small holes like these are safe from most nest predators, including pine martens.

A Pygmy Owl attracts a mate by its advertising song, a clear, fluty whistle. The relationship between members of a pair can be fierce, with much chasing and aggression at first. Also, later in the season, a female Pygmy Owl sometimes attacks her mate to stimulate him to go out hunting.

adults

Little Owl

Athene noctua (ath-**ee**-nee **nok**-too-a)

length 21–23 cm

This owl has a reputation for being active during the day, perching on a post fully awake or making a switch from tree to tree with its up-and-down, bounding flight. Yet, curiously, it rarely if ever hunts by day, even when feeding young. For this, its normal active times are between dusk and midnight and then again from 2 a.m. until dawn, and you would think that, when daylight came, it would be needing its sleep. Presumably it gets by on short cat-naps.

This bird is very common in the warm climate of Greece, as well as in Spain, Portugal and Italy, where there is a healthy supply of food and many natural holes and crevices available for nesting. Its distribution in northern Europe is patchier and the intensification of agriculture so prevalent there has set it on the path of severe decline in many areas.

There is a shift in this bird's ecology north to south, with insects becoming more and more important in warmer climates. Little Owls are particularly fond of beetles, crickets and earwigs, which they usually catch by dropping down to the ground from a low perch. They will also hunt on the ground for earthworms, which they tug at with such vehemence that, when the worm finally gives way and slips out of the ground, the momentum may cause the birds to fall over backwards! Besides these staple foods, mammals (especially voles), amphibians and birds may all find their way on to the menu. Most unusually for an owl, the Little Owl also takes a small amount of plant material, including leaves, fruits and berries.

Pairs of Little Owls tend to remain within their shared territory throughout the year and, indeed, probably for life. They are quite demonstrative about the pair bond, regularly indulging in bouts of mutual preening ('allopreening'), while perched in close contact; divorces are unusual. In early spring the males defend their borders with a clear, upwardly inflected hoot, and then indulge in a brief period of nest-showing. This procedure, which is common among owls generally, involves a male entering several potential nest holes, looking outside each one questioningly, perhaps nibbling at the interior and calling to the female outside.

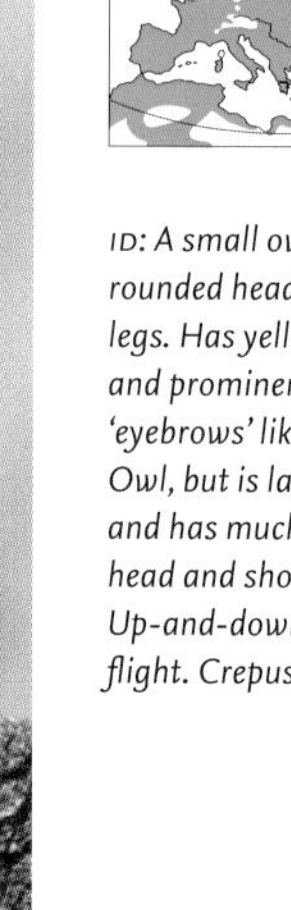

ID: A small owl with a rounded head and long legs. Has yellow eyes and prominent white 'eyebrows' like Pygmy Owl, but is larger, paler and has much bigger head and shorter tail. Up-and-down bounding flight. Crepuscular.

adults

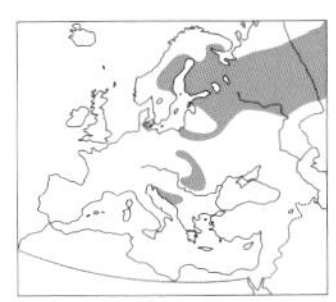

ID: *Considerably larger (half as big again) and longer-tailed than Tawny, and much paler in colour, but has same large head and black eyes. Neatly streaked on breast. Flies in a similar manner, but note the wedge-shaped tail. Nocturnal.*

Ural Owl

Strix uralensis (**striks** yoo-ral-**len**-siss)
length 50–62 cm

There are not many birds in Europe that could be considered dangerous to people, but the Ural Owl is definitely one of them. If a human intrudes closely upon an occupied nest, this large predator will readily make diving attacks and attempt to slash the person's head or shoulders with its talons.

The Ural is a highly secretive member of the guild of owls living in the northern coniferous forest belt, although a relict population also breeds in montane deciduous forests in central Europe. It is less noisy than many other species of owl; breeding pairs may be almost silent throughout the year. Urals breed at low density and are mainly nocturnal. Locating them is a challenge.

In contrast to most other owls at high latitudes, Urals remain within one territory throughout their lives. This is made possible by a catholic diet that includes not just those hard-pressed, boom-and-bust voles, but also rabbits, amphibians, insects, carrion and a range of birds from finches to Black Grouse. Nevertheless, vole numbers seem to determine breeding success. In good vole years 76 per cent of females breed, as opposed to 24 per cent in poor years: the eggs that they lay are larger and they begin breeding earlier. Small mammals and other food items are procured mainly during the night by the 'perch and pounce' method.

The stability of the Ural's life is also exemplified its faithfulness, mostly leading to a lifelong pair bond. The divorce rate for established pairs is only 2.7 per cent.

Tawny Owl

Strix aluco (**striks** ah-**loo**-ko)
length 37–39 cm

Young Tawny Owls have a tough initiation into adult life, as jolting as the shift between a warm bath and a cold shower. Having being looked after devotedly by their parents for as much as three months after leaving the nest, during which time they are gradually weaned off food deliveries and learn hunting skills for themselves, they are suddenly thrust into an urgent search to find a territory. If they fail they will surely starve. If they succeed – usually by replacing an incumbent that has died – the territory will be theirs to keep for the rest of their lives. Most spend a while searching and may travel as far as 20 km, but seldom further, to find one. The months between August and November will determine their future.

The Tawny Owl benefits from stability. Territories are often traditional, changing hands without any alteration of boundaries. Once they have settled in, birds soon get to know their patches intimately and learn about the distribution of food from month to month. This experience and a catholic, variable diet enables them to survive even the harshest conditions.

In broad-leaved woodland, which is the Tawny Owl's prime habitat, small mammals form the bulk of their prey. In more open areas, however, and especially in areas of human settlement, birds take over. A bewildering number of species of both have been recorded in the diet, including voles, mice, shrews and rats, even edible dormice among the mammals, and Starlings, finches, pigeons, thrushes and especially House Sparrows among the birds. Tawny Owls also regularly hunt for worms on lawns and may take insects, frogs and fish as well. Their typical method is to sit on a perch, watching for opportunity and then grabbing what they see by means of a dive to the ground. Birds may be attacked at their roosts, however, and Tawny Owls will also quarter the ground in a slow, searching flight. Adaptable both in diet and feeding method, the Tawny is the most numerous European owl.

Males make their familiar hooting advertising call in the autumn and early winter, aiming primarily to attract females. Recent research has shown that a male's sound is remarkably revealing of its performer, enabling a potential mate to be well informed before making an approach. Males with a greater body weight make lower-pitched and more tremulous hoots, and the hoots of those with a parasite infection are both higher in pitch and shorter in length. The more aggressive the males, the more frequently they hoot.

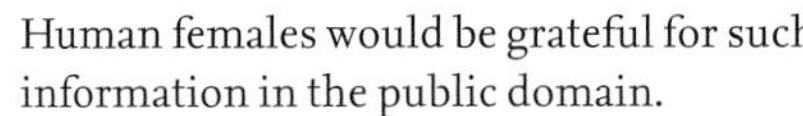

Human females would be grateful for such information in the public domain.

Although the Tawny Owl is common in many areas inhabited by people, it is not easy to see, being primarily a nocturnal species, hunting between dusk and dawn. By day it hides away, usually in thick cover high up in a tree.

ID: *Widespread, rather plump, nocturnal owl with dark eyes and a large facial disc; no 'ears'. The size of a crow. Flies on straight course, with strong flaps interspersed with glides.*

ID: Large owl with huge, rounded head. In flight recalls a heron – slow flaps interspersed with long glides. Crepuscular.

Great Grey Owl

Strix nebulosa (**striks** neb-byoo-**loh**-sa)
length 59–69 cm

An alarmed Great Grey Owl stretching itself up as high as it will go, with its feathers fluffed out and its yellow eyes offering a determined stare, is a pretty formidable sight. Its feats of daring are impressive, too, with reports of it banishing mighty Goshawks from their territory and even attacking bears in defence of the nest. Yet the birds themselves are only half the weight of the comparably sized Eagle Owl, and the only animals they routinely terrorise are voles.

These are birds of the far north, where their prime habitat consists of lichen-sprinkled spruce and pine forests. Some birds remain on their territory all year and they have a talent that enables them to survive, even when their patch is under deep snow – they can detect small mammals by sound. The birds hover over the snow, listening, and then, 'clenching' their talons, they drop down, smash through the crust and grab their prey from as much as 45 cm below the surface. When using their more normal 'perch and pounce' technique, they are able to detect prey from 100 m away.

Nevertheless, the prey needs to be there in the first place and some birds are forced to move around semi-nomadically, following the vole populations. As a result Great Greys may change partners from year to year and may also practise what can only be described as speed-dating, pairing up a mere two weeks before egg laying. The nests are usually placed in the abandoned structures of other birds such as Sparrowhawks and Buzzards.

adults

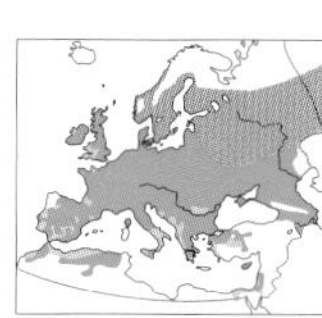

ID: Medium-sized owl, smaller and slimmer than Tawny; usually perches very upright in a tree (see Short-eared). Flies low over ground with wavering wingbeats with heavy action interspersed with glides. Long 'ears' and red eyes diagnostic if seen well. Widespread and often common. Nocturnal.

Long-eared Owl

Asio otus (**ay**-zi-oh **oh**-tuss)
length 35–40 cm

In common with the Short-eared Owl, the Long-eared eschews the normal 'perch and pounce' hunting technique favoured by most owls in favour of active hunting flight. It flies low over the ground at a height of 0.5–1.5 m, steadily checking the ground below for food and often hovering briefly above it before a pounce led by the talons. This checking is done almost entirely by ear; the Long-eared Owl is capable of locating prey in complete darkness this way and, in contrast to the Short-eared, hunts only during the night. The rustle of wind tends to reduce its effectiveness, as well as making prey more difficult to catch, so under these conditions it might have to resort to more sedentary techniques.

With a wider distribution in Europe than any other owl, the Long-eared is an adaptable species. Its requirements for breeding are simple enough, just somewhere with some thick tree cover adjacent to open ground. The nature of the woodland is not important, with both pure deciduous and pure coniferous stands utilised, but there must be old Crow or Magpie nests available for secondhand use. Many Long-eared Owls live in small copses and shelterbelts where, despite being quite large birds, they are easily overlooked.

A good many Long-eared Owls, especially the Fennoscandian birds, evacuate their breeding areas in the winter and may travel some distance, occasionally as far as Egypt in the east. They are more sensitive than forest owls to snow cover, and the males, without the need to defend scarce tree holes for a nest site, are under less compulsion than many other species to sit out the harsh conditions. The birds often migrate in small groups, and, upon arrival, may be drawn to the same rodent-rich wintering areas; if this happens the birds gather by day to sleep in thick bushes, each owl just a few metres from the next. A good roost site like this is essential for survival and many are traditional, with years of use behind them.

In common with most owlets, young Long-eared Owls usually leave the nest itself before they are able to fly – in this case, nearly two weeks before. This stage of development is known as 'branching' and it is probably an adaptation to reduce predation. The youngsters spread out and roost some distance from their siblings, meaning that if one is discovered and killed by a marten, for example, the rest of the brood will not necessarily be slain along with it.

adults

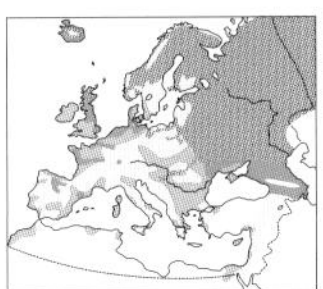

ID: *Slightly larger than Long-eared but similar, especially in flight. If perched, has distinctive horizontal profile; usually on the ground or a low post. Generally crepuscular but may be seen during the day.*

Short-eared Owl

Asio flammeus (**ay**-zi-oh **flam**-mee-uss)
length 37–38 cm

The Short-eared Owl has longer, narrower wings than most others of its family, giving it the ability to fly close to the ground at low speed with a minimum of flapping, reducing the noise it makes while doing so and enabling it to detect prey by ear more efficiently. It can also make supremely quick in-flight adjustments while hunting.

This is a bird of tundra, moorland, grassland and marshes, places where there are few if any trees. In these barren habitats the Short-eared Owl is unusual in laying its eggs on the ground, usually in a shallow scrape excavated by the female. The site chosen is generally on a slightly raised, dry patch with copious low vegetation, but occasionally the birds must make do with wetter sites where they will do something almost unique among owls: build a nest.

Another unusual piece of behaviour is a tendency to roost on the ground. In winter, when Short-ears are drawn in numbers to food-rich sites, these roosts are community affairs, with a membership that often reaches 20 and may touch 100. Owls are rarely sociable so, once again, the Short-ear defies owl norms. Roosts may be occupied at varying times, because the Short-eare hunts regularly at any hour of the day or night.

In the breeding season male Short-ears perform an impressive display flight, rising high into the air and clapping their wings together. If approached by a rival instead of a potential mate they switch to the 'underwing display', lifting their wings high to show off their pale coloration.

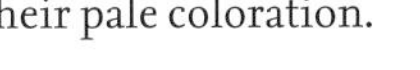

adults

Tengmalm's Owl

Aegolius funereus (ee-**goh**-li-uss foo-**nee**-ri-uss)
length 21–28 cm

Generally speaking owls prefer rather open woodland, as opposed to dense forest, in which to hunt, with plenty of glades and edges rather than closed canopy, but the Tengmalm's Owl is an exception, being equally efficient in both environments. In fact, in summer it is an advantage to hunt in deep forests, because the lack of light restricts the vegetation cover under which prey can hide, making it more vulnerable.

The Tengmalm's Owl is found mainly in the boreal coniferous forest belt, being especially common in stands of spruce. It will, however, also breed in mixed woodland, especially where there are beech trees. It is a nocturnal species with exceptionally good hearing, aided by having asymmetrical ear openings which permit the detection of sound in the vertical as well as the horizontal plane; it is almost certainly able to hunt in complete darkness. It is very much of the 'perch and pounce' school and observations have revealed that, even when it has detected prey, it will make a strike only once the meal is out in the open. Its favourite food items are – inevitably for an owl – voles, although it will catch birds and insects, too.

Many Tengmalm's Owls breed in the far north of Europe and for those that remain during the winter food may be unpredictable in its appearance. For this reason the birds may cache food in holes and nest boxes when they have a good day, with up to seven items recorded. In the prevailing cold climate cached prey often freezes and when this happens a hungry Tengmalm's Owl might have to sit on its next meal, as if incubating it, in order to defrost it prior to consumption.

Males are more willing to sit out the winters than females – they are probably under more pressure to hold on to their territories, while the females or young birds have only their own survival to think about. Those that migrate often lead a nomadic lifestyle in search of prey and it then becomes doubtful that they will meet up with the same partner the following spring. On the contrary, female Tengmalm's Owls have been known to breed in one season 680 km away from where they were in the previous one. In fact, relationships in this species of owl are much more fluid than most. Both males and females may have more than one mate; the latter, indeed, may lay two clutches of eggs in a season, each fathered by a different male.

In many parts of its range the Tengmalm's was once heavily reliant on the excavations of Black Woodpeckers for its nest holes. Now, though, it often uses nest boxes instead.

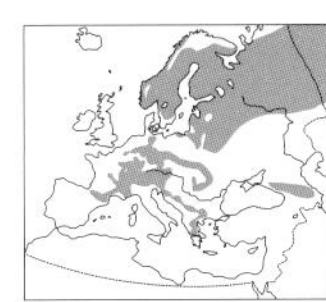

ID: *Not much bigger than Little Owl, but a forest bird. Wide facial disc and yellow eyes give permanent surprised expression. Nocturnal.*

adults

Nightjars family *Caprimulgidae* (kap-ri-**mool**-jid-ee)

Habitat Open woods and forest edge, heathland, chalk downland, young plantations.
Food Insects, taken in flight, including moths, beetles and mosquitoes.
Movements Both migratory, wintering in Africa (Red-necked in West, Nightjar also in East). Depart by late October, return in late April and May.
Voice Both have loud, distinctive voices (see text).
Pairing style Monogamous.
Nesting Solitary and territorial.
Nest None; eggs laid on the ground. They may be moved around the nesting area.
Productivity 1–2 broods a year.
Eggs 2.
Incubation 17–18 days, mostly by female, although the male may take short stints at dusk and dawn.
Young Semi-precocial, downy.
Parenting style Both adults feed the young.
Food to young Regurgitated insects.
Leaving nest Young fledge at 16–17 days and are independent at about a month.

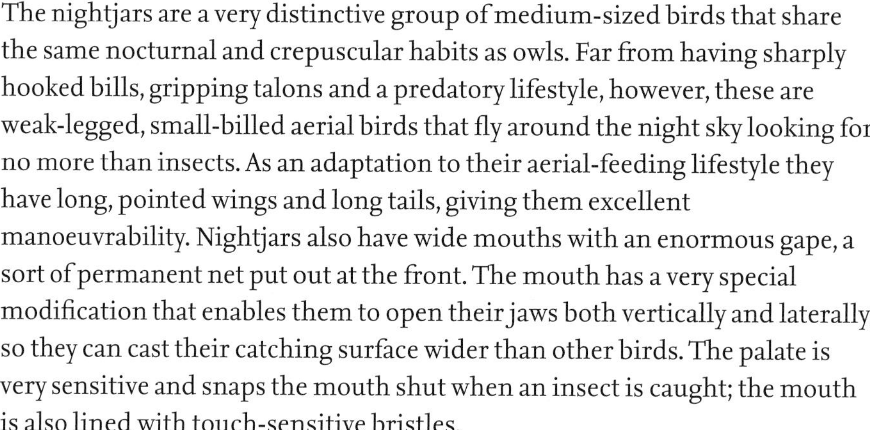

The nightjars are a very distinctive group of medium-sized birds that share the same nocturnal and crepuscular habits as owls. Far from having sharply hooked bills, gripping talons and a predatory lifestyle, however, these are weak-legged, small-billed aerial birds that fly around the night sky looking for no more than insects. As an adaptation to their aerial-feeding lifestyle they have long, pointed wings and long tails, giving them excellent manoeuvrability. Nightjars also have wide mouths with an enormous gape, a sort of permanent net put out at the front. The mouth has a very special modification that enables them to open their jaws both vertically and laterally, so they can cast their catching surface wider than other birds. The palate is very sensitive and snaps the mouth shut when an insect is caught; the mouth is also lined with touch-sensitive bristles.

It would be incorrect to assume from the above, though, that nightjars simply fly around using their open mouth to trawl randomly as they fly. On the contrary, they have effective night vision and catch food with targeted strikes, usually coming from below so that the insect's silhouette is visible against the night sky or moon. Nightjars have large eyes with many rod cells in the retina that detect sharp detail and contrast, and even a small plate called a tapetum that reflects light back from behind the retina so that it has a second chance to be detected – the same feature that make cats' eyes glow in a torch beam. These attributes help nightjars feed in low light conditions, but they do not work on the darkest nights, when feeding is much reduced. As a result these birds are crepuscular – most active at dawn and dusk.

With their highly cryptic plumage, nightjars are very difficult to find when they are at roost by day. The same applies at their ground nests, where their plumage blends in with the pattern of rough ground, and their young are also covered with down. They don't build a nest structure, but simply lay their eggs on the soil, occasionally moving them around.

Not surprisingly, given their diet, both our species of nightjars are confirmed migrants, arriving rather late in the spring and departing with the first whiff of autumn. Their loud, unearthly advertising calls are thus mainly a feature of warm, still summer nights.

Nightjar

Caprimulgus europaeus

(kap-ri-**mool**-guss yoo-roh-**pee**-uss)

length 24.5–28 cm

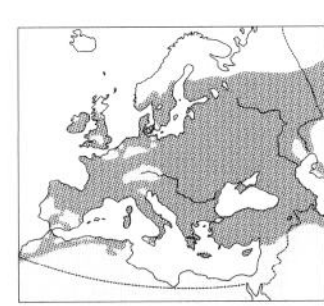

ID: *Easily identified as a nightjar with its horizontal posture, large head and minute bill. For differences from very similar Red-necked, see below. About the size of a Kestrel, with similar long wings and tail. Flies with deep wingbeats on irregular course, with regular turns, jinks and hovers. Strictly nocturnal.*

The unearthly advertising call of the Nightjar is one of the most remarkable of all European bird sounds. It is a very rapid succession of somewhat wooden notes strung together in a long series, shifting from one pitch to another intermittently; it has been compared to the engine of a two-stroke motorcycle!

The males make this 'churring' sound at dusk and dawn, to delineate their territories and advertise their presence to females. It may be delivered from several song posts and when the performer is shifting stages the 'song' will cease in favour of a brief frog-like 'kru-ick' flight call. If a female shows interest the male resorts to display flights, in which he may lift his wings and glide along, fly with exaggerated beats, or – and this is diagnostic of pair formation – sharply clap his wings.

Being on the ground, Nightjar nests are highly vulnerable, although both adults and young are cryptically coloured, so predators are unlikely to come across a family except by chance. If this happens the parents perform distraction displays in which they pretend to be injured or disabled, and deflect the danger. The chicks, meanwhile, can walk within a few hours of hatching and tend to leave the vicinity of the nest for the nearest cover.

In good seasons Nightjars may have two broods, but their season is relatively short and labour must therefore overlap. The feeding and care of the first brood is allocated to the male alone as soon as the young are two weeks old, while the female begins incubating a second clutch. By the time the first set of young is independent, after 31–34 days, the next eggs are on the point of hatching.

Nightjars catch most of their food in airborne sessions, but at times, especially if there are fewer insects around, they will operate by short sallies from a perch. One study has shown that sallying nets them about five captures a minute, whereas continual flight may lift that figure to twelve.

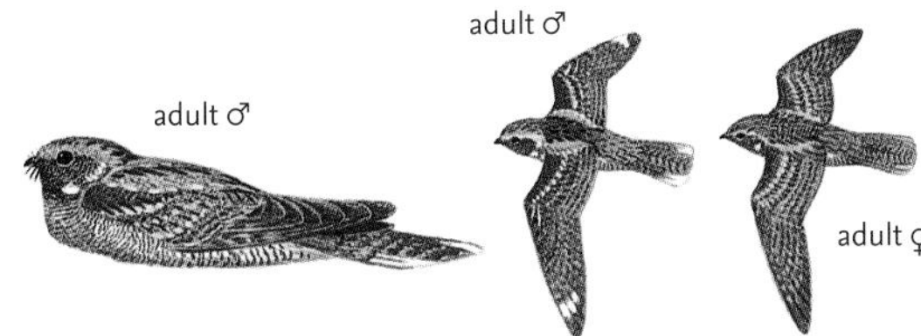

Red-necked Nightjar

Caprimulgus ruficollis

(kap-ri-**mool**-guss roo-fi-**kol**-liss)

length 30–32 cm

You might have difficulty distinguishing a Red-necked Nightjar from a Nightjar by eye – the Red-necked is a little bigger and has a more powerful-looking flight, but it requires a trained eye to tell – but you would never confuse the two by ear. While the Nightjar makes its well-known 'churring' sound (see above), the Red-neck repeats a 'kut-ok' note, like somebody beating wood or using an exotic percussion instrument. The sounds are the musical versions of chalk and cheese.

This species has a restricted range, breeding only in Spain, Portugal and North Africa. It migrates to tropical West Africa for the winter, returning in mid-April, earlier than the Nightjar. It breeds in open woodland and forest with bushy areas intermixed; the *dehesas* – open forests of oaks and umbrella pine – represent typical habitat. Where the Red-neck and the Nightjar coexist, the former takes the valleys and the latter occupies the higher plains.

Few differences in behaviour from the Nightjar have so far been uncovered, but it seems that this species feeds on the ground rather more often and possibly has a preference for larger prey. It also begins calling later in the evening than the Nightjar and carries on more regularly at night.

ID: *Similar to Nightjar but larger. Has a longer tail and is said to have a more powerful flight, with more swoops and fewer twists and turns. Distinguished by warm rust-red colour in ring all around neck, and also on throat and upper breast. Advertising call, habitat and range are best pointers.*

Swifts family *Apodidae* (ap-**poh**-did-ee)

Habitat Aerial, so the ground below is relevant only insofar as it affects insect prey. The birds need buildings, cliffs or trees on which to nest.
Food Aerial insects and spiders procured in flight. Over 500 species have been recorded in the diet of Swifts. Aphids, ants and flies are important.
Movements Long-distance migrants wintering in Africa. They have different lengths of stay in Europe: Swift May–July, Alpine and Pallid Swifts March–October.
Voice High-pitched squealing or screaming sounds. Pallid makes harsher sound than Swift. Alpine makes a trilling call.
Pairing style Monogamous and faithful from year to year.
Nesting Usually colonial. Pallid Swifts and Swifts may form mixed colonies together.
Nest Open nest of straw, leaves and feathers cemented with saliva. Placed on flat surface (Swift and Pallid Swift) or adhering to side of crevice (Alpine).
Productivity 1 brood a year except Pallid, which has 2.
Eggs 2–3. Swift lays 3 eggs only when the weather is hot.
Incubation 17–23 days; longer if it is cold. By both adults, beginning with first egg.
Young Nest-bound, altricial. Highly resistant to starvation (see Swift).
Parenting style Both adults tend and feed the young.
Food to young Tiny insects, delivered up to 1000 at a time in food boluses. In good weather the young may be fed every half-hour.
Leaving nest Fledging period varies greatly according to the weather, with the range 37–56 days. The young of Swifts (and perhaps others) leave on their chosen day before 8 a.m. and without their parents' knowledge; they are henceforth independent.

No other birds in the world spend a higher proportion of their life flying than the swifts. They never come to ground voluntarily, instead using high ledges on cliffs, trees or buildings for their nests, and drinking by making low passes just over the surface of the water. They are capable of sleeping on the wing and at least sometimes probably copulate while aloft as well. They collect nest material either by breaking sticks off trees or by collecting straw, grass, leaves and feathers blown into the air by the wind. These materials are bound together by copious saliva into a cup or saucer shape. The birds don't land at a potential nest site until they are about two years old, which means that, from the time they first leave the nest at about two months old, they do not touch a hard surface before clocking up about 500,000 km under their own steam.

A swift's wing is modified for effortless, manoeuvrable flight. It is long and sickle-shaped, allowing the birds to glide for long periods without having to flap. It is essentially composed only of the 'hand' bones, with the arm very much reduced – so swifts fly with their fingers, one might say.

The feet are tiny and are arranged so that all four toes point forwards. This means that swifts cannot perch, unlike their aerial colleagues the swallows, but they can cling to vertical surfaces, much as we might cling on to a fence that we wish to peer over.

All members of the family feed exclusively on relatively small aerial invertebrates, not just flying insects but also the army of web-borne spiders that is wafted aloft by summer air currents like mini-parachutists. Although the birds have wide gapes to act a bit like nets, their strikes are targeted and intentional, rather than random and trawling. As a rule swifts tend to sweep around for insects at higher elevations than swallows or martins.

Alpine Swift

Swift

Apus apus (**ap**-puss **ap**-puss)
length 16–17 cm; wingspan 42–48 cm

The weather is an important factor in the lives of all birds, but for few is it such a critical day-to-day issue as for the Swift. This bird depends for its livelihood on a good population of insects being available in the sky all the time, so the moment inclement weather strikes – be it wind, rain or cold – food is whisked away or fails altogether to emerge and the Swift is in trouble. It will hunt over water when rain is in the air, for here there will always be some insects hatching, and it will take to the shelterbelts in a wind. But the fact is that fickle meteorological conditions do it no good at all.

Part of the problem is the Swift's own fault. It has the widest distribution of Europe's four species and is the only swift in the world that reaches the Arctic Circle in summer. In many of the places where it occurs it is simply asking for dodgy conditions and it's no wonder that hereabouts the skies are as thick as soup with flying insects one day, but empty the next.

The Swift, though, has some extraordinary adaptations, physiological and behavioural, to unpredictable conditions, and perhaps the most remarkable – and logical – is its habit of simply flying away from bad weather. When a cold front is approaching, the number of insects drops, even when the disturbance is still 500 km away, giving the Swifts advance notice of a change. They prepare to leave and, as the depression arrives, they make escape movements away from the wind and cold. In Europe depressions usually arrive from the west, so the Swifts head off to the southeast, flying against the wind and making a short cut to warmer air. They then circle round, clockwise, keeping away from the edge of the depression, and loop back to the breeding areas when the poor weather has moved away. During these escape movements a Swift may fly as much as 2000 km, all to get a bit of warmth and sun.

Of course, if these escape movements occur in the middle of summer, it is likely that the refugees will include breeding birds which have to abandon young in the nest in order to survive. One might expect that leaving progeny behind would be a calamity, but it is not necessarily so. Young Swifts are used to unpredictable food deliveries. When feeding is good they put on a lot of weight and build up fat reserves to tide them over while the adults are away, which may be several days. In addition they may lower their metabolic rate and become torpid, like miniature reptiles, burning up as little fuel as possible.

The Swift is celebrated for its very unusual habit of sleeping while airborne, something suspected, although unrecorded, in some other birds, too, especially seabirds. The individuals that do this in Europe will mainly be year-old birds that are attending colonies but not breeding, because the adults usually sleep in the nest. At dusk groups of them scream loudly and rise into the sky, probably searching for a warm layer. They may go up to 1000–2000 m in altitude and, in the half-light of dusk, they are lost to view. They spend the night circling, alternating glides with slow flaps, and take catnaps as they do so.

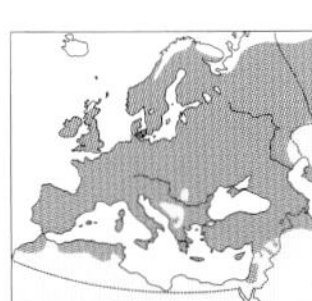

ID: This and all the swifts are easily distinguished from members of the swallow and martin family by their long, pointed, narrow-based wings. Fly with long sweeps often high above ground, with less fluttering than any swallow. Virtually always seen flying; unable to perch at all, so never seen on wires or on the ground. This species is dark sooty-brown all over except for a small and subtle whitish bib.

ID: Very similar to Swift, but has larger white throat patch and its dark eye patch clearly contrasts with rest of head. Has paler and scalier plumage than Swift. From above, trailing edge of wing is noticeably paler than leading edge of wing or back (a surprisingly obvious feature) and, from below, outer "hand" is clearly darker than inner "hand". Has broader, blunter wings than Swift.

Pallid Swift

Apus pallidus (**ap**-puss **pal**-lid-duss)
length 16–17 cm; wingspan 42–46 cm

The Swift and the Pallid Swift are undoubtedly closely related and their differences in lifestyle are slight. They will, in fact, regularly mix together in the same breeding colonies and even club together into the screaming flocks that demonstrate a colony's solidarity.

Nevertheless, there are differences. The Pallid Swift is confined to southern Europe, where it is mainly coastal, breeding especially on cliffs and islets and being less dependent on buildings than the Swift. It does venture inland, though, especially to urban areas, and Europe's largest colony, with 8000 pairs, is in Seville. Throughout its range it seems to be a common sight in gorges and in towns next to lakes, but strangely the Bulgarian population is found largely at high altitudes, between 1200 m and 1600 m.

Breeding in a warmer climate has enabled the Pallid to be less in thrall to weather conditions than the Swift. It will, for example, delay breeding for much longer in periods of inclement weather and its clutch size, unlike that of the Swift, will be unaffected. It is also, uniquely among European swifts, double-brooded, fledging its first brood in July and its second as late as October. Concomitantly it tends to leave its breeding areas later than the Swift and, although most Pallids migrate, a few have been recorded overwintering.

There seem to be few differences in diet between Swift and Pallid Swift, and no obvious differences in how the food is obtained. The Pallid is also known, like the Swift, to roost on the wing.

White-rumped Swift

Apus caffer (**ap**-puss **kaf**-fer)
length 14 cm; wingspan 34–36 cm

This is the smallest and much the rarest swift in Europe, with a breeding population of only around a hundred pairs, all in Spain (but expanding slowly). The birds are not colonial here and for breeding they invariably appropriate old Red-rumped Swallow nests, so the population is found in exactly the same habitats as its 'landlords'. The swifts line old nests with feathers and lay two eggs.

This bird can be a very late migrant. The first arrive at the beginning of May, but many don't appear until mid-June; they leave, presumably for Africa, in October.

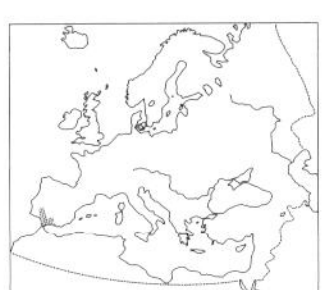

ID: Small rare swift with cleanly defined white rump and white throat patch; the secondaries are white-tipped, producing a narrow bar along the trailing edge of the inner wing. Tail longer than on other swifts.

Alpine Swift

Apus melba (**ap**-puss **mell**-ba)
length 20–22 cm; wingspan 54–60 cm

As the largest of Europe's swifts, one might expect the Alpine Swift to deal in superlatives, and so it does. Using its powerful flight and high speed, it is known to travel at least 600 km, and up to 1000 km, every single day. The Alpine Swift also forages higher up in the sky than other swifts – to 3700 m in the Himalayas.

Essentially a bird of moderately high mountains, and despite its name usually breeding below altitudes of 1000 m, only occasionally reaching up to 2300 m, the Alpine Swift is mostly associated with rocky outcrops, caves and sea cliffs, wherever there are abundant crevices for nesting. In the last century, however, it has taken, as the other swifts have, to breeding on buildings in settlements, even large cities, especially in the east of its range. It is a colonial species, with an average of about 15 pairs per colony in some areas at least, although this may vary. Some colonies are known to have been in existence for hundreds of years on the same spot. In contrast to the Swift, Alpines do not sleep in the air above their colonies, but instead roost in the nest or cling to vertical surfaces.

The Alpine Swift's nest is often stuck on to a vertical surface, too, rather than being placed on a ledge; it depends on the nature of the site. It seems that the male secures rights to the ledge first and that the female, arriving slightly later in the spring, is wooed by lots of bouts of mutual preening. In one study, about half the pairs in a colony used the same site from year to year and in another a single pair remained together for eleven years.

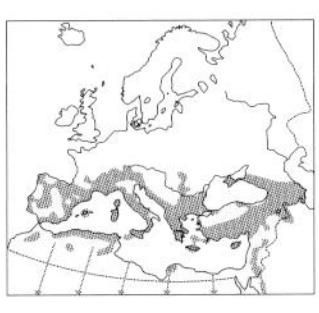

ID: Unmistakable owing to its large size, bold white throat, dark breast band and white belly.

Kingfisher *Alcedo atthis* (al-**see**-doh **at**-thiss) family *Alcedinidae* (al-see-**die**-nid-ee)

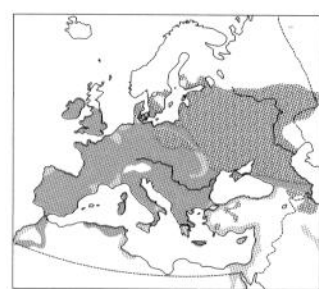

length 16 cm
ID: *Unmistakable. Male has all-black bill; female has orange base to lower mandible.*

Habitat For breeding, fresh still or slow-flowing water, especially rivers. In winter may be found on the coast and by large lakes.
Food Fish are mainstay, plus some crustaceans, insects, amphibians and molluscs, all caught by plunge-diving. Fish are beaten on perch to stun them and are invariably swallowed head first.
Movements Migratory in central, east and north Europe, but resident in the west and southwest.
Voice High-pitched whistle, of same pitch as squeaking car brakes.
Pairing style Monogamous, but regularly change partners, both year to year and between broods.
Nesting Solitary and territorial.
Nest Chamber at the end of a burrow dug by the birds themselves, 50–90 cm long.
Productivity 1–2 broods a year, exceptionally 3.
Eggs 6–7.
Incubation 19–21 days, by both sexes (mainly female at night).
Young Altricial; naked at first.
Parenting style Young are fed by both parents, at first using the 'carousel' system (see text).
Food to young Fish, regurgitated at first, but soon whole.
Leaving nest Young fledge at 23–27 days, then are fed by the parents for about 4 days before becoming independent.

Catching fish is no easy matter if you start from a perch. For one thing you have to spot the shy creatures in the first place, which may not be easy, especially if light is glinting off the surface or the water is stirred up by wind. Then, before you strike, you must estimate how far down the target is, a process rendered tricky by refraction, which makes underwater objects look closer than they are. And then, of course, you must plunge in and grab them, which requires considerable skill.

Somehow, though, the Kingfisher makes a living in this way, and its prime weapon is its remarkable eyesight. It has exceptional colour vision produced by oil droplets in the retina, and that helps to detect the fish amidst the subtle and shifting colours of a river. It also has an unusual arrangement of the eye that gives it highly sensitive all-round vision with one position of the head and equally sensitive overlapping or binocular vision, to help judge distance, with another. When a Kingfisher is watching below it, with its head angled down at 60 degrees, it can shift between the two types of vision with a small turn of the head, thereby first spotting a fish and then measuring how far away it is. The rest – allowing for refraction and adjusting its dive accordingly – is probably mostly down to practice. It certainly works, because one study found that 50 per cent of all dives were successful.

Although the Kingfisher feeds primarily on small fish, it does eat some other food items as well. In Britain, for example, the diet in one survey was found to constitute 60 per cent fish and 20 per cent insects, whereas in Spain a survey came up with 78 per cent fish and 10 per cent crustaceans. Frogs sometimes hop on to the menu, as do molluscs and butterflies, and the latter may actually be caught in flight, without recourse to a plunge dive. Although Kingfishers usually obtain their food from a perch, they are perfectly capable of hovering above the water instead.

Kingfishers breed beside still or slow-flowing water with an abundant supply of small fish, together with plenty of waterside vegetation to provide lookout perches over the water. Another necessity, of course, is a suitable earthen bank in which to excavate the nest. For this, both birds dig on and off for between four and seven days before they finally complete a tunnel with a slightly raised chamber at the end that is 12–15 cm across, onto which the eggs are laid directly. Just before it is complete the male begins a rigorous regime of plying the female with food, ritually presenting a fish to her while they are sitting side by side on a perch.

The young are fed in a remarkable way. Instead of the unseemly free-for-all seen in most nests of young birds, the nestlings are fed in strict rotation, literally. The chicks sit in a circle back to back with only one of them facing the light coming from the tunnel entrance; when a parent comes in with a fish, that chick is fed and then, democratically enough, it stands aside for the next to be fed and everyone moves round, like slides in a carousel.

Bee-eater *Merops apiaster* (**mer**-rops ay-pee-**ass**-ter) family *Meropidae* (mer-**rop**-pid-ee)

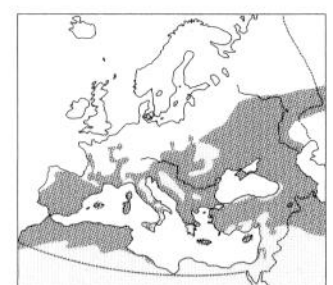

length 28 cm
ID: Unmistakable.

Habitat Open areas with plenty of insects and high perches. Particularly fond of river valleys.
Food Flying insects, especially bees and wasps. Often obtained by aerial sally from perch.
Movements Summer migrant, wintering in western or southern Africa. Departs between August and October and arrives back in March and April.
Voice A liquid, rolling 'prrt' is the main call. Calls are individually recognisable.
Pairing style Monogamous.
Nesting Usually colonial, but sometimes as single pairs.
Nest A chamber at the end of a tunnel 1–3 m long, excavated by both birds. No material.
Productivity 1 brood a year.
Eggs 4–7, sometimes up to 10.
Incubation 20 days, by both parents.
Young Nest-bound, altricial and naked.
Parenting style Young are fed and tended by both parents and often by an extra helper or two.
Food to young Flying insects, similar to adults' diet.
Leaving nest Young fledge at 25–30 days, and will then be fed outside the nest chamber for a few days. The family often departs together on migration.

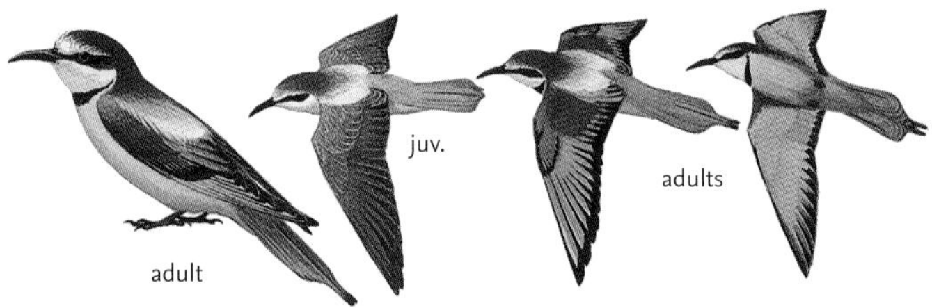

These gorgeous birds are popular with just about everyone, with the exception, perhaps, of apiarists. As their name implies, bees are their main source of food, especially honeybees – the sort you get in hives – and bumblebees. But they take other flying insects as well and these include just about everything you could find in the summer skies: wasps, flies, ants, mosquitoes, grasshoppers, mantids and dragonflies, for example; these are caught on the wing, on a long- or short-haul sally from a perch.

Bees and wasps do, of course, sting, and Bee-eaters have a very thorough way of dealing with this problem so as not to ingest the toxin. They take the insect by its midriff and hammer its head on the perch beside them, disabling it. They then transfer their grip to its rear end, lean over to their other side and rub it on the perch up to ten times, a process which causes the venom to be discharged as the abdomen is crushed. Finally, they revert to the first side and, once again, subject the insect to a beating on its head. Stingless insects are spared the abdomen crushing, but they are beaten about the head vigorously, the larger ones up to 80 times. Each individual Bee-eater will invariably beat a bee on one side and rub it on the other, a bit like being right- or left-handed.

Most Bee-eaters live in colonies and studies on their vocalisations have shown that individuals in the colony can tell everyone else apart by their unique calls. This helps social cohesion and makes pair formation easier (the birds have few ostentatious displays). In addition it allows non-breeding first-year birds to recognise their parents and help in the breeding attempt. These supernumeraries are usually males and they may help their father and mother with feeding the young and possibly with other nest duties as well.

Bee-eaters lay a lot of eggs, one every day for about a week, but they begin incubation with the first. Since each egg needs the same amount of time to develop, this means that the ages of the nestlings are invariably staggered when they hatch. There is no democracy in a Bee-eater nest – every chick must compete to be fed, something that the younger chicks do less vigorously than the older. So the older birds get the lion's share of the food deliveries and only when food is abundantly available do the younger birds have a chance of survival.

Roller *Coracias garrulus* (koh-**ray**-see-ass **gar**-oo-luss) family *Coraciidae* (koh-ray-**sie**-id-ee)

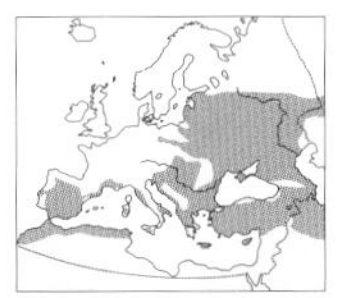

length 31–32 cm
ID: If seen properly unmistakable, but looks like a Crow or Jackdaw in silhouette.

Habitat Open forests (especially of oak and pine), steppe and grassland in warm, sunny climates.
Food Invertebrates and small vertebrates such as lizards and snakes. Indigestible parts are ejected from the mouth as pellets, about 10 times a day.
Movements Summer migrant wintering mainly in East Africa. Departs in August and returns in May.
Voice A guttural 'rak', often repeated.
Pairing style Monogamous. Some pairs apparently tolerate a third bird in the territory, but its role, if any, is not yet understood.
Nesting Solitary and territorial.
Nest A hole, usually in a tree, but sometimes among rocks or even old buildings. Holes made by Black or Green Woodpeckers are most popular. No material.
Productivity 1 brood a year.
Eggs 4–5.
Incubation 17–19 days, by both adults, but only by female at night.
Young Nest-bound, altricial and naked.
Parenting style Young fed by both adults.
Food to young As adult food.
Leaving nest Young fledge at 25–30 days, and become independent 3 weeks later.

If a crow went on a makeover TV show to overhaul its looks and turn around its popularity, it would probably end up looking like a Roller. The shape is essentially the same, the voice is just as harsh, but the colours are fabulous and there is none of that insalubrious carrion eating and messing about at rubbish dumps.

The Roller is a 'perch and pounce' predator of the warm, sunny, insect-rich parts of Europe. It sits on a lookout point 3–6 m above ground, observing the comings and goings of prey below, and then goes after whatever it has spotted by means of a shallow, leisurely glide down and a quick grab. The meal is then brought back to a perch and beaten senseless against a hard surface before being swallowed. The prey sought is typically between 10 mm and 30 mm long. Large beetles usually dominate the menu, but it is possible to make a long list of the items that might be consumed. Most of them are various insects, but scorpions are important in places, and frogs, lizards and even snakes are caught sometimes. The snakes may be as long as 35 cm and may take some time to despatch and eat.

Rollers pair up in their winter quarters, which is just as well, because they are late arriving in Europe. They settle into a territory and the male defends it vigorously, using the flight display that gives this bird its English name. He flies up at a sharp angle, beating his wings hard, stalls at a height of 200 m or more, then dives down, calling, rolling his body from side to side until he almost touches the ground, whereupon he swoops up again and the sequence is repeated. The display is directed at any strange bird and sometimes at other intruders, such as people, too.

Rollers migrate in the autumn to East and Central Africa, where they join all the birds that breed anywhere from Europe to China, making the Roller an abundant bird there. They travel by day in small groups, apparently averaging 67 km per day overall.

Hoopoe *Upupa epops* (oo-**poo**-pa **ee**-popss) family *Upupidae* (oo-**poo**-pid-ee)

adults

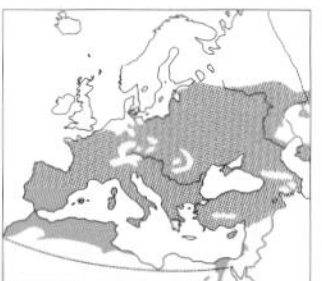

length 25–29 cm
ID: Unmistakable!

Habitat Open country with a combination of trees or walls for nesting, and bare or sparsely vegetated ground. Includes low-intensity farmland, open woodland, orchards and olive groves.
Food Mainly insects taken from the ground or by probing in the soil.
Movements Migrates to Africa for the winter. Movement in autumn not rushed, starting any time between mid-July and late October. Returns in March and April.
Voice A far-carrying, dove-like, evenly paced 'poo-poo-poo', the sort of sound you might coo to a baby.
Pairing style Monogamous.
Nesting Solitary and territorial.
Nest In a hole, usually in a tree, but also in rocks, walls etc or in the ground.
Productivity 1–2 broods a year.
Eggs 5–8.
Incubation 16–18 days, by female, fed by the male.
Young Nest-bound, altricial and downy, with some remarkable forms of defence (see text).
Parenting style Female broods young, but both adults bring food.
Food to young Insects, often including many larvae and pupae of butterflies and moths.
Leaving nest Young fledge at 24–28 days and are fed by the adults for a few days thereafter.

The Hoopoe is the sort of bird that looks as though it should be rare, but it isn't. On the contrary, it is common in the warmer and drier parts of Europe and is tamer than many more run-of-the-mill birds, contentedly living alongside people, nesting in their walls and feeding in their gardens.

With its long, slightly curved bill, the Hoopoe is adapted to feeding on the ground, both by picking insects off the surface and by probing underneath it. Despite looking fragile, the bill is toughened and the bird has a special adaptation of the jaw that enables it to open the bill while it is still in the ground, thereby making space to grab hold of a larva or grub embedded in the soil. Hoopoes are especially fond of mole crickets and cockchafer larvae, which are found in the ground but leave visual clues above it, such as a recognisable entrance to a burrow. Hoopoes also eat beetles, including stag beetles, plus grasshoppers, crickets and other creepy-crawlies, occasionally adding the odd lizard or frog.

Hoopoes regularly probe into dung heaps, rubbish dumps and patches of animal excreta, a practice which looks unsavoury but no doubt yields a good crop of insects. But it has given them a reputation for being unhygienic which, regrettably, is amply enforced by the fact that their nests stink. Both female parent and young are able to secrete a foul-smelling odour from their enlarged uropygial (preen) gland, which carries more than a whiff of rotting meat, enough to make you recoil violently at the entrance.

If the smell doesn't deter predators from the nest, the youngsters have several other tricks up their sleeve. They can eject faeces with deadly accuracy towards an intruder, sometimes hitting it from 60 cm away. If this doesn't work they can hiss like snakes and jab with their sharp bills. Not surprisingly, the nesting success of this eye-catching and nose-catching species is higher than most.

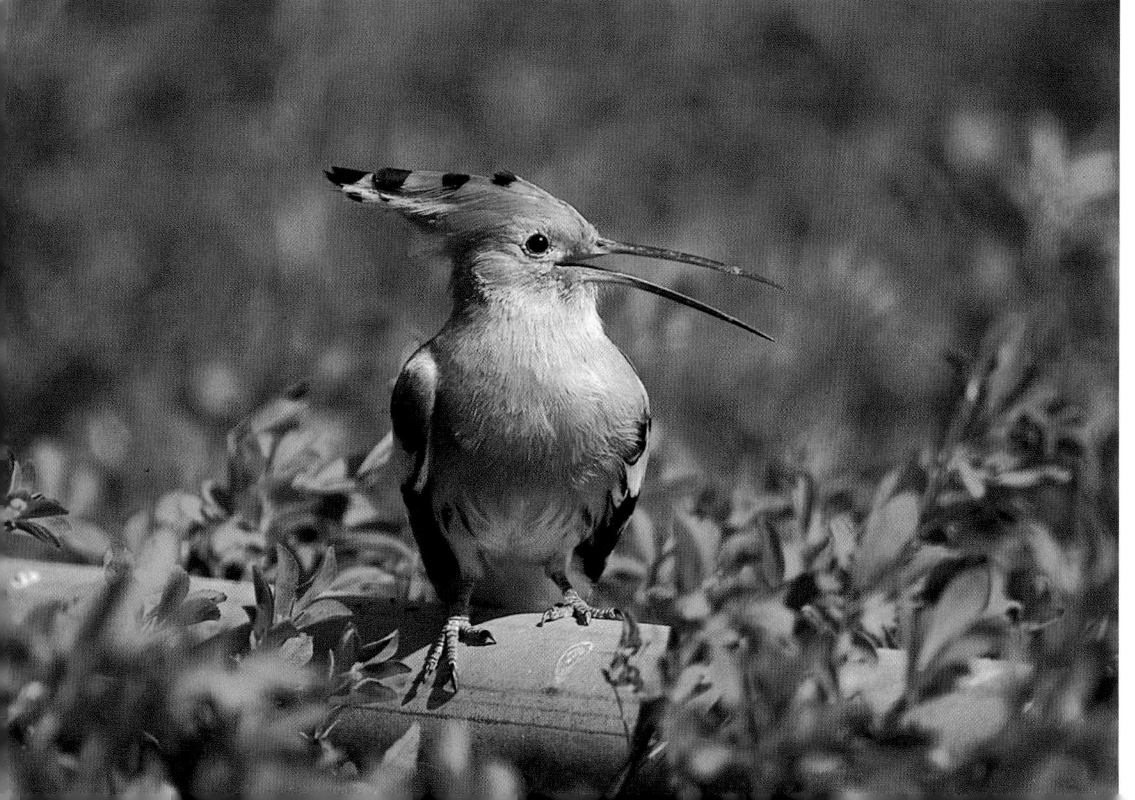

Woodpeckers family *Picidae* (**pie**-sid-ee)

Habitat Mainly woodland and forest. Several species require open ground.
Food Mainly invertebrates, especially wood-boring beetles and ants. Also nuts, seeds.
Movements Most are resident. Wryneck is a long-distance migrant to tropical Africa.
Song Most species tap bills rapidly on wood to make 'drumming' noise (but not Wryneck or Middle Spotted Woodpecker; Green only rarely).
Pairing style Most are monogamous, but both Lesser Spotted and Great Spotted females may have 2 mates.
Nesting Territorial and solitary.
Nest All species except Wryneck (see entry) excavate their own nesting holes. Eggs are laid onto a platform of wood chips.
Productivity 1 brood a year (Wryneck 2).
Eggs 3–10 (Wryneck 7–12).
Incubation 9–17 days. Often only the male incubates at night.
Young Nest-bound, altricial young hatch blind and naked.
Parenting style Both parents feed young by regurgitation.
Food to young Mainly insects, especially ants. Some young are given fruit or berries.
Leaving nest Young leave nest at 18–28 days, but remain in parents' care for 2–7 weeks afterwards.

Three-toed Woodpecker

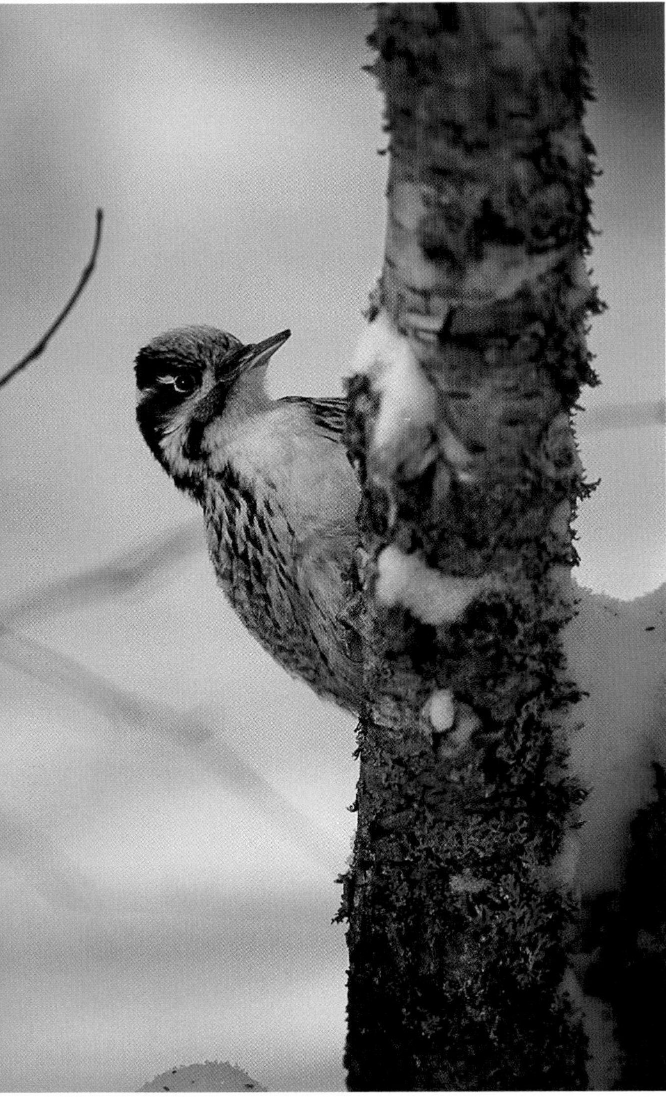

Few birds are as instantly recognisable as woodpeckers. They live up to their name, and their distinctive shape is entirely a consequence of their unusual lifestyle, which consists of clinging on to vertical trunks and using their bills to excavate holes in bark and wood. For this they have special adaptations of the skull, feet and tail.

A woodpecker's bill is powerful and chisel-shaped, not too sharp (because it would get stuck in the wood) and not too curved (it would break). The act of hammering puts great strains on the skull, so the woodpecker has an enlarged brain case for extra protection, and both the bones and the muscles at the base of the bill act as shock absorbers. The nostrils are often covered with feathers for protection from flying chips and sawdust, and the eyes are shut each time the bill strikes the wood. Not surprisingly, the bill wears as it hammers and probes, keeping it sharp.

A woodpecker's feet are arranged with two toes facing forwards and two backwards, a system known as zygodactyl, which helps the birds to cling and grip. The feet are short and strong, with sharp claws. They work in tandem with the tail to keep the woodpecker on the tree, the latter acting as a prop while the claws hold on. The woodpecker's tail is also especially stiffened for the purpose.

The act of hammering is useful in two ways. First of all, it enables most species of woodpecker to obtain food by uncovering wood-boring insects in the bark and timber. Secondly, it enables the birds to make holes for nesting or roosting. They simply select a stretch of timber, often on a dead trunk or branch, and excavate it as required. A nesting chamber is usually completed after about two weeks of work.

Most woodpeckers have sedentary lives, enabling them to learn the best feeding sites in their territory over years of occupation. Some, including the Black and White-backed Woodpeckers, have enormous territories covering many square kilometres. To get from place to place most fly in a distinctive way, regular bursts of a few wingbeats carrying them on a steep up-and-down course. The exception to this is the Black Woodpecker, which flies on a straight but unsteady course, a little like a Jay.

Great Spotted Woodpecker

Dendrocopos major (den-**drok**-oh-poss **may**-jor)
length 22–23 cm

ID: The commonest woodpecker. Medium-sized, with mainly black back offset by large white 'blob of paint' on shoulders (shared by Syrian and Middle Spotted). Underside largely unstreaked white with brilliant crimson undertail coverts. Crown black, with white forehead. Male has red spot on nape, lacking in female. Beware juveniles (early summer) which have red crowns and pink undertail coverts, making them resemble other species.

Over most of Europe the Great Spotted Woodpecker is the most common species in its family. It is also the most adaptable, living in almost any wooded habitat, from pure deciduous forest to pure coniferous forest, in large or small stands of trees, and in many different climatic zones, from the Mediterranean to the taiga. It employs a wide variety of feeding techniques to take a whole range of foods and, in the light of its dominance and adaptability, every other woodpecker species has to specialise.

The Great Spotted Woodpecker's diet, like that of most woodpeckers, varies greatly during the course of the year. In summer the birds will probe into fissures in the bark for invertebrates and glean them from branches and leaves. In autumn and winter they will hammer into dead timber for wood-boring insects and also harvest seeds and cones. From early spring onwards they will make rings of holes 3–8 mm deep around trees and drink the sap exuding from them. And in summer they have the unexpected habit of feeding on the eggs and chicks of hole-nesting birds such as tits.

More than any other woodpecker, the Great Spotted has developed the habit of using 'anvils', special crevices where items such as seeds can be wedged firmly while being worked on. Sometimes the birds simply open an existing crack in the bark, but at other times they will construct the anvils from scratch by chiselling into a vertical surface. Cones are gathered in the canopy and brought to the anvil from some distance away, and large piles often build up below, having been dropped from the high-rise workshop.

In the winter many northern populations of Great Spotted Woodpeckers rely almost completely on the seeds of conifers for their food. But cone crops are unpredictable and if they fail many thousands of individuals are forced to move south to search for food, in special migratory movements called irruptions. Birds caught up in these movements have been known to travel as much as 3000 km.

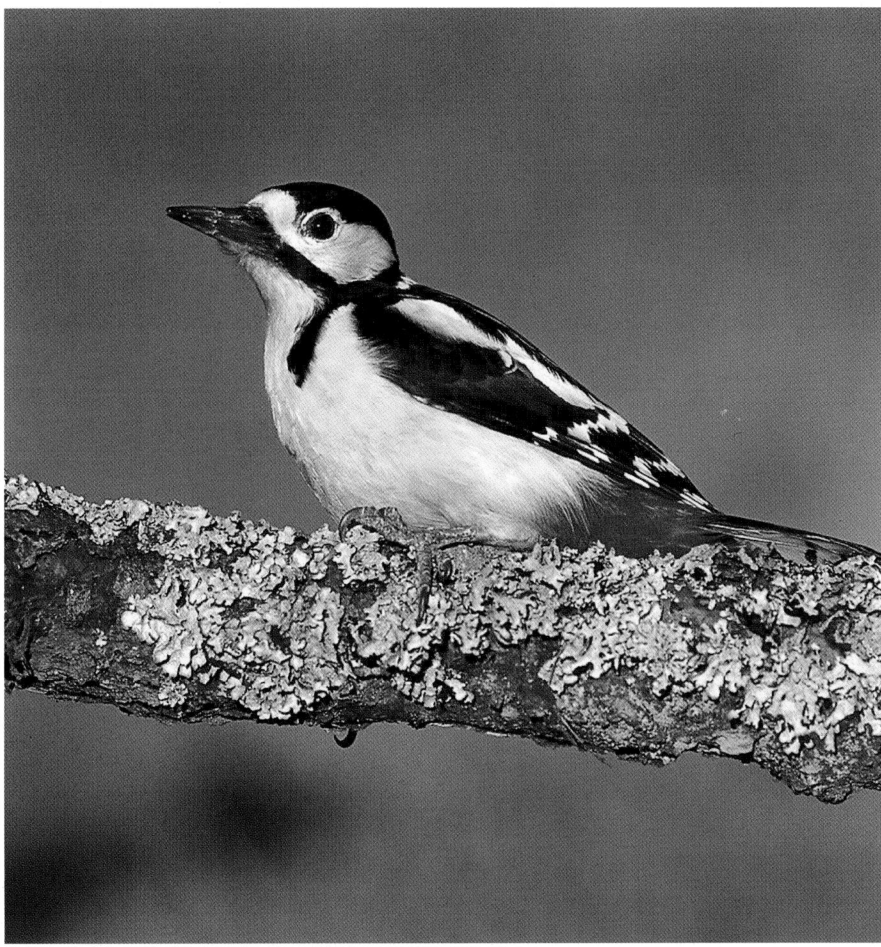

From early spring, both sexes 'drum', striking wood with rapid blows in quick succession to make a sound like a drum roll. In doing this they are not excavating a hole – that requires a much slower rate of strikes – but advertising their presence to other woodpeckers in the vicinity. Drumming both proclaims a territory and can bring potential mates into contact, so acts as a kind of song. Once attracted, pairs cement their relationship with various displays, including special 'fluttering' flights around the trees, and pursuits.

Both sexes excavate a hole in almost any kind of tree, either dead or living. They begin by carving a horizontal entrance a few centimetres deep, then work inside the hole, boring downwards to make the nest chamber. The chamber is between 25 cm and 35 cm deep and has a floor of wood chippings as a platform for eggs and young. When the eggs hatch, both sexes feed them by regurgitation.

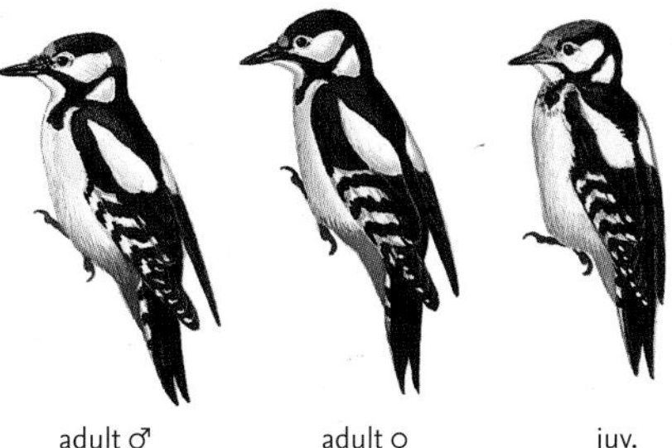

Lesser Spotted Woodpecker

Dendrocopos minor (den-**drok**-oh-poss **mie**-nor)
length 14–15 cm

This dainty bird is the smallest member of its family in Europe, not much larger than a House Sparrow. Its size enables it to forage on thin vertical twigs 1–3 cm in diameter, usually right up in the forest canopy and too small to support other woodpeckers.

In summer the Lesser Spotted Woodpecker feeds on such insects as ants and aphids, but in winter, despite its size, it is perfectly capable of hammering into timber to obtain wood-boring insects. Nevertheless, it is found mainly in areas with plenty of softwood trees, especially near water. When not breeding it has the habit of joining flocks of small woodland birds, such as tits, as they roam through the woodlands. On its wanderings it may even end up visiting reedbeds, clinging to the vertical stems.

This is one of the quieter woodpeckers. Although it drums and has a 'peep-peep-peep' call, it uses these sounds sparingly. As a consequence, it is very easy to overlook.

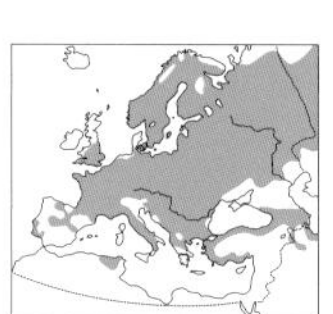

ID: Restless, flitting movements lack jerky style of other woodpeckers. Has smaller, shorter bill. Easily distinguished from Great Spotted by white bars going down black back, like a ladder, and by complete lack of red on undertail. Male has red crown, female has white forehead and black crown.

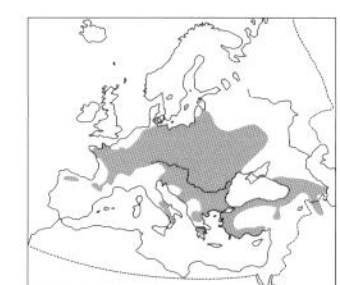

ID: Slightly smaller than Great Spotted Woodpecker, but has a much shorter bill and unusual habit of perching across branches. Uniquely, both sexes have bright red crowns. Further distinguished from Great Spotted by yellowish and profusely streaked underside and by only pale pinkish-red on undertail.

Middle Spotted Woodpecker

Dendrocopos medius (den-**drok**-oh-poss **mee**-di-uss)
length 20–22 cm

One of the few woodpeckers regularly to perch across branches as well as cling on to them, the Middle Spotted Woodpecker is a bird of broad limbs and trunks. In contrast to most species it hardly hammers at all, but concentrates almost entirely on gleaning insects from the surface throughout the year. Much of its foraging is done high up in the crowns of tall trees.

Ecologically speaking this is a sensitive species, heavily dependent on mature deciduous forest with a good proportion of large oaks. Oaks have particularly insect-rich, furrowed bark, ideal for gleaning. About a third of all foraging is also from dead wood, so the Middle Spotted Woodpecker does not do well in intensively managed woodlands.

In the spring Middle Spotted Woodpeckers advertise their presence mainly by vocal sounds. Although they do occasionally drum, this is an unusual event.

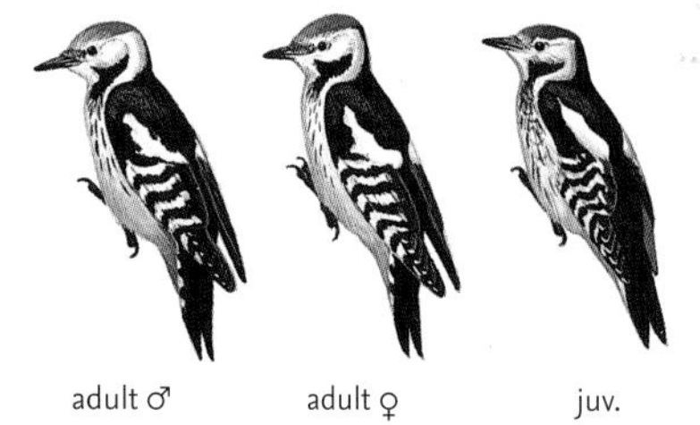

Syrian Woodpecker

Dendrocopos syriacus
(den-**drok**-oh-poss sir-ri-**ah**-kuss)
length 22–23 cm

Although the Syrian Woodpecker is almost identical to the Great Spotted in appearance, it has a quite distinct ecology. Where the Great Spotted is mainly a woodland bird, the Syrian thrives in more open country, with scattered plantations, orchards and gardens. The two species also have slightly different foraging styles, the Syrian being less inclined to hammer than the Great Spotted and more inclined to probe the bark for food. And while the Great Spotted tends to prefer woodland canopy, the Syrian is more often found on the ground or on low tree trunks.

The Syrian is also the most vegetarian of all the woodpeckers, taking seeds, nuts and berries throughout the year, even feeding berries to its young on occasion. It seems particularly fond of walnuts and almonds, and in some parts of its range can be a minor agricultural pest. Although it was once confined in Europe to the extreme southeast, the Syrian Woodpecker has benefited from the clearance of forests for agriculture and has expanded its range westwards in the last hundred years.

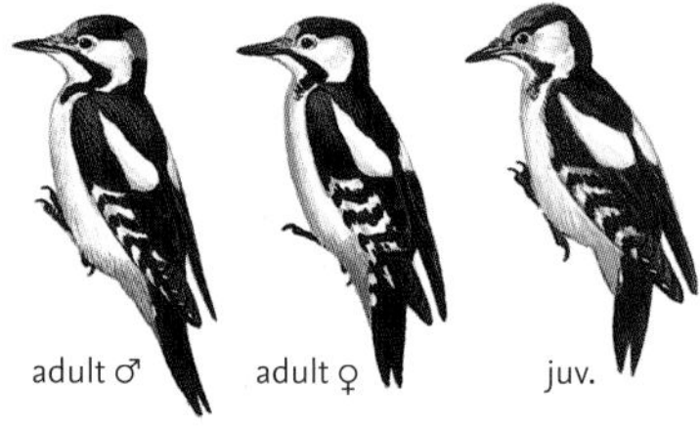

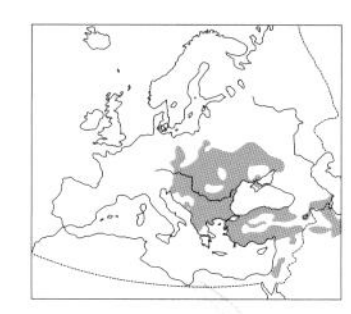

ID: Similar to Great Spotted in plumage and habits, but with paler red undertail, a few streaks on the flanks and a whiter face, without the black bar seen in Great Spotted.

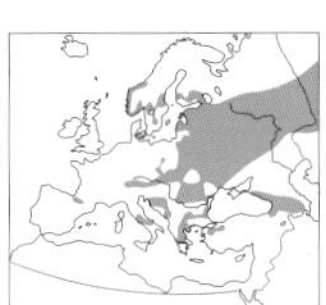

ID: Slightly larger than Great Spotted Woodpecker, with longer neck and longer bill giving distinctive shape.

White-backed Woodpecker

Dendrocopos leucotos
(den-**drok**-oh-poss loo-**koh**-tuss)
length 24–26 cm

It's often easier to find signs of the White-backed Woodpecker's activity than to see this elusive bird itself. An expert excavator, it leaves large, oval-shaped gashes in the timber up to 23 cm deep where it has been hammering for the wood-boring beetles and moth larvae that make up its diet. It will also completely strip off the bark from whole trunks and branches. But foresters need not worry: this largest of Europe's black and white woodpeckers is drawn only to rotten wood and fallen trees, not to live timber.

In contrast to the Three-toed Woodpecker, which has a similar diet, the White-backed is confined mainly to deciduous trees, including beech, aspen, oak and birch. It is a fussy species, requiring stands at least 80 years old, in large, unbroken tracts little affected by management. These requirements are at odds with most human use of forests, so not surprisingly this bird is declining in much of its European range.

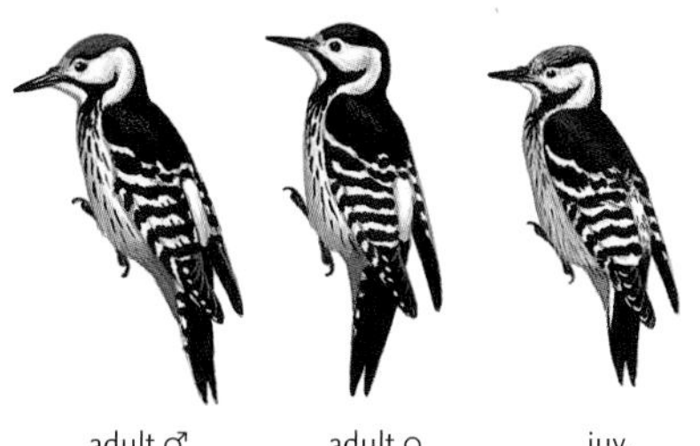

adult ♂ adult ♀ juv.

Three-toed Woodpecker

Picoides tridactylus (pik-**koy**-deez trie-**dak**-til-lus)
length 21–22 cm

Not for nothing is this successful woodpecker given its common name, for it has indeed lost one of its hind toes and climbs trees using only three. It is an elusive bird that lives in old dense forests with lots of dead and fallen trees. Here it specialises in eating the larvae and pupae of wood-boring beetles, pecking, hammering and tearing away strips of bark to get at them. It is strongly drawn to areas where the forest has been affected by heavy insect infestation, fire or wind and avalanche damage – anywhere where foraging has been made easier. It is also especially fond of making holes in wood and drinking sap from them.

The Three-toed Woodpecker is found from northern Europe right across Siberia and into Japan. There are two discrete populations in Europe, one in the lowland spruce and fir forests of the northern taiga belt, the other on steep, high-altitude, spruce-covered slopes on central European mountainsides. It is just possible that these geographically isolated populations represent different species.

adult ♂ adult ♀ juv.

ID: Distinctive black and white woodpecker, the only one in Europe with a golden-yellow crown (lacking in female).

ID: Unmistakable once the familiar woodpecker shape is seen. Can be confused with similar-sized crow, but flight very different, flappy and jerky rather than smooth and steady.

Black Woodpecker

Dryocopus martius (drie-**ok**-oh-puss **mar**-shuss)
length 45–57 cm

Although this is the largest of Europe's woodpeckers, as big as a crow, it can nonetheless be a very difficult bird to see, because each individual ranges over a huge area and remains shy of human contact. The Black Woodpecker is a forest species, inhabiting large tracts of tall trees with plenty of open glades intermixed. Feeding mainly on or near the ground, it is particularly drawn to tree stumps, where it will remain busily feeding for up to two hours at a time, hacking away at the rotten wood to reveal its favourite prey, ants.

Whilst the ant-loving Green Woodpecker has a long tongue to pry into cracks, the Black Woodpecker is less subtle and simply uses its powerful bill to break into the ants' habitat. Its tongue has a hard tip and is equipped with backward-pointing barbs, like a harpoon, making it an effective adhesive weapon for the bird's soft-bodied prey.

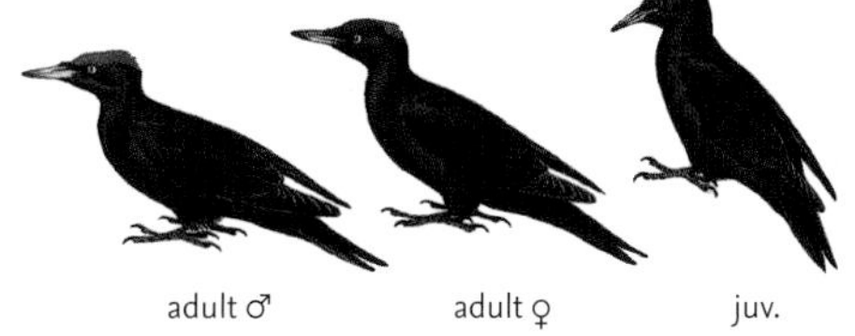

adult ♂ adult ♀ juv.

Wryneck

Jynx torquilla (**jinks** tor-**kwil**-la)
length 16–17 cm

ID: Odd-looking bird not easily appreciated as a woodpecker; doesn't cling in the same way, often perching across a branch as 'normal' birds do. Also rather small, not much larger than sparrow. Short but very pointed bill. Very distinctive when seen well. Complex bark-like pattern on plumage, predominantly grey above with several dark stripes. Barred below, this being especially obvious on the throat.

At first sight the Wryneck does not look like a woodpecker, with its cryptic brown plumage, soft tail feathers and habit of perching across branches. But it has zygodactyl feet and a long, woodpecker-like tongue, ensuring its place in the family. Ants are the most important component of its diet, obtained mainly on the ground.

The Wryneck is the only European woodpecker that is a regular long-distance migrant, moving between tropical Africa and Europe, and travelling by night. It arrives on its breeding grounds in March and April, settling in open woodland, parks and orchards, anywhere with old trees and patches of turf exposed to sunlight.

With its short, sharp, slightly curved bill, the Wryneck is unable to drum, hammer or excavate its own nest hole. Instead, it breeds in natural cavities or old woodpecker holes, brazenly removing the nests of other birds if they are occupying its chosen site.

The name Wryneck arises from the threat display of cornered adults or nestlings. These make hissing sounds and turn their heads around slowly, somewhat like a snake.

adults

Grey-headed Woodpecker

Picus canus (**pie**-kuss **kay**-nuss)
length 25–26 cm

adult ♂

adult ♀

juv.

A close relative of the larger Green Woodpecker, the Grey-headed is another ant specialist, but is perhaps a little less dependent on them. It spends less time on the ground than the Green Woodpecker and more time in the trees. It has a shorter tongue and probably a broader diet.

In Europe the Grey-headed Woodpecker is found in subtly different habitats to the Green. It prefers smaller woods and is often found near water. It is more tolerant of high altitudes and more confined to deciduous stands. Even so, the precise habitat differentiation of the two species is obscure in Europe. The Grey-headed is actually the more successful species worldwide, with a huge range encompassing not just temperate forests but also the rainforests of southeast Asia.

ID: Smaller than Green Woodpecker with slightly shorter bill; more arboreal. Distinguished from Green Woodpecker by predominantly ashy-grey head, with narrow black moustache and eye patch.

Green Woodpecker

Picus viridis (**pie**-kuss **vir**-rid-diss)
length 31–33 cm

The Green Woodpecker is green for a reason. The colour is ideal camouflage for a bird that, rather than feeding in the trees as most woodpeckers do, forages on the ground among swards of grass and turf. It is a specialist, spending most of its year at the nests of various species of meadow ants, which it catches by digging funnel-shaped holes in the ground up to 12 cm deep. Such holes often cut through the ants' underground tunnels and the insects simply march along them to their doom. At other times the ants are intercepted as they pour out in defence of their nest and are lapped up by the Green Woodpecker's tongue.

A woodpecker's tongue is a remarkable instrument, capable of movement in any direction at the tip, and often very long – the Green Woodpecker's, for example, extends 10 cm from the end of the bill. The 'hyoid apparatus', the arrangement of bones that provide support and attachment for the tongue, is so long that it must arch completely around the woodpecker's skull to fit in. Most woodpeckers have barbs at the tip of their tongues for spearing prey, but the Green Woodpecker has a flat, wide tip instead and relies on the adhesive properties of the secretions from its enlarged salivary glands to hold on to its prey.

Turf does not present much of a hammering challenge, so a Green Woodpecker 's bill is weak compared to those of other species. One probable consequence of this is that the Green Woodpecker rarely drums. Instead, when spring approaches the birds produce a loud laughing call to advertise the territory.

Despite their weaker bills Green Woodpeckers do excavate their own nest hole. It is usually bored into dead wood, and this means that, for a territory to be ideal, it must contain mature trees as well as suitable open areas for feeding. Many such places suffice, including open forest, heathland and gardens, making the Green Woodpecker a common and familiar species.

ID: Easily identified as a woodpecker by its large-headed, short-tailed shape and heavily undulating flight; only confusion is with Grey-headed Woodpecker. Ground-loving. Both sexes have red crowns; male has red centre to moustache, female has black moustache.

adult ♂ adult ♀ juv.

Larks family *Alaudidae* (al-**low**-did-ee)

Habitat Open areas of various sorts, especially grassland and steppe; warm, arid places carry the most species. Most, except Wood Lark and Thekla Lark, shun trees and bushes.
Food Mainly seeds and insects, obtained on the ground by picking and, in some species, digging.
Movements Most migratory in some form, but move relatively short distances, staying within Europe (e.g. Shore Lark, Wood Lark). Some make local movements at most (Dupont's, Thekla). Short-toed Lark long-distance migrant to Africa. Skylark may evacuate wintering areas in severe weather (escape movements).
Voice Each lark has its own individually recognisable song, often high pitched and sustained; often given in song flight. Calls are often 'extracts' from the song.
Pairing style Usually monogamous.
Nesting Normally solitary and fiercely territorial, but pairs may form neighbourhood groups.
Nest A cup of grass, lined with smaller fragments. Placed in a scrape on the ground made by the female and usually sited next to a tuft, herb, bush or rock.
Productivity 1–3 broods a year (Skylark sometimes 4).
Eggs 2–6.
Incubation 11–16 days, by female only.
Young Nest-bound, altricial, downy on head and upper parts for camouflage. Young have distinctive spots on the tongue and inside tips of the mandibles.
Parenting style Both sexes tend and feed the young.
Food to young Fed insects at first but diet rapidly changes to vegetarian. As a result juvenile larks have poor plumage and undergo a complete moult in the autumn (most other small birds retain their wing and tail feathers).
Leaving nest Young may leave the nest a day or so before they can fly. Fledge at 10–20 days.

Crested Lark

With the larks we enter the vast assemblage of birds known technically as passerines; all the remaining species in this book belong to that group. Passerines share a common arrangement of the foot, with three toes pointing forwards and one back, which helps them to perch effectively on twigs, branches and so on. Passerines also all have quite sophisticated internal singing apparatus, so as a group they may be summed up as 'perching birds and songbirds'. Although they include crows in their number, most Passerines are rather small and a good many are inconspicuous.

Larks, the family that introduces the passerines, are very much of the 'little brown bird' ilk, the ones with similar coloration that terrify those new to birdwatching. Their plumage is streaked and pretty dreary, but that suits them fine. They rely on their plumage for camouflage when they are feeding, roosting and incubating, all of which they do on the ground. If they were too conspicuous they wouldn't survive for long.

They may not look much, but larks are special. They are different in a couple of anatomical respects from every other set of small brown birds. For one thing they lack a bone in their song-producing apparatus, the syrinx, which every other passerine family in Europe has. And their feet are scaled both at back and front, whereas every other passerine has scales only at the front. This protects the lark from wear when it is walking around.

And larks do walk. They run, too – but they don't hop, in contrast to most other passerines. A lark's foot is also characterised by a long claw on the hind toe, which enables the bird to run around on sand and other soft surfaces, distributing its weight over a wide area, a bit like a snowshoe. A lark's wings are long, its body tends to be thickset and its neck is short. The bill may be long and slightly curved, or it may be short and thick, rather like that of a finch.

For all their structural uniqueness, it is doubtful that anyone but a specialist would notice larks much except for one thing – their song flights. In the breeding season male larks take to the skies and, as they follow a choreographed routine of rising or falling, hovering or drifting, they blurt out their high-pitched monologues. These are primarily territorial in function and when one male sings rivals often join in to drive home their own message. These sounds may dominate the open countryside in which larks live, and shout their way into the consciousness of those who may otherwise be indifferent to them.

ID: *Usually easily identified by its long, slightly decurved bill and lack of any crest; no other terrestrial bird looks quite like it. Rounded crown has dark stripes. Neck is thin and long for a lark. Often runs fast and far.*

Dupont's Lark

Chersophilus duponti
(ker-**soff**-fil-lus doo-**pon**-tie)
length 18 cm

Traditionally, an early start is required to hear the varied and twittering song of the Dupont's Lark, a bird that performs best at dawn and dusk and is highly secretive for the rest of the day. Actually to see one is a real challenge. When starting to sing, males quickly rise up to 150 m above ground in the half-light, soon disappearing from view, and they remain aloft for an exceptionally long time for any singing bird, between half an hour and an hour in total. Once they have lulled the observer into a lack of concentration they suddenly plummet down, without warning and at great speed, breaking their fall only at the last moment before disappearing into thick bushes. Binoculars are rendered useless.

In Europe this species breeds only in Spain, with a total population of around 15,000 pairs. This scarcity is down to its very particular choice of habitat, which is best described as shrub-steppe – dry, bare ground with scattered thick bushes no more than 30–60 cm high. To a Dupont's Lark it is vital that this habitat is on flat ground with a gradient of less than 25 per cent; otherwise it is unsuitable. And although the bird may occur anywhere between sea level and 1600 m, most are found on plateaux at about 1000 m. The Dupont's dislike of intensive agriculture renders its populations isolated and vulnerable.

Within its special habitat the Dupont's Lark feeds on the ground, using its strikingly long bill to dig into the hard surface of the soil, where it finds insects and seeds, or into tarantula burrows. It has a strong pecking action that has been likened to that of a woodpecker. The nest is placed under a thick bush or stone.

adults

Calandra Lark

Melanocorypha calandra
(mel-lan-noh-**kor**-riff-fa kal-**lan**-dra)
length 18–19 cm

It doesn't take much for a Calandra Lark to burst into song. When one bird starts, it seems to act as a signal, compelling all the males in an area to rise up into the air themselves and make it a group effort. Birds flushed aloft by people also readily begin singing, evidently deciding that, since they have become airborne, they might as well make the most of it.

It's a good song, too, very like that of a Skylark, but a little less exuberant and overstated, with many richer notes. The birds sometimes perform from the ground or a perch, but the song is typically delivered in a choreographed display flight, with the birds describing definite and regular circles in the air, sometimes to a great height. In contrast to many larks, Calandras are hard to miss in the air; their smart black underwings are obvious against the sky, and they usually beat their wings relatively slowly and deliberately, sometimes with a few glides in between.

This is a bird of grassland and fields, including cereal crops; towards the east of its range it will also inhabit rank grass and even bushy areas. It feeds mostly on the ground, using its heavy bill as a blunt instrument to despatch rather more formidable insects than those eaten by other larks – crickets and large beetles, for instance – as well as seeds. The bill can also be used for digging and, as a useful trick in the winter, to break through the crust of snow.

After breeding, Calandra Larks are highly sociable, gathering in flocks with other larks and, especially, Corn Buntings. These flocks probably wander widely and it's possible that some birds actually spend the winter in Africa, since their numbers are much lower then than in the breeding season.

adults

ID: *Large lark with a heavy bill and rounded head with no crest. White supercilium and half-collar around neck; distinctive black smudge on the side of the neck. Easily recognised in flight by dark underwing with white trailing edge.*

Short-toed Lark

Calandrella brachydactyla

(kal-lan-**drel**-la brak-ki-**dak**-til-la)

length 13–14 cm

If you were to take a long-distance walk over the arid grasslands and steppes of southern Europe where the Short-toed Lark occurs, you would find that its song, far from being a constant presence ringing in your ears, would drift in and out of your hearing. You would walk into 'zones' where these birds were concentrated, with up to 10 or 20 males displaying in the air at one time, but it would be another 10 km before you stumbled upon something similar again. This experience shows that, of all birds, few are more clumped into 'neighbourhood groups' than Short-toed Larks.

These are not colonies, though. The birds are vehemently territorial and exclude other birds from their substantial defended patch, with none of the communal feeding or loafing that is common in true colonies. Rival males often sing just a few metres away from each other, keeping to the same height above ground, facing off like two boxers before a bout, and there are frequent fights. Each territory is about 40–50 m in diameter and serves all purposes, including courtship, nesting and providing for the young. So the birds may be concentrated, but they are not sociable.

The primary method of defence, the song flight, is most distinctive. Birds fly up to 30 m or so with rapidly beating wings while singing a prologue and then, having attained an acceptable height, launch into the main song, which is phrased and imitative. On reaching the end they descend on closed wings and, just before they touch the ground, give a hesitant little upward flutter before resuming the prologue on another ascent. And so it goes on, the birds looking with their repeated ascents and descents like animated, feathered yo-yos.

After breeding, differences are forgotten and Short-toed Larks gather into tight-knit flocks, often consisting of hundreds of birds, which fly around in a co-ordinated unit. They leave Europe in September for Africa and return again in March.

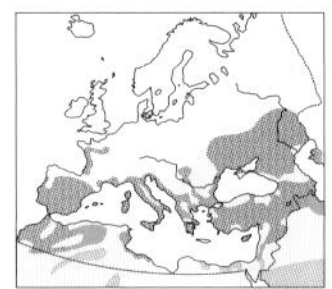

ID: Small, finch-like lark with a short and thick but pointed bill. Reminiscent of much larger Calandra Lark in having a white supercilium, white half-collar around neck and variable smudge on the sides of the breast. Often looks very pale and washed-out, with almost completely unmarked white underparts.

Lesser Short-toed Lark

Calandrella rufescens

(kal-lan-**drel**-la roo-**fess**-enz)

length 13–14 cm

One way of discovering which birds are present in an area is to listen to the song of a Lesser Short-toed Lark – if you can find one! These birds incorporate expert imitations into their performances and can reproduce the sounds of, for example, such local exotics as Black-bellied Sandgrouse, Stone Curlew and Spectacled Warbler. They are even occasionally kept in captivity and can imitate human whistles and other household noises, among much else. It may not be advisable to use the song to help you distinguish these larks from other members of the family, such as Crested Larks and Short-toed Larks, either, because they steal phrases from them, too. Incidentally, the song flight of this bird is generally agreed to be less incessantly undulating than that of the Short-toed Lark and ranges over a slightly wider area.

Where both species of Short-toed Larks occur, they often overlap in habitat and may even share territories. Nevertheless the Lesser Short-toed avoids the grassy plains and low-crop areas beloved of the Short-toed, and it tends to occur in drier and more saline terrain, with plenty of stones or bare ground. Although it may occur in hotter places in summer than the Short-toed Lark, it is clearly hardier and does not migrate away from the breeding areas in the winter. Instead the birds form into flocks and roam the area in search of seeds, feeding communally on the ground.

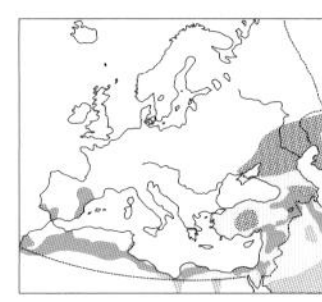

ID: Usually quite easy to distinguish from Short-toed by its decidedly short and stubby bill, by its streaks on the breast and by its lack of any black smudge on the side of the breast. May resemble Skylark in plumage, but latter is much larger with longer, sharper bill.

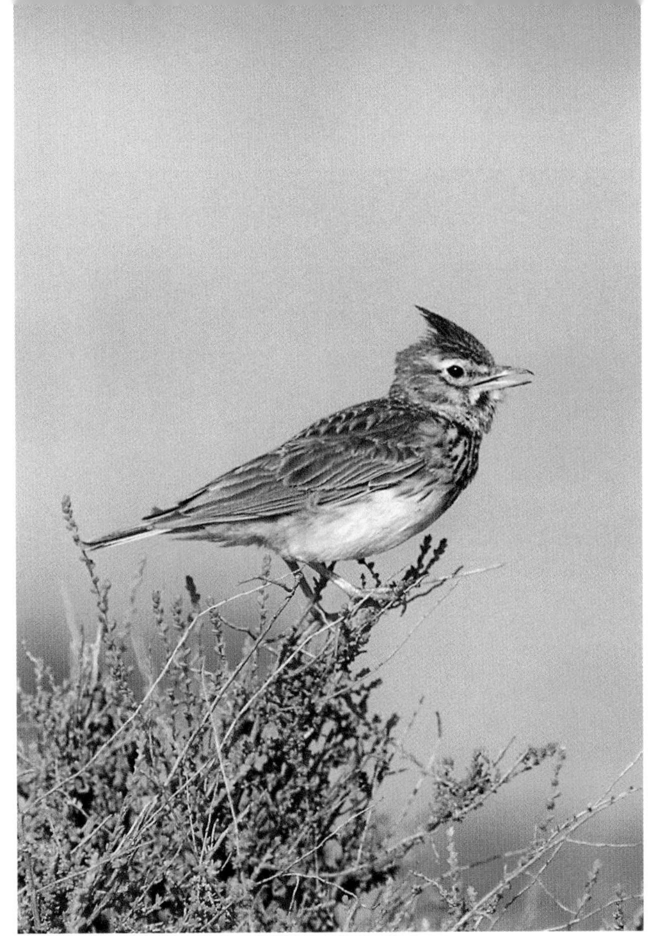

Thekla Lark

Galerida theklae (gal-ler-**rie**-da **thek**-lee)
length 17 cm

More smartly streaked, bespectacled and with a more neatly combed crest than the Crested Lark, the Thekla is a better turned-out species than its slightly larger close relative. In common with the Crested Lark, it exhibits the unusual habit of smashing snails against an 'anvil', Song Thrush-like, to open them. It also, distinctively, flicks stones over to see what lies underneath.

The Thekla is a species of the edge, encompassing in its territory the interfaces between elements of a habitat. It will occur, for example, where bare rock lies next to low vegetation or go where a road or track passes through cultivation. In contrast to the Crested Lark it is content with slopes and rocky ridges, and tends to be more at ease at higher altitudes. Bushes are no problem and, indeed, the Thekla often perches on them, which the Crested rarely does.

Both species are notable for their communal roosts of three to six members. The birds make small hollows in the ground by scratching with their feet and shuffling their bodies, as if dust-bathing, and then drawing leaves towards them – as camouflage, though, not as bedding. The hollows may be only a few centimetres apart, but more usually a metre or so, so the birds are packed together like campers at a crowded site. They often use the same hollows for a week or so before moving on.

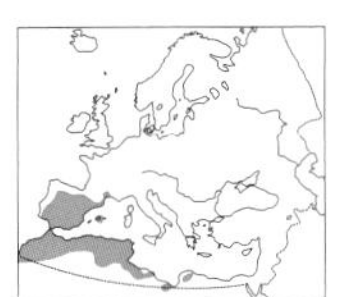

ID: Confusingly similar to Crested Lark and most differences are a matter of fine judgement. Shorter bill with convex lower mandible; shorter crest. Streaking on breast is usually darker and more clearly defined; white supercilium is clearer. Rump tinged reddish.

Crested Lark

Galerida cristata (gal-ler-**rie**-da kriss-**tay**-ta)
length 17 cm

Not one of Europe's more elegant birds, the dumpy Crested Lark is an unsubtle feeder, using its bill as heavy equipment to bash, dash and dig. It excavates small holes up to 2 cm deep in the soil to look for insects and seeds, and rather than trying to split the latter with its bill using the skilled art of mandibulation, it will hit them against a hard surface instead. Insects, too, may suffer in this way, the larger ones being struck against the ground or a rock so hard that their wings and legs eventually fall off. All in all, this is not a bird to invite round for a polite meal.

It's a success, though. The Crested Lark has a wide distribution but, being essentially a bird of semi-desert or steppe, it is commonest in the warm south. Back in the mid 1800s though, it began an expansion north that followed the burgeoning road and railway network, taking to the fallow ground beside the workings, these urban wastelands offering a parallel with the dry terrain the birds were used to. It is present up to the edge of the Baltic to this day.

The Crested is less sociable than many other larks, being usually found only in small groups of a handful of individuals, even in winter. The birds do not breed particularly close together either and, despite being fierce in defence of their territory, males do not skirmish as often as many other larks. The song flight is given less exhaustively, too, although the Crested Lark makes up for this by being incessantly 'conversational', continually calling and uttering song phrases from ground or bush. Its song flight involves less hovering than that of the Skylark, with much more wandering about the skies, often in wide circles.

When breeding, Crested Larks often place their nests right under the branches of an overhanging bush and may even incorporate these into the structure, like a lean-to. This roof protects the nest from the hot sun. For second broods, however, the birds are much less conscientious in their construction, sometimes neglecting even to build a floor.

ID: Often very abundant large lark, with most obvious spiky crest, always visible. Plain brown wings without white trailing edge, distinguishing it in flight from Skylark. Bill long and sharp-pointed. Streaking on underside often weak.

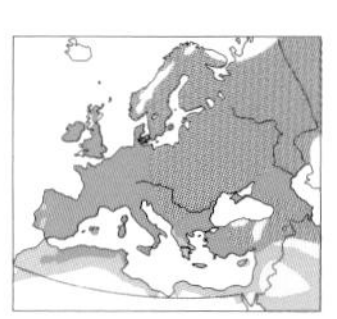

Skylark

Alauda arvensis (al-**low**-da ar-**ven**-siss)
length 18–19 cm

ID: Very widespread large lark, almost as big as a Starling, but slightly smaller than Crested Lark. Crest is not always apparent, and is never as pronounced as on Crested and Thekla Larks. Has white outer tail feathers (brown on Crested and Thekla) and white trailing edge to wings. Plumage predominantly brown and streaky, with few clear distinguishing features; mainly whitish from lower breast downwards.

When people talk about 'a lark', they are almost invariably referring to the Skylark. This bird is a cultural icon, its song celebrated both in music (for example, Vaughan Williams's *The Lark Ascending*) and in poetry (Shelley's *To a Skylark*). Its habit of singing to the first dawn light is proverbial, captured in phrases such as 'up with the lark' and in the description of a person who is at their best in the mornings as a 'lark' rather than an 'owl'. To most people, there is one species of lark, and one only.

The reason for this familiarity is simple. As people have cleared forests and other habitats to make way for fields and farmland, the adaptable Skylark has followed along with them. Over the centuries this bird's ecstatic song has poured down onto those working the land, so much so that it has become lodged in a common consciousness and sense of place.

The song is sweet enough on the ear, with its high pitch, exuberant tone and effortless delivery. It is varied, too, incorporating motifs from other birds as well as the Skylark's own repertoire. But its special property is its sustained nature; when a Skylark is singing – usually in a display flight – there is no break, no real phrasing, just a stream of unbroken sound like the flow of a small brook. The sound starts just after the bird lifts off at a steep angle to the ground, continues on its rise to 50 m or more, is maintained for a period of hovering (at 10–12 wingbeats per second) and accompanies the display's slow, spiralling descent. Only during the final plummet to earth does it fall silent, so that the bird can reach the ground with a degree of privacy.

It is easy to imagine, when you walk along the edge of a field densely populated by these birds, that each song is interminable. But this isn't true. The average song flight goes on for just two and a half minutes, and even a more passionate performance rarely stretches beyond five. The reason, then, that one's ears may ring with lark song at the end of a summer afternoon is that Skylarks often hold contiguous territories and one male may simply follow another into the sky, without any interval.

It is certainly true that larks rise early. In June in continental Russia, for example, there is a sustained period of song between 2.30 and 11 a.m., and at the same time of year in southern Sweden most birds are underway by 3 a.m. The males, who are the main performers, are under pressure to keep singing to maintain their territorial boundaries, working hard like city workers afraid of the sack. Singing is surrounded by a macho culture. If a dangerous predator such as a Merlin attacks, the best males carry on singing regardless of the risk, and suffer fewer casualties as a result of their cheek – perhaps the predator recognises their audacity as strength and seeks out cowering birds instead. So there is little vocal respite, for any reason. Birds holding territory all year will even sing in January on mild days.

The Skylark is a bird of fields and grasslands, much more tolerant of low growth than other larks. Its diet through the year tends to follow the agricultural cycle: cereal grain and weed seeds in autumn, leaves and seeds in winter, recently sown cereal grain again in spring and then insects in summer when the crops are growing. All food is obtained on the ground, by visual searching and digging. The latter method is put to use to find newly sown grain, much to the chagrin of farmers.

Skylark breeding is a cut-price, rushed affair. Male and female may bring up four broods in a season, and so they usually stick together and shun the time-consuming process of changing mates. The nest is a simple lined scrape, the sort of structure that a secondhand store might sell. The clutch is incubated for a mere 11 days (one of the shortest periods among European birds) and the young leave the nest half-ready, sometimes after only eight days. They are looked after for about 25 days after hatching and are then sent out, with bargain plumage, into the wild to fend for themselves.

Wood Lark

Lullula arborea (**lull**-yoo-la ar-**boh**-ree-a)
length 15 cm

No other lark perches in trees quite as much as the Wood Lark, and very few choose to sing from such elevated perches – except perhaps, on occasions, the Thekla. Even that species, though, does not demand that its territory has suitable high singing posts from which, if it is in the mood, the Wood Lark will perform.

Yet the Wood Lark is just as liable to sing in flight and its song flight is just as good as those of other larks. It rises from its high perch, lifting into the sky in wide spirals, until it eventually finds its preferred height and makes circles and loops there. It often threatens to return to earth and then lifts up again, in full song all the while, stretching out the aerial performance to two minutes or more. The mellifluous song, aptly transcribed in its generic name *Lullula*, is a series of liquid trills dropping down in pitch, recalling the fall in tone of a siren as it passes by (the Doppler effect). Few bird songs are as easy on the ear.

The Wood Lark is a bird of sunny places that have a combination of scattered trees, sparse vegetation and close-cropped turf on which the birds can feed. In the north and west of Europe this often means heathlands and moors, while in central Europe open pine woods fit the bill best. Recently cleared ground is often occupied for a while before the ground vegetation gets too tall. In the north of their range Wood Larks may be migratory, but they don't go far, simply melting into the populations of resident birds a little further south.

Male Wood Larks often come back to the same territories year after year; their attachment to these is greater than to their females, whom they change each season. Breeding begins early, with eggs often in the nest in March, and most pairs can then raise at least two broods. The youngsters apparently stay close to the territory even when a second brood has been started, and the birds form family flocks in the autumn.

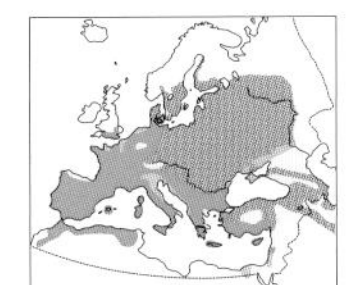

ID: Small plump lark with very short tail. On the ground distinguished by 'zebra crossing' of two dark and two pale stripes on the primary coverts; and by the broad supercilium that reaches to the back of the head to meet its opposite number on the other side. Cheek pale reddish-brown. Slight crest.

Shore Lark

Eremophila alpestris
(er-rem-**mof**-fil-la al-**pess**-triss)
length 14–17 cm

Most of Europe's larks are found in the south of the continent in warm, sunny climates. That makes the Shore Lark, a bird of the Arctic, sub-Arctic and Arctic-Alpine zones, an outstanding exception. Only the Skylark reaches as far north, and it is abundant in hot climates as well. The Shore Lark occurs in uninviting habitats, the open lichen-covered tundra, cold barren steppes and the tops of mountains, where the weather can turn nasty at any moment. In winter it doesn't have much of a respite, either, with Fennoscandian birds travelling the short distance to the chilly coasts by the North and Baltic Seas, and the Balkan population essentially staying put.

For a Shore Lark, breeding requires contingencies. To protect its nest from the wind, the bird places small stones around it and may even make itself a 'drive' with them – a path to the hollow it has excavated. In suitable sites the nest may also be placed underneath a tussock. And if it snows, the bird simply scratches the white stuff away with its foot to reach the ground beneath, and then it is business as usual.

Shore Larks otherwise act much like other larks. The male has a towering song flight, sometimes rising up as high as 250 m and singing while he intersperses bursts of flying with downward glides. The song is less vehement than those of most other larks, and blows away somewhat in the wind. On the ground Shore Larks may also sing and show off their raised 'horns' to other males.

The two populations in Europe are experiencing contrasting fortunes. In Fennoscandia numbers are in sharp decline; the bird has become almost extinct in Finland. In southeast Europe, however, it is flourishing and spreading. Nobody, it seems, knows the reasons for either change.

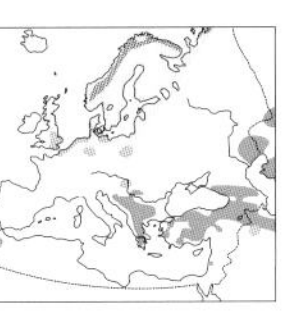

ID: Probably the easiest lark to identify owing to its bold face pattern; whitish below, without any streaking. Yellowish head with black mask going down cheek and a bold black collar; breeding male has black 'horns'.

Swallows and Martins family *Hirundinidae* (hir-run-**die**-nid-ee)

Habitat Feed on the wing almost anywhere, but especially over water. Habitat parameters defined by nest sites, e.g. buildings for Swallow and House Martin, mountains and cliffs for Red-rumped Swallow and Crag Martin, riverbanks and sandy cliffs for Sand Martin.
Food Aerial insects, obtained on the wing.
Movements All except Crag Martin long-distance migrants, commuting to and from Africa, and migrating by day, often in large groups.
Voice Songs are unimpressive though pleasing twitterings, often with grating quality. Swallow's song includes a harsh rattle, the loudness, length and regularity of which reflects the singer's size and dominance.
Pairing style Socially monogamous, but extra-pair copulations rife in several species, especially among colonial pairs.

Nesting Most colonial, but Swallows, Red-rumped Swallows and Crag Martins may nest singly. The colonies of Crag Martins may be loosely defined.
Nest Most species build nests out of mud pellets, often reinforced by straw, feathers and other organic materials. Each species has slightly different construction, Sand Martin digs a burrow.
Productivity 2–3 broods a year.
Eggs 4–7.
Incubation 11–20 days, varying according to the weather, by female.
Young Nest-bound, altricial, naked.
Parenting style Both sexes feed and tend the young.
Food to young Aerial insects, delivered in bundles.
Leaving nest Young fledge at 17–30 days and are looked after by parents for some time afterwards.

Crag Martin

Several members of the swallow and martin family are so common in Europe that it is easy to forget what specialised birds they are. Adapted for catching flying insects on the wing, they spend less time on the ground or perching than any other group of land birds except for the unrelated Swifts. They have long, pointed wings and small and short legs, reflecting the bias in their lifestyle. Even so, their claws are strong for gripping on to nests or banks or wires.

Swallows and martins have short, flattened bills but a very wide gape, enabling them to open their mouths and snatch at prey; but they don't trawl through the skies randomly – each insect is seen and targeted before being caught. Their flight is light and highly manoeuvrable, enabling them to twist and turn in pursuit of insect traffic, and they can swoop and soar according to need. The tail, which is fairly long to long and often forked, helps in this manoeuvrability.

Swallows have been emancipated from being too closely tied to particular nest sites by using mud as their primary building material. This enables them to place their constructions in locations out of reach of other birds, such as vertical surfaces. In contrast to swifts, swallows and martins collect most of their building materials from the ground, making short forays down to the sides of rivers or puddles. Since the House Martin, for example, often uses over a thousand pellets in the framework of its nest, it is not surprising that most members of the family breed not far from water.

Apart from the Crag Martin, all the species are highly migratory, disappearing into the vastness of Africa for the winter months. The Swallow, in particular, is often seen as the herald of spring and is welcomed back with great enthusiasm by many Europeans. This is a bit hard on the Sand Martin, which usually arrives earlier than the Swallow, in the first week or two of March.

Swallows have no obvious close relatives. The family is well defined, and all the members have complete bronchial rings on their voice-producing apparatus, the syrinx – never mind the technicalities, it is a unique feature, illustrating how unusual these birds actually are.

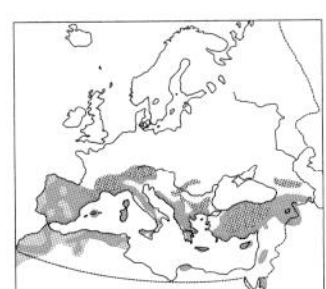

ID: *Compact, heavy swallow with brown plumage and barely a trace of a forked tail. Wings broad and held out straight, giving triangular shape. Makes rapid sweeps like Swallow, and often flies high.*

Crag Martin

Ptyonoprogne rupestris

(tie-an-oh-**prog**-nee roo-**pess**-triss)

length 14.5 cm; wingspan 32–34.5 cm

If you see an aerial bird in Europe in the winter, it is most likely to be a Crag Martin, the only member of its family not to migrate to Africa in bulk in the autumn. That's not to say that none travels south after breeding – there is a wintering roost on Gibraltar, for example. But in many parts of their range Crag Martins remain close to their nesting areas all year round.

This species has quite a restricted habitat, occurring only in hilly areas in the dry Mediterranean zone, most commonly between 500 m and 1000 m above sea level (although up to 2500 m in the Sierra Nevada in Spain). For nest sites it selects more or less vertical cliff faces which are well sheltered from the worst of the weather, and there it builds a half-cup under an overhang. The cup is made up of mud pellets, and it differs from that of the House Martin in not being connected to a 'ceiling' above.

Crag Martins nest singly or in small colonies of 2–20 pairs. The nests are well dispersed, being on average 30 m apart, and the males defend them very aggressively, chasing birds of any kind away from an area of about 200–300 sq m around the entrance. If other Crag Martins intrude they will be first chased and then attacked, the assailant grabbing the offending bird by the nape. Fighting birds often remain interlocked and fall to the ground, still scrapping, like a pair of actors in a Hollywood film.

The Crag Martin is the champion glider among swallows and martins, often soaring on thermals and mountain updrafts. In common with the rest it feeds on small flying insects, but unusually it will sometimes pick these, mid-flight, from the rock surface.

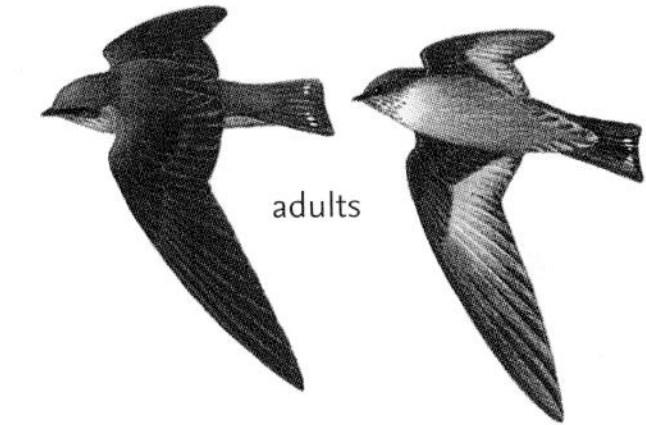

adults

Sand Martin

Riparia riparia (rie-**pay**-ri-a rie-**pay**-ri-a)

length 12 cm; wingspan 26.5–29 cm

The Sand Martin, with its small size and weak flight, would seem an unlikely candidate for undertaking an ambitious piece of engineering work. Yet the tunnel that it excavates for its nest is just that. Dug out by both members of a pair with their bare claws, it may reach 100 cm (average 65 cm) in length, which is very roughly equivalent to a person digging a tunnel 20 m into the soil. Each tunnel inclines upwards into the ground and ends in a nesting chamber 4–6 cm in diameter, safe from the elements and from almost every predator. And it may be completed in only five days.

The tunnel is important not just for the eggs and young, but for the initial pair formation as well. The male arrives first at the colonial breeding site, which may be a riverbank, a sandy cliff or a human excavation, and quickly selects a site for a hole. He then sets about digging, reaching some 30 cm into the sand before deeming it appropriate to attract a mate. The males perch conspicuously at the entrance to their abode and sing their buzzing songs, ruffling their feathers and vibrating their wings; they may also take off from the hole, circle and return, hoping to lure a female in. If all goes well the female inspects the burrow and the two birds join forces to complete it.

In common with most members of the family, the Sand Martin readily succumbs to extra-pair temptation. Males especially will try to mate with almost any female within range, chasing them whenever they are out of the burrow and attempting to copulate on the ground, on wires or even in the air. If a male sees that his mate is being chased by other suitors, he may banish her into the burrow out of harm's way.

Young Sand Martins hatch after 14 days and are then brooded and fed underground for another three weeks. By the twelfth day, rather than meekly remaining in the nest chamber to be fed, they come to the hole entrance to meet the parent when it arrives. After they emerge they join a crèche, where the adults continue to feed them, recognising their calls; siblings recognise each other's calls, too.

adults

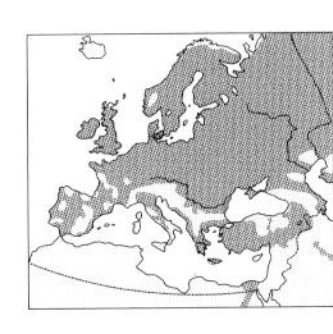

ID: *Small, weak-looking swallow, with fluttering flight lacking the regular glides and sweeps of other members of the family. Wings often held close to body in flight. Plain brown above, without white rump.*

Swallow

Hirundo rustica (hir-**roon**-doh **roos**-ti-ka)
length 17–19 cm; wingspan 32–34.5 cm

With most birds it is difficult, if not impossible, for us to distinguish the more attractive individuals from the ones that are less desirable. But with Swallows it is easy. The sexiest males are those with the longest tail-streamers. Tests have shown that having a long tail is a slight impediment to flying, so a male showing off such a characteristic is beating the odds and proving himself strong enough to overcome them. More specifically, a long tail is an indication of the efficiency of an individual's immune system, since both are directly linked to the amount of testosterone present.

Another trait for sexual selection in Swallows is the symmetry of a bird's tail. If a bird 'tries' to grow a long tail, but the two streamers don't quite add up to the same length, it is patently inferior and may well have a higher parasite load than a bird with a symmetrical tail. Birds that have streamers of equal length are also more efficient fliers than those that don't, and they are better able to escape from predators such as Sparrowhawks. All in all, an even tail is a reliable and honest indicator of survivability.

Yet another trait that female Swallows use to select a male is his nest-building ability. Good nest-builders invariably make good fathers, investing a great deal of time in finding food for the young. But these New Men, showing their feminine side, are not necessarily those with the best tails – and if a female has the choice she will normally opt for a long-tailed, symmetrical, macho type, even though it will cost her some attention. She goes, therefore, for good genes over good parenting, knowing that her offspring will benefit in the long term by being fit and healthy. This is known as the 'sexy son' hypothesis.

Of course, one way round the problem of selecting the ideal mate is to be formally and socially monogamous with a good carer, but to slink away for a bit of better genetic material on the side. And indeed, both sexes of Swallows frequently indulge in extra-pair copulations on the occasions when they are apart. Most breeding Swallows are social nesters, and colonial living especially presents plenty of opportunity to get to know the neighbours in the most profound sense. Aware of this, male Swallows invest a great deal of effort watching over and protecting their females during the latter's fertile period, rarely letting them out of their sight.

Despite all the shenanigans, Swallows do eventually get round to building a nest and bringing up young. Their nests are made, typically for the family, out of pellets of mud, often with straw and other harder materials intermixed. The latter allow the nest to expand or contract without collapsing if it dries out or becomes moist. Swallows try to select mud without too much sand content, as well, since this could make the structure liable to crumble in mid-brood. The nest is saucer shaped and placed on a horizontal surface, often the beam of a building such as a barn, shed or garage. Swallows are unusual in preferring to nest inside a man-made structure rather than outside it.

When the young hatch they are fed mainly on large flies such as bluebottles and horse-flies. These the Swallow catches in its usual style, flying fast and at a low height over fields or water. The birds often feed in the vicinity of livestock, taking advantage of insects disturbed by grazing animals; they may also follow people walking across fields for the same reason. The adults themselves feed on similar food to the young, but often take smaller items for their own nourishment.

However well they are fed, some young Swallows face an unusual danger. If a male is left unpaired or bereaved during the breeding season, he may take the exceptional step of killing off a healthy brood by picking them out of a nest and dropping them, one by one, to certain death on the ground below. This infanticide always splits up the bond of the parents, and the murderer frequently pairs up with the divorced female – his intention all along. This occurs in about 3 per cent of breeding attempts.

Once they have bred once or twice, Swallows migrate in September and October to central and southern Africa for the winter. They tend to travel by day since, being aerial feeders, they can provision themselves en route. By night they usually roost in reedbeds, often in enormous numbers. When crossing the Sahara, however, Swallows migrate by night rather than by day, to avoid the risk of overheating.

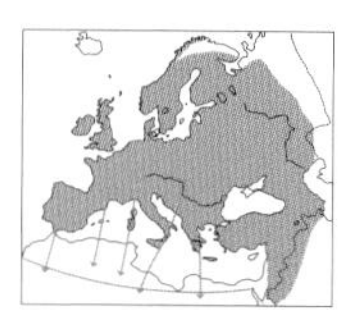

ID: The typical swallow, with long, swept-back wings and long tail streamers. Always looks longer-tailed than any martin. Wings are broader-based than on Swift (see page 203). Often flies low, with long sweeps over ground on 'rowing' wingbeats. Glossy blue above, without white rump. Mainly pale creamy-white below, but has royal-blue breast band and reddish throat and forehead.

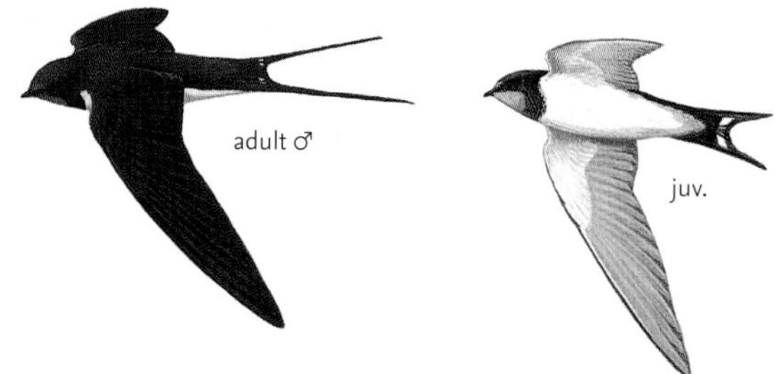

Red-rumped Swallow

Hirundo daurica (hir-**roon**-doh **dow**-ri-ka)
length 16–17 cm; wingspan 32–34 cm

ID: Bulkier than Swallow with shorter wings; otherwise similar. Flies with slower wingbeats and glides and soars more. Pale buff below with fine streaking, lacking red throat and breast band.

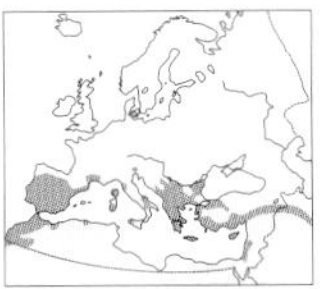

This is much more of a 'wild' bird than the familiar Swallow, occurring mainly in dry, rocky habitats such as cliffs and mountains. The main reason for the difference is that it is far less dependent on buildings for nest sites than the Swallow, using caves and rock faces; if it does use man-made structures, it tends towards ruins and abandoned sites. Against this trend it does, however, have something of a weakness for bridges, and in Bulgaria and Romania, to which it has recently spread, almost a third of all nests are on these artificial constructions.

The nest itself is more elaborate than that of the Swallow or House Martin. Made up from pellets of mud, it is shaped like a bowl and is attached to a ceiling or overhang, so it has no support at all. The entrance is funnel-shaped and built out to make a lobby, although this is always the last section to be made and is often not finished until after the eggs are laid. On average the structure takes about two weeks to build and is used for all the broods in a year, and also in subsequent years. For entirely practical reasons the birds need a supply of mud within 150 m of their site if they are to embark on a serious building programme.

Many Red-rumped Swallows nest singly, but small colonies containing up to four pairs can be found in some places, especially in the east of the bird's range. In early season these sites are the scene for the male's courtship display, in which he flies in circles around the female and calls, sometimes vibrating his wings and diving steeply down to vary his programme. At other times, as both birds fly together, he will lift his head up and raise his tail instead. If all goes well the pair will raise two broods in a season; less than 25 per cent go on to have a third.

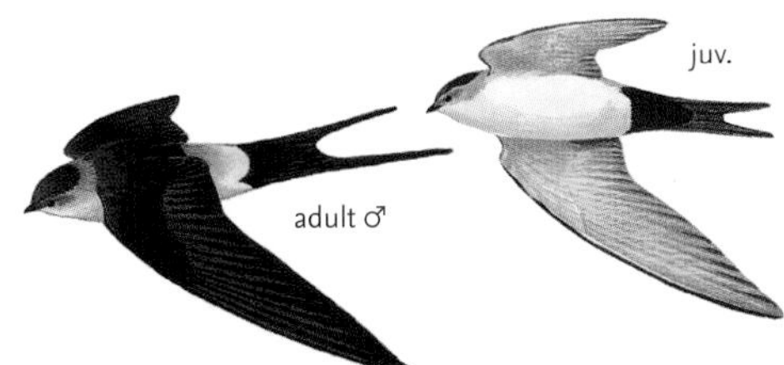

House Martin

Delichon urbica (**dee**-li-kon **urb**-bi-ka)
length 12.5 cm; wingspan 26–29 cm

One of the most intriguing puzzles yet to be resolved in European ornithology is where the 90 million or so House Martins that leave our shores each autumn on their southbound migration are heading. We know that, in common with Sand Martins and Swallows, they are long-distance commuters to Africa, but where exactly on that continent all the populations go, and how they live when they get there, is almost a complete mystery. Although over a million House Martins have been ringed in Europe so far, a mere 20 have been recovered in sub-Saharan Africa, from widely scattered locations. Similarly, there have been many sight records, but nothing like as many as there should be for such a numerous bird. Tantalisingly, some records have involved House Martins flying very high, at the limit of binocular reach. Perhaps they all remain up in the sky, catching insects at a great height? And since there are virtually no records of roosts, perhaps they sleep up in the air, as Swifts do? For the moment, we must be content with speculation.

On its 'home' ground in Europe the House Martin is a moderately high aerial forager, plying the skies at an average height of 21 m above ground in the breeding season (in comparison to 7–8 m for the Swallow). These birds take smaller insects than Swallows, mainly aphids and small flies, and they catch them one at a time, by sight. When hunting, the House Martin glides more than the Swallow and moves around in small arcs rather than long sweeps. But in common with all aerial foragers, it flies much lower in bad weather and is also drawn to rivers, lakes and other freshwater sites in cold weather to catch emerging insects.

House Martins are colonial, collecting to breed in small groups of five to ten pairs, but sometimes more (over a thousand is known). The males tend to return to the same colony and nest site each year, but females are less attached to their natal area and when they first return as yearlings they may wander several kilometres away. The older males invariably arrive first in the spring, usually in April, and immediately choose and guard a nest site (often on an old half-completed nest) by perching on it and threatening intruders with a special call. Once the females arrive, the males give an enticement call instead and pair formation effectively takes place by the female choosing site and male at the same time.

The nest of a House Martin is a remarkable structure, a half-cup attached to a vertical wall immediately below an overhang. The entrance is just a narrow slit at the top of the cup, which can be a bit of a squeeze, and it usually faces away from next door's entrance, out of neighbourly respect. The nest is made from between 700 and 1500 mud pellets, plus a few feathers, and depends entirely on the adhesive property of the mud to hold it together and keep it in place. Both sexes build it, and if they are starting from scratch it will take about two weeks to complete. Most nests these days are found on buildings, especially at the top of walls under eaves, but originally the House Martin nested on cliffs, rocky outcrops and even tall trees. Nest sites need to be close to water and rich feeding areas, because the birds prefer not to commute much further than 450 m when provisioning their young.

However flimsy the nest might look, young House Martins are often reluctant to leave it. The adults sometimes take many hours to coax the recalcitrant fledglings out to make their first flight, and they may have to swoop up to the entrance time after time, calling in encouragement. If things are slow, other members of the colony, young and old, may join in as well, until the fledglings are shamed out. Even this departure is temporary, however, because the young will return to the nest regularly for roosting and shelter for their first few days.

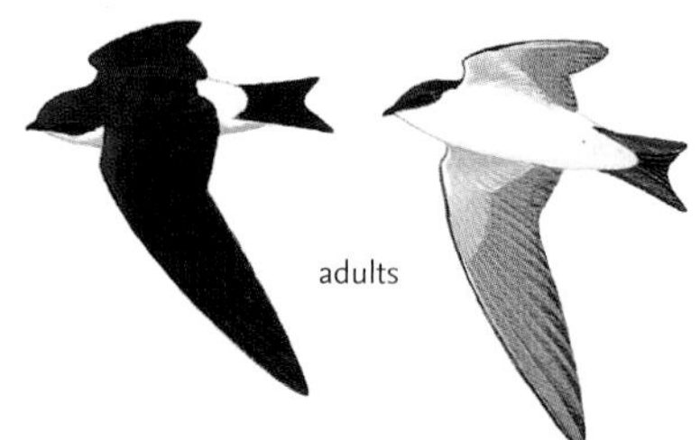

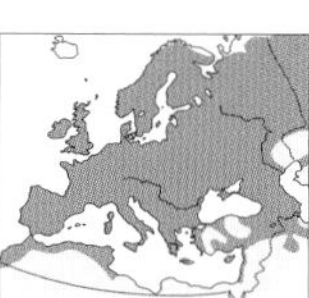

ID: Much shorter tail than Swallow, with shallower fork. Wings also shorter, more stubby than those of Swallow. Flight is more fluttering, with fewer sweeps and more turns. Easy to identify by being pure white below (no breast band) and very dark blue above, with prominent white rump.

Pipits and Wagtails family *Motacillidae* (moh-ta-**sil**-lid-ee)

Habitat Predominantly open areas, many species (including all the wagtails) near water. Most forage on turf or bare ground. There seems to be a pipit for every habitat: meadows, trees, rocks, tundra and mountains.
Food Primarily insects and other invertebrates (crustaceans, spiders), usually picked from the ground while the birds walk. Wagtails may take items from the water, and they also catch insects in aerial sallies, which some pipits sometimes do.
Movements Some long-distance migrants to Africa (e.g. Yellow Wagtail, Red-throated Pipit); others migratory, but tending to remain within Europe (e.g. Meadow Pipit, Grey Wagtail). Some resident (e.g. some Pied Wagtails and Rock Pipits).
Voice Pipits have distinctive songs of repeated syllables: 'tsip-tsip-tsip...' that alter in pitch and detail as the birds perform their song flights. Wagtails have rambling or sweet songs, also uttered in song flight.
Pairing style Usually monogamous, but some pipits may be polygynous (e.g. some Rock Pipits and Tawny Pipits).
Nesting Territorial and usually solitary, but Yellow Wagtail and several pipits form small neighbourhood groups.
Nest Nest on the ground (pipits) or in cavity (wagtails except Yellow, which is a ground-nester) such as hole in rocks, buildings, bridges or tree roots. Nest is well-hidden cup of grass and leaves.
Productivity 1–2 broods a year.
Eggs 3–7.
Incubation 11–14 days, by female only in pipits and by both sexes in wagtails (although female does most).
Young Nest-bound, altricial, downy.
Parenting style Both adults feed and tend the young.
Food to young Insects, delivered in bill.
Leaving nest Leave nest at 10–16 days, and then parents (or parent) feed fledged young for another 2–3 weeks.

The pipits and wagtails are sprightly, ground-dwelling songbirds with long, slender legs and equally long, slender tails. In contrast to most passerines they walk rather than hop and they often do so with a slight nod of the head on each step, a bit like a chicken. Many have an extended hind claw to help balance on the ground. Their bodies are slender and attenuated, and their bills thin and pointed. Many wag their tails up and down, sometimes incessantly, but some do this very little.

Technically, the wagtails and pipits share anatomical features, including details of their feet, which are diagnostic. Of more interest, though, are the similarities in behaviour. All are strongly territorial and the males deliver their songs either on the ground or in stereotyped display flights; these performances include the longest bird flight display known, performed by an American species called the Sprague's Pipit (*Anthus spragueii*), which reputedly may last for three whole hours. All species forage principally on the ground and nest either there or in various cavities, never in a tree. All migrate by day and all gather together to form communal roosts at night.

The pipits are not the sort of birds to feature on a poster on your bedroom wall. They are small, brown and streaked, and have pale, usually white, outer tail feathers; they look rather like miniature versions of a thrush. The sexes are alike and so are the species, often making separating them difficult for birdwatchers.

The wagtails, on the other hand, have bright or contrasting plumage. Three of our four species show a lot of yellow. The males and females have slightly different plumage patterns. As their name implies, wagtails wag their tails habitually, but nobody has yet come up with a definitive answer as to why they do so.

Tawny Pipit

Anthus campestris (**an**-thuss kam-**pess**-triss)
length 16.5 cm

Most European pipits forage by wandering somewhat aimlessly over the ground and pecking now and then, but the Tawny Pipit adopts a much less serendipitous approach. Its foraging is more akin to that of a plover or Blackbird, in that it will interrupt its walking or running with regular time-outs at a standstill to observe what is about. If it sees something, it will then run towards it. This pipit is somewhat more formidable than the rest, and will at times stand on a particularly large prey item such as a cricket and hack it to pieces with its bill.

Tawny Pipits are unusual among pipits in being regularly polygynous. The incidence is at least 10 per cent, and all males studied so far have had just the two partners in the same territory, rather than any more. In some nests the female alone feeds the young, but in others the male contributes, although it is not known whether this is related to the pairing system. Whatever happens, it seems that young Tawny Pipits have a luxurious amount of parental care in comparison with most small birds, having been observed being fed when over two weeks out of the nest.

Another distinctive aspect of the Tawny Pipit is its song display. Accompanied by just two or three syllables endlessly repeated, it follows a definite undulating course, rising and falling in time with the song. It may also have a more abrupt ending than other pipit song flights, with a rapid plunge to the ground replacing the more leisurely glide down, although this happens, too. The sight of a neighbour singing is seemingly too much for a territorial bird to witness and a song duel between the two rivals is soon joined.

The Tawny Pipit represents the warm end of the pipit climatic spectrum, occurring mostly in the south of Europe. Its habitat requirements are open, sandy areas with some taller grass, shrubs and a few trees. The maquis of the Mediterranean region is ideal.

ID: Large, leggy, wagtail-like pipit which often wags tail. Much plainer than most pipits, with hardly any streaks on white underparts and mainly unstreaked pale-brown back. Strong white supercilium. Flight feathers dark with pale fringes; conspicuous dark bar near shoulder.

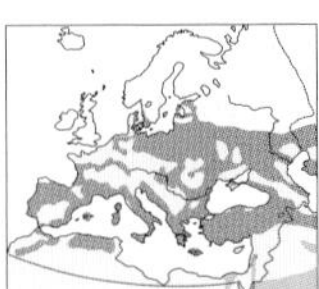

adult

juv.

Meadow Pipit

Anthus pratensis (**an**-thuss pra-**ten**-siss)
length 14.5 cm

When the wind blows hard and wild on the open terrain where Meadow Pipits live, there is sometimes a truce between the territory-holding male birds. If one holds a more sheltered patch of ground than the rest, he will, for once, tolerate a small band of neighbours taking refuge within his borders, without trying to evict them. But when the weather calms down tempers hot up again and the birds return to their paranoid ways.

Normally a Meadow Pipit territory has three zones. The inner one is like a house, where the birds place the nest and spend most of their time; the middle zone is like their garden, where they find most of their food. Outside this is a much larger zone that is sometimes shared by neighbours. It is equivalent to the shops, where the birds go foraging further afield when under pressure to provide for their young. The inner two zones form a vigorously defended core area.

As with all pipits, the male Meadow Pipit performs a spirited, essentially stereotyped song flight for the purpose of proclaiming site ownership. He rises from the ground with rapid, fluttering wingbeats and then, sometimes after a short excursion, glides gently to ground with wings held firm, tail raised and legs dangling. During this flight he utters a song of considerable tedium, endlessly repeating short notes like bleeps from an alarm clock, although at least they change pitch a bit. Overall the displaying bird may resemble a paper aeroplane, powered by clockwork.

When song flights fail to prevent intruders from violating boundaries, owner-occupier Meadow Pipits quite naturally take umbrage. A song duel on the ground may follow, or the birds will ruffle their plumage and droop their wings while facing each other; they might even trample their feet, too, in irritation. If nothing is resolved the birds fight, sometimes flying up to 20 m as they peck and scratch with their feet, like flying Coots. Conflicts are quite common among Meadow Pipits, partly perhaps because these birds often nest at high density.

It is difficult to escape the impression that the Meadow Pipit is rather an aimless bird. Its foraging technique is simply to run or walk over the grass, pecking every so often for insects and small seeds, like a shopper without a list. It never does anything innovative, such as flying from a perch and snatching insects in flight, or turning objects over. It also has a weak and indecisive flight, sometimes being noticeably capricious about where it will land, changing its mind and direction several times before finally coming to ground. But, of course, this is only an impression, and the bird is an effective feeder and a capable flier – many of the northern populations are migratory.

The Meadow Pipit is the commonest of its kind in western and northern Europe. It prefers longer grass than other pipits and occupies a wider range of habitats, including grassland, tundra, moorland, salt marshes and certain types of arable or pastoral land.

ID: Typical 'miniature-thrush'-like pipit with long hind claw. Walks in long grass with shuffling, creeping gait; may perch on trees and wires. Often in flocks. When flushed, flies around hysterically, often circling about.

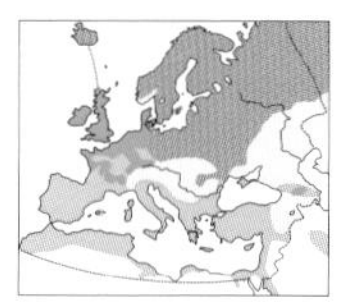

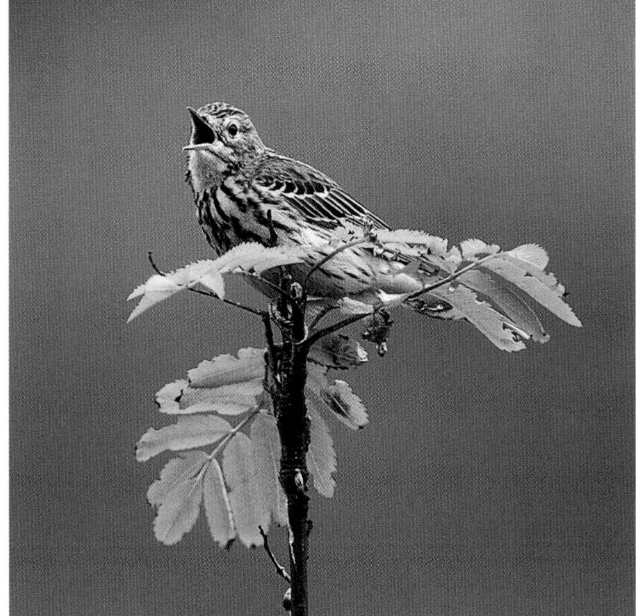

Tree Pipit

Anthus trivialis (**an**-thuss triv-vi-**ay**-liss)
length 15 cm

If you do something well, it pays not to do it too often; you don't want its impact to be reduced. This seems to be the attitude of the male Tree Pipit: he performs an excellent, compact song flight, differing from that of all other pipits by setting off from a perch at the top of a tree and ending there, or on another high perch. But he does it only sparingly. In one study, birds started their song at 3 a.m. but remained resolutely planted for the first hour, and they performed about ten times as many songs from a high perch as in flight display. In fact, these birds spend over 15 hours of the day on their perches and just five feeding on the ground or attending the nest, which does not sound like a very busy breeding season.

The song of the Tree Pipit is much better than the rest, with superior tone and a definite beginning, middle and end. The start, begun near the top of the bird's ascent into the sky, is decidedly Chaffinch-like; and the end, coinciding with his parachuting, gliding descent, with wings steady, feet dangling and tail up, is full of expert final flourishes, like the musings of a gifted musician. This pipit is top of the tree, in every sense.

This is a successful species with a wide range in Europe. It reaches both to the Arctic and to high altitudes – up to 2300 m in the Alps, for example, just above the tree line. Its requirements are a coincidence of open, sparsely vegetated ground dotted with suitable trees; various habitats, including open woods, heaths and scrub, all fit the bill. The Tree Pipit both nests and feeds on the ground, taking insects in the breeding season and a few fruits in the autumn.

Very much migrants, all populations of this species evacuate Europe in the autumn to spend the winter in Africa. Every bird west of longitude 15°E appears to fly southwest for a refuelling stop in Portugal before setting out on the longest part of its journey.

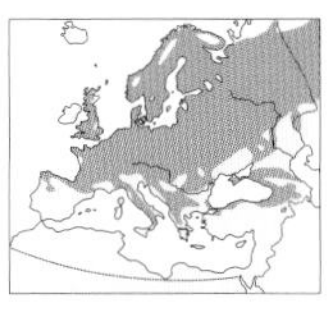

ID: A little heavier and less sociable than similar Meadow Pipit, with broader, blunter bill and short hind claw. Often 'pumps' tail up and down. Has smoother walking action and more often perches in trees than Meadow Pipit.

Rock Pipit

Anthus petrosus (**an**-thuss pet-**troh**-suss)
length 16.5–17 cm

The Rock Pipit is the maritime specialist among pipits, never breeding far from the rocky seashore. It is found in two areas of Europe: the coast of Britain, France and the Faeroe Islands; and the Baltic Sea and Fennoscandian coast – it does not breed anywhere else in the world. The birds from each area look slightly different, especially in spring, when the northern male is a lot smarter than his southwestern counterpart, and there are some differences in behaviour, too. The southwestern birds are mainly resident, not moving far from their territories in winter. The northern birds are migratory, travelling to the North Sea coast and sparingly elsewhere; they are sometimes recorded some distance inland.

A more intriguing difference, not yet entirely confirmed since it is hard to prove a negative, is that southwestern birds are monogamous while their Fennoscandian counterparts are regularly polygynous. About 50 per cent of individuals may be doubly attached, and the males concerned tend to help feed the brood of their first female with enthusiasm, but don't help much with their second.

Perhaps not surprisingly, Rock Pipits are highly territorial and attempt to keep their borders intact with the up-and-down song flight typical of pipits. This is not very different from that of the Meadow Pipit, although at certain stages the wingbeats are apparently slower in rhythm. Most territories contain either some cliffs or a large rock, somewhere for concealing the nest in a hole or hollow, and they can be very evenly distributed along a coast. Birds feeding their young spend their time foraging both on the seashore and in nearby short grassy swards. The nest itself may be only 2 m above the high-water mark and, perhaps predictably, is often made up from seaweed as well as other materials.

Feeding in the intertidal zone, Rock Pipits eat fewer insects than other pipits and more exotic items, including molluscs, worms, tiny crabs and even small fish.

ID: Large dark-looking pipit with dark red or black legs. Outer tail feathers grey-brown, not white like other pipits'. Underparts darker than those of other pipits and are usually heavily streaked with slightly smudged pencil-lines. Upperparts and wings also distinctively dark.

ID: *Small pipit usually easily distinguished by the orange-brown coloration on the head and breast (lacking in first-winter birds), white stripes down the back and streaks on the rump.*

Red-throated Pipit

Anthus cervinus (**an**-thuss ser-**vie**-nuss)
length 15 cm

Mostly breeding above 66°N, this is very much Europe's Arctic pipit, although both Tree and Meadow Pipits may overlap its range. It is one of the commonest and most noticeable birds of the tundra in the summer months, continually performing noisy song flights which are hard to overlook. More specifically it is most abundant in mires and bogs with willow and sedge.

Not surprisingly, the Red-throated Pipit has to be able to withstand cold and wind; it has been recorded singing unconcernedly when the temperature was –12°C and, on another occasion into a raging gale. Its nest is usually placed on the side of a mossy hummock or bank, sheltered from the prevailing wind, and there may even be a small tunnel in the grass leading up to the entrance, a bit like a driveway.

The song flight of the Red-throated Pipit, a better effort than that of the Meadow Pipit, ascending to a greater height and with a richer, more structured vocal accompaniment, is mainly used as a territorial flag. When the males arrive on the breeding grounds they sing for several hours a day, with occasional fighting also breaking out to resolve neighbourly issues. Despite all these efforts members of a pair often subsequently share a communal feeding area and, in a quirk that is hard to explain, the males invariably search for food for their young over a wider area than the females.

After breeding, the Red-throated Pipit embarks on a migration to East Africa, giving it the longest journey by far of any European pipit. Western birds travel east before turning south and some, rather sensibly, remain in Italy or Greece for the winter instead.

Water Pipit

Anthus spinoletta (**an**-thuss spin-noh-**let**-a)
length 17–17.5cm

The Water Pipit is one of Europe's truly montane birds, breeding most abundantly between 1400 m and 2500 m in the central European mountains, but venturing as high as 3000 m and as low as 615 m. It breeds in open areas which have a combination of short grass for foraging and either rocks, bushes or trees for lookout posts; it also needs rocky cavities for nesting, although apparently the hoof-print of a cow will also do. The territories sometimes overlap those of the Meadow Pipit, but the two birds don't compete because the Meadow Pipit forages in tall, dense vegetation in the breeding season, not on the short turf beloved of this species. The Water Pipit feeds on small insects, which it finds on the grassy surface in the uncomplicated foraging manner typical of pipits. In severe weather, it will feed at the entrance to marmot burrows, which are relatively sheltered.

Males of this species have a song flight that is very much in the vein of most pipits, and a song that is very similar to that of the Meadow Pipit. To us it is a simple long series of repeated notes and indeed, the average male sings only three different kinds of notes, in various sequences. One of these syllables, the so-called 'snarr' syllable, is highly significant, though. The heavier the body size of the male, the more he uses snarr syllables; his territorial boundaries are firmer and he experiences enhanced mating success. It appears that female Water Pipits recognise snarr syllables as a sign of a good male, regardless of the quality of his territory.

The migration of the Water Pipit is sometimes merely altitudinal in nature, taking the birds on the short drop from the hills to the valleys. A significant proportion of birds, however, spread out over the central European lowlands in winter, some reaching as far as Britain and thereby, quirkily enough, actually travelling north when most European birds are going south. They settle on freshwater meadows and other damp habitats.

ID: *Large pipit with black or dark red-brown legs, like Rock Pipit. Stance often strikingly upright. Shares long bill and grey-brown upperparts with Rock Pipit but has white outer tail feathers.*

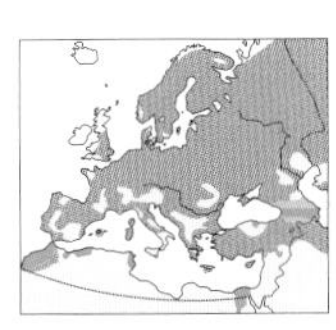

Yellow Wagtail

Motacilla flava (moh-ta-**sil**-la **flah**-va)
length 17 cm

ID: The shortest-tailed wagtail and probably the one that wags its tail the least – certainly not incessantly. Black legs and bill and almost always buttery-yellow underparts (paler in female) and greenish back. Flight feathers are fringed with olive-green or narrowly fringed white. Males don a bewildering range of head patterns according to origin and race. First-winter much duller than adult, light olive-brown on upperparts and similar on underparts but for yellowish vent. Wing pattern as adult.

The Yellow Wagtail is not, one might say, a single product. It comes in a variety of subspecies that differ mainly in the head pattern of the male. Each is found in a different part of Europe: the 'Yellow' Wagtail breeds mainly in Britain, the 'Blue-headed' Wagtail widely in continental Europe, the 'Black-headed' Wagtail in the Balkans and the 'Ashy-headed' Wagtail in Italy; there are, however, zones of overlap. These birds, it seems, may not be just geographical variations, though: recently both Yellow and Blue-headed Wagtails have been found in the same area but not interbreeding, so it is possible that all the forms should be considered as separate species.

Even so, it is difficult to separate the subspecies in terms of habitat or behaviour. The Yellow Wagtail is, throughout its range, a bird of meadows and wetland fringes, being especially fond of wet grassy areas with a vegetation height of 45–60 cm, much higher than that preferred by other wagtail species. It consistently differs from the others, too, in its nest site, choosing to use the ground rather than hiding the structure in some kind of crevice. The nest is usually placed by the side of a tussock for concealment. In recent years the Yellow Wagtail has taken to nesting widely in arable areas, among crops, often quite some distance from water.

Everywhere within its broad range the Yellow Wagtail has a close association with grazing animals, especially cattle. As the animals feed, their foot and tail movements displace insects, which the birds duly snap up. The birds often use the backs of cows or horses as vantage points for their aerial sallies, and they also pick blood-sucking insects direct from their hosts' skin. It is not uncommon to see dozens of these birds waiting at the animals' feet as if they were followers hanging on every word of some wise guru. The association is even more favourably enforced by the animals' frequent bowel motions. Dung heaps are prize properties for Yellow Wagtails, and individuals will spend hours around them, picking off the lively insect fauna.

These birds are long-distance migrants, wintering in sub-Saharan Africa. They depart Europe in August and September and return in March, travelling by day and roosting in large numbers in reedbeds and other wetland sites. It is thought that some northern European birds overfly the Mediterranean on their southward journey, moving on a broad front and not concentrating at short crossing points. It is also presumed that returning birds make the Saharan crossing in a single flight. Having increased their body weight by a third or more in West Africa, they depart in the evening at the southern edge of the desert and fly for the next three nights and two days, a total of about 70 hours of non-stop flying.

Yellow Wagtails have a lively song flight, delivered in undulating fashion, as if the bird were at the end of a long string. The males arrive at the breeding grounds well before the females, and courtship begins when the latter arrive. Intriguingly, though, 'engagement' pairs may form on autumn migration, with juvenile males and females becoming inseparable, at least for a while. Whether these associations blossom later into breeding units is not yet known.

Blue-headed Wagtail

Yellow Wagtail

ID: *The longest-tailed wagtail. Distinguished from all Yellow Wagtail races by grey back and pink legs. Wings mainly dark but tertials have white fringes, making large white band in centre of wing visible above and below.*

Grey Wagtail

Motacilla cinerea (moh-ta-**sil**-la sin-**nee**-ri-a)
length 18–19 cm

This is the white-water wagtail, the member of the group most associated with fast-flowing streams and torrents. It skips from rock to rock in mid-stream, and feeds on the shore, picking at insects and snapping them in mid-air. The faster the water, the greater the gradient, the more the water is stirred into rapids, the higher the population of Grey Wagtails will be. That's not to say that they shun slower-flowing rivers entirely; they don't. And in winter they may occur in gentle lowland areas, near weirs and even sewage farms. But at heart the Grey Wagtail is a bird that needs the roar of rushing current nearby.

Not surprisingly, given that they breed along rivers, Grey Wagtail territories are linear, with a stretch 'belonging' to each pair. To be viable a territory needs plenty of feeding sites, some trees for perching and for song posts, and a suitable cavity for the nest – a rocky crevice, for example, or a hole in the roots of a tree by the river. Each pair's patch is fiercely defended from rivals, so much so that Grey Wagtails have occasionally been seen fighting to the death, one bird holding another's head under the water to drown it. Grey Wagtails also attack their reflections in glass. When two male birds are in opposition they lift up their heads to expose their smart black chins.

Family life in Grey Wagtails is strong. The pair remains together for at least the season, and may rear up to three broods during that time. Both sexes co-operate in incubation, brooding and feeding the young in the nest. Their youngsters are given an extended period of parental care after they have fledged, which may add up to three whole weeks, unusually long for such a small bird. Furthermore, once they have become independent, the young from a brood often stick together for several months, joining other birds at favoured feeding sites before finally splitting up.

Citrine Wagtail

Motacilla citreola (moh-ta-**sil**-la sit-tree-**oh**-la)
length 17 cm

You won't get a Citrine Wagtail wandering far from water. It is more of a wetland species than either the Pied or the Yellow Wagtail, and its longer legs help it to wade into water more frequently. It has even perfected the trick of thrusting its head into water to pick food from beneath the surface, something the other wagtails rarely if ever do. It will often, however, feed at the feet of cattle, in Yellow Wagtail style.

This is a rare bird in Europe. It occurs among osier thickets in the tundra, breeding at the daring latitudinal range of 71–75°N in the extreme east of our region. In a separate population farther south it occurs in mires, meadows and bogs and is sparsely distributed but well established in the Ukraine and Belarus. In recent years it has been advancing west, breeding in the Baltic States, Finland and Poland. One bird has even hybridised with a Yellow Wagtail in Britain.

The small European population is scattered, but where it occurs the nests are usually bunched together into neighbourhood groups, with perhaps 50 m between them. Grouped or not, the males defend their patch vehemently, at first with a very simple up-and-down song flight, hovering at the top, and then, all negotiations over, by fighting. The nest is built in a hollow in a bank and, especially in northern regions, is a sturdy structure. In keeping with the Citrine Wagtail's paddling lifestyle, the young tend to be fed aquatic insects, including dragonfly larvae; if Yellow Wagtails feed their young on dragonflies, these are usually the free-flying adults, obtained on land.

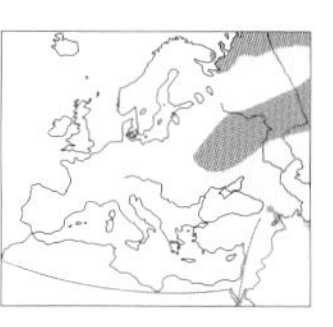

ID: *Longer-tailed than Yellow Wagtail, similar to Pied. Breeding male distinctive, with brilliant lemon-yellow underparts and head; both sexes distinguished from Yellow Wagtail by grey back and from Yellow and Grey by bold white fringes to flight feathers.*

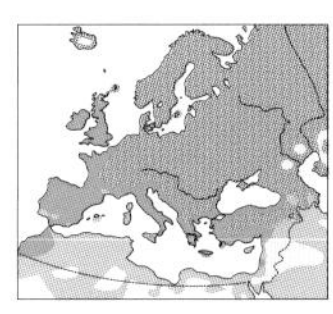

Pied Wagtail

Motacilla alba (moh-ta-**sil**-la **al**-ba)
length 18 cm

ID: Plumage lacks any yellow, in contrast to most plumages of other wagtails. Both races have bold black and white head pattern in breeding plumage, and black breast band in non-breeding plumage. Two races: Pied Wagtail (mainly Britain) has black back in male and dark grey back in female; White Wagtail (elsewhere) has lighter grey back, with the male showing a sharp transition at the nape between the black crown and the grey back.

The Pied Wagtail's life revolves about extreme territoriality and extreme sociability. In the breeding season it requires privacy, occupying its own patch of ground next to some sort of water – a river, a lake, a mountain stream or a sewage farm, for example. In the winter, though, it has a choice; it can either maintain a feeding territory of its own, or it can join a flock. Flocks consist of up to 20 birds, each of which picks the ground for small insects, spiders, seeds or crustaceans, and keeps its individual distance from the rest. Solitary birds feed more slowly, but employ a wider variety of techniques in their searching, including quick aerial sallies to catch flying insects, and running hard and fast towards a morsel seen from a distance, methods that are inhibited by the need to keep apart from others in a party. The composition of flocks may vary day by day, or even hour by hour, depending on how rich the feeding is.

Sometimes there is a halfway house between solitary feeding and flock feeding. Certain normally territorial males may tolerate a second bird on their patch, when there is plenty of food available and the benefit of enlisting additional defence for the territory outweighs the cost of sharing food with another. The extra birds are known as 'satellites', and may be employed for a week or more by a particular male. Like home helps, they may be virtual professionals and move from territory to territory, wherever they are needed. Satellites are usually society's subordinates, first-year birds or adult females. The latter, in fact, quite regularly pair up with one of their employers at the beginning of the breeding season.

Whether they are flock members or territory holders, all Pied Wagtails join with their peers on winter nights to roost communally. They use a variety of sites, including reedbeds, trees, sewage farms, greenhouses and buildings. They may gather in their hundreds, even thousands (a roost of 5000 has been recorded), arriving about an hour and a half before sunset for a quick wash and brush-up, accompanied by much calling, before entering the roost itself. Once darkness has fallen and the birds have spaced themselves out so that they are on average 17 cm apart, the roost falls silent. So far, nobody is entirely sure why these birds gather together so religiously.

The Pied Wagtail is a familiar bird throughout Europe. It occurs over a breathtakingly broad climatic range, from the edge of the desert to the Arctic tundra. It also breeds up to an altitude of 3000 m. Its requirements are very simple: it just needs some short turf, preferably near water, for feeding and, in the breeding season, any kind of cavity for its nest. It is very comfortable in human company and may be found in both rural and urban areas, exploiting greens, gardens, roadsides and car parks, as well as farmland and rivers. Of all the wagtails and pipits, it is by far the most adaptable.

Compared to other wagtails, the Pied Wagtail has little interest in singing or song flights. It will sometimes give a rather ecstatic babble of call notes strung together to make a song, like an avian version of James Joyce's *Ulysses*, but that's about it. A few call notes, plus the occasional upward tilt of its head to show off the throat, are usually enough to make its territorial and sexual intentions plain.

White Wagtail

Pied Wagtail

Waxwing *Bombycilla garrulus* (bom-bie-**sil**-la **gar**-oo-luss)

family *Bombycillidae* (bom-bie-**sil**-lid-ee)

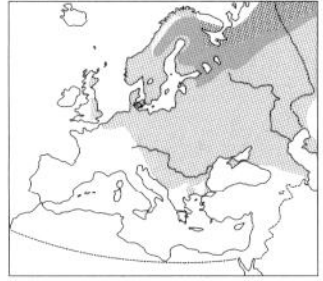

length 18 cm
ID: *Unmistakable. Starling-sized bird with soft plumage and crest.*

Habitat In breeding season boreal forest, especially of old trees well spread out and with a copious layer of ground vegetation.
Food Insects in summer, especially mosquitoes and midges; in winter, almost entirely fruit – unusual for subsisting on little else at this time.
Movements Partial migrant subject to southward eruptions from time to time (see text).
Voice Call a high-pitched trill; song an elaboration of this.
Pairing style Monogamous.
Nesting Usually solitary but not very territorial; pairs often nest close together.
Nest Cup of thin conifer twigs, reindeer moss and grass, lined with grass. Placed in conifer tree 3–15 m above ground, usually close to stem.
Productivity 1 brood a year.
Eggs 5–6.
Incubation 14–15 days, by female only, fed by male.
Young Nest-bound, altricial and naked.
Parenting style Both adults tend and feed the young.
Food to young Regurgitated insects and berries.
Leaving nest Young leave at 14–15 days.

adult

juv.

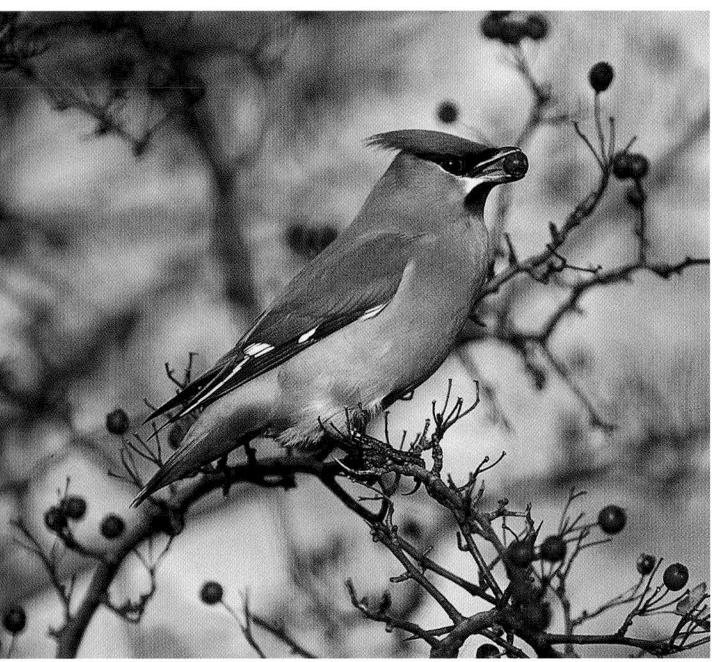

The silky-plumaged Waxwing, as well turned out as a Parisian lady leaving a beauty parlour, with its black eye-shadow, hair-dried crest and wings duly waxed, is the only European bird that can subsist for months on end entirely upon fruit. A good many other birds eat huge quantities of berries in the autumn and winter, among them thrushes, starlings and warblers, but every one of these must take in some invertebrates as a supplement during this period. Not so the Waxwing – it is a specialist, single-minded frugivore.

It has one main adaptation to its unusual diet, and that is a remarkably wide gape for a bird of its size – 11 mm, the same as that of a Fieldfare, although the latter is twice as heavy. This enables it to pluck just about every type of fruit available in the wild, and those it cannot pluck, such as apples, its thick bill enables it to pick at, taking chunks out of them where they grow. On an average winter day a Waxwing will eat between 600 and 1000 berries, approximately double its body weight.

In the breeding season the Waxwing's diet alters considerably. In the northern taiga where it nests, mosquitoes and midges are exceedingly abundant, and for a few months the bird subsists largely upon these instead. It obtains them by fly-catching, leaving a high perch on an aerial sally and snapping them up in flight. Later on, it may use this same skill to catch falling snowflakes, since its usual diet requires it to drink a considerable amount of fluid.

Waxwings nest very late in the season, rarely before June. This is because the birds need to await the arrival of summer fruits – which both adults and young need in addition to insects, during and after breeding. As a result of relying on food that is patchily distributed in their environment, Waxwings eschew territoriality and often forage together, well away from the nest, in groups.

At the end of the breeding season the shift back towards a solely frugivorous diet happens slowly and is dependent on weather conditions and insect supplies. Eventually, though, as autumn bites, the birds once again acquire their tunnel vision and become particularly dependent on rowan berries. The supply of these will determine their movements for the following months. If stocks are high the birds will remain in the taiga zone, not far from where they bred. If stocks are poor, however, and the Waxwings have also had a good breeding season, the density of birds competing for the same resource becomes untenable, and large numbers then evacuate south in search of berries in temperate regions of Europe. These evacuations are known as 'eruptions' and often take the birds well to the south of their normal wintering range.

The Waxwing's unusual coloration is related, as is so much of its biology, to its diet. The yellow and red patches – the latter looking like waxy blobs on the tips of the secondary feathers – are made from carotenoid pigments present in fruit. Older birds have more coloration than younger birds, and males more than females, so it is likely that the feature is connected with sexual selection.

Dipper *Cinclus cinclus* (**sink**-luss **sink**-luss) family *Cinclidae* (**sink**-lid-ee)

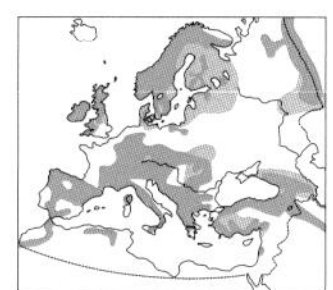

length 18 cm
ID: Very distinctive small bird of rushing torrents.

Habitat Fast-flowing rivers and streams.
Food Various aquatic insects, acquired by swimming and diving underwater. Mayfly adults and nymphs, caddis-fly larvae and stonefly nymphs are important.
Movements Many resident, but others move downstream in winter.
Voice Usual call a sharp 'zit!' Song a warble of strained quality.
Pairing style Monogamous, but occasional bigamy by males.
Nesting Solitary and territorial.
Nest A bulky (often football-sized), circular, domed structure made out of moss (usually several different species), with an inner cup of grass stems and rootlets, lined with leaves. Usual dimensions: 16–23 cm high, 13–22 cm wide. Hole faces downwards, usually over water. Nest placed on rock ledge by river, also under bridge. Sometimes behind waterfall.
Productivity 2–3 broods a year.
Eggs Usually 4–5.
Incubation 15–18 days, by female alone.
Young Nest-bound, altricial and downy.
Parenting style Young fed and tended by both parents.
Food to young Insects.
Leaving nest Young leave nest at 19–25 days. They can dive and swim immediately, before they can fly.

adult black-bellied race

Dippers are the world's only truly aquatic songbirds, the only ones given to habitual total immersion as a way of life. With few obvious external adaptations to diving – no webbed feet, for example – one might expect it to take the soft option and be somehow half-aquatic, swimming around in still, gentle water like a toddler at a baby pool. But no, this extraordinary bird likes the fast, highly oxygenated stuff. It lives on rivers with strong, challenging currents and white water, where even the ducks are few and far between.

The Dipper does have some features to help it in this wild environment. It has very dense plumage to keep out the icy water, and its feathers are heavily waterproofed with oil from its large preen gland. Its body is streamlined so that the water flows easily past it, and its legs and feet are strong, for gripping rocks under and above the water. The wings, which help to power the bird when it is swimming, have strong muscles.

The Dipper acquires most of its prey from the stream bed, by turning over pebbles with its strong, short bill and fielding what morsels of food dwell beneath them. To do this effectively it uses its wings to 'fly' against the current and keep it down at the bottom, and it also grips with its feet, fighting its own buoyancy. Remarkably, a Dipper about to dive doesn't need to fly up and plunge in, like a portly Kingfisher, using its momentum to immerse. It can simply walk into the water until submerged, barely making a wake.

Dippers are, like most river birds, highly territorial. In their turbulent habitat communication can be a problem, and it is thought that this is the reason why Dippers dip. The dipping is a quick flexing of the legs, like a rapid curtsey, and Dippers do it repeatedly, especially in territorial encounters; so it is almost certainly a signal advertising a bird's presence. Another signal is blinking. Dippers are unusual in having completely feathered eyelids, which happen to be white – highly conspicuous when a bird blinks. Blinking tends to occur alongside the dipping display and is also probably a signal.

Some Dippers keep both breeding and winter territories, which may be the same. They are defended from about September onwards, and may be owned by a pair, or by an individual of either sex. Both sexes sing. The song is adapted to be heard amidst roaring water, as one might expect, and is a strained warble, often with scratchy, harsh and sweet notes all mixed together. Regardless of their territorial bent, Dippers in autumn may roost in small groups in traditional locations, such as beneath bridges.

Dippers seem almost immune to cold. They sometimes hunt for food under the ice and can be found in temperatures down to –45°C, although rivers are abandoned if they freeze over completely and the birds may move up to 1000 km to the south, or simply downstream. The breeding season starts very early, with territories maintained or established in January or February. Courtship also starts at this time of year, and there may even be construction and refurbishment of nests. Even migratory Dippers in the far north of Europe are back on site by March.

Wren *Troglodytes troglodytes* (troh-glo-**die**-teez troh-glo-**die**-teez)

family *Troglodytidae* (troh-glo-**die**-tid-ee)

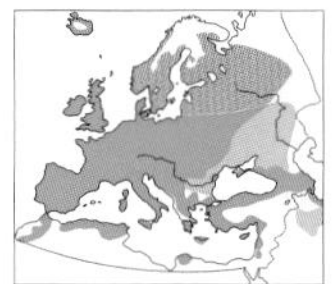

length 9–10 cm

ID: One of Europe's smallest and most abundant birds. Easily identified by shape: tiny body, long, slightly downcurved bill and short tail. Plumage brown with darker bars; long, pale supercilium.

Habitat Anywhere with tangled undergrowth, particularly woods, riversides, gardens; also cliffs and moorland.
Food Small invertebrates, especially beetles.
Movements See main text.
Voice For song, see main text. Call is a staccato, spitting 'tek, tek'.
Pairing style About half of males monogamous, the rest attempt to mate with at least two females. Pairs often break up after only one brood.
Nesting Solitary and territorial.
Nest Dome of moss, leaves and grass, bundled into some kind of hollow.
Productivity 2 broods a year.
Eggs 5–8.
Incubation 16 days, by female only.
Young Nest-bound, altricial and downy.
Parenting style Female feeds young, with variable help from male.
Food to young Various small insects, but fewer beetles than on the menu of adults.
Leaving nest Young leave at 14–19 days, but may be fussed over for up to another 18 days more.

adult

juv.

One of Europe's smallest birds, the Wren has its own unique shape, with a plump body, a short and often upturned tail and a long, slightly curved bill. Its plumage is mostly light brown, with darker barring.

Although the Wren is often abundant, especially in the lush woodlands of central and northern Europe, this small, ball-shaped bird can be very difficult to see. It spends its life close to ground in forest, scrub, waterside and garden, in places where leaves, shoots and branches are densely clustered, forming a labyrinthine mass of concealing and sheltering vegetation. Here it hides, a true skulker, spending many hours quietly working the ground or the surfaces of leaves for food, staying mostly in deep shade and rarely venturing higher than 3 m above ground.

Only when singing is the Wren obvious, and then mainly to the ear, not the eye. Its song is extraordinary for its vehemence and seems to any listener to be far too strong to come from such a small bird. Each Wren repeats one long phrase with as many as fifty separate notes, delivered with great speed and gusto. It appears to throw its whole body into the song, opening its bill wide and trembling, like a miniature opera singer.

In early spring the males embark upon a curious nest-building programme which will play an important role in attracting a mate. They set about constructing between five and eight (occasionally up to ten) nest 'shells' in different parts of the territory. These so-called 'cock nests' are complete but for the inner lining. When a female intrudes into the territory the male immediately directs her to one of his cock nests, displaying on or near it with loud song. If this nest or a subsequent exhibit meets with a female's approval, this goes a long way towards pair formation. The female will mate with the male, then complete the nest by adding a lining of fine materials such as hair or feathers.

After this there may be little contact between members of a pair. The male continues to defend his territory, while the female incubates the eggs and feeds the young, with only occasional assistance. In fact, some males attempt to attract a second or even a third female to breed in one of their unused cock nests, and so become polygynous.

Being so small, Wrens are vulnerable to the effects of cold weather. This problem is partly offset by their choice of well-sheltered habitat, but long periods of extreme cold do cause high mortality. For this reason populations in Fennoscandia and the Baltic states are migratory, evacuating their breeding areas in the autumn and returning in spring. Meanwhile, resident populations are sometimes forced into extreme measures to aid their survival: on bitter winter nights these unsociable, highly strung birds may cluster together in bodily contact to keep warm. Up to 60 or more Wrens have been recorded using a single small nest box, their bodies packed in rows one on top of the other.

Accentors family *Prunellidae* (proo-**nel**-lid-ee)

Habitat Dunnock in woodland and scrub, usually in lowlands. Alpine Accentor in mountains.
Food Insects taken on the ground; some seeds in autumn and winter.
Movements Dunnock resident in much of western and central Europe, migratory in the east and north, but only going as far as southern Europe. Alpine Accentor mainly an altitudinal migrant, but some move much further.
Voice Main call of Dunnock a plaintive 'seep', that of Alpine Accentor a rippling 'chirrup' very like Skylark. Song of Dunnock a cyclical phrase resembling the sound of the wheels of a squeaky trolley; Alpine Accentor's song similar, but slower and more musical.
Pairing style May be monogamous or practise all the versions of polygamy (see text).
Nesting Dunnock solitary and territorial, although several males and females may share territories (see text). Alpine Accentor groups live together in a shared home range.
Nest Cup of twigs, stems and roots, lined with fine materials such as hair and moss. Dunnock in bush or hedge, Alpine Accentor in rock crevice.
Productivity 1–2 broods a year.
Eggs 4–6 in Dunnock; clutch larger in polyandrous trios if both males have copulated with the female. 3–4 in Alpine Accentor.
Incubation 12–15 days, by female only.
Young Nest-bound, altricial and with some down.
Parenting style Both sexes feed and tend the young, the males on condition that they have copulated with the female concerned first.
Food to young Small insects, a few seeds. Alpine Accentor grinds seeds up in its crop before feeding them to young.
Leaving nest Young Dunnocks fledge at 11–12 days, but sometimes leave nest a day before they can fly. They are fed by the adults for 14–17 days thereafter. Young Alpine Accentors leave at about 16 days, also largely flightless.

Accentors are a small, somewhat obscure family of small, brown, superficially sparrow-like birds that feed on the ground. Not many people on the street have even heard of them and even fewer would know that they are any different from lots of other small brown birds.

But accentors are different, for two reasons, one anatomical and one behavioural. The anatomical feature that stirs the juices of specialists is the unique bill. It has a very sharp point, allowing the birds to eat rather small food items, but is wide at the base, and the upper mandible is so swollen in shape that it is actually round in cross-section – very strange. It is often used for flicking leaves dismissively aside as the birds feed.

Accentors may be modestly coloured and retiring in habits, but their sex life is extraordinary, if not unique. Put simply, it involves many different options for pair-bonding, not just monogamy but also various forms of polygamy, including polygyny (one male, more than one female), polyandry (one female, more than one male) and both of these at the same time, so-called polygynandry (a male paired to two or more females, the latter in turn paired to two or more males, including the first). Not only do Dunnocks exercise all these options, but their copulatory behaviour is also unique – see the individual account below.

The odd name 'accentor' simply means 'singer', from the Latin *cantor.*

Alpine Accentor

Prunella collaris (proo-**nel**-la col-**lah**-riss)
length 18 cm

In several respects the Alpine Accentor differs greatly from the Dunnock. It is far less skulking, for example, tending to forage right out in the open among grass and boulders on mountain slopes, and sometimes making uninhibited aerial sallies to catch flying insects. It has a quite different habitat, occurring only on mountains between the tree line and the snow line, ranging from 1800 m right up to 3000 m, where it commonly feeds at the edge of melting snow. It also, in contrast to the self-conscious Dunnock, has a song flight. The male rises steeply into the air, hovers or soars, and then drops down, sometimes in a pipit's 'paper aeroplane' fashion, to land a little higher than its lift-off point.

In its unusual breeding behaviour, however, the Alpine Accentor fully rivals the Dunnock. Alpine Accentors live in polygynandrous groups of 3–6 males and 3–5 females, in which there is a competitive free-for-all. The dominant males in each group attempt to monopolise access to as many females as possible, as in the Dunnock's social system. To protect their paternity the males copulate with great frequency, perhaps a hundred times a day, and their testes, to cope with the strain, may constitute 8 per cent of their body weight. Copulation is exceedingly rapid, lasting only 0.15 seconds, but is aided by the male having a large sperm duct that hangs down as a sac and may be activated simply by contact with the female.

The females, meanwhile, live in a stable hierarchy competing for the attentions of males, knowing, as in the Dunnock, that copulation equals parental help. The females actually sing during their fertile period to mark themselves out from the competition. Within the hierarchy, high-ranking females frequently interrupt the copulations of low-ranking ones, preventing any 'contract being signed' and thereby monopolising the males' charms and later parental assistance for themselves.

adult

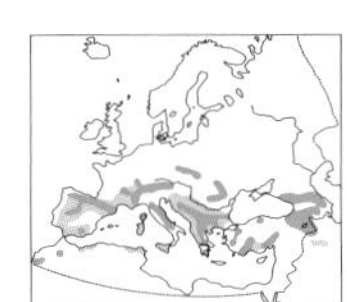

ID: Shares shuffling gait and wing-flicking of Dunnock, but is larger and chunkier. Strong undulating flight, unlike feeble flight of Dunnock. Also more colourful, with reddish-brown flanks, whitish throat with black bars and two white wing bars well separated by dark wing panel.

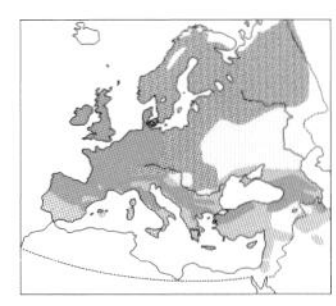

Dunnock

Prunella modularis (proo-**nel**-la mod-yoo-**lah**-riss)
length 14.5 cm

ID: Small, unobtrusive brown bird usually seen on the ground, moving along with creeping gait and constant flicks of the wings and tail. Rounded head, thin bill and red legs. Streaky plumage a bit sparrow-like, but mainly ashy-grey around the head. Juvenile streakier still. Rather common in western Europe.

The Dunnock, also known helpfully but not euphoniously as the Hedge Accentor, is the best studied member of its small family. It is also the only one to have forsaken the mountains to adopt lowland woodland, scrub and gardens as its habitat. Here it forages under cover of foliage, or nervously in the open, pecking in a continuous and somewhat robotic fashion, always moving forwards. It doesn't so much hop as shuffle along, with a creeping, rather mouse-like gait; it crouches down, too, as if embarrassed about its legs, which are hardly visible below the breast feathers. To add to the appearance of nervousness, it constantly flicks its wings. In much of Europe the Dunnock, despite its retiring nature, is a familiar if somewhat overlooked bird, but its range peters out towards the Mediterranean region, where it occurs only in winter.

Dunnocks have a pretty spicy sex life, something that was worked out as recently as the 1980s in the humble setting of the Botanic Garden in Cambridge, England. These birds exhibit monogamy, polygyny, polyandry and polygynandry, and any individual may embark on any one of these possibilities in any season, sometimes actually changing its arrangement in between broods. Few other birds enter such a realm of choice. How this list of options arises requires some explanation.

Female Dunnocks break the small-bird mould by skirmishing over territories in the spring, rather than leaving such things to the males. Once these border disputes are settled the owner-occupiers make it known that the services of males are required. Gleefully, the males move in and it becomes their task to take over the defence of the female's territory. If this happens successfully the pair will be monogamous.

Unfortunately, Dunnock sex ratios are such that there are usually fewer females around than males, and hence feminine territories are larger than most males can cope with. When this happens a male has to enlist the help of another to keep the territory's boundaries safe, and the two may share singing posts and give the impression of teamwork. They are, however, in competition to serve the sexual needs of the female. An awkward hierarchy develops, with one male at least nominally dominant over the other and, in theory, having full and exclusive paternity rights. The dominant bird is termed the alpha-male; the subordinate the beta-male.

This is all very well, but the female does not necessarily buy into the arrangement. In Dunnock society, a male that is permitted sexual relations with a female effectively signs a contract undertaking to help her feed her subsequent young, and this can be of great survival value to the chicks. In short, it is in any female's interest to copulate with both available males. So she readily undermines the dominance hierarchy by seeking out the beta-male behind the alpha-male's back. In these polyandrous trios, therefore, three birds will contribute towards feeding the young. Sometimes it's even four, because it may take three males to protect the larger female territories.

Occasionally a male comes along that is a little bit superior. He not only finds it ludicrously easy to defend one female's borders, but he can actually encompass two. In these unusual cases such a male may obtain exclusive access, and exclusive paternity rights, to the reproductive efforts of two females in a polygynous trio. Although this is not advantageous to either female in the short term, they do at least know that their progeny will be formed from superior genetic material.

Finally, sometimes these superlative males bite off more than they can chew and, despite monopolising the two territories in the beginning, find it difficult to keep the borders intact; they then reluctantly recruit further male help. In these cases two males are now sharing a territory with two females, or they may collectively be sharing the defence of three female territories. At this point, where polygynandry enters the scene, things become a little complicated.

This remarkable set of arrangements is probably related to quality of habitat. Dunnocks take very small food items, and only where these are truly abundant in optimal habitat can a single monogamous pair cope with feeding their young. In any kind of sub-optimal habitat it then becomes advantageous for a female to buy in more help by soliciting to more than one male.

The mating display of the Dunnock is also unique. In a climate of uncertain paternity, the male begins copulating by pecking at the female's cloaca up to 30 times. This effectively causes the most recent sperm to be summarily ejected, and is performed most often when the male suspects his female of cuckoldry. In addition, male Dunnocks mate with their partners at least twice an hour throughout the females' ten-day fertile period.

Thrushes family *Turdidae* (**tur**-did-ee)

Habitat Wide range, but notably woodland, woodland edge, gardens and rocky areas. Bluethroat and Thrush Nightingale prefer vicinity of water.
Food Insects and other invertebrates, especially worms, mainly acquired from the ground. Almost invariably feed on fruit in autumn and winter.
Movements Most long-distance migrants, wintering in Africa; Northern Wheatear and Rock Thrush particularly celebrated in this respect. Robin and the larger thrushes may be resident, or make relatively short-distance movements within Europe. Ring Ouzel also winters in North Africa.
Voice Many have superb, loud, musical songs, which clearly differ from individual to individual and may even improve with the age of the bird. Several are practised mimics e.g. rock thrushes, wheatears, Redstart, Whinchat.
Pairing style Usually monogamous (but some indulge in extra-pair copulations). Male Bluethroats and Stonechats may acquire two mates.
Nesting Solitary and territorial, except Fieldfare, which is frequently colonial. Robin famous for its territorial aggression.
Nest Usually a bulky, somewhat loosely constructed cup of grass and dead leaves, sometimes with mud. Usually placed low to the ground or on it, but Mistle Thrushes build high in trees. Several use cavities, from rodent burrows (Isabelline Wheatear) to trees (Redstart) and rock crevices (rock thrushes, Black Redstart).
Productivity 1–4 broods a year.
Eggs Usually 4–5.
Incubation 10–17 days, by female.
Young Nest-bound, altricial, partly covered with down.
Parenting style Both sexes feed and tend the young.
Food to young Almost invariably invertebrates, especially insects and earthworms.
Leaving nest Young fledge at 8–19 days.

Well known though the thrushes undoubtedly are, they defy an easy definition as a group. They all (or most) have ten primary flight feathers and twelve tail feathers, and they have slender but somewhat blunt bills – hardly headline stuff. Almost all species have strong legs and feet, and most, but not all, feed by hopping along the ground. Many of our species also have comparatively large eyes for feeding in shady environments and this may encourage some to sing earlier in the morning and later in the day than many other species. The Robin, Nightingale, Black Redstart and Whinchat commonly sing at night.

The trouble is that thrushes come in two size categories, which are not instantly recognisable as close relatives. These are the 'true' thrushes, such as the Blackbird and Song Thrush, and the smaller versions, which are collectively known as 'chats'. The latter group includes nightingales, the Robin and wheatears as well as the birds actually called 'chat', the Stonechat and Whinchat. They are smaller than true thrushes, often not much larger than a Great Tit, and because they feed less slavishly on the ground, and also on account of morphological similarities, it has been trendy in the last few years to place the chats together with flycatchers in their own separate family.

On the whole, the European thrushes have excellent songs. Some of these are rightly celebrated, such as those of the Nightingale, Blackbird and Song Thrush, whereas others, such as the Bluethroat, are almost as good but less well known.

Another feature shared by almost all our thrushes is that the juveniles are cryptically coloured and spotted. Even young Robins are spotted and do not acquire the orange-red colour until their first moult. The larger thrushes, of course, also have copious spots on the breast and it is this feature, perhaps, that most clearly defines a 'thrush' in many people's minds.

Red-flanked Bluetail

Tarsiger cyanurus (**tar**-si-jer sie-an-**noo**-russ)
length 14 cm

This elusive Robin-like bird just qualifies as a breeding species in Europe, with only 10–50 pairs nesting each year in the taiga forest of eastern Finland. The figures are subject to great fluctuations between years, and there are often significant numbers of unpaired males (up to 250) present. The species inhabits undisturbed, mossy spruce forest with plenty of fallen trees, usually on slopes.

In contrast to most small members of the thrush family, the males of this species usually sing from the very top of a tall tree, rather than from an inconspicuous perch further down; their song is a short phrase with a slightly melancholy, lost feel, like that of a depressed Redstart. The birds often forage in the branches of trees, too, as well as on the ground.

Red-flanked Bluetails are migrants, arriving in Finland in late May and departing for the long trip to China in September.

ID: Robin-like in profile, but with longer tail and remarkably small bill. Constantly flicks wings and jerks tail. Male highly distinctive, powder-blue above with apricot stain on flanks, and white throat. Female lacks blue coloration, but shares white throat and apricot flank wash; white eye ring also conspicuous.

Robin

Erithacus rubecula (er-**rith**-a-kuss roo-**bee**-koo-la)
length 14 cm

Highly strung and hot-tempered, the Robin is one of Europe's most famously territorial birds. The red (actually orange) breast is a permanent signal to other birds to keep their distance, and intruders that breach the defended borders of territories are asking for trouble: battles over land can be tense and violent, very occasionally resulting in death. In the spring and summer it is mostly males that snarl and skirmish, but females join in in the autumn and winter. And their ire may be expressed not only towards rivals. A Robin may become bothered by other small skulking species such as Dunnocks, too, and even by mice on occasions.

So why do Robins guard their patch so jealously? The answer is at least partly to do with their feeding method. The Robin is a professional exponent of the art of 'perch and pounce', habitually sitting still on a low, often shady perch near the woodland floor, waiting for insects or worms to come into view below it. If they do, the bird flits down to catch them; if they don't it will go hungry or adopt another method such as hopping along the ground. And what a Robin needs for 'perch and pounce' to be effective is privacy. If silence prevails, the small creatures of the ground layer will show themselves, but if another Robin or passing bird intrudes into the feeding arena it might cause a good meal to scuttle back into the leaf litter, scratching its name from the Robin's menu – and that simply won't do. Hence the territory holder's need to keep its boundaries intact.

In the main a territory is defended by song. The Robin is one of the few birds that sings almost throughout the year, with a lull only during the moult in July and August. It is a shrill, wistful effort with a deceptively relaxed tone. Usually there are pauses between each song phrase, and each song is different from the last, as if the bird was answering questions from an inaudible interviewer. When birds are fired up, however, they alternate their phrases, one quickly following on from the other, or one bird may overlap its rival's phrase. These song duels may last for hours and signify the last attempts at a negotiated settlement in a contest between two birds.

Vocal rivalry then develops into visual display. The opponents face each other and show off their red breasts to maximum effect. On the ground they will puff themselves up and point to the sky, while on a perch they will lean forwards if the rival is below them or back if it is above. Most visual encounters prompt a quick withdrawal by a rival, but occasionally these lead to fast and vicious fights, with much kicking and pecking directed at the other bird's face and eyes.

In the middle or late winter a quite different song display begins to be heard. A male Robin no longer sings from medium height on a half-concealed perch, as is his norm. Instead he operates from higher up, in a more conspicuous position and sending forth an allegedly more cheery song. This is the mate-attraction song, and aims to advertise the bird to local females. The latter indicate interest by intruding on the territory, initially to the usual hostility from the male. But after a few attempts the territory holder gets the message and the two birds engage in the so-called 'song and following' ceremony, the male singing and the female chasing. The pair bond is formed, the male resumes his usual song and it may then be several months before nest building begins.

Robins build their cup of dead leaves, moss and grass in a concealed site low to the ground, or on it. A hollow in a bank is a favoured site, as are the roots of trees. In the west of Europe, where Robins are common garden birds, they often use unusual sites such as shelves in greenhouses, coat pockets or flower pots.

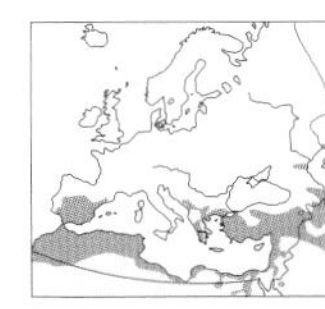

ID: Unmistakable if seen well, a small brown bird with a large blob of orange on the breast and forehead. Juvenile lacks orange and is spotted.

ID: *Small distinctive tapered brown bird, with long, thick bill and very long tail with diagnostic black and white tip. Strong eye stripe; supercilium also conspicuous. Often jerks tail upwards and holds it above back; also fans it.*

Rufous Bush Robin

Cercotrichas galactotes
(ser-koh-**trie**-kass gal-lak-**toh**-teez)
length 15 cm

There are two populations of the Rufous Bush Robin in Europe, one in Spain and Portugal, the other in Albania and Greece, and ne'er the twain shall meet. Each winters in a different part of Africa, the Iberian population in the western Sahel region, and the Balkan population in the northeast. Both are late arrivals in their breeding areas, showing up in May or June.

This is a bird of warm, lowland regions, occurring mainly in man-made habitats such as vineyards, orange and almond groves, and gardens. Despite an apparent ease with people and cultivation, the population is patchy and declining, for reasons that are unclear. The species has quite a wide diet and many means for finding it. It will dig for earthworms like the best Blackbird, snatch butterflies in flight like a flycatcher, hover in front of flowers to get flies, and chase ants and grasshoppers on the ground like a wheatear. So lack of dietary adaptability is unlikely to be the problem.

Rufous Bush Robins are territorial birds, singing their pleasing, Robin-like songs both from prominent song posts and in flight. When rivals meet they behave like miniature peacocks, spreading their wings open to almost touch the ground and fanning their long tails behind them.

This bird builds its nest low down, usually just 1–2 m above ground, in a bush or shrub. Occasionally nests have also been found in tin cans left on the ground, into which the untidy cup of twigs, grasses and rootlets has been squeezed. Another more common site is among prickly pear cactus and, as if to embellish the desert theme, the nest is sometimes decorated with an old snake skin.

adult Western   adult Eastern

Thrush Nightingale

Luscinia luscinia (loo-**sin**-ni-a loo-**sin**-ni-a)
length 16.5 cm

The trouble with famous relatives is that you are inevitably compared with them. Could the Thrush Nightingale possibly sing as well as its more celebrated western counterpart? In a word – yes. The songs are very similar, and perhaps the greatest tribute to the Thrush Nightingale's efforts comes from the rival itself: Nightingales are antagonistic to mouthy Thrush Nightingales, and vice versa. There are subtle differences to the practised ear, though: the Thrush Nightingale's song is a little louder, slower and clearer; the phrases always begin with a 'pew' note and often end in a rattle (the Nightingale rarely rattles); and there are fewer of the Nightingale's grandiose, sobbing crescendos.

Pair formation is similar in both nightingale species. The female is attracted by the male's song and, having entered his territory, apparently gives him a quiet summoning call to express interest. The male approaches on the ground and displays by lifting and fanning his tail and shivering and drooping his wings; he then dashes towards the female and, having almost reached her, jumps backwards and does the same again several times. There is then a chase. Once paired, the female builds the nest, beginning with a layer of dead leaves on the ground, then adding grass and twigs to make a cup. Both sexes feed the subsequent young, often splitting care of the brood between them once it has fledged, with the father having sole responsibility for half the young and the mother for the rest.

This species has a more limited habitat than the Nightingale, almost always occurring in thickets near water, especially if these have a rich layer of earth and leaf litter. It likes the vegetation to be quite patchy and between 3 m and 16 m tall. Preferring dampness, it shuns the warm, dry locations favoured by Nightingales, and apparently it sings more freely in bad weather. In common with the Nightingale it usually feeds on the ground, scouring the leaf litter for small invertebrates and hopping around well within the shady undergrowth.

adult   juv.

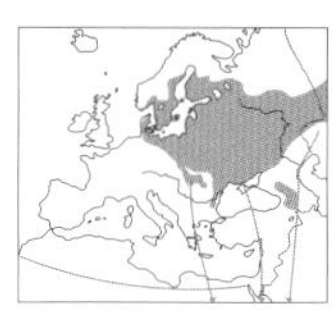

ID: *Extremely similar to Nightingale, but less warm brown in general tone, with some individuals lacking any rusty-red colour except on the tail (and even this is less intense than on Nightingale). Underparts usually faintly streaked or mottled. There may be the suggestion of a breast band and sub-moustachial stripe.*

Nightingale

Luscinia megarhynchos
(loo-**sin**-ni-a meg-ga-**ring**-koss)
length 16.5 cm

The Nightingale has quite a reputation as a songster. Its outpourings have inspired great human music and great literature, from a short but starring role in Beethoven's 6th Symphony (the Pastoral) to sonnets by Milton and odes by Keats. The scientific name *Luscinia* means, roughly, a 'singer of lamentations', and the name Nightingale itself means 'night singer'. The bird is synonymous with its song.

That is a lot of fuss for a performer with a remarkably short singing period, which we Europeans hear for only about eight weeks a year. Nightingales arrive in Europe from Africa in April and start singing immediately, but their efforts decline in mid-May and have petered out by the first week of June. From as early as mid-July the birds begin to migrate south again and all have departed by the end of September. They probably overfly the Mediterranean and Sahara in one go and they reach their winter quarters in October, where they hold winter territories and resume singing, but less lustily than when on their breeding grounds.

On their annual fleeting visits to Europe, therefore, Nightingales have attracted a lot of attention. So is the song worth the hype? Emphatically, yes! It is remarkable for its power, range, clarity and variety, the work of a real virtuoso. It is not relaxing to listen to – it's too urgent and demanding for that – but it is undoubtedly gripping. The song is delivered in short phrases lasting two to four seconds each, which are separated by much the same length of pause. The character of each phrase is different, with various clear bell-like notes, liquid notes and sobbing notes all intermingled, plus the odd chuckle and squeak as well. The whole performance is delivered with great fluency and ease, and is characterised by remarkable changes in volume mid-phrase – some phrases start with long crescendos and end so fast and so emphatically that they are like exclamations! Each male has a repertoire of between 100 and 300 different phrases or song types, which he delivers in regular cyclic succession, up to 400 times per hour. The sheer effort and persistence are a marvel.

Of course, one reason why the Nightingale's song is so enjoyed is that it is often heard at night, when most other birds are silent. Contrary to popular myth, though, it is not an exclusively nocturnal sound. Males often sing by day and, interestingly, their motivation and method differs at this time. The point of the song is more territorial, more directed to rivals, and the bird shifts perches more often. At night the male is appealing more towards female listeners and he remains rooted to the same song post.

As for the bird itself, it is disappointing to look at, just like a big brown Robin. In much of its range it is difficult to see, remaining hidden in thickets even when singing, and feeding unobtrusively on the ground. It is a bird of woodland edge and scrub, especially favouring growth that enables it to move along unobstructed, without the clutter of herbs and grass. In southern Europe it also occurs in very small patches of undergrowth, and here may break cover to sing from high branches and telegraph poles.

ID: Warm brown-coloured chat with large black eyes. Larger than Robin with longer tail, less plump profile. Hops along with wings drooped and tail cocked. Generally rusty-coloured on upperparts, especially on rump and tail. Underparts very pale and plain, with whitish throat and belly and no hint of streaking.

Black Redstart

Phoenicurus ochruros
(fee-nik-**koo**-russ oh-**kroo**-ross)
length 14.5 cm

There are two species of redstart in Europe, both of which have the curious habit of continually quivering their bright orange tails, a form of self-advertisement. They are ecologically quite separate, with the Redstart being a woodland bird and the Black Redstart inhabiting rocky places with lots of bare, open ground.

In fact the Black Redstart lives something of a double life as a species. Most birds are indeed found where rocks are plentiful, in mountains and ravines and along cliffs and ruins. In the Alps they are found up to an elevation of 2400 m, amidst stunning mountain landscapes. Another population, though, has taken to living among buildings, often within deeply urban centres, where the air is anything but bracing and few other bird species go. Instead of choosing rock fissures these birds breed on concrete ledges, sometimes up to 45 m above ground. They forage on waste ground, running or hopping between weeds and rubbish like streetwise Robins, instead of between wild flowers and lichen-covered rocks. And they sing over the din of traffic and engines rather than the trickle of mountain streams.

Wherever it occurs, the Black Redstart is an indefatigable singer, regularly repeating its phrases 5000 times a day, especially at dawn and dusk. Its song has two parts, often labelled as 'question' and 'answer': the first part is upwardly inflected, with an enquiring tone; the second is longer and trails off into a sound like crumpling a piece of paper. A little plaintive but far-carrying, it is sung from a characteristically high perch, either a rock or the roof of the loftiest building around.

ID: Both species of redstarts habitually and incessantly shiver their bright orange tails. Male easily recognised by coal-black body colour intensifying towards upper breast and head, and by contrasting white wing patch. Female sooty brown, darker than similar female Redstart, with redder undertail coverts.

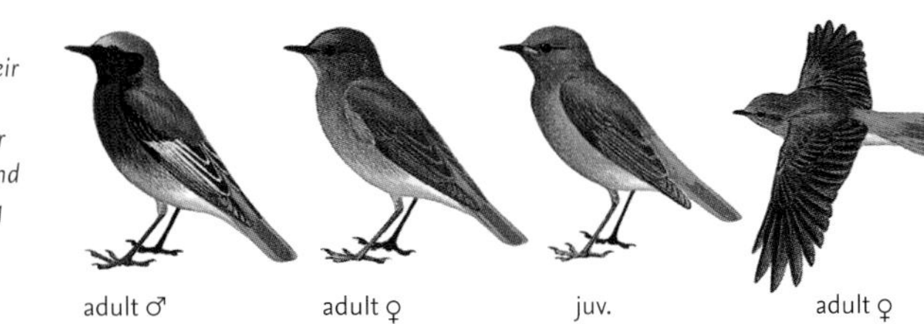

Redstart

Phoenicurus phoenicurus
(fee-nik-**koo**-russ fee-nik-**koo**-russ)
length 14 cm

The Redstart is the jack-of-all-trades amongst its peer group of chats, at least in terms of seeking food. While Robins, Stonechats and Whinchats hunt their insects primarily by 'perch and pounce', and the other chats forage mainly on the ground, the Redstart is less married to one particular method. In contrast to the others it also regularly forages among the leaves of trees for its beloved caterpillars and beetles, well above ground, even hovering at the end of branches to pick insects. In one study, Redstarts performed three operations to an almost equal degree: feeding in the trees, foraging on the ground and taking off into the air to catch insects in flight. It also showed that male Redstarts were more likely to feed in trees, and females on the ground.

In contrast to the other chats, Redstarts nest in holes in trees and have an elaborate nest-showing display. A male first selects a likely hole for a stage and then has three ways of advertising it to his mate (or potential mate). He will sing from inside the hole with his head out, thereby showing his prominent white forehead; he will fly in and out of the hole with feverish frequency; and he will perform a short flight display outside it, showing off his fanned orange tail. Apparently the last of these three is a bit of a desperation tactic, most commonly performed by a male without a mate or any immediate prospect of acquiring one. Female Redstarts are choosy, careful creatures; even the best males may have to sing for several weeks before they detect a spark of interest.

The song is a gentle ditty that always begins the same ('hey-diddle-diddle…'), but ends differently each time, the latter half often featuring highly competent mimicry of local birds. The bird tends to sing from just a few elevated and highly favoured perches, where it feels comfortable. The nest-showing song, however, uttered from the quite different stage of the nest cavity, is a much more rushed, nervy affair.

The Redstart is as much at home in sub-Arctic coniferous woods as in the richly layered broad-leaved forests further south. It is not, though, as common as it used to be. Around 1968 the population crashed almost throughout the continent and has never regained its former levels. It is probable that the cause was a drought in its wintering grounds in the Sahel region of Africa.

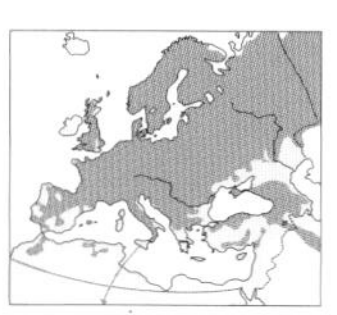

ID: Orange, constantly shivered tail diagnostic of both redstarts. Male easily recognised by white forehead, black throat and orange underparts. Female similar to female Black Redstart, but paler brown, with a more obvious contrast between darker upperparts and paler, orange-stained underparts. Eye ring obvious, undertail coverts and chin off-white.

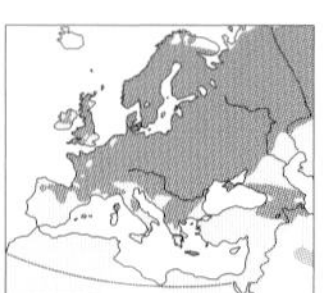

ID: Small upright-perching chat, similar to Stonechat but may lean a little more forward when perching and show flatter crown. Wings also longer than Stonechat's. Easily distinguished from Stonechat by prominent white (male) or buff (female, immature stages) supercilium and by white at base of tail (not on rump). Male has more orange breast and blacker white-edged ear-coverts than female; also white wing patches.

Whinchat

Saxicola rubetra (sak-sik-**koh**-la roo-**bee**-tra)
length 12.5 cm

The Whinchat is one of those birds that birdwatchers love, the sort that actually sits still for a while on a prominent perch so that it can be identified and admired at leisure. Mind you, the perches it selects are usually low and flimsy ones: whereas the Stonechat sits on robust perches, such as fence posts, the Whinchat is often seen on the swaying stems of weeds and fresh growth of bracken. In general it prefers more grassy sites than the Stonechat, with less attendant cover. It is also found much further to the north in Europe, in moorland, bogs and clearings.

As might be guessed from the fact that it possesses longer wings, the Whinchat is also much more of a migrant than the Stonechat. The whole population begins its southward migration in July and August and disappears from Europe to winter in tropical Africa south of the Sahara. Its return is quite protracted, lasting from February until May, and this may cause problems. Male Whinchats are faithful to the sites they have used in previous seasons and, should one return a little late to find his space occupied, a potentially violent quarrel may ensue. Whinchats are not afraid to fight, and if a spat is settled in this way, the winning male quite often performs a special song flight, with roll and somersault included. Normally he performs only the up-and-down sort, so these extra manoeuvres can be put down purely to triumphalism.

If males are faithful to their breeding sites, the same cannot be said for their attachment to the females. Indeed, both sexes commonly change partners between broods, leaving just as the chicks have hatched or left the nest and dumping the remaining parental care on their erstwhile mate. In complete contrast, some unattached birds of either sex may also tender their parenting services to a pair and help feed the young. Clearly, Whinchat relationships are not of the strongest sort.

The female Whinchat builds a nest well concealed in the grass – indeed, grass is integral to its structure – and incubates the eggs on her own. When the chicks hatch, though, responsibilities are usually divided – often literally, with each parent taking charge of one half of the brood.

Stonechat

Saxicola torquata (sak-sik-**koh**-la tor-**kway**-ta)
length 12.5 cm

The Stonechat is a sit-and-wait predator. It selects an elevated perch, watches the ground below and waits for something to show up in its line of sight; when this happens it flies down and snaps the morsel up, usually an insect. On average it waits for 25 seconds on each perch before moving on, and the average perch height is 1 m in spring and 1.6 m in summer. Possibly the higher figure is due to a slight change of tactics, because at this time of year the birds frequently leap into the air to catch flying insects.

The Stonechat itself is not the only beneficiary of its feeding method. Groups of birds, including Meadow Pipits, Whitethroats, Dartford Warblers and Reed Buntings, will sometimes follow Stonechats along as they feed, knowing that these birds are excellent at spotting predators and will give alarm calls, allowing everyone to flee. In return it is possible that the Stonechat gains through fielding any insects that are fleeing the foragers further down.

Stonechats are nervous and noisy at the best of times. When they have young in the nest, though, this turns to paranoia and the birds incessantly give off two calls: a 'wheet' sound which suppresses the begging calls of the young and a 'chack' to distract attention from the nest. The latter call, which has very similar equivalents in other closely related birds, gives rise to the English name 'chat'.

Stonechats sing, too, a pleasing enough, somewhat slurred but scratchy phrase noticeably reminiscent of that of a Dunnock. It has been discovered that males with higher song rates are better providers of food for young, so presumably they are more attractive to females. For singing, a male will perch higher up than when he is scanning for food and he sometimes indulges in a short, very whirring song flight. The song seems entirely aimed at seducing or pampering the female, because it is seldom heard in aggressive encounters with other males.

In contrast to Whinchats, Stonechat partners usually remain together throughout the breeding season. Their relationship may last into the following autumn and winter, too, and they may live more or less in the same place all year round, as long as weather conditions allow. Some individuals, though, migrate short or long distances, many going south into the Mediterranean basin for the winter. Resident birds, beginning their breeding season early, often squeeze three or even four nesting attempts into the year.

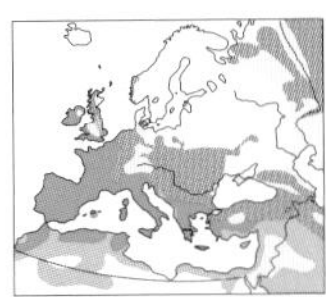

ID: Rounder-headed than Whinchat and with more upright posture; also more demonstrative, with incessant wing-flicking. Male distinctive, with blackish head and obvious white half-collar. Female a washed-out version of the male, easier to confuse with Whinchat, but lacks supercilium and white sides to tail.

Bluethroat

Luscinia svecica (loo-**sin**-ni-a **svee**-sik-ka)
length 14 cm

The Bluethroat has more than just a glorious, cobalt-blue badge on its throat to beguile the opposite sex. It also has a small, intriguing spot interloping amidst the blue. When a Bluethroat sings, its full-throttle throat ruffling may cause the spot to enlarge – and even, it is said, to 'twinkle' – to add an irresistible visual element to an already very fine, varied and mimetic vocal performance. Moreover, the spot is sometimes orange-red and sometimes white, according to where the bird comes from (see illustration).

Needless to say, the blue throat is a feature for sexual selection. Bluethroats are nominally monogamous, but both sexes frequently indulge in extra-pair liaisons; about 35 per cent of all nests contain some young lacking the genetic material of their nest-attending father. Recent experiments have shown that some males' throats are more impressive than others in the ultraviolet spectrum, and the well-endowed birds are more successful than less 'colourful' birds, both in obtaining a social mate and in gathering an extra-pair portfolio. Females also have some blue on the throat, and the larger and heavier they are the more colour they exhibit. All this would seem to lead to a simple enough conclusion – more blue, more sex – but it appears that birds seeking extra-pair liaisons are looking more for genetic compatibility than for quality. The more closely the birds match in their DNA, the better the young will be in resisting disease.

Male Bluethroats defend their territory by singing from a concealed perch, although excitement will tempt them into the open and sometimes into a display flight, too. When the challenge becomes more serious, they show off their blue throats – raising them for a head-on challenge, and assuming a leaning-over posture to display to a bird perching below. In addition, the rivals may also fan their tails to show off the chestnut sides.

As a rule, the Bluethroat is a skulking species, feeding and building its nest on the ground. Red-spotted *svecica* birds are pretty common and will occur where there are thick, lush patches of vegetation amidst open ground. Birds of the race *cyanecula* are much less common and more dependent on marshes and other wetlands.

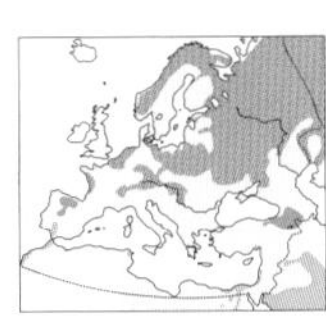

ID: Slightly smaller and longer-legged than Robin, but usually unmistakable, with blue on throat (less or missing in female), prominent white supercilium and, diagnostically, orange-red sides to base of tail.

Isabelline Wheatear

Oenanthe isabellina (een-**an**-thee iz-za-bel-**lie**-na)
length 16.5 cm

ID: Large, leggy, pale wheatear with sexes virtually alike. Has shorter tail than Northern Wheatear which does not reach ground when bird is standing upright (seems to brush ground in Northern). Upperparts sandy brown, including wings, with only the black alula providing contrast; tail has broader black band than Northern. Male lacks face mask, but has black lores, lacking in female.

This is the largest of the wheatears and is dominant over all the others; even the highly strung Northern Wheatear will allow migrant Isabellines to feed unmolested in its territory. It is a rare bird in our area, breeding only in Greece, European Turkey and the wheatear hotspot of southern Bulgaria. Here it lives in dry, open habitats such as steppes and plains where there is plenty of level ground and only a few scattered rocks, bushes or herbs – these would cramp its feeding style.

This wheatear is much more 'cursorial' than the others, seeking most of its prey by a series of rapid runs along the ground. It has longer legs than other wheatears and uses these to dash after ants or beetles located during a sentry-like scan from a rock or a rise in the ground. It also takes insects from the entrance and 'lobby' of rodent burrows.

In its meagre habitat there are few places to nest – hardly any rock crevices or thick bushes, for example – so most pairs of Isabelline Wheatears have to use the burrows of steppe-living rodents (or sometimes Bee-eaters). These may be in short supply, so the territories of these birds are either very widely spaced or, where colonies of rodents occur, closely packed. A male Isabelline Wheatear attracts females by performing a short song flight that ends, unsubtly, at the entrance to such a hole, where he stands upright and cocks his tail.

These birds operate an unusual and variable mating system. Many birds are monogamous but some males may be habitually bigamous, much to the irritation of their mates, who vigorously attempt to exclude the second female. The mating rituals are highly elaborate. Prior to copulation the male may flutter-leap over the female, back and forth, up to 50 times, or roll from side to side on the ground.

Pied Wheatear

Oenanthe pleschanka (een-**an**-thee pleh-**shan**-ka)
length 14.5 cm

Being one of the least weighty wheatears, the Pied is able to perch on flimsy vegetation as well as rocks. As a result it slavishly adheres to the 'perch and pounce' method of capture, waiting on a lookout post about 1 m above ground, scanning for prey below and then making a rapid pounce before returning to the same spot, hopefully with a bill full of food. The idea of spending more than a few seconds on the ground is anathema to it, as if it were afraid of burning its toes if it did.

This is a rare species in Europe, with a restricted distribution along the Black Sea coast. It is the eastern counterpart of the Black-eared Wheatear and the two species are so closely related that they readily interbreed in the zone of overlap. There are differences, though, including the Pied Wheatear's preference for more desolate, unfriendly habitats, such as sea cliffs, dry steppes and stony slopes, places where there are plenty of rocks and some short turf.

The process of pair formation in the Pied Wheatear can be astonishingly brief, lasting just an hour or so, and is usually undertaken in the romantic half-light of dusk. This species is less of a show-off than the Black-eared Wheatear, the male performing far fewer song flights and the female being evidently less enamoured of displays and posturing. As a rule, territories are smaller than those of other wheatears and the males will sometimes share the airspace above them when performing song flights.

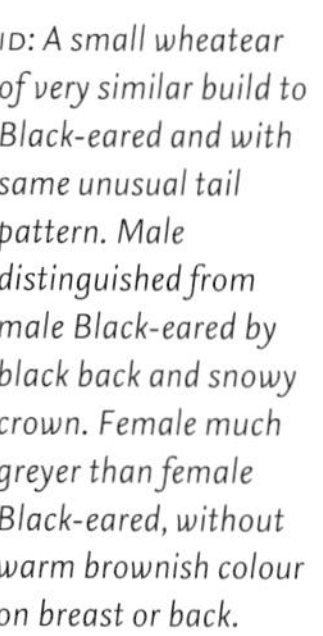

ID: A small wheatear of very similar build to Black-eared and with same unusual tail pattern. Male distinguished from male Black-eared by black back and snowy crown. Female much greyer than female Black-eared, without warm brownish colour on breast or back.

ID: *Highly distinctive black mountain bird with white rump, undertail coverts and tail with black T pattern at the end; unlikely to be confused with anything else. Female sooty brown, not black.*

Black Wheatear

Oenanthe leucura (een-**an**-thee loo-**koo**-ra)
length 18 cm

No one could accuse the male Black Wheatear of not trying hard in his pursuit of a mate and the maintenance of the pair bond. Not only does he perform a pipit-like up-and-down song flight and a beguiling dancing display in which he paces on the spot with feathers ruffled and tail spread, he also goes to considerable trouble to build a platform of stones at the sides of the nest site. This 'monument' is no incidental detail; it may be 10–15 cm wide and consist of hundreds of items (usually stones, but also pieces of wood or earth). Where several years' collecting accrues at a suitable site (e.g. a cave) there may be as many as 9000 in all in one spot. The stones are not integral to the nest structure, but are purely for show.

The process of collecting stones has two functions. Firstly, it draws a female's attention so that, when a male is performing song flights, he will each time land closer and closer to the nest entrance to lure the female there. And secondly, because the stone collection carries on after the pair bond has been formed, it is used as a measure of the two birds' sexual quality and thereby helps them to adjust to each other.

The Black Wheatear is a large species found in Spain and Portugal and is unusual among wheatears in being non-migratory, although some birds in mountainous areas retreat to lower altitudes in winter. It is also less antisocial than the rest; the birds regularly feed in dispersed groups of about half a dozen, without conflict. They eat larger insects than most other wheatears and are armed with a heavy bill and protective stiff feathering about the chin and forehead.

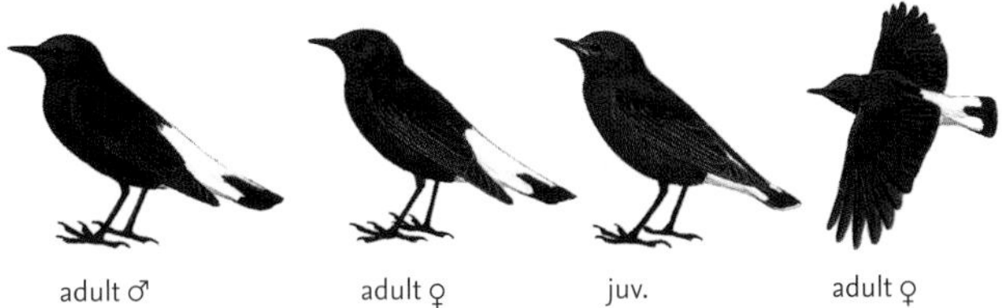

Black-eared Wheatear

Oenanthe hispanica (een-**an**-thee hiss-**span**-ik-a)
length 14.5 cm

This slim wheatear is something of an all-rounder when it comes to feeding techniques. Its light frame allows it to perch on flimsy lookout posts, so the 'perch and pounce' method, in which it flies down to the ground from an elevated position (up to 3 m) to catch whatever it has spied from above, is probably its favourite.

Where the vegetation is thick, however, it will hover into the wind 1 m or so above the ground like a mini-Kestrel, and when the vegetation is sparse it will hunt by running along the ground. When most prey is aerial it will snatch it in flight, and when prey is hidden it will clap its wings to flush it into the open. This impressive range of skills is primarily put to use to catch insects, and it works best in habitats which combine bushy cover with open ground, such as maquis, Mediterranean heathland, rocky limestone hillsides and woodland edge. The warm, invertebrate-rich climate of southern Europe provides the best possibilities.

Male Black-eared Wheatears are territorial, showy birds. They sing incessantly in early season, often all day long, alternating between several different elevated song posts. They also regularly launch into prolonged display flights, rising up to about 20 m and describing circles or arcs in the air, often making sharp turns as if they were following an invisible racetrack; these performances may last for over a minute which, for any species, is quite a long time. As if feeling left out, the female sometimes takes to the air to enjoy the fun, too, flying low, slowly and provocatively just in front of the male.

In a fit of bashfulness the male's display at a potential nest site is quite different, for he will often enter a deep hole and sing from the 'lobby', partially or fully concealed. Once the site has been decided, the bird often makes a small platform of twigs at the entrance.

ID: *Small, with relatively short legs and fairly horizontal posture when perched. Black going up the sides of the tail from the T. Male variable in plumage pattern and has completely black wings; in both races, forms with black throats or just black face masks occur. Females have mottled throats/masks.*

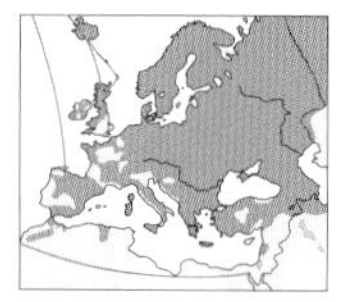

ID: Large wheatear with diagnostic grey back, duller in female than male (lacking in non-breeding birds). Male has black ear coverts, butterscotch-yellow throat and white belly; female lacks face mask. Dark wings contrast with rest of body (see Isabelline). Often told from other small ground birds by its prominent white rump. Tail is white with black band at end and central column making T shape.

Northern Wheatear

Oenanthe oenanthe (een-**an**-thee een-**an**-thee)
length 14.5–15.5 cm

The Northern Wheatear is by far the most widespread of the wheatear group and master of a bewildering range of climatic conditions – from the Arctic to the Mediterranean, from the damp west to the dry east and from sea level to at least 2500 m. All it demands within those parameters is a suitable nest site among rocks or in a burrow, and short-grass turf with a rich insect life easily harvested by ground foraging. Habitats as diverse as tundra, grassland and mountain tops are all suitable, although cultivated areas generally are not – otherwise we would probably be knee-deep in Northern Wheatears.

This bird is a consummate migrant and a living essay on the origin of migration. Despite having a wide range covering most of Eurasia and spilling both west to Greenland and Canada and east to Alaska, all populations winter in tropical Africa. The migration from Europe is substantial enough, but some of the birds from these peripheral populations make mind-bogglingly long journeys of up to 15,000 km in order to meet up with the rest of their species; logic would dictate they would be better served flying due south, to India or to South America, to spend the winter. But that logic does not take account of the gradual development of this bird's migratory patterns. The Northern Wheatear probably originated in Africa and started migrating regularly only in response to the gradual thawing of Europe after the last Ice Age. It will have followed the climatic amelioration little by little, first commuting to southern Europe each year, then gradually creeping further north, west and east as new habitats opened up. It is easy to imagine that, as it spread, it never 'occurred' to the Northern Wheatear not to go to Africa, even when the journey became excessive. The long-distance travellers are victims, then, of history nullifying expedience.

Remarkably, too, the smartly attired males tend to be the first long-distance bird migrants to arrive in Europe in the spring, often turning up at the end of February, even in the northern half of their range. Migrants often travel in bulk, so to speak, and if they are becalmed by harsh weather en route they will soon descend, in true *Lord of the Flies* style, into bickering over temporary feeding territories. The feeding methods of this bird, scanning its surroundings at head height on the ground and chasing after any insect prey it spots, demand a certain amount of space to be effective.

Northern Wheatears have a pipit-like display flight which is mainly territorial in function. They rise into the air on fluttering wings, attempt to maintain their height for a while and then plummet or glide down. Run-of-the-mill performances take them only 2–3 m off the ground, but if a male is embroiled in a fierce dispute with a neighbour he may rise to 10 m or more, just to make a point. In the presence of an intruder or rival male he also has a delightful dancing display, in which he flies repeatedly over the other bird from one side to another, as if he were a tennis ball in mid-rally.

Male Northern Wheatears guard their females carefully just before egg laying, in an attempt to protect their paternity. Occasionally, though, their concentration wanes and their mates slip away from this stifling supervision. Although this opens up the prospect of extra-pair copulation, all may not be lost; recent studies have shown that, even if they do escape their mate's attentions, female Northern Wheatears are very choosy about affairs, opting to succumb only to the most superior of males.

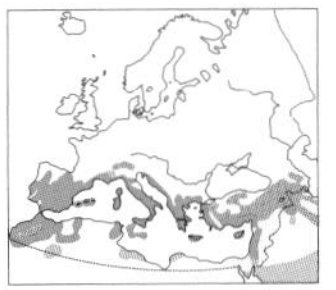

ID: *Larger than Rock Thrush, with slim body, long tail, and characteristic long-nosed profile; bill longer than that of Rock Thrush. Male distinctive with bluish hue all over. Female differs from female Rock Thrush by plain back and lack of reddish colour on underparts.*

Blue Rock Thrush

Monticola solitarius
(mon-**tik**-oh-la soh-lit-**tare**-ee-uss)
length 20 cm

Looking like a Blackbird with a blue cast, the Blue Rock Thrush is more familiar than the Rock Thrush. This is partly because it tends to occur at lower altitudes, and partly because it more regularly nests on man-made structures, such as ruins, castles, towers and quarries. It tends not to occur much above 1000 m and the breeding birds at the highest altitudes descend lower in winter. In contrast to the Rock Thrush, it is not a long-distance migrant, with some birds staying put in the breeding areas and some simply making the short transfer from hills to coast.

Both species of rock thrush feed in a similar way, using an elevated perch as a lookout point to monitor the activity of prey on the ground. Once they detect something, they nimbly slip down and snap it up, sometimes gathering two meals in one go. The main food is invertebrates, but lizards of up to 10 g in weight, small rodents and even snakes may be captured, too. If insect food is especially abundant the birds may fly up to catch it in a short sallying flight. In order to provide enough food, a Blue Rock Thrush territory usually encompasses a rock face some 100 m long by 40–60 m high.

Blue Rock Thrushes do have a song flight, although it tends to be used more sparingly than that of the Rock Thrush. The start is usually different, with a gliding rather than a fluttering ascent, and with a variety of ways of descending, including both gliding and plummeting. The birds imitated in the song are also different, with Willow Warblers and Cirl Buntings being top of the pops. Female Blue Rock Thrushes sometimes sing, too, but they never launch into a display flight to do so.

Rock Thrush

Monticola saxatilis (mon-**tik**-oh-la sak-**say**-til-liss)
length 18.5 cm

It can be hard work to see a Rock Thrush. It is a bird of high altitudes, breeding on sunny, south-facing grassy slopes dotted with plenty of rocky outcrops, where it can easily hide. Extremely nervous and ever on the lookout from atop a rock, it is usually the first in the bird community to give an alarm call and it can then make rapid ascents or dashing descents over the rocks to get away. Most birds are found between 500 m and 2000 m above sea level, usually at low density, and their nest sites, hidden away in rock crevices or under boulders, are often highly inaccessible.

In contrast to the Blue Rock Thrush, this species always migrates away from Europe for the winter. On migration it seems no easier to pin down than elsewhere, and it just slips away, almost unrecorded, into Africa, perhaps using rocky massifs as stepping stones on its way through the Sahara.

The birds return to the breeding grounds as early as February and at once the males start performing their spirited song flights, which are primarily territorial in function. The birds lift sharply into the air with rapid wingbeats and begin singing on the way up, soar for a moment, keep a level or slightly undulating course and then plummet unexpectedly toward the ground, only to use their downward momentum to swoop up and repeat the manoeuvre. A Chaffinch song is mimicked for the peak of ascent, but the spectacular Nightingale routine is given during the plummet, for maximum effect.

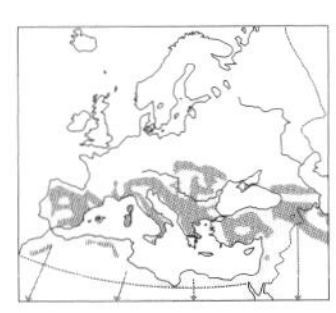

ID: *Shy, starling-sized thrush of mountains with long body and bill, but short orange tail. Sits with upright posture. Male very distinctive and colourful, with large white patch on back. Female speckled by pale spots on head and back; underneath has rusty tones, and barring.*

ID: *Similar in shape and size to Blackbird, but slightly slimmer, with distinctly longer and more pointed wings; much shyer. Male easily recognised by white 'napkin' across breast, still present but generally less bright in female. Both sexes have white edges to wing feathers.*

Ring Ouzel

Turdus torquatus (**tur**-duss tor-**kway**-tuss)
length 23–24 cm

The Ring Ouzel is found in mountainous and tough habitats, where the townie Blackbird gives way. There are two main populations in Europe – one in the high mountains of central Europe, the other on the oceanic fringe in the British Isles and Fennoscandia – and, interestingly, these two factions have diverged in several ways. The birds of the northwest live mainly on moorland and rough ground above tree level (250 m+) and tend to nest on the ground. Those of central Europe occur in high-altitude (600–2000 m) open conifer or conifer-beech forest and almost always nest in trees. They winter just north of the Mediterranean whereas northwestern birds winter in Spain and North Africa.

This bird is the shyest of the larger thrushes, usually flying off at the slightest disturbance and proving hard to locate. Undemonstrative, it sings its mournful, Song Thrush-like song from only slightly elevated perches and generally performs only at dawn and dusk. Display, as in other thrushes, is somewhat understated, with just a few chases, interspersed by the male raising his head daringly a few times to show off his white collar. Males are, however, highly aggressive in defence of their territory.

The nest is a complex and quite large structure with three definite layers: an outer shell and foundation of sticks, a bottom layer of mud mixed with grass and moss, and an inner lining of much finer, 'designer' grass stems. Nests on the ground are usually in a crevice, where they have side or back support; nests in trees are usually close to the trunk and supported by branches.

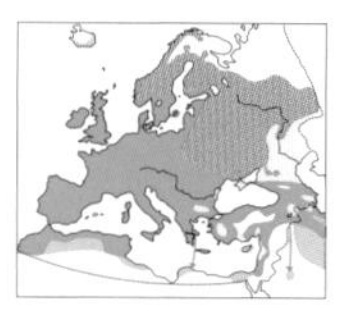

Blackbird

Turdus merula (**tur**-duss **mer**-roo-la)
length 24–25 cm

ID: Familiar well-proportioned thrush with long tail. Male easily recognised by black plumage relieved only by orange bill and eye ring (first winter males have dark bill). Female dark brown, often paler on throat and with streaks on breast; still darker than any other thrush. Juvenile covered with copious buff spots.

The Blackbird is such a familiar sight to people living in towns and cities that it is difficult to appreciate that only 150 years ago it was very much a forest bird. Its dark coloration and low-pitched, melodious song are both signs of a species that is used to deep shade, the latter because sounds of deep pitch are less easily dampened by foliage than high ones, and therefore travel further. But from about 1850 it began a remarkable spread into urban and suburban areas, one that continues to this day in the northeast of its range. The takeover has been so complete that Blackbird densities in suburban areas are higher than those of deep forest, or of anywhere else.

Blackbirds are easily seen feeding on lawns or field edges, where they have a distinctive way of operating. They stand still, looking or listening for signs of movement and then, if nothing registers, they make a quick run or hop in a linear direction to another lookout point so that they scout from a different place. If they still draw a blank they may change direction, but if something shows they will run towards it and attempt to grab hold. Blackbirds are the most successful of garden birds at eating earthworms from lawns, having acquired the remarkable skill of pulling them out intact, even after a struggle.

The Blackbird's success is underpinned by adaptability, so it is not surprising that it employs many other methods of feeding, too. Alone among the thrushes that root around in leaf litter the Blackbird is able to scratch the ground with its feet, like a chicken, to reveal morsels just underneath the surface, and it will also take detritus in its bill and toss it aside with a contemptuous flick. In the late summer and autumn its attention turns to fruit and it has occasionally been recorded snatching it in flight. The Blackbird also readily feeds from bird tables and other artificial sites. In difficult weather conditions its catholic diet enables it to find and consume unusual emergency foodstuffs, such as faeces, tadpoles, fish, kitchen scraps and carrion, when a less adaptable bird such as a Song Thrush would perish.

The Blackbird is an irascible character. Rival birds frequently confront each other over territory, meeting on the ground face to face, with feathers ruffled, tail fanned and wings drooped. Fights take place quite regularly and consist of an unseemly flurry of kicks and pecks, with the protagonists sometimes leaping into the air, as if they were miniature stuntmen playing a scene. But it's not pretend, and some individuals die of their injuries.

This general testiness extends to the Blackbird's roosting habits. Outside the breeding season the birds roost communally, usually sharing the same bush, but well spaced. Before settling down, though, there tends to be an almighty discussion about who goes where, with all the birds exchanging angry 'chink' calls. A similar volley of abuse is offered to owls being mobbed.

From late winter the males sing their highly complex and euphonious songs. Each bird's song is distinct and there is good evidence that the repertoire of older birds is better than that of their younger counterparts. Cold weather impedes singing whereas, at least in its early stages, mild, damp conditions promote it. During incubation, however, song is at its peak and may be heard from well before dawn till after dusk.

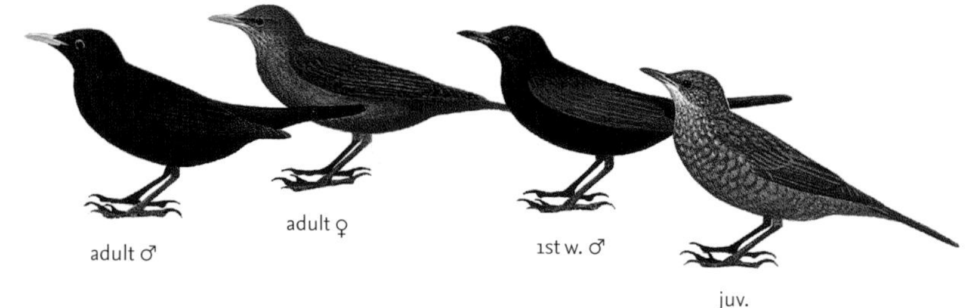

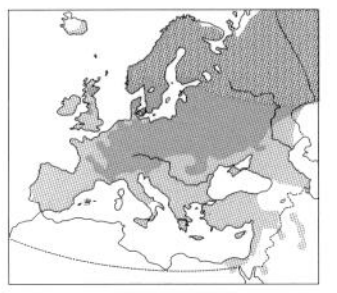

ID: *Large thrush with unmistakable colour scheme, including smoky-grey on head, back and rump; mantle violet, tail black. 'Thrushy' spots turn to chevrons on flanks.*

Fieldfare

Turdus pilaris (**tur**-duss pie-**lay**-riss)
length 25.5 cm

In the woods, parks, hedgerows and farmlands of central and northern Europe where the Fieldfare breeds, it could be described as something of a folk hero. A whole range of other birds attempts to nest alongside it, like acolytes inveigling their way into a neighbourhood rendered fashionable by the presence of a star name. These include such disparate characters as Bramblings, Redwings, Great Grey Shrikes and Merlins, and some of these species may deliberately seek out Fieldfares each year and attain greater breeding success as a result. The reason? Fieldfares have a nest-defence strategy like no other and can stand up to the largest and most dangerous predators.

These large thrushes are colonial, although the nests are always at least 10 m apart and an occupied area can cover many hectares of woodland; perhaps it would be better to view them as suburbs. If a large raptor such as a crow or Buzzard approaches such a settlement, then, it may face the wrath of many birds. In any case, the action is co-ordinated. The birds take to the air and, calling angrily with a loud, discordant screech, they dive-bomb the predator, one by one, each time delivering a well-aimed shot of excrement. Within a short period a large target can be hit many times, becoming matted with the stuff and, if it is not careful, grounded. Not surprisingly, the attacker soon retreats, and one would imagine never returns.

The Fieldfare is one of northern Europe's most abundant birds, relishing any type of countryside that provides both trees or scrub for nesting and open pasture for feeding. In the summer it feeds on the ground in typical thrush style, stop-starting across the turf and digging into the soil when it detects a worm or other creature. It is also an enthusiastic consumer of berries at all times of year, but this tendency is usually most marked in the autumn, when it leaves most of its breeding sites to travel south and west for the winter.

This is the only large thrush to perform a song flight, an unspectacular effort at no great height and on a horizontal plane, not much more than a perch-to-perch transfer on slow wingbeats. In contrast to the exultant efforts of other thrushes, its song is hard on the ear, unmusical, disjointed and not very varied.

Song Thrush

Turdus philomelos (**tur**-duss fil-loh-**mee**-loss)
length 23 cm

With its clear, urgent, perfectly enunciated phrases, each repeated a few times, the Song Thrush has one of Europe's best-known and most appreciated songs. Heard right from October through into early summer, the song is extremely variable and each bird may call on between 138 and 219 song types. At times when the song dominates a neighbourhood, being proclaimed almost incessantly throughout the day, the singer can be confidently labelled as unpaired. Paired Song Thrushes sing very little, usually just for a short burst at dusk, and this is one reason why this species sometimes appears much less common than it actually is.

It is at heart a forest bird, occurring in just about every type of treed habitat from unbroken coniferous stands to wall-to-wall deciduous. It is at home in the shade, where it flicks away the leaf litter in its search for a wide range of invertebrates, but also requires open ground, particularly grassy swards where, keeping close to cover, it will search for earthworms and soil-living invertebrates, detecting them visually from surface movement and also by listening. Whenever possible it will also feed on fruit and it is one of the few thrushes that regularly eats yew berries.

In times of hardship, including winter cold and summer drought, the Song Thrush's fallback position is to look for snails. It is the only thrush that can open them, which it does by bashing them on a hard surface with a downward thrust and a deft, last-moment turn of the head. Appropriate surfaces are often used repeatedly, and these 'anvils' may gather an accumulation of broken shells. Rocks make ideal anvils, but in gardens the birds have been known to use bottles.

The Song Thrush tends to shun the warmest and driest parts of Europe, because it is unsuccessful in foraging on hard, dry ground, and because it requires mud for its nest. Uniquely, the mud (or dung) makes up the lining, and the blue eggs are laid onto it.

In some parts of Europe the Song Thrush is a resident, where it may start breeding early and make up to four attempts a year. Birds in the north and east, though, are migratory, and differ from Redwings and Fieldfares in returning to the same wintering areas every year.

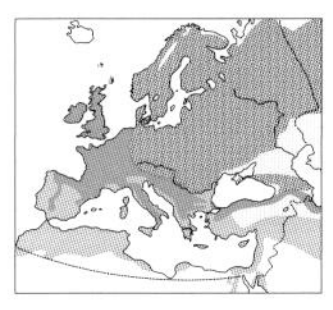

ID: *A small thrush, better proportioned than similarly plumaged Mistle, with proportionally larger head and shorter tail. Upper parts relatively warm brown compared to Mistle. Spots on breast on buff background, at least on upper breast and flanks; tend towards being arranged in lines. Tail unmarked; underwing sandy brown.*

Mistle Thrush

Turdus viscivorus (**tur**-duss viss-**siv**-or-uss)
length 27 cm

This, the largest of Europe's thrushes, is a bird of tall open forest. It is less cover-hugging than the Blackbird or Song Thrush, feeding boldly on large swathes of grass out in the open, although it is shy and will take flight at the slightest disturbance. It uses its powerful bill to dig into turf and is perfectly capable of turning over stones and other heavy objects to inspect what is revealed underneath. In common with other large thrushes its main summer food is invertebrates gathered from the soil, but it does not scrabble among leaf litter or seek deep shade.

A highly strung species, the Mistle Thrush reacts to any sort of fear or irritation with loud, rattling calls. Being one of the few birds to place its nest high in tree forks, it is constantly on the lookout for crows and other predators, which it will attack or harry away from the territory as soon as it spies them. It often lays eggs as early as March, and it has been suggested that this is a strategy to get a breeding attempt in before the predators find nest-robbing fashionable and profitable.

The scientific name *viscivorus* means 'consumer of mistletoe', referring to the bird's love of this delicacy. From October onwards, in fact, the long-lasting berries of this and other plants such as yew or holly become the focus of Mistle Thrush attentions. Single birds or pairs commandeer isolated trees or clumps as their own, defending them against all other berry-eating birds with considerable aggression. This strategy allows the birds to ensure that plenty of berries remain on the plants long into the winter and following spring, making the trees a living larder for the Mistle Thrush's exclusive use in times of hardship. Being good stewards of their berry supply, Mistle Thrushes eat the produce only when necessary, feeding on invertebrates whenever conditions allow and keeping an eye out for interlopers. However, their strategy can fail if, during harsh conditions, large flocks of hungry nomadic thrushes overwhelm their defence by sheer weight of numbers.

The Mistle Thrush's song is a melodious, wild-sounding series of short phrases with a distant, melancholy air. It often performs when other birds do not, such as during the afternoon and in spells of inclement weather, including rain and high winds.

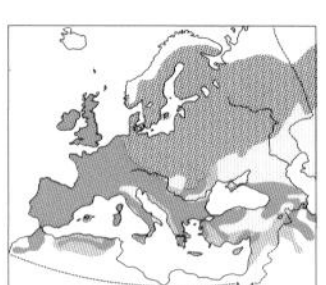

ID: The largest thrush, a good deal bigger than similar Song Thrush; also has odd proportions, with small head, barrel chest and long tail. Much colder, paler brown than Song Thrush; wings show pale panel on coverts. Spots on underparts have white background, but on the breast sides the 'ink has smudged' to give dark patches. Spots rounded, rather than upward pointing as in Song Thrush. Tail has white terminal spots; underwing white.

Redwing

Turdus iliacus (**tur**-duss eye-li-**ay**-kuss)
length 21 cm

The last thing one might expect from a relative of those accomplished performers the Song Thrush and the Mistle Thrush is a bird with just one song. But although what the species sings as a whole is variable, male Redwings in a particular area do indeed recite just one slogan each, over and over again. Their proclamations differ from those of birds in other areas, so they can be viewed as dialects. In Norway, the area occupied by birds singing a particular dialect averaged out at 41.5 sq km and there were clear boundaries differentiating one dialect from another.

This small thrush requires the same combination of forested or scrubby areas with some open ground as the other larger thrushes. It is, though, a little more restricted than the others, being found mainly in the boreal zone of the north. Typically it likes mosaic habitats, including open forest, forest edge, parks and tundra scrub, but it shuns closed canopy. As a bird that tends to benefit from woodland management thinning the trees out, it has increased in numbers recently in Fennoscandia, especially since the 1950s.

After breeding, Redwings evacuate south to spend the winter in southern and western Europe, with a few going as far south as North Africa. The wintering area varies drastically from year to year, and there are records of birds wintering in Britain one year and Greece the next. Early in their travels they subsist mainly on berries and become essentially nomadic in their search for them.

In contrast to the Fieldfare, the Redwing often feeds among leaf litter, as well as out on open pasture and fields. But to many people in Europe the most familiar view of Redwings is of a flock moving across a field on a broad front, running forwards little by little in stop-start fashion, like an invading army.

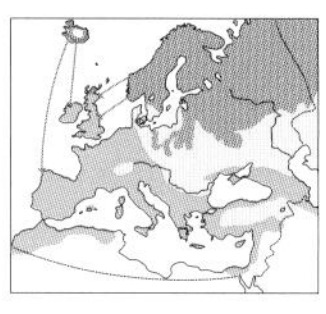

ID: Small, Starling-sized thrush with shortish tail. Superficially like Song Thrush; most easily distinguished by prominent white supercilium. Breast and flanks striped rather than spotted, and lower flanks reddish where colour appears to have 'leaked' from underwings.

Warblers family *Sylviidae* (sil-**vie**-id-ee)

Habitat Most well-vegetated habitats, but especially marshes, woods and scrub.
Food Insects and other invertebrates, which may include small snails. Great Reed Warbler takes fish fry. Many eat berries in the autumn, especially prior to migration.
Movements As small insectivores, almost all species are long-distance seasonal migrants, wintering in Africa. A few are resident (Cetti's, Moustached, Sardinian and Marmora's Warblers and, in places, Goldcrest). Most migrate by night.
Voice Warblers are defined by their many and varied songs, many of them easily recognisable; few 'warble' as such. Some songs are short (e.g. Cetti's, Dartford), others long and rambling (e.g. Sedge). Females may select males with better song repertoires.
Pairing style Usually monogamous, but several species regularly practise polygyny, including Cetti's Warbler, Zitting Cisticola and Great Reed Warbler. Aquatic Warbler virtually promiscuous, with no formal pair bond at all.
Nesting Usually solitary and territorial, but several species (notably in genus *Hippolais*) form clusters of pairs known as neighbourhood groups.
Nest Variable, but usually a tightly woven cup of grass and plant stems, lined with finer materials. Nests of *Phylloscopus* warblers dome-shaped. Zitting Cisticola nest unusual (see entry). Goldcrest nest deep pocket lined with feathers. Some *Sylvia* warblers build several nests for female to inspect.
Productivity 1–2 broods per year, occasionally 3 (e.g. Zitting Cisticola).
Eggs 2–7 (but Goldcrest and Firecrest 7–11).
Incubation 9–17 days, usually by female alone, but sometimes both parents contribute (especially in *Sylvia* warblers).
Young Nest-bound, altricial and naked.
Parenting style In most species both parents feed and tend the young, but in some polygynous species the male offers little (e.g. Cetti's Warbler, Great Reed Warbler) or no (Aquatic Warbler) help.
Food to young Insects, delivered bill to bill.
Leaving nest Most fledge at 10–16 days, but some leave nest a day or two earlier. Goldcrest and Firecrest take longer, 16–21 days.

Balearic Warbler

The warblers are mainly small birds, no bigger than a tit. Most have thin, straight bills of no great length, which are used to pick and glean from the foliage. They are highly active foragers, moving through the foliage with great speed and expertise, and although they have rather slender legs, their feet are strong and enable the birds to perform the gymnastics necessary to make their feeding effective. Most species are highly capable of catching insects in flight, but they tend to do this 'on the hop', flitting from perch to perch, rather than in the formal sallying manner adopted by flycatchers and several members of the thrush family.

Being insectivorous, most warblers are migrants, vacating Europe in the autumn to spend the winter in Africa. Some travel considerable distances to do this, several thousands of kilometres. Just before departure, many species eat berries to help fuel them for their journeys.

It's hard to overlook warblers when they return, for most have very distinctive songs which they sing with great gusto in order to sort themselves out territorially. A good many species sing at all hours of the day and night before they are paired, but abruptly cut their output once they have acquired a mate. For birds that are unimpressively coloured and hide away amongst the foliage, it is hardly surprising that songs play a prominent role in their social and breeding activities. In most species (but less so in *Sylvia* warblers) the sexes look alike, so it helps that, in general, only the males sing.

Warblers are divided into various groups with different characteristics. The groups are named after their scientific generic names. Not all members of the family are assigned to a group, though, so only the main ones are listed here: ***Locustella*** warblers are almost paranoid in their cover-haunting habits, rarely showing themselves except when singing – and even then not being highly visible. They have strong legs and feet and walk or run, rather than hop, on the ground, where they normally feed. Their tails are long and rounded at the tip. Their songs are insect-like and often continuous. ***Acrocephalus*** warblers are relatively strongly built birds clad in dull brown, some with streaks. They tend to have long bills and somewhat peaked crowns, giving rise to the scientific name, which means 'sharp-headed'. Almost all live in waterside vegetation and are often skulking, feeding near the ground. Their songs are in continuous phrases, and many have a chattering quality. ***Hippolais*** warblers are mainly tree-haunting birds that forage well off the ground. They closely resemble *Acrocephalus* warblers in shape and size, but are not found in marshes. Their nests are neat cups placed on and attached to the fork of a tree. Their songs are long-winded and babbling. They have no ritualised advertising song flight. ***Sylvia*** warblers are birds of bushy, scrubby and woodland habitats. By far the most colourful warblers, they are unusual in exhibiting some differences in the plumage of the sexes. Their songs are often scratchy and harsh, and usually rather short. ***Phylloscopus*** warblers are predominantly small green birds with short bills. They are more arboreal than other warblers, often foraging high in the crowns of trees. The domed nests are, however, usually on the ground. Many sing quite musical, wistful songs in short phrases, and only a few perform song flights.

Cetti's Warbler

Cettia cetti (**set**-ti-a **set**-tie)
length 13.5 cm (males up to about 20 per cent heavier than females)

Most people's first experience of a Cetti's Warbler is of a disembodied shout from the depths of a waterside bush. Few birds are so skulking and yet so noisy. And few follow such a distinctive method of singing: there will be a sudden burst of rich, sweet song and then silence; after several minutes another round will be fired, but from a spot some distance away, and so on. The male Cetti's Warblers sings on patrol, one phrase from each favoured perch, the silence coinciding with a rapid but concealed sprint through the tangle of vegetation from one singing post to another.

Male Cetti's often sing all year round – this is a perk of being one of the few European warblers not to be a long-distance migrant. Their territories are typically long and linear, following the course of a ditch, stream or path, for example, and may cover 100 m or so. By early spring, after a winter's negotiation, most border disputes have been settled and there is little obvious conflict between the males; instead the competition turns to the acquisition of females.

Whereas many a warbler is basically monogamous, with the odd instance of polygamy, Cetti's Warblers do things the other way round: most breeding males attempt to acquire more than one mate and only a few settle for one. Perhaps not surprisingly some males are better at attracting females than others; in one study from England, about 20 per cent procured one mate, 30 per cent two mates, 20 per cent three and a few even managed to hold on to four. Many of the rest remained unpaired in this evidently meritorious system.

Intriguingly, there is some evidence that the uneven distribution of pairing is related to the size of the males. The Cetti's Warbler shows exceptional variability in body weight, both between male and female (the male is up to about 20 per cent heavier than the female, the greatest discrepancy of any small European bird) and between individual males. Some studies have suggested that the heavier males tend to acquire the most mates; and not only that, but their females also lay larger clutches of eggs.

Not surprisingly, with its attention divided, the male Cetti's Warbler does not contribute to the domestic tasks of incubation or brooding the young, although he will feed nestlings at times. He will, however, be enthusiastic over providing for all of his fledglings before they become independent. Most male Cetti's Warblers ensure that their females' nesting cycles are not entirely concurrent, giving them the chance to devote some care to each brood, one at a time.

ID: Very skulking, usually sings unseen from cover. Medium-sized warbler with large tail, often cocked; noticeably short wings, rounded crown. Rich warm brown on back, with distinct grey wash to sides of neck.

ID: *For a warbler, pretty unmistakable – very small and streaky, with plump body, short wings and rather plain face. Tail has black and white tips.*

Zitting Cisticola

Cisticola juncidis (sis-**tik**-oh-la yoon-**kie**-diss)
length 10 cm

The Zitting Cisticola is our only representative of a group of small warblers that are found mainly in the tropics, and it brings with it quite an exotic lifestyle. It is, for example, highly polygamous – a male Zitting Cisticola who was unable to furnish himself with at least four female mates in an average year would consider himself a bit of a failure. Acquiring just a single mate is not up to standard; it is simply polygamy gone wrong. The average breeding male Zitting Cisticola sires between 10 and 16.5 fledglings every season.

To attract females, the male performs a song flight of unrelenting tedium. Taking to the air, he flies widely around his territory and beyond (sometimes as far as 1 km), often describing a wide circle. En route he follows an undulating course, bouncing up and down as if attached to a piece of elastic. On his way up to the highest point of each swing he sings 'zit', and when he reaches the same point on his next swing he goes 'zit' again, and so on, *ad nauseam*. The name is appropriate enough, therefore, but that does not make listening to a Zitting Cisticola any more interesting.

Male Zitting Cisticolas have more than just themselves to offer; they are also keen to show a prospective female a nest – or, at least the beginnings of one, the so-called 'courtship nest'. A female approaching the territory is introduced to its owner by the 'pendulum flight', a series of swoops towards her from the side. If she maintains interest the male will then switch to a more direct 'zigzag flight', indicating the nest's position, and alternate this with the pendulum flight from time to time as the female hops toward the nest. Finally, once she reaches the goal, the male switches to flying in horizontal circles. The female's acceptance of nest and male is usually signalled by her crossing the threshold and entering the nest.

A Zitting Cisticola nest is highly unusual. It is roughly bottle shaped, with the entrance at the top. It is built within the close-knit vertical stems of a clump of grass and is usually fixed between 10 cm and 50 cm above ground. Construction involves weaving grass leaves together using cobwebs, and the bird will actually make holes in leaves with its bill so that it can pass gossamer cords through and sew them together. The male makes the outer part, and then the female lines it with more cobwebs, grass flowers and plant down. The resulting structure may be 20 cm tall.

The Zitting Cisticola is very much a bird of grassy places and low growth, occurring, for example, in pastureland, crops and marshes. It is found primarily in the Mediterranean, but in recent years has spread north along the Atlantic coast of France, where its limit is set wherever a region experiences more than 15 days of frost per winter. The population here fluctuates greatly, but the mere presence of the Zitting Cisticola is impressive for a bird that is found mainly in very hot places indeed.

adult

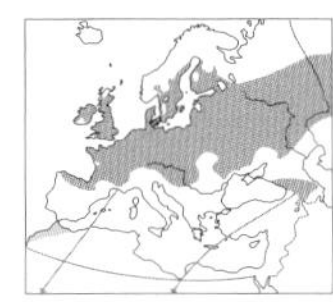

Grasshopper Warbler

Locustella naevia (loh-kuss-**stel**-la **nee**-vi-a)
length 12.5 cm

ID: Small skulking bird with quite Dunnock-like profile and olive-brown ground colour. Has spiky bill, gently rounded crown, curved primaries and heavy tail of other Locustellas. *Upperparts, though, are uniquely peppered with dark brown spots, and bird is streaked on whitish undertail coverts, flanks and, sometimes, on the chest. May look vaguely Sedge Warbler-like but lacks prominent supercilium.*

The widespread but mysterious Grasshopper Warbler is a very skulking species that lives in short, thick vegetation up to 1 m high, with the odd taller bush or thicket interspersed. It spends most of its time on the ground or within the tangle of foliage, either creeping along stems or branches or running over the ground with an odd but highly distinctive, high-stepping gait, like that of a hurdler. It is a fastidious forager, often spending some moments in one place thoroughly checking the possibilities before moving on, and it may deal at some length with larger prey items as if relishing every moment of their consumption. Living so low down in such a tangle of vegetation, it is notorious among birdwatchers for disappearing into a bush or tussock never to be seen again.

The only time Grasshopper Warblers are easily detectable is when they are singing. The males like to perform from higher above ground than they would normally go in the course of their foraging lives, so they often use the side branch of a low bush, or even the top, as a singing post. The song is a reeling sound, like that of an angler bringing in a catch, or like a freewheeling bicycle. Consisting of double notes repeated at the astonishing speed of 26 per second, it is easily blown away by any breath of wind, and when singing the birds have a habit of turning their heads around, so that the song appears to vary in volume, muffled when the bird is looking away and strong when it is facing the hearer. The song may be heard at any time of the day or night.

When a female approaches the territory of a male, Grasshopper Warblers throw off the shackles of their retiring life for a while and indulge in a spirited chase, often accompanied by excited singing. Male pursues female vigorously, and he may even fly around her in a low, silent display flight, using moth-like wingbeats. When on a perch he may flap his wings in a slow and exaggerated manner, a display known as wing-waving, and he may perk up all his efforts by carrying a leaf as well, which may be passed to the female. Mating takes place on or near the ground.

Grasshopper Warblers have a widespread distribution in northern and central Europe. Their habitat of dense, low growth is not shared with many other species. Recent evidence suggests that, at least on the edge of their range, Grasshopper Warblers may be partly nomadic, their distribution being affected by spring temperatures and the presence or absence of warm easterly winds.

adult

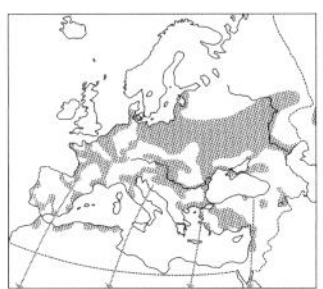

ID: The plainest Locustella, *without streaks on either upper or underparts; undertail coverts may show the merest hint of light spotting. Most similar to habitat-sharing Reed Warbler, but slightly darker and lacking contrasting warm coloration in rump. Also has shorter bill, heavier, rounded tail and curved primaries (the outermost with pale edge).*

Savi's Warbler

Locustella luscinioides
(loh-kuss-**stel**-la loo-shin-ni-**oy**-deez)
length 14 cm

For a *Locustella* warbler the singing performance of a Savi's is an act of audacious showmanship. It actually sits up high on top of a reed stem, in full view of an observer, usually by day. Outrageous! At least when feeding, though, it reverts to generic type, walking, creeping or hopping down near the ground, often deep within cover.

In contrast to the Grasshopper or River Warbler, the Savi's has a well-defined and somewhat restricted habitat. It occurs mainly in large to very large reedbeds, especially mature ones with lots of layers of growth. It avoids reed monocultures, however, preferring an understorey of sedge and other waterside plants where it can feed, and here the population is at its densest. Some populations are tolerant of alders and other trees growing nearby.

Where they occur, Savi's Warblers are usually found in bulk, with many birds sharing the same reeds at high density. The males, however, are extremely territorial and often sing at each other, not far apart, across their invisible boundaries. These borders are seldom crossed, although later in the season the birds often seem to shift about and may alter their boundaries for second broods, making them notoriously difficult to census. The song is typical for the group, sounding more insect-like than bird-like (it is almost identical to the stridulation of the Roesel's bush-cricket), but it also sounds distinctly like a miniature drill.

Savi's Warblers obtain most of their food deep down in vegetation close to the water, or even from the surface. The latter has been confirmed by the presence of significant numbers of aquatic larvae and water-snails in the diet. As a rule Savi's Warblers take fewer fast-moving prey items than their reed bedfellows, the Reed Warblers, and they creep rather than flutter about to take them.

adult

River Warbler

Locustella fluviatilis
(loh-kuss-**stel**-la floo-vi-**ay**-til-liss)
length 13 cm

It is quite possible that someone could have breeding River Warblers on their doorstep and not know it. This is a very secretive, skulking species, extremely difficult to see, and the male's song sounds more like a cricket or cicada than a bird, so it is easily mistaken for something else. The sound is almost mechanical in tone, like the rhythmic 'zip-zip-zip' buzzing of a sewing machine, and it is normally performed at night: one study revealed that 90 per cent of all output was in the dark. Moreover, males stop singing as soon as they are paired, so after the brief vocal season they vanish into the scrubby hinterland and many are never detected at all.

River Warblers are birds of eastern and central Europe, and found in such habitats as wooded swamps, marshes, bogs and willow scrub, not necessarily near water or rivers. They require very dense but low undergrowth, often including grasses and nettles, and this needs to be interspersed with bushes (often hazel) whose leaf layers are 0.5–1.5 m above ground, leaving bare ground underneath where the birds can forage. They thus occupy rather different habitats to Grasshopper and Savi's Warblers. In common with other *Locustella* warblers, though, River Warblers walk and creep around under cover, well hidden in their own mini-forest. They will also forage along streams and other watercourses.

The nest is typical for a *Locustella* warbler, a loose cup of dead leaves and grasses about 10 cm in diameter. It is well hidden on or near the ground in dense vegetation, and can usually be approached only along some 'tunnel' in the vegetation, like a secret spy hideaway.

adult

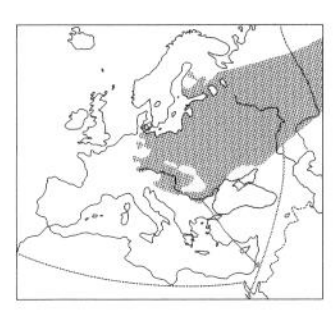

ID: Spiky bill, flattish head, curved outer edge to primaries and broad, heavy tail and with very long outer tail coverts. Easily distinguished from Grasshopper Warbler by mainly plain, unspotted plumage. Darker than Savi's Warbler, a sort of olive-brown, and usually shows some streaking on the throat and chest; also has pale tips to undertail coverts, giving spotted effect.

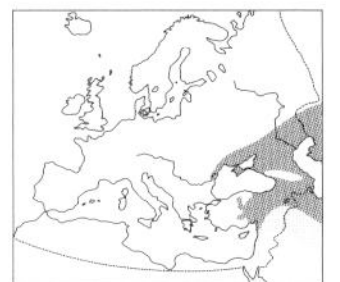

ID: *Small for an* Acrocephalus *warbler, with very short wings and long tail. Size, relatively short yellowish bill with black tip and pronounced supercilium recall a* Phylloscopus *warbler, but Paddyfield is warm brown with a reddish-brown rump.*

Paddyfield Warbler

Acrocephalus agricola

(ak-ro-**sef**-fal-luss pal-loo-**dik**-oh-la)

length 13 cm

The Paddyfield Warbler is really an Asian species reaching into Europe at the extreme western edge of its range. It replaces the Reed Warbler east of the Caspian Sea and is a common bird of waterside vegetation in the scattered marshlands of the Asian forest-steppe belt. It is often found by small lakes, and typically likes rather sparse, low vegetation beside thicker bushes, preferring such micro-habitats to those of unbroken reedbeds. Not surprisingly, given its name, it also occurs in rice fields. On its wintering grounds in India and Asia it is abundant in this habitat and, in the 1960s, having been a scarce and scattered species in the Ukraine, it spread to rice-growing areas and began to prosper.

In much of its behaviour the Paddyfield Warbler seems to be similar to the Reed Warbler; it builds, for example, a similar nest bound to vertical reed stems and placed over standing water. The nest is made up from grass stems, reed fibres and some reed flowers. The male's song also resembles that of the Reed Warbler, although it is somewhat more musical and fluent. But when performing the Paddyfield Warbler is a little more ostentatious, typically singing from the top of a reed in clear view.

Aquatic Warbler

Acrocephalus paludicola

(ak-ro-**sef**-fal-luss pal-loo-**dik**-oh-la)

length 13 cm

The Aquatic Warbler has an unusual mating system, which begins and ends with the act of copulation. Unusually for a small bird, this is considerably prolonged, lasting about 30 minutes instead of a few seconds. Once this has been achieved, the male contributes absolutely nothing to the rearing of the young, leaving this task entirely in the hands of the female – which is very unusual. Furthermore the female, it seems, habitually mates with more than one male; the six eggs from a normal clutch are sired by between two and five different fathers. Males usually attempt to copulate in the evening, when their chances of fertilising the egg to be laid the next morning are highest, but they do not always succeed.

Males advertise their presence by song, which is mainly delivered from a perch and, less often, during a song flight in which the bird lifts up to a height of 3 m to 30 m and then raises his fanned tail, causing a steep plummet. The male has at least two types of song: a short, blunt one used for territorial encounters with other males, and a longer, more complex one designed to impress the females.

This unique warbler is confined to eastern Europe and Russia, and breeds mainly in marshes dominated by clumps of sedge up to 80 cm tall, with water in between a few centimetres deep. The presence of willow bushes is also popular. Such habitats provide the female with sufficient insects and spiders to feed her young that the one-parent-family option can succeed. Despite large populations having been found recently in Belarus, the Aquatic Warbler is still Europe's rarest small migratory bird.

ID: *Buff stripe over top of crown and pronounced black and buff 'tramlines' down the back. Has pronounced supercilium and fine streaks on the flanks or even the chest. Tail has noticeably spiky tips.*

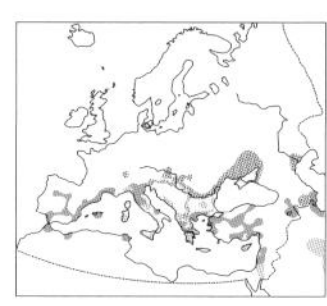

ID: *Typical* Acrocephalus *shape, with long bill and slightly raised crown. Plumper than Sedge Warbler, with shorter wings, slightly heavier tail, and darker crown on head. White throat contrasts with the brown breast and belly.*

Moustached Warbler

Acrocephalus melanopogon

(ak-ro-**sef**-fal-luss mel-lan-**noh**-poh-gon)

length 12–13 cm

This is a reedbed bird that is very choosy about its nest site. It always builds among the broken, fallen stems of last year's reed growth, rather than amidst the new stuff. This confines it to older, denser stands of reeds, but frees it from depending on any new growth to support its nest. It is therefore able to begin breeding much earlier in the year than, say, a Reed Warbler or Great Reed Warbler, with some pairs laying eggs before the end of March.

In many parts of its range, it is also one of the few warblers not to be migratory. It can stay put because it is specially adapted to pick very small items from the surface of leaves and stems, the sort that remain available all year but carry little interest for its competitors. Its large feet, with long claws, make it nimble in its foraging, allowing it to hold on to vertical and horizontal stems alike and to reach into nooks and crannies unavailable to many other birds. It feeds mainly on insects (frequently beetles), and about 20 per cent of all its food is grabbed from below the water surface.

The male Moustached Warbler has the usual lively song typical of its close relatives, but before entering into the usual chatter the bird repeats several pure notes in sequence, a prologue quite similar to the throbbing 'pu-pu-pu…' crescendo heard from the Nightingale. This distinctive sound can be heard almost throughout the year, even in winter, when the reedbeds are otherwise mostly silent.

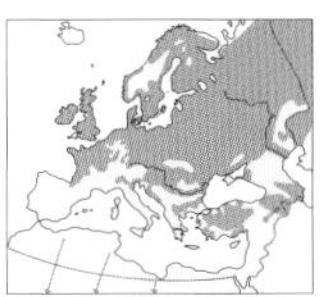

ID: *About Reed Warbler size with similar long bill, sloping forehead and longish, narrow tail. Has pronounced broad supercilium above narrow dark eye stripe, and faint dark streaks on back (more pronounced on Moustached and much more on Aquatic).*

Sedge Warbler

Acrocephalus schoenobaenus

(ak-ro-**sef**-fal-luss shoo-noh-**bee**-nuss)

length 13 cm

There are not many patches of damp marshy vegetation in Europe that lack breeding Sedge Warblers, except those around the Mediterranean, where this species is replaced by the much more localised Moustached Warbler. The Sedge is a common and widespread bird, the only member of its genus to occur well up into the Arctic Circle. Besides its climatic advantage it is less choosy in habitat than the rest, not confined to reedbeds or the margins of water, but also found in quite dry, scrubby habitats with scattered trees. It does not tend to build its nest over water, but instead hides it away in thick vegetation within 50 cm of the ground.

The lively song of the Sedge Warbler is a rambling paragraph of fast, harsh notes, characteristically dispensing with the Reed Warbler's rhythmic pattern in favour of passages that speed up or slow down at will. The song often contains a good deal of mimicry, and when the singer wishes to produce maximum effect it will launch into a short, up-and-down song flight. Recently it has been shown that the prevalence of these song flights is a good indicator of health: the bird that indulges in plenty of aerial songs tends to carry a lower parasite load than a more perch-bound individual.

Within a complex song like that of the Sedge Warbler there is plenty of room for variation, and it was from studies of this bird that scientists were able to prove for the first time that, at least in some species, females preferred to pair with males with a wider singing repertoire. Using birds in captivity, they showed that female Sedge Warblers performed more sexual displays when played recordings of birds with good songs than for those with less varied songs. Furthermore, additional experiments have shown that a male with a better repertoire is also a better provider, bringing food to the chicks more often than a less inventive male.

The Sedge Warbler forages mainly in the lower stratum of vegetation and specialises on taking slow-moving or stationary prey, shunning the faster-moving insects chased by the Reed Warbler. It tends to feed most at dusk and dawn, when insects are slow paced because of the low temperature. It catches most by simply picking them from the surfaces of leaves or twigs, but is not averse to the odd spot of leap-catching, nabbing a flying insect while moving between perches.

In the autumn Sedge Warblers suddenly feast themselves upon an unusual food fad – aphids. These seem to have a special ingredient that helps the birds fatten up prior to their migration to West Africa; they manage to do this journey in a single flight lasting three days and three nights, covering 4000 km in all.

ID: *Very similar to Reed and Marsh Warblers, so best distinguished by song and habitat. Bill is longer than Marsh's and shorter than Reed's. Supercilium reaches behind eye and more obviously pale. Slightly greyer wash on underparts, and darker legs.*

Blyth's Reed Warbler

Acrocephalus dumetorum

(ak-ro-**sef**-fal-luss doo-mee-**toh**-rum)

length 13 cm

This mainly Asian species is unusual for an *Acrocephalus* warbler in several respects. It is not confined to marshy or swampy vegetation, as most of them are, but occurs even in clearings among woods and in bushy areas far from water. Nor does it keep low down when foraging, as most of them do, but is instead perfectly at home in the tops of small trees. And it has a most unusual song: a clear, relatively slow, very musical number which has echoes of the Song Thrush's performance, with that same clarity and including the same insistent, lucid repetitions.

It is not, though, a familiar bird to most Europeans, breeding mainly in Russia, the Baltic States and Finland. It arrived in the latter only in the 1930s, having spread from further east, and it continues to make progress, having recently reached Sweden, where it breeds annually. But Europe is on the edge of its range and, at the end of the breeding season, our migrants fly to Pakistan and India for the winter, rather than to Africa.

Birds arrive in mid to late May and the males immediately start singing, by day and by night. They choose higher perches than most of their relatives, including the very tops of bushes and even overhead wires. When a female approaches a male in his territory she gives a call as a cue, and he immediately launches into an excited song flight, taking him up and down, with his body angled almost vertically, to land close to where the female has just perched. This exuberant display is typical of this uncharacteristically showy species.

Marsh Warbler

Acrocephalus palustris

(ak-ro-**sef**-fal-luss pal-**lus**-triss)

length 13 cm

Few birds take to migrating as enthusiastically as the Marsh Warbler, a bird that is 'on the road' for at least half the year. It arrives on its European breeding grounds later than most migrants, in late May or even June, and is one of the first to leave. The vanguard migrates south in July and all have left us by the end of August. The breeding season is squashed into a couple of short months. Pity the poor youngsters, then, who have to migrate within three weeks of leaving the nest. Completing their juvenile development and preparing for migration in that ludicrously short time must be quite a strain on their biochemistry.

All Marsh Warblers leave Europe by the southeasterly exit, passing through the eastern Mediterranean and down the Arabian Peninsula, eventually crossing into Africa and settling for some time in Ethiopia and the Sudan. They then continue south, and some may turn up in the southern half of Africa in November and December, only to veer north again a couple of months later. The Marsh Warbler's is one of the longest of all European songbird migrations.

The travellers don't waste their time on the road: they learn songs. The Marsh Warbler is outstanding among warblers, and among European birds generally, in constructing a song that is almost entirely mimetic. It has its own character all right – chatty, lively, sweet and silvery – and is always thoroughly recognisable as a Marsh Warbler, but it is unquestionably the sum of many parts. The bird learns snatches of material both in Europe, where it grows up, and in Africa, where it soon arrives. The average individual copies from 45 African and 31 European species, making for quite a cross-cultural mix!

This is a bird of rank, wet places. It is not a reedbed bird, like the Reed Warbler, nor can it abandon marshy areas at will, as the Blyth's Reed Warbler can. Its niche lies somewhere between the two. Ideal habitat consists of tufty vegetation 1 m or so tall, typically incorporating nettles, meadowsweet and willowherbs. A few patches of reed within the mix are appreciated, too.

The nest is built part way up some close-knit plant stems, as is the nest of a Reed Warbler. The work of a Marsh Warbler can easily be recognised, though, by the rim extending around the outer edge of the supporting stems to give the appearance of 'handles'.

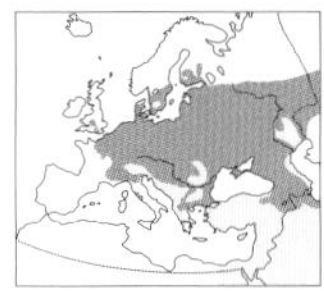

ID: Frighteningly similar to Reed and Blyth's Reed Warblers, but has slightly shorter and thicker bill and head is slightly more rounded. Wing is longer than Blyth's Reed Warbler and, in comparison to Reed Warbler, the pale tips to the primaries are more crisply marked. Slightly colder in colour than Reed Warbler, lacking contrast between back and rump. Legs pink.

adult

Reed Warbler

Acrocephalus scirpaceus

(ak-ro-**sef**-fal-luss sir-**pay**-see-uss)

length 13 cm

Some birds are very much associated with a particular habitat, and the Reed Warbler is very strongly attracted to reedbeds. These may be almost any size, from vast swathes beside shallow lakes to tiny waterside patches of only 1 sq m or so in extent. Within this habitat it particularly likes the plants to be at least 120 cm high and growing at a minimum density of 40 stems per square metre. This will enable the Reed Warbler to build its well-crafted nest, which is a cup suspended around an average of 3.5 stems and placed c.50 cm above the water surface.

For foraging, the Reed Warbler is somewhat less skulking than many of its close relatives, or at least it feeds more out in the open than they do. While most other warblers feed near the base, the Reed Warbler forages about in the middle levels of plant growth, and often catches its prey in flight. Two of its favourite methods are 'leap-picking', in which it jumps or flits from one stem to the other to catch an insect it has seen from a distance, and 'leap-catching', in which it catches a flying insect in mid-air as it swaps perches. The method used often varies throughout the day. At first light, when it is chilly, Reed Warblers tend to pick insects from the surface of the vegetation, since the prey is still sluggish. In the middle of the day, however, with the insects warmed up and ready to fly at a moment's notice, the birds resort to more active methods.

The Reed Warbler's song is characterised by being highly rhythmic, a series of chirpy phrases uttered in a dancing tempo that remains fairly constant. The average male has two or three favourite perches on which to sing; these may be low and screened by the reed tops, for delivery of the territorial song, or sung from a higher clump, in which case they are advertising songs aimed to be picked up by females. An unpaired male may sing for 8–12 hours a day although, in contrast to many similar warblers, things usually quieten down at night. Once paired, a bird will usually sing much less frequently. However, throughout the season, males in an area often indulge in so-called 'social singing', a brief communal burst at dawn and dusk.

Perhaps because of their restricted habitat, Reed Warblers are usually found in clusters of pairs, almost in a colony. Within this area each couple occupies an area of about 330 sq m, which is about one-sixth of the territory size of the Sedge Warbler.

Reed Warblers arrive relatively late in Europe, usually reoccupying their breeding areas from the second half of April onwards. They leave again from mid-July and winter in Africa south of the Sahara. Once there they leave behind their close attachment to reeds and may be found in all sorts of bushy areas.

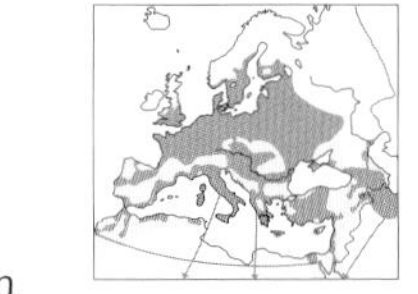

ID: Shares characteristic long bill and sloping forehead of all Acrocephalus *warblers, but is the 'longest-nosed'. Mainly plain brown above with warmer colour on rump (see Marsh); and pale buff below. Pale supercilium ill-defined and does not noticeably stretch behind eye (see Blyth's Reed). Legs greyish.*

adult

Great Reed Warbler

Acrocephalus arundinaceus
(ak-ro-**sef**-fal-luss ar-run-din-**nay**-see-uss)
length 19–20 cm

The Great Reed Warbler is the largest of the warblers, almost as big as a Song Thrush. It clambers about the reeds in a clumsier manner than the smaller reed-haunting species, with heavy hops and slow movements, and it also has a tendency to crash-land somewhat after a short flight. When a Great Reed Warbler is moving about, the reed tops shake, giving the bird's presence away.

It has the most extraordinary song, a powerful, rhythmic and yet fitful series of croaking and grinding sounds, with high and low notes often juxtaposed so that the voice appears to be breaking like that of a human adolescent. The song is loud, but not very pleasing to our ears, yet it is an extremely important factor in how female Great Reed Warblers choose their mates. Some males have better repertoires than others, and it is these that are the most desirable. Many Great Reed Warblers live as monogamous pairs, but cuckoldry is common. The females invariably seek out extra-pair copulations with males with a higher vocal repertoire, and it has been shown that the nestlings produced by such clandestine pairings tend to have a better survival rate than their half-siblings.

Many of the more desirable males acquire more than one mate. If this happens there tends to be a difference in social status between the females, with the individual that paired first being of higher rank than the later-acquired 'mistresses'. Normally it is only the primary female that can expect assistance from the male in feeding the nestlings; the others must raise their broods alone. Intriguingly, though, evidence has recently emerged that some females of lower rank might actually prick the eggs of the primary female to ensure that they don't hatch, ensuring that the male's attention turns to them instead.

The Great Reed Warbler is quite selective in its habitat, being drawn mainly to tall, thick-stemmed reeds above shallow water. More specifically, it likes the reeds to be at least two years old and with an average stem diameter of at least 6.5 mm. Moreover, these stems should be not too densely packed, showing a range of only 34–62 stems per square metre. Despite being so fussy, the Great Reed Warbler is a common marshland bird, especially in eastern Europe.

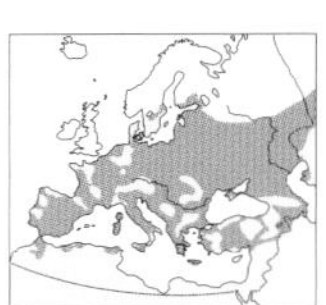

ID: Quite easily distinguished from other plain Acrocephalus *warblers by having similar colour and shape, but by being much larger – almost as big as a Song Thrush. Bill is also much heavier than the rest. Has broad buff, slightly messy supercilium, mainly in front of eye.*

adult

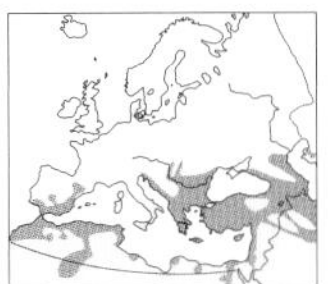

ID: Small (eastern) or medium-sized (western) warbler that looks more like a Reed Warbler than another Hippolais*. Has habit of constantly flicking tail downwards. Shares long bill and sloping forehead with Reed, but has cleanly square-ended tail with white outer feathers. Also lacks any warm brown tones on plumage, and especially lacks russet on rump.*

adult

Olivaceous Warbler

Hippolais [pallida] (hip-poh-**lay**-iss **pal**-lid-da)
length 12–13.5 cm

The Olivaceous Warbler has been setting taxonomists' hearts a-flutter recently, with the revelation that the populations of Iberia on the one hand and southeast Europe on the other are almost certainly genetically distinct enough to be considered as separate species. The two forms are slightly different structurally, with the Western Olivaceous Warbler (*Hippolais opaca*) being larger than the Eastern Olivaceous Warbler (*Hippolais pallida*) and also possessing a bigger, broader bill. The rival populations occupy slightly different habitats, too, with the western form confined to dry sites with trees and the eastern having a broader habitat range, encompassing both wet areas and bushy places without trees. The populations are both migratory, but one winters in the western Sahel region and the other in the eastern Sahel.

This is a restless bird that tends to forage in the canopy of trees and bushes well above ground. It will pick insects from the surface of leaves and twigs, and will commonly flit from perch to perch, snaring an aerial insect en route. It will also drop down to collect items that have fallen to the ground. Whatever it is doing, every few moments it will enact a quick down-flick of the tail, its trademark quirk. In another habit, an Olivaceous Warbler often sings as it moves about, much as we might hum when we are busy and absorbed.

These are late migrants over their range, the first birds appearing at the end of April and the last not settling down until June. In common with the other *Hippolais* warblers, Olivaceous Warblers habitually form neighbourhood groups of pairs that nest at high density. The males, though, are still very territorial, and will sing at each other and fight where necessary in defence of their patch. Proximity does not necessarily breed amity. The males' babbling songs may be heard right through into late summer, long after other species have fallen silent.

Icterine Warbler

Hippolais icterina (hip-poh-**lay**-iss ik-ter-**rie**-na)
length 13.5 cm

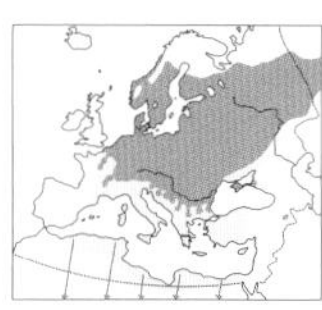

ID: *Medium-sized warbler with typical* Hippolais *profile – long, broad bill, sloping forehead and 'blank' expression caused by pale lores. One of two similar bright yellowish* Hippolais, *but larger and longer-billed than Melodious Warbler, with pale edges to secondaries and tertials producing relatively conspicuous wing panel. Also has longer wings and blue-grey legs.*

The marvellously manic song of the Icterine Warbler may be heard locally over a large part of Europe, including most of the centre and up to the fringes of the Arctic, mainly along woodland edges where the vegetation is well lit and the undergrowth copious. In the southwest, however, this species is replaced by the very closely related Melodious Warbler and the battle lines between the two run down through northern and eastern France and along the southern edge of Switzerland and Austria. In at least some places where the two occur together, breeding success is apparently impaired, so where one species replaces the other, the transition tends to be total.

This is a restless bird that moves around rapidly in the foliage of trees, often snapping up insects as it flits from perch to perch. The name *icterina* translates as 'jaundiced', and its yellow coloration often invites comparison with the Willow Warbler, which often occurs alongside. In contrast to that dapper, fast-moving bird, however, the actions of the Icterine Warbler are just that little bit clumsy, with the odd inelegant landing and a habit of stretching forwards slightly awkwardly to pick up an insect. In the autumn these birds eat quite a few berries, and their upward lean and downward tug to pluck these fruits form another distinctive habit.

Icterine Warblers are aggressive on arrival at their breeding grounds. The males sing loudly and often fight, fluttering upwards face to face and sometimes tumbling to the ground. They also have a special flight display when faced by an opponent; known as the 'butterfly flight', it consists of a simple horizontal transfer from one perch to another with the wings beating especially fast. The birds also snap their bills when angry. Sometimes, in fits of aggression, they may chase completely unrelated birds away as well.

The females make an unusual nest that is typical of the genus *Hippolais*. It is a very neat cup placed on a fork, well above ground, sometimes high in a tree; the branches of a fruit tree are a favourite site. The nest is woven onto the supporting sides of the fork, using bark fibres, plant down and spiders' webs, and it may be decorated on the outside with more bark or even with such incongruous materials as paper or rags.

adult spring   adult autumn

Olive-tree Warbler

Hippolais olivetorum
(hip-poh-**lay**-iss oh-liv-**vee**-toh-rum)
length 15 cm

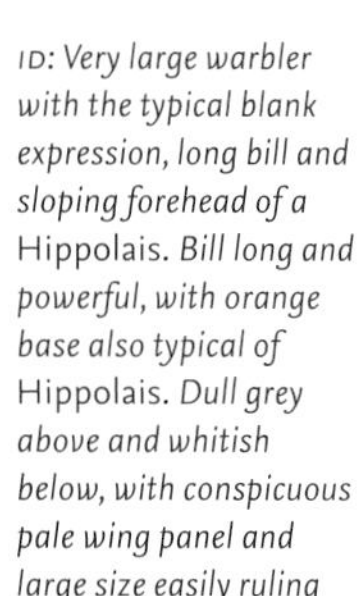

ID: *Very large warbler with the typical blank expression, long bill and sloping forehead of a* Hippolais. *Bill long and powerful, with orange base also typical of* Hippolais. *Dull grey above and whitish below, with conspicuous pale wing panel and large size easily ruling out Olivaceous Warbler. Very long, pointed wings with white outer feathers.*

The entire world population of the Olive-tree Warbler is found in southeast Europe and Turkey. It adds up to no more than 25,000 pairs in all, of which about half are in our area. This bird is a migrant, arriving on its breeding grounds in May and departing between July and September, to spend the winter in a surprisingly wide area of Africa from the tropical east to the south. Breeding birds are found on dry, often stony hillsides covered with bushes and trees, the latter normally being important. In Bulgaria, though, where the population is expanding northwards, it also occurs in scrubby areas without trees. Throughout its European range the Olive-tree Warbler sticks largely to coastal areas and is often found on offshore islands.

One of the more secretive of the *Hippolais* warblers, the Olive-tree tends to keep out of sight. This doesn't mean, though, that it skulks in the undergrowth. Far from it – it is comfortable foraging in the canopy of trees such as oaks and olives (of course), and it may also sing from a high perch. It is presumed to feed largely on insects and spiders, and in autumn has been recorded eating figs, which is no doubt indicative of a wider habit of taking fruit before migration.

The song of the Olive-tree Warbler is deeper and slower than that of the other *Hippolais*, and on its day can almost resemble the lurching, retching feel of the Great Reed Warbler's output. The song is often heard in the middle of the night, as well as by day.

adult

ID: *The smallest* Hippolais, *with buttery-yellow plumage that might recall a* Phylloscopus *but, like all members of this genus, has a 'blank' expression owing to its pale lores. Usually easily distinguished from similarly plumaged Icterine Warbler by shorter bill and shorter wings, by lack of pale wing panel and by brownish, not grey legs.*

Melodious Warbler

Hippolais polyglotta (hip-poh-**lay**-iss pol-li-**glot**-ta)
length 13 cm

This species is smaller and shyer than its irrepressible close relative, the Icterine Warbler, tending to feed more quietly in the canopy of bushes and trees. That does not, however, mean that it is a shrinking violet; far from it – this bird is on the march. From its stronghold in the southwest of Europe it is expanding northwards, having begun its spread in the 1950s from central France to encompass the Netherlands (one pair) by 1990. Characteristic of this spread have been remarkable takeovers: in Belgium, for instance, the Melodious Warbler increased from 17 pairs in 1983 to about 100 in 1995; and in Germany it exploded in the area of Saarland from a single pair in 1984 to 100 or more the very next year.

This is a bird of warm climates, occurring in bushy areas and on the edges of woodlands. It requires at least some trees within its territory, and it does not like small, isolated patches of vegetation. In France it is characteristic of sites that are in the process of regenerating after being cut down, whereas in its heartland of Iberia it is rather more flexible and widespread, occurring in all sorts of scrubby areas.

The scientific name *polyglotta* is appropriate because, within its highly distinctive song, the Melodious Warbler incorporates some excellent mimicry copied from local birds. These imitations are often included in the first section of its two-part song, an introductory series of repeated motifs that then lead into a much faster series of babbling notes. There appears to be considerable variation in the males' song repertoire. Some enter into the second section with polished gusto, whereas other, lazier types leave out the second half altogether. In some parts of its range the Melodious Warbler is noted for singing in the middle of the day, when other species are silent in the heat.

In common with other *Hippolais* warblers the Melodious often nests in neighbourhood groups, with clusters of pairs occupying one part of a site while the other is left vacant. Such togetherness is not a sign of peace, however, as male Melodious Warblers are just as aggressive in defence of their territory as any other small bird.

Marmora's Warbler

Sylvia [sarda] (**sil**-vi-a **sard**-da)
length 12 cm

Of all the *Sylvia* warblers, this one spends its time in the lowest scrub and feeds closest to the ground. This preference for foraging close to the ground or on the ground itself, together with their liking for more uniform types of low scrub than those occupied by other warblers, keeps them separate from competitors such as Sardinian Warblers, Dartford Warblers or even Stonechats.

Recent studies on this bird have shown conclusively, and excitingly, that it isn't a single species, but two. Birds on the Balearic Islands are smaller and longer-tailed than those on Corsica and Sardinia, and the males have whiter throats. Tellingly, birds of each population have different contact calls and fail to respond aggressively to recordings of the other species' songs, which means that they do not understand each other's 'language'. This would act as an isolating mechanism preventing the two species hybridising – strong evidence that they are separate entities.

The Balearic Warbler (*Sylvia balearica*), which occurs on all its namesake islands except Menorca, breeds in *Cistus* or *Erica* scrub less than 2 m tall, and most populations are resident, with at least some birds maintaining pair bond and territory all year round. Marmora's Warblers (*Sylvia sarda*) of Corsica and Sardinia occur in similar habitat up to an altitude of 1800 m.

ID: *Very small warbler with a long tail that is cocked upwards, Wren-like. Coral-red eye ring; red base to bill. Only likely to be confused with similarly shaped Dartford Warbler, but plumage is grey all over, without wine-red underparts.*

Dartford Warbler

Sylvia undata (**sil**-vi-a un-**day**-ta)
length 12.5 cm

Most of the small, sun-loving, scrub-loving *Sylvia* warblers are confined to the Mediterranean region, but the Dartford Warbler is an exception. Alone among its near relatives it has broken away from the climatic norm and also colonised the temperate zone of northwest Europe as far as Britain, aided by the ameliorating effects of the Atlantic Ocean. And it doesn't just flirt with this climate; it sticks it out even in the cold, damp days of mid-winter, when it ekes out a living by foraging in dense heath and keeping its head down. The majority of Dartford Warblers are therefore resident and remain resolutely in their territory throughout the year. Only extended periods of snow cover or sharp frost can displace them or wipe them out.

One of the Dartford Warbler's strategies for surviving poor weather would appear to be communal roosting, a habit not seen among any other *Sylvia* warblers. There are several records of six to eight birds sleeping in the same bush at night, and even sharing their site with two other small-bodied species, Wrens and Goldcrests.

The Dartford Warbler's case is also no doubt helped by the fact that not many other birds choose to skulk in uniform low, thick, heathy vegetation in winter, so it has little competition. In these well-sheltered thickets it feeds almost exclusively on arthropods, including insects and spiders, picking them off vegetation at a height of 50 cm–2 m above the ground. It rarely ventures onto the ground itself, in contrast to, say, the Marmora's Warbler, and it rarely feeds in trees, although it will readily accept small trees in its territory, as singing perches, for example.

Stability seems to be a feature for this species. As well as living in the same territory all year round, birds also, where possible, remain with their mates from year to year and throughout the year (in France, about 16 per cent were able to do this, a high figure given the inevitably high mortality for such a small bird). The only time they have to move is when, as youngsters, they disperse from their natal areas; some individuals undoubtedly migrate considerable distances, but in the main they tend to settle only a few kilometres from where they were born.

The Dartford Warbler is a productive species. Even on the northern fringes of its range it can fit in three broods a year, with the first clutch (in April or May) averaging four eggs and later clutches five. Both birds feed the young but, because the male does not have a brood patch, the female performs the lion's share (75 per cent) of incubation duties. Nest building is shared, but the male may build several incomplete structures as part of his mate-attraction routine.

ID: A very small, dark, Wren-sized warbler with longer tail than any other European species; tail often held raised. Red eye. Upperparts brown-grey, underparts red-wine coloured; male also shows white spots on throat. Female has whitish throat, duller underparts and slightly brown-tinged back.

Spectacled Warbler

Sylvia conspicillata (**sil**-vi-a kon-spiss-sil-**lay**-ta)
length 12.5 cm

If any bird demonstrates an uncanny ability to disappear into the sparsest of cover and remain unseen, it is the Spectacled Warbler. Its habitat encompasses lower (1 m tall or so), more open, broken-up vegetation than that utilised by other *Sylvia* warblers, but this does not make it any less skulking. Indeed, its impoverished habitat, lacking any of those sumptuous, thick bushes in which to hide that are beloved, for example, by the Sardinian Warbler, simply underlines its ability to keep out of sight. It often feeds on or close to the ground, under the shade of vegetation and, in contrast to many other warblers, it rarely if ever leaps into the air in pursuit of flying insects.

The Spectacled Warbler is a bird of warm or very warm areas, including those that could be described as arid – in some places, in fact, it will occur in salt flats and semi-desert. In most of its European range it is a summer visitor, but in contrast to some close relatives it does not go far in winter, only to the northern fringes of the Sahara down to Mauritania.

The male has a short song which is quite sweet and polished, certainly easier on the ear than the scratchy, strained efforts of Sardinian or Dartford Warblers. He sings all year round, but especially between February and May, when he will even perform in a brief, dancing song flight like that of a Whitethroat. In spring some males are such vigorous vocalists that they will even sing while being held in the hand prior to ringing!

Spectacled Warblers lay eggs with an unusual greenish hue, quite different to those of other *Sylvia* warblers. These are placed in a well-built cup-nest in a bush or matted grass up to 70 cm above ground.

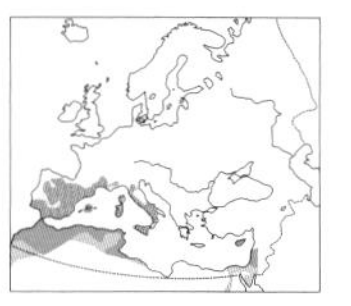

ID: Small warbler of low vegetation, very like Whitethroat, but smaller with a finer bill and shorter wing tips. Male distinguished from male Whitethroat by darker pink breast and darker grey head, especially between eye and bill (accentuating white eye ring). Female distinguished from female Whitethroat by more uniform chestnut brown wing, with fewer dark centres to tertials or secondaries (this difference shared with males).

Sardinian Warbler

Sylvia melanocephala
(**sil**-vi-a mel-lan-noh-**sef**-fa-la)
length 13.5 cm

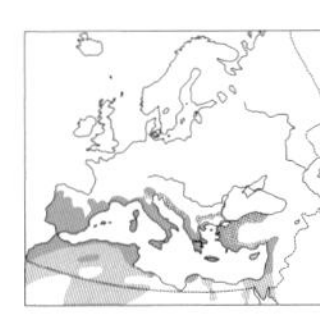

ID: Common slim Mediterranean warbler with comparatively large head, short wing tips and long tail. Male has smart black head and white throat, plus flame-red eye ring; otherwise mainly grey. Female has dark-grey rather than black head and has brown rather than grey body plumage, but shares male's white throat and red eye ring. Female easily distinguished from Whitethroat or Spectacled Warbler by lack of rich chestnut colour on wings.

A loud burst of sound like the fast shaking of a child's rattle often announces the presence of what is generally the most abundant of the small, scrub-loving Mediterranean *Sylvia* warblers. The Sardinian Warbler is a familiar garden bird in parts of southern Europe and, by being the most adaptable of any of its close relatives, has been known to share space with seven other *Sylvia* species throughout its wide range in all their different niches. For example, it can occur in low scrub less than 1 m high, as occupied by the Spectacled Warbler, yet also share the same habitat as the wood-haunting Blackcap, feeding up in the crowns of trees. Its only real requirement seems to be that the bushes in its many habitat types should be relatively thick, so that it can hide away.

The majority of European Sardinian Warblers are non-migratory and occupy their territories year round. Those individuals that do migrate tend not to go very far and the species as a whole shows little tendency to deposit fat for fuel. Captive birds also exhibit limited migration restlessness – the 'energy' that drives migrating birds – in the autumn, confirming their largely sedentary character.

In common with other *Sylvia* warblers, the Sardinian feeds mainly on insects and other arthropods, gathering these directly from the vegetation by picking, normally working in private beneath the canopy. While foraging in such places it also takes a great deal of fruit, especially in the autumn and winter, with olives apparently being one of its favourites, although a good number of berries are also eaten – it will even occasionally feed berries to its young. In addition, at times when fruit or insects are scarce, it will drink nectar from flowers.

From late January onwards resident males begin to utter their fast, warbling song phrases to confirm their ownership of a territory. Although the song is hurried and not particularly rich to the ear, the phrases are highly varied and, on average, a male has 84 different notes in his repertoire. In one study each song lasted on average 3.8 seconds and was separated from the last by a pause averaging 4 seconds, but this may vary according to season and the stage in the nesting cycle. The male usually chooses an elevated perch from which to sing, but if a territorial dispute is ongoing he will often sing in flight as well, lifting 4 m or so into the air and then gliding down with wings held up. Once the breeding season is over the song declines markedly, but then, in September, it has a brief resurgence as the territorial pack reshuffles in time for the winter.

Subalpine Warbler

Sylvia cantillans (**sil**-vi-a **kan**-til-lanz)
length 12 cm

The Mediterranean scrubland is full of closely related, colourful, perky warblers, but each of them has its own niche, slightly different from that of the rest. For its part the Subalpine Warbler is found in higher, more luxuriant, more typically evergreen scrub (1–4 m high) than most of the others and, in contrast to Marmora's, Dartford and Spectacled Warblers in particular, it thrives in the presence of scattered trees such as oaks, where it often feeds up in the crowns, well above the normal sphere of operation of the other species. The Subalpine Warbler also has a fondness for thick scrub along streams in valleys and, as its English name implies, it often breeds at higher altitudes than other *Sylvias* – up to 1500 m in Spain and Greece.

These birds begin their migration unusually early, in mid-July, when some populations make significant short-distance movements to places rich in food. Here they may remain for up to three weeks, fuelling themselves for the next, longer stage that may take them right over the Mediterranean and perhaps beyond. When preparing for migration, Subalpine Warblers eat large amounts of fruit, including small berries that they can swallow easily and bigger fruits, such as figs, that they simply pick at. This fruit, combined with some insects to provide essential amino acids, nourishes them until they reach the southern edge of the Sahara, where they spend the winter.

Upon their return in April, males defend their territories by vigorous singing, often launching into the air on a short, up-and-down song flight. During courtship the males build several incomplete nest structures which, curiously, seem to be largely ignored by the female. Instead, both sexes work on the official nest, a cup built of dry grass and leaves and placed up to 1.3 m above ground (high for a Mediterranean *Sylvia* warbler).

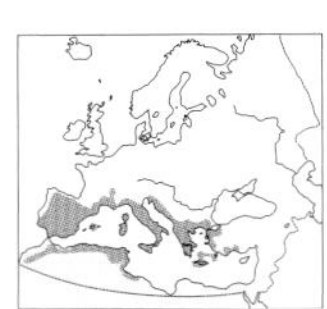

ID: Small, slim warbler with fairly long tail and red eye ring. Male easily distinguished from Whitethroat by reddish underparts and white moustache. Female a washed-out version, with pink underparts and only a hint of a moustache; bluish-grey on head, with white eye ring.

Orphean Warbler

Sylvia [hortensis] (**sil**-vi-a hor-**ten**-siss)
length 15 cm

The Orphean Warbler's visit to its breeding grounds in Mediterranean Europe is astonishingly short. The first birds arrive in mid-April, which is by no means early for a spring migrant, and major departures begin in July, making this one of the very first bird species to leave Europe in the autumn. The whole population, both adults and youngsters, then makes its way down to the sub-Saharan Sahel region from Senegal to Yemen, where the birds spend a long winter.

The Orphean Warbler is a large but elusive species, breeding at lower density than most other warblers, with each pair having a relatively large territory at least 200 m away from their nearest neighbours. In fact the birds are as likely to breed near Woodchat Shrikes as other Orphean Warblers; in southern France (and perhaps elsewhere) there is a clear association between the two, parallel to that between the Barred Warbler and the Red-backed Shrike. The two species often breed in the same bush, and the warbler often forages close to the shrike, presumably taking advantage of the latter's vigilance while feeding.

In contrast to most other Mediterranean *Sylvia* warblers, the Orphean prefers tall bushes and trees to lower vegetation. It occurs in warm, dry, open woodland made up from broad-leaved trees, and it spends most of its time in the canopy, picking insects from leaves in a slower, more deliberate way than the smaller, hyperactive *Sylvias*.

Recent research has confirmed that what we know as the Orphean Warbler is in fact two closely related species, one occurring in southwest Europe as far east as Italy (Western Orphean Warbler *Sylvia hortensis*) and the other from Slovenia eastwards (Eastern Orphean Warbler *Sylvia crassirostris*). The two species winter in different places, they have quite different songs (that of the eastern bird is much richer, almost like a Nightingale's), and the eastern form also has a longer bill – possibly an adaptation for feeding among *Acacia* thickets in the winter. They do, however, look almost identical, masking what has been revealed in the laboratory as a considerable genetic difference.

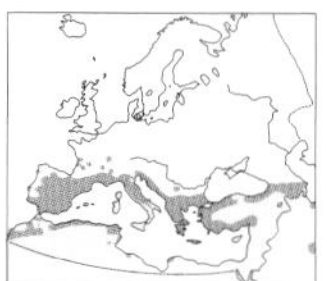

ID: Unique combination of black head and white throat with pale staring eye. Large tree-haunting warbler with pale (often white, sometimes tinged pink) underparts and grey upperparts. Female similar to male, but slightly browner on the back. Black on head may be most intense on ear coverts.

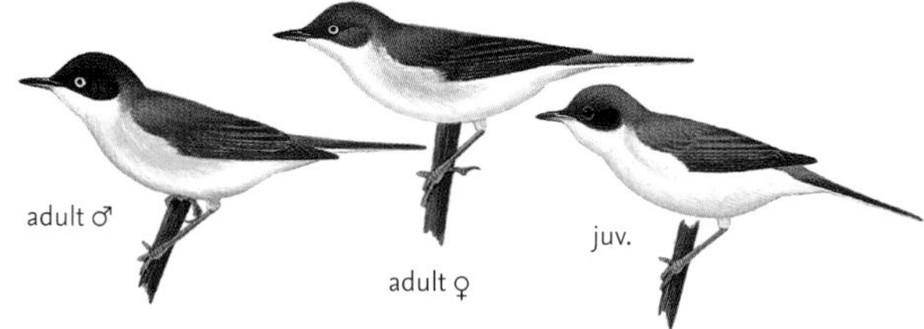

Barred Warbler

Sylvia nisoria (**sil**-vi-a nie-**soh**-ri-a)
length 15.5 cm

When Barred Warblers arrive on their central European breeding grounds in the late spring, they seek out a suitable place to nest. There is nothing unusual about this – they pick a thick, thorny bush like many a warbler – except that, in 85–93 per cent of cases in the western part of the range, the site is very close to that occupied by a quite unrelated bird, the Red-backed Shrike, often in the same clump of bushes. The relationship extends to the two having similar timings to their respective breeding seasons, and to the female Barred Warbler looking remarkably like the female Red-backed Shrike, as if one were a fashion icon and the other a follower. It appears that the two species benefit from each other's vigilance to the presence of predators, while the Barred Warbler no doubt also profits from the shrike, itself a predatory bird, being particularly aggressive in defence of its nest. At least one study has shown that shrike-groupie Barred Warblers have a higher rate of breeding success than birds that breed on their own.

A smaller bird than the Barred Warbler would probably find itself threatened by a shrike, but this is the largest of the *Sylvia* species and it can hold its own. It is also one of the most skulking, feeding under cover of vegetation. With its relatively heavy bill the Barred Warbler takes larger, more solidly built insects than many other warblers, including crickets and beetles. In the autumn it also takes large quantities of fruit.

Male Barred Warblers have a song that is very similar to that of the Garden Warbler, although with shorter phrases. The song is sometimes given in a brief song flight, in which the bird either loops over a bush or flies from one bush to another, progressing with slow, very full wingbeats and fanning his tail to reveal its white sides. Unsurprisingly, the song often contains mimicry of the Red-backed Shrike.

Males build several incomplete nest platforms and show them off to visiting females as part of their courtship routine. Females probably use these platforms to assess a male's quality (or that of his territory), because, once pairing has taken place, they are partially dismantled to provide material for the breeding nest. Once the female is incubating, two-thirds of males then occupy another territory and attempt to mate with another female. If this happens successfully, the male will return to his primary mate as soon as his second mate is incubating; the latter will then have to rear her young alone. In another twist to this bird's breeding biology, some pairs are helped at the nest by year-old males that are not yet ready for breeding.

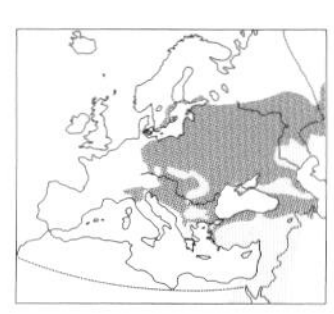

ID: Large sluggish warbler with diagnostic black bars across white underparts, like a miniature Cuckoo (less obvious and more diffuse in female). Male has staring yellow eye, brown in female. Both sexes have a double white wing bar and spots on the end of the tail.

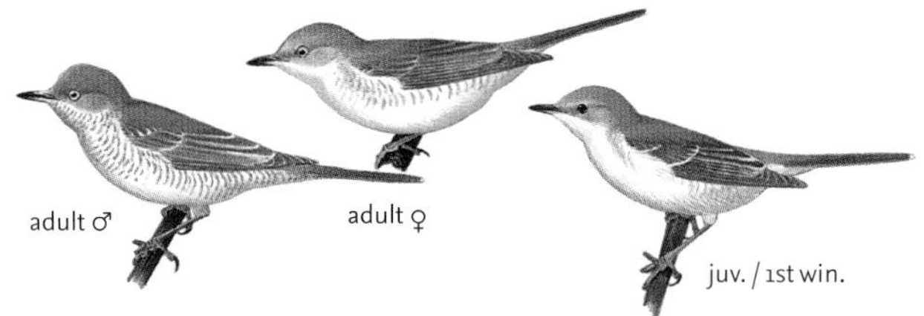

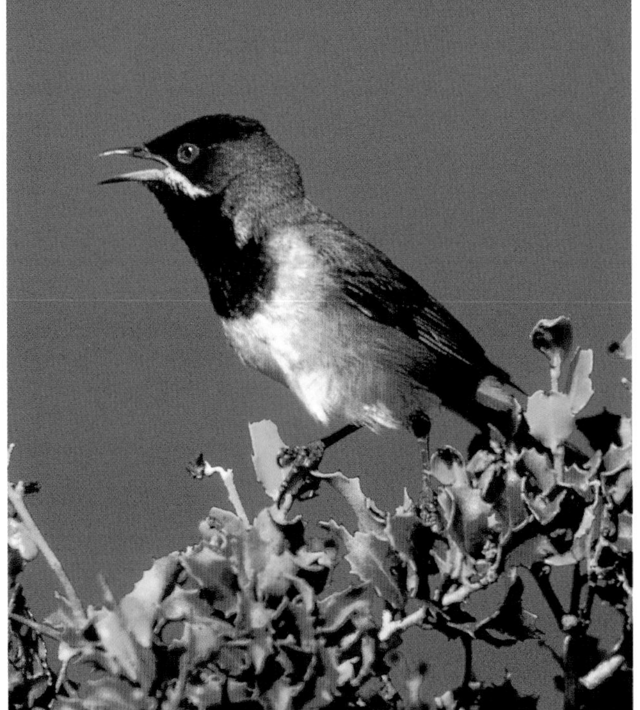

Rüppell's Warbler

Sylvia rueppelli (**sil**-vi-a roo-ep-**pel**-lie)
length 14 cm

In the small southeastern corner of Europe where the Rüppell's Warbler occurs, it is one of the very earliest migrants to arrive in the spring. Some males turn up in the first week of March and the rest come before the end of the month, setting up their territories by means of vigorous singing and a zigzagging song flight. The females arrive about ten days after the males, amidst this burst of territorial activity.

The Rüppell's Warbler is a member of the Mediterranean scrub-loving *Sylvia* group, overlapping with, for example, the Sardinian, Orphean and Subalpine Warblers. In contrast to the rest it occurs almost entirely in very dry, rugged, undulating terrain and needs a combination of rocks and low, thorny scrub to suit its requirements, singing regularly from both. It ranges to higher elevations than most of the rest, up to 1600 m, and often occurs along ravines and gullies. It usually forages within the canopy of a bush or low tree, keeping out of sight.

In keeping with other *Sylvia* warblers, the males build several unlined 'cock' nests for the purposes of display. This habit seems to be more developed in Rüppell's Warblers than in several other species, although few detailed studies of the Rüppell's have been made. The nest itself is placed 45–75 cm above ground, in thick, thorny scrub.

After breeding, Rüppell's Warblers migrate south to winter in northeast Africa between Chad and Sudan.

ID: Distinctive Sylvia *of similar size and shape to Whitethroat. Male easily recognised by diagnostic combination of black head and throat separated by white moustache, together with red eye ring. Otherwise grey, with white fringes to flight feathers. Female head pattern duller and more mottled, but still distinctive.*

Garden Warbler

Sylvia borin (**sil**-vi-a **boh**-rin)
length 14 cm

This famously featureless bird is the epitome of the tricky warbler, hard to see but easy to hear. It has a fine, rich, warbling song imbued with a hint of the Skylark's ecstatic timbre, but the phrases are easily confused with those of the Blackcap. In fact its song is far more even and babbling than that of the Blackcap, without the poor start and fine finish characteristic of that bird.

The two birds don't help by living in very similar habitats. Both occur in richer, higher vegetation than other *Sylvia* warblers, the sort characteristic of woodland or woodland edge. Their territories often overlap. Nonetheless the Garden Warbler, unlike the Blackcap, can occur in scrubby areas without trees and it prefers a more open canopy and richer undergrowth. It is also found in moister places and, tends to forage slightly lower down among denser vegetation.

The Garden Warbler is a confirmed migrant, more so than its colleague, with the entire population evacuating the breeding areas in the autumn and not returning until April or May. Experiments with hand-reared birds have provided fascinating insights into the nature of their migration; early in the migration season central European Garden Warblers have an innate tendency to orient southwest, whereas later on, in October, in the same experimental cages, their preferred bearing is south or southeast. These tendencies precisely reflect what birds do in the wild: they first head down to Iberia to cross the Mediterranean near Gibraltar, and then change direction to take them into the heart of Africa. Clearly their migration route is predetermined and internally controlled.

It is also fuelled by a combination of fruit and insects. Prior to migration Garden Warblers may double their body weight, by eating more often and by taking in a wide variety of berries – those of 35 species of plants have been recorded as being consumed in central Europe. The berries provide ready access to fats, and the insects contribute essential proteins. This type of feeding is abandoned in the breeding season, when the birds spend their time foraging for small, soft-bodied insects, which they pick from foliage and twigs.

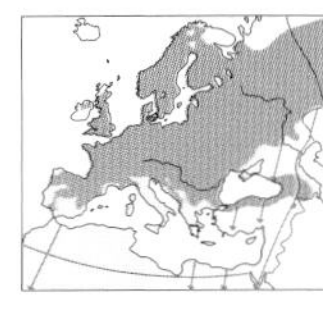

ID: Famously featureless warbler, mousy brown above except for a hint of grey on the neck sides, and paler below. Staring brown eye looks out from featureless face. For a warbler, has surprisingly short, stout bill.

ID: *Small skulking warbler easily distinguished from Whitethroat by its black legs, relatively clean white underparts, brownish wings same colour as back and darker head with blackish ear coverts. Sexes much alike.*

Lesser Whitethroat

Sylvia curruca (**sil**-vi-a koo-**roo**-ka)
length 12.5–13.5 cm

For its song the Lesser Whitethroat seems to have borrowed a phrase from a completely different bird. Although it can give the usual mumbled, fast-paced warble typical of its genus, it also has a loud, far-carrying, rattling trill that is more like the efforts of a Cirl Bunting than a warbler. This gives away its progress as it skulks in the thick but tall vegetation found on the edges of woodland and along hedgerows (in contrast to its close relative the Whitethroat, it doesn't have a ritualised song flight). This song is remarkably similar almost throughout its European range, lacking much of the exotic variation shown by its congeners.

At heart this is a central and eastern European bird. It does breed as far west as Britain and France, but its true leanings are revealed by its migration strategy, which takes it to Africa by way of the eastern Mediterranean. Having bypassed the sea, many birds then somewhat incongruously turn sharply southwest and may winter as far west as northern Niger and Mali, more or less due south of where they started! That amounts to one long detour, which is repeated on the return migration in spring.

On its breeding grounds the Lesser Whitethroat inhabits taller vegetation than the Whitethroat, and often encompasses trees in its territory – even conifers, which are shunned by other *Sylvia* warblers. It nests higher up than the Whitethroat, Blackcap or Garden Warbler, to about 3 m off the ground, and may also forage higher up than the Whitethroat. It tends to select thorny trees for its nest, since these provide a better 'scaffolding' for its cup-like structure.

The male Lesser Whitethroat builds several incomplete 'cock nests' for the female to inspect, a practice which forms an important part of the pair-bonding process. Once formed, the pairings are more adhesive than in the more fickle, indecisive Whitethroat.

Whitethroat

Sylvia communis (**sil**-vi-a com-**myoo**-niss)
length 14 cm

The Whitethroat is one of Europe's commonest and most widely distributed warblers, occurring in all kinds of open country where there are scattered bushes, including such habitats as hedgerows, heathland and large gardens. It is an effervescent species, the male tirelessly singing his short, scratchy song from a prominent perch in the early part of the breeding season and both sexes readily investigating disturbances with irritable, slightly croaking calls. Its curiosity and energy somewhat undermine its inborn need to skulk, making it a much easier bird to see than, for example, a Lesser Whitethroat, Blackcap or Garden Warbler.

These birds are summer migrants, arriving in late March and April. The males appear about ten days before the females, and delineate territories by means of their perched song, which averages 1.5 seconds in length, and, when they are excited, by song flights, which may last ten seconds or more. During the latter the birds rise steeply into the air and may then dance up and down for a short while, like puppets on a string, before dropping down to earth.

Whitethroat territories are highly flexible. For a start, those used for courtship are much larger than the final breeding territory, which means that boundaries change as the season progresses. It is also common for a male to hold several territories at once, sometimes, but not always, with a separate female in each. It appears that the Whitethroat population contains a shortage of females and, in an average season, only 50 per cent of territories play host to a breeding attempt. Some males, evidently those of highest quality, are double-brooded, fathering two sets of young, each by a different female.

This is very much a bird of low scrub. The nest is rarely higher than 1 m above ground and is usually well concealed among brambles, nettles or other plants that predators find troublesome. Whitethroats also keep low when foraging, rarely entering the foliage of trees and instead keeping to the lowest stratum of vegetation, the herb layer.

Although common, the Whitethroat was once much more so. In the period from 1960 to 1970, and especially in 1969, the population crashed almost Europe-wide by anything from 100 per cent to 50 per cent. A long drought in the Sahel region of Africa, where Whitethroats winter, is thought to have been the cause, and although the species has made partial or strong recovery in many places, it has never again reached its population levels of previous decades.

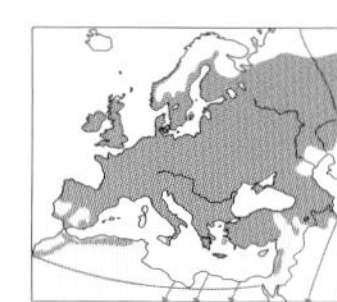

ID: *About size of Great Tit, with long tail and peaked crown. Lives up to name, with bright white throat that looks like shaving foam when bird is singing. Male has grey head with white split eye ring and pink breast; female has grey-brown head and buff breast. Both sexes have brown back and rich rufous fringes to most flight feathers, a useful distinction from Lesser Whitethroat and others.*

Blackcap

Sylvia atricapilla (**sil**-vi-a at-tri-**kap**-pil-la)
length 13 cm

The Blackcap is one of the most familiar and recognisable of European warblers and in some parts of its range is numbered among the ten commonest breeding birds. It is principally a species of open forest with a lush understorey, but it has also colonised such places as riverine woodland, olive groves, parks, gardens and urban areas. No other *Sylvia* occupies such a broad spectrum of habitats.

The song is a rich, fluty warble with a noticeably mumbling, uncertain beginning and a strong whistling finish. It is a familiar sound at almost any time of year where the bird is resident, except during the moult in late summer. A male usually delivers his phrases from a favourite concealed perch 4–13 m above the ground, and he often does so amidst bouts of busy foraging. The song is quite variable and may include imitations, even of the Garden Warbler with which this bird is so often confused.

When a Blackcap male sings, he is passing on information of great significance to a female. It has recently been discovered that the males with a high song rate, between 160 and 180 phrases per hour, are those that possess the best territories, with a high density of vegetation suitable for nesting. Males that sing at a lower rate, uttering 80–100 phrases per hour, hail from territories with more open vegetation, where a potential nest is more vulnerable to predators. The males disclose this information honestly by their song rate, allowing the females to choose the best possible mate. But that's not the whole story. Males that sing a lot contribute much less to feeding the young than their less voluble colleagues. A female, therefore, that places her nest in a lower-quality territory at least gains the benefit of having more help in providing for her chicks.

After breeding, Blackcaps take up a bewildering variety of different migratory strategies. The population breeding in northern Europe follows the typical pattern of a long-distance migrant, flying down to sub-Saharan Africa for the winter; some may travel as much as 6000 km to their wintering grounds. Further south, birds tend to migrate much less far, so that in the Mediterranean part of their range they are partial migrants at best. This means that their northern relatives actually fly over and beyond them, a phenomenon known as leap-frog migration.

The Blackcaps of western Europe tend to start their migratory journey by heading southwest, towards Iberia, whereas those breeding east of 12–13°E fly southeast, towards the eastern end of the Mediterranean. In the overlap between this so-called 'migratory divide' it appears that some birds fly south, some north and some northwest. There are records, for example, of birds from central Europe wintering in Fennoscandia, 2000 km to the north, and, in recent years at least, some German Blackcaps that formerly went to Spain have taken to wintering in Britain and the Low Countries instead. This movement was unknown before the 1960s and is now recorded in about 10 per cent of the relevant population. This goes to show how flexible a bird's migratory strategy can be.

The Blackcap is a typically insectivorous warbler in the breeding season, but in the autumn and winter it takes considerable numbers of berries, which tend to form the bulk of its diet. Over 90 species of plants have been recorded as providing food for Blackcaps, although only a few, notably ivy, are of particular importance. Berries and fruit may, of course, run out locally, so Blackcaps wintering in Europe tend to be nomadic, travelling around in search of supplies. Many individuals wintering in southern Spain hop across to North Africa in January and February as stocks become low in mainland Europe.

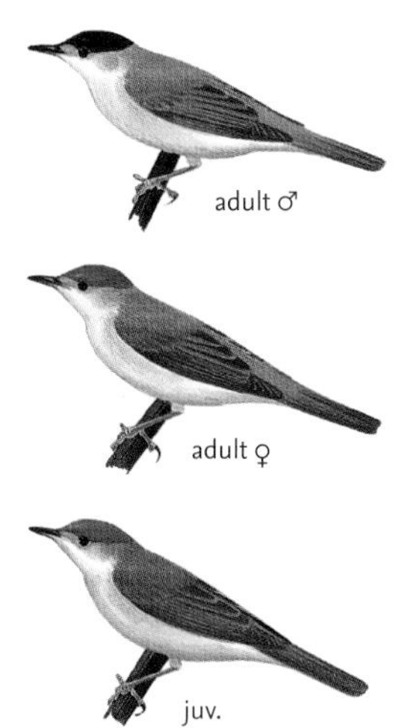

ID: Pretty unmistakable – largely grey-brown tit-sized bird with clearly defined black skullcap, reddish-brown in female. May be confused with Marsh Tit, but lacks that species' black bill and white cheeks.

Greenish Warbler

Phylloscopus trochiloides
(fil-**loss**-koh-puss tro-kil-**loy**-deez)
length 10 cm

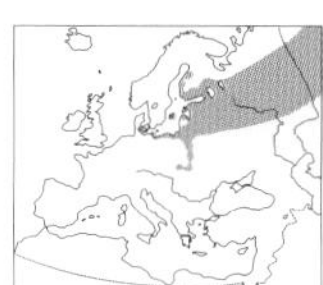

ID: *Small tit-like warbler with short bill, as with other* Phylloscopus. *About size of Chiffchaff, with large head and still more rounded crown. Main colour rather neat olive-green, contrasting with clean white underside. Has small white wing bar. Well-defined black eye stripe (usually a bit broken up on lores) and broad whitish supercilium. Similar to Arctic, but has darker legs.*

adult spring   adult autumn   juv.

Only in comparatively recent times has the Greenish Warbler – at heart an Asian bird – attained a foothold in Europe west of Russia. In the 1900s it began to be recorded for the first time in the lands east of the Baltic, and only since the 1970s has it been seen regularly in Poland, the Czech Republic and Germany. This gradual spread has been marked by considerable fluctuations, with large numbers in good years and almost none in poor years. Good years inevitably coincide with high temperatures in April and May and with persistent warm air masses coming from the southeast. These whisk the birds further west than usual.

This is a highly active, arboreal bird that feeds on insects on the hop, so to speak, often picking them from foliage as it flies from one branch to another, or fielding insects disturbed by its wingbeats. It forages over the complete range of forest strata, from the thick undergrowth just above ground to the very top of the canopy. It also shows an equally wide tolerance of woodland types for breeding. In northeast Europe and in the central European mountains, for example, it breeds in spruce forests sprinkled with scattered deciduous trees, whereas in the central lowlands it occupies rich, broad-leaved woods containing many types of tree, each contributing to a multi-layered structure. The Greenish Warbler also occurs in gardens, parks and small copses. The nest is placed on the ground in tall vegetation.

This species is unusual among warblers in that both sexes readily sing in the breeding season, typically from well above ground. They give a song phrase that would be pleasing if it were not so rushed – the notes seem to trip over one another and muffle the overall effect. The song period in Europe lasts from the second half of May to the end of July, but birds of both sexes begin again as they take up their winter territories in the Indian subcontinent.

Bonelli's Warbler

Phylloscopus [bonelli]
(fil-**loss**-koh-puss boh-**nel**-lie)
length 11.5 cm

It's trendy among the various Asian *Phylloscopus* warblers to breed in lowlands in the north of their range and in hills and mountains in the south, but the Bonelli's Warbler is the only European member to follow this trend slavishly. Thus in west and central Europe it is a lowland bird, and in the Mediterranean region it is associated with high altitudes. And this isn't its only ecological dichotomy. In some places it breeds in open deciduous woodlands characterised by large trees such as oak, beech and sweet chestnut, and in other places it is equally at home in stands of pure conifers. Furthermore it seems to like rather dense ground vegetation in some regions and a sparse understorey in others. Among its few consistencies, the Bonelli's Warbler likes a light, open canopy with at least some undergrowth, and it breeds only in warm continental climates.

Given this bird's schizophrenic tendencies, you probably won't be surprised to learn that there are two separate populations in Europe, geographically isolated from one another both in breeding and in wintering ranges. In recent years DNA analysis has shown that they are perhaps best regarded as separate species. The eastern Bonelli's Warbler (*Phylloscopus orientalis*) of the Balkans and Turkey is longer winged than the western bird (*P. bonelli*) and has a different call, a monosyllabic 'sip' to the western bird's 'tu-eep'. Apparently, the song is also minutely different.

The song itself is little more than a short trill on one note, a bit like that of a Blue Tit or Cirl Bunting. The male makes up for this unimpressive effort by singing almost non-stop in early season, making the Bonelli's Warbler an easy bird to detect. Once he has chosen his mate and nest site, he stops. But there is a short period before his breeding life settles down when everything can go wrong; females in the process of seeking a nest site sometimes change territories, and partners, at the last moment.

The nest itself is placed on the ground, always well hidden. Many can be found beneath overhanging tussocks or logs and fallen branches. The female often makes a small hollow first, and then constructs a dome-shaped structure largely out of grass.

adult spring   adult autumn   juv.

ID: *Similar to Chiffchaff but head and neck look strangely bleached out, leaving dark staring eye in blank face. Underparts clean white and back may be grey-green (western birds) or distinctly grey (eastern birds). Wing feathers and edge of tail fringed by yellow-green; rump distinctly yellowish.*

Wood Warbler

Phylloscopus sibilatrix
(fil-**loss**-koh-puss sie-bil-**lay**-triks)
length 12 cm

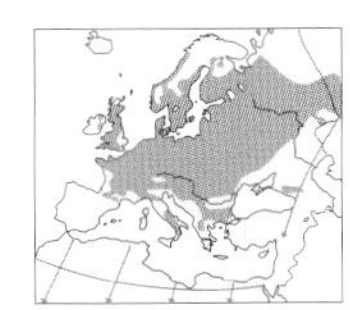

ID: Broad-beamed, short-tailed Phylloscopus, *usually easily identified by its very bright yellow supercilium, face, throat and upper breast. Lower breast and belly are clean white, sometimes meeting the yellow abruptly, to make a band. Most flight feathers have bright green fringe; upper parts also pleasingly beech-green.*

No other warbler in Europe is so much a bird of the forest interior as the Wood Warbler, which is unusual in requiring a shady area beneath a closed canopy for successful breeding. Most populations are found in tall, mature oak, beech or chestnut woods or a combination of these, but the Wood Warbler will also breed in conifer forests, so long as these have at least some deciduous trees. Along with the closed canopy this fussy operator also needs minimal undergrowth (once this has risen above 2 m it is deemed unsuitable) and light cover at every possible stratum between the two. The former is required for the nest and the latter to provide perches for singing and displaying, and for approaching the nest with food.

It seems odd that a bird living in mature woodland should practise song flight, since presumably the space for such aerobatics would be rather limited. Nonetheless this is exactly what the Wood Warbler does, following a horizontal course from perch to perch while flying with fast but shallow wingbeats. The song is uttered either just before or just after the bird becomes airborne and carries on until he lands. It consists of two parts which may be sung independently of one another. One is an accelerating, shivering trill that sounds like a spinning coin coming to rest and the other is a series of mournful piping notes.

Having made all these efforts, male Wood Warblers don't always settle for a single mate. Depending on the location and, evidently, upon the year, up to 40 per cent of the population may acquire two mates, hogging the available talent and leaving some competitors unpaired. This tends to happen when a male has acquired a mate and she is incubating; finding himself independent and not especially busy, such a male solicits for another mate, either on the edge of his territory or, sometimes, by moving to a different one. If he is successful, he will then give the lion's share of his attention to one mate or the other (usually the first), helping to feed and tend the chicks, although occasionally the neglected female may bring her offspring towards the rival's nest and the male divides his attention.

Wood Warblers must fit all their arrangements into a short breeding season. Having arrived towards the end of April, they are early returnees to their wintering grounds in central and east Africa, with the main departure occurring in August.

adult spring — adult autumn — juv.

Arctic Warbler

Phylloscopus borealis
(fil-**loss**-koh-puss boh-ree-**ay**-liss)
length 10.5–11.5 cm

Like an entrepreneur with little time, the ultra-successful Arctic Warbler is an energetic, active bird, the sort that can be exhausting to watch. In common with other *Phylloscopus* warblers it is an arboreal species, feeding mostly well above ground and picking insects from leaves as it moves rapidly around. Its brief visit to Europe is like an appointment squeezed into a busy schedule. It arrives as late as the second half of June, crams in a quick breeding attempt in the taiga forests of the north and is gone by mid-August, back to its wintering grounds in Southeast Asia.

The Arctic Warbler is not an Arctic bird at all, instead occurring in tall, well-grown coniferous forests well south of the tundra, especially stands with a few deciduous or scrubby trees intermixed. In many places it breeds along rivers and beside water courses. The main population occurs in European Russia, where it is very common; small numbers are also found in Fennoscandia. This species has the distinction of being the only Old World warbler to have colonised the North American continent, having established a foothold in Alaska.

In social situations Arctic Warblers are highly demonstrative, marking their excitement with various types of wing-flapping, like an overexcited professor waving his arms. This may be so fast as to produce a loud whirring sound when males fly from tree to tree in territorial confrontations, or it may be slow and full, as when a male and female are in close proximity and are engaged in courtship.

adult spring — adult autumn

ID: Large for a Phylloscopus *(bigger than Willow Warbler) and long-bodied. Similar olive-green coloration and white wing bar to Greenish, but larger and with dusty colour, or even faint streaking, on breast. Face pattern is even stronger, with distinctive long supercilium that arcs down towards back of head. Dark eye stripe does not peter out on lores. In further contrast to Greenish, bill has black tip.*

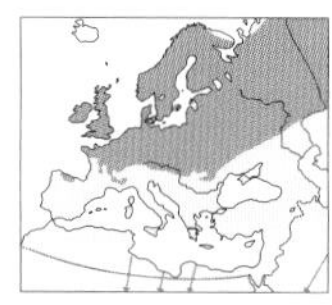

Willow Warbler

Phylloscopus trochilus
(fil-**loss**-koh-puss **trok**-kil-luss)
length 10.5–11.5 cm

ID: *Very common* Phylloscopus *warbler, with relatively flat crown and long wings and body. Very similar to Chiffchaff, but usually has much cleaner whitish breast that may even be yellow-tinged. Upperparts dull olive-green, offering stronger contrast to underparts than seen on Chiffchaff. In addition, Willow has longer, better-defined supercilium, and usually flesh-coloured legs. Bill often yellowish at base.*

The soft, descending scale of the Willow Warbler is one of the dominant sounds of Europe in spring. Everywhere from the fringes of the Mediterranean to deep into the Arctic Circle this small, sprightly, foliage-gleaning warbler arrives from Africa to become a common bird of scrub and low trees. It is much associated with transitional habitats, be it new growth appearing in previously cleared areas or the last substantial vegetation at the tree line in mountains and tundra. The Willow Warbler is commonest in the north and is the most numerous bird in Fennoscandia, with at least 24 million breeding pairs. It is possible, indeed, that no other summer visitor from Africa outnumbers it in total population. It wasn't always so, of course. The activities of people opening up Europe's vast forests have no doubt benefited this pioneering edge-habitat species.

The Willow Warbler is the epitome of the *Phylloscopus* or 'leaf' warblers, a tit-sized, plain, yellowish bird that forages actively among the foliage (*Phylloscopus* means 'examiner of leaves') well above ground. Were it not so fidgety in its movements it would be a difficult bird to detect among the backdrop of a million leaves. It feeds from the surface of these, plus twigs and branches, principally taking soft-bodied meals such as aphids and caterpillars, and besides gleaning it will also make short aerial sallies to catch flying insects.

Male Willow Warblers arrive about ten days before the females and immediately set up territories by song. These territories are important, since they will provide everything a bird, its mate and young may need, including a nest site and all their food. Not surprisingly, competition is strong and Willow Warblers can become extremely aggressive in defence of their patch. It appears that prior residence is an advantage because, when a male returns to his territory of last year to find it occupied by an early-arriving interloper, he always seems to win his precious land back.

Territories are no less important to the females, of course, and members of the fairer sex are highly judicious in their choosing of a potential site and its owner. It seems that each will visit several potential mates before she pairs up, spending 10–20 minutes in each territory and monitoring the incumbent's song output. She will pay particular attention to how often the male sings and how much he forages. If a male has a high song output and does not forage much, this implies that he finds food easily in his territory and does not have to search very hard. A bird in a lower-quality territory will spend more of his time foraging, and will consequently have a lower song output. Thus, simply by listening in, a female can make value judgements about a male and, in particular, about the patch of ground where she might potentially hunt for food for her young.

This latter aspect is especially significant because, as with the closely related Chiffchaff, the female Willow Warbler often finds herself in the role of main provider for the family. Male Willow Warblers are probably not as indifferent to mates and family as Chiffchaffs, but they are more regularly polygynous, with some males taking two and others three different mates; such birds cannot provide for all their offspring.

The hard-pressed female also builds the nest, although the male often accompanies her when she is doing so and provides moral support. As with other *Phylloscopus* warblers, the Willow Warbler's nest is a domed structure made out of grass and leaves, and whilst that of the Chiffchaff is usually constructed above ground, the Willow Warbler's is placed on it.

adult spring · adult autumn · juv.

Chiffchaff

Phylloscopus collybita
(fil-**loss**-koh-puss kol-li-**bie**-ta)
length 10–11 cm

Few birds have a more distinctive song than the even-paced, metronomic 'chiff-chaff, chiff-chaff...' of this, one of Europe's commonest warblers. The utterance would never be placed in anyone's Top Ten musical favourites, but this apparently repetitive refrain is a lot more variable than is widely appreciated. The number of units in the song can vary between 3 and 20, and the order of the respective 'chiff' and 'chaff' elements is changed with every phrase. Furthermore, in the breeding areas the males often interpose a series of stammering 'tett' notes between the more familiar phrases, something they do not do on migration or in the wintertime.

In Iberia the Chiffchaff's song is quite different from that heard everywhere else. It is a three-part phrase, beginning with a few chiffs, carrying on with a few 'hweet' notes (similar to the call) and ending with a silvery trill. This vocal distinction, together with a somewhat brighter plumage, has led scientists to consider the Iberian birds as a different species, the Iberian Chiffchaff (*Phylloscopus ibericus*). This form also occurs in southern France.

As a rule, the Chiffchaff is more of a woodland bird than its very similar relative the Willow Warbler. It tends to occupy mature lowland woodland with an open canopy and healthily copious understorey. Throughout most of its range it prefers deciduous woodland, but it is no stranger to coniferous forest in places, so long as there are some broad-leaved trees as well. Riverine forest is often densely occupied and in central Europe this species also has a strong attachment to cemeteries and parks.

The Chiffchaff's habitat requirements of open canopy and rich but not stifling understorey reflect a remarkable distinction between the two sexes. Almost everywhere it occurs, the Chiffchaff seems to allocate the canopy to the male and the understorey to the female, where they respectively spend most of their time. The bond between the sexes is not very strong, and members of a pair effectively live 'in different houses'. They seem to meet largely for display purposes and at the nest when they are feeding young.

The male Chiffchaff, though, is often a real slouch when it comes to parenting. His contribution to feeding the chicks varies between an even share and almost nothing. It seems that most females are perfectly capable of looking after the young themselves and the pair bond often splits at this time, or even before. Despite the lukewarm relationship, male Chiffchaffs seem to be strangely reluctant to acquire more than one mate, though they have ample opportunity to do so.

The female's low-level life includes building a domed nest just above or on the ground. It is always carefully concealed in tall vegetation and is also made from inconspicuous materials such as dried grass, moss and various leaves. Interestingly, when a female builds her second nest of the year for another brood, she often places it higher up than the first.

The Chiffchaff is a migrant, wintering from southern Europe down to West Africa, with a few individuals braving conditions further north. In the northern parts of its range it is often one of the first migrants to appear in spring, from early March onwards.

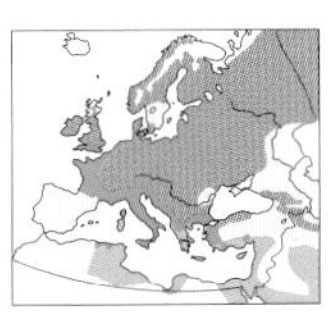

ID: Small green warbler about size of Blue Tit, with small bill, greenish plumage and noticeable supercilium. Famously similar to Willow Warbler, but has rounder crown, shorter primary projection, and legs are usually black, not flesh-coloured. Also, looks a bit grubbier than Willow, with slightly dusky breast offering less contrast with upperparts; cheeks darker, accentuating white eye ring split by dark eye stripe. Bill often dark. Flicks tail downwards, which Willow Warbler does very little.

adult spring

adult autumn

Firecrest

Regulus ignicapillus
(**reg**-yoo-luss ig-ni-**kap**-pil-lus)
length 9 cm

The Firecrest is as small as the Goldcrest and clearly very closely related to it, but the two species can coexist because of their subtly different ecological requirements. So, whereas the Goldcrest is essentially arboreal and drawn to conifers, the Firecrest often feeds at lower levels over a less restricted range of habitats, including both coniferous and mixed woodland. In addition, the Firecrest takes larger food items on average than the Goldcrest and forages with less fastidiousness, changing perch more often.

The Firecrest is also a less hardy bird than the Goldcrest, being found mainly in central and southern Europe and not occurring in Fennoscandia. In the north and east of its range it is primarily migratory, whereas southern birds are resident. Overall, the indomitable Goldcrest has a much broader world range than the Firecrest, being found as far east as China, while the latter is almost confined to Europe.

There are some interesting behavioural differences between the two species. The nest of a Firecrest, for example, is built only by the female, not by both sexes, and is it somewhat smaller than the Goldcrest's substantial structure. It is often sited in ivy or other creepers, as well as sometimes high up in a conifer. And when Firecrests are displaying, they don't nod like a Goldcrest to show off the crown. Instead, presenting their stripy heads as their most prominent feature, they simply look straight towards each other.

adult ♀ juv.

ID: Same size and shape as Goldcrest, and equally agile. Easily distinguished by highly patterned face: black eye stripe and bold white supercilium give unique 'expression' to Firecrest. Also shows paler underparts than Goldcrest, contrasting with greener back; bronze patch at 'shoulder'.

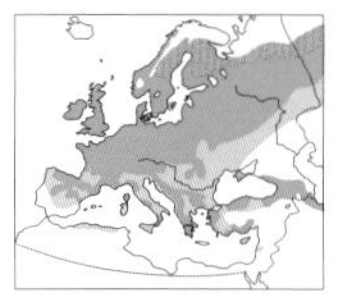

ID: *Along with Firecrest, smallest European bird. Round-bodied and short-tailed, mainly olive-green, paler below; wing has strong white bar. Active and agile in branches, often hovers. Crown is yellow, with a black bar either side; in male yellow intensifies to orange towards nape. Face little marked, with dark staring eye.*

Goldcrest

Regulus regulus (**reg**-yoo-luss **reg**-yoo-luss)
length 9 cm

There is no smaller bird in Europe than the Goldcrest and it lives in a niche unoccupied by any other species except the Firecrest, a place where only the miniature can go. It forages for insects among the leaves and branches of thick conifers, particularly spruce and fir, disappearing into the dense needlework and working its way to the very tips of delicate branches. It does this with relentless energy, never stopping for a moment, not even to sing, and it combines its searching of surfaces with regular hovering, making it look like a somewhat portly hummingbird. For a birdwatcher the Goldcrest is easy enough to see, but difficult to follow around in the binoculars.

Despite its size the Goldcrest is found primarily in the north of Europe. Here, after all, is the greatest abundance of conifers, although on the other hand the winters are long and harsh. Goldcrests do evacuate some of their more extreme haunts from October onwards, especially those inside the Arctic Circle, but some can still be found all year beyond 65°N. Indeed, experiments have shown that even when it is –25°C outside Goldcrests can maintain their internal body temperature of 39–41°C for 18 hours, so long as they can obtain enough food and can huddle up to another Goldcrest at night. But in order to survive they must simply feed all day without stopping.

Goldcrests eat mainly insects and other arthropods of various sorts, especially the smallest (up to about 40 mg in weight). These include scale insects, aphids, flies and mites, for example, although many other groups have been recorded as well. The Goldcrest's thin bill is specially designed to take these small-bodied creatures from confined spaces.

Goldcrests also have special adaptations for breeding in less than kind climates. The nest, for example, is an ample cup of three layers suspended from a twig. The outer layer is made up of a mixture of cobwebs, moss and lichen, and inside this is another layer of moss and lichen. Finally, for the lining, the birds stuff feathers in, often in large quantity. A few of these feathers are specially fixed in to form a sort of umbrella over the entrance, trapping the warm air inside. The entrance itself is rather narrow and often placed flush against the twigs from which the nest is suspended. All in all, the nest is well designed to keep out the cold.

Despite their audacity in the face of conditions that would make most small birds move out, Goldcrests do inevitably suffer in the very worst conditions. Mortality is high, and small groups of Goldcrests that form in the winter and hold their own communal territory often dwindle to trios or pairs by the following spring. Nonetheless, the Goldcrest is a highly productive species, capable theoretically of bringing up two broods of nine chicks each in a season, so any losses are soon made up. Goldcrests ensure that they can raise two broods in the short northern season by overlapping them. Both sexes build the first nest together, and while the female is incubating the first brood the male embarks on a second structure. The eggs hatch and both adults feed the chicks at first, but this soon changes as the female moves to the second nest and lays a second clutch while the male takes over sole responsibility for feeding the first brood. Once these chicks are independent he joins the female in feeding the second clutch, and the division of roles ceases.

Despite its size the Goldcrest is a fearless and pugnacious bird. When two rivals meet they don't necessarily exchange pleasantries, but instead ruffle their respective crown feathers to show off the attractive yellow and orange coloration, flick their wings and bob their heads. This showing-off of the colourful crown is a more or less universal display among these birds, for something very similar takes place when male and female meet.

Flycatchers family *Muscicapidae* (moo-si-**kap**-pid-ee)

Habitat Mainly open woods; also gardens and orchards.
Food Invertebrates, especially flying ones that are snatched in a short sally from a perch; also fruit, especially in autumn.
Movements All migratory, arriving late in the spring (May) and departing early (August onwards). Go to sub-Saharan Africa except Red-breasted, which winters in India.
Voice Less accomplished songsters than thrushes or warblers; the song is generally simple and not very loud. Red-breasted Flycatcher is the best songster.
Pairing style Mostly monogamous, but males of Pied, Collared and probably Semi-collared Flycatcher may have 2 or more mates in separate territories.
Nesting Territorial and solitary.
Nest Usually a loose cup of dead leaves and stems, grass, moss and rootlets (Spotted Flycatcher also uses twigs), lined with finer materials. Placed in a hole or cavity, or close beside a tree trunk.
Productivity 1 brood a year except Spotted, which regularly has 2.
Eggs 4–7, hatching synchronously.
Incubation 12–15 days, by female (although male Spotted occasionally contributes).
Young Nest-bound, blind and sparsely covered with down when first hatched.
Parenting style Both parents feed young.
Food to young Small insects, especially caterpillars.
Leaving nest Young leave nest at 11–18 days, but may be fed by parents for several weeks afterwards.

The flycatchers would look much like any other group of small, plain-coloured birds were it not for their eye-catching method of procuring food. Starting from a still position on an elevated perch, they suddenly launch into the air on an acrobatic sally, making darting movements in rapid pursuit of a flying insect. Snapping their bills, often audibly, on their prey, they then return to the same or another perch. This feeding style gives them their name.

Flycatchers have long wings and long tails for extra manoeuvrability in the air, but their feet, needed only for long periods of perching, are short and weak. Their bills are flattened and very broad, with a wide gape, and small touch-sensitive bristles grow beside the bill to help detect prey. With their upright posture and habit of sitting still waiting for prey, the flycatchers invite comparison with the smaller thrushes or chats; recent DNA evidence has confirmed the close relationship.

Since they depend on a good supply of flying insects to feed themselves and their fledged young, all flycatchers are late migrants to Europe, arriving well behind most other birds. Their breeding success is highly dependent on the weather, with cold and rain causing widespread failures.

Semi-collared Flycatcher

Ficedula semitorquata
(fie-**see**-doo-la sem-mi-tor-**kway**-ta)
length 13 cm

The black and white flycatchers of the Balkans, Turkey and the Caucasus have long been known to be slightly different in plumage from the more widespread Pied and Collared Flycatchers, but only recently have these populations been considered a species in their own right, the Semi-collared Flycatcher. The most important distinction is in the song, a series of notes like a Collared Flycatcher's delivered at the speed of a Pied's, but there are other subtle differences, too.

The Semi-collared, for example, seems to catch more food in sallying flight than the foliage-gleaning Pied, and it can be found in mixed woods. It is less demonstrative than either at the nest when danger threatens, flicking its wings less often. It also has a unique call uttered when the male shows a potential nest site to the female, quite different from those given in the same situation by the other two. But otherwise its behaviour is very similar to the commoner species.

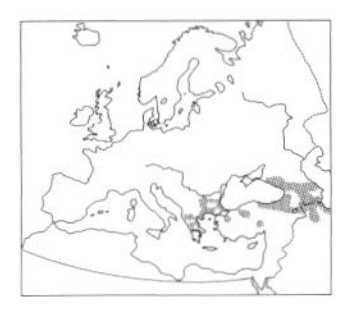

ID: Male has half-collar across neck, and much white in tail; also white at base of primaries and on median coverts. Female has narrow pattern of white in wing.

Collared Flycatcher

Ficedula albicollis (fie-**see**-doo-la alb-bi-**kol**-lis)
length 13 cm

Tall, verdant, deciduous woods are the habitat of the Collared Flycatcher, a canopy species that hunts the rich insect life high above ground. In contrast to the very similar Pied Flycatcher, it feeds mainly by sallying from a fixed perch and snapping up passing insects, rather than picking from leaves; for this aerodynamic reason it has fractionally longer wings than its close relative.

This is the continental counterpart of the Pied Flycatcher, replacing it in warmer climates. The two species do sometimes overlap and where this happens the Collared is dominant, forcing neighbouring Pieds into marginal, less productive habitats.

In common with Pied Flycatchers, Collared Flycatchers sing to attract a mate to a nest site, and an element of the population will attempt to acquire a second mate and a second territory once their primary mate has begun laying. In fact, some Collared males have been recorded trying to keep up five territories at once. Extra-pair copulations are common but, interestingly, males don't always visit their rivals' nests for this purpose alone; apparently they also tour the neighbourhood assessing the productivity of different territories, presumably with a view to occupying these in later years if they get the chance.

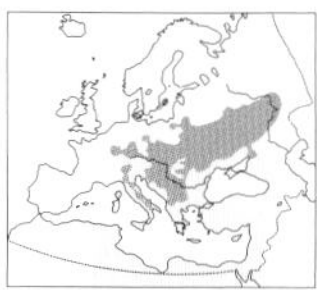

ID: Male smart, with full collar of white around neck and much white in wing, including primary bases; also large white spot on forehead. Female shares white primary bases; also paler brown than Pied Flycatcher.

Pied Flycatcher

Ficedula hypoleuca (fie-**see**-doo-la hie-poh-**loo**-ka)
length 13 cm

This small, restless flycatcher takes its food primarily from the leaves and bark of trees, rather than darting into the air to catch it; it even picks from the ground from time to time. It is found in mature deciduous and mixed woods without too much of a closed canopy, and occurs further north and west than its two sibling species, the Collared and Semi-collared Flycatchers.

The Pied Flycatcher is famous for an exceptionally unusual mating system, found only among a minority of individuals. All males sing to attract females to the centrepiece of their territory, a potential nest hole, and then form a pair bond. Most males then stop singing and play their part in feeding the young, as do many other small birds. But others, once their mate begins incubation, start to sing at another, completely different nest hole well away from the first, in an effort to attract another mate. Remarkably, this secondary territory may be as much as 3.5 km away from the primary one, although 200 m is more common; clearly the intention is to deceive both females into thinking that she is the sole partner. If a male does attract a secondary female, he will desert her as soon as the clutch is laid and redirect his attention to his primary mate. The secondary female suffers from lack of help with feeding the young, but may still manage to fledge some chicks, thus increasing the productivity of her wayward mate.

This system has its disadvantages to a potentially bigamous male. Studies have shown that, if a territory holder strays any more than 10 m from his primary female, neighbouring males will take advantage of his absence. Thus Pied Flycatcher society is rife with extra-pair copulations and on average only 75 per cent of chicks in a nest will carry the genetic material of the 'rightful' father.

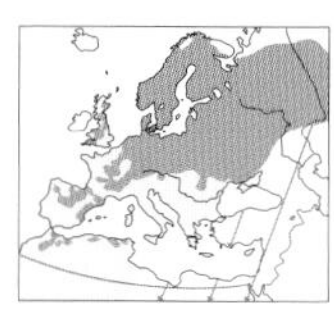

ID: Small black and white flycatcher with less white on wing than close relatives, minimum white at primary bases. Female darker brown than other species, especially on back.

Red-breasted Flycatcher

Ficedula parva (fie-**see**-doo-la **par**-va)
length 11.5 cm

A tricky bird to see, the Red-breasted Flycatcher is usually found around the middle levels of tall deciduous forests, especially those with rich undergrowth. Here it gleans most of its food from leaves, moving rapidly under cover of vegetation and using the perching and sallying technique less often than other flycatchers. When it does perch, it often flirts its long tail up and down, showing off the white sides.

Perhaps because of its inconspicuous nature, this bird has a far-carrying song and, alone among our flycatchers, will sometimes perform it during a brief display flight independent of the nest, in which it flies from perch to perch with a whirr of wingbeats. Otherwise it will sing from close to a trunk, lifting its head high to show off the red breast to best effect. The male normally stops singing as soon as the female begins incubation. But then, strangely, song will often start up again in the autumn, perhaps to help the bird establish a territory in which to feed.

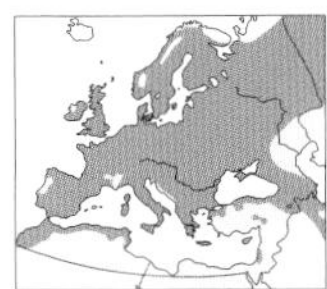

Spotted Flycatcher

Muscicapa striata (moo-si-**kap**-pa stri-**ay**-ta)
length 14.5 cm

ID: Plain brown, Robin-sized bird best identified by upright posture and flycatching habits. Only the young have spots. Adults have streaks on throat and crown, otherwise grey-brown above, pale below.

Few small birds in Europe have such a wide breeding range as the Spotted Flycatcher; in summer it is found all the way from the fringes of the Arctic to the Mediterranean region, and from the Atlantic coast east to Russia. Here it occupies open, usually deciduous woods, favouring those with plenty of glades and edges offering ample airspace. This is because, of all its small family, the Spotted Flycatcher is the most wedded to the signature technique of darting repeatedly into the air from a perch to catch a flying insect. When doing this it habitually waits on a high perch just below the canopy, bolt upright and alert, and then launches into a pursuit flight every 20 seconds or so to snare a blowfly, bee or wasp. Curiously, the Spotted Flycatcher is alone among its relatives in habitually returning to the perch it has just left. In bad weather it reluctantly searches the canopy, gleaning smaller insects from leaves, often hovering to do so.

For nesting, a Spotted Flycatcher seeks out a site that is sheltered but easily accessible and enjoys a commanding view of the surroundings. It shuns small holes, instead selecting natural platforms of close-growing twigs near the trunk of a tree, or the cross-branches of a creeper. It also uses open-fronted nest boxes, especially in gardens. Indeed, gardens, with their open design and banks of showy flowers, are ideal for this bird, which can often become quite used to people.

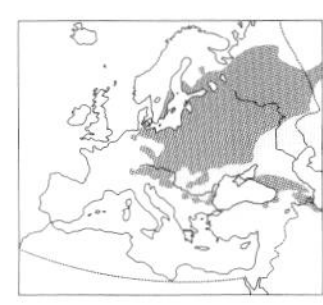

ID: Small, round-headed bird with obvious white in tail. Adults have reddish throat and grey head.

Tits families *Paridae* (par-rid-ee) and *Aegithalidae* (ee-jith-al-lid-ee)

Habitat Woodlands of various kinds, and scrub; also parks and gardens. Azure Tit in wetlands.
Food Mostly insectivorous in spring and summer (especially caterpillars); fruits and nuts added in autumn and winter (less in Long-tailed).
Movements Most are resident. Great and Coal Tits (and sometimes other species) may leave northern areas if food supplies are short.
Voice Most have loud songs, often based on repeating a double note. Vocabulary complex: Great Tit is said to have at least 50 different calls!
Pairing style Mainly monogamous, but there is often infidelity. Pair bond may be lifelong.
Nesting Solitary and territorial.
Nest Typically placed in holes either in trees or on the ground; in most cases simple cups made chiefly of moss, lined with hair and, on occasion, feathers. Nest of Long-tailed Tit elaborate and unusual (see entry).
Productivity Usually 1 brood, though 2 frequent in the south in several species.
Eggs 4–16, more in older birds in better habitats. Clutch size may be inherited, at least in Great Tit
Incubation 12–17 days, by female only, fed by male.
Young Nest-bound, altricial, downy.
Parenting style Both sexes feed young in and out of nest (Long-tailed Tit may also have nest helpers). Female broods.
Food to young Usually caterpillars. The two adults may make 1000 visits to the nest each day, each time bringing a single caterpillar.
Leaving nest Young fledge at 16–23 days. After leaving the nest, they are fed and looked after for about a week.

Siberian Tit

Tits are among the commonest, boldest and most intelligent of birds and among the most numerically successful in Europe. Two species, the Great Tit and Blue Tit, would find a place in the top ten of the most abundant woodland birds in Europe, and the Coal Tit and Long-tailed Tit are not far behind. Tits are among the first birds with which novice birdwatchers become familiar, since most species visit gardens and readily take food from bird tables and feeders. Wherever they occur they are usually easy to see, and most have loud, cheery voices, with an exceptionally wide vocabulary.

Most members of the family are small, no bigger than a Chaffinch, and they specialise in feeding up in the trees. They have strong legs and feet for clinging (some have ridges on the underside of their feet to help with this) and frequently hang upside down or perform other acrobatics. Their arboreal expertise notwithstanding, most species also readily feed on the ground, especially in autumn when seeds are widely available.

Most tits have bold patterns on the head, usually with a black cap and bib. The Blue and Great Tits are brightly coloured, but the rest are a mixture of black, white and brown. Oddly, the brown tits are great collectors and storers of food, while the colourful Tits acquire what they need on a daily basis.

Tits are gregarious in autumn and winter, but territorial in the breeding season. Species often mix together in flocks that roam woodlands and hedgerows between July and February, and it has been shown that members of flocks watch other members feeding and pick up new foraging techniques.

The Long-tailed Tit is placed in a different family from the rest of the tits on account of its odd pink plumage, its minute bill, its habit of roosting in the open in small huddles, and the details of its nest, which is domed and not placed inside a hole. Nonetheless, its appearance and demeanour are so tit-like that it is included here.

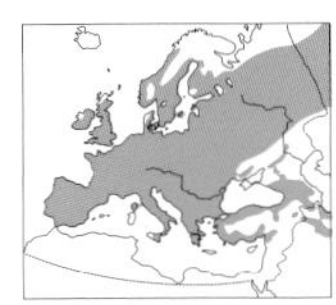

ID: Unmistakable tiny pink, black and white bird. Juveniles have more dull black on face than adults.

Long-tailed Tit

Aegithalos caudatus (ee-jith-**ay**-loss kow-**day**-tuss)
length 14 cm (of which tail 9 cm)

It is almost impossible to see one Long-tailed Tit without seeing another, and between June and February you would be unlikely to see only two. For this is a highly sociable species, living in groups with strong and significant ties. Moreover, Long-tailed Tit flocks tend to attract other species that join them in roaming deciduous woods, scrub and hedgerows.

At the end of the breeding season the young don't leave their parents' territory, as most small birds do, but remain alongside them into the winter; hence the flocks. Together parents and progeny hold a group territory and they may be joined by some of the unattached blood relatives of the adult male, who help defend the borders. As the season progresses things change slightly: young males remain with their parents, but the females leave for neighbouring flocks, sometimes defecting during skirmishes between the two, and others come in. At night in colder weather, all members of the flock may sit on one branch and huddle together in bodily contact, something that very few other birds do.

Once spring arrives, the flock splits up into its constituent pairs, senior adults and male progeny with their new partners; each pair selects a nest site within the borders of the winter territory. For up to a month in March and April, the pairs construct a remarkable domed nest with an entrance to the side. It is made up mainly of moss and bound into shape by thousands of strands of cobweb, which make it flexible enough to expand as the nestlings grow. On the outside the nest is camouflaged with lichens, and the inside is stuffed with 800–2500 feathers, possibly usually obtained from the corpses of birds. The nest may be placed in one of two puzzlingly different locations: either low down in a dense bush, preferably thorny; or 10–20 m up in the fork of a tree.

When the young hatch they are brooded by the female and fed by both parents; but that isn't the whole story of their care. At many nests there are supernumerary helpers, which bring in extra food for the young; there may be as many as eight of these auxiliaries, but generally only one or two. These helpers are usually, once again, siblings of the male bird; many of them are probably failed breeders, coming to promote their genetic material by proxy rather than twiddling their thumbs. The young of nests with helpers stand a much better chance of survival than nestlings that have only the parents present.

The 'reward' for a nest helper is a place in the winter huddle at night. Having participated in helping to rear the young, it is accepted into the winter flock. Long-tailed Tits are very small-bodied birds and when it is cold a huddle is an important survival mechanism.

Long-tailed Tits are, unlike typical tits, mainly insectivorous throughout the year. They feed on a variety of small creatures, but especially butterflies and moths, feasting on adults, larvae, pupae and, with their minute bills, even the eggs.

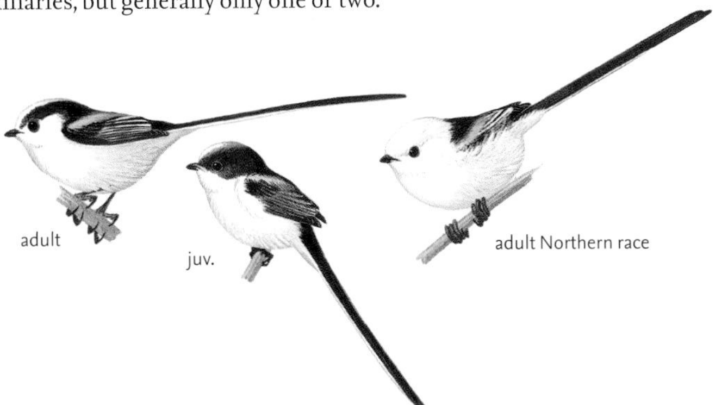

Sombre Tit

Parus lugubris (**par**-uss loo-**goo**-briss)
length 13–14 cm

Lacking some of the exuberance of other tit species, the Sombre Tit is a noticeably quiet, unobtrusive bird. Even in early spring, when most tits are singing lustily, the Sombre Tit can manage only a few phrases every hour. And while other tits can be hard to miss, the Sombre Tit has a habit of remaining undercover within the vegetation, working methodically in a small part of its territory before moving on, not dashing from place to place. It is found in a broad range of habitats, including mountain woodland (with deciduous or coniferous trees), scrub and cultivated areas such as orchards, and it is entirely restricted in our area to the southeast. Pairs are invariably well spread, suggesting that they have large territories and that these are occupied all year round.

With its powerful bill, the Sombre Tit can reach some items unavailable to the smaller tits. It is often seen holding large nuts and seeds in its feet while it hammers them open, and it will wedge the more reluctant ones into the bark and work on them there. It will perch on seed heads and tear them to pieces. This power compensates for its general lack of finesse and agility.

The nest is usually placed in a hole in a tree, but also regularly among rocks and on the ground. It contrast to those of most tits, the nest is made not of moss but of dry plant fragments and wool.

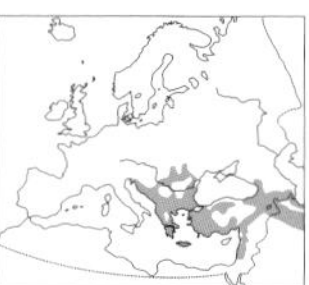

ID: Largest tit, plumper than Great Tit, but most recalls that species. Sombre coloration: tired grey-brown above, greyish below. Usual black cap, white cheeks and black bib of other tits.

Marsh Tit

Parus palustris (**par**-uss pal-**loo**-striss)
length 11.5 cm

Don't look for a Marsh Tit in a marsh. Despite both its English and scientific names, it is a species of broad-leaved woodland – the name originated out of confusion with the Willow Tit. Moreover, it particularly favours oak and beech woods, especially those with a generous understorey of holly and other shrubs. It will occur in patches of alder in damp places, but it can normally tolerate only quite extensive stands of trees, with little in the way of tidying and management.

This is a very sedentary bird which, once settled into a territory in young adulthood, never leaves it. Marsh Tits in their first few months of life wander with flocks of other birds, but by the next spring their travels cease. Cold weather doesn't shift them and neither, it would appear, do vagaries of food supply. They live as pairs in a territory that can be 2.5 ha in extent. When parties of other tits pass through their area the incumbent pair may join them, but leave as soon as they reach their borders.

In common with other tits, the Marsh Tit feeds on invertebrates in spring and summer, and nuts and seeds in winter. Within this generalisation it is actually the most vegetarian of all the species, taking plant material in preference to insect food even when the latter is still available outside the peak breeding season. Many food items are stored for brief periods immediately after discovery, largely to avoid piracy from Blue or Great Tits when the species are foraging in the same area.

The Marsh Tit prefers to use natural holes for nesting, although it can also be persuaded into nest boxes. It is dominant to the Willow Tit where the two coexist and, once the latter has excavated its nest hole, the Marsh Tit may take it over.

ID: Small tit with glossy black cap, neat bib and plain wings; no wing bars; no pale patch on secondaries. Slighter than Willow Tit and less heavy around back of neck. Outer tail feathers longest, so tail may look slightly forked (on Willow Tit central tail feathers are longer than outers, making tail look rounded).

Siberian Tit

Parus cinctus (**par**-uss **sink**-tuss)
length 12.5–14 cm

The boreal forests of northernmost Europe play host to the scarce Siberian Tit. It is found mostly in pine and spruce forest, in places where there is a thick canopy and plenty of old and rotting trees. It searches each tree as it feeds, and is surprisingly agile for a large tit, covering the trunk, small twigs and topmost needles with equal facility. It also likes to feed among lichen.

In the harsh climate of the extreme north, it pays to be prepared, so Siberian Tits spend a great deal of their time collecting food to be stored away for the winter. About 65 per cent of everything they find in spring is stashed away, in the needle clusters at the tips of coniferous branches, in crevices or in clumps of lichen. Most of it is insect food, especially caterpillars, which are killed before storage, but a few seeds are secreted, too. In the autumn there is more storing still, ready for the approach of winter, when the temperature may plunge to –45°C on cold nights and food may be needed urgently.

The social structure of the Siberian Tit includes several unusual quirks. Essentially, pairs live in large territories throughout the year. But in winter they may be joined by up to seven first-year birds that help to defend the territory. In spring, most leave, but the odd one will remain in the pair's territory, and possibly breed if one of the original pair dies. In addition to this, spring territories, so vigorously defended by other tits, are sometimes shared by two breeding pairs.

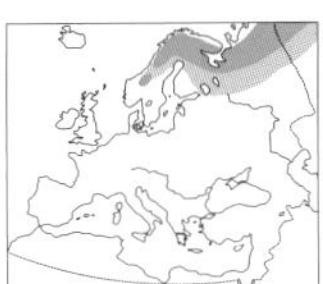

ID: Large tit with fluffy plumage. Rusty-brown on flanks and chocolate-brown on back. Cap is grey-brown, not black as in other similar tits.

adult

juv.

Willow Tit

Parus montanus (**par**-uss mon-**tay**-nuss)
length 11.5 cm

It might be remarkably similar to the Marsh Tit in appearance, but the Willow Tit is very different in many aspects of its life history. For one thing, a major part of its European population breeds in conifer woods, something that the Marsh Tit never does. It also excavates its own nest hole which, again, the Marsh Tit does not do. The Willow also feeds on finer and smaller items, especially in the seeds that it takes. And, at least in some parts of Europe, the composition of its winter flocks is quite different.

Besides boreal and montane evergreen forests, Willow Tits occur in two other distinct habitats: small clusters of trees or bushes in damp areas; and birch forests. The first habitat gives the bird its English name, as willows, along with elders, birches and alders, are ideal for it; these are all thin, weak-barked trees that are likely to provide nest sites. Birch forests are occupied chiefly in the far north.

The Willow Tit is not the only European tit to excavate a nest hole; the Crested Tit does, too. But while the Crested Tit will sometimes not bother with the whole rigmarole and will simply modify an existing hole, the Willow Tit must excavate a new one every year; otherwise it will not breed. Even nest boxes must be filled with removable wood chippings if they are to be accepted. Interestingly, excavation is carried out by both sexes of Willow Tit, but in the Crested Tit solely by the female.

Once breeding is over and winter beckons, Willow Tits fall into various social camps according to where they occur. Paired adult birds remain on their territory all year, and in some areas they remain just as a twosome in winter. In other places they will accept two first-year birds into the territory to share its defence, and in still other areas they will accept four tenants, to make a group of six. Within all the social groupings adults are dominant over first-year birds; but if one adult dies, a younger bird tends to move in to take its place.

ID: Exceedingly similar to Marsh Tit, but cap is sooty, not glossy, and most birds show definite pale panel on wing, made by pale edges to the secondaries. Bib is often larger than that of Marsh Tit and less neatly defined.

ID: Unmistakable. The only small brown woodland bird in Europe with a prominent crest.

Crested Tit

Parus cristatus (**par**-uss kriss-**stay**-tuss)
length 10–12 cm

Most tits have life histories geared for mass production and high mortality, but not the Crested Tit. Each year it lays a modest clutch of between four and eight eggs, and once the young have survived the post-fledging period, their winter mortality rate can be as low as 8 per cent, exceptional for such a small bird (30–50 per cent is more typical). Adult pairs live in the same territory year round and the bond between them lasts for life.

An advantage of living in a fixed territory is the possibility of storing food for later consumption. Crested Tits don't just eat what they need for the day; they also collect seeds when they are plentiful and store them away in crevices above ground, for example in fissures in bark, one item per hiding place. These can then be retrieved when times are hard, which may be as much as several months later.

The social organisation and pairing of Crested Tits is unusual. It seems that first-year birds wander around after fledging and eventually latch on to an established pair with whom they will subsequently spend the winter and share the territory, defending it collectively. Several of these drifters may become 'tenants' of the same pair, and if they are of the opposite sex, there is a high chance than they will become an 'item' themselves.

Crested Tits are found in pine woods in the north of their range, but are more common in mixed woods, and then deciduous woods towards the south: beech in the Pyrenees, cork oak in Spain. Ideal habitat contains rotten tree stumps for nesting. Although some holes prove suitable for nesting, others are refurbished and still others are excavated from scratch, by the female working on her own.

ID: *May recall Blue Tit, but with white underparts and crown, broad white wing bars and edges of tail; tail is also longer.*

Azure Tit

Parus cyanus (**par**-uss sie-**ayn**-uss)
length 12–13 cm

This powdery-white and delicate blue tit is rare in our area: the only significant populations are in Belarus. From time to time, though, nomadic wanderers turn up in Fennoscandia and Central Europe from Russia. The local Blue Tits may be affected, too, because the two species quite often form mixed pairs, and a hybrid version, the so-called 'Pleske's Tit', is well known.

On its home turf the Azure Tit is a bird of riverside broad-leaved woodland, damp thickets, marshy scrub and floodlands. It can be difficult to see, because birds have a habit of foraging from top to bottom and soon disappearing behind a screen of dense foliage. When foraging in a willow, for example, they begin with the small twigs and work their way down to the ground, and in reedbeds they methodically extract caterpillars from the stems, roof to ground floor. In common with most tits, they feed mainly on seeds in the winter.

Blue Tit

Parus caeruleus (**par**-uss see-**roo**-leh-uss)
length 11.5 cm

Effervescent and bold, the Blue Tit punches above its weight. When competing with the much larger Great Tit over food at a bird table or other source, it is not bullied into submission, and the two species are well matched. In spring, though, when the birds compete for nest sites, the Great Tit usually wins out, relegating the Blue Tit to less desirable sites.

The Blue Tit is an exceedingly common bird over almost all of Europe, excluding the far north and Iceland. It prefers deciduous woodland and forest to any other habitat, but is adaptable enough to thrive in gardens, shrubbery and other sites with fewer trees. It is highly acrobatic, moving from a perched to a hanging position with considerable ease, and effortlessly reaching to the very tips of branches. As far as the tit family goes, the Blue Tit is the dominant species of the broad-leaved canopy.

In the winter, Blue Tits usually go about in mixed-species flocks; indeed, groups of this species often form the nucleus of such aggregations. Ringing studies have shown that the constituent Blue Tits come from two different social backgrounds: some are residents, moving around with the flock close to their territory or birthplace; others are nomads, enjoying only temporary membership of any flock. At bird tables and other concentrated food sources, flock behaviour tends to break down.

From early spring Blue Tits begin to sing and pair up. Perhaps surprisingly for such a small bird, individuals that can do so tend to re-form relationships from the previous year. There are many different songs, but the most typical and recognisable is a long drawn-out trill preceded by a couple of shorter notes. A common display added later in the season is a brief whirring display flight, terminating close to a potential nest site.

Blue Tits lay a lot of eggs. In woodland the average size of a clutch is 11 and can be as much as 18, which is as high as for any small bird in the world.

ID: *Unmistakable small, brightly coloured tit with cobalt-blue crown and dark eye stripe. Blue crown shows ultraviolet reflectance, the intensity of which varies individually and is a measure of a bird's quality.*

Great Tit

Parus major (**par**-uss **may**-jor)
length 14 cm

Not many species are candidates for the commonest bird in Europe, but the familiar Great Tit has a good case, occurring throughout our region except in Iceland. It is essentially a woodland bird, thriving most when there is a mixture of tree types and the cover is not too dark and cramped. But it has also readily adapted to using many different kinds of edge habitats, including scrub, farmland copses and gardens, and it even penetrates into the heart of cities and sprawling suburbs. Not only is it familiar, but it is also one of the most intensively studied birds in the world, aided partly by its almost fanatical use of nest boxes. If these are provided, the Great Tit will soon abandon its heritage of nesting in natural holes in favour of these new-fangled artificial constructions.

The Great Tit differs ecologically from other tit species in typically feeding close to the ground, or on it. In winter it rarely strays above 7 m, habitually searching for food on large branches and on trunks, where there is little competition from other tits. It has a powerful bill and can open large nuts, including those of hazel and beech, by hammering. Studies have shown that beech mast may be crucial to this bird's prospects of winter survival; populations tend to be high in spring after a good autumnal beech crop, then poor the year after a moderate one. In summer the Great Tit abandons its low niche in favour of gleaning caterpillars, which at that time seem almost to drip from the canopy.

In winter, most Great Tits forage as part of a roaming mixed-species flock. These flocks, which form each day in the morning and may have some consistency of membership, at times attract dozens of individuals of such species as various tits (including Long-tailed Tits), Nuthatches, Treecreepers and Goldcrests. The main reason for gathering loosely like this is to create a communal vigilance against predators, but for a dominant bird such as a Great Tit, there is the added advantage of the opportunity for theft. It is easy for a Great Tit to persuade a Coal Tit, for example, to surrender any food that it has had the temerity to find, thus making stealing a cost-effective way to feed for the larger bird. Just as human pickpockets or muggers benefit from a high density of population, so Great Tits benefit from being in flocks.

From January onwards, Great Tits take up territories by singing; if they leave it too late, they may be unable to acquire a patch of ground. The male's song is a very cheerful repetition of two notes, with something of an attack at the beginning; it has been likened to the sound of a saw sharpening, a foot pump or the word 'TEA-cher' repeated quickly. It is a dominant sound of the season.

The pair bond between male and female is monogamous, but often somewhat strained by infidelity, real and potential. At times a male Great Tit feels the need to watch his mate literally from dawn to dusk, from the time when he sings during the dawn chorus to when he escorts her back to her roosting hole. If all goes well, the 8–13 eggs and resulting nestlings will be his, but spring can be an anxious time.

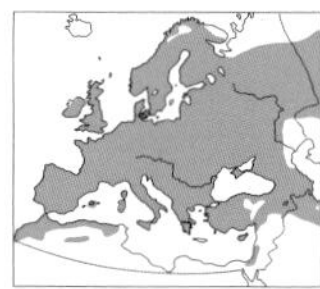

ID: Easy to identify, with yellow breast bisected by broad black vertical line, broader in the male (particularly from legs to tail). Bold white cheek, glossy blue-black crown, greenish back.

Coal Tit

Parus ater (**par**-uss **ay**-ter)
length 11.5 cm

The Coal Tit is perhaps the nearest of the tit species to being a specialist, because it almost invariably occurs in coniferous woodland, especially when breeding. It has long toes and an extremely narrow bill, the former ideal for acrobatics high in branches, the latter an adaptation for poking among conifer needles. It is the smallest of the true European tits and the most agile, forever hanging upside down, slipping from branch to branch with quick flutters and also, in contrast to most other tits, regularly hovering. It is essentially a tree-top bird, feeding preferentially in the crowns and upper branches.

Not surprisingly for a bird with such a fine bill (rivalling that of the Goldcrest, living in the same habitat), the Coal Tit takes the smallest average food items of any European tit. These are principally invertebrates in spring and summer, and include aphids, caterpillars and far more spiders than are taken by any other species. Seeds of spruce are particularly important, too, and may form the mainstay of the diet in the winter. In common with most tits with brown (or nearly brown) plumage, Coal Tits collect and cache large amounts of food, partly for winter survival and partly to keep them hidden from competitive Blue and Great Tits. That is what a Coal Tit is doing when it visits a bird table frequented by the other two – in great haste, flying in, grabbing a nut and zooming away. It is taking its prize away for storage, privately.

At times Blue and Great Tits can be the bane of a Coal Tit's life. If all three species mix in winter flocks, Coal Tits are frequently attacked by the other two, and have their food stolen. Should they coexist in breeding areas, Coal Tits will find themselves literally at the bottom of the tree when it comes to nest sites. Blue or Great Tits take the safer, higher holes, while Coal Tits are condemned to mouse holes and crevices among the roots. Deep in coniferous forest, where the others are rare or absent, Coal Tits hold sway and rarely compete much among themselves for territories.

Coal Tits are more likely to be double-brooded than other members of the family and they are unique in occasionally making three nesting attempts. It is likely that, where both survive, Coal Tits keep their partners from year to year. They probably stay together in winter flocks, even though they do not remain on their breeding territory.

Every so often Coal Tits from northern populations respond to acute food shortages by erupting south and west. But apart from these instances, the Coal Tit is not migratory.

adult

juv.

ID: Smallest of the true tits and may recall miniature Great Tit at first, but much less colourful. Large-headed and short-tailed. Blue-grey above, with two rows of white dots making wing bar; crown black but nape white.

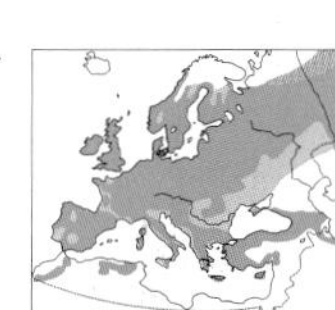

Bearded Reedling family *Timaliidae* (tim-mal-**lie**-id-ee) and Penduline Tit family *Remizidae* (ree-**mie**-zid-ee)

Habitat Wetlands. Bearded Reedling found exclusively in large reedbeds and their immediate surrounds; Penduline Tit in waterside vegetation, requiring a mixture of reeds, shrubs, small trees and herbs.
Food Bearded Reedling eats invertebrates (beetles, caterpillars, midges, spiders and snails) and seeds of reed. Penduline Tit eats larval insects, spiders and a few small seeds.
Movements Penduline Tit migratory in the north (arrival February–May, departure August–September), sedentary in the south. Bearded Reedling mainly sedentary, but eruptive (see text).
Voice Distinctive: Bearded Reedling has metallic, lively 'pching' note, like mini cash-register. Penduline Tit has high-pitched whistle that drops in pitch, like a sigh.
Pairing style Bearded Reedling monogamous, but Penduline Tit's arrangements very complicated (see text).
Nesting Bearded Reedling loosely colonial; Penduline Tit solitary and territorial (but territories rather clustered).
Nest Bearded Reedling builds cup of dead leaves, usually of reeds, near ground; lined with reed flowerheads. Nest of Penduline Tit extraordinary (see text).
Productivity Bearded Reedling highly productive, with 2–4 broods a year; Penduline Tit usually 1 brood a year, rarely 2.
Eggs Bearded Reedling 4–8, Penduline Tit 6–8.
Incubation 11–14 days, by both sexes (Bearded Reedling); 13–14 days, by one adult of either sex (Penduline Tit).
Young Nest-bound, altricial, naked.
Parenting style Tended by both parents (Bearded Reedling) or 1 (Penduline Tit).
Food to young In both species, small invertebrates, including caterpillars.
Leaving nest Fledge at 12–13 days (Bearded Reedling) or 21–25 days (Penduline Tit).

These two species are both superficially tit-like in behaviour, being small, lively and active, and expert in clinging on to small branches or stems, often hanging upside down to feed. Both have earned the epithet 'tit', although the Bearded Tit is now usually called the Bearded Reedling. Neither, however, are true tits. They differ in many aspects of their behaviour, not least in the construction of their nests.

Bearded Reedling

Panurus biarmicus (pan-**noo**-russ bie-**arm**-mi-kuss)
length 12.5–14.5 cm

The common reed provides the Bearded Reedling with everything it needs. The birds forage on reed stems in the spring and summer, looking for caterpillars and other insects; they eat the seeds of reeds in the winter; and they build their nests out of reeds (and sometimes sedges). It amounts to complete dependence on one plant species for this specialised bird.

The transition from eating soft-bodied, nutritious insects to hard seeds in autumn requires a certain change in the Bearded Reedling's gut. The stomach acquires special hard plates and greatly increases in mass. In addition, the birds swallow up to 600 minute stones to aid in the breaking down of vegetable food. Once spring returns the plates disappear and the birds eject their small grinding agents, replacing them with a few larger stones instead.

Individual Bearded Reedlings may live in one reedbed for their whole lives, but in some autumns, perhaps due to population pressure, a proportion of birds get up and leave an area. They go off in all directions, stopping only when their urge to travel is halted by the sight of a reedbed. The birds travel in even numbers, sometimes twos of the opposite sex, but these 'pairs' do not necessarily breed together in the following season after their shared journey.

These irregular eruptions are preceded by an eye-catching display known as 'high flying'. It is just that – a very fast climb several hundred metres into the air, accompanied by loud calling. Several times the birds rise, only to plummet back to their own reedbed. Eventually they will ascend again and fly off to pastures new.

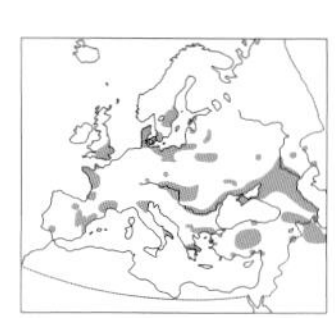

ID: Distinctive small reedbed bird with long tail. Male has grey head and black moustache (not a beard!), which female lacks. Juvenile has black patch on back, and some black on edge of tail.

Penduline Tit

Remiz pendulinus (**ree**-miz pen-doo-**lie**-nuss)
length 11 cm

The Penduline Tit may be small, but in its way it has an effect on its immediate surroundings. You can tell when Penduline Tits are in an area, not by seeing the birds, but by seeing the results of their handiwork – nests will hang from branches everywhere.

The social organisation of the Penduline Tit revolves around these amazing structures. They are made up entirely of plant fibres and down, and hang suspended from the end of a branch of a tree or thicket, usually 1–10 m above the water. They are domed in shape, but have a downward-facing tube-like extension on one side, near the top, which acts as the entrance lobby. When constructing the nest, the builders begin by attaching a strong loop of plant fibre underneath the branch tip, and then build out the sides. Plant fibres used include those of nettles and grass, and they are compacted into shape by plant down, giving the overall structure a felt-like feel. More plant down is stuffed inside.

Nest-building is the only time when the relationship between male and female Penduline Tits is sustained. They work together – often with one concentrating on the outside and the other on the interior – and that's about it, a two-week fling. They don't co-operate in bringing up the young, but one or the other takes sole charge. Who it is depends on the bewildering sexual politics of the species. Males are sometimes polygynous, each with several mates with whom they share nest-building duties and contribute genetic material; the most successful male birds, the ones that attract most females to their partially completed nests, are those whose structures are least infested with parasites such as mites. Females are regularly polyandrous, building with and then copulating with a succession of relatively 'clean' males. There are records, for example, of female Penduline Tits having six partners in a season, with each of whom they will build a nest and for whom they may lay a clutch of eggs to incubate. Other females incubate their first clutch themselves and stick to one partner, notwithstanding the fact that the partner himself may be building a nest with another female at the same time. Few birds have such a convoluted breeding system.

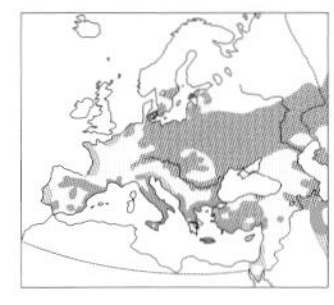

ID: Unmistakable tiny bird of wetlands and waterside trees. Male has larger black face mask than female.

Creepers families *Sittidae* (**sit**-tid-ee), *Certhiidae* (ser-**thie**-id-ee) and *Tichodromadidae* (tik-ko-dro-**mad**-id-ee)

Habitat Treecreepers, Nuthatch and Corsican Nuthatch in woods and forests; Rock Nuthatch and Wallcreeper on rock faces and buildings.
Food All eat insects and spiders in spring and summer. Nuthatches take nuts and seeds in winter.
Movements Nuthatches and Treecreepers sedentary. Wallcreeper makes altitudinal movements.
Voice Nuthatches fluid whistles and trills; Wallcreeper slurred piping whistle; Treecreepers very high-pitched sibilant songs.
Pairing style Nuthatches monogamous, Treecreepers almost always so, but occasionally polygynous.
Nesting Solitary and territorial.
Nest Most Nuthatches nest in holes; Wallcreeper in rock crevice; Treecreepers behind bark flaking away from tree, or similar sites. See individual entries for details.
Productivity Wallcreeper single-brooded and Nuthatches usually so. Treecreepers double-brooded.
Eggs Nuthatches 5–10; Wallcreeper usually 6 (range 3–9); Treecreepers 6–7.
Incubation Nuthatches 14–18 days; Wallcreeper 18–20; Treecreepers 13–15. All by female only, often fed by male.
Young Altricial and slightly downy.
Parenting style Young are fed by both sexes, female broods.
Food to young Invertebrates.
Leaving nest Young Nuthatches fledge at 22–30 days, Wallcreepers at 28–30 and Treecreepers at 14–17. Young can often climb well as soon as they leave the nest and may be independent in a week.

The 'creepers' are a small group of birds that don't perch in the conventional sense, but adhere closely to tree limbs and rock faces, climbing up (or down) them with a jerky motion. They come from three families:

The **Nuthatches** can move up or down surfaces with equal facility. When stationary they cling with one foot well above the other, the upper one carrying the weight (so the bird is effectively hanging), the lower one supporting; their short tails are not used in climbing. They often adopt a unique head-down posture. Nuthatches have long bills which they use for probing into cracks and for hammering open nuts. They are insectivorous in the breeding season, but mainly vegetarian outside it.

The **Treecreepers** recall miniature woodpeckers, with their upright posture on the tree trunk, their feet held at the same height and the tail used as a support, like a brace. They creep up trunks and branches in a mouse-like manner. They have long, thin, down-curved bills that are no good for excavation, but ideal for probing and prying among fissures in the bark. They are mainly insectivorous.

The **Wallcreeper** resembles the nuthatches in general habits and in having a short tail, but it progresses upwards only and has a long curved bill, like a treecreeper. It is a specialist bird of high altitudes.

Short-toed Treecreeper

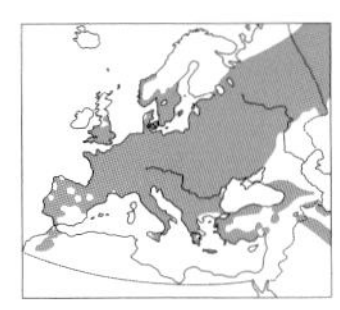

Nuthatch

Sitta europaea (**sit**-ta yoo-**roh**-pee-a)
length 14 cm

ID: Distinctive plump, large-headed, short-necked and short-tailed bird that hugs tree trunks. Blue-grey above, buff below, the latter intensifying from breast to undertail coverts and flanks (especially male). Bold black eye stripe.

This is by far the most widespread nuthatch in Europe, occurring throughout the continent except for the far north. It is a woodland bird, preferring large deciduous trees with airy crowns and complex networks of branches and twigs where it can climb along, up and down, foraging over surfaces with its rather hurried, jerky action. It will also tolerate more open parkland habitats, so long as the trees are not too far apart, when they might put a strain on its rather weak, heavily undulating flight.

In spring and summer Nuthatches eat a variety of insects and spiders gleaned from the surfaces of trunks. Their unique way of descending trees head first may give them a different perspective from other insectivorous climbers, enabling them to exploit food overlooked by competitors.

Once the breeding season is over, though, Nuthatches resort to feeding on seeds and nuts, which they break open by sharp pecks of the long, thin bill. Harder fruits may be held by the feet while being worked on, or wedged into a suitable bark crevice so that the birds can strike them with full force. The tapping sound so made can easily be confused with the efforts of woodpeckers. When autumn food is available in quantity, some will be hoarded away, wedged into the bark and covered over by moss or other debris up in the trees, ready to be retrieved during lean periods later on.

A winter food store is useless, of course, if its owner does not stay put within its territory to exploit it, and most Nuthatches are jealous of their borders all year round. Intruders are chased away, although the occasional young bird may be tolerated as an unpopular tenant in the winter, relationships remaining tense for months. For territorial defence Nuthatches have loud voices, making cheerful-sounding whistles, rapid trills and slow down-slurred notes, which may be a common soundtrack to the woodland atmosphere of early spring.

More tension erupts later, when Nuthatches compete with other species for that precious commodity, a nest hole. But these birds have a secret weapon that enables them to win some battles with, for example, Starlings. When a pair of Nuthatches finds a suitable hole, the female plasters mud all over the entrance so that, eventually, the opening is made to measure – ideal for a Nuthatch, too small for a Starling, keeping the competing birds out. More mud may be affixed to the roof or sides, too, to shelter the chamber from rain and draughts.

Corsican Nuthatch

Sitta whiteheadi (**sit**-ta wite-**hed**-die)
length 12 cm

The pride of Corsica, this small nuthatch is found nowhere else on earth. It isn't confined just to the island itself, but more specifically to mountain forests of Corsican Pine, almost entirely between 1000 m and 1500 m. It is most abundant in unmanaged stands of its favourite tree, with plenty of rotting timber and clearings created by tree fall. It is pretty fussy, then, and the total population is not much more than 2000 pairs.

Corsican Nuthatches are often seen nosing around in the tops of the trees at the end of branches, among the dense foliage of needles. They may hover to reach outlying branches or make darting sallies to catch insects in mid-air; in many ways, they act more like Coal Tits than nuthatches. In winter they revert to type, gleaning trunks and larger branches for insects, and also taking seeds from cones. The latter are often cached for use in hard weather.

In its nesting habits the Corsican Nuthatch is quite unlike the Nuthatch. It does not plaster its hole with mud; and it sometimes excavates its own nest hole, which the Nuthatch doesn't do. The nest itself is a cup of needles, bark and wood chips, lined with moss, lichen and other softer materials.

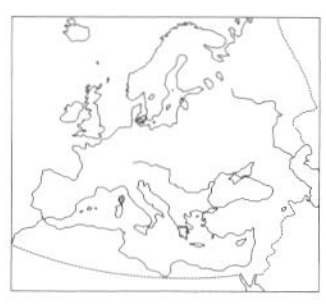

ID: Unmistakable small nuthatch with white eyebrow and thinner bill than the prototype. The only nuthatch in Corsica.

Rock Nuthatch

Sitta neumayer (**sit**-ta **nyoo**-mie-er)
length 13.5–14.5 cm

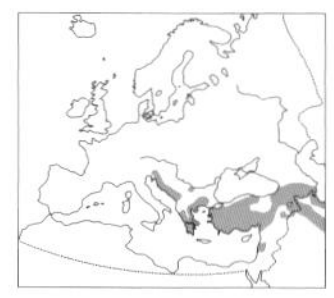

ID: Like a pale version of Nuthatch with longer bill and found in different habitat. Virtually white below, undertail coverts faint buff; no markings on tail.

Many birdwatchers see their first Rock Nuthatch when visiting archaeological ruins, in Greece or elsewhere in southeast Europe. The first sighting is usually of a small bird perched upright on a rock, peering over to investigate an invasion of its territory and perhaps giving its trilling call. Old buildings are ideal for Rock Nuthatches, as are rocky slopes and mountains, their 'natural' habitat. The birds feed on the ground and investigate nooks and crannies on steep cliff faces and outcrops; they do visit adjoining trees, but mostly in winter, and cannot be considered as woodland birds at all. They occur in warm, dry places, usually on calcareous soils, up to about 1000 m in altitude.

The nest is an extraordinary structure, not placed in a hole as is typical for a Nuthatch, but built out from a slight depression in a rock face, usually beneath an overhang. The finished flask shape juts out some way from the rock and is rounded off at the end, where an entrance tunnel as much as 10 cm long is added like an extension tube. This architectural marvel is made from a concoction of mud, animal dung, hair, feathers and plant resin. The bodies of insects are entombed within the mixture, and berries are added, too, each apparently to give binding strength. Inside, the birds build a cup of moss, grass, feathers and other debris, and lay their well-protected eggs.

Wallcreeper

Tichodroma muraria (tik-**kod**-roh-ma moo-**ray**-ri-a)
length 16.5 cm; wingspan 27–32 cm

This is a stunning bird found at high elevations, often amongst magnificent scenery. It is unique in form, colour and habits, and difficult to locate in its rarefied habitat. It is such a draw to birdwatchers that, remarkably, holiday packages have been arranged with the sole purpose of seeing it.

It is certainly eye-catching, for although the body colour is mostly grey and black, the broad, butterfly-shaped wings are patterned with brilliant crimson, jet-black and white. It flies with a distinctive erratic flutter and skip, with brief glides, so at times it can resemble a leaf blowing in the breeze high on the rock face. When foraging, the Wallcreeper moves upward in a series of hops, as if it were climbing a ladder, and it incessantly flicks its wings open to reveal their startling red centres, a contact signal to other birds.

Most Wallcreepers breed 1000–2000 m above sea level. They are thinly spread, occurring mainly on large, precipitous rock faces and vertical walls, especially near streams and torrents. They feed on insects and spiders gleaned from the rocks or captured in a rapid mid-air chase. If it is raining, which it frequently is in Wallcreeper habitat, the birds will descend to forage over streamside boulders and pebbles instead. The cup-shaped nest is hidden in a deep crevice or rock fissure, often moistened by permanent spray. It has two entrances, one each for entry and exit, or sometimes one for the male and the other for the female.

After the breeding season Wallcreepers descend to much lower altitudes, and may swap their remote habitat for castle walls and church towers, even within towns. Each bird, male or female, holds its own winter territory, proclaiming it by song and vigorously chasing off any intruders.

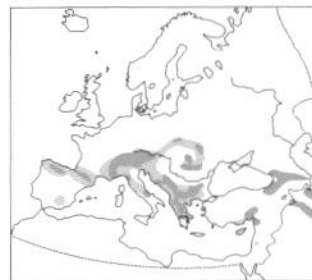

ID: Unmistakable. Female lacks black throat of male. Sexes similar in winter.

adult ♂ br. adult ♀ / non-br. ♂

Short-toed Treecreeper

Certhia brachydactyla (**ser**-thi-a brak-ki-**dak**-til-la)
length 12 cm

There are perhaps no more similar species to look at in the whole of Europe than Treecreepers and Short-toed Treecreepers. They are almost impossible to distinguish by sight but, fortunately for us, their songs and calls are very different. While the Treecreeper tends to whisper its sibilant calls and song phrases, the Short-toed makes loud, confident whistles and has a song phrase that penetrates the woodland. As if assured of its vocal prowess, the Short-toed Treecreeper sings much more regularly, and for a longer part of the year, than its quiet counterpart.

The two species are ecologically separate, a fact that is easiest to appreciate when both occur in the same area. The Treecreeper, tougher by nature, tends to be found at higher elevations, including mountains, and often in conifer forests, which are generally shunned by the Short-toed Treecreeper. It has a more northerly distribution and is the only treecreeper found in Britain and Fennoscandia. The Short-toed Treecreeper occurs mainly in broad-leaved woodlands and copses, especially around oak trees, and is dominant in lowland central Europe, Iberia and Italy, where the Treecreeper is almost absent.

The foraging habits of the two species are very similar, although the Short-toed is said to feed more slowly and methodically, and to spiral less. It also requires more rugged bark, being less able to cope than its longer-toed relative with smooth-trunked trees. Few differences in breeding behaviour have been reported, although the Treecreeper is said to be more pugnacious than the Short-toed in the defence of its territory.

adult juv.

ID: Almost identical to Common Treecreeper, but with longer, more bent-looking bill, less clear-cut white supercilium, dustier underparts and different detail to wing pattern. Also significantly noisier.

Treecreeper

Certhia familiaris (**ser**-thi-a fam-mil-li-**ay**-riss)
length 12.5 cm

The Treecreeper is a specialist, with just one main way of foraging, but a very successful one. Starting from the bottom of a tree trunk, it simply climbs up the bark, often following a slightly spiral trail. As it ascends it peers and probes into the many tiny holes, crevices and irregularities on the surface, picking insects off the bark and disturbing them from their hiding places. In this way it nourishes itself all day long, not departing from its upward progress except perhaps to work along the underside of a branch or to flit down from high in each tree to the base of the next when its exploratory trail has been exhausted. As a feeding technique it might be one-dimensional, but it is effective.

The Treecreeper's simple method enables it to work trunks and branches all year round, feeding on insects and spiders even in the midst of winter. Snow does not normally cover all its potential feeding sites and, because the Treecreeper can reach hidden places unavailable to other birds, it has little competition. It takes a very wide variety of insects, including beetles, earwigs, moths and lacewings. It does pick up a few seeds, mainly very small ones such as spruce or pine, but it cannot survive for long without invertebrate food.

Treecreepers often join flocks of other small birds moving through the woods, taking advantage of the collective vigilance against predators. At night they settle into a small crevice, lying as flat as possible for shelter. In very weak-barked trees a Treecreeper might excavate a hollow for itself, and on cold nights several birds may congregate, huddling together to benefit from each other's body heat.

In the breeding season, Treecreepers build their nests in sites that they must come across frequently every day – small splits caused by bark flaking away from a tree trunk. In such fragile places they make a boat-shaped nest out of small fragments of twigs, roots, moss and grass. The nest may be so narrow that the incubating bird cannot turn around. Sometimes the birds will use similar sites, for example in the small pits created by ivy and other creeping plants, or where small depressions are found on the bark itself.

Although most Treecreepers are monogamous, a few males are known to take more than one mate; there has even been one observation of two females sitting side by side in the same nest, but on different clutches. Many Treecreepers have two broods and sometimes, in order to speed things up, the female will begin incubating a second clutch before young from the first have left the nest.

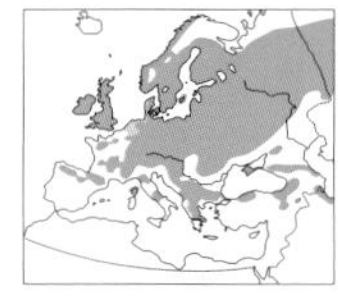

ID: Treecreepers are unmistakable as such, with long, decurved bills, mottled brown backs and clean white underparts. Hug closely to branches, upright. See Short-toed Treecreeper for differences between two species.

Golden Oriole *Oriolus oriolus* (oh-**rie**-oh-luss oh-**rie**-oh-luss)

family *Oriolidae* (oh-**rie**-oh-lid-ee)

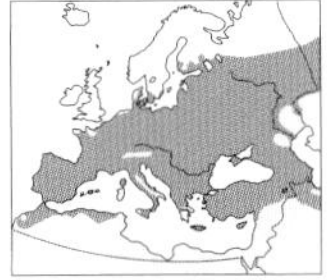

length 24 cm
ID: *Black and yellow male unmistakable. Female less contrasting and less fulsomely yellow, being almost green on the back and whitish below, with streaks on the breast. First-summer male similar to female, but more streaked. All have bright pink bills.*

Habitat Open woods and forest edge, usually but not always deciduous. Often drawn to linear woodland, especially by water.
Food Insects, especially caterpillars and beetle larvae, gleaned from foliage in the canopy. Also eats berries in autumn.
Movements A summer migrant, arriving from late April and departing for Africa in August.
Voice Wide vocabulary includes male's song, a melodic, exotic-sounding whistle. Both sexes have a growling, cat-like call.
Pairing style Monogamous.
Nesting Solitary and fiercely territorial.
Nest Unusual structure slung from high branches (see text).
Productivity 1 brood a year.
Eggs 3–4.
Incubation 16–17 days, mainly by female. Young hatch synchronously.
Young Nest-bound, altricial, downy.
Parenting style Both sexes feed the young, helped occasionally by one or several wandering immature birds. Parents are exceptionally aggressive in defence of the nest.
Food to young Insects, especially caterpillars, plus a little fruit (including cherries).
Leaving nest Young fledge at 16–17 days, and may then be looked after for another 2–3 weeks. The family party may begin migration together, and young have even been recorded begging for food in transit.

There are plenty of birds in Europe that are more easily heard than seen, but few offer such a visual feast when they are finally glimpsed as the Golden Oriole. It belongs to a family that is mostly found in the tropics and it both looks and sounds the part. The male's plumage is bright buttery yellow and its fluty song would make a good soundtrack for a film about rainforests.

Nonetheless, the Golden Oriole is a widespread and often common breeding bird in many parts of Europe, occurring from the shores of the Mediterranean to the fringes of the boreal zone in Fennoscandia. It is arboreal, living in the canopy of tall deciduous trees, which may be in linear groups or within a wood spaced well apart – Orioles require plenty of freedom of movement within and between the crowns.

The nest of a Golden Oriole is highly unusual. Although it could be described as a cup, it is not placed on a network of branches, as most cup nests are. Instead it is slung from two horizontal supports, often close to a fork, hammock-like. It is made up of strips of bark, grass and plant wool 20–40 cm long, which are bound to each support, being looped around or stuck with saliva. Within the hanging cup the birds place a lining of softer materials. In all, the nest may take almost two weeks to build.

Golden Orioles are very vigorous in defence of their nest and eggs. Their main enemies are Jays, Magpies and Carrion Crows from the air and squirrels and martens in the branches. All may be attacked with repeated dives and attempted blows, with the defenders making loud squealing noises during their resistance. At times several pairs from the neighbourhood may take part in a concerted attack. As a result of all this, Golden Oriole nests are rarely plundered.

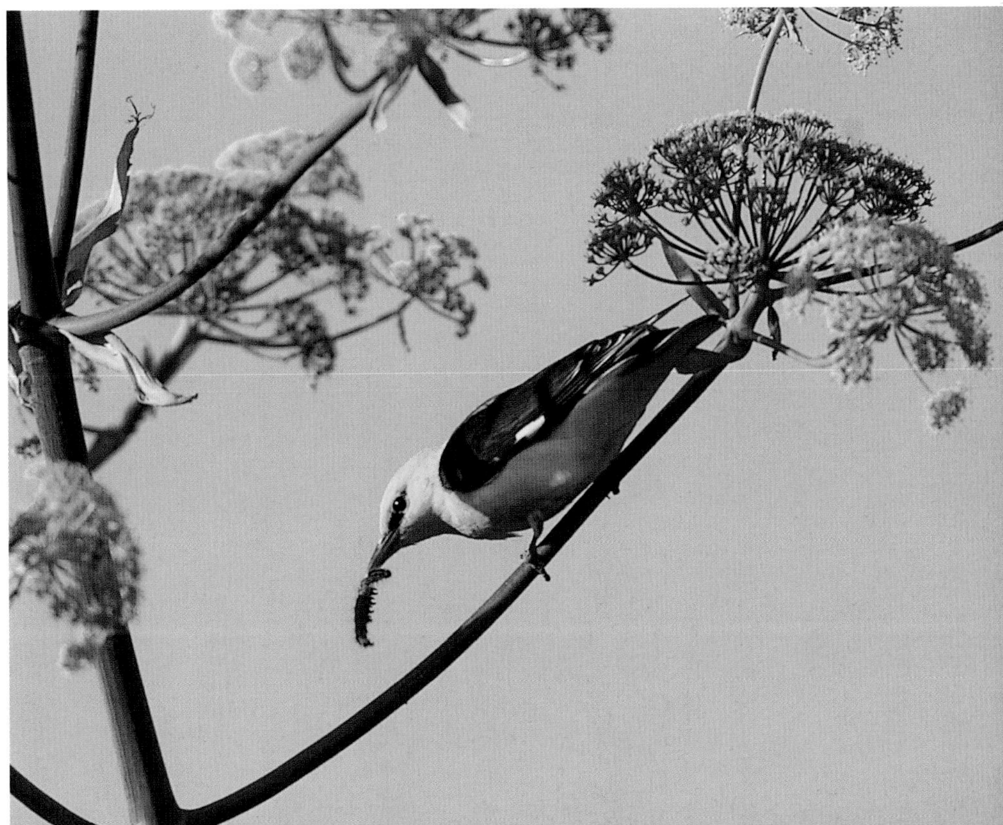

Shrikes family *Laniidae* (lan-**nie**-id-ee)

Habitat Mainly areas with a mixture of bushes and more or less open ground.
Food All eat insects, especially beetles, and some also take small vertebrates. In Red-backed, Masked and the two Grey Shrikes food is often impaled on thorn of tree for storage or dismemberment.
Movements Most are exclusively summer visitors, wintering in sub-Saharan Africa. Great Grey Shrike is partial migrant, not moving out of Europe. Southern Grey Shrike mainly resident.
Voice Undistinguished songs are babbles or quiet warbles, with some harsh, scratchy notes. Birds usually stop singing once paired.
Pairing style Monogamous.
Nesting Solitary and territorial, although nests of Lesser Grey Shrikes or Woodchat Shrikes may be close together ('neighbourhood groups'). Some species nest close to raptors and to Fieldfare colonies, presumably for protection.
Nest Quite bulky constructions of roots, green stems (sometimes of aromatic plants), leaves, grass, lichens etc., lined with finer materials. Often decorated with flowers, string or litter. Usually built near the top of a small tree, but in Red-backed Shrike low in dense bush.
Productivity Most single-brooded, but Masked Shrike often double-brooded.
Eggs 3–7.
Incubation 14–15 days, by female, fed by male.
Young Nest-bound, altricial, naked.
Parenting style Both adults feed young, and may be helped by local unpaired males.
Food to young Mainly invertebrates.
Leaving nest Young fledge at 14–20 days.

Although they are classed as songbirds, the shrikes are more like birds of prey in their feeding habits: they are bold and persistent predators, subsisting on large insects and small vertebrates, including other birds. They have powerful, sharply hooked bills and strong legs and feet with sharp claws. In contrast to true raptors they kill their prey not so much with the feet as by wounds or blows from the bill.

The shrikes are especially noted for their habit of impaling captured prey on sharp thorns, spines or even barbed wire. Sometimes several prey items may be stored near each other in 'larders', leading to the nickname of 'butcher birds'. There are two reasons for impaling prey: if the feeding conditions are good, the shrike can cache excess food for later use should things deteriorate; and impaling can also help a shrike to dismember larger food.

Southern Grey Shrike

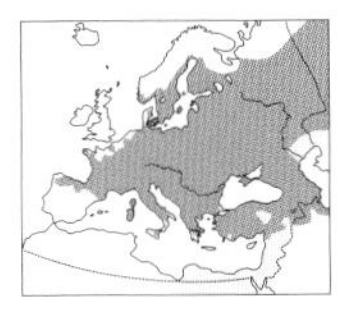

Red-backed Shrike

Lanius collurio (**lan**-ni-uss kol-**loo**-ri-o)
length 17 cm

ID: A small shrike, the male with distinctive smart chestnut, pink and grey plumage, with a black face mask. Female a washed-out version of male, with strongly barred underparts.

When looking for prey, the Red-backed Shrike waits patiently on a perch a few metres off the ground and scours its surroundings for movement below. If nothing happens for a while, it will switch lookout posts, flying from one to another with a brief, whirring, slightly undulating action. It customarily gives a slow wag or sideways flick of the tail as soon as it has landed, letting any neighbours know of its continued right to the new perch. Then, should a beetle or other large insect appear anywhere within 30 m, the shrike will glide over to the spot and grab the insect on the ground with its sharp claws. After a brief struggle it duly picks it up and returns to another perch to dismember and consume it. It will crush smaller insects in its jaws and hold them in its feet while the bill pulls them apart. This is the typical feeding method of most members of the shrike family. In common with several other species, the Red-backed often impales its prey and will catch small mammals and birds as well as insects.

The Red-backed is the commonest and most widespread of the smaller shrikes. It occurs in a variety of habitats with a suitable combination of shrubs and small trees for look-out posts and nest sites, and bare soil or short grass where insects come out from their hiding places. Like other members of the family it needs shelter to aid hunting, and a warm climate to bring out its food. It does not do well in areas where agricultural intensification has taken hold, since this reduces the numbers of insects and the richness and variety of potential habitat; like many shrikes, it is in serious decline.

The Red-backed Shrike is a summer visitor to Europe, wintering in southern Africa, and has a most interesting migration route. It appears that virtually all birds, including those from western Europe, fly down to the eastern side of the Mediterranean, to pass over Greece and Egypt on their way south. Then, on their return, they follow a more easterly route still, through Arabia and the Middle East, before coming back into Europe – a good example of a 'loop migration'.

Male and female Red-backed Shrikes are somewhat different to look at, whereas most shrikes only show minor differences between the sexes. In some populations there seems to be a surplus of males. At any rate, every population seems to contain plenty of unpaired birds, the majority of which cannot hold territories, laying claim only to the odd hunting perch. Once a breeding pair's boundaries begin to creak under the strain of parenthood, these single males, no longer hounded out from a territory, often amuse themselves in an otherwise unproductive July by helping to feed young at the nests of their neighbours, travelling up to 1 km away to do so.

Lesser Grey Shrike

Lanius minor (**lan**-ni-uss **mie**-nor)
length 20 cm

Very much an insect-eater, this is perhaps the most specialised of the shrikes. It hardly ever takes birds or small mammals and does not impale prey on the thorns of bushes. Its favourite foods are beetles, which have been found to constitute 90 per cent or more of the summer diet. Where beetles swarm in the evening, Lesser Grey Shrikes will keep hunting almost until dark. More typically they will practise the usual shrike method of perching up high (often on overhead wires) and watching for movement below.

This species is found in warm, sunny places, usually in the lowlands. In common with most shrikes its ideal habitat will include bare ground, low grass and a few scattered bushes, but it also seems to need some tall trees nearby, although not enough to form woodland. One of these trees will be used for the nest site, which is out on a branch some distance from the trunk. Fruit and walnut trees are often used.

The Lesser Grey Shrike has a distinct tendency to be sociable when nesting, both with its own kind and with unrelated species. Although some pairs are territorial, most nest in a loose association of between three and seven families known as a neighbourhood group. Sometimes the Lesser Grey will nest near other shrike species, including Woodchats and Great Grey Shrikes, and it will make use of the proximity of other aggressive, vigilant species such as Red-footed Falcons, Kestrels, Fieldfares and Golden Orioles.

The Lesser Grey Shrike is a late migrant to Europe, arriving in early May. It often seems to turn up in small concentrations, leading some to suggest that migrant birds may make their entire migratory journey together – if so, that would be very unusual.

ID: Smaller than Great Grey, with longer wings and shorter tail. Breast is tinged pink and the black on the face mask reaches up onto the forehead.

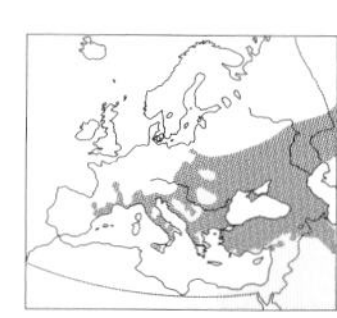

Great Grey Shrike

Lanius excubitor (**lan**-ni-uss eks-**koo**-bit-tor)
length 24–25 cm

If you were to come across a shrike anywhere north of the Mediterranean basin in the wintertime, it would surely be this species, the largest, toughest and most predatory shrike of all. In complete contrast to its sun-loving relatives, the Great Grey braves the edge of the taiga in summer and wet, draughty places in winter, not withdrawing very far to the south of its breeding range even in harsh climates. It is found in all sorts of open country, including marshes, heaths and grasslands, so long as there are some lookout posts and a reasonable supply of food. So it is far more adaptable than the other shrikes, and more widespread, too.

When hunting, the Great Grey perches higher up than most other shrikes, regularly on the tops of trees. From here it has a commanding view and is able to use its excellent vision to detect prey: it can spot an invertebrate in flight at 100 m and a small mammal on the ground at 260 m. Its repertoire of prey items is varied. It is principally insectivorous, like most shrikes, but it takes a higher proportion of small mammals and birds than the rest do. When dealing with vertebrates the Great Grey has to modify its normal 'perch and pounce' method of hunting. Mammals, for example, must be approached carefully, to avoid bites, so the hunter lands near them, not too close, and then performs a bizarre dance with its potential victim, dodging the mammal's teeth but endeavouring to bite the back of its neck to cut the spinal cord. There is a record of a shrike biting a rat 117 times before the latter was subdued. One can only imagine the scrap that must have occurred when a Great Grey Shrike took its largest recorded victim, a stoat.

Birds are a much rarer food item because they are so difficult to catch – the Great Grey Shrike has no great flying prowess. But where possible it uses its feet to grab them in flight, then takes them to the ground and kills them in the same way as mammals.

In the fickle climates where these birds hold their winter territories, the hunting conditions are highly unpredictable, so Great Grey Shrikes are notable for the amount of food they cache. Much is impaled on thorns or in branches, usually scattered about the territory, where it is left for a rainy day.

ID: *Large, ashy-grey, black and white shrike. Underparts whitish, crown and back grey.*

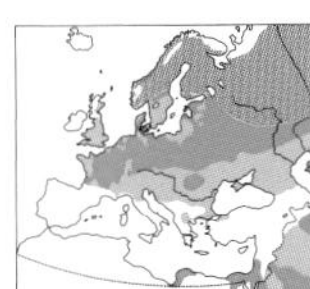

ID: *Similar to Great Grey Shrike in plumage, but slightly darker grey on crown and back, and with definite pinkish tinge on underparts.*

Southern Grey Shrike

Lanius meridionalis (**lan**-ni-uss mer-rid-di-on-**a**-liss)
length 24–25 cm

Only recently has the Southern Grey Shrike been elevated to full species status, separate from the Great Grey. It is probably an even more formidable predator than its northern counterpart, since it is armed with a still longer and heavier bill. Another characteristic that separates it from the Great Grey is its shorter wings, a trait consistent with its reduced tendency to migrate. Southern Grey Shrikes may make dispersive movements south after the breeding season, but most populations are probably resident and there is evidence that some pairs might remain together outside the breeding season.

The Southern Grey Shrike lives in warm, dry, open areas. Its typical habitat is characterised by a mixture of open ground and small bushes and trees, the *maquis* and *garigue* vegetation types so prevalent in the Mediterranean region. These places abound in large insects, but a feature of the Southern Grey Shrike's diet is the abundance of small reptiles such as lizards. When hunting, in contrast to the Great Grey Shrike, this species doesn't perch in tall trees; instead it starts lower down, in the tops of bushes.

Woodchat Shrike

Lanius senator (**lan**-ni-uss sen-**nay**-tor)
length 18 cm

ID: *Smart, high-perching small shrike with chestnut crown and black back.*

In some parts of its range the Woodchat Shrike overlaps with other species of shrike, occurring in similar habitats, apparently with little enmity or competition. Certainly it tends to hunt from higher and more exposed perches than the other small species, including overhead wires and taller trees, and also catches much of its food in flight – perhaps this makes the difference. The Woodchat Shrike is primarily insectivorous, taking very few small vertebrates and rarely impaling its prey.

In common with the other species of similar diet, the Woodchat Shrike is a migrant, arriving in Europe any time between late March and early June, and departing for Africa in August and September. During its stay it inhabits partly open areas with well-spaced bushes and trees – typical shrike country.

Many Woodchat Shrike populations have a surplus of males and there are reports of hybridisation with other shrikes, which seems to be a feature, if an occasional one, of this family. In several studies as many as 23 per cent of all males in a population remained unpaired and a high proportion of these helped at the nests of successful pairs later in the season.

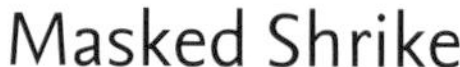

Masked Shrike

Lanius nubicus (**lan**-ni-uss **noo**-bi-kuss)
length 17–18 cm

A rare shrike of southeast Europe, the Masked Shrike has a different habitat from the other species, being found in open woodland or even in glades amidst more substantial tree cover, often in the hills. It can be a difficult bird to see, because it uses inconspicuous side branches of small trees as lookout posts, and generally keeps quiet and hidden. Yet when it does make an appearance it can be markedly tame. It will allow a close human approach even during the breeding season, and there are records of individuals flying down to people's feet to snatch insects disturbed by their walking.

Its main food in the breeding season consists of large insects. But despite being the smallest shrike in Europe it can be highly predatory, taking lizards and birds. In contrast to most shrikes, which concentrate on fledglings or nestlings, the Masked Shrike apparently eats fully grown birds, many of these being tired migrants taking a break in their journey. These and other prey items may be impaled on thorns.

The Masked Shrike is a migrant itself, wintering in sub-Saharan Africa. It arrives from mid-April and departs in August and September. It contrast to other shrikes, it sometimes fits in two broods during its short stay.

ID: *Smallest and slimmest shrike, with long tail. Black and white, with apricot-tinted breast. White supercilium, black on crown.*

Crows family *Corvidae* (**kor**-vid-ee)

Habitat Almost any habitat, in any climate and any altitude up to 3000 m.
Food Omnivorous. Several species collect food in autumn for long-term storage; others cache for short term.
Movements Most are sedentary, not moving any great distance.
Voice Many have harsh or deep voices, with chatters and caws prevalent. Most make complex sounds, including high musical notes, often audible only close up.
Pairing style Monogamous long-term pair bonds, but extra-pair copulations and rape are known.
Nesting Some are solitary and territorial (Carrion Crow, Magpie, Nutcracker, Jay, Raven); others nest in colonies (Rook, Jackdaw). Some can sometimes, but not always be colonial (Alpine Chough) and others are not strictly colonial but live in groups (Siberian Jay, Azure-winged Magpie).
Nest Quite large and made up of sticks of various sizes, often in layers. Earth may be mixed in, and grass, roots, lichens, plant fibres, feathers or hair may be used for the lining. Mainly open cup, but Magpie's has a roof.
Productivity 1 brood a year.
Eggs 2–8, hatching at slight intervals.
Incubation 15–23 days, by female only (except Nutcracker, in which both sexes incubate).
Young Nest-bound, altricial and downy (Jays and Nutcrackers naked).
Parenting style Fed by both parents (and by nest helpers in Azure-winged Magpie).
Food to young As parents', fed by regurgitation from crop.
Leaving nest Fledge at 14–49 days, then parental care for up 3–4 weeks.

Magpie

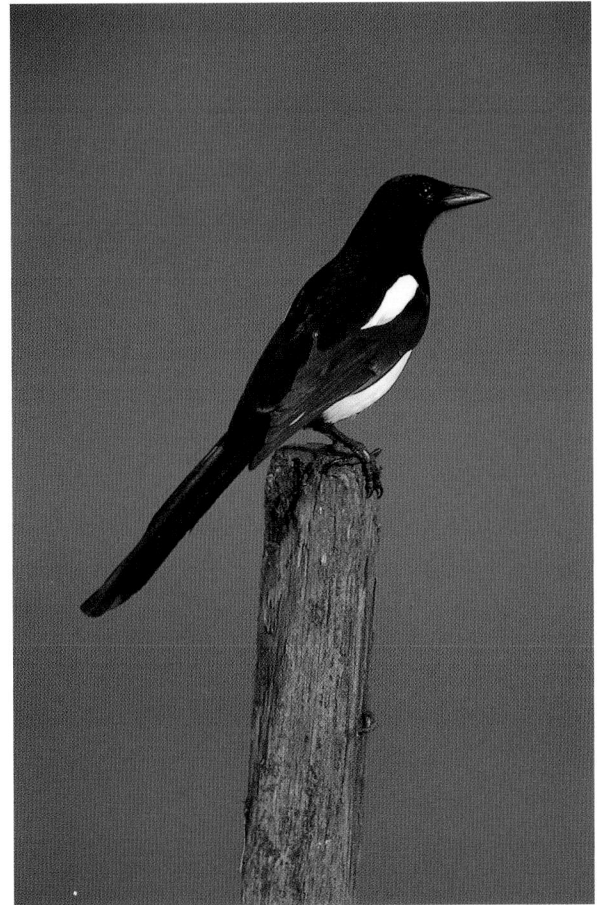

Everyone recognises a member of the crow family – or do they? We are all familiar with the large black birds we see in our towns and countryside, but many people do not realise that the crow family also includes some more intricately patterned species such as Jays, Nutcrackers and Magpies.

Members of the crow family have strong bills, relatively long legs (they feed a great deal on the ground) and bristle-like feathers that cover the nostrils. They are larger than most other 'perching birds' (passerines), and the Raven, the largest member of this grouping, is as big as a Buzzard. The legs are very strong so that a crow can, for instance, tear apart a food item by standing on it and pulling with its bill. The plumage of male and female can be strikingly similar, so much so that it is impossible to tell them apart by sight. Most species have short tails and broad wings.

A crow's bill is a multi-purpose tool that enables its owner to be truly omnivorous. Most crows have a food preference – one may be primarily a scavenger, whilst another, such as the Nutcracker or Jay, may depend upon fruits or nuts for most of the year – but at the same time they are flexible enough to dip into other dishes when needed. Crows are sometimes predatory, taking small mammals, invertebrates, adult birds, eggs and young, but the importance of live meat is usually exaggerated. For the Magpie, for example, small birds are a seasonal tipple and make up only a fraction of its annual diet. Crows are notable for their habit of placing food in caches, often for long-term storage.

This is a very successful family of intelligent, gregarious and noisy birds. Their boldness and adaptability often make them numerous and dominant in a location, but they are seldom popular. People see them as too successful, not pretty enough and a danger to other birds. These are value judgments based on little firm evidence, but the truth is that crows often do look menacing and that they will never find their way to people's hearts.

Most crows form stable, long-term pair bonds maintained by intricate and intimate nuances of behaviour. Within this framework all species are also highly sociable, with well-organised societies containing pairs, non-breeding flocks or co-operative groups. Such behaviour is facilitated by a surprisingly complex vocabulary, often understated and difficult to hear – a far cry from the proverbial harsh notes and caws so often associated with this largely misunderstood family.

ID: *Unmistakable pink-brown crow with black, white and kingfisher-blue wing pattern. Distinctive floppy flight.*

Jay

Garrulus glandarius (**gar**-roo-luss glan-**day**-ri-uss)
length 34–35 cm

Much can be learnt about the Jay simply from its English and scientific names. The name 'Jay' spoken angrily in a loud voice approximates to this bird's harsh call, a familiar sound that often breaks the silence of a wood in autumn and winter. *Garrulus*, the Latin word for talkative, might seem a little exaggerated, but in fact the Jay has a wide and well-used vocabulary besides its screech. In spring it utters a sweet warble under its breath, a song containing many imitations of local birds.

As for *glandarius*, that means 'of the acorn' and it refers to the intimate relationship between the Jay and the oak tree. The link is most obvious between late September and early November, when Jays collect acorns for their winter stores. Each Jay or pair of Jays lives in a permanent home range that may or may not include a good stand of oaks. If it doesn't, the birds must commute to the nearest wood to get their provisions, which may involve a one-way journey of 4 km or even more. They arrive at the wood and generally fetch the acorns straight off the trees, before they have fallen. They pick up between three and nine (nine for long journeys, some carried within the oesophagus) and return to the home range, where they hide each one in a separate site. An acorn may be worked under leaf litter, among roots, into the soil or sometimes into a bark fissure, then the evidence is concealed and the precise spot memorised. In all, a Jay may collect and hide up to 5000 acorns.

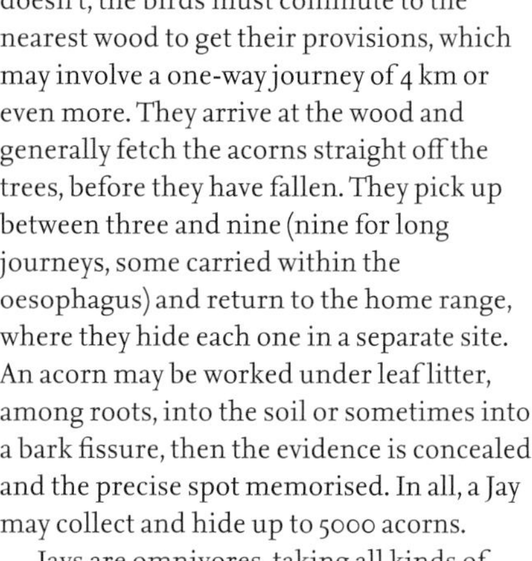

Jays are omnivores, taking all kinds of food throughout the year. In spring and summer they eat chiefly insects, especially caterpillars and beetles, plus a few eggs and nestlings of woodland birds. In autumn and winter they will feed on a wide variety of nuts and fruits besides acorns. One might be tempted, then, to wonder why they store so much food of a particular type (though they do sometimes store other fruits). The answer must be that the caches are a useful insurance against general food shortage; buried acorns do not spoil quickly, and Jays can retrieve them as and when required; indeed, they often feed them to their young after more than six months in the soil.

ID: *Distinctive and unlikely to be confused with anything else in its habitat. Flight less floppy than Jay's.*

Siberian Jay

Perisoreus infaustus
(per-ris-**soh**-ree-uss in-**fow**-stuss)
length 30–31 cm

Few Siberian Jays ever see people. They are birds of the mighty coniferous forest belt, the taiga, where human settlements are separated by hundreds of kilometres and the inhabitants seldom penetrate the dense, pristine stands of Scots pine and Norway spruce favoured by the birds. But that does not mean that Siberian Jays avoid people; far from it – they are drawn to us. Humans bring food when they enter the wilderness and offer an opportunity for easy pickings.

Siberian Jays live in small groups that hold a communal territory. The flocks contain between three and six birds, and are composed of an adult pair plus one or more 'hangers on' – offspring from the most recent clutch or unrelated juveniles from elsewhere. The flocks move around the forest silently, one bird following another in no formal order, although the adult male is dominant. In spring and summer, when the adult pair breeds, one or more of these youngsters often remains in the territory and may help with nesting duties.

Siberian Jays are omnivores, eating insects, small birds and mammals, carrion and much plant material, including berries. They are inveterate storers of food, too, putting items aside at all times of the year by hiding them in cracks in the bark. The birds often place lichen or other materials over them to conceal them from other would-be consumers. It has been suggested that this habit enables them to live and breed in the harsh environment of the far north.

Magpie

Pica pica (**pie**-ka **pie**-ka)
length 44–46 cm, including tail

ID: *Unmistakable.*

A Magpie perched high in a tree, flirting its tail, is saying nothing, yet saying a lot. Since these birds have no real song, 'treetop sitting' is the way that territorial birds proclaim ownership of their patch of land and keep intruders out. There's not much movement, no sound, only a confident presence.

Magpie society is a divided one. On one side are the 'haves', the paired birds living and breeding in their own territory and remaining settled for long periods of time. On the other are the 'have-nots', members of the local non-breeding flock, birds without territories, mostly youngsters, but a proportion of adults, too. This state of affairs is reasonably fluid, with some territory owners being demoted from time to time and some non-breeders acquiring territories.

Territories change hands in various ways. There is some natural mortality and consequent replacement, as one might expect. Secondly, some birds manage to acquire small territories on the edge of existing ones at the end of the breeding season, when territorial defence is low; having 'squeezed in', the newcomers eventually expand their boundaries, little by little, to make the territory viable for breeding. And thirdly, in early spring the dominant males in the non-breeding flock sometimes make an audacious bid to take over a territory. They gather together, make a great deal of noise and display and posture, challenging the incumbents. The commotion attracts an audience of all local birds, breeders and non-breeders, up to a total of about 25 spectators. The disturbance is usually futile, with the challengers being ousted, but these 'ceremonial gatherings' do sometimes result in new pairs gaining a foothold in the disputed area.

Once settled, Magpies build an unusual nest for a crow – a dome with a roof and a side entrance, made out of sticks. It takes both birds a lot of effort to build it, and they sometimes begin on mild winter days. It seems that the dome is necessary to keep out predators, especially Carrion Crows, with which Magpies have a mutual enmity. After all, the nest is extremely easy to find.

The Magpie is a celebrated omnivore. It actually eats more insects and nuts than anything else, but finds itself in hot water over its fringe dietary activity. In spring Magpies utilise the glut of eggs, nestlings and fledglings in gardens and hedgerows to feed themselves and their young, much to the disgust of birdwatchers and householders who side with their hapless victims.

Azure-winged Magpie

Cyanopica cyanus (sie-an-**noh**-pi-ka sie-**ayn**-uss)
length 34–35 cm

The extraordinary world distribution of the Azure-winged Magpie causes scientists to scratch their heads. How can a bird possibly live in two such widely separated places as Iberia and the Far East without any populations in between? It just doesn't make zoogeographical or evolutionary sense. People speculated that perhaps the Azure-winged Magpie was introduced to Europe by man, but then sub-fossil remains were found recently on Gibraltar, proving that this bird is definitely native. So the puzzle remains.

The bird itself occurs in various types of woodland in Spain and Portugal, especially of stone pine – another riddle, because in Asia it is confined to deciduous forest. It also spills over into open country with hedgerows, olive groves and orchards. It is notable for living all its life in small, stable flocks, which are often seen flying in single file from one tree to another, or on to the ground, giving their high-pitched 'vree' calls.

The flocks consist of between 3 and 16 families, adults and young, which defend a large group territory. In the breeding season only a relatively small proportion breed and these are helped in their many tasks by other flock members. Remarkably, these duties include building the nest and feeding the sitting female, as well as the more usual feeding of young carried out by nest helpers of other species. The nests are in dispersed colonies, often in neighbouring trees, and they are built a long way out from a tree trunk, just below the crown – a very inconspicuous position, safe from predators.

ID: *Slimmer than Magpie; unmistakable given reasonable view.*

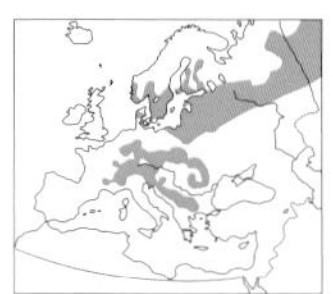

ID: Flight and shape similar to Jay, but longer and thinner bill and shorter tail. Otherwise the unusual plumage is unmistakable.

Nutcracker

Nucifraga caryocatactes
(noos-si-**fray**-ga kar-ri-oh-kat-**tak**-teez)
length 32–33 cm

In its zeal for storing away seeds and nuts in the autumn, the Nutcracker very much resembles the Jay. If anything, though, good supplies are even more critical than they are for the more omnivorous Jay, both for winter survival and in preparation for breeding. Nutcrackers nest earlier in the spring than other woodland crows, often when snow is still on the ground, so they need to remain in good condition throughout the winter. The Nutcracker doesn't store acorns, but has other favourites: montane birds in central Europe store seeds of the Arolla pine or, if these are absent, the nuts of hazel; birds further east prefer the seeds of the Siberian stone pine. So important is the collection of fruits that young Nutcrackers in their first autumn must obtain a territory soon after becoming independent in order to survive; their mortality rate is high.

From time to time poor feeding conditions in their Russian range force Nutcrackers of the Siberian (thick-billed) race to erupt west and south into Europe. Curiously these are mostly one-way movements, with the birds either dying in their wintering grounds or breeding in a new place. Small populations in the Low Countries originated from such invasions and have persisted for many years since.

The family life of Nutcrackers is strong. The male takes a major role in feeding and incubating, the latter behaviour unique among European crows. The young, too, have a long period of dependence, not leaving until four months after they have fledged.

Alpine Chough

Pyrrhocorax graculus
(pir-roh-**koh**-raks **gray**-koo-luss)
length 38 cm

The Alpine Chough lives and breeds at altitudes beyond the reach of most other European birds. It is comfortable at 3000 m and almost never descends below 1500 m; nest sites are at heights where many species would perish. Within its limits the Alpine Chough moves effortlessly up and down mountains, feeding at the snow line one moment, descending to the tree line another; it has been known to range 1600 m in a single day. It has an ease of flight that makes this possible; it can soar in good weather or ride tempestuous winds. It gives the impression at times of simply playing with whatever weather the mountains throw at it.

Alpine Choughs are sociable birds. Most people see them for the first time on mountains with ski lifts or restaurants, where the choughs search for scraps of food.

Despite their tendency to associate in flocks, most Alpine Choughs nest singly (though colonies of up to 20 pairs are known) on a cliff ledge, in a cave or on a building, away from ground predators. The nest can be placed deep in a crevice up to 10 m from the outside world, in complete darkness.

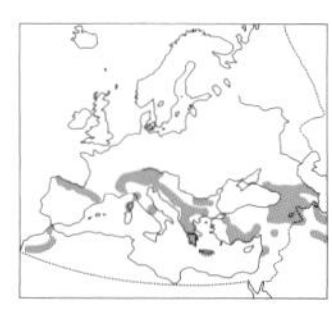

ID: Small black crow with red legs and short, yellow bill. High-altitude species. In flight similar to Jackdaw but (like Chough) has two-toned underwing and obvious 'fingers'.

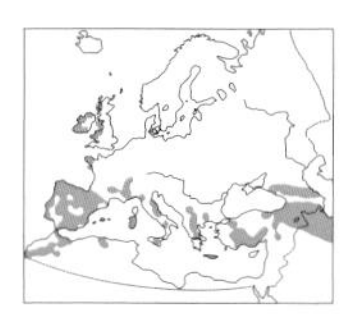

ID: Very different from usual crow. More acrobatic in flight than other crows, except Alpine Chough. If seen well, unmistakable. Choughs rarely, if ever, perch on trees, in contrast to other crows.

Red-billed Chough

Pyrrhocorax pyrrhocorax
(pir-roh-**koh**-raks pir-roh-**koh**-raks)
length 39–40 cm

The Red-billed Chough is a highly specialised feeder, concentrating on probing the soil for beetle larvae, ants and other invertebrates, and lacking the predatory habits of the rest of the family. It is also the most aerially able, demonstrating a wide array of aerobatics. A typical routine is to stall in the air and plummet down, wings closed, only to pull out of the dive just in time and then regain height to repeat the process. But this is only one manoeuvre among many. Choughs ride air currents in flocks, soaring, tumbling and twisting, and uttering their distinctive 'chee-ow!' call. Many crows are good in flight; Red-billed Choughs are exceptional.

Red-billed Choughs are found in two main habitats: rocky coasts and mountains. They have a highly fragmented range in Europe, with many rather small outlying populations, for example in Sardinia and Crete. Their need for a rich fauna in the soil, combined with access to sea caves, deep rocky crevices or crumbling ruined buildings for safe nest sites has limited them, but agricultural intensification, along with the persecution that comes with being a crow, has made them scarcer still.

Choughs pair for life but, even when breeding, waste few chances to join flocks for communal feeding and aerobatics. The core of a flock tends to be made up of non-breeding youngsters and may number a hundred birds. But membership is informal, with birds coming and going as they please.

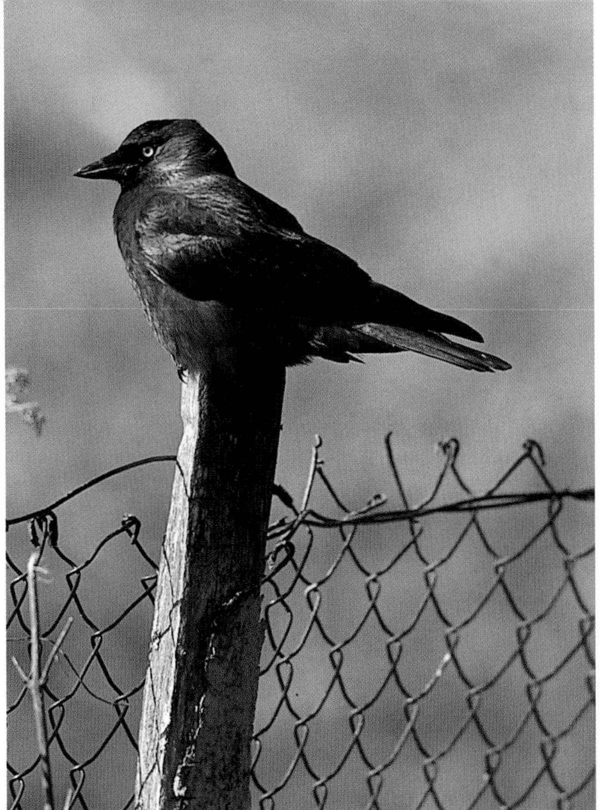

ID: *Smallest crow, with noticeably shorter bill than others. Ash-grey colour on nape diagnostic.*

Jackdaw

Corvus monedula (**kor**-vuss moh-**nee**-doo-la)
length 33–34 cm

Within a flock of Jackdaws, it is usually noticeable that birds are flying in pairs. The impression doesn't lie: these small crows are extremely faithful to their partners and once two birds have been together for more than six months they almost never divorce, even after several unsuccessful nesting attempts. Such failures would split most pairs, but the consequences of becoming single for a Jackdaw are severe – both sexes would lose their nest site and slide down the social scale.

Jackdaws are extremely sociable. Most breed in colonies, albeit somewhat dispersed ones. Their need for holes in which to place their nests limits them to such habitats as cliffs, towns (where there are rows of chimneys), quarries and patches of wood with old trees, so the density of nests can be highly variable.

The Jackdaw feeds on many different foods, although it concentrates on invertebrates. With their short bills, Jackdaws cannot probe far into the ground, so they sometimes follow Rooks around and work over the soil that the latter have disturbed, or take rides on sheep to see what can be stirred up. But they are perfectly capable of finding their own food and are unusual among crows in gleaning caterpillars from high in trees.

Rook

Corvus frugilegus (**kor**-vuss froo-jil-**lee**-guss)
length 44–46 cm

Throughout its range the Rook is often confused with the Carrion Crow, but it is a far more sociable species than its rather sinister-looking cousin. The Carrion Crow does form non-breeding flocks and gather to roost in large numbers, but it always nests singly, within its own extended territory.

The Rook, on the other hand, gathers in colonies, and members of those colonies feed together, roost together and engage in preening and loafing together. Most colonies, called 'rookeries', contain up to about 25 pairs, but rookeries of a thousand pairs are well known and the record for Europe is one of 16,000 pairs in Hungary.

The Rook requires quite a specialised habitat. It feeds over pastureland and other ground covered by short vegetation, but needs high trees in which to nest – a juxtaposition of habitats that must once have been quite unusual. It has benefited, though, from man's clearance of forests and is now mostly considered a farmland bird.

Young Rooks acquire their territories in the autumn because the breeding season begins early. They build a complex but open, cup-shaped stick nest, made up of several layers, in the highest branches of a tall tree. Most pairs have eggs in March and the young hatch in April; at first they are fed exclusively by the male. The reason for the early start is that the young depend on soil invertebrates, such as earthworms and various larvae, which are plentiful in early spring, but become much more difficult to uncover from drier ground later on.

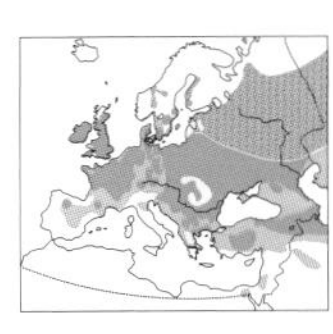

ID: *Similar to Carrion Crow, but with more peaked forehead and shaggier feathers on lower belly. Diagnostic whitish bill; no feathering on nostril.*

Carrion Crow

Corvus [corone] (**kor**-vuss kor-**roh**-nee)
length 45–47 cm

There are two distinct races of this crow in Europe, which may be separate species. One is the all-black Carrion Crow (*Corvus corone*), which is predominantly found in western and southwest Europe and tends not to migrate very much. The other is the grey and black Hooded Crow (*Corvus cornix*), found east of a line between Denmark and Italy; northern populations of this form are migratory and have a marked preference for travelling along coastlines. Some consider the two forms to be separate species, but where the two meet there are invariably zones of hybridisation, with individuals thereabouts sporting intermediate patterns. Interestingly, although the hybrids are fertile, there are suggestions that they lack the fitness to survive for long.

Whatever appearance it takes, this is an abundant and successful species. It subsists on many sorts of foodstuffs (not just carrion) and, like other adaptable species, concentrates on what is easily found locally, to the exclusion of variety. Thus some crows feed along the tide line on shellfish and other animals, others roam over fields looking for insects, and still others take nuts from trees.

Crow society is marked by a shortage of territories, with conflict and tension between paired territory holders and members of non-breeding flocks. If a bird dies, its mate may be ousted within hours or even find itself in a new attachment, such is the pressure for space. Aggression between Carrion Crows and Magpies is also fierce, and each species routinely disturbs the other or robs it of eggs or nestlings.

The nest of a Carrion Crow is a complex structure made up of four layers, from an outer shell of large sticks mixed with soil and leaves, to a thin inner lining of soft materials. Man-made objects such as paper, tin foil and clothing often find their way into the structure as well. The nest has to be strong and flexible. It is placed near the topmost branches of a tree and must not fall apart when the wind blows.

Carrion Crows are good parents, with both sexes contributing to feeding the young well beyond fledging. Some youngsters indeed remain in their parents' territory for the whole of their first winter before they taste the harsh world outside.

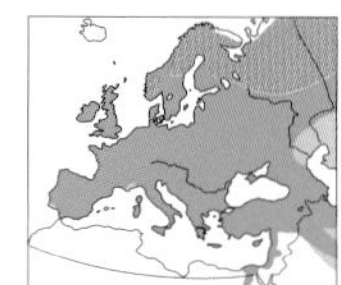

ID: Carrion Crow is the familiar all-black crow with a dark bill. Similar in size to the Rook, but with a much flatter forehead with an even slope down to the bill. Also has closely feathered upper legs. Hooded Crow is distinctive.

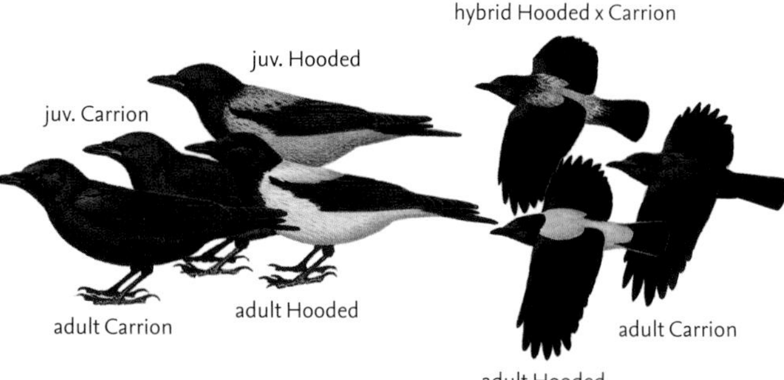

Common Raven

Corvus corax (**kor**-vuss **koh**-raks)
length 64 cm, the largest perching bird

There has to be something special about a bird that can breed anywhere from the edge of the Sahara to deep into the Arctic, and any elevation from sea level to over 2400 m. No other bird in Europe embraces such a range of climatic conditions as the hardy, adaptable and exceptionally intelligent Raven.

To understand the Raven's adaptability to different habitats, we need to appreciate how it can modify its behaviour to suit a situation. So, for example, in cold weather it tends to tuck its eggs and young up in the soft lining of the nest to keep them warm. Conversely in very hot weather it can make ventilation holes in the side of the nest structure; it will also, incidentally, bring water to the young in its bill, and give them an impromptu bath by soaking its belly feathers and sitting on them. It is similarly resourceful when seeking food. When it wants to, the Raven can be highly predatory, flying low over the ground to catch rabbits. At other times it can hawk for insects in mid-air or perch on trees to feed on caterpillars.

Ravens pair for life, and over the course of time they get to know each other as a couple so well that they develop a language, both of sounds and of gestures, that is uniquely theirs. Other species of birds are more given to stereotyped, rigid behaviour patterns. Another powerful demonstration of the Raven's intelligence is in its undoubted capacity for play. Birds often seem to 'enjoy' performing aerial acrobatics, rolling over on to their back in flight, diving at each other and tumbling to earth. Young birds in captivity have been known to slide down slopes repeatedly, like children at a playground, and they quite frequently indulge in 'upside-down hanging', clinging to their perches like bats. Not many other birds do that!

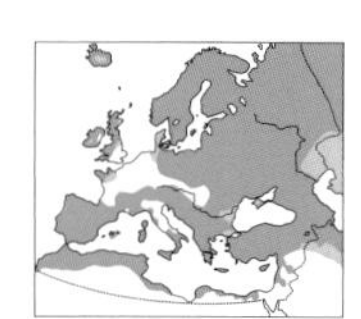

ID: Very large crow with distinctive flight profile of long, wedge-shaped tail and long wings. Huge bill is diagnostic.

Starlings family *Sturnidae* (**stur**-nid-ee)

Habitat All require combination of cavity nest sites (e.g. trees, buildings) and some open pasture for foraging. Spotless Starling and especially Starling often in densely settled areas.
Food Invertebrates, fruits and seeds.
Movements Spotless Starling and some populations of Starlings resident. Many Starlings from north and east Europe migrate to south of Europe for winter. Rose-coloured Starlings summer visitors, May–October, migrating to India.
Voice Unusual rambling songs, fast and with many repetitions of elements, mixed in with whistles and clicks. The Common Starling is also famed for its mimicry.
Pairing style Monogamous, but a few male Common Starlings are polygynous, acquiring up to 5 mates.
Nesting Rose-coloured Starling colonial; others usually colonial, but not always.
Nest In holes in trees, rocks or buildings.
Productivity Usually 1 brood.
Eggs 4–5. Some females lay more eggs and dump them in the nests of neighbours.
Incubation 11–15 days, mainly by female.
Young Nest-bound, altricial and almost naked.
Parenting style Both sexes feed the young.
Food to young The 3 species have different principal or important foods: Starling soil invertebrates such as beetle larvae; Spotless Starling adult beetles; Rose-coloured Starling locusts and grasshoppers.
Leaving nest Young leave nest after 21–24 days. The juveniles then form their own large flocks, independent of the adults.

The starlings are a small group of easily recognised and familiar medium-sized songbirds with spiky bills, short tails and strong legs and feet. In contrast to most passerines they walk or run along the ground rather than hop. They have characteristically triangular wings and fly on a straight course with rapid wingbeats and occasional glides, although they are also capable of wheeling in circles and turning in tight corners. Feeding mainly on invertebrates that are found in the soil, starlings have stout bills powered by very strong muscles, and they have the special knack of making holes in the soil by inserting the bill and then opening it, a process known as prying. The front part of the skull is narrow and, once a starling has made a hole with its bill, the eyes rotate forward to give the bird overlapping 'binocular' vision, helping it to judge distance.

Starlings are extremely sociable birds and generally nest in colonies.

Spotless Starling

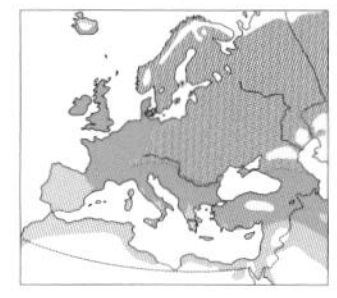

ID: In most of Europe the abundant starling. More spotted and more metallic green than breeding plumage of Spotless Starling, with pale edges to flight feathers. Male has blue colouring at base of bill, female pink/yellow. Still more spotted in winter, all over head and body.

Starling

Sturnus vulgaris (**stur**-nuss vul-**gay**-riss)
length 21.5 cm

Not always the most popular of birds on account of its abundance, rowdiness and tendency to gobble its food down with indecorous speed, the Common Starling nonetheless exhibits so much unusual behaviour that it really should have earned our admiration. There is hardly an aspect of its lifestyle that has not thrown up some surprise for the scientists.

It is, for example, a rare exponent among smaller birds of intraspecific brood parasitism – that is, it will lay eggs in the nests of strangers of its own species. This is a cheap way for a female to add to her productivity without having to make any more effort than laying an egg, thereby leaving it in the care of unwitting foster parents. In some colonies as many as 46 per cent of nests have been found to contain eggs lacking any genetic material from the sitting bird or its partner. Remarkably, on her visits to a neighbour's nest, a female Starling will sometimes actually eat or destroy an egg to even up the clutch numbers, mimicking the destructive habits of the Common Cuckoo.

The nest, placed in a hole in a tree or building, was for a long time considered nothing special. But then it was discovered that, in choosing suitable material for the structure, the Starling actually uses its sense of smell as a quality-control tool, presumably in order to detect material that could aid nest sanitation or have some other benefit.

The breeding cycle is unusual in that, when birds in a colony are laying their first clutch, all do so in a highly synchronised manner, the eggs being laid within a few busy days. When it comes to second clutches, however, the egg dates are all over the place, with little or any synchronisation, which presumably reduces opportunities for parasitism.

The young take about three weeks to fledge, and once they have done so they are determinedly independent. They leave the parents' territory within hours and form their own special flocks, like gangs of adolescents. These flocks may number hundreds or even thousands of birds, every one of them a juvenile; meanwhile the adults remain, as is their custom, in much smaller, quite intimate parties.

Outside the breeding season Starlings are also famed for their commuting habits and enormous roosts. Roosts form in places such as low scrubby bushes, reedbeds and buildings in town centres, and suitable sites attract birds from as much as 50 km away, flying in from all directions in the evening. The commuting flocks coalesce into vast swarms of up to 2 million birds, which may indulge in spectacular aerial manoeuvres. Starlings are often very noisy at night and, when dawn breaks, they are ready to depart for their feeding grounds. The departure is staggered, with birds leaving at intervals of about three minutes; how each bird knows which departure is allotted to it is unknown.

Finally, Starlings also have interesting voices and their effervescent songs often contain remarkably accurate mimicry, not just of other bird species (the Golden Oriole is a favourite), but of other environmental noises. In urban areas individuals have copied crying babies, telephone rings and doorbells, among other things. Each individual male has his own personal repertoire of 20–70 song segments.

Rose-coloured Starling

Sturnus roseus (**stur**-nuss **roh**-zee-uss)
length 21.5 cm

The splendid Rose-coloured Starling is an erratic summer visitor to Europe, breeding somewhere most years, but in abundance only in infrequent 'invasion' years, when it arrives in large numbers from its core distribution on the Central Asian steppes. If it does come it will normally settle only in the eastern half of Europe, arriving very late in the spring, at the end of May.

The breeding of Rose-coloured Starlings is timed to coincide with an abundance of its favourite foods, locusts and grasshoppers. In the summer these insects have a non-flying immature stage and are easy to catch on the ground. When feeding, a flock of Rose-coloured Starlings moves on a broad swathe across the grassland, the lead birds running, the ones at the back periodically overflying them to regain the lead – thus the flock 'rolls' along. The same pattern is followed by other Starling species.

The business of mate selection is brief, so where other European Starlings are given to a spot of polygamy, Rose-coloureds don't usually have time! Potential mates display on the ground, the male circling the female and, unusually, singing (other Starlings confine their singing to high perches). Nests are always in colonies, sometimes of hundreds of pairs, and usually sited on a rocky outcrop within cultivated or grassland country.

ID: Adults unmistakable in summer. Juveniles paler in plumage than Starling, and with shorter, pale (not dark) bill. First-winters and winter adults always show contrast between dark wings and paler body plumage.

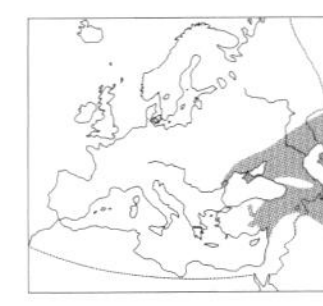

ID: Less spotted than Starling, especially in winter. Adults black with oily look to plumage.

Spotless Starling

Sturnus unicolor (**stur**-nuss **yoon**-ni-kol-lor)
length 21–23 cm

Something about the climate of the western Mediterranean favours the Spotless Starling over the usually more abundant Starling. Spotless Starlings are year-round residents in Spain, Portugal and some Mediterranean islands, whereas the Starling visits these places only in the winter. The Spotless is doing well and increasing, but anywhere north of the south of France it disappears.

Much of the behaviour of the two species is similar. The Spotless has a different song to the Starling, with much louder and frequent whistling noises, a bit like the whistle you make when relieved about something. But like the Starling it feeds mainly on the ground, pushing its bill into the turf and then opening it. It also similarly nests in holes in trees and buildings.

There do seem to be a few differences in feeding. Spotless Starlings are more closely associated with cattle and cattle country.

And the food given to the chicks is different: adult Starlings collect soil invertebrates, especially soft-bodied ones, whereas the Spotless Starling feeds its young on high numbers of large adult beetles caught on the surface.

Sparrows family *Passeridae* (pas-**ser**-id-ee)

Habitat From forests to farmland, arid areas to watersides, lowlands to high mountains. House Sparrow is almost indifferent to climate.
Food Principally seeds, berries and a few invertebrates.
Movements House Sparrow and Tree Sparrow mainly sedentary; Rock Sparrow and White-winged Snowfinch altitudinal migrants; Spanish Sparrow true migrant in east.
Voice Unmusical cheeping and chirping.
Pairing style Mainly monogamous, but House Sparrow may be polygamous or promiscuous and male Rock Sparrows often acquire two or more mates.
Nesting Usually colonial, except for White-winged Snowfinch.
Nest Ball-like mass of grass or straw with a roof and with hole to one side. Nests in cavities tend to expand to fill the available space.
Productivity 2–3 broods a year, although the House Sparrow could in theory fit in 4.
Eggs 4–5.
Incubation 9–16 days, by both sexes.
Young Nest-bound, altricial. Downy in Rock Sparrow, naked in others.
Parenting style Both sexes feed the young.
Food to young Invertebrates.
Leaving nest Fledge at 11–21 days, values towards higher end for Rock Sparrow and White-winged Snowfinch.

The sparrows are small, thick-billed birds that differ from the other main families of seed-eaters (finches and buntings) in building somewhat messy, dome-shaped nests out of grass and straw, a little bit like the weavers of Africa. They are generally short-tailed and large-headed, and feed mainly on the ground. In contrast to the other seed-eaters the song is somewhat rudimentary and unmusical, although that of the White-winged Snowfinch, often delivered in flight, is much better than the rest.

Two species, the House Sparrow and Tree Sparrow, have proved exceptionally successful in colonising urban areas, the latter mainly in Asia.

Spanish Sparrow

House Sparrow

Passer domesticus (**pass**-er doh-**mess**-tik-uss)
length 14–15 cm

This irrepressible species is one of the world's best-known birds and one of the most numerous, too. It is familiar to city dwellers the world over as the epitome of a small brown bird. It is perky and resourceful, and whilst it can be outrageously bold, coming to feed on people's hands and squabbling with pigeons over bread in town parks, it has enough wildness to treat humanity with caution. So, while the House Sparrow lives in intimate association with people, it has never become domesticated or acquiescent. It has also kept its identity intact, so that House Sparrows the world over have very similar plumage patterns, in contrast to Mallards or Feral Pigeons, for example, which show endless variations.

The conjecture is that the House Sparrow first came into contact with people about 12,000 years ago in the Middle East, attracted by the activities of grain farmers. Presumably the birds soon found it convenient to breed close to their source of food, and took to nesting on buildings. From then on the House Sparrow came to rely on its human benefactors for food and shelter and, as people and their settlements spread, so did House Sparrows. Through deliberate introduction, this bird now occurs on every continent of the world. And everywhere it goes, it keeps close to people and buildings. It is hard, if not impossible, to find an emancipated 'wild' House Sparrow anywhere.

House Sparrows are sociable birds that live in small, discrete colonies. Once a young sparrow has been accepted into a colony and has obtained a nest site, the course of its life will be set. It won't be 'thrown out' and it will have little need ever to go outside the communal boundary. Many of the important duties of its life, such as feeding, preening and loafing, will be group affairs with close 'friends'. The sparrow will acquire a mate and keep it, from year to year, within and outside the breeding season. In the colony order is kept by a dominance hierarchy, in which the male birds with the largest throat patches are senior to the rest. Few small birds have such stability in their lives and in all their relationships.

Of course, behind this front of respectability House Sparrows have a darker side. Both male and female are regularly promiscuous outside of their pair bond, and it seems that casual solicitation of males by females is a routine event. These liaisons do not affect the pair bond, but they do, of course, lead to quite an input of genetic material to each clutch. A more sinister piece of behaviour that is occasionally recorded is infanticide. This happens when a member of a pair is suddenly bereaved during the breeding season. Robbed of potential breeding success, the widowed bird is driven to the extreme measure of killing the young of a neighbouring pair. This act of murder usually has the effect of splitting up the chicks' parents, leaving one of the couple available, remarkably, to pair up with the killer of its offspring.

House Sparrows do, in fact, leave their group territories once a year. In late summer, when grain is ripening in arable fields, they suddenly abandon the breeding areas and join in large foraging flocks. Few travel more than 2 km, but they are nonetheless, briefly, away from home. They remain on this feeding binge for a few weeks and then, in September, they return. Among the returnees are a handful of young birds that are applying to join the colony. They will be recruited mainly where vacancies arise through the death of colony members. Females pair with widowed males, and young males can occupy the nest sites of missing males. Youngsters that fail to acquire mate or site will leave the colony the following spring and try their luck elsewhere.

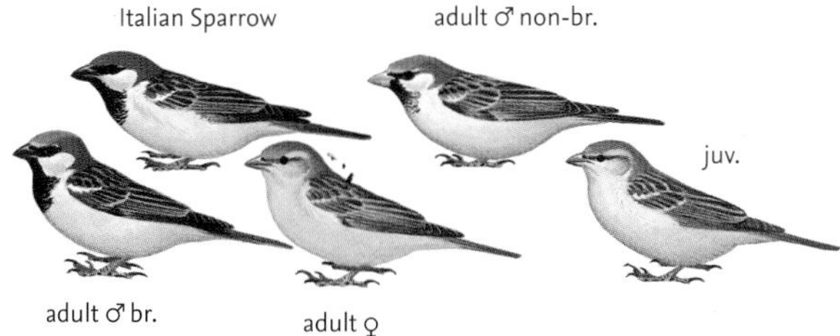

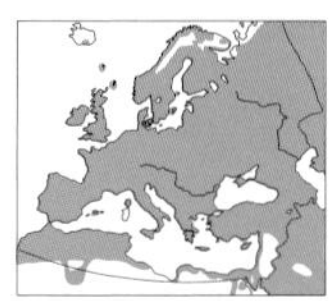

ID: Identified as a typical sparrow by its large head, thick bill, short tail and somewhat over-fast flight on direct, not particularly undulating course. Has a tendency to look dishevelled and grubby. Male has grey crown and cheeks; underparts also grey. Female very similar to Spanish Sparrow (see that entry), with grey underparts and pale stripe running back from behind eye.

Tree Sparrow

Passer montanus (**pass**-er mon-**tay**-nuss)
length 14 cm

If the House Sparrow is clearly associated with people and their buildings, it is much more difficult to understand the needs of the Tree Sparrow. Apart from requiring a hole for its nest, usually in a tree, it can occur in a wide range of different habitats. It is also prone to erratic numbers and distribution, appearing and then disappearing from places for no obvious reason, sometimes over the course of many years. Although in Europe it is considered very much a countryside and farmland bird, living in wilder places than the House Sparrow and free from the influence of man, the Tree Sparrow takes over completely as the urban sparrow of the Far East. In short, it is ecologically something of an enigma.

The Tree Sparrow usually lives in small colonies. Towards the end of the breeding season, the young disperse from these colonies and form flocks that tend to concentrate at good feeding areas. Later on, the adults join them and for a few weeks all the birds concentrate on feeding well and getting into shape, emancipated from any attachment to the colony site. Then, in late September and October, they begin to go back to a colony roost site each night, experienced birds returning to their old haunts and youngsters applying for 'membership' there. For a short period in the morning, each male sings near a potential nest site and pair formation may well occur; for the rest of the day the birds fly off to feed. By the end of November the morning song ceases and, although the colony's roost site is occupied each night, the birds range widely all day, often in large flocks, scouring the countryside for seeds.

In February singing starts again. It seems that this is not to promote pair formation, which is usually done in the autumn, but to stimulate the females to get into breeding condition. Some weeks later, the birds build a nest in their chosen site and may raise two or three broods in a season.

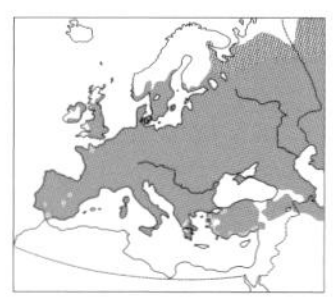

ID: Uniquely among typical sparrows, sexes alike. Distinguished from other sparrows by being smaller and neater, and by black spot on white cheek. Underparts also paler, and unstreaked.

Spanish Sparrow

Passer hispaniolensis
(**pass**-er his-span-ee-oh-**len**-siss)
length 15 cm

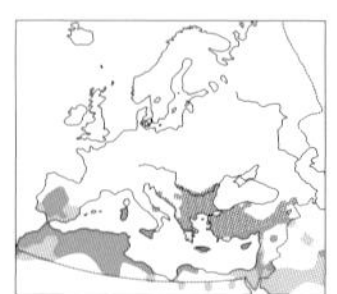

ID: Male differs from House Sparrow in his reddish-brown crown, white cheeks and heavy black streaking on back and underparts (less obvious, but still present, in winter). Female almost identical to female House Sparrow, but tends to have more distinct narrow streaks on underparts.

In some ways Spanish and House Sparrows are extremely similar. They are alike in plumage and in much of their behaviour. They regularly interbreed, and where this happens stable hybrids may occur.

There are differences, though. The Spanish Sparrow is less dependent on human activity and artefacts than the House Sparrow, occurring in 'wilder' areas, especially in moist and marshy habitats. It also usually builds a free-standing nest in a tree, rather than packing one into a hole. In Spain, though, birds in forest areas often breed in the 'basement' of the nests of large raptors or storks, regardless of whether or not the rightful owners are present upstairs.

In its social and migratory habitats the Spanish Sparrow is spectacularly different. It is much more colonial and nests may be densely packed. Colonies in Spain may number 2500 pairs (in Asia 800,000!) with nearly 200 in a single tree. And while the House Sparrow is mainly sedentary, the Spanish is often highly migratory, with birds departing south out of Europe for the winter. Males and females often migrate separately, and when they arrive back they form a colony and pair up at the same time. Occasionally after completing one brood, the birds leave and go north, some forming a new colony and breeding again in a new location.

Rock Sparrow

Petronia petronia (pet-**troh**-nee-a pet-**troh**-nee-a)
length 14 cm

A Rock Sparrow resembles a 'normal' sparrow on the ground, with its thick bill, short tail and brown patterned plumage. But when it takes to the air it is very different – the flight is undulating and swooping, not straight and over-fast, and there is a definite look of power and elegance completely lacking in other Sparrows.

These birds live, not surprisingly, in rocky places, usually dry and lifeless-looking sites with only short plant cover, typically on slopes, anywhere between sea level and about 2000 m. They subsist on seeds through most of the year, with berries entering the diet in quantity in the autumn. They feed mainly on the ground, often in large flocks of their own species (up to 2000) or mixed in with other seed-eating birds.

In spring male Rock Sparrows lay claim to several potential nest sites (crevices in rocks) and advertise for mates by their chirpy singing. When a female arrives, the male performs a nest-showing display and then, bizarrely, drives his visitor away. If a female returns a few more times a brief union is formed and the female begins to build a nest. The male now loses interest somewhat and the roles reverse, with the female repeatedly keeping the male away. In a sense the male is happy to oblige, because this enables him to start displaying at another potential nest site to attract a second and even a third female. Curiously enough, there seems to be little or no tension between these 'shared' females.

ID: A thickset sparrow with a very heavy pale bill. Plumage pale and washed-out compared to other sparrows; sexes alike. Note strong brown streaks running down breast; also pale supercilium and crown stripe.

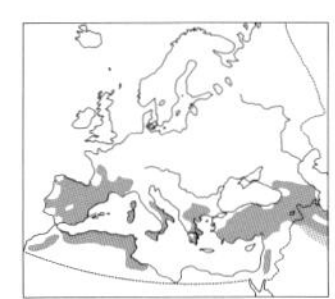

ID: Distinctive high-mountain sparrow-like bird, confusable only with Snow Bunting, which does not overlap in range.

White-winged Snowfinch

Montifringilla nivalis (mon-ti-frin-**jil**-la ni-**vay**-lis)
length 17 cm

The White-winged Snowfinch fills the sparrow niche high in the mountains of central Europe, between 1500 m and 3000 m. Its 'natural' way of surviving at such altitudes, especially in winter, is to look for seeds on high mountain pastures, but it has readily adapted to the presence of people and will take scraps from ski centres and lodges, even in the middle of sizeable towns.

In spring the diet changes, more completely so than for other sparrows. Invertebrates take over, and the birds typically spend time close to the edges of snowfields. If wind-blown insects land on snow they are rendered immobile by the low temperature, and make easy pickings. Moreover, the damp ground around melting snow is ideal for foraging.

Snowfinches nest in cavities, often high up on crags far out of reach of predators. They also use buildings, including ski lifts and avalanche protectors. The female builds a bulky structure out of grass and other materials specially selected for their dryness. When the young hatch they beg with unusual gusto, lifting their rudimentary wings so high that they are almost vertical.

Finches family *Fringillidae* (frin-**jill**-id-ee)

Habitat Finches go where their seeds are found: woods and forests, scrub, fields, open country.
Food Specialist seed-eaters or fruit-eaters, with each species having particular preferences. Most also take insects during the breeding season.
Movements Most are partial migrants, with some of a given population migrating and others remaining on site. The only species in which the entire European population migrates are Brambling and Common Rosefinch. Several, including Bullfinch and Pine Grosbeak, are irruptive. Crossbills are nomadic.
Voice Most have loud voices. Chaffinch and Brambling have stereotyped songs, the carduelines have rambling, non-territorial songs, often delivered in flight. Individuals within a species often have distinct flight calls.
Pairing style Typically monogamous, but several species are sometimes polygynous (see Greenfinch).
Nesting Some are solitary and territorial (e.g. Chaffinch), but the majority nest in small neighbourhood groups of a few pairs.
Nest A cup of grass, moss and other vegetation; Bullfinch uses sticks. Built by female, except Bullfinch and Pine Grosbeak, in which male may help.
Productivity 1–3 broods a year (Common Rosefinch and Pine Grosbeak usually only 1).
Eggs 2–7, hatching synchronously.
Incubation 10–16 days, by female only, provisioned by male in all species except Chaffinch and Brambling.
Young Nest-bound, altricial, downy.
Parenting style Both adults feed the young in the nest. Once the young have left, the male sometimes takes over while the female re-nests.
Food to young Chaffinch and Brambling feed their young exclusively on invertebrates; the rest primarily on regurgitated plant material (usually with a smattering of insects).
Leaving nest Young fledge at 11–18 days, then are fed by one or both adults for a further 15–30 days.

No European birds are so closely associated with a diet of seeds than the finches. Broadly speaking, each finch has a bill adapted for extracting the seeds from a particular plant: so Goldfinches have thin bills to reach into thistle heads, Crossbills have crossed mandibles to open conifer cones and so on.

A finch bill is special. On the roof of the mouth are two grooves, one either side of the mid-line. When a finch is dealing with a seed it lodges it in one of the grooves and then brings the sharp edge of its lower mandible to bear and pierce the husk. Once the lower mandible is in, the tongue rotates the seed, peeling off the husk as it goes round (a bit like the action of a tin-opener). The seed's kernel is thus exposed and can be swallowed, while the husk is discarded. Whatever its bill shape and dimensions, this is the unique technique common to all finches.

Within the finch family is a major division that is so fundamental that the family is now generally split into two. The Chaffinch and Brambling (the 'fringillines') have relatively unspecialised bills and, in contrast to all the others, feed their young exclusively on invertebrates, not seeds. The rest of the family, the 'carduelines', feed their young wholly or mainly on plant material, usually seeds. The result of having different baby food is that fringillines and carduelines differ in many aspects of their breeding behaviour, which are summarised in the Chaffinch entry below. One of the more interesting differences is that the cardueline finches, uniquely among small songbirds, concentrate on defending their mate rather than a fixed territory.

Finch nests, in contrast to those of sparrows, are neat and well built. However, the finches do rather spoil their handiwork after their young hatch. Most parent birds remove the youngsters' waste in faecal sacs throughout the nestling period. Finches give this up after 8–10 days, allowing a distinctive white build-up on the rim of the nest.

Finches are very vocal: members of a pair use their voices for one-to-one communication, and may even match their calls, as if adopting mutual small talk. Canaries, which are members of the finch family, are apparently able to generate new nerve cells to aid song production. This is the first time that large-scale birth and death of nerve cells has been seen in an adult animal, and it has potentially profound applications in the study of human neurological wasting diseases, such as Alzheimer's.

ID: Distinctive small brown finch with swollen bill and white eye ring.

Trumpeter Finch

Bucanetes githagineus
(boo-kan-**nee**-teez gith-a-**jie**-nee-uss)
length 12.5 cm

In recent years a small population of this desert species – currently about 300 pairs – has colonised Spain from North Africa. This finch is notable for its remarkable nasal calls, said to resemble a child's toy trumpet. Parent Trumpeter Finches develop sacs on either side of the mouth to carry food for the young, much as the Bullfinch does.

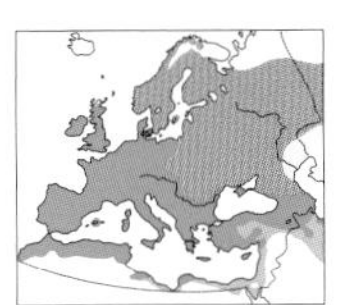

ID: *Very common slimline finch with long tail and prominent white shoulder patches. Wing bar complicated and distinctive. Male colourful in spring, more subdued in winter, but always has pink flush to breast and belly, lacking in female.*

Chaffinch

Fringilla coelebs (frin-**jil**-la **see**-lebs)
length 14 cm

The Chaffinch and Brambling are distinct in many ways from the cardueline finches. As mentioned in the introduction, much of the difference is related to their summer diet, which consists not of seeds but entirely of invertebrates, which are also fed to the young. With their unspecialised bills and feet, neither Chaffinch nor Brambling is adapted to clinging on to seed heads, and with their typically rapid pecking style, neither is proficient at long, patient operations to extract recalcitrant seeds, either. Instead they glean insects from leaves and branches, and can also catch them in rapid aerial sallies. As far as seeds are concerned, they are limited to ground foraging. So Chaffinches and Bramblings are ecologically more like tits than other finches, swapping their main diet between summer and winter.

In the summer, insects are so abundant in woods or woodland edge that an adequate supply is always available close at hand. This enables the Chaffinch, unlike other finches, to defend a territory in the spring which, in theory, carries all the resources it needs for breeding. Male Chaffinches become highly protective of their patch from about February onwards and sing their cheerful, accelerating songs as a message of ownership and mate attraction. Each has his own repertoire of three to six song types; young males in their first year learn songs from their father and other local males. As a result, Chaffinch songs show distinct dialects, with birds from different locations having recognisably different mixtures of song types.

When male and female Chaffinches meet, the male conducts several displays to show off his colourful plumage to the full. One of the less subtle ones is called the 'crouching lopsided' display, in which the male perches close to the female and leans towards her, tilting up his closed wing to reveal the colourful pink flanks and belly underneath. Another display is a brief fly-past below the female, designed to show off the colourful wing pattern. Chaffinches, incidentally, do not moult in the spring, but allow natural wear and tear to abrade the dull tips of their feathers, revealing brighter subterminal colours underneath.

Once it has formed, the relationship between male and female is not especially close. Other finches practise courtship feeding, in which males bring collected seeds to the female and exchange them mouth to mouth, but Chaffinches don't do this; with so many insects around the female can easily sustain herself without such extra provision. In fact, a female Chaffinch's lot appears to be a hard-working one, since she carries much of the burden of feeding the young, in addition to laying the eggs and brooding the chicks. The male, meanwhile, is quite often absent, indulging in sexual antics with nearby females, although these rarely if ever develop into formalised bigamous pair bonds.

ID: Shape similar to Chaffinch, but tail shorter and more forked. Male distinctive. Both sexes always have orange wash to underparts and shoulders, and diagnostic white rump.

Brambling

Fringilla montifringilla (frin-**jil**-la mon-ti-frin-**jil**-la)
length 14 cm

Birch woods and the edges of conifer forests form the core habitat of the Brambling, the northern equivalent of the Chaffinch. This species is abundant in Fennoscandia and Russia, breeding mainly north of 60°N, where it can be the commonest bird alongside the Willow Warbler. Its dry, wheezing song, very different from the chatter of the Chaffinch and delivered with the head raised slightly higher, is a familiar sound at these latitudes.

In common with Chaffinches, Bramblings turn insectivorous in the breeding season. They feed their young mainly on caterpillars at first, and then on adult beetles as the nestlings grow. The need to be territorial, so important to Chaffinches, appears to be less developed in Bramblings; they defend nest and female rather than resources, and quite often cluster their nests in neighbourhood groups. The nest itself is bulkier than that of a Chaffinch – perhaps to be expected for the more northerly bird – and contains many more feathers for its lining. Most pairs in the far north raise only one brood and this seems to be the case in late springs as well, when Bramblings may interrupt their migration to breed further south than usual.

Most of Europe knows the Brambling only as a winter visitor; the whole population evacuates the breeding areas in the autumn, reaching as far down as southern Spain. Wintering Brambling tend to specialise on the mast of beech trees and may congregate in enormous numbers at rich sites: a winter roost may contain millions of birds.

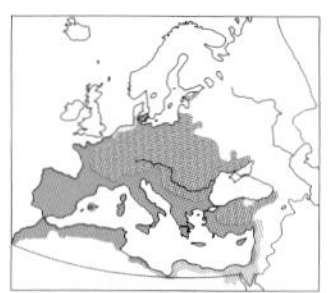

ID: Tiny finch with minute, stubby bill. Smaller than Siskin, with narrower yellow wing bars and lacking marks on face. Heavily streaked above and below. Rump bright yellow. Male has strong lemon tint to head and breast.

Serin

Serinus serinus (se-**rie**-nuss se-**rie**-nuss)
length 11.5 cm

Once confined to the Mediterranean region, the Serin has spread to the north and northeast of Europe in the last hundred years or so, reaching the fringe of the taiga in the Baltic States and Russia. It would have spread further were it not for its reluctance to cross wide stretches of water, ensuring that it has never managed to establish a proper foothold in Britain or Fennoscandia. Nevertheless it is still doing well for a bird whose world range encompasses only Europe and North Africa.

The Serin's recent successes have stemmed from a switch in its habitat preferences from woodland and forest edge to man-made environments such as gardens, churchyards and suburban streets. It absolutely revels in the availability of overhead wires, where it can perch and sing, and in the mixture of vegetation types, tall and short, that is found in such places. Typically it feeds on the ground, on various seeds such as dock, shepherd's purse, nettle and chickweed. But it also makes excursions into broad-leaved trees such as birch and elms to take buds and catkins in the spring, and it prefers to place its small, neat cup-nest in the branches of a conifer. Variety is a key for this species.

Serins sing all year, a delightful fizzing, over-fast phrase sounding like the jangle of tiny keys. The song is usually delivered from a high perch, but the male requires little encouragement to launch into the air and follow an arc in flight, flapping his wings slowly and tilting from side to side.

Citril Finch

Serinus citrinella (se-**rie**-nuss sit-rin-**nel**-la)
length 11.5–12.5 cm

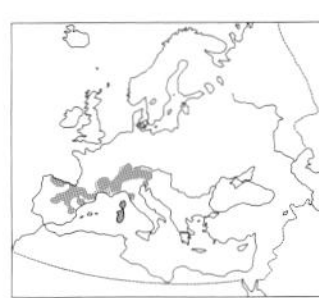

ID: Small but slender, fairly long-tailed finch with distinct greyish tint to head and neck. Wing has two broad yellow-green wing bars; underparts are entirely unstreaked. Island birds have brown back.

(Mainland race illustrated)

The Citril Finch is one of the few bird species entirely confined to Europe and, idiosyncratically, the only one that inhabits upland conifer woods in central Europe but is missing from the boreal forests of the north. But is it one species or two? There is a race found on Corsica, Sardinia, Capri, Elba and Gorgona that has a different colour pattern, different song and different nest site from the continental form, surely enough to merit its being treated as a separate bird entirely.

The Citril Finch usually feeds on the ground. It will go aloft into the trees, but prefers to perch rather than cling, and is much less acrobatic than most other small finches. It is not a bird of large, dense tracts of forest, even of its favourite tree, spruce. Instead it prefers to feed on adjacent meadows and clearings, or near human habitation, including gardens.

On the continent the nest is placed on a conifer, usually near a trunk and surrounded by thick branches. It is a well-built cup of grass, wool, roots and lichen. On the Mediterranean islands, though, it is placed in a bush of tree-heath or juniper, often only 1 m above ground. The structures here are much flimsier, being shallow and made up only of fine grasses.

The Citril Finch is normally found between 700 m and 1500 m when breeding on the continent, although it is something of an altitudinal migrant and will descend and spread out lower in winter. On the Mediterranean islands it inhabits rocky and scrubby places from sea level to 1650 m all year round.

Greenfinch

Carduelis chloris (kar-doo-**eel**-liss **kloh**-riss)
length 15 cm

The Greenfinch is familiar throughout Europe as a large, thick-billed, boisterous and slightly bullying finch, its aggressive tendencies seemingly embodied in the slight but permanent frown of its dark eyebrow. Of all the finches that specialise on seeds, this one probably takes the greatest variety, using its heavy bill to break open all but the hardest shelled. It evidently has several niches to itself: few other finches take seeds from sunflowers or rosehips, or fruit from blackberries. These birds can even cope with yew berries, which are highly poisonous; they remove the seed coat, the dangerous part, by mandibulation. This flexibility allows the Greenfinch to live in a wide range of habitats, including woodland edge, gardens, cemeteries, scrub and farmland. In one study in a cultivated area with plenty of hedges, Greenfinches were found to utilise the seeds of every one of the 30 commonest plants of the area.

Greenfinches are at their most obvious in the spring, when the males utter their canary-like trilling songs from the tops of trees and bushes; the usual run of phrases is regularly interrupted by an emphatic wheezing note, sounding a bit like the word 'green'. Every so often the males break off from perch-bound singing to launch into a song flight, in which they flutter at about tree-top height with heavy wingbeats, pitching to and fro and often describing circles or figures of eight.

Recent studies have shown that the Greenfinch's pairing system is quite complicated. Although monogamy could be considered the rule, about a quarter of males in a population may be polygynous, with two or even three mates each. This leaves some males unpaired and it is not uncommon for them to display to attached females and even to help with feeding the young. Although this does not benefit an unpaired male in the short term, it may help him to ingratiate himself to the female concerned and make her sympathetic to his advances the following year.

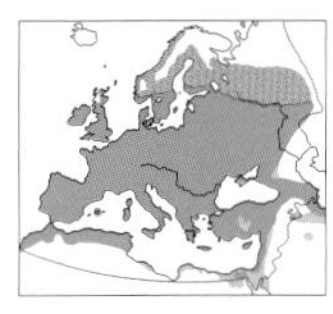

ID: Large, upright, perching, short-tailed finch with heavy, pale bill. Strong yellow edge to wing. Male apple green in body colour, female duller and with some faint streaks.

Siskin

Carduelis spinus (kar-doo-**eel**-liss **spie**-nuss)
length 12 cm

The Siskin is a little more specific in its habitat requirements than many other finches, and in the breeding season it is highly dependent on forests of spruce. It feeds its young on the seeds of these trees as they begin to ripen, harvesting them from cones by inserting the closed bill between the scales and then opening it. This is the same method often used by the Goldfinch, although the Siskin has a shorter bill. The Siskin also nests in spruce trees, often very high up. Most small birds build their nest low down, but conifers such as spruces grow their densest foliage in the canopy and here the Siskin constructs its neat cup out near the end of a branch.

The Siskin's association with spruce trees can be shown by the variability in its breeding season. In good years with a healthy crop of seeds, Siskins may lay their eggs as early as the middle of March, even in the far north of Europe, and then be in a position later in the season to begin a second brood (which, incidentally, is often nurtured on pine and herb seeds). In poor years, however, Siskins may have to wait until other types of seeds become available before attempting to breed at all, in May or possibly even June. The abundance of their favourite tree crop also affects their migration. In years of high population level but poor pickings, large numbers erupt from the northern forests to seek food further south.

In winter, however, the Siskin indulges a different passion – for alder seeds – and follows it to the damp habitats and riversides where these trees thrive. Siskins are sociable by nature and, in the few places where alders are really plentiful, flocks of hundreds or even thousands of birds may gather together. Most pairs of Siskins apparently meet and form couples in these flocks and, at the end of winter, migrate back to the northern spruce forests together.

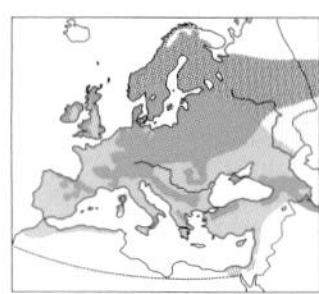

ID: Small forest and waterside finch, similar in colour to Greenfinch, but much smaller and with thinner bill. Yellow wing bars go across, not down edge of wing; flanks streaky.

Twite

Carduelis flavirostris
(kar-doo-**eel**-liss flay-vir-**ross**-triss)
length 14 cm

The Twite is a bird of cold, wet and windy places, living out in the open, far from the ameliorating shelter of bushes and trees. As a breeding bird it is found on mountains, hills and rugged coastlines, and in winter it extends to coastlines, cultivated areas and waste places. It has a remarkably disjunct distribution, with two distinct centres, one in northwest Europe, including Fennoscandia and Britain, the other encompassing the mountains of west and central Asia. Presumably the Twite was once much more widespread when the climate was colder, and retreated in two directions when things changed.

If the Twite is a relic, it is a very successful one. It has a habit of embracing new opportunities, for example in Poland and Germany, where wintering birds quickly took advantage of the growth of weeds in bomb sites after the Second World War and these days are often found in fields of introduced alien plants. The Twite is never afraid of marginal habitats and is the only finch that will virtually get its feet wet when feeding on sea aster and *Salicornia* on salt marshes.

In the breeding season male Twites perform a splendid song flight over the nest site, making circles in the sky and alternating flaps with glides. The pairs, once formed, often nest on the ground.

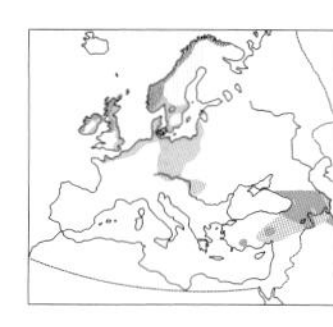

ID: Similar to Linnet, but with longer tail. Bill usually yellow, not grey as in Linnet. Face has distinct warm buff tinge at most times.

Arctic Redpoll

Carduelis hornemanni

(kar-doo-**eel**-liss **hor**-ne-man-nie)

length 13–15 cm

The Arctic Redpoll can look a bit like a Common Redpoll wearing a winter overcoat, because of its fluffed-out appearance and denser feathering, especially about the head, neck and lower belly. It is one of the few small birds that can remain at extreme latitudes during the winter, when it is able to survive temperatures down to –67°C. Apart from this impressive hardiness, it is similar in behaviour and ecology to the Common Redpoll, which winters in gentler climates.

Redpolls have a special feature of their alimentary canal to help them survive the cold, a small pocket halfway down the neck known as an oesophageal diverticulum, which can be thought of as an internal store of food to keep the fires burning inside. During the short Arctic days the birds feed on small, highly calorific seeds and are able to ingest far more than most small birds at a single sitting, putting the extra rations in their 'pocket'. Once night falls they retreat to a sheltered place (sometimes a tunnel in the snow), fluff out their feathers and move food from store to gut as and when required.

adult ♂ br. adult ♀ / 1st w. juv.

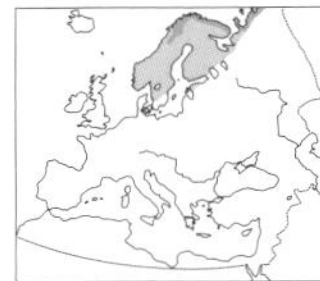

ID: Very similar to Common Redpoll, but fluffier and with smaller, 'pinched in' bill. Rump with very little or no streaking, and usually white. Pink colour on breast usually very subtle.

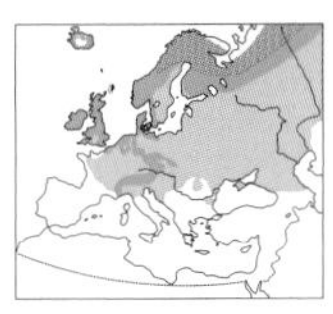

ID: Small, tree-living and acrobatic. At all stages, shows diagnostic combination of black bib, raspberry-red forehead and very small, yellow bill. Streaky brown, with whitish or buff wing bar.

Common Redpoll

Carduelis flammea (kar-doo-**eel**-liss **flam**-mee-a)

length 11.5–14.5 cm

The Common Redpoll, more than any other finch, comes in all shapes and sizes. Some are small and slim, others much larger and fatter; the latter could be separate species or simply subspecies – the debate is raging. Along with their physical differences come habitat variations and feeding preferences, making the Redpoll a pretty knotty problem for ornithologists.

The smallest race, the Lesser Redpoll (*C. f. cabaret*), was originally found almost entirely in Britain, Ireland and the Alps, but has recently undergone a significant and quite unexpected expansion of its range east into lowland continental Europe. It is a bird of commons and scrubby hillsides and is primarily arboreal, feeding in various small trees, including birch. The northern race, sometimes called the Mealy Redpoll (*C. f. flammea*), is much larger, paler and mainly an inhabitant of birch woods. The race from Iceland and Greenland, the Greenland Redpoll (*C. f. rostrata*), is larger still and, like the Mealy Redpoll, will compete at the limits of its range with the Arctic Redpoll in low tundra vegetation and on the ground. The northern races sometimes erupt southwards when their populations are high.

Whichever form they take, Redpolls eat very small seeds, especially those of birches, alders and spruces. As suggested above, they feed primarily up in the trees, exhibiting an acrobatic feeding style akin to that of a tit, often hanging upside down as they work the catkins. In one comparative study their foot-to-bill co-ordination was measured as superior to that of two other species that feed in similar trees, the Goldfinch and the Siskin. Nevertheless, when the seeds begin to fall from their favourite trees in late winter, flocks of Redpolls commonly find themselves feeding on the ground or resorting to taking unusual foods such as leaf- and flower-buds and even insects.

A Redpoll's nest is placed at varying heights in such trees as spruce and juniper, although it is often somewhat higher up than for many other finches. It is a thoroughly messy cup of twigs and stems, rounded off by so much plant down in the lining that it can appear distinctly white from a distance.

juv. adult ♀ br.

adult ♂ br. adult ♂ non-br. adult ♀ br.

Goldfinch

Carduelis carduelis

(kar-doo-**eel**-liss kar-doo-**eel**-liss)

length 12 cm

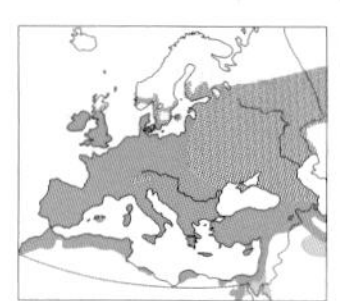

ID: Adults unmistakable. The plain-headed juveniles are perhaps best identified by the adults in their company.

The sprightly Goldfinch has the longest and sharpest bill of the finches and as a result can reach into seed heads unavailable even to close relatives. Its particular aptitude is for feeding on thistle seeds, which can account for a third of its annual diet. It likes the milky, half-ripe versions, which it can extract by probing down into the seed head and opening its bill using the strong muscles in its jaw, thereby forcing the head apart, as one might use a pair of tweezers. Besides thistles, the Goldfinch works on burdocks, dandelions and other members of the plant family Compositae. It can also extract the seeds from teasel, the only species of finch to do so. The seeds of these plants are at the bottom of spiked tubes and a Goldfinch's bill is just long enough to reach them.

Since the Goldfinch extracts most of its food directly from the plants themselves, it needs to be acrobatic just to hold on when foraging. Feeding birds often hang upside down and will use their wings to flutter and balance if certain seed heads are positioned in a particularly awkward place. Being small and light helps them to be agile. In the winter months many thistle heads die and fall to the ground, so the Goldfinches can then abandon their tricky balancing operations and feed without frills.

Goldfinches are, in common with most finches, highly sociable. In the breeding season most pairs nest together in neighbourhood groups of up to nine couples. Each pair holds territory only in the close vicinity of the nest, freeing birds to flock together and make expeditions to neutral ground in search of food, usually travelling no more than 800 m or so from their nest sites. After breeding, adults and young from neighbourhood groups wander more widely, often mixing with similar groups from elsewhere and coalescing into huge flocks of up to a thousand birds. These make quite a sight as they feed on ripening thistle heads, a mixture of bright colours with a twittering background.

These small birds are careful about where they place their nests. The most typical site is right at the end of the branch of a tall tree such as a sweet chestnut,concealed by leaves and inaccessible to predators, not always very high above ground. Such nests are usually safe from disturbance, but vulnerable to the wind. To combat the danger of the eggs or young tipping out, the nest is extremely well made, lined with compact plant wool and with an unusually high rim.

Goldfinches may have several broods a year, but their peak breeding season is unusually late, in August or even September. This, of course, coincides with the height of the thistle season.

Linnet

Carduelis cannabina
(kar-doo-**eel**-liss kan-na-**bie**-na)
length 13.5 cm

One might guess that the Linnet was a consumer of plant seeds simply by its names. 'Linnet' comes from the scientific name for flax (*Linum*), Carduelis from thistles (*Carduum*) and cannabina from hemp (*Cannabis*). As a matter of fact, none of these plants is overweening in importance to Linnets, but the association holds good nonetheless – this is a seed-eater *par excellence* and one of the few European birds to feed its young entirely on plant material (at least in the majority of cases), to the exclusion of invertebrates.

The Linnet relies mainly on the weeds of open ground, waste places and the edges of fields. Typical of its diet are seeds from docks and bistorts, mustard-like plants such as charlock , pinks such as chickweeds, and relatives of the daisy such as dandelions and groundsel. These tend not to be much-loved or admired plants and so the Linnet's fortunes can sway this way and that with the trends in modern farming and land use. The tidying up and increasing efficiency of arable cultivation is to the Linnet's detriment; yet ironically, one trendy new crop, oil-seed rape, is very much to its liking.

In contrast to most finches, Linnets seldom feed in trees, or even bushes. They are far more likely to be seen perched on seed heads or on the ground, where they will trample down the stems of short plants in order to get at the seeds at the flower head. They almost invariably feed in groups, large or small, and are not averse to joining other species with a common interest such as Chaffinches, House Sparrows or buntings. If a large mixed flock is disturbed, however, the Linnets will break away from the other fleeing birds and form their own exclusive group. When they do so their tight flocking style, with the birds seemingly attached to one another by means of elastic as they wheel to and fro, can be appreciated to the full.

The Linnet nests earlier than most other finches, often laying eggs by mid-April, at the beginning of the seeding season. At such a time there may be little foliage available in which to conceal its nest, so the Linnet has a preference for making its constructions in evergreen shrubs such as gorse. It is also atypical among most of its family in nesting very close to or even on the ground.

ID: Small, slender finch with very short, small bill. Breeding male distinctive, but females and non-breeding males best identified by grey bill, whitish markings on face and white edges to wings and tail.

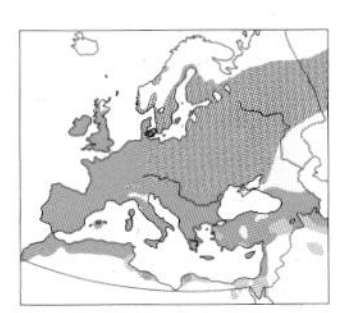

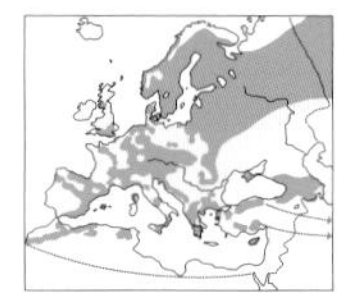

ID: *Distinctive stocky finch with large head and short tail. No wing bars or markings on most birds, just an orange-red (male) or green (female) coloration. Distinctive if crossed bill can be seen. Often feeds silently amidst canopy of conifers.*

Common Crossbill

Loxia curvirostra (**lok**-see-a kur-vir-**ross**-tra)
length 16.5 cm

The Crossbill, if one may use the analogy, made a 'career move' early on in its life that has shaped every aspect of its development. At some point it 'decided' to specialise in harvesting the very abundant, but awkward-to-obtain seeds of coniferous trees, and all its peculiarities have resulted from that specialisation. The Crossbill is clearly closely related to other finches (with similar displays, territorial and nesting habits, for example), yet differs from the rest in many ways that would appear to be fundamental.

The crossed mandibles are used for extracting seeds from ripening cones. Conifers don't give up their seeds easily, shielding them behind tightly closed scales; most birds cannot reach them until the cones are well open. But the Crossbill steals a march on the rest by getting at the seeds before this happens. Put at its simplest, the crossed bill is a tool for forcing scarcely opened scales back so that the seeds can be scooped out by the tongue. By the act of inserting its open bill between two scales and then shutting it, the Crossbill makes an opening. This happens because, when the bill shuts, the mandibles fit to the side of each other; thus the bill is wider shut than open, and this is what forces the scales back.

It is the lower mandible of the bill that is twisted and, perhaps surprisingly, this twist may be either to the right or to the left of the upper mandible (just as we are right- or left-handed, individual Crossbills are left- or right-billed). Birds whose bill twists to the right approach the cone from the right-hand side; and if the cone has been snipped off to be worked on, it is held in the right foot. The reverse happens in left-billed and left-footed birds. At birth, incidentally, the Crossbill's bill is straight, for it is not the internal bone structure that is twisted, but the horny surface layer, which develops later. Only when youngsters are 27 days old does the twisting begin to show, and only after 45 days are the birds able to feed themselves effectively.

The Crossbill's adaptation is all very well if there are plenty of seeds ripening, but no amount of specialisation works if there is no food to be had. The Common Crossbill's main food comes from spruce, and this tree has the annoying habit of producing its seeds in great abundance in some years, only for the crop to fail in others – worse still, this may be spread over a wide area. As a result, Crossbills often have to evacuate breeding areas in search of better food supplies. They may leave in large numbers and there may not be any clear directional movement; flocks can become virtually nomadic. The evacuations may occur at any time of year, but are particularly frequent in late summer. At this time Common Crossbills can be seen in unusual places and may reoccupy sites after an absence of many years. What is interesting about these movements is that, if they could be considered as migrations, they would be one-way trips, without a seasonal return ticket.

Another difficulty of slavishly following seed supplies is that your breeding seasons can be highly inconvenient. Birds must breed when food is abundant and if that means mid-winter – which it frequently does – then so be it. There is a celebrated record of a female Crossbill near Moscow incubating eggs while the outside temperature was –19°C. When the temperature beneath the incubating bird was measured it was found to be a cosy 38°C, which just goes to show that, if food is around, birds, insulated as they are by their feathers, can still thrive.

The closely related **Scottish Crossbill** (*Loxia scotica*) of the Caledonian pine forest of northern Scotland is identical except for the dimensions of the bill. This species has shunned the Common Crossbill's favourite spruce in favour of feeding on pine seeds. As a result its bill is broader and heavier than that of the Common Crossbill, but less swollen than that of the Parrot Crossbill. Among other differences between Common and Scottish Crossbills are the latter's softer voice, its tendency to be found in smaller flocks and its lack of any long-distance migratory or nomadic movements.

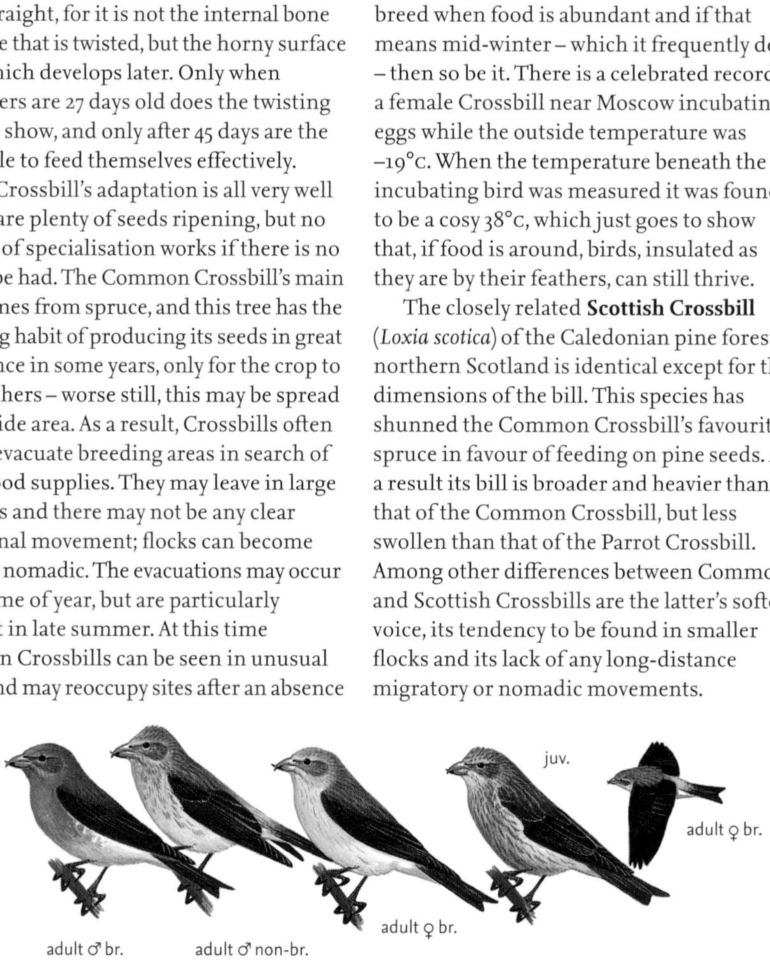

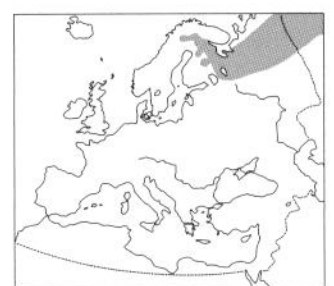

Two-barred Crossbill

Loxia leucoptera (**lok**-see-a loo-**kop**-ter-ra)
length 15 cm

ID: Easily distinguished from Crossbill by its two prominent bright white wing bars. Male is brighter, more cherry-red than male Common Crossbill.

Each species of Crossbill is adapted to exploiting the seeds of a particular conifer and for the Two-barred Crossbill it is the larch. The bird's relatively thin bill is ideal for the narrower, shorter scales of this tree's cones and also for those of spruce. It has the same general feeding technique as the Common Crossbill, although some say that it prefers to cling on to cones and work on them *in situ*, rather than snipping them off. But the technique of squeezing seeds out by closing the bill still applies.

This species seems to be less restricted in ecology than the other Crossbills. It often feeds on the seeds of broad-leaved trees – Crossbill sacrilege – and takes berries when these are available. On the other hand, it is more climatically limited. It is found only at high latitudes and in Europe seems unable to colonise vast areas of apparently suitable habitat further south. In our area it breeds regularly only in Russia and Finland, although in years of poor seed supply and high population pressure, large numbers do erupt towards the south and west.

Much of this bird's behaviour is typical of crossbills generally, but it has a far superior, sweeter, rambling song than the others.

Parrot Crossbill

Loxia pytyopsittacus
(**lok**-see-a pie-ti-oh-**sit**-ta-kuss)
length 17.5 cm

Only with considerable practice is it possible to tell a Parrot Crossbill from a Common Crossbill, so similar are these two closely related species. Given a good view, though, the heavier, less crossed bill and slightly pot-bellied appearance of this species is moderately noticeable, particularly in the larger and heavier-billed males. The call note is definitely lower in pitch, too.

Whereas the Common Crossbill specialises in extracting the seeds of spruce and is widely distributed in Europe, the Parrot Crossbill is a specialist on pine seeds and is confined to the northern taiga belt; but although this distinction holds good as a generalisation, both species will use the other's favourite tree on occasions. It seems that pine is a rather more dependable crop than spruce, because Parrot Crossbills only rarely erupt from their breeding range in any numbers, with their movements having nothing like the frequency and volume of Common Crossbill 'invasions'.

Parrot Crossbills always breed on the edges of forest, never in dense ones. Nests on pine are well out from the trunk, but nests in spruce (apparently the majority) are close to it. They are typical crossbill nests, if a little bulkier than the rest, made up from dry conifer needles, bark, twigs and moss.

ID: Very similar to Common Crossbill, but bill as deep as long; lower mandible tip not visible above upper mandible. Lower mandible bulges. Head larger.

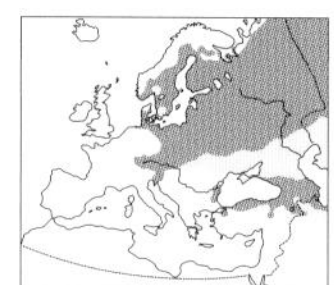

Common Rosefinch

Carpodacus erythrinus

(kar-**pod**-da-kuss er-rith-**rie**-nuss)

length 14.5–15 cm

ID: Mature male distinctive, bright red on head, chest and rump, other plumages brown. Somewhat short, bulbous bill and dark, staring eye.

Most Common Rosefinches seen in Europe are the descendants of pioneers. This bird was once a great rarity here, but from the second half of the 19th century a major westward expansion began which has continued, with ups and downs, ever since.

They may be special visitors, but Common Rosefinches don't hang around in Europe much. They are very late arriving, sometimes in the first week of June, and equally early in their departure. Unusually for European birds, their wintering grounds are not in Africa but in India and Pakistan.

The Common Rosefinch seems unable to decide on its favoured habitat. In the east of Europe it is a dry-country bird, inhabiting scrub and woodland edge; in the pioneering west it is confined to wet areas, especially where there are small bushes of willow or alder. It takes all sorts of plant parts – berries, buds, flowers – and not just seeds. It feeds both on the ground and in trees and bushes.

The song of the Common Rosefinch is a very cheery phrase sounding a little like 'pleased to meet you!' and it may be sung throughout the bird's short breeding season. Sometimes the singer is brown rather than red; curiously male birds mature sexually, breeding in their first year, before they acquire their colourful plumage.

Pine Grosbeak

Pinicola enucleator

(pie-nik-**koh**-la ee-noo-klee-**ay**-tor)

length 18.5 cm

The Pine Grosbeak has attracted some unflattering nicknames. Its tendency to remain in one tree for some time, working with great deliberation as it picks off berries one by one, a little like a koala on a eucalyptus, has led to it being called a 'mope' in Canada; and one of its Fennoscandian names – conferred on account of the tameness of Russian birds when unusual visitors were more likely to be shot than admired – translates as 'silly idiot'.

The northern taiga belt is the home of this hardy species, although it is thinly distributed and seems to be extremely picky about the conditions it needs – in Lapland, it seems to thrive in the presence of juniper scrub below coniferous trees. Its fussiness is all the more surprising because it makes excellent use of a wide range of foods during the year. In winter it usually feeds on berries in trees; in spring and summer it takes buds and berries from the understorey. And at various other times it will nourish itself upon a variety of seeds, shoots and flowers.

The Pine Grosbeak often remains at high latitudes in winter, protected by its unusual fluffy plumage. However, if the crop of rowan berries is poor in Russia, birds may erupt from these high latitudes and be found in large numbers further south than they usually go.

ID: Largest and tamest of the European finches, with fluffy plumage, long tail. Too big to be confused with other finches.

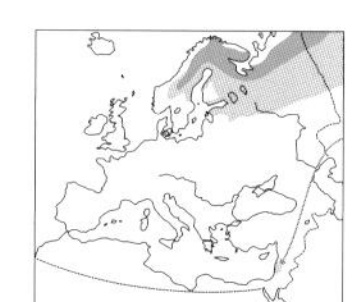

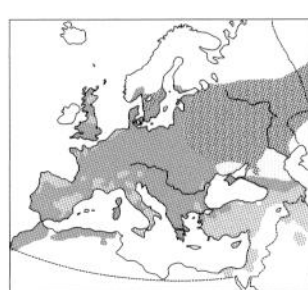

ID: Huge head and bill and short tail are usually enough to identify it. Female has grey, not bluish wing bar made by secondaries, and is usually of duller hue than male.

Hawfinch

Coccothraustes coccothraustes
(ko-ko-**throw**-steez ko-ko-**throw**-steez)
length 18 cm

In a family famed for its radiation in bill structure, the Hawfinch appears at the power – rather than the precision – end of the spectrum. Its bill is a remarkable tool. The bird weighs 55 g, while the load its bill can generate touches 45 kg, enough to crush the hardest tree seeds, including cherry and olive stones; and also enough to do severe damage to anyone who mishandles a Hawfinch while trying to ring it. In theory, a Hawfinch could probably sever a little finger.

The bill's internal structure enables the considerable strain of exerting such forces to be distributed to the muscles on both jaws, thus spreading the load. Both mandibles are fitted with two horny and serrated knobs that meet each other at the midline and overlie the other pair. Hard seeds are held between the four knobs, which concentrate the pressure and rupture the hard coat without damaging the bill.

It isn't easy to see a Hawfinch. It lives primarily in the canopy of tall deciduous trees, especially oaks and hornbeams, and is very shy. When flying from one place to another it tends to lift very high up, even on short transfers. It is also a quiet species without much of a formal song, and only makes easily missed, if somewhat penetrating, 'pix' or 'seep' calls.

For breeding, Hawfinches show an interesting polarisation: some are highly territorial, while others nest in small neighbourhood groups. The reason for this divergence is unclear.

Bullfinch

Pyrrhula pyrrhula (**pir**-roo-la **pir**-roo-la)
length 14.5–16.5 cm

In its social behaviour the Bullfinch is very different from the other finches. For example, it does not gather into large groups like the rest, even outside the breeding season. The most you'll see together is about half a dozen, and many observations will simply be of pairs; for a finch, that is hardly any at all. These pairs, furthermore, appear to persist as such throughout the breeding season and beyond into the winter – perhaps even for life; at any rate, the pair bond is much stronger and more intimate than in other finches. Sexual behaviour occurs at all times of the year, not just during the breeding season. On regular occasions birds approach each other and then turn away, moving their tails to one side, a display unique to the Bullfinch. At other times the couple touch bills and the male may offer a stick to the female.

The Bullfinch is a quiet bird. Individuals give a soft but penetrating 'pew' note to one another, and both sexes sing a quiet song sounding like the creaking of a rusty sign blowing in the wind. But it is easy to miss all these vocalisations, in contrast to the merry chattering of other finches.

Bullfinches do eat seeds, as would be expected of a finch, but a considerable part of their diet (up to 30 per cent) consists of buds and other soft parts of plants, including flowers. They have a short and rounded bill that is sharp edged, making it ideal for snipping these off, and the birds usually feed up in the trees.

In the spring, both sexes develop pouches on either side of the mouth that are used for transporting food to the young. Between them they hold a cubic centimetre of extra provision, allowing them to make fewer visits to the nest than they otherwise would.

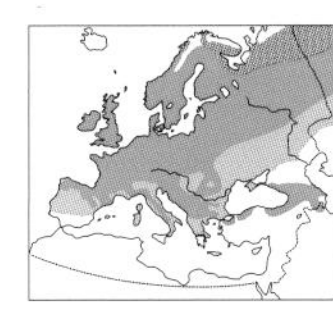

ID: Boldly patterned, with black cap, black tail and black wing with large white bar. Prominent white rump in flight. Not a streak to be seen anywhere on the smart plumage.

Buntings family *Emberizidae* (em-ber-**rie**-zid-ee)

Habitat Found in a variety of open and bushy country, including fields and hedgerows. Many species are northerly in distribution and inhabit marshy or tundra habitats.
Food Seeds of grasses and other plants. Invertebrates mostly in breeding season.
Movements Most are long-distance migrants. This family contains a higher proportion of birds wintering in Asia than any other European bird family.
Voice Not as vocally sweet as finches, with dry or slightly strained songs. Often make up for quality with exceptionally long singing periods and high output.
Pairing style Usually monogamous, but Corn Bunting and Snow Bunting regularly polygynous.
Nesting Usually solitary and territorial, but some species form clusters (neighbourhood groups) of pairs.
Nest Cup nest of grass, stems, moss and suchlike placed on or near the ground amidst thick vegetation; built by female.
Productivity 1–3 broods a year.
Eggs 3–6, usually hatch synchronously.
Incubation 11–14, by female.
Young Nest-bound, altricial, downy.
Parenting style Usually fed by both parents, but in Corn Bunting often by female only.
Food to young Invertebrates.
Leaving nest Young buntings often depart the nest unusually early, well before they can fly – sometimes at only 5 days old. All have fledged by 14–15 days.

At first sight a bunting looks very much like a finch and the most important distinctions are technical: the details of bill, skull and palate are quite different. Although the short, conical shape of the bill is similar from the outside, the buntings lack the grooves inside a finch's bill and most have a bony hump in the roof of the mouth to help crush seeds; in addition, the cutting edges of the bill are curved slightly inwards. There is less variation in the beak and no buntings show outlandish adaptations such as crossed mandibles.

Several behavioural and ecological distinctions between the two groups are easier to appreciate than any physical characteristics. The buntings, for example, have a broader diet than finches, invariably feeding on insects in the breeding season and taking them to their young whole, not regurgitated. Buntings feed on seeds in autumn and winter, but they take a much narrower range than finches, usually sticking to grass seeds. To obtain these they feed on the ground, rarely if ever venturing to herbs or trees. And since grass seeds are most easily found in open habitats, buntings are not, on the whole, forest or woodland birds.

Many buntings have distinctive songs, but these are usually short and stereotyped (although there are dialects), and no bunting sings in a rambling way like a finch. The songs are largely for territorial proclamation, and pair formation occurs when a female approaches a male's territory. Curiously, the apparently welcome visitor is usually aggressively rebuffed before being beguiled by displays on the ground. Most finch pairs form in winter flocks and their displays are much more protracted and intimate.

Buntings tend to build their cup-shaped nests on or close to the ground. A notable family trait is that the young often leave this vulnerable birthplace well before they can fly, sometimes only five to eight days after hatching.

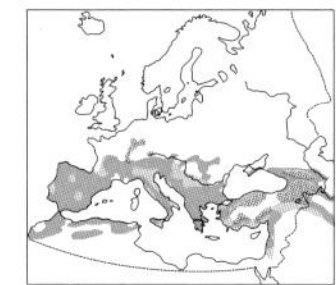

ID: *In contrast to most Buntings, male and female similar. Grey head with neat black stripes diagnostic.*

Rock Bunting

Emberiza cia (em-ber-**rie**-za **see**-a)
length 16 cm

Like two ladies attending a wedding in the same outfit, the Rock Bunting and Dunnock seem to coexist on their breeding grounds with almost the same song. Although their songs are meant to be directed only to their own species, there are times when male Rock Buntings and Dunnocks sing against each other, seemingly unaware of their 'mistake'.

The Rock Bunting occurs in open areas dominated by rocky features, often at altitude. However, rocks are not enough; every Rock Bunting territory also requires trees and bushes, in which the birds can forage and from which the male can sing. In fact males are much easier to see than females, the latter tending to hide away in low vegetation or on the ground. When singing, or at least in between phrases, the males commonly spread their tails to show the white tips, as if they were not conspicuous enough on the tree tops.

In common with other Buntings, the Rock Bunting primarily feeds on grass seeds, although it will take insects and occasionally makes a brief flutter above ground to catch one in flight. It keeps to the same diet in winter. Many Rock Buntings are altitudinal migrants, leaving upland areas in favour of gentler climates lower down. They are rarely found in large flocks at any time of year.

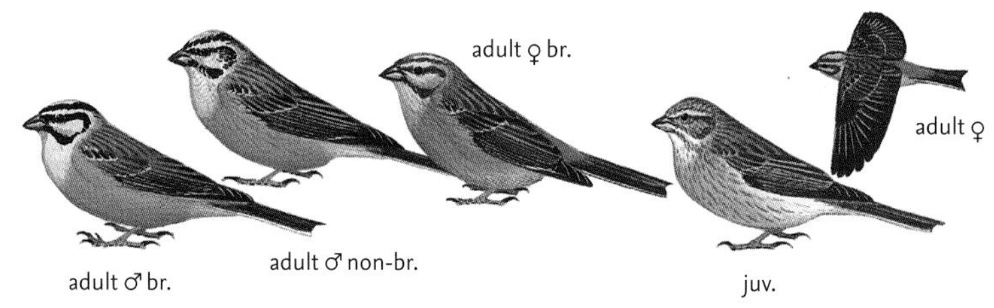

Lapland Bunting

Calcarius lapponicus
(kal-**kay**-ri-uss lap-**pon**-ni-kuss)
length 15–16 cm

The extreme northern latitudes of the world play host to two of the toughest of all the songbirds, the Lapland Bunting and the Snow Bunting. Both are large, densely feathered birds that need to tolerate exceptionally cold weather, especially upon their arrival on the breeding grounds in spring, when not much snow has melted. The Snow Bunting is marginally the tougher of the two: it seeks out harsh, bare, rocky areas for its habitat, while the Lapland Bunting prefers mossy and scrubby tundra slightly further to the south.

On their breeding grounds pairs of Lapland Buntings are often found in close proximity to one another, brought together by their habitat requirements, but male birds still defend their own exclusive territory from their neighbours. Surprisingly, and in complete contrast to several other bunting species, they are remarkably lazy singers, often not bothering to use their voices for hours on end, and then only upon sighting an intruder or a visiting female. Many birds only have one or two song posts and their entire singing period may last no more than a couple of weeks. Nevertheless the song is sweet and musical, and when the males' hearts are in it they will launch into a showy song flight, rising steeply from the ground to about 10 m, then swinging from side to side before gliding downwards in a spiral.

Near to the nest, and also in threatening situations at any time of year, Lapland Buntings use a distraction display to fool predators. They pretend to be injured and may lead intruders well away from the nest, walking rather than flying. Such a distraction technique is unusual among small birds.

ID: Big bunting whose shape recalls a lark (long body, long wings) more than a bunting. Breeding male unmistakable. Otherwise distinguished by its pale yellow bill and wing pattern, with the central brown panel bordered by narrow wing bars either side.

Yellowhammer

Emberiza citrinella (em-ber-**rie**-za sit-trin-**nel**-la)
length 16–16.5 cm

The Yellowhammer's is one of the most familiar of all bird songs, a simple dry rattle ending in a wheeze, and has attracted many colloquial renditions such as 'a little bit of bread and no cheese!' In fact, anyone living in a rural area should have plenty of time to make up their own version, for few birds have such an extended singing season or perform so indefatigably; they simply cannot be missed. From the time that a male takes up a territory from February onwards, right on into the early autumn, he begins with the dawn, then has a short bout of foraging before starting up his song once again for a few more hours until mid-morning. This is followed by a lull until another peak towards the late afternoon and evening. Only darkness and the need to roost cut off the flow. By the end of the day a male Yellowhammer may have sung 7000 times.

This is a territorial species and, because breeding sites are usually along hedgerows or other thin strips of vegetation, the defended areas are linear. In a study in England, for example, each male's territory was found to be on average about 60 m long, and stretched up to 10–15 m into the adjacent fields either side. Although defended vigorously, territories are used only for pair formation and nesting, with the birds travelling to neutral areas to find food.

As far as feeding is concerned, the Yellowhammer is a species thoroughly set in its ways. It almost always forages on the ground and most of its pecking movements are directed downwards. It has a diet of seeds that it favours, such as grasses, but there are others, such as crucifers, that it simply will not touch. It hunts for insects during the breeding season and will pick up berries in late summer and autumn, but that is the extent of its dietary adventure.

Males and females are socially monogamous, although extra-pair copulations are frequent. The most desirable males, and those most likely to sire young outside their formal relationship, are those with the largest amount of reddish plumage on the face. These are usually older birds that have learnt to seek out plants containing carotenoids, the chemicals that produce this hue. Most display is on the ground. The female builds a nest low down, well hidden in vegetation, and after a short incubation period the young leave the nest early, usually before they are able to fly.

A close relative of the Yellowhammer – so close that the two species occasionally hybridise – is the Pine Bunting (*Emberiza leucocephalos*), a rare bird in Europe. It breeds on the tundra to the east of our area, but a few individuals regularly winter in northern Italy and perhaps elsewhere.

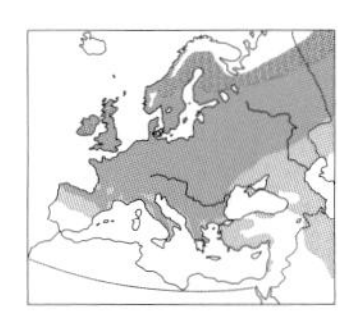

ID: Common and widespread. Easily identified by yellow head and chestnut rump. Female much duller than male and more streaky.

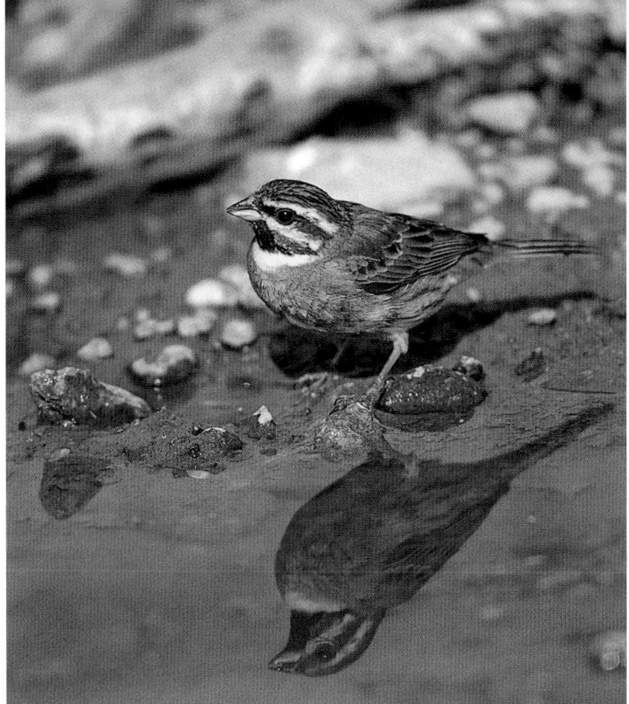

Cirl Bunting

Emberiza cirlus (em-ber-**rie**-za **sir**-luss)
length 15.5 cm

Like the sort of awkward and exacting guest most dreaded by hoteliers, the Cirl Bunting is a fussy species, for whom everything must be just right if it is to settle down. A study in Germany found that Cirl Buntings would thrive only where there was a slope of 20–35 degrees, an aspect facing south to southeast and an altitude of 200–300 m; the type of vegetation was also a factor. This pernickety nature is typical. Throughout their range these birds occur only in regions with warm, dry summers and short, frost-free winters, and may be shifted by the slightest alteration in microclimate. Perhaps surprisingly, though, the species as a whole has quite a wide range and can be locally common. Its heartland is in the warm southwest.

These are skulking and secretive birds, spending much time hidden by thick vegetation. Even on the ground where they feed, they rarely if ever venture onto bare soil, using short or trampled pasture instead. But for a Cirl Bunting to be content its feeding sites must be no further than 30 m from the nearest cover. This excludes it from the more open, agricultural areas inhabited by Yellowhammers.

The only time a Cirl Bunting is conspicuous is when the male is singing his territorial song, a sort of poor-man's Yellowhammer without the 'cheese' ending. This song is uttered from a high perch, often very persistently, and for a long period between March and August. Cirl Buntings are exceedingly territorial and will see off rivals with considerable aggression anywhere within 150 m of the nest.

ID: Male highly distinctive. Female distinguished from Yellowhammer by olive-green rump, clean thin pencil lines on underparts, and more sharply patterned head.

Ortolan Bunting

Emberiza hortulana (em-ber-**rie**-za hor-too-**lay**-na)
length 16–17 cm

Most buntings are seed-eaters that have a seasonal preference for invertebrates and feed them to their young; but if there is a species that turns this rule around a bit, it is the Ortolan Bunting. This bird is as likely to be seen scouring the tops of trees and bushes for insects as it is to be foraging for seeds on the ground, and its sharply pointed bill is equally suitable for picking invertebrates off leaves with tweezer-like precision or for crushing and de-husking small seeds. The Ortolan, then, could be described as the all-rounder of the bunting family.

It is widespread in Europe, occupying places with low rainfall and plenty of sun and typically avoiding the Atlantic seaboard. Within this limit it can occur in a bewildering variety of habitats, from clearings in forests to bare rocky hillsides. In some places it will occur on farmland and in orchards, but as agricultural practices change and insect numbers decline, its range in northwest Europe is diminishing and becoming more fragmented. Ecologically its requirements are hard to pin down.

In spring male Ortolan Buntings sing a perfunctory phrase, often with a striking resemblance to the opening four notes of Beethoven's Fifth Symphony, although there is much variation and birds from specific regions have their own dialects. Ortolan Buntings also have several ways of delivering their song. They may sing from a perch or in two types of song flight, one taking them up and down from a bush top, the other describing a circle in the horizontal plane.

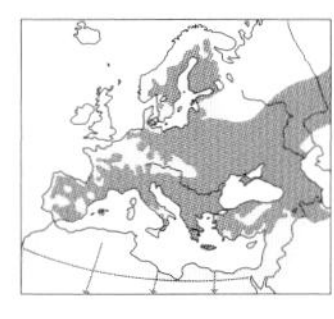

ID: Pink bill is a key feature, distinguishing it from other buntings. Prominent yellowish eye ring at all stages. Pink wash to plumage.

Cretzschmar's Bunting

Emberiza caesia (em-ber-**rie**-za **see**-zi-a)
length 16 cm

The rule is, if you wish to see a Cretzschmar's Bunting, don't look upwards. Of all the Buntings, this is probably the most terrestrial, carrying out the most important tasks of its life on the ground. It forages there for small seeds and a few invertebrates, especially favouring bare patches, rocks or stones and very short grass. It nests on the ground, building a cup of stalks, roots and grass within a shallow depression, under a rock rose or among the network of roots of a shrub. And the male even sings his four-note extravaganza on the ground, from a low rock or stone, or even from where he stands on the bare earth. On the odd occasion he might make a daring visit to a metre-high bush and utter a few phrases, but this is not usually his style.

The Cretzschmar's Bunting is, though, a relatively long-distance migrant, so it isn't afraid to fly. It leaves its breeding areas in July and August and travels to northeast Africa (perhaps flying over the eastern Mediterranean) or to Arabia (presumably travelling overland via Israel) for the winter. It returns in late March, with the males forming the advance guard, about ten days before the females.

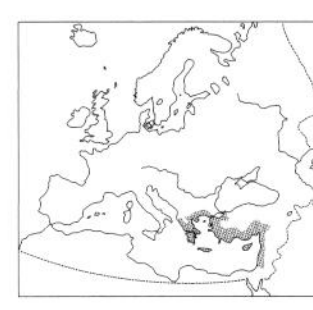

ID: Distinguished from Ortolan by white eye ring and slightly redder bill; stripe running down side of face is rusty red, not yellow.

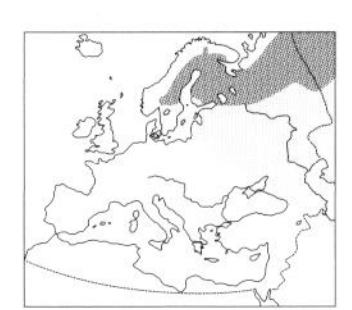

ID: Usually easy to identify in breeding plumage by the black face pattern and reddish-brown breast band and flanks. Flank colour retained outside breeding season, as are chestnut nape and narrow white wing bars.

Rustic Bunting

Emberiza rustica (em-ber-**rie**-za **roos**-ti-ka)
length 14.5–15.5 cm

The Rustic Bunting is a member of the club of buntings that have expanded their range west into Europe in the last hundred years. It was first recorded in Sweden in 1897 and now breeds over most of that country, having crept further and further south with each passing decade; it is also found in parts of Norway, Finland and Russia that were previously unoccupied. This must be a little inconvenient, since the pioneering birds still use southern Asia for their wintering grounds, making their migration a long and convoluted one. With an ardent dislike for dry habitats, Rustic Buntings skirt the steppes of Europe and Central Asia as they travel east, hugging forested habitats to the north as far as they can.

For breeding, Rustic Buntings are drawn to ground that is boggy and sprinkled with pools, with heavy undergrowth and a few trees; this might sound fussy, but suitable habitats abound in the hinterland of Fennoscandia. The birds feed mainly on the ground close to water, but also sometimes within thick bushes. In common with other buntings, they eschew their non-breeding diet of seeds in favour of invertebrates, the exclusive diet of the young. In their rich habitats, such food is not hard to find.

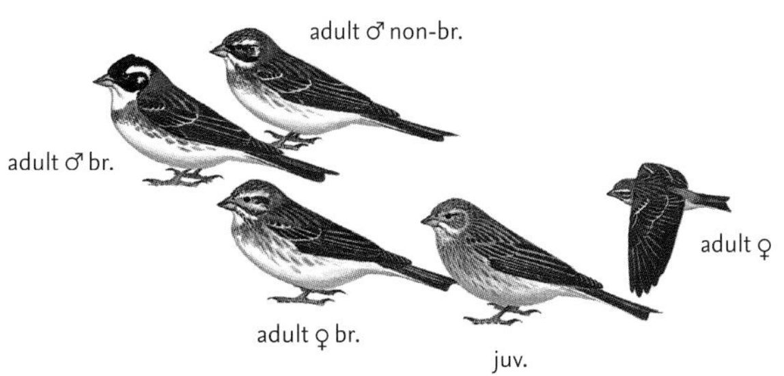

Little Bunting

Emberiza pusilla (em-ber-**rie**-za poo-**sil**-la)
length 13–14 cm

If you made a list of European buntings in order of how far north their core breeding range fell, you might be surprised to find that the Little Bunting, the smallest of the group, was third behind the large, hardy Snow Bunting and the equally hefty Lapland Bunting. That suggests that this bird with its small, sharply pointed bill is a tough customer. And so it is, eking out a living in the dwarf willow zone within the northern tundra. It is found in more scrubby habitats than the Lapland Bunting, including those with a few tall trees; but if the tree growth becomes too thick the Rustic Bunting takes over.

The doughty Little Bunting makes a formidable journey even to turn up in Europe. It winters in China and Southeast Asia and when it sets off after the breeding season it must first fly a long way east before heading south. It tends to arrive late on the breeding sites, often the first week of June.

The Little Bunting is well known for being tame, both on migration, when it will often flock with other small birds, and on the breeding sites, where it shows none of the paranoia of several other buntings. Birds can be approached closely as they sing their buzzy songs, throwing such effort into them that they almost overbalance on their perch.

ID: Small, with distinctively straight upper mandible, black crown with brown central stripe, and chestnut cheeks bordered with black at rear.

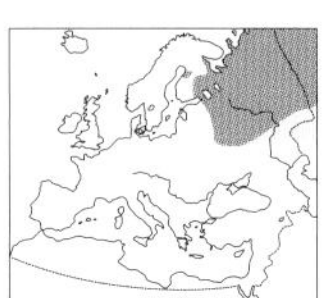

ID: Male unmistakable. In other plumages shows distinctive stripy head pattern, yellowish breast.

Yellow-breasted Bunting

Emberiza aureola (em-ber-**rie**-za ow-ree-**oh**-la)
length 14–15 cm

One of several buntings to have reached Europe from further east in the last hundred years, the Yellow-breasted Bunting is still a rare bird here. It breeds only in Russia and Finland, with only about 300 pairs in the latter. It winters in Southeast Asia and arrives very late on its breeding grounds.

Its favoured habitats are valley bottoms covered with tall, thick grass and dotted with willow or alder bushes. Where these occur pairs have a marked tendency to gather into neighbourhood groups.

Snow Bunting

Plectrophenax nivalis
(plek-troh-**fee**-naks nie-**vay**-liss)
length 16–17 cm

The Snow Bunting breeds further north than any other small bird in the world, right up to the permanent ice of the northern hemisphere. It has thick plumage for insulation and often walks in something of a crouch, with the upper parts of the legs warmed by the fluffed-out plumage of the belly, a behavioural adaptation to prevent heat loss.

Many Europeans see Snow Buntings only in the winter, when they visit steppes and windswept coastlines far to the south of their breeding range. Here they gather in sizeable flocks and have a dynamic way of feeding: the flock walks forwards as a unit, but the back markers continually take off and fly to the front, leapfrogging the front runners to roll the flock onwards.

The first male Snow Buntings return to their breeding areas as much as a month earlier than male rivals and females. They establish territories by singing, mainly from the ground. As soon as a female lands on a male's patch he performs the so-called 'mannequin display', spreading and drooping his wings and tail and shuffling away for a short distance, only to return quickly and repeat the process, making him look like a small machine. Some males, particularly in the southern parts of the range, may obtain more than one mate, but at high latitudes the short breeding season does not allow for extra dalliances.

The nest of a Snow Bunting is a robust open cup of moss and grass, usually placed in a rock crevice, and also often among seabird colonies. It is often lined with feathers from another inhabitant of the far north, the Ptarmigan.

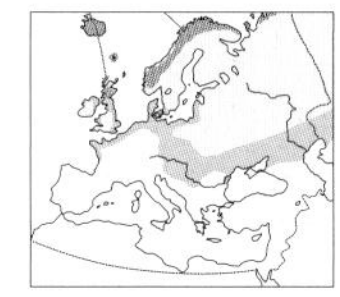

ID: Large, long and with thick plumage. Usually easy to distinguish by the amount of white on it, especially on the wing.

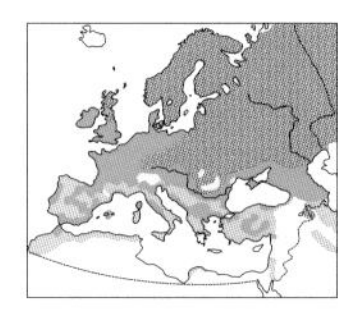

ID: Male distinctive, with jet-black head and white collar. Other plumages show prominent pale 'moustache' bordered by dark streak on side of chin, grey bill with slightly curved sides.

Reed Bunting

Emberiza schoeniclus (em-ber-**rie**-za **shee**-nik-luss)
length 15–16.5 cm

The song of the Reed Bunting is a simple affair, just a few notes strung together to make a staccato phrase that sounds a bit like 'Three Blind Mice'. But it is also variable: it may be sung fast or slow. A bird singing the fast phrase is announcing that it is unattached, but as soon as it pairs up the song switches to the slow version. Even birdwatchers, then, can easily tell the marital status of the bird they are hearing.

Despite having such clear signals among themselves and being socially monogamous, Reed Buntings still manage to indulge in much extra-pair intrigue. In one study in England, up to 86 per cent of all nests had at least one egg that contained different male genes from those of the 'official' father. It is supposed that this is a particular problem for Reed Buntings because, in the environment of thick, marshy vegetation where they live, the females can easily give their guarding males the slip and form clandestine liaisons with neighbours. In a way, though, the official mates have the last laugh. Somehow aware that their paternity has been compromised, they devote less effort to their share of feeding the young than males that have prevented these happenings.

The Reed Bunting shows remarkable variation in body and bill size. In northwest Europe the birds are comparatively small and have unremarkable bills; but in southeast Europe they are much larger (as big as Yellowhammers) and have greatly swollen, bulbous bills adapted to biting through reed stems to get the insects inside, especially in winter.

Corn Bunting

Miliaria calandra (mie-li-**ay**-ri-a kal-**lan**-dra)
length 18 cm

ID: Large, round-headed, barrel-chested bunting. Streaks on breast often coalesce to form spot. Bill pink.

Not even its most ardent admirers would claim that the Corn Bunting was a stunning species: it is plump, dull and streaky. But its plain looks cover up a private life that is vivid and colourful, and has made it a favourite subject for study among scientists in search of a whiff of scandal.

Even the bald statement that males are 20 per cent heavier than females is an eye-opener. Such a distinction is unusual among songbirds generally and is a classic sign of a bird that does not always adhere to the norm of monogamy. And indeed, between a quarter and a third of males in a population wholeheartedly embrace polygyny; many pair up with two or three females at the same time and there are individuals on record that have paired with 18 females in a season! It sounds unfair and it is – not surprisingly, a significant proportion of males are unable to acquire any mate at all. For their part the females tend to remain paired to the same male all season.

A male's desirability is at least sometimes related to the quality or size of his territory. It appears that, when a female has to choose between a bachelor in a poor territory and a polygamous male in a good one, she will tend to opt for the latter. Where Corn Buntings are migratory or partially migratory, males arriving early have a greatly enhanced chance of breeding success, presumably because they have the pick of the territories. The quality of territory is, of course, related to its ability to provide plenty of food, which is high on a female Corn Bunting's list of priorities.

Male Corn Buntings defend their patch with a very distinctive song that sounds like the jangling of a bunch of keys and is repeated at frequent intervals, even in the middle of the day. A performer may sing from a bush top or an overhead wire, but he might equally be content to sit among the tops of crops or herbs where he can be very difficult to spot. Every male uses a number of different perches and, when moving from one to another, takes the opportunity to indulge in a little self-advertisement, dangling his legs conspicuously.

The Corn Bunting is very much a bird of arable country, with a particularly strong attachment to fields of barley; these apparently host a higher proportion of polygynous males than anywhere else. The species also seems, for little apparent reason, to prefer rolling terrain to a flat landscape, and is drawn to places by the sea. It is widespread in Europe.

Black-headed Bunting

Emberiza melanocephala
(em-ber-**rie**-za mel-lan-noh-**sef**-fa-la)
length 16–17 cm

During their short summer stay in Europe Black-headed Buntings are conspicuous birds, showing off a combination of confident behaviour, large size (they are the second-largest bunting in Europe after the Corn Bunting) and, in the male, gaudy plumage. In the warm southeast where these birds occur, the male's short but melodious song (at times approaching a Garden Warbler in tone, although always preceded by dry 'zit' calls) is a common sound, very much part of the agricultural landscape. The singers often perch as high as they can, on the top of a bush, tree or overhead wire, and perform for hours on end. At times, as if to break the monotony, they may launch into a brief song flight, singing as they transfer between one perch and another, dangling their legs as they do so. More rarely they may lift exuberantly into the air and descend with a flutter, like plump yellow Tree Pipits.

This is one of the buntings that migrates – not to Africa, as most European migrant birds do, but to Asia and, in this case, India. Its long journey probably dictates that the breeding season is unusually brief. It arrives right at the end of April and leaves as early as late July, condensing its breeding activities into a mere three months. Usually this is time enough only for a single brood, raised on a loose untidy nest often placed in a vine.

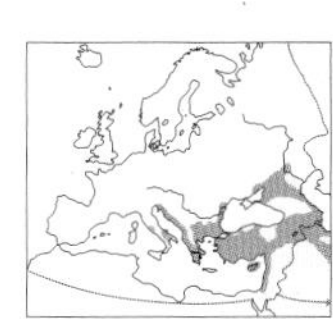

ID: Large and plump. Male unmistakable. Female has unmarked yellowish breast, unstreaked head.

Glossary

Advertising call a vocalisation given by a bird other than a Passerine, to declare ownership of a territory or to attract a mate.
Altitudinal migration a seasonal movement not so much of latitude as of altitude, birds moving less between places than between heights.
Arboreal living in the trees, above ground.
Arm in identification parlance (but not literally) the inner part of a bird's spread wing. The outer part is called the hand.
Altricial helpless at hatching, with eyes closed. Usually naked or sparsely downy.
Aspect ratio a measure of flight performance defined by the length of a wing divided by its width.
Asynchronous hatching hatching that takes place over several days, leading to different ages within the brood.
Auntie a bird, which may or may not be related to any of the young, enlisted to tend a crèche.
Bigamy (bigamous) breeding relationship in which one sex, usually the male, is paired to two of the opposite sex.
Binocular vision a type of vision in which the fields of the two eyes overlap. Since the eyes can see an object from two slightly different angles, binocular vision makes it easier to judge distance.
Bivalve a type of mollusc with two shells that can be tightly shut together, like a glasses case.
Bolus a lump of food made up from many small items, such as insects.
Boreal associated with the northern coniferous forest belt.
Breeding grounds a broad term for the geographical range over which a species normally breeds.
Breeding site fidelity the act of returning to the same breeding site year after year, usually for a bird's whole lifetime.
Brood a collection of young constituting a single breeding attempt.
Brooding the act of an adult bird sitting on young, rather than eggs, to maintain their body temperature.
Brood parasite a species that lays eggs in the nest of another species (interspecific) or another individual of the same species (intraspecific). Intraspecific brood parasitism is sometimes known as egg dumping.
Brood patch an area of skin on the belly that has lost its feather covering and can therefore be in contact with the eggs during incubation.
Brood splitting the act of assigning particular chicks within a brood to each adult, for their exclusive care.
Cache a store of food, usually containing many items.
Call broadly, any bird vocalisation that isn't a song. Calls are usually short (one or two syllables) and immediately address a particular situation e.g. alarm, flock contact.
Canopy the more or less continuous network of branches and foliage forming the topmost layer in a forest.
Carotenoid pigments organic compounds primarily responsible for red or orange colours in the plumage and taken in as part of the diet.
Carrion the bodies of dead animals.
Cephalopods a group of molluscs including squids, cuttlefishes and octopuses.
Cloaca the terminal opening of a bird's reproductive (and digestive) system to the exterior.
Club usually applied to a gathering of non-breeding or pre-breeding seabirds on the edge of a colony, used for activities ranging from purely loafing to active courtship.
Clutch a set of eggs constituting a full breeding attempt.
Cock nest a nest structure, usually unlined, built by a male bird to show to a female as part of the pair-bonding process.
Colony a clearly defined gathering of pairs for breeding, each pair with its own small territory immediately around the nest.
Communal courtship courtship displays performed by several adults (usually males) at once.
Co-operative breeding a breeding system in which birds other than the parents help with feeding and tending the young. Helpers are often called supernumeraries.
Courtship the act of performing ritualised, standardised displays to attract a mate or maintain a pair bond.
Courtship feeding provisioning of food by a male to an adult female. The offering helps to maintain the pair bond, but also helps the female to keep in good condition while forming eggs.
Crèche a gathering of unrelated young birds brought together for protection.
Crepuscular active at dawn and dusk.
Cryptic coloured, patterned or behaviourally inclined to be concealed.
Cursorial liable to run along the ground.
Dabbling the act of placing the bill into water, usually at the surface.
Decurved curved downwards (opposite: recurved)
Differential migration the migration of a species in which different age and sex classes have different destinations, routes and/or times of flight.
Dispersal (post-juvenile dispersal) the movement of juvenile birds away from their parents' territory and beyond once they are independent, in no particular direction and often not very far.
Distraction display a stereotyped set of postures or behaviours performed by parent birds in order to distract the attention of a potential predator away from nest or young.
Diurnal active by day.
Down small feathers characterised by their fluffy structure, found, for example, on chicks and on the breast of wildfowl.
Drumming the sound made by the beating of a woodpecker's bill on wood for the express purpose of advertising; also used for the vibration of a Snipe's outer tail feathers during display flight.
Dust-bathing a form of bathing in which a bird uses earth instead of water, to remove parasites, oil and detritus from the plumage.
Eclipse plumage a cryptic, female-like plumage acquired by male ducks for concealment whist they are moulting their flight feathers.
Egg dumping see Brood parasite.
Emergent vegetation vegetation that is rooted underwater but has foliage extending above the water surface.
Ericaceous refers to a plant in the heather family (Ericaceae).
Eruption the periodic but irregular arrival of a species or population well out of normal range, usually in response to overcrowding and/or lack of food. From the point of view of the areas that receive the visitors, it is known as an irruption.
Escape movement a movement of a bird in response to untenable weather conditions.
Extra-pair copulation (EPC) copulation outside the pair bond in socially monogamous species.
False nest a nest-like structure built or created for copulation or feeding the young, for example, rather than for incubating the eggs.
Family a grouping of closely related genera and species.
Fingered refers to the tip of a wing in which the main flight feathers (the primaries) are spread out.
Fledging the act of acquiring the first set of (juvenile) feathers, often a prerequisite to leaving the nest for the first time.
Fledgling a bird that has fledged and left the nest.
Flight song a song that is specifically delivered as accompaniment to a ritualised display flight.
Flush to scare off a previously hidden bird or other animal.
Fly catching specifically, a food-gathering technique involving short aerial sallies from a perch to catch prey in flight.
Foot paddling (pattering) applying fast pattering movements of one foot to the surface of a substrate such as mud, in order to attract food or render it visible.
Fringing vegetation vegetation on the side of a body of water.
Gape the opening created when the mouth is opened wide.
Genus (pl. genera) a grouping of closely related species. In a scientific name the first word is the genus, and the second the species.
Gliding the act of moving forwards in the air with the wings held still.
Gonydeal angle a sharp deflection upwards of the ridge of the lower mandible near the tip of the bill.
Hand in bird identification, the outermost part of the wing (see Arm).
Harem a collection of females bound together by allegiance to a breeding male.
Herbivore (herbivorous) having a diet composed of plant material.
Home range an undefended area (thereby not a territory) where a bird lives and spends its time.
Hover to fly on the spot, maintaining position over the same patch of ground, usually sustained by fast flapping flight.
Immature any bird that has left the nest and has not yet acquired full adult plumage.
Incubation the act of sitting on a clutch of eggs to warm them and allow them to develop.
Intertidal zone the ground covered by high tide and exposed at low tide.
Introduced refers to a non-native species that is present in an area as a result of human activity, including deliberate release.
Invertebrate a general term for the vast assemblage of animals that have no backbones (i.e. anything that isn't a fish, amphibian, reptile, bird or mammal). Includes arthropods such as insects and spiders, crustaceans, molluscs and worms.
Irruption see Eruption.
Juvenile a bird sporting its first set of true feathers.
Leapfrog migration migratory journeys that take some populations further than others, the former overflying the latter.
Lek a set of displaying males at a communal arena, gathered together for the purpose of mate selection by visiting females.
Littoral living by the shore of a lake or the sea.
Loop migration a migration in which the outward and return journeys take different pathways, although they have the same departure/arrival points.
Lumbricid worms the group that includes most of Europe's common earthworms, mostly in the genus *Lumbricus*. Technically these worms are in the phylum Oligochaeta.
Mandibulate to work with the bill.
Marsh tern one of the three dusky-plumaged terns of the genus *Chlidonias* that breed mainly in freshwater habitats.
Migrant in one sense, a bird species that migrates; alternatively, an individual bird in the act of migrating.
Migration a regular movement, usually seasonal, between one place or another carried out by a population of birds. Does not refer to daily movements or feeding trips for the young.
Migratory divide a divergence of initial migratory direction taken by members of the same species living in different geographical areas, in order to avoid a common barrier such as a mountain range or water body.
Mobbing individual or communal harassment of a predator by birds with a view to forcing it away from the immediate vicinity.
Monogamy (monogamous) a mating system in which one male is bonded to one female and both sexes have a role in the breeding attempt. In genetic monogamy the eggs are the genetic product of both parents only; in social monogamy the adults play their roles must may also indulge in extra-pair copulations.
Morph one or more distinct and consistent plumage patterns or colours seen within a species, independently of an individual's age, location or sex. Also Phase.
Moult the act of replacing worn-out feathers, usually carried out at a specific time each year.
Moult migration a journey undertaken to a special place with the express purpose of moulting.
Mutual preening the act of preening another individual, usually but not always the mate. Often performed in pair-bond maintenance.
Neighbourhood group a group of pairs of birds whose territories are clustered more closely than would be expected by random dispersal, but do not form a colony.
Nestling a young bird confined, by virtue of its early stages of development, to the nest.
Nocturnal active at night.
Nomad a bird that moves in response to the availability of suitable breeding or feeding conditions, not normally predictably and not necessarily returning to where it started.
Offal waste or rejected parts of a carcass.
Omnivore (omnivorous) a species that will eat any category of food, typically referring to both plant and animal matter.
Opportunist (opportunistic) a bird that can adapt to the immediate prevailing availability of food, rather than having specific limitations of diet.
Order a high rank of classification grouping families together (see Family).
Partial migration migration in which only certain individuals of a population or species migrate, while the rest don't.
Passage migrant a bird passing through a place, of a species or population that neither breeds nor winters there.
Passerine a member of the order Passeriformes, characterised by its foot arrangement (see Perching bird) and by its well-developed vocal apparatus, the latter giving the ability to 'sing'.
Pectoral flight muscles the large muscles that are found under the breast of birds and power the bird for flight.
Perch and pounce a feeding technique involving an initial watch from an elevated perch, followed by a rapid plunge down to grab any prey sighted.
Perching bird a specific term sometimes used for members of the order Passeriformes, all of which have a foot arrangement (three toes pointing forwards, one back) that aids perching.
Phase see Morph.
Picking (surface-picking) obtaining food direct from a surface (mud, leaf etc).

Plunge-diving the act of diving into the water from any distance above the water, rather than from a swimming position.
Polychaete worms a group of worms of the segmented type (phylum Annelida), most of which are marine.
Polyandry (polyandrous) a mating system in which one female is mated with two or more males, either at the same time (simultaneous) or one after the other (successive).
Polygamy (polygamous) a general term for a mating system in which a member of one gender is paired to two or more individuals of the opposite sex.
Polygynandry (polygynandrous) a mating system in which both the birds forming a pair bond may be polygamous at the same time.
Polygyny (polygynous) a mating system in which one male is mated to two or more females, either simultaneously or successively. See Polyandry.
Precocial a chick that is well advanced and mobile at hatching, usually downy, with eyes open; usually quickly able to feed itself.
Probing the act of searching for food below a surface (e.g. mud)
Promiscuous refers to a mating system with exclusively sexual, rather than social pair bonds.
Quartering the act of flying slowly and low above ground, searching for food below.
Raptor a general term for a diurnal bird of prey.
Redhead a term for the female and immature male plumages of certain ducks (e.g. of genera *Mergus* and *Bucephala.*)
Regurgitation the ejection of partially digested food from the crop or gizzard to feed the young.
Reintroduction a conservation measure involving the release of captive birds into the wild in areas where they have become extinct.
Relict generally refers to a population left isolated (from another) by the action of an ice age or similar climatic or geological event.
Resident a bird that remains all year in the same area.
Role reversal a rare breeding system in which the males have taken on most of the duties often associated with females, such as incubating, brooding and tending the young, while the females often initiate display.
Roosting a term referring in birds to sleeping and often also to those activities associated with sleeping – pre-roost behaviour, settling down and presence at the roost site while awake.
Sahel the region of Africa on the southern fringes of the Sahara Desert.
Sawbill a term referring to the ducks of the genus *Mergus*, which have bills with serrated edges.
Scavenger a bird that eats carrion or rubbish, typically not killing for itself.
Scrape a shallow depression in the ground created by a bird for its nest.
Sea duck a duck that is customarily seen on the sea, either in the breeding season or, more often, in the winter.
Sedentary non-migratory (but the juveniles may disperse)
Semi-precocial having the characteristics of a precocial chick (e.g. well-developed, downy) but remaining confined to the nest or nesting territory.
Skulking customarily remaining hidden low down in thick vegetation.
Sky dance an elaborate display flight, usually referring to one carried out by a bird of prey.
Snorkelling the act of holding the head underwater while swimming before a dive, to check for prey or suitable conditions.
Soaring flying upwards, usually in circles.
Solitary nesting in its own territory separate from other birds.
Song a pattern of sounds, often repeated, that is used by a species to proclaim territorial ownership and/or to attract a mate. Usually longer and more complex than a call.
Song flight a stereotyped aerial routine for advertising purposes, always accompanied by a song.
Species a population of birds sharing a common phenotype (i.e. the same appearance and genetic make-up) and usually able to interbreed with one another but not with a member of another species.
Speculum the colourful bar on the secondary flight feathers of a duck.
Staging area an area, usually traditional, used by a bird or population of birds in mid-migration, often for refuelling, moulting and fattening.
Steppe treeless and often waterless lowland grassland, typically found in Eastern Europe in a continental climate.
Stoop normally a vertical or near-vertical dive in the air, usually for catching prey.
Stop-run-peck feeding a method of feeding by sight employed by several birds, notably plovers, characterised by regular pauses while the bird is motionless scanning for food, followed by a run towards any prey sighted.
Sub-colony a subdivision of a colony, normally defined by closely synchronised breeding stages (e.g. egg-laying and incubation periods).
Subspecies a phenotypically distinct population within a species, usually defined by distribution but not genetically isolated enough to be called a species.
Surface seizing a method of feeding employed by birds swimming on the water, in which food is gathered on or from the surface without a dive or upending.
Switchback flight the name given to many display flights, especially by waders, involving regular rising and falling in the air.
Synchronous hatching hatching in which all chicks emerge from the eggs within a 24-hour period, leading to all the brood being of roughly the same age.
Syrinx the sound-producing apparatus of birds, located at the base of the trachea where the bronchial tubes are attached.
Taiga the northern coniferous forest belt.
Talons the feet of a bird of prey or owl.
Terrestrial living primarily on the ground.
Territory an area defended by a bird or birds for breeding or feeding purposes, or both.
Tertial step a bulge seen on the closed wing of gulls behind the primary flight feathers.
Thermal a bubble of air heated by the sun and rising from the ground, composed of swirling updrafts that can be used by birds for lift.
Trill the rapid reiteration of one note.
Tundra the zone of low vegetation found beyond the tree line at high latitudes and altitudes.
Upending a feeding technique used in water, in which the neck is immersed so far that the front of the body is under water and the tail points up into the air, the position maintained by paddling with the feet.
Vertebrate an animal with a backbone. Includes fish, amphibians, reptiles, birds and mammals.
Wader also known as a shorebird, a specific term referring to the generally long-legged birds of the sandpiper family *Scolopacidae*, the plovers *Charadriidae*, Oystercatchers *Haematopodidae*, Stone Curlews *Burhinidae*, Avocets and Stilts *Recurvirostridae*, Pratincoles *Glareolidae* and Stone Curlews *Burhinidae*. In contrast to the terminology used in North America, does not refer to the larger long-legged birds such a herons and storks – these are sometimes known as wading birds.
Wing loading a measure of flight performance defined by the ratio of total body weight to wing area.
Wintering grounds the broad area where a species resides during the non-breeding season (also known as resting areas).
Wreck the large-scale beaching or blowing inland of birds that are usually found far out at sea. Usually occurs in response to extreme weather.

Photography Credits

All images © David Cottridge apart from the following:

pp. 105t, 272t, 329br Arnoud van den Berg; 73b Arnoud van den Berg/ Windrush; 201b Nigel Blake; 40, 50, 51t, 58b, 63b, 88t, 98b, 104t, 112b, 116, 117b, 129, 155, 164t, 171t, 174t, 199t, 202, 220b, 225t, 251tl, 254t, 256, 278t, 278b, 282t, 289, 290, 295, 309b, 324t Richard Brooks; 102b, 224, 264b Richard Brooks/ Windrush; 97 Peter Cairns/ Windrush; 258, 293b Kevin Carlson/ Windrush; 200, 201t Colin Carver/ Windrush; 56 Bill Coster/ Windrush; 317t Mike Crewe; 29t, 82, 296 Paul Doherty/ Windrush; 94b G.Downey/ Windrush; 26t, 35t, 66b, 67t, 72t, 76t, 77b, 99t, 104b, 130b, 132b, 138b, 167b, 214bl, 214br, 260tr, 323t Goran Ekstrom; 170, 172t Tom Ennis; 221t Tom Ennis/ Windrush; 41b Rory Glenn/ Windrush; 27, 86t, 96, 124t, 124b, 138t, 140r, 148, 152t, 190, 219b, 284 Chris Gomersall; 156b Michael Gore/ Windrush; 191, 197b, 203, 246b, 251tl, 299t, 325t, 325b Dave Kjaer; 62b, 75t, 112t, 144b, 174b, 178t Chris Knights; 25t, 29bl, 237, 244b, 259t, 259b, 260b, 326 Mike Lane; 12, 32t, 94t, 99b, 137, 151r, 158b, 215tr, 280, 293t, 294, 306b, 313t, 316b Gordon Langsbury; 103t Gordon Langsbury/ Windrush; 41t, 152b, 185, 330tl Tim Loseby; 14, 64t, 65b, 101, 103b, 119, 147, 168b, 184, 186t, 188, 222, 223t, 230, 238, 276, 304tr, 327b, 330tr; 113 D.Mason/ Windrush; 288 George McCarthy/ Windrush; 89b, 231t Mike McKavett/ Windrush; 75b, 109b, 173b, 197t, 211, 215tl, 216b, 283t, 285t, 299b, 329t Jari Peltomaki; 76b, 78b, 90, 105b, 149, 158t, 162b, 262t, 263t Rene Pop; 34b J.Roberts/ Windrush; 95t Paul Rogers/ Windrush; 26b, 327t Chris Schrenk/ Windrush; 32b Brent Stephenson; 33b, 86b, 219t, 225b, 265t, 303b Roger Tidman; 98t, 106, 135b, 146, 168t Roger Tidman/ Windrush; 34t, 74, 79, 83, 91, 95b, 100, 107, 122, 123, 143, 164b, 179t, 189, 205b, 215b, 223b, 229, 257, 261r, 283b, 307, 309t, 316t, 319t, 319b, 330b David Tipling/ Windrush; 205t Ray Tipper; 14, 64t, 65b, 101, 103b, 119, 147, 168b, 184, 186t, 188, 222, 223t, 230, 238, 276, 304tr, 327b, 330tr Alan Williams.

All illustrations by Norman Arlott © HarperCollins apart from pp. 8r, 9l © Lizzie Harper.
All maps © HarperCollins.

Index

Bold page numbers refer to main entries